The New York Times
Chronicle of American Life

From the Crash to the Blitz
1929-1939

Also by Cabell Phillips

The Truman Presidency
Dateline: Washington (Ed.)

The New York Times
Chronicle of American Life

From the Crash to the Blitz
1929-1939

by Cabell Phillips

Art Directed by Harris Lewine

Fordham University Press

New York   2000

With a new introduction by Herbert Mitgang

Library of Congress Cataloging-in-Publication Data

Phillips, Cabell B. H.
    From the crash to the blitz, 1929–1939 / Cabell Phillips; with a
new introduction by Herbert Mitgang.
        p.   cm.
    Originally published: New York : Macmillan, 1969.
    Includes bibliographical references (p.   ) and index.
    ISBN 0-8232-1999-2.—ISBN 0-8232-2000-1 (pbk.)
    1. United States—Civilization—1918–1945.   I. Title.
E169.1.P543   2000
973.916—dc21   99-16824
                                                          CIP

ACKNOWLEDGEMENTS

Excerpts from the following books are reprinted by permission:
Depression Decade by Broadus Mitchell, copyright © 1966, reprinted by
permission of Holt, Rinehart & Winston, Inc.; *Four Prominent SO & SO's*,
by Ogden Nash, copyright © 1934, 1962 by Ogden Nash, reprinted by permission of Curtiss Brown, Ltd.; *Spending to Save*, by Harry L. Hopkins,
copyright 1936 by W. W. Norton & Company, Inc., copyright renewed 1964
by David, Stephen and Robert Hopkins; *Roosevelt and Hopkins* by Robert
Sherwood, copyright 1948, reprinted by permission of Harper & Row, Publishers, Inc.; *Roosevelt & Frankfurter*: Their Correspondence by Max
Friedman, copyright © 1967 by Max Friedman, reprinted by permission of
Atlantic-Little, Brown and Company; *Middletown in Transition*, by Robert
& Helen Lynd, copyright 1937, reprinted by permission of Harcourt, Brace
& World, Inc.

Printed in the United States of America

For Sy,
who for so long has made
so many things possible

About Roosevelt, one writes of the past and thinks of the future. You cannot say with assurance what he will do but only what he has done. We write our history of these times in twenty-four hour installments.

—Raymond Clapper in
Current History,
October 1938

CONTENTS

attitudes and a widening sophistication about the world; popular taste in movies, radio, music, reading, and other diversions. With a little luck, one could surmount the bleakness of the times.

16 THE SECOND NEW DEAL: HIGH NOON to DUSK 481

Much of the ardor and drama had gone out of the New Deal by 1937; the great period of innovation was past and a reviving prosperity blighted the spirit of reform, embittered the political climate. Although Roosevelt had achieved his greatest electoral victory in 1936—he took every state except Maine and Vermont —his luck ran out a year later as he attempted to "pack" the Supreme Court, failed him even worse in his ill-fated "purge" in the by-elections of 1938. A recession and persistent unemployment added to his woes. As the decade ended he seemed almost a leader without a following.

17 A NEW DEAL for LABOR _____ 511

Organized labor in the U.S. belatedly comes of age with a strenuous assist from the New Deal—and, tardily, from the Supreme Court. Armed with new legislative weapons, it makes a whirlwind assault upon the open shop, faces rebellion in its own ranks. Birth of the CIO and the sitdown strike; the lengthening shadow of John L. Lewis. Recognition at last.

18 UP from ISOLATIONISM _____ 527

As war clouds gather over Asia and Europe this country becomes obsessed with an almost fanatical determination not to be drawn into the maelstrom. Senator Nye, among others, whips up the notion that wars are started by and fought for the benefit of international bankers and "munitions kings." Isolationism becomes a pervasive, militant cult. As fighting flares in China, Ethiopia, Spain; as Hitler menaces Central Europe, Congress passes a stiff neutrality law. "Hands off" becomes core of U.S. foreign policy; the President's hands are tied. But the pace of aggression quickens, terror spreads until many Americans feel threatened. Roosevelt's call at Chicago for "measures short of war" to halt aggressors brings new note of rationality into the nation's thinking. With the Austrian *Anschluss* and Czechoslovakia's "betrayal" at Munich, the myth of isolationism is punctured, slowly deflates.

19 THE DAYS of PEACE RUN OUT: 1938-1939 ___ 551

The chronology of a year of nightmares, Sept. 1938–Sept. 1939: Hitler institutes systematic persecution of the Jews; Franco crushes the Spanish Loyalists; Germany seizes all of Czechoslovakia, thrusts new demands upon Poland. The U.S. Neutrality Act is extended over Roosevelt's protest, further weakening British-French stance toward Hitler. Germany and Russia sign pact, agree to dismemberment of Poland and Baltic States. The *Blitzkrieg* smashes across Poland; Britain and France declare war on Germany as Second World War begins.

Organization, as well as confounding the idealistic struggle to strengthen the rule of law through an International Court of Justice.

The 1930s were a wakeup decade in many lands. Expectations rose. Class differences became more apparent. Benevolent governments realized that there was a large gap between the way their own citizens lived and worked. The lack of equality for women at home and in the workplace became more visible. Inequality for minorities existed on the job, in the classroom, and in the courthouse. Civil- and human-rights legislation would have to await the post–World War II years in the United States.

The greatest theoretical experiment to bring government closer to the people and increase production without capitalism took place in Russia. The system was rooted in Marxist economic theory. At first, many Americans applauded the Russian Revolution that ousted the czar, though during the 1920s the Republican administrations continued President Woodrow Wilson's nonrecognition policy.

In 1933, the Roosevelt Administration realized that nonrecognition had failed and that improved relations might help to pull the United States out of the Depression and deter Japanese expansion in Asia. Diplomatic relations were established with Russia. The Soviet Union became an ally of the Western nations during World War II and suffered huge casualties. After the defeat of the Axis Powers, the Cold War froze relations, and what Winston Churchill called an "Iron Curtain" descended over Eastern Europe.

"So you've been over into Russia?" said Bernard Baruch, the American financier and presidential adviser, to Lincoln Steffens, the respected American author, in 1931. And Steffens famously responded, "I have been over into the future, and it works." It did not. After the downfall of the czarist regime, the Soviet Union soon turned into a dictatorship—not of the proletariat but of the Politburo in the Kremlin. Russia turned into a police state that lacked any semblance of democracy. After seventy years, the state-run economic system collapsed. The old Soviet Union splintered into several states, but at least there were elections and freedoms to help guide Russia into the new millennium.

The Great Crash on Wall Street that began in the fall of 1929 led to the Great Depression. How did it happen? Manufacturers invested to capacity to meet the demands of the postwar boom. People lived on credit; consumers bought durable goods in quantity for the first time. The Federal Reserve tried to raise interest rates to discourage small and large investors from "playing the stock market." Buying on margin eventually led to even greater debt when investments slid downward. Companies cut back on their own plans to produce durable goods. The fall in prices triggered cutbacks in demand—and loss of jobs. It was a vicious circle: workers were idle because manufacturers could no longer afford to hire them; there was no market for goods because workers didn't have any income to remain consumers.

When the Great Crash struck during the presidency of Herbert Hoover, there was no federal social legislation—no safety net—to help the unemployed and their families.

While Washington was doing little to solve the crisis of unemployment, Governor Franklin D. Roosevelt in Albany saw the need for government to intervene and provide assistance to the jobless and poor. In a direct critique of Hoover's reliance on the familiar "trickle-down theory"—the benevolence of big business to solve the unemployment and wage problems—Roosevelt said:

Let us face the facts. In the field of private endeavor we have retained in large degree the personal liberty of the individual, but we have lost the economic liberty of the individual. This has been swallowed up in the specialization of industry, of agriculture and of distribution, and has meant that the cog can move only if the whole machine is in perfect gear. We thus see, on one hand, an overproduction of food and clothing and close by many millions of men and women who lack the medium of exchange—money—with which to ward off starvation and nakedness.

We know now from bitter experience that the theory that a Nation could lift itself up by its own bootstraps was not sound. That the cheering thought that the larger the number of people engaged in manufacturing commodities the more these commodities would be used could be carried too far. That just because a piece of paper was labeled a share of stock or a bond did not of necessity give it value. That an increasing concentration of wealth and of power that wealth controls did not guarantee an intelligent or a fair use of that wealth or power.

F.D.R. called for labor legislation to keep step with the newest developments in industrial life and the newest conceptions of social welfare. His recommendations for New York State foretold what would occur when he took office as president in 1933. These included:

- Establishment in the Labor Department of a special means for the enforcement of the provisions of the Labor Law relating to the eight-hour workday, the prevailing rate of wages, and the need to give preference to citizens of New York State on public-works projects.
- A genuine eight-hour day and forty-eight-hour week for women in industry.
- The establishment for women and children of an advisory minimum- or fair-wage board.
- The raising of the limit for compensation in all classes of disabilities to $25 a week.
- Coverage by the Workmen's Compensation Law of all diseases arising from occupational tasks.

In the same legislative message, F.D.R. made this idealistic statement that seemed more like a cheerleading comment than a practical piece of legislation: "A declaration in the form of a statute that the labor of human beings is not a commodity or an article of commerce." Never mind. It was the kind of inspiring remark that gave heart to people in New York and the nation.

President Hoover was a stolid man, imbued with Quaker morality and with faith in the economic philosophy of laissez-faire. But the old doctrines would not help the Okies and the farmers in the desolate Plains states, heading westward in jalopies to some promised land in California. As depicted by John Steinbeck in his novel *The Grapes of Wrath*, they moved in a dispirited human tide. They named their ramshackle roadside homes "Hoovervilles." The country was ripe for change in the 1932 elections. Governor Roosevelt became President Roosevelt. The federal government took direct action to create jobs and extended new forms of social security to the populace.

The author of *From the Crash to the Blitz* boldly and accurately titles his chapter on the change in the White House from Hoover to Roosevelt a "Coup d'État." It was not a silent revolution; it was a real, but bloodless, revolution. It became known as the New Deal. After the American Revolution and the Civil War (the Second American Revolution), the New Deal could rightly be branded the Third American Revolution.

In his acceptance speech to the Democratic National Convention in Chicago on

July 2, 1932, Roosevelt said, "I pledge you—I pledge myself to a *new deal* for the American people. Let us all here assembled constitute ourselves prophets of a new order of competence and of courage. This is more than a political campaign; it is a call to arms. Give me your help, not to win votes alone, but to win in this crusade to restore America to its own people."

There is little dispute among historians that F.D.R. was the twentieth century's greatest president. The patrician from the Hudson River Valley somehow formed a common bond with the common man. He hit the ground running in his fabled first "Hundred Days" in office. That metaphor is used advisedly: Roosevelt's legs were encased in braces. He could not walk unaided. Sometimes he used a wheelchair, sometimes a crutch or canes; most often he leaned on the arms of one of his sons or of a military aide in his public appearances. Here was a man who, with the brilliant inspiration of Eleanor Roosevelt, was determined to overcome his polio infirmities. In this respect, he displayed superhuman courage—and that same courage became the talisman of his administration.

During the "Hundred Days" he proposed a number of emergency measures that altered the nation's social and political direction. At the heart of these changes was the National Recovery Act, which came complete with a slogan that captured the attention of workmen and businessmen: "N.R.A.—We Do Our Part." (The letters had nothing to do with the National Rifle Association!) With the slogan came a drawing of a Blue Eagle.

Out of the N.R.A. grew the W.P.A.—the Works Progress Administration. This was the bureaucracy that brought jobs to the unemployed. With a maximum thirty-hour work week, paying an average of between $50 and $60 a month, this became a living wage that enabled breadwinners to support their families until real jobs began to open up. Cabell Phillips knew what the W.P.A. meant to people; he himself worked in its press section between 1936 and 1939 as information director of the N.Y.A.—the National Youth Administration, another one of the so-called "alphabet agencies."

At the same time that the social legislation was approved by Congress, President Roosevelt began a direct line of communication with the American people. They became known as "fireside chats." These radio talks brought Roosevelt into nearly every American kitchen and living room.

From the Crash to the Blitz is not a total tale of despair and political revolution. The book includes lively sections on popular culture and what the federal government did to encourage the arts by direct subsidies.

The most exhilarating development in the theater was the creation in 1935 of the W.P.A.'s Federal Theater Project. Actors, playwrights, composers, directors, scenic designers, and all the elements of theater came together to pursue their muse and craft. Orson Welles, John Houseman, Marc Blitzstein, and hundreds of performers and technicians honed their skills with federal assistance. One of the daring innovations was *The Living Newspaper*, which combined the technique of the radio and the newsreel. One such production, titled *One Third of a Nation*, took its theme from President Roosevelt's memorable phrase that one-third of the nation was "ill-fed, ill-housed, ill-clothed."

The middle of the "low dishonest decade" saw the birth and growth of a notable theatrical company, The Group Theater, whose poet laureate–playwright was Clifford Odets, writing plays with social significance. Brooks Atkinson, *The New York Times* drama critic, gave rave reviews to *Waiting for Lefty, Till the Day I Die,* and

Awake and Sing. Waiting for Lefty aroused the passions of the censors, who banned it in Boston, New Haven, and Philadelphia because of its "obscenity and blasphemy." Actually, the bluenoses found it objectionable because it was a broadside in favor of union activity. Atkinson called the play "one of the best working-class dramas that have been written."

The Spanish Civil War, considered a warmup for World War II, united writers and artists to warn against the rise of Fascism in Spain and Italy and anti-Semitism in Germany. Could it happen in the United States? That was the cautionary tale offered by Sinclair Lewis, the American Nobel laureate in literature, in his sardonic novel *It Can't Happen Here.* The Federal Theater Project mounted his novel as a drama. On Broadway and in theaters in seventeen states, the play ran for 260 weeks. Such daring subject-matter aroused the House Committee on Un-American Activities. Congress cut off the funding for the Federal Theater Project in 1939, and it was disbanded, but not before the left-wing themes and anti-Fascist diatribes brought new audiences into the theater.

The Roosevelt Administration also supported literature—that is, starving authors. The W.P.A. Federal Writers Project paid distinguished writers to produce the American Guide series—regional guides to all the states. Among those who contributed to these and other writing projects were Ralph Ellison, Richard Wright, John Cheever, Conrad Aiken, Alfred Kazin, and Nelson Algren. Photographers and painters also availed themselves of government largesse. The Farm Security Administration sent out photographers to illustrate how people lived and worked. The Treasury Department established a Fine Arts Section to decorate the walls of public buildings. The W.P.A. Federal Arts Project had more than five thousand artists and allied workers on its payroll. They produced murals, sculptures, and prints for everything from county courthouses to one-room school buildings.

After President Roosevelt was reelected in 1936 to a second term and the country slowly began to emerge from the Depression, another world war threatened in Europe and Asia. Eventually, World War II would cost the lives of some sixty million combatants and civilians. When Japan bombed Pearl Harbor on December 7, 1941, F.D.R. called the attack "a day that will live in infamy," and Congress declared war against the Axis nations. President Roosevelt then exercised his constitutional role as commander-in-chief of the armed forces.

Before Pearl Harbor, the general mood of the nation was to stay aloof from distant wars. Liberal and conservative spokesmen and publications warned against foreign entanglements. The New Deal Congresses were more concerned with domestic issues, passing a Neutrality Act in 1935 that prevented the United States from shipping arms to any country. With misgivings, President Roosevelt signed it. But he and other statesmen recognized the danger of isolationism and began to increase the national defense budget.

On September 1, 1939, an "extra" edition of *The New York Times* carried this banner headline:

GERMAN ARMY ATTACKS POLAND;
CITIES BOMBED, PORT BLOCKADED;
DANZIG IS ACCEPTED INTO REICH

The story went on to say that German planes swooped out of the morning mists to dump bombs and machine-gun fire on the cities of Poland, and German troops and tanks smashed across the Polish border from Slovakia on the south and East Prussia in the west. From the Kroll Opera House in Berlin, Hitler addressed his cheering millions: "I have put on my old soldier's coat [he had been a corporal in World War I] and I will not take it off until we win victory for the Fatherland!"

Two days later, Prime Minister Neville Chamberlain, the sad leader who had promised "peace in our time" and failed, declared that a state of war existed between Britain and Germany. The ill-prepared Western nations had caved in to the dictators. Soon the Luftwaffe would begin its blitz of London, making no distinction between military and civilian targets. World War II had begun.

Time was on Hitler's side; country after country fell as all Europe was occupied. It was not until the United States entered the war at the end of 1941 that victory over Germany and Japan became a possibility; and it was a hard-won victory, not becoming reality until 1945. At last it was possible to dream again of the "Four Freedoms" that President Roosevelt had promised the people of the United States and the world in his message to Congress on January 6, 1941:

We look forward to a world founded upon four essential human freedoms. The first is freedom of speech and expression—everywhere in the world. The second is freedom of every person to worship God in his own way—everywhere in the world. The third is freedom from want—everywhere in the world. The fourth is freedom from fear—anywhere in the world.

New York   HERBERT MITGANG
February 1999

PREFACE

IT HAS BEEN TWENTY YEARS since I first came upon Mark Sullivan's *Our Times.* I needed, for something I was writing at the time, clarification of an incident during the Harding Administration. I found it in the concluding volume, *The Twenties,* of his excellent six-volume history of the first three decades of this century. But a good many hours elapsed before I put that bit of information to use, for I was so fascinated by the book that I spent the rest of the day on a delightful tour of exploration through the six volumes, which I had obtained from the library. As rapidly as I could afford them (at about six dollars a copy), I bought the entire set for my own library. My enjoyment—and occasional dependence on them professionally—has diminished but little over the years.

It seemed to me that this is the way contemporary history ought to be written—with the intimate perspective of an observer at or close to the scene, and with a good reporter's judgment of what is and what is not important to his story and his instinct for significant detail and color. Mark Sullivan was for almost fifty years a distinguished correspondent for, among other publications, the New York *Herald Tribune.* (The final volume in his series was published in 1937.) His skilled rewriting of the major news events of his epoch, and his evocation of dramatic sidelights and of the social and political context in which they occurred, give to his narrative a freshness and piquancy not often found in conventional histories. These books can be opened almost at random and read for an hour or more with keen enjoyment.

I never attained Mark Sullivan's professional eminence, but I have been a newspaperman for most of the last forty years and have been based in Washington since 1935. For a long time I have had the immodest desire to rewrite the news of *my* epoch in a fashion somewhat similar to Sullivan's, picking up at the point in time where he left off. *The New York Times,* my employer for the last twenty-four years, and The Macmillan Company generously provided me with the opportunity.

I call this "a journalistic *reprise*" of the revolutionary decade that ran roughly from the stock market crash of 1929 to the onset of the Second World War in 1939. It is a *reprise* rather than a scholarly social history. Scholars in great number have had their go at it and have drawn, I suspect, the last measure of scholarly conclusions and deductions from it. I have sought, rather, to describe the thirties in the round and to recreate the sense of involvement and propinquity that so many of that generation experienced in the midst of those stirring times. The framework of my narrative is necessarily political, since the big story throughout was the New Deal in its many exciting, exasperating convolutions. I have tried to fill out the framework by setting the events in the context of contemporary human experience. Mass unemployment is both a statistic and an empty feeling in the stomach. To fully comprehend it, you have to both see the figures and feel the emptiness.

So it is as a reporter that I have gone back to where the action was a long generation ago and try now to tell you not only what happened but what it was like to be there at the time.

My basic source of information from beginning to end has been the files (in microfilm) of *The New York Times*. I chose this not only because it was the most easily available to me but because it is incomparably the best record extant of past events and their setting. I have drawn quite heavily also on such leading periodicals of the period as *Literary Digest, Time, Today, Collier's, The Nation,* and *Harper's.* In addition I have consulted a large number of published works such as histories, memoirs, diaries, government reports and books dealing with particular phases of the decade, most of which are appropriately identified in the bibliographical notes at the end of the volume.

Among my most valued co-workers have been the staffs of the Library of Congress, the District of Columbia Public Library and the libraries of a number of government departments, trade associations and private organizations. I owe a particular debt of gratitude to my colleagues on *The New York Times* and to a large number of other friends and contemporaries of mine on the Washington scene for helping out so generously on this project with their specialized knowledge and their reminiscences. In a number of instances they have read parts of the manuscript and given me many helpful suggestions. I am also indebted to three young graduate students from local universities— Richard McMasters, James Oswald, and Ruth E. Armstrong—who at various times have served so ably as research assistants.

Much that the text in this book fails to state is dramatically conveyed by the illustrations. The liberal and sensitive employment of graphics here tells what some aspects of life were like in the Thirties in a way that words could only approximate. Michael O'Keefe, a picture editor for the Sunday Department of the *Times,* made the laborious preliminary search for many of the pictures used. The final selection, captioning, and layout of the illustrative material are the handiwork of Art Director Harris Lewine and his Designer, Robert Aulicino. The excellence of their craftsmanship is self-evident and cannot be enhanced by further encomium from the author.

CABELL PHILLIPS

Washington, D.C.
March 1969

CHAPTER 1
Winter of Despair
1932–1933

NO NEW YEAR EVER DAWNED with less hope than 1933. The Great Depression, having grown progressively worse for three long years, had spread a pall of fear and desperation across the whole land. The new year brought no promise of abatement, only the prospect of more of the same. The physical signs of distress were everywhere. You encountered them with wearying monotony day after day: clusters of hungry men and women waiting like docile peasants for food handouts at the relief stations; the smokeless chimneys and rusting sheds of factories standing mute and empty behind their locked gates; the abandoned shops and stores, their doorways littered with trash, their grime-streaked windows staring vacantly upon half-empty streets; the drooping shoulders of a father, husband, brother, or friend whose pride had been battered into lethargy and dejection by months of fruitless job hunting; the panic and anger of the crowd milling before a bank entrance on whose door a typed note stated, "Closed until further notice by order of the Board of Directors."

But even worse than this visible evidence of breakdown was the knowledge that it was everywhere—not just in your town or your state or your part of the country. The blight spread across the whole nation—big cities, small towns, the limitless countryside—like a deadly plague of the Middle Ages. Nor were its victims just certain kinds of people. They were farmers, bankers, carpenters, lawyers, factory workers, preachers, chorus girls. Every class, it seemed, except the poor Negroes in the slums who had never known anything but hard times anyway, was stricken in some degree. But even those who still had jobs or income lived with a hot ball of fear in their gut that tomorrow their luck would run out. "What will I do then?" sprang equally from the tortured clerk behind the counter and the merchant behind his desk.

Worse still was the knowledge that there was nothing you or your boss or the governor of your state or the President of the United States could do about it. All the towers of wisdom and strength on which you were accustomed to lean had crumbled. The roots of your faith in the American Way and even, perhaps, in the benevolence of God, had begun to wither like a vine too long deprived of rain. You felt trapped, like an animal in a cage, as some malevolent force that you could neither comprehend nor fend off inexorably worked to destroy your whole scheme of life. And in these early weeks of the new year 1933 you felt that the climax was approaching. Things were happening that seemed to warn, like thunderclaps in the hot night sky, that the storm was about to loose its furies.

Such things as——

It was bitterly cold in the little town of Lemars, Iowa, on the morning of January 4, 1933. On the snow-packed ground before the entrance to the Plymouth County Courthouse, eight hundred roughly dressed farmers and townsmen were packed shoulder to shoulder. They had begun assembling before daybreak. They were restless and in an ugly mood, the breath from their mutterings and occasional catcalls congealing in gray wisps of fog above their heads.

The farm of one of their neighbors, John A. Johnson, was posted to be auctioned from the courthouse steps at ten o'clock. The sale was to satisfy a $33,000 mortgage held by a New York insurance company. After two summers of searing drought and with the price of corn dropping to 10 cents a bushel (the actual cost of raising it had been about 80 cents), Johnson had fallen hopelessly behind in his payments. The court had granted the company's petition to foreclose, as it had on a score of other debt-ridden farms in the county in the preceding months.

The people gathered at Lemars did not intend to prevent the sale of John Johnson's farm (mobs in other communities had tried to prevent such sales). But they were going to see to it that the property was bid at the full face of the mortgage, so that the Johnson livestock and family possessions would not have to be sacrificed to make up the deficiency. So, when Sheriff Ripley stood up on the portico, read off the court order, and asked, "What am I bid?," the only response came from an obvious "city fellow" standing at his elbow, Herbert S. Martin, an attorney representing the insurance company.

"Thirty thousand," Martin said in a nervous, scarcely audible voice.

"No! No!," the crowd yelled. Individual voices cried out: "Full value!" "Thirty-three thousand or nothing!" "Stop the sale!"

The sheriff held up his hands to restore quiet. "Mr. Martin says that is as high as the mortgage holder has authorized him to go," he shouted. "Unless I hear another offer I'll be forced to knock it down to him. Do I hear another bid?"

Again the crowd broke out into a bedlam of shouts. "No! No! Full value or no sale! Let's show 'em we mean business. Get Martin! Get Ripley!"

As the mob surged forward up the steps, the sheriff and the lawyer made a dash for the courthouse door, but not in time. The two men were roughly seized and pushed out into the center of the seething, pummeling mob. A heavy rope with a hangman's noose was slipped over the distraught lawyer's head. "We'll hang him from the highest tree in town," someone yelled, and the crowd took up the chant.

Frantically, Martin implored for time to telegraph his principals asking permission to raise his bid. His wire ended with this desperate plea: "Rush answer. My neck at risk." Two hours later his bid of $33,000 for the Johnson farm was accepted with the grudging consent of the mob, and the crisis of law and order at Lemars, Iowa, was ended.

Such things as——

Ever since the first of the year, unsettling gossip that the city's banks were in trouble had flowed through financial circles in Detroit, and from there to the little business firms and on into the rumor-ravaged residential districts of Hamtramck and Dearborn. The whole city was in trouble, and everybody knew it. Auto production had been skidding downward for three years. More than 100,000 people were out of work, and some 5,000 families were in acute distress, which the public welfare agencies were unable properly to cope with. "Agitators" had begun to organize the jobless and the destitute into unemployed councils and to stage demonstrations at the office of Mayor Frank Murphy.

The rumors about the banks added a new dimension to the anxiety the city was already suffering. From time to time "runs" developed—first at one and then at another as panicky groups of depositors withdrew their funds— but the banks managed to hold up through January and on into February. The Mayor and other civic leaders called for confidence and steady nerves, and their reassurances were bolstered by news that the Ford Motor Company had opened a new account with a deposit of $7 million in the Union Guardian Trust Company, one of the city's largest but most suspect banks.

Actually, Union Guardian was shakier than most Detroiters realized. Seventy percent of its assets were all but frozen in real estate loans. It had borrowed to the limit from other banks and from the Federal Reserve to replenish its liquid reserves. Early in January it had applied to the Reconstruction Finance Corporation (a government agency created in 1932 for the specific purpose of bailing out foundering banks and insurance companies) for a $60-million loan. Now, early in February, its application was turned down. The harassed officials of Union Guardian, ninth largest bank in the country, faced the awesome reality when they opened for business on Monday, February 12, that they had only enough cash to meet two days of normal withdrawals. Union Guardian was insolvent—the most hated word in the banker's lexicon—but if it admitted the fact and went under it would draw half the other banks in Detroit, and maybe in the state, down with it. It would be a catastrophe such as the city had never experienced.

All that day and the next the bank's officers met secretly with a handful of financial leaders and representatives of the state banking department. Secretary of Commerce Chapin, a Detroiter, was summoned from Washington, and he brought with him the Under Secretary of the Treasury, A. A. Ballantine. Late Tuesday, Michigan's Governor William A. Comstock slipped away unnoticed from the Capitol at Lansing and joined the band of worried men in the Union Guardian boardroom. Their presence there was shrouded in the deepest secrecy, for if the fact of the crisis became known hordes of panicky depositors would storm the doors of every bank in the city before the next noon.

It was past midnight when the session broke up. The Governor drove back to Lansing, but he did not go to bed. Instead, he summoned a corps of aides to hammer out the last legal defense against the pending financial storm. At three o'clock on the morning of February 14 he proclaimed an eight-day "public holiday" throughout the State of Michigan during which "all banks, trust companies and other financial institutions shall not be open for the transaction of trust or banking business."

Most Detroiters were at breakfast or on their way to work when newsboys screaming "Extra! Extra!" brought them the first word that the banks were shut. For a week at least they would have to live on whatever cash they had in their pockets or cash registers, and, more ominously still, they might never retrieve what they had entrusted to the banks for safekeeping. There were some 900,000 depositors in Detroit, with accounts aggregating more than $700 million frozen in the vaults by the Governor's orders.

The initial impact of the news produced shock and anger, and then, strangely, a kind of bewildered amusement as if the people were saying to one another, "Imagine finding ourselves in this impossible predicament!" For a day or so they laughed when a vice president asked an office boy, "Brother, can you spare a dime?" or when a luncheon party offered the cashier a million-dollar check in settlement of a ten-dollar food bill. The *Free Press* sought to boost the public morale with a story headlined, "Detroit Stays on the Job with Valiant Smile." But the smile faded as the week wore on. It turned to grimness as thousands of families, particularly in the middle-class and poorer districts, ran out of credit with the grocer and even out of small change for smokes and carfares. By week's end misery had bitten deeply into every segment of the city's life. There was hunger where hunger had somehow been staved off until now; promised jobs evaporated suddenly in the crisis; marginal businesses, unable to stand one more financial strain, slid into bankruptcy. And for those who were still relatively secure, there was the gnawing specter that a part, at least, of their assets would forever be lost to them in the debacle of the banks.

Detroit was not alone. Banks had been collapsing like dominoes all across the country for three years; 1,400 had gone down in 1932 alone. But Detroit's crisis was the most spectacular and the most unnerving to date; proof positive, it seemed to many, of the inevitable breakup of the nation's financial structure. In the week that followed, a dozen other governors adopted Michigan's last-ditch stratagem of declaring a bank holiday.

Such things as——

NEW YORK, Jan. 6 (AP)—After vainly trying to get a stay of dispossession until Jan. 15 from his apartment at 46 Hancock Street, in Brooklyn, yesterday, Peter J. Cornell, 48 years old, a former roofing contractor out of work and penniless, fell dead in the arms of his wife.

A doctor gave the cause of his death as heart disease, and the police said it had at least partly been caused by the bitter disappointment of a long day's fruitless attempt to prevent himself and his family being put out on the street.

Just before he died Cornell had carried a bag of coal he had just received from the police upstairs.

Cornell owed $5 rent in arrears and $39 for January, which his landlord required in advance. Failure to produce the money resulted in a dispossess order being served on the family yesterday and to take effect at the end of the week.

After vainly seeking assistance elsewhere, he was told during the day by the Home Relief Bureau that it would have no funds with which to help him until Jan. 15.

Such things as——

In Richmond, Virginia, a city unaccustomed to strife since its sacking by the Yankees in 1865, a delegation of fifty whites and Negroes representing the local Unemployed Council called at the office of Mayor J. Fulmer Bright a few days

Dip Your Brush In The Sunshine

And Keep On Painting Away

Fox-Trot Ballad

Words by
Andy Razaf

Music by
J.C.Johnson

Successfully Featured by

Ted Lewis
and
His Band

Exclusive Columbia
Record Artists

At left: For the unemployed and destitute, a day in "this life" was often just a "bowl of cherries." (Above) Ted Lewis, with the help of some 1931 Andy Razaf lyrics, exhorts and exhorts . . .

At left: (top) 10/28/31. Police Reserves maintain order as some of the 750,000 New York City jobless register at the Emergency Unemployment Relief Registration Agency. (Bottom, left) The jobless often resorted to "homemade" Sandwich Boards in seeking work. (Bottom, right) Photographer Dorothea Lange's memorable *White Angel Breadline*, San Francisco, 1933. (Below) John Howard Lawson's *Success Story:* mediocre box office, divided critics, and a Luther Adler bravura performance for the 1932 season. (At right) Eddie Cantor's hit version of the "cockeyed optimism" of Tin Pan Alley.

(Following spread) Bank Failure. New York City, 1932. (Inset) 1932 Pulitzer Prize Cartoon by John McCutcheon of the *Chicago Tribune.*

BEGINNING
MONDAY EVENING,
DECEMBER 5, 1932

MATINEES
WEDNESDAY AND
SATURDAY

THE GROUP THEATRE, INC.,

PRESENTS

"SUCCESS STORY"

By JOHN HOWARD LAWSON

PRODUCTION DIRECTED BY LEE STRASBERG

SETTING DESIGNED BY MORDECAI GORELIK

CAST

(In the order of appearance)

SARAH GLASSMAN . . . .*Played by* STELLA ADLER
DINAH McCABE . . . . " " RUTH NELSON

(Top) Members of the Iowa National Guard protecting Judge C. C. Bradley from farmers protesting over mortgage foreclosures. (Middle, bottom, and at right) Hunger Marchers pause in Newark, N.J., for some *Internationale* before moving on to Washington, D.C. In New York City it was Apple Sellers on West 42nd Street and Breadlines, Soup Kitchens, and Depression Restaurants from Times Square to the Bowery.

Hunger March
(1933)

Translated by Abe Little
From the Yiddish by I. Rontch

Music by
Jacob Schaeffer
(1933)

In march time (M.M. ♩ = 120)

VOICE

1. We do all the buil-ding, Our hands all the plow-ing; And
2. Black com-rades a - wa-ken! Come, steel your dark shoul-ders! Your

PIANO
f (loud)

yet do we starve, Have no homes of our own, Have no homes of our own.
slave driv-ing boss Our foe we meet face to face, We meet face to face.

We do all the wea - ving, Our hands all the sew-ing; Our
Strong red rows are mar-shalled, All com - rades and broth-ers, No

work feeds the boss, We get on - ly the bone, We get on - ly the bone.
ter - ror, no lynch can ham-per can slack-en our pace, Can slack-en our pace.

after Thanksgiving in 1932. They had come to petition the Mayor to recommend a $750,000 relief appropriation to the City Council, and to halt the eviction of the unemployed from their homes. The Mayor and his Chief of Police were ready for them.

Take these men by the scruff of the neck and the seat of the pants and throw them out," the Mayor ordered. Members of the delegation were rudely hustled out of the building, and their spokesman, one Abe Tompkin, said to be a New York Communist, was arrested on a charge of vagrancy.

Defending his action, Mayor Bright said: "The best indication I see that our people are not starving is the fact that so few men made any effort to get jobs

shoveling snow during the last few days. The danger of the situation is that we will breed new indigents and make utterly worthless the workers we have been forced partially to support.

Such things as——

WASHINGTON, Feb. 15 (from *The New York Times*)—Samuel Insull, Jr., told the Senate Banking and Currency Committee today how members of his family had made a paper profit of $25 million through a contract enabling them to buy stock in the Insull Utility Investment Co., Inc., at a price far below the market quotation.

CHAPTER 2
Collision Course–and Crash!
October 24, 1929

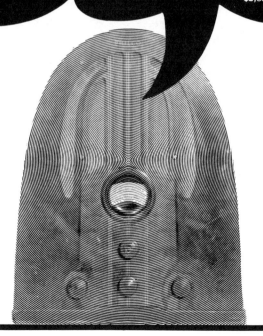

Sixteen Leading Issues Down $2,893,520,108;
Tel. & Tel. and Steel Among Heaviest Losers

Issues.	Shares Listed.	Losses in Points.	Depreciation.
American Radiator	10,096,289	10¾	$104,748,997
American Tel. & Tel.	13,203,093	34	448,905,162
Commonwealth & Southern	30,764,468	3¼	96,138,962
Columbia Gas & Electric	8,477,307	22	186,500,754
Consolidated Gas	11,451,188	20	229,023,760
DuPont E. I.	10,322,481	16¾	169,080,625
Eastman Kodak	2,229,703	41⅞	93,368,813
General Electric	7,211,484	47½	342,545,490
General Motors	43,500,000	6¾	293,625,000
International Nickel	13,777,408	7⅞	108,497,088
New York Central	4,637,086	22⅝	104,914,071
Standard Oil of New Jersey	24,843,643	8	198,749,144
Union Carbide & Carbon	8,730,173	20	174,615,460
United States Steel	8,131,055	17½	142,293,446
United Gas Improvement	18,646,835	6	111,881,010
Westinghouse Elec. & Mfg.	2,589,265	34½	88,682,326
			$2,893,520,108

IF MILLIONS UPON MILLIONS OF AMERICANS were desperate, frightened, and even rebellious, they had good cause to be. The Great Depression was the most pervasive, the most persistent, and the most destructive economic crisis the nation had ever faced. If, in perspective, scholars today minimize the threat of this crisis to the fundamental institutions of American life—the capitalist free-enterprise doctrine in particular—few were so sanguine at the time. When that desolate winter of 1932–33 settled in, most people believed, with a sort of fatalistic despair, that the world they had known was dead and that the world ahead was unknowable. And some said, "Good riddance."

How had we reached this fearful dilemma?

The roots of the Great Depression can be traced back to the world war of 1914–18 and even beyond. Some authorities describe it as the ultimate collapse of the industrial revolution, with the machine devouring man. It is, indeed, a fact that technology made enormous strides during the first two decades of the century and then took another giant step forward under the impetus of the war. The automobile came into its own, the production line replaced the craftsman's bench in thousands of factories and shops, the radio was developed and flourished like a weed in the sun, machines dug coal five times faster than miners with picks and shovels, food processing revolutionized the grocery business and the dinner table, electrical energy multiplied human energy a hundred times over and in hundreds of different ways, and families by the tens of thousands fled the drudgery and loneliness of the farms for the drudgery and lonelines of the cities. Between 1920 and 1930 economists ceased pondering the question of "America's capacity to produce," which had preoccupied them for fifty years, and turned belatedly to "America's capacity to consume," about which they had much to learn.

It is a pity they didn't turn to it sooner, because their classic postulate about the automatic balancing of supply and demand had begun to fall apart before their eyes. For in that same decade, while productivity per man-hour in manufacturing went up 43 percent (two and one-half times as fast as the population), factory wages went up less than 20 percent. The profits of a hugely productive industry went not into higher wages or lower prices but into dividends, into more machines and factories—and into speculation. The money didn't go where the people could use it to buy the things they had produced.[1]

Income distribution was further restricted by the rapid growth of monopoly in a dozen fields. There were more than a thousand mergers of local utility companies in 1926 alone, and by 1930 one-half of the total electrical output in the country was controlled by *three* huge holding companies. A study made in 1930 indicated that nearly one-half of the nonbanking corporate wealth in the country was held by the 200 largest corporations, which in turn were under the interlocking control of some 2,000 individual executives and financiers. In the corporate society that mushroomed during the twenties the worth of the individual as a free agent and master of his economic destiny took a nose dive in the marketplace. Laissez-faire was an incompatible bedmate for an Economy of Abundance.[2]

Meanwhile the whole farm sector of the economy was allowed to stagnate and even to fall backward during this dizzying decade. No one except the farmers seemed to care, least of all President Coolidge (a farm boy himself), who proclaimed, "The business of government is business," and acted accordingly in countless official decisions. While net farm income remained static at about $9 billion during all the years that corporate and speculative profits were zooming off the charts, the value of farm lands decreased from $80 billion to around $55 billion, and the rate of farm bankruptcies multiplied six times over. Farmers were the first victims of the Great Depression. They fled their sterile acres in droves, at the rate of 600,000 annually during the closing years of the twenties, and crowded into the towns and cities, where, before long, they would fall under another kind of blight—namely, unemployment.[3]

Although the tinder that fueled the Depression had been gathering undetected for a decade, the spark that set it off was struck in a single week in October, 1929, when the stock market crashed. This is a chronological oversimplification, of course, because the ultimate crash itself, like the climax of a Greek tragedy, was preceded by an inexorable and prophetic chain of events extending over many weeks. But that was when the roof finally fell in. The New Economic Era, so devoutly extolled by a whole generation of statesmen, savants, and moneymen, disappeared forever in the debris. In the popular mind at least, and in the minds of some experts as well, the Great Depression dates from the Great Crash.

How did it happen?

The psychological virus that set off the orgy of speculation in the last half of the decade of the twenties has never been isolated. There is, of course, a strong susceptibility to the fast buck in the American bloodstream, and it had broken out in epidemic proportions before, as in the Crédit Mobilier scandal of the nineteenth century and the "panic" of 1907. What triggered this speculative madness in about the year 1926 is uncertain, but this time the seizure was to be of heroic proportions.

The focus of the infection was the New York Stock Exchange, and a few facts about that institution will help to set up the picture.

The volume of trading on the Exchange (the total number of shares bought and sold) rose by a series of unprecedented leaps from 451 million in 1926 to over 1.1 billion in 1929. In these same four years the daily average top price for twenty-five leading industrials rose from $186.03 to $469.49 per share. That meant a "paper profit" of about 250 percent, or a real profit of the same pleasing amount if one had bought at the low and sold at the high levels.

A large proportion of the trading, possibly a third or more, was done on margin. A broker required only about a 10 or 20 percent down payment by the customer on a block of stock and in effect loaned the customer the

The Victor record label:

Victor

For best results use
Victrola Tungs-tone Needles

Comedian with ukulele

Everything is Hotsy Totsy Now
(Irving Mills-Jimmy McHugh)
Gene Austin
Ukulele and Jazz effects by Billy ("Yuke") Carpenter
19656-A

The Gambling Scene from
The Gold Diggers of Broadway. Warner Brothers, 1929.
Ann Pennington (atop table),
and Nick Lucas (with guitar).

At left: The Golden Age of Sports. (Clockwise) Bronko Nagurski; Knute Rockne; Rockne and his boys; Paul Waner; From left to right: Walter Johnson, Doug Fairbanks, Sr., Babe Ruth; From left to right: Jimmy Foxx, Gordon Cochrane, Al Simmons. Bobby Jones; Babe Ruth and daughter, and (inset) the Babe into the wood.

William T. "Big Bill" Tilden. U.S. Champion, Men's Singles, 1920–1926, 1929. Runner-up, 1918, 1919, 1927.

Mickey Walker, the "Toy Bulldog." Welterweight Champion, 1922–1926. Middleweight Champion, 1926–1931. Fought Light Heavyweight and Heavyweight, 1931–1935. Drew in 15 with Jack Sharkey; won from King Levinsky and Paulino Uzcudun in 10 rounds each; and stopped by Max Schmeling in 8.

At left: (clockwise) Al Capone, 1929; Paul Whiteman's *Rhythm Boys*, left to right: Harry Barris, Bing Crosby, Al Rinker; Cornelius Vanderbilt, Jr., (left) and F. Scott Fitzgerald (right) judge a Beauty Contest; Charles Lindberg and his *Spirit of St. Louis*; George Gershwin; and Herbert Hoover. (Above) Governor Franklin D. Roosevelt and Al Smith. (Below) St. Valentine's Day Massacre, 1929. (At right) "Heigh-Ho, everybody, Heigh-Ho." Rudy Vallee fronting the band from the Heigh-Ho Club, midtown New York, over radio station WABC, 1928.

remaining portion of the purchase price. This easy-payment plan (it wasn't so easy if the value of your stock went down and you had to put up more margin) naturally excited the gambling instinct not only of unwary amateurs but of professional speculators as well. Buying on margin was established practice, but under the feverish scramble to "get into the market" the volume of these loans rose prodigiously, from $3.2 billion in September 1926 to $8.5 billion in September 1929. This was equal to about one-half the entire public debt of the United States Government, which stood that year at $16.9 billion. So intense was the demand for this Wall Street "call money," for which the brokers were willing to pay as much as 15 percent interest (charging their margin customers four or five points more), that many banks and corporations across the country sent their surplus funds to Wall Street to cash in on the bonanza.[4]

By the beginning of 1928 speculating in the stock market had become almost a national mania. It was not true that "everybody" was "in the market," as was commonly said at the time; it just seemed that way. Actually, only about a million persons owned stocks on margin in September 1929—chiefly the amateur and professional speculators—and about two million owned shares outright. But the mania, like the national obsession with a seven-game World Series, had made most of the citizenry vicarious speculators. Next to crime, the most engrossing news on any day's front page was likely to be what had happened on the market: Radio up another 6⅜; bears rout bulls in raid on Anaconda; Cleveland's Van Sweringen brothers reported buying heavily to extend their rail empire; an unknown newcomer, Frisbee Consolidated, startles the analysts with a meteoric rise, and so on. Nearly everyone could translate the esoteric language of the financial specialists into the patois of Main Street. Your barber or streetcar conductor was as emphatic in his expertise as your banker or lawyer. Enough people whom you knew, or knew of, were dabbling in the market to give verisimilitude to the impression that everybody was doing it: a spinster aunt, a school principal, the clerk at the post office, the taxi driver, the typist in the office pool. Everyone was prepared to believe such stories as that of the banker's chauffeur who had held on to his fifty shares of something-or-other after the banker had dumped his, and cleaned up a cool $1,500. Exploits such as these were the talk of the town—any town—the stuff of exciting folklore.

To satisfy this urge for fast riches, brokerage offices proliferated across the country, in cities, suburbs, and small towns, like recruiting stations in wartime. Most branch offices had direct wire connections with New York or other big city establishments, and bore the outward marks, at least, of respectability. Others consisted of no more than a battery of rented telephones installed in a vacant store or hotel suite, manned by a squad of confidence men who kept their packed suitcases handily by their sides. These "bucket shops" and "boiler factories," dealing in the shards of unlisted, unknown, and even nonexistent securities, differed from the starched-collar establishments mainly in that they offered their victims a faster, closer shearing.

To accommodate the timid and the skeptical, there was a sharp revival of the investment trust in the late twenties. An investment trust was a company that owned nothing but the stock of other companies. An investor with as little as ten dollars could buy a share in the trust in the expectation that he would profit proportionately as the trust reaped dividends from its portfolio. He was assured of the additional advantage over the freelance speculator that the trust's operations were guided by Wall Street experts of great wisdom; there was usually an impressive roster of bankers, corporation executives, and financiers on the letterhead.

There were fewer than a hundred investment trusts in existence in 1926; by the summer of 1929 there were more than 500, with more than $3 billion worth of shares held by an unnumbered legion of principally small investors. It was usual practice for the organizers to cut themselves and their friends in for sizeable blocks of the new stock at less than the opening price. If the trust had prominent backing, as many of them did, an almost instantaneous rise in price was assured. Thus, in January 1929 J. P. Morgan and Company, the most impeccable name in high finance, launched an investment trust called United Corporation. The partners and their friends bought in at $75 a share in advance of the public offering. When the shares went on sale the price was $92; before the first week was out they had been bid up to $100.

Inevitably, many of these trusts were tacked together on the shakiest of foundations, but it seemed not to matter. The public demand for their stock was insatiable. In many instances the value of the shares offered exceeded by two or three times the total value of the stocks and other assets on which they were based.

New investment trusts were spawned by a process of inbreeding that almost guaranteed a sterile offspring. In the summer of 1929, for example, the New York financial house of Goldman, Sachs and Company floated the Shenandoah Corporation, a third of whose assets was stock in another investment trust, the Goldman Sachs Trading Corporation. Within a few weeks, the same company announced the creation of still another and larger trust, the Blue Ridge Corporation, 80 percent of whose capital consisted of stock in the Shenandoah Corporation. Thus one investment trust could be built atop another, and the people who bought nearly $250 million worth of stock in Shenandoah and Blue Ridge owned virtually nothing that represented real wealth: no factories, no airlines, no oil wells, nothing but a ticket in a lottery. There were few laws in 1929 about how the sucker trap could be baited.

The dazzling pace of the investment splurge was not without its Cassandras. "It is perfectly well recognized by 'insiders,' " the *Journal of Commerce* observed late in 1928, "that a market of the kind that has been going on cannot last indefinitely but must undergo a readjustment." Possibly the "insiders" did know it, but few of them, even those in positions of responsibility in government, wanted the unpleasant task of saying so. Secretary of the Treasury Andrew W. Mellon was no man to spread the alarm; he and his family had profited handsomely in the great bull market. President Hoover could not bring himself to rock the boat, although he confessed years later in his pub-

STOCK PRICES SLUMP $14,000,000,000
IN NATION-WIDE STAMPEDE TO UNLOAD;
BANKERS TO SUPPORT MARKET TODAY

At left: (top) The tape runs out. Will Nigh's
production of *Born Rich* and Rollin Kirby's
cartoon "Sold Out," October 25, 1929.
(Bottom) "Black Thursday" on Wall Street,
October 24, 1929. Cartoonist O. Soglow sums it all up!

lished *Memoirs* that he realized it was sailing in perilous waters. When the Federal Reserve Board issued a cautious and ambiguous warning that speculation was approaching the danger point, Arthur Brisbane, the widely read Hearst columnist, reproached it scornfully: "If buying and selling stocks is wrong, the government should close the Stock Exchange. If not, the Federal Reserve should mind its own business."

Up and up the market soared, gaining speed and spinning off miracles as it went. Between 1928 and 1929 the value of new capital issues offered jumped from $9.9 to $11.6 billion. Between June and the end of August of the latter year there was a gain of an unprecedented 110 registered on *The New York Times* average of 25 industrials, reaching an all-time high of 449 on September 3. To better illustrate what this meant, here are the gains made by a few blue-chip issues in the eighteen months between March 3, 1928, when many thought mistakenly the peak had been reached, and September 3, 1929, when the peak actually was reached: American Can, 77 to 181⅞; American Telephone and Telegraph, 179½ to 335⅝; General Electric, 128¾ to 396¼; Montgomery Ward, 132¾ to 466½; Radio Corporation of America, 94½ to 505; United States Steel, 138⅛ to 279⅛; Electric Bond and Share, 89¾ to 203⅝.[5]

September 3, 1929, was not a crisis day except in retrospect. The market was strong with more than four million shares being traded but no important new pinnacles were reached. The next day prices began gently to soften, and a day later the *Times* index showed a drop of ten points. Roger Babson, a financial prophet of the period, proclaimed that the slide was on and that the country was headed for a depression. Few took alarm, but it was apparent that some large traders were quietly unloading, and the experts agreed that a "technical readjustment" in the market was under way. The "readjustment" continued all the rest of that month and on into the first weeks of October. It was the bears and not the bulls who now dominated the financial news. The emphasis was on selling instead of buying.

The crisis day that no one failed to recognize was Thursday, October 24, the wildest day the New York Stock Exchange had ever experienced. This was the "Black Thursday" of historic fame.

Over the preceding weekend brokers had sent out thousands of margin calls. Some of their customers responded; others did not or could not. The holdings of the delinquents were dumped on the market. Some investors, made apprehensive, decided on their own to get out while the getting out was good. There was a mad scramble of selling: six million shares on Monday, six million on Tuesday, eight million on Wednesday. Prices plunged in wild disorder. *The New York Times* index lost fifteen to twenty points each day. The tickers ran as much as two hours behind. And thousands of investors, packed shoulder to shoulder in brokerage offices all across the country, watched in helpless misery as the racing figures on the blackboard or the Trans-Lux spelled out their ruination.

Thursday was even worse. As the starting bell clanged on the Exchange floor, great 20,000-share chunks of blue chips were offered "at the market."

United States Steel, opening at 205½, skidded before noon to 193½. General
Electric went from 315 to 283, RCA from 68¾ to a dismal 44½, and so on
straight across the board. The scene on the floor and the galleries of the
Exchange was one of shoving, yelling chaos as traders and clerks swarmed
over one another like a colony of excited ants. An unheard-of total of 12.8
million shares were to change hands before the day ended.

There was a dramatic and briefly successful rescue operation that afternoon. A group of the city's largest bankers—Charles E. Mitchell of National
City, Albert H. Wiggin of Chase National, William C. Potter of Guaranty
Trust, Thomas W. Lamont of J. P. Morgan and Company, and Richard
Whitney, vice president of the Exchange—met secretly at the Morgan offices
shortly after noon to consider what could be done to halt the stampede. The
rumors that such a meeting was being held had, in themselves, a moderately
calming effect. When later the rumors of the meeting were confirmed and
Whitney was seen to stride confidently out onto the teeming floor from one
trading post to another, placing orders for sizable blocks of their stocks at
the last quoted figure, the effect was that of a cooling shower on a summer
day. The word was out that the bankers had formed a pool of unknown magnitude (estimates went as high as $240 million, but a more likely figure is $90
million) to steady the market—that is, to peg some of the perilously sinking
bellwether issues like steel, motors, radio, etc., at the asking price to prevent
their being driven down to more ruinous levels.

The stratagem worked, for that day at least. The market steadied during
the afternoon, and a few issues climbed a point or two back toward their opening prices. But it had been a disastrous day. Tens of thousands of investors all
across the country, only dimly aware of the how and why of the bankers'
rescue, had either been wiped out or been frightened into a permanent state of
panic. Not all the reassurances about the "fundamental soundness" of the economy that flowed from Washington and other seats of the mighty could restore
their fortunes or their faith. If they had not already been washed out, they
wanted to get out fast with whatever they had left. Their selling orders continued to flood the Exchange during the next two days, driving prices further
and further down.

"Black Thursday" (October 24) is something of a misnomer in pinpoint-
ing the great stock market crash. It was a day of unparalleled frenzy, but it
was the beginning rather than the climax of a five-day cycle of headlong disintegration. Equally "black" but considerably less frenzied was Tuesday,
October 29, when the speculative boom ended in a last, great convulsion.
Perhaps it was simple exhaustion, or resignation to the inevitable, that damp-
ened the spirits of the traders on the floor and the crowds of the curious who
congregataed around the intersection of Broad and Wall streets that day. As
the *Times* reported the next morninng: "The Exchange resembled Grand Central Terminal at commuting time, with orderly crowds lined up before each
post, talking in subdued tones, without any pushing or crowding. . . . Richard
Whitney, hat tilted on his head at a jaunty angle, sauntered nonchalantly across
the floor half an hour before closing and left the room with a debonair smile

at Post 2, where traders in United States Steel were waiting to dispose of shares at 175. It closed Monday at 186."

That Tuesday, too, was a day for the history books. Within the first half hour 3,250,800 shares, a good average day's business in normal times, were offered for sale. By the end of the day, 16.4 million shares had been traded— a record that would stand for over thirty years. Blocks of 10,000, 20,000, and 50,000 shares were thrown helter-skelter on the market, many at asking prices below the previous day's closing. *The New York Times* average, which had dropped 49 points on Monday, went down another 43 on Tuesday. General Electric was off 48 for the day, Westinghouse 34, AT&T 34, U. S. Steel 18.

The investment trusts, meanwhile, had sunk almost out of sight. The holdings of many of them had long since become worthless. Among the relatively few listed on the Exchange (most such shares were sold over-the-counter), Goldman Sachs Trading Corporation skidded during this dreadful day from 60 to 35, and its offspring, Blue Ridge, which had sold at a respectable 24 at the peak of the bull market in September, opened at 10 this day and plummeted almost at once to 3.

This time the bankers did not come to the rescue. They could not, because many of them were, if not actually wiped out, perilously close to it and paralyzed by fear. "In the first week the slaughter had been of the innocents," J. K. Galbraith has written. "During this second week there is evidence that it was the well-to-do and the wealthy who were being subjected to a leveling process comparable in magnitude and suddenness to that presided over a decade before by Lenin." [6] From the peak of the bull market in September to the debacle of October 29, over $32 billion worth of equities had simply vanished from the earth. It may be said that this sum represented only paper wealth or gambler's wealth; true, but it was real enough to make paupers of tens of thousands of men and women.

The great stock market boom, a real-life fantasy that for four years had bewitched scholars and statesmen as well as knaves and fools into a common illusion of easy riches, had incontestably collapsed. The New Economic Era, so proudly hailed from the days of Coolidge to the day before yesterday, was gone with the wind too. In its place stood the gaunt specter of the Great Depression.

CHAPTER 3
Crash and Aftermath
1929–1932

WHETHER THE STOCK MARKET CRASH begat the Depression or the Depression begat the crash is a question that economists still argue over. What is unarguable, however, is that in the three years following the crash the whole American economy ran steadily downhill at a quickening and disastrous pace.

The index of manufacturing production, which had hit a dramatic peak of 127 in June 1929, had slipped to 97 one year later, to 82 in 1931, and to 58 in the same month of 1932 (it pulled up to 64 before the end of the year). What these index figures meant in terms of specific industries was this: Steel production, which had been a respectable 40.6-million tons in 1930, was a feeble 13.6-million tons in 1932; automobile production, which had been valued at $1.5 billion in 1930, a peak year, was down to $608 million in 1932; retail trade, which had grossed $8.1 billion in 1930, had been cut almost in half, to $4.2 billion, by the end of 1932. Corporations reported gross profits (before taxes) in 1930 of $3.3 billion, reflecting the tail end of the great boom. The next year they reported a *loss* on operations of $800 million, and in 1932 a loss of $3 billion, almost equal to the gain of two years before.

Virtually every important industrial group suffered the same devastating sort of erosion. Each responded in the only way it knew how to respond: by cutting dividends, reducing inventories, laying off help, cutting wages and salaries, abandoning capital improvements, and going on reduced schedules. Like a snake eating its tail, the process of economic stagnation fed upon itself.

In the same three years small and marginal businesses, even the big marginal ones, toppled like dominoes. A staggering total of 86,000 business enterprises failed and closed their doors: 26,355 in 1930; 28,285 in 1931; and 31,822 in 1932. The last figure represents the largest number of business failures ever recorded in a single year, with a total of $928 million in liabilities outstanding.

Farm income went the same way: $4.1 billion in 1930, $3.2 billion in 1931, $1.9 billion in 1932—a 50 percent drop in three years. Farm debt increased in reverse ratio to the decline in farm income, and thousands of farm families were forced off the land either by foreclosure or by destitution.[1]

Naturally the cost of living went down too, not only because prices were being cut but because the people had less to spend. The Department of Labor consumer price index, based on 1929 as 100, was at 80.8 in 1932 and destined to go lower still. The Piggly-Wiggly Stores (the first self-service chain) advertised in the Washington *Post* on June 25, 1930, that they had Land O'Lakes butter at 54 cents a pound, Green Bag Coffee at 29 cents, prime rib roast at 35 cents, and country fresh eggs at 35 cents the dozen. Seventy-five dollars was about tops for a man's Hickey Freeman or Rogers Peet suit, but there were some good buys of Richman suits at $29.50. The Thom McAn chain sold passable shoes at $4 the pair. Comparable advertisements three years later showed that the food items were all five to fifteen cents lower (eggs two dozen for 41 cents), but prices for men's wear were about the same. Average family income, which had been about $2,300 in 1929, was down to $1,600 or less in 1932. Only one family in five had as much as $3,000 a year to spend.[2] On

March 15, 1930, 513 persons paid taxes on personal incomes of $1 million or more, a record that was to stand for many years. Three years later the number of acknowledged millionaires had shrunk to 20.

But most poignant and meaningful of all in this dismal record were the statistics of unemployment: 4,340,000 in 1930, 8,020,000 in 1931, 12,060,000 in 1932. The 1932 figure meant that about one in every five persons in the labor force, or about one of every seven adults in the population, was out of a job. And this did not take into account other millions who were "underemployed," that is, working only two or three days a week or one or two weeks a month. In some cases the reason was that only part-time work was to be had; in others, it was the well-intentioned one of "sharing the work," of making two jobs out of one. But to a large extent this amounted to little more than "sharing the misery," because even a full week's wages in many instances was insufficient to take care of an average-sized family. Average weekly earnings in manufacturing, for example, slid from $24.77 in 1930 to $16.21 in 1932, a drop of approximately one-third. Dividing such a paycheck between two families could do little more than to make both ineligible for charity or public welfare.

The poor of that desolate winter of 1932-33 were not merely the familiar prisoners of the local ghetto or the down-at-heel whites from working-class neighborhoods. People had been out of work because not only factories and mines and construction projects had shut down but also banks and stores and shops and architects' offices and insurance agencies and business enterprises of every kind. The man who knocked at your door at night and asked apologetically if he could "interest you" in his line of brushes or encyclopedias or Christmas cards or cemetery lots might be the same fellow who a few months or a year ago had cheerfully O.K.'d your loan at the bank or had written the editorials in your newspaper or had been the vice president of a leading real estate company. When the city put out a call for a hundred men to shovel snow at fifty cents an hour, the throng of maybe a thousand who lined up at the employment office in the cold dawn had a scattering of men in homburgs and chesterfield overcoats. On Long Island a sturdy mother of six picketed the town hall protesting her exclusion from the snow-shoveling gang. She was hired to drive a truck.

Distress cut indiscriminately across all economic and social barriers. If anything, it cut most cruelly at those who were least familiar with hard times, for pride and self-esteem bruise more easily than flesh. The middle-class or well-to-do breadwinner who is suddenly deprived of his ability to preserve his status, or even to make a living, suffers a degradation far more intense than the working-class man who has lived with insecurity most of his life. He dwells less on his hard luck than on his failure as a man; he feels cut off from the tribe.

Maybe you or your father or a cousin or neighbor were out of a job— possibly preserving a shabby gentility in a threadbare suit and polished shoes

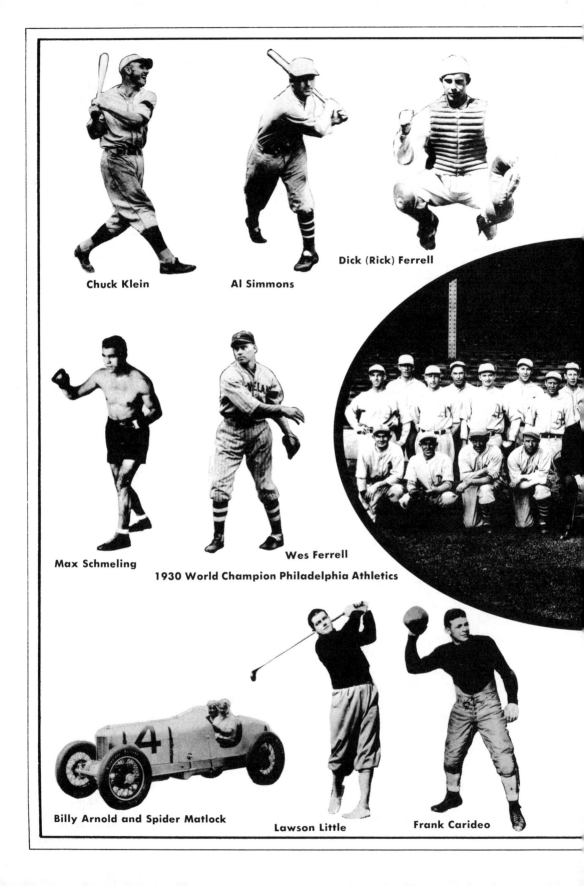

Chuck Klein

Al Simmons

Dick (Rick) Ferrell

Max Schmeling

Wes Ferrell

1930 World Champion Philadelphia Athletics

Billy Arnold and Spider Matlock

Lawson Little

Frank Carideo

Jimmy Foxx

Johnny Goodman

Ellsworth Vines, Jr.

Eleanor Holm

George Lott

Fred Perry

Gene Sarazen

Lou Gehrig

At right: (top) Mayor James J. Walker and Knute Rockne attending the December 13th, 1930, Army-Navy game. Army won 6–0. (Middle) Jockey Earle Sande and 1930 Triple Crown Winner *Gallant Fox*. (Bottom) Clarence "Buster" Crabbe after breaking the Olympic record in the 400-meter free style, Los Angeles, 1932.

"I joined the cops purely for the adventure of the thing."

that let the wet through; leaving the house with a contrived gaiety each morning to try again for a job and to hide out most of the day in the public library; avoiding or being avoided by friends and fellow workers who have managed to hold on and might assume that you want to make a "touch"; sneaking like a culprit into a pawnshop to hock a watch, a wedding ring, or the family radio; or experiencing the ultimate humiliation of the registered letter with the eviction notice (the postman knows what it is; he's delivered dozens like it).

The jobless were the most conspicuous feature of that dismal social landscape, particularly in the cities. They clustered about poolrooms and taverns, sat in the parks when the weather was fair, stood in empty doorways to get out of the wind, panhandled for nickels and dimes on the streets, haunted their union halls or the clubrooms of the Moose and the Elks and the Redmen, sat for hours over a nickel cup of coffee in dingy restaurants, staring out the window. (A passable cup of tomato soup could be made by ordering an extra cup of hot water for your coffee and dousing it with ketchup from the bottle on the table. If there was a free tray of crackers on the counter, you had a meal that would do you for a day.)

Every morning a shuffling, tattered, dispirited group of fifty, maybe as many as a couple of hundred, congregated around the hiring halls, the docks and railroad yards, the construction sites, or the public employment offices, wherever casual labor might be needed. When the word went out in Pittsburgh or Detroit or Los Angeles that one of the big factories was hiring, the cops got to the gates ahead of the applicants to put down the rioting as hundreds of desperate men fought and shoved to be numbered among the two or three score of lucky ones at the head of the line. The unlucky ones gathered in tight knots around speakers who stood on park benches or soapboxes and harangued them about the failure of the capitalist system, the greed of the bosses and bankers in their big houses uptown, the need for common men to unite to claim their rights. "There's no unemployment in the Soviet Union, comrades," the speakers said. "And there wouldn't be any here either if we workers owned the means of production."

It was not only in the cities that the jobless congregated. Like lemmings forced to seek new feeding grounds, they dispersed in a great, aimless migration across the countryside. Singly, in pairs, in groups of a dozen or more they drifted from town to town, from state to state, with no hope beyond something to eat each day or occasionally to pick up a dollar or two pushing a wheelbarrow, harvesting wheat, washing dishes or at whatever came to hand. They were a forlorn and familiar sight along almost every highway, lugging old suitcases or bundles of duffel, their thumbs upraised in the universal supplication of the hitchhiker, watching dejectedly as most motorists (frightened by recurrent tales of hijackings and robberies) passed them by. In the fall of 1932 these transient jobless were estimated at about a million of whom almost a fourth were under twenty-one and many thousands were women and girls.

But more of them took to the rails than to the slower and often inhospitable highways. Every passing freight had its complement of deadheads watching the countryside whirl by from the open door of a boxcar or crouching in peril under the sloping end of a gondola. (Only youngsters who didn't know better rode the catwalk, where a hand or a face could be cut to ribbons by the wind and cinders or crawled into the ice chute of a reefer [refrigerator car] and risked freezing to death.) Near every large freight yard there were hobo jungles where these weary vagrants congregated to exchange intelligence about travel conditions up and down the line, and to test the prospects for scrounging a meal, a bed, or a few days' work in a neighboring town. The railroads got to be rather tolerant toward the deadheads, probably because there was nothing they could do to stem the multitudes of free riders wherever the freights ran. But the local police often took a harsher attitude when the colonies of drifters got too large or too settled. The solution was not to jail them but to apply enough terror to drive them on.

Many in this population of floaters were veterans of the Bonus Expeditionary Force (BEF)—the ragged army of some 25,000 World War veterans who had converged on Washington in June 1932 to try to pressure Congress into passing legislation to pay them a cash bonus for their military service. Their demands were not granted; instead they were driven from their burlap and tar-paper encampment within sight of the Capitol dome, by regular Army troops acting on direct orders of President Hoover (it was perhaps the worst political blunder of this hapless man's career). Now hundreds of these BEF men, penniless, jobless, embittered in some cases to the point of violence, joined the army of drifters, enjoying a certain melancholy status among them as "old pros" who had at least flung a fist in the face of the oppressor.

And on the highways leading west from the Plains States, which had been parched into lifeless windrows by three summers of drought, the migrant horde was swollen by thousands of destitute and dispossessed farm families. These were the Okies, countless replicas of Ma and Pa and Tom Joad, whose flight to the Promised Land of California was later to be chronicled by John Steinbeck in *The Grapes of Wrath*. In their jalopies and trucks and mule-drawn wagons, piled high with children and bedsteads and cooking pots and often a crate of chickens or a live pig for rations, they moved in a dispirited human tide along the main routes west, settled briefly in ramshackle "Hoovervilles" along the roadsides, and suffered harassment and indignites at the hands of sheriffs' deputies and police who wanted no alien Okies adding to their woes.

The government at Washington was neither blind nor indifferent to this mass suffering. Its concern was vitiated, however, because it did not comprehend the nature of the disaster that had struck. Herbert Clark Hoover, the President, was a stolid, humorless man, as deeply imbued with Quaker morality as with faith in the economic philosophy of laissez-faire. At his right hand in the Cabinet sat Andrew W. Mellon, one of the world's richest men, who had been Secretary of the Treasury continuously since the Presidency of Harding in 1921. Neither Hoover nor Mellon was without compassion. Hoover had first distinguished himself in organizing an international relief program to abate hunger in Europe in the wake of the World War, but his

At right: (top) A show of strength. Bonus Marchers gather in Union Square, New York City, before their start for Washington, D.C. (Insets) From left to right: Hunger Marchers give the clenched fist in their demands for Winter Relief; The Battle of Anacostia Flats: Battling, Bonus-seeking veterans push the line forward and then, in bitter hand-to-hand fighting, succumb to Washington, D.C., police and eviction from "Tent City."

Bonus
Marchers

and Mellon's response to the crisis was postulated on two inviolable articles of faith.

Their first article of faith was that periodic depressions are an inevitable by-product of the capitalist system and have to be borne with patience and fortitude until corrected by the "natural laws" of economics. It was permissible to apply a bit of grease to the squeaky axle now and then, but not to tamper with the design of the wagon or its motive power.

Their second article of faith was that unemployment and its accompanying distress, like an outbreak of measles or the unpredictable flooding of a river, are a local problem to be met by local authorities. While the central government might properly intervene to pump money into a shaky banking system or to subsidize a faltering industry with protective tariffs, the buying of food for a hungry family would be an intolerable descent into socialism. The answer to human destitution was charity.

Thus restricted, the Administration had only a few options open to it with which to combat the deepening crisis. In the main these were directed at patching up the central economic structure on the conventional theory that restoratives applied at the top would ulimately trickle down to the wage earners and consumers at the bottom.

As Washington saw it, the most critical area of need was the nation's banks, which were toppling at an alarming rate, tying up not only personal assets but funds and credits of business firms as well. Loath to have the Federal bureaucracy seem to dictate to the bankers how they should run their business, President Hoover first tried for voluntary cooperation among them. In the fall of 1931 he set up the National Credit Corporation and invited the bankers to pool their resources so that the big strong banks could help the small weak ones when these got in trouble. It didn't work. Banks that still had a safe measure of solvency were unwilling to stretch their luck by taking on the burdens of the less solvent.

So it fell to the government to assume the risk, partially at least. In January 1932 Congress created the Reconstruction Finance Corporation, capitalized it at $2 billion, and set it up in business as a "banker's bank." Its earlier operations often had some of the excitement of a fire brigade. In February 1933, it chartered a plane to fly $24 million in currency from New York to New Orleans to enable the Hibernia Bank and Trust Company, one of the city's largest, to open for business on a Monday morning. A decision on whether or not the agency would bail out a foundering bank was often awaited in a community with the cliff-hanging suspense of a movie serial. The RFC proved to be an effective antidote in many individual bank crises. The rate of failures in its first year of operation was cut by almost a third (from 2,298 in 1931 to 1,404), and 280 banks that had closed during 1932 were enabled with RFC assistance to reopen. Before the year was out, RFC capitalization was increased to $3 billion, and a number of railroads, insurance companies, and other large corporate enterprises were admitted to shelter under its protective wing.

Other efforts made by the Hoover Administration to prime the economic pump included reductions in the discount rate by the Federal Reserve Board to make bank credit more available; a stepped-up program of purchases by the Federal Farm Board in a largely futile effort to stabilize the prices of wheat and cotton; enactment of a stiff tariff act that resulted unexpectedly in almost obliterating what was left of the nation's export market; and increased appropriations for such traditional public works as post offices, bridges, and river and harbor developments. These programs were all in accord with the orthodox 'trickle down" theory of economic recovery. Whatever value they had, it would be months, even a year or more, before their benefits would percolate down to where the starved roots of the problem lay: the critical and rapidly worsening shortage of purchasing power in the hands of the consuming public.

Meanwhile the President remained adamant in his opposition to anything resembling a "dole" for the jobless and the destitute. He regarded this not only as economically unsound but as morally offensive, sapping the initiative and independence of the working class, whom he suspected of being all too ready to become wards of the government if given the chance. The "rugged individualism" of the American character, Mr. Hoover believed, was too cherished an asset to be contaminated by exposure to such "Socialistic schemes" as the "dole" (a form of unemployment relief adopted by the British).

"We cannot squander ourselves into prosperity," he told a press conference in January 1932. "The people will, of course, provide against distress, but the purpose of the national government must be to restore employment by economic recovery. The reduction of government expenditures and the stability of government finance is the most fundamental step toward this end."

His comment was directed particularly at legislation then pending in Congress to appropriate $500 million for grants to the states for relief and public welfare. The bill failed, but later that year the RFC was authorized to make limited loans to the states for the same purpose, a circumvention of the "dole" system to which the President reluctantly agreed.

Mr. Hoover's only solution for meeting human needs was the old-fashioned one of charity, "neighbor to neighbor, community to community," as he put it. To stimulate the public's charitable impulses, he created late in 1930 the President's Emergency Committee for Employment ("unemployment" was eschewed as a bad word in this context), with Col. Arthur Wood, a prominent industrialist, as its head. The committee was not to do anything directly about employment or unemployment; its sole function was to promote through propaganda and publicity interest in local community chests and similar campaigns and to stimulate local authorities to extra efforts in behalf of the jobless and the destitute.

Some states, and many of the smaller cities and counties, had no organized welfare departments in 1932. Often the poorhouse was the only institution maintained for the poor at public expense. Therefore the job of ministering to the destitute jobless fell as an ever growing burden on the churches and private social agencies. Where public funds were appropriated, they were

(Above) The 1931 Le Baron-bodied Marmon V-16. Inspired by Ettore Bugatti's 16-cylinder aircraft engines, Howard Marmon produced a car that held the American Class A 24-hour speed record of 76.43 m.p.h. until beaten by a 1953 Chrysler averaging 89.89 m.p.h! (At left) One of the high points of Lincoln history. The first V-12, Model KB, for 1932. Note the outside horns.

NEW 8

THE new Eight embodies our ideas of a truly modern motor car . . . . styled for the modern trend, engineered for modern conditions and priced to meet 1932 standards of value.

Joseph L. Graham
Robert C. Graham
Ray A. Graham

A TRULY MODERN MOTOR CAR

1 DEEP BANJO FRAME . . . An entirely new and stronger type of frame, lowering both frame and body without affecting road clearance, increasing riding ease and reducing frame-weave and side-sway.

2 OUTBOARD SPRINGS . . . An equally new type of spring mounting, giving a spring spread 8 inches wider in front and 6 inches wider at rear—further reducing side-sway and increasing stability.

3 SILENCED CHASSIS AND BODY . . . New quietness, obtained by rubber mounting of engine and springs, new resonator type exhaust silencer, carburetor silencer, and the use of rubber dough and sound-deadening material throughout the body.

4 OIL TEMPERATURE CONTROL . . . Engine designed to automatically control oil temperature within the limits necessary for maximum life and efficiency.

5 DASH REGULATED SHOCK ABSORBERS . . . A new convenient button on the dash controls shock absorber action, stiffening or softening ride to suit any load or road.

6 DASH CONTROLLED FREE WHEELING . . . A new improved Free Wheeling control button, making possible instant shifting from Free Wheeling to conventional drive or back again. Use of the reverse gear does not affect Free Wheeling.

7 SUPER-HYDRAULIC BRAKES WITH NEW CENTRIFUSE DRUMS . . . Rigid shoe, self-equalizing brakes with fixed diameter ribbed steel drums, having centrifugally cast braking surfaces, provide much longer lining life and increased efficiency.

8 SYNCHRO-SILENT GEAR SHIFT . . . A new transmission, in which both gear shifting and driving are silent in second and third speeds. This silence is obtained by the use of gear synchronizers and helical gears.

SPECIAL "BLUE STREAK" ENGINE WITH ALUMINUM HEAD

90 HORSEPOWER   123 IN. WHEELBASE

$995
AND UP AT FACTORY

GRAHAM

Warm...
Dependable
Coats...for
Small
Budgets
•

$9.98 $7.98

1931 Fleetster, Model 17, Type 1 Demonstrator.

Bob Hall's 1932 Wasp-powered, gull-wing "Bulldog."

1933 single-engined, four-passenger Lockheed Vega.

The hairiest, most romantic, and most dangerous racing plane of all time. Jimmy Doolittle and the Gee Bee R-1. 1932 Thompson Trophy Winner at 252.686 m.p.h.

Marlene Dietrich in Josef von Sternberg's *Dishonored*, 1931.

The first Gee Bee (Granville Brothers Aircraft).
Designer Bob Hall and the Model Z in flight.

BEGINNING TO FLY

The Book of Model Airplanes 🖉 🖉

By Merrill Hamburg
Secretary of the Airplane Model League of America

'This book will be not only
a service to every model-
builder, but a worth-while
spur to the development of
aviation in this country.'
— *Commander Byrd.*

With an Introduction by Richard E. Byrd

At left: Poster for the 1932 National Air Races, Cleveland, Ohio. (Inset) Wiley Post and Harold Gatty in the *Winnie Mae* over Lower Manhattan at the start of their record-breaking 'round-the-world flight. (Top) The Gee Bee again. Jimmy Doolittle taking the flag in the R-1 to win the 1932 Thompson Trophy Race. (Middle) 'Round the world in 8½ days! Post and Gatty touch down in New York after 15,474 miles and a total elapsed time of 8 days, 15 hours, and 50 minutes. (Bottom) An early thirties United Air Lines departure. The Ford Tri-motor carried 12 passengers and cruised at 125 miles per hour.

soon exhausted, and intensive drives were organized to extract contributions from the public. In November 1932 a Citizens Committee in New York sought $15 million in private contributions to be matched by like sums from the state government and the RFC to care for an estimated 150,000 to 200,000 families in distress. In many cities where the fund drives failed to reach their quotas, mayors turned to the banks for loans but were often rejected because the city's credit was exhausted. Various barter schemes were devised under municipal auspices: The unemployed might cut wood or shovel snow and be paid in script exchangeable for food. Schoolteachers and other public employees were assessed a part of their pay each month—pay that was already depleted in most instances by successive salary cuts—to finance public soup kitchens. Chicago, virtually paralyzed by a taxpayers' strike ($300 million in uncollected city taxes were outstanding in November 1932) was even paying its police and other employees in scrip based on the hope of future tax collections. Governor Gifford Pinchot of Pennsylvania urged the citizens of his state to contribute their old clothing to the unemployed, and a city official in Oklahoma proposed a nationwide program whereby restaurants would put their food scraps into covered metal buckets for distribution to the "deserving poor." Public relief payments, where they existed at all, were on a pitiably frugal scale. The standard for a family of four in New York in the winter of 1931–32 was $15 a week, probably the highest in the nation. It was $5.50 a week in Philadelphia, and even less in some other cities.

"It is becoming increasingly true," a spokesman for a national Jewish social research agency told a Senate committee in Washington that winter, "that the efforts of local relief agencies do not go much beyond the objective of seeing that nobody will starve." He added that deaths from undernourishment were being reported from many cities.

The President and his spokesmen tried desperately to coax good times back by incantation. It was firmly believed in most important quarters in Washington and Wall Street that if confidence could be restored the banks would lend money again, factories would open their doors, businessmen would buy and sell, workers would be hired, and life would return to normal. The word "confidence" acquired an almost mystical quality, like the key to a magic formula. It was entreated and evoked and simulated by every imaginable device.

"The economy is fundamentally sound," the President kept reminding the people. Time and again he returned to the theme (as expressed in a broadcast speech in October 1931) that the Depression was just "a passing incident in our national life." Repeatedly he predicted an upturn by a given date or month, only to have his prediction turn sour. Secretary Mellon was an equally indefatigable and equally erring prophet: "I see nothing in the present situation that is either menacing or warrants pessimism," he said as the Depression dragged toward the end of its second year. Myron C. Taylor, board chairman of the U.S. Steel Corporation, told a gathering in New York in October 1932 that the general industrial situation was "more promising" than at any time in the previous two years, and that the recovery is "definite and progressive."

Many private organizations pounded away at the same theme. The National Association of Manufacturers, for example, felt that if people stopped talking about hard times the hard times would go away. Late in 1932 it sponsored a weekly radio program called "America at Work," which featured local business enterprises around the country that were going great guns—depression or no depression. "Many of the bad effects of the so-called depression," a NAM spokesman explained, "are based on calamity howling." The newspapers, too, did their bit in the propaganda war. Scores of them used unsold advertising space to plug such currently popular slogans as, "Spend $20 and start the return of prosperity." The Raleigh *News and Observer* urged explicitly: "Let's buy something! It makes no difference what—a hat or a suit of clothes, a new automobile or furniture for your home or office. What you buy people will have to make. It will put them back to work, and they will have money to spend for what you have to sell."

But no amount of exhortation and chins-up propaganda could conceal the grim fact that the Depression was deepening, that millions of people were suffering acute privatation, and that a spirit of anger and disillusionment was sweeping across the land.

President Hoover and his men had been trapped by the failure of an out-dated philosophy. The capitalist system as they had known it was incapable of adjusting automatically to the mountainous stresses that had piled on it since 1929. The adjustment required by the events of 1929–32 was unlike the cyclical readjustments of the past, the postwar depression of 1920–21, or the money panic of 1907. The "natural laws" of the marketplace so precisely defined by the classical economists were inoperable—if, in fact, they had ever had more than superficial validity. The dawning of this bitter truth in mid-1932, as the election campaign got under way, left the President saddened, dismayed, and helpless.

CHAPTER 4

Coup d'Etat 1932

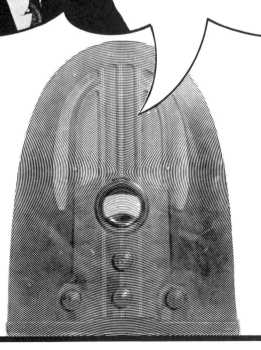

I pledge you—I pledge myself to a new deal for the American people. Let us all here assembled constitute ourselves prophets of a new order of competence and of courage. This is more than a political campaign; it is a call to arms. Give me your help, not to win votes alone, but to win in this crusade to restore America to its own people.

— Acceptance Speech
Democratic National
Convention
Chicago. July 2, 1932

THE REPUBLICAN CONVENTION, held in Chicago the second week of June 1932, renominated President Hoover and Vice President Charles Curtis, as it was expected to do. Inevitably, it was a lethargic affair and contained little of drama and no surprises.

Among the Old Guard stalwarts who were in control, confidence ran high that, in spite of the Depression, their administration would be returned to power. The Democrats, having been soundly trounced in 1928, were apparently still badly split and demoralized. Mr. Hoover believed that a couple of major speeches was about all the effort he personally would have to invest to assure victory. The platform adopted at the convention was conveniently vague and platitudinous. It promised an early deliverance from economic misfortune and straddled the red-hot prohibition issue in a manner designed to evoke the least displeasure from both the wets and the drys.

The litter produced by the Republican convention was still on the floor of the Chicago Stadium, and the beds were still warm at the Congress and other hotels, when the vanguard of the Democratic hosts piled into the city to start the wheels of their convention, scheduled to begin a week after the departure of the Republicans. In place of lethargy and decorum they brought with them, as was their immemorial custom, exuberance, intrigue, and a satchel-full of knives. For this was to be one of the rowdiest and bitterest conventions in Democratic history and a landmark in the nation's history as well.

It is hardly needful at this late date to retrace the aristocratic lineage and early career of Franklin Delano Roosevelt, who was to be the hero of the piece. He had been a liberal state senator representing his native Dutchess County at Albany, an Assistant Secretary of the Navy under President Wilson, and a makeweight candidate for the Vice Presidency on the foredoomed Democratic ticket of 1920 before he was crippled by poliomyelitis the following year. With his intense vitality and ambition, he reemerged on the public scene in 1928 to nominate New York Governor Alfred E. Smith for the Presidency at the Democratic convention in Houston; and, somewhat to his own surprise and contrary to the wishes of his wife, he ran for and was elected Governor that same year in Smith's stead. He was reelected two years later by a record plurality of more than 700,000 votes.

Though his record had not endowed him with a commanding public image by 1932 (Walter Lippmann described him after the convention that year as "an amiable . . . pleasant man who, without any important qualifications for the office, would very much like to be President"), Roosevelt himself and at least two other important figures sensed his Presidential potentialities.

One of these was Louis MacHenry Howe, a disheveled, asthmatic, and incurably dour little gnome of a man, a former newspaper reporter who had become Governor Roosevelt's personal aid and confidante. The other was James Aloysius Farley, genial, outgoing, big-framed and tough as a draft horse, who had risen through the ranks of New York State politics to manage the Governor's 1930 re-election campaign and to become Democratic state chairman. What these two dissimilar men had in common besides an unquenchable faith in the destiny of FDR was a deep and intuitive grasp of the mystique of partisan politics. Howe, with a subtle insight into the mass mind, was the strategist; Farley, shrewd, resourceful, and disarmingly gracious, the tactician. On the day after the 1930 victory these two combined their talents for an ambitious venture: the making of a President.

Sitting amid the day-after shambles of their headquarters in the Biltmore Hotel with a cluster of reporters in the waiting room demanding some sort of postelection news, Farley and Howe put their heads together to concoct a statement. "It should be," Farley has recalled, "something more than the usual routine patter of words that the press and public had been led to expect on such occasions, because it was intended for consumption not only by the voters of New York but by the voters in every state in the Union." The key paragraph of the statement, issued in Farley's name as state chairman, read as follows:

I fully expect that the call will come to Governor Roosevelt when the first presidential primary is held, which will be late next year. The Democrats in the nation naturally want as their candidate for President the man who has shown himself capable of carrying the most important state in the country by a record-breaking majority. I do not see how Mr. Roosevelt can escape becoming the next Presidential nominee of his party, even if no one should raise a finger to bring it about.

Roosevelt, who had not previously been consulted in the matter, happily gave his assent to the statement when it was read to him over long-distance telephone in Albany. "Whatever you say, Jim, is all right with me." A couple of weeks later, writing to commend Farley for the manner in which he had conducted the gubernatorial campaign, Roosevelt took an appreciative look into the glowing future. "You have done a wonderful piece of work," he wrote. "It is not merely a fine record but a great opportunity for us to consolidate the gains. When I think of the difficulties of former State Chairmen with former Governors and vice versa, I have an idea that you and I make a combination which has not existed since the days of Cleveland Lamont." [1]

If Roosevelt, Farley, Howe, and Company sensed so promptly the presitial potentialities of the New York Governor, the message was slow in getting through to some other important quarters. Not the least of these was Alfred Emanuel Smith, the colorful, gravel-voiced, and widely popular Happy Warrior who had been smothered under an avalanche of "dry" and anti-Catholic votes in the 1928 Hoover landslide. As titular leader of his party, Smith had a valid prior claim to consideration for a second try. The option undoubtedly would be a good deal more valuable in 1932 than it had been in 1928, for the Depression was beginning to rub the shine off the image of the Great Engineer in the White House. The "wet" forces were gathering strength in every part of the country for modification or repeal of Prohibition, and the conscience of the nation had been pricked, to some extent at least, by the religious bigotry that had cost Smith votes in many states.

Moreover, Smith regarded his somewhat younger successor in the governorship as a protégé, and an ungrateful one at that. He had been irked by Roosevelt's failure to consult with him on political and legislative affairs, and now the Governor's open flirtation with the Presidency, without so much as a by-your-leave to the party leader, was a piece of intolerable effrontery. Smith, now making a second career in New York real estate, snorted for all to hear that the Albany upstart might have a surprise in store for him before the nominating convention came around. Among a number of party stalwarts sharing this view were the sachems of Tammany Hall and the chairman of the Democratic National Committee, John J. Raskob. To the old-line party professionals Roosevelt seemed an undependable sort.

Undismayed, Farley and Howe set to work to build a campaign and a campaign organization for Roosevelt. They compiled lists of Democratic officials and party leaders in every state and, as an opening gambit, sent each a copy of a restrained but subtly effective little pamphlet telling how the party had organized for victory in New York in 1930. From this start a lively and copious correspondence was developed, each letter bearing Farley's distinctive signature in green ink. In the spring of 1931 a modest campaign fund was accumulated from half a dozen prominent donors, such as former Ambassador Henry Morgenthau, Sr., Herbert Lehman, a wealthy banker, and attorney Frank C. Walker, and a small headquarters was set up in a suite of offices on Madison Avenue. Roosevelt was already fairly well known among party leaders throughout the country because of his service in the Navy Department and on the Democratic ticket in 1920. Farley and Howe used every opportunity to impress upon these leaders his accomplishments as governor and his larger potentialities in statecraft.

The letters brought encouragement, but more direct assurances were needed on what the political climate was really like out through the country. Accordingly, on a hot Sunday in mid-June 1931, Farley, bearing a Rand McNally atlas, a double handful of railroad timetables, and state lists of Democratic party functionaries, journeyed up to Albany for a conference with Roosevelt. Farley, an enthusiastic member of the Benevolent and Protective Order of Elks, had planned to attend the annual Grand Lodge convention in Seattle early in July. He now proposed to expand this pleasure jaunt by taking firsthand political soundings in a number of key states west of the Ohio River. The Governor and Howe fell in wholeheartedly with his plan, and for two hours the three of them sat in shirtsleeves around a table in a wing of the executive mansion working out schedules and contacts.

Farley's odyssey as a "political drummer" took him into eighteen states in nineteen days, with only a stopover for the Elks' fiesta in Seattle. From Indiana to Illinois to Minnesota to South Dakota to Montana to the three states of the Pacific Coast and eastward again by way of Colorado and the Plains States, he lived in sleepers by night and met and talked with politicians by day. His approach was adroit. "I never talked to individuals about the presidential nomination unless I was certain of the other fellow's position," he explained later. "Usually I sparred around a bit by suggesting we had three outstanding potential candidates in New York State—Alfred E. Smith, Owen D. Young, and Franklin D. Roosevelt—and that it was my purpose to find out what the public thought of them as possible standard bearers."

If his listener seemed committed to someone other than Roosevelt, Farley did not risk offending him by a "hard sell." But if he was receptive or merely neutral, the talents of one of history's most gifted political evangels were turned on like a gentle benediction to draw him into the fold of true believers.

Bill Howes, national committeeman for South Dakota, got "the treatment" during a lunch at Aberdeen. "Farley, I'm damn tired of backing losers," he said. "In my opinion Roosevelt can sweep the country and I'm going to support him." He thumped his big fist on the table for emphasis, and Farley beamed.[2]

And so it went with scores of leaders with whom the big genial New Yorker talked on his journey. (He recorded in his memory the names and features of approximately 1,100 large- and small-bore politicians he met on this trip so that he could call them by name when he saw them again a year or five years later.) The reports he sent back to Roosevelt and Howe by special-delivery mail each night glowed with optimism. Midway on his journey back from Seattle, he wrote: "There is apparently an almost unanimous sentiment for you in every one of these states and the organization in every instance is for you wholeheartedly." At another point he wrote that he had encountered some scattered sentiment for Smith or Newton D. Baker, Wilson's Secretary of War, or for Governor Albert Ritchie of Maryland. But, he added, "it doesn't appear at the moment they are getting anywhere." A hopeful portent, he noted on another occasion, was the number of prospective candidates for governor and senator who said it would be a boon to have Roosevelt heading their ticket in 1932. And in a final burst of optimism he wrote: "The sentiment [for FDR] is so general that, to be frank with you Governor, it is almost unbeliev- able. . . . My statement upon reaching New York will be so enthusiastic that those who read it will think I am a fit candidate for the insane asylum."

Roosevelt's campaign for the nomination was now on in earnest and gather- ing momentum as it rolled. Although the nominating convention was a year off, he and his backers decided against that stratagem of coyness usual in the circumstances and made their intentions clear. Al Smith fumed, and Chairman Raskob and his first deputy on the national committee, Jouett Shouse, set quietly about throwing up some roadblocks to the Governor's ambitions. They favored Smith and encouraged Democratic governors to sew up their state delegations as favorite sons to keep them out of Roosevelt's grasp. Meanwhile Farley redoubled his missionary endeavors around the country, nailing down hard commitments of support wherever he could, and building his fences with such important Democratic leaders in Congress as Cordell Hull, Burton K. Wheeler, and Homer Cummings. Roosevelt, for his part, was attracting national attention by his advocacy of more strenuous and direct efforts by government to meet the worsening effects of the Depression, giving the Hoover Administration a hard time in the process.

Consequently, the formal announcement of his candidacy on January 21, 1932, surprised no one. Al Smith's official entry into the race two weeks later quickened the pulse of the nation, for clearly a scrap of magnificent proportion was shaping up.

It was stiflingly hot in Chicago in the last week of June 1932. Such breezes as there were blew from the scorched plains of the west, bearing clouds of gritty dust that clung to sweat-drenched bodies. The dust filtered through closed windows onto desks and into bedclothes and bureau drawers, and drifted in eddies along the trash-strewn streets of The Loop. Chicago was spiritually stifling too that summer. Its enormous, gusty vitality, of which Carl Sandburg and other poets had sung, was shrouded in hopelessness and despair. Acres of lifeless factories and rail yards, unswept streets and parks overgrown with weeds, rows of vacant stores with blackened windows, and the ragged, apathetic jobless—50,000 or more—in the flophouses along West Madison Street and in the ghettos of Halstead and South State, gave to the city an overwhelming sense of desolation. Chicago, that summer, was Skid Row, U.S.A., the symbol of the nation's debauch. Only the inkeepers and the bootleggers were glad to see the Democrats come to town.

Farley arrived in Chicago early in the week preceding the opening of the convention, which was scheduled for Monday, June 27. With a small complement of aides (Howe remained for the time being in New York), he set up headquarters in the choice suite on the top floor of the Congress Hotel, overlooking Lake Michigan. In the corridor facing the elevator bank he mounted a large splashily colored map of the United States showing the states claimed for Roosevelt. It was an impressive instrument of psychological warfare, for it added up to 551 first-ballot votes. This was short of a winning total, of course, but it was far more than any other real or probable candidate could claim this far in advance.

All told, there were to be nine claimants to the nomination at this convention. The ones that counted, in addition to FDR, were Smith, with an equally elaborate suite on the floor below, Governor Ritchie, and, most enigmatically of all, crusty old John Nance Garner of Texas, Speaker of the House of Representatives. He had not only the large and solid Texas delegation behind him, but, with the backing of William Randolph Hearst, the powerful California delegation as well.

Hearst's principal aim in backing Garner was to block Smith and thus to satisfy a grudge that had rankled in the millionaire publisher's heart for a decade. In 1922, when Smith first ran for Governor, he refused to have Hearst, then a New Yorker, on the ticket with him as a candidate for United States Senator. This demolished Hearst's soaring political ambitions for good, and he moved west. Now, to reinforce his prospect for revenge, he put William Gibbs McAdoo, Wilson's Secretary of the Treasury, in charge of the 1932 California delegation. McAdoo also had a score to settle with Smith: The two had fought one another to a standoff for the presidential nomination at the memorable Madison Square Garden convention of 1924. Thus the Garner bloc of 90 delegate votes, double-brassbound against Smith, was a valuable prize for any candidate who could capture it.

In the preliminary maneuvers of the convention Jim Farley played most of his cards well. He managed to get a majority of Roosevelt men on two key committees, platform and credentials, and to slyly outwit his foes by sewing up the permanent chairmanship of the convention—a critically important post analagous to that of a "bought" referee in the prize ring—for Senator Tom Walsh of Montana, another firm Roosevelt partisan. But he nearly blew his chances by trying to force a change in the traditional voting procedure of the convention.

For half a century Democratic conventions had been bound by a rule requiring a two-thirds majority for nomination. This device, so cherished by Southern conservatives, literally put a veto power in the hands of a minority of the delegates. At a caucus of some sixty Roosevelt leaders on the Thursday preceding the convention opening in Chicago, a resolution was adopted calling for abrogation of the two-thirds rule. The motion was offered and pushed through by a raucous and flamboyant newcomer to national politics, Huey Pierce Long, the freshman Senator from Louisiana and no darling of the conservatives of Dixie. Such a rules change, if forced upon the convention, would almost certainly assure a first-ballot victory for Roosevelt, but with equal certainty it would draw torrents of anger from the camps of the other candidates.

Farley claims that the motion was adopted over his protest, and that as chairman of the caucus he allowed the proceedings to get out of hand.[3] While he favored a simple instead of a two-thirds majority rule, he felt that it was tactically unwise to attempt so revolutionary a change at the time. However, he went along with it after checking the question out with the Governor by telephone. On Saturday he issued a statement: "This thing must be done, should have been done before, and will be done now," which hardly conveyed any reluctance he may have felt.

As predicted, a storm of denunciations and charges of bad faith erupted. They reverberated through the Chicago hotel lobbies and on the front pages of the nation's press. A spokesman for Al Smith decried the move as "a gambler's trick." Testy old Carter Glass of Virginia said, "I cannot support any candidate who takes a short cut to the nomination that way." The reserved and dignified Newton D. Baker, whom many regarded as a promising dark horse in the event of a deadlock, protested: "Sensitive men will find it difficult to defend a candidate who starts out with a moral flaw in his title." Indeed, so vehement and widespread was the reaction, that the Roosevelt managers suddenly found elements of their coalition coming unstuck. Arthur Krock predicted in *The New York Times* that Roosevelt's chances of capturing the nomination, which only days before had seemed so bright, now hinged precariously on the outcome of this single issue.

Farley and Howe (he had arrived in Chicago on Sunday) were badly shaken. They took counsel with the other Roosevelt leaders at headquarters and concluded that they were in a hopeless box and that the only way out was to back out. Accordingly they advised the Governor to this effect. On Monday he issued a public statement in Albany saying that in the interest of preserving harmony within the party, "I am asking my friends at Chicago to cease their activities to secure the adoption of the majority rule at this time."

This renunciation was met with shouts of glee among the anti-Roosevelt forces, who felt their prospects had been enhanced by the front runner's humiliation. The Baker and Ritchie stock in particular seemed to have gained buoyancy from the event. Farley, however, yielding none of his imperturbability and optimism in public, continued to predict a first-ballot victory for his man. He was a good deal less certain about it, though, than he had been. His candidate's prospects had been severely damaged.

Monday was the official opening day of the convention, and the influx of delegates, alternates, hangers-on, and plain spectators reached a high-water mark. "Cowboys from the Texas plains, elderly statesmen from the South and heavy-jowled Tammany braves swarmed into Chicago in holiday mood today," F. Raymond Daniell reported in *The New York Times*. "They crowded the furniture out of the lobbies of the big hotels, swamped the elevators and the cracked ice service at the Congress Hotel and provided more amusement for Chicago since this city put [former Mayor] 'Big Bill' Thompson on the shelf."

From Al Capone's red-hot Cotton Club on the South Side to the more sophisticated Dill Pickle in an alley off Rush Street uptown, to the swank dining room of the Palmer House in The Loop, to the myriad big and little speakeasies and girly joints sequestered in the dimly lit catacombs of downtown Chicago, the entrepreneurs of the city prepared for a busy and prosperous week. Five floors of the elegant Drake Hotel on the Gold Coast were blocked out for the special trainload of Tammany chieftains and braves who arrived from New York with seventy cases of bottled goods labeled "ginger ale." A whooping delegation of Oklahoma cowboys supporting the Presidential aspirations of their shaggy and profane Governor, "Alfalfa Bill" Murray, dominated the cavernous Stevens Hotel as though it were their home corral. A forty-piece girl band attached to the Oklahoma entourage and costumed in hip-high kilts and scarlet jackets proclaimed reveille for the Governor at six o'clock each morning from the sidewalk in front of the hotel, contributing greatly, it was believed, to his failure to make much of a political dent on the other delegates. A striking figure about town was the sartorially resplendent Mayor Jimmy Walker of New York (even then under investigation for misconduct in office). His sidekick on many a visit to the town's leading night spots was that familiar habitué of the Sunday rotogravure pages, Cornelius Vanderbilt, who during daylight hours was First Deputy Doorman at Roosevelt headquarters. "If this convention stopped right now, two days before the voting starts," Will Rogers wrote admiringly from the scene, "it's been a better convention than the Republican one."

For Farley and Howe, however, and for scores like them in the other candidate camps, there was no time for gaiety and hell-raising. They ate sandwiches from trays, slept when they could, and sweated in limp shirts through long arduous hours of scheming, arguing, pleading, threatening, and promising. FDR clearly was "the man to beat," so "Stop Roosevelt" coalitions were secretly hammered together in one room at midnight, only to be pulled apart by dawn in another room. Meanwhile state delegations were caucusing, disagreeing, getting into fist fights, reuniting, changing their minds. Every fresh rumor of a disaffection in the Roosevelt ranks sent Farley scurrying to the scene of trouble, just as a hint that a Smith or a Ritchie delegation was weakening sent him scavenging for their votes. His own state delegation was a major irritant: It was split 67 for Smith to 27 for Roosevelt and he could not budge it.

As Thursday, the day of decision, approached, Farley was confident that Roosevelt's first-ballot strength would hold at around 650. But unless there were some switches he would be at least 120 short of the needed two-thirds majority, and that would mean a second ballot, maybe a third and a fourth, and maybe a deadlock. Farley saw that as the real danger, because the Roosevelt forces were short of commitments for second- and third-ballot switches. Favorite son delegations like those for Governors Harry F. Byrd of Virginia and George White of Ohio were stubbornly resistant, and Baker's stature as a dark horse was growing by the hour. Where could the reserve troops be found to throw in midway of the battle that would start a victory stampede? The most promising corps was the 90-vote Texas-California bloc tied to Garner.

The scene in the bleak barnlike Chicago Stadium was one of noisy chaos as the contestants lined up at the starting gate on Thursday, when the nominations began. Miles of red, white, and blue bunting—originally put in place for the Republicans—hung in tattered festoons or dangled loosely from their moorings. Hundreds of balloons and an occasional pigeon drifted high up in the torpid air or nestled against the naked girders under the dark ceiling. An enormous pipe organ rumbled and throbbed continuously. The galleries were packed shoulder to shoulder with noisy, undisciplined spectators, a majority of them an organized claque recruited by the Smith forces. On the floor facing the vast curtain-draped platform and the ranks of crude workbenches for the press, three thousand delegates, half-delegates, quarter-delegates, and their alternates and flacks squirmed and shoved aimlessly like a colony of restless ants among the tight rows of red folding chairs. Brilliant Kleig lights for the photographers and newsreel cameramen added to the intolerable heat and created a harsh miasmic glow compounded of smoke, dust, and the fetid expirations of thousands of sweating bodies. But not one of those who had fought or faked his way into the Stadium that day would willingly have been anywhere else.

The nominating speeches, each with two or more seconders, began shortly after noon and droned on past a brief dinner recess to midnight and beyond. As each candidate's name was offered, the organ began fortissimo to boom out his theme song, his gallery claque screamed, and his backers on the floor began a serpentine march through the aisles of the convention floor, yipping and yelling in synthetic delight. The loudest demonstration of all, lasting nearly an hour, was for Smith, and his army of galleryites almost shook the building from its foundations. Roosevelt's nominating speech, a rather dull effort, was made by an old Dutchess County friend, John E. Mack. The organist struck up "Anchors Aweigh," a huge crowd of marchers took to the floor, and the Roosevelt gallery claque began to cheer. The cheers were soon smothered under the boos and catcalls of the Smith contingent. Under promptings from Edward J. Flynn, a Roosevelt manager from the Bronx, the organist attempted to throw off the protesters by switching to the currently popular tune "Happy Days Are Here Again." The boos were not stilled, but a political anthem was coined that was to serve the Democratic party for twelve years.

On, on, on through the sweltering exhausting night went the speeches and the hoopla. It was 4:28 Friday morning before Chairman Walsh could gavel down the racket and call for the first poll of the states.

Meanwhile, at the Congress Hotel, Farley, Howe, and other Roosevelt managers engaged in a frantic series of conspiracies and negotiations to crack some of the untapped sources of delegate strength. The Garner bloc was their main objective. A day earlier, Joseph P. Kennedy, a longtime friend of Hearst, had called the publisher at his San Simeon palace from the Roosevelt headquarters, urging him to instruct McAdoo to release the California delegation on the second ballot at least. Kennedy warned that if a deadlock occurred, the probable winner would be Newton D. Baker, whom Hearst loathed almost as much as he did Smith. Hearst was noncommittal, but he pointedly did not reject the suggestion.

At every opportunity and under every pretext Farley buttonholed Sam Rayburn, a fellow Texan and Congressional colleague of Garner's and leader of the Texas delegation. Earlier in the week Farley had learned from sources in Washington, where Garner had remained because Congress was still in session, that the Speaker might be receptive to an offer of the Vice Presidency. Farley had gotten Roosevelt's tentative consent to such a deal, and now he dangled this possibility before Rayburn. The enigmatic Rayburn seemed unimpressed, but, like Hearst, he stopped short of a clear negative. "We have come to Chicago to nominate Jack Garner for the Presidency if we can," he said bluntly. "We are not against any other candidate and we are not for any other candidate. But we don't intend to make it another Madison Square Garden." [4]

Throughout all his hectic negotiations of Thursday, Farley had not been able to change a thing. And now, as the moment of truth approached, there hung the Garner prize, ninety votes that would spell almost certain victory, dangling temptingly just beyond reach.

The big Irishman was near exhaustion and despair as he hurried out to the Stadium in the Friday dawn to make his own tally of the voting. As he sat on the platform during the interminable roll call, he waited tensely but not quite hopefully to see if some wavering state would switch. None did. The final vote was not disappointing in itself; his lines had held firm and on the first ballot Roosevelt had a commanding lead of 661¼ to 201¾ for Smith and 90¼ for Garner. But Farley was more than 100 votes short of fulfilling his prediction of a first-ballot victory, and he had only token reserves with which to meet any defections on the next go-around. He signaled Chairman Walsh to ignore the clamorous calls for adjournment, and the roll call for the second ballot began as the morning sunlight streamed through the eastern skylights and the delegates slumped wearily in their chairs with mouths agape. An hour later the second tally showed little change from the one before: FDR inched ahead with 16½ reserve votes Farley had committed for psychological effect, Smith dropped by 7½, and Garner's total stayed where it was. On the third ballot there was even less of a change, and it looked as though the most dread contingency of all had occurred—a deadlock. But now human endurance had run out, for Farley and everyone else, and at 9:30 o'clock he signaled the chairman to adjourn the convention until evening.

There was, however, no rest that day for the scores of managers and submanagers clustered around the leading contenders and dark horses. For most of them there was, in spite of their weariness, a tense and heady sense of elation, for Roosevelt, the front runner, had been stopped in his tracks. Now to put together a coalition that would surge out on the next couple of ballots and take the lead away from him. Smith, Ritchie, and, particularly, Baker—all looked like good rallying points. Could the Garner camp be enticed into some such combination?

At the Roosevelt headquarters the tension was equally high but spirits were dulled by exhaustion. Howe lay on the floor of the suite, his head on a pillow with two electric fans blowing over his frail body, his voice coming in asthmatic whispers. Farley fell asleep in a chair with the telephone in his hand while waiting for a call to Albany to be completed. His most pressing objective was to find Sam Rayburn. At midmorning he arranged a secret rendezvous with the stubby Texan in the suite of Pat Harrison, leader of the Mississippi delegation. The time for maneuver and jockeying was past, and both men knew it.

Farley told Rayburn that he could definitely commit the Governor's choice of Garner as Vice President if Rayburn would now commit the Texas delegation to Roosevelt. Such a switch would mean certain victory for both men on the next ballot, he said, and without it there would certainly be a deadlock, with Baker the probable beneficiary. Rayburn heard him out in silence, then rose to leave. "We'll see what can be done," he said cryptically, slapping his Panama hat on his bald head with an air of determination. To Big Jim Farley that was assurance enough. He raced upstairs to tell Howe, Flynn, and the other insiders of the headquarters group, "Texas is ours!" But the secret had to be guarded like a holy relic from the ravening newspapermen and the spies of the other candidates.

Rayburn had his work cut out for him. His unruly delegation had widely split among those who had sworn to stick with Garner to the bitter end and those who would be willing, *in extremis*, to switch to Roosevelt, to Smith, or to Ritchie, in about that order. He also knew, as the only man in Chicago who could get a phone call through to hard-nosed old "Cactus Jack" Garner in Washington (a personal call from Al Smith had gone unanswered for

At left: Al Smith in his earlier "Happy Warrior" days. The bitterly defeated 1928 candidate lost the 1932 Democratic nomination to Franklin D. Roosevelt on the fourth ballot as William Randolph Hearst influence swung both the Texas and California delegations. (Middle) Chicago, 1932. An ecstatic nominee! (Left to Right) Franklin D. Roosevelt, James Roosevelt and, (behind mike) Will Rogers. (Below) Election night crowds in Times Square, November 8, 1932.

VICTOR

24270-A

HAPPY DAYS ARE HERE AGAIN-Fox Trot
(Dia: Alegres)
(Jack Yellen-Milton Ager)
Lec Reisman and his Orchestra
with vocal refrain

" HOOVER "

(THE MAN FOR UNCLE SAM)

Words and Music by L. L. WILLIS

Pub. Agts. VosBurgh's Orchestration Service
1547 BROADWAY
NEW YORK CITY, U. S. A.

twenty-four hours), that the Speaker was less than enthusiastic about the Vice-Presidency. In the face of these uncertainties he called a caucus of the Texas delegation late Friday afternoon at their headquarters in the Sherman Hotel. His proposal that they switch to the New York Governor created an uproar. As the Texans squabbled loudly among themselves, almost coming to blows at one or two points, Rayburn was called from the room to take a long-distance telephone call. It was from Garner.

"Sam," the caller said, "I think it's time to break this thing up. This man Roosevelt is the choice of the convention. He has had a majority on three ballots. We don't want to be responsible for tying up this convention and bringing on another Madison Square Garden."

"Do you authorize me to release the Texas delegation from voting for you for the presidential nomination?"

"Yes," came the firm reply.

Rayburn strode back into the noisy meeting room. "Well, John is out," he told the delegates. "He tells me to thank you from the bottom of his heart. He releases you without any strings whatever." [5]

This news created a new uproar that rivaled in miniature the earlier scene on the floor of the convention hall. Rayburn's efforts to guide the group to a decision for Roosevelt were fought by Garner bitter-enders as well as by advocates of the other contenders. At last, after an hour of turmoil and hysterics, a vote was called for. By the harrowing margin of 54 to 51, the Texas delegation, bound by the unit rule, agreed to cast its 46 votes for Roosevelt. Rayburn hurried out to convey the news to Farley, and, most importantly, to McAdoo.* The prize was in the bag for the New York Governor.

In retrospect at least the concluding act of the Chicago drama was anti-climatic, though it was hardly that at the time. When the convention reassembled Friday night, the air crackled with rumors that a break was imminent, but there were a dozen superheated versions of when and for whom it would come. As the clerk began the ritualistic call of the states—Alabama . . . Arizona . . . Arkansas—it appeared that the new tally would be a monotonous repetition of what had gone before. But at the call of "California," the tall, spare frame of William Gibbs McAdoo rose from the delegates' section, and he asked permission to address the convention. Taking the microphone, as a sudden hush fell over the huge assemblage, he said:

"California came here to nominate a President of the United States. She did not come here to deadlock this convention. . . . We believe that when any man comes into a Democratic national convention with the popular will behind him to the extent of almost seven hundred . . . "—the galleries

---

* In some published versions of the Texas switch it is contended that Mr. Hearst, through a Washington emissary, prevailed upon Speaker Garner to withdraw and to release his delegates to Roosevelt. This is not supported by Mr. Farley nor by Mr. Garner's biographer, Bascom N. Timmons (*Garner of Texas,* New York, 1948), nor by Arthur Krock of *The New York Times,* who was an on-the-spot observer of the scene.

erupted in a roar of yells and boos—"he is deserving of the nomination. Accordingly, California casts forty-four votes for Franklin D. Roosevelt."

Rayburn had declined McAdoo's offer to yield California's position on the roster to Texas. But this formality mattered little. The rush for the band-wagon was on, and in spite of the raucous protest of the Smith galleryites, one state after another switched to Roosevelt. On the fourth and final tally he had won a more than two-thirds majority of 945 to 190½ for Smith, who, in bitter disappointment, refused to concede the winner the traditional cour-tesy of unanimity.

Garner's nomination for Vice President followed as a matter of course. The next day, Saturday, Roosevelt broke precedent by flying to the scene of the convention to accept the nomination in person. He presented a buoyant, smiling, confident figure and the gallant effort he made to stand on his metal-braced legs achieved a sympathetic relationship with his audience. His very appearance on the platform seemed to erase almost instantly the bitterness and weariness through which his nomination had been won. And when, in ringing tones, he told them, "I pledge you, I pledge myself, to a new deal for the American people," he evoked a thunder of the most spontaneous and genuine cheers heard in Chicago all week.

The election campaign of 1932 was hardly a contest. Franklin D. Roosevelt, vetoing the suggestion of some of his party elders that he confine himself to a "front porch" campaign (Garner told him, "All you've got to do to be elected is stay alive"), moved out aggressively to show himself to the voters in every part of the country. He not only enjoyed these exhibitions of his political skill but demonstrated to the world that his affliction was no barrier to his goal. The result was all that he could have hoped for. The country gained a picture of him as a smiling, warmhearted man with the grace and good looks of a patrician and the poise and self-assurance of an ex-perienced politician. However one translated the words he spoke or the ideas he espoused (this was not always easy), one found a sense of vitality in the way his head sat upon the muscular shoulders, in the outthrust chin and strong nose and intelligent eyes, in the clear diction and confident voice that glided so easily from sober exhortation to subtle wit. The thousands who saw and heard him found his reasoned optimism infectious and exhilarating.

The Democratic platform, a model of brevity as platforms go, was well tailored to his needs. On prohibition, the overriding popular issue of the day (or so it was believed), the party's stand was clearly for repeal, whereas the Republican position was murky. Other planks repeated, in substantially the same clichés used by the Republicans, the Democrats' allegiance to the sacred doctrines of economy in government (specifically, a 25 percent cut in spending), a balanced budget, a sound currency, and a tariff "for revenue." The Democratic platform then moved briskly into more radical territory by calling for Federal expenditures for relief, a large public works program, old-age and unemployment insurance, regulation of holding companies and security exchanges, and a fuller measure of government responsibility for "human welfare." This was an area the Republicans had touched on in the most gingerly fashion. How the Democrats planned to retrench on federal expenditures at the same time that they proposed massive new programs for "human welfare" was not spelled out. But since a political platform is made "to run on, not to stand on," it served the party's purpose admirably.

If the Democratic platform contained ambiguities and if its declarations in favor of laissez-faire were in conflict with those for the welfare state, it only reflected the confusion in the minds of many in the party, including the candidate himself.

Roosevelt was no student of economics, and such ideas as he had were of the orthodox and conventional sort. He believed in the balanced budget, for example, as the chief bastion of government stability. Even in his campaign speeches he would liken federal fiscal management to the family bank account. At the same time he had a highly developed social consciousness and a liberal attitude toward popular democracy and the rights of labor that seemed to be a blend of Midwest Populism and the aristocrat's *noblesse oblige*. He installed one of the country's first state relief administrations during his second term as Governor of New York, and in his preconvention campaign for the nomination he made the plight of the Forgotten Man a staple of his dialectic. In the pre-Keynesian days of 1932 (the British thinker's concepts had not gained currency outside elite academic circles here at the time), the seeming incompatibility between economic laws and social ends troubled many a seeker after justice.

In his election campaign, and even afterward, Roosevelt was subject to many conflicting pressures in the formulation of his ideas and his program. From the Right and the Center he was besieged by traditionalists and conservatives, many of them the most influential leaders of his party, to hew to the old familiar lines. Garner warned him that Hoover had already gone too far in "leading the country down the path of socialism." Al Smith snorted publicly that the candidate's preoccupation with the Forgotten Man was breeding "class warfare." Carter Glass cautioned him against trying to buy back prosperity "by picking the pockets of the American taxpayers."

From the Left and Left-of-Center there were contrary forces pulling him in the direction of progressivism and the New Economics. Some, like Senator Burton K. Wheeler of Montana, "Young Bob" LaFollette of Wisconsin, and Hiram Johnson of California, born to the Populist tradition and weaned on the liberalism of Teddy Roosevelt and Woodrow Wilson, urged him to lash out at the ogres of monopoly capitalism. Another group, younger and more sophisticated, who had read in Veblen and Commons and Marx and even Keynes, tried to lead him to think more about the inadequate structure and function of the econmic system than about patching its leaks. Their nucleus was a small body of economists and university professors, such as Rexford Tugwell, Raymond Moley, Adolf Berle, and a few others, who had been attracted to Roosevelt's banner as "idea men" during the preconvention phase and were to stay on to become key men in the fabled Brain Trust. It was their counsel and their speech-writing that came in time to give the most luster and excitement to Roosevelt's campaign, but they did not have a monopoly on the candidate's ear.

It took Candidate Roosevelt many weeks, in fact, to get the liberal community, or its spokesmen in the press at least, to look seriously at his credentials, and many continued to regard him skeptically. "It is difficult to see just what the progressives find so attractive about [him]," Oswald Garrison Villard wrote in *The Nation* a week after the convention. "As in the case of Harding, it is an unearned honor that has gone to Franklin Roosevelt. Certainly no one would dare to assert that he achieved it by courage, by outspokenness or by a passionate defense of the right of the American citizen to life and liberty." Columnist Heywood Broun derided him as "the corkscrew candidate." H. L. Mencken wrote that "Roosevelt Minor fails somehow to measure up to the common concept of a first-rate man." And Paul Y. Anderson, another liberal commentator, grumbled as the campaign reached its midpoint: "Mr. Roosevelt's flashy smile and flashier phrases have become almost as tiresome as the muddy and interminable sentences of Mr. Hoover." The tone of these jibes softened markedly as the campaign neared its end, but many liberal spokesmen carefully kept their fingers crossed whenever they wrote about the Demorcratic candidate.

Roosevelt's campaign trail zigzagged back and forth across the country from about the middle of September onward. It included an expedition to the West Coast and back in October with a dozen major speeches and countless appearances from the back platform of his train along the way. Everywhere he met ever larger and more enthusiastic receptions. In a period of national gloom he was a bearer of hope and good tidings even if many were uncertain what those tidings meant. But at least he promised to do *something,* and to a citizenry that had become appalled by the bewildered inaction of the Hoover Administration, this was promise enough.

Roosevelt told midwestern audiences, for example, that his farm program would include an overhaul of the Joint Stock Land Banks through which so many of their farms had been sold under foreclosure. At Seattle he called for laws regulating the public utilities, and in Denver he proposed a great network of publicly owned hydroelectric facilities stretching from the Colorado River to Muscle Shoals in Alabama. In Boston he reiterated his call for federally financed unemployment relief programs, unemployment insurance, and old-age pensions. In Pittsburgh he again solemnly promised a balanced budget and a slash in Federal expenditures. In the course of a speech on his economic program at St. Louis, once the beer capital of America, a loud voice from the packed audience interrupted him to ask: "What about repeal? Will you bring back beer?" Roosevelt hesitated for a moment, looked up with that sly smile that always presaged a witticism, and continued in mock solemnity: "And in the meantime I propose to increase the Federal revenue by several hundred million dollars a year by placing a tax on beer." The crowd roared its approval and began to chant in unison: "We want beer! We want beer!"

The most widely accepted public opinion poll of the period was the mail "straw vote" conducted by the weekly *Literary Digest*. From the outset of the campaign this poll had shown Roosevelt leading Hoover, but as October wore on the Democrat's margin became overwhelming—55.9 percent to 37.5 percent in the final tally just before election—and the betting odds on a Roosevelt victory climbed to 7 to 1. Nothing succeeds like success in politics, and as the bandwagon gathered speed former foes of the candidate, such as Al Smith, John Raskob, Mayor Frank Hague of Jersey City, Governor Ritchie, and a host of others, swung aboard. Dissident Republicans, too, such as Hiram Johnson, Borah of Idaho, and George Norris of Nebraska, added their prestige to the cargo. If not actually fellow travellers with Roosevelt, they were conspicuous nontravelers with Hoover. The "Republicans for Roosevelt" clubs were an important adjunct of the Democratic campaign.

Meanwhile anger, frustration, and a growing foretaste of defeat plagued the Hoover camp. The President, a man of conscience who had only a limited tolerance for the wiles of the politician's game, was being besieged on a number of fronts besides the political. Even as he acknowledged his party's nomination for a second term in the White House, he was confronted by the embarrassing arrival of the Bonus Army on the doorstep of the capital. His harsh solution of that dilemma late in July brought torrents of criticism (and some praise) upon his head. Congress, already under effective control of the Democrats—in 1930 they had won a majority in the House and a 48-47 standoff in the Senate—was at its balkiest. The President was also engaged in a series of international negotiations involving a moratorium on the Allies' war debts as well as reparations and arms limitations. The domestic economy was showing some slight stirrings of recovery that summer, particularly in the stock market, and he was much concerned lest its delicate respiration be disturbed by the tumult on the political front.

It was inconceivable to Mr. Hoover that the Chief Executive of a great nation caught in the grip of crisis should have to absent himself from his post and squabble in the gutter like an ordinary politician. But the thrusts and jibes of the opposition candidate drove him to anger, and the policies espoused by the Democrats seemed to him so patently dangerous to the nation's welfare that he could see no alternative but to move out into the hustings himself.

If making that decision was painful, its execution was even more so. As the earnest, plodding defender of a *status quo* that was so clearly in disarray, Hoover was no match for Roosevelt's glib and fast-paced offensive. If he met warmth and understanding in one community as his campaign train rolled across the country in mid-October, he was likely to encounter apathy and sullenness in the next. In Detroit, where Henry Ford had posted notices throughout his factories saying, "To prevent times from getting worse and to help them get better President Hoover must be reelected," throngs along the parade route greeted the President with jeers and with placards proclaiming "Hoover—Baloney and Apple Sauce," "Down with Hoover," and similar sentiments. The worried Secret Service halted the procession long enough to switch the President and Mrs. Hoover from an open to a closed car. Following his major farm speech in Des Moines, the Omaha *World-Herald* editorialized: "Mr. Hoover deepens the impression that four more years of Hoover would be just four more years of Hoover."

Like a harassed fighter who sees the referee's decision going against him, Hoover sought desperately to move onto the offensive. He deployed his Cabinet out on the firing line and stepped up his own campaign schedule almost to the point of exhaustion. Having spent three years minimizing the depth and seriousness of the Depression, he now depicted it as a worsening conflagration which only experienced Republican firefighters could control, and which a Democratic victory would certainly spread.

"My countrymen," he pleaded before an audience in Indianapolis, "the fundamental issue is whether we shall go on in fidelity to American traditions or whether we shall turn to dangerous innovations. This campaign is a contest between two philosophies of government." In Pittsburgh he said the country had been within two weeks of being forced off the gold standard during the preceding winter, and warned that this dire crisis would return in more threatening form if the Democrats came to power. In Chicago, where ten thousand hunger marchers had paraded noisily through The Loop a few days before, the President, in obvious reference to the Bonus Army, proclaimed: "Thank God there is a government in Washington that knows how to deal with a mob." And in his final appeal to the voters of New York he uttered a dark prediction that was to haunt him for years to come. If the Democrats, he said, were permitted to carry through their intention of scrapping the Smoot-Hawley Tariff Act, "grass will grow in the streets of a hundred cities, a thousand towns; the weeds will overrun the fields of a million farms." (Four years later, in the first blush of the New Deal recovery, the Democrats in convention at Philadelphia sent a huge harvesting machine rumbling through the narrow streets looking for "Hoover's grass" to be mowed.) Mr. Hoover, the liberal press said, had resorted in his extremity to a "scare campaign."

The outcome of the election on November 8 had been foretold long before the first ballot was cast, but not the outsized margin by which the electorate would repudiate the Old Deal and welcome the New.

Hoover carried only six states—Connecticut, Delaware, Maine, New Hampshire, Pennsylvania, and Vermont—with 59 electoral votes; Roosevelt carried the remainder with 472. In popular votes the Democratic total was 22.8 million; the Republican, 15.7 million. The Republicans in Congress and in a score of statehouses across the country were also engulfed in the Democratic landslide. Measuring the carnage in the next morning's edition of *The New York Times*, Arthur Krock wrote: "A political cataclysm unprecedented in the nation's history and produced by three years of depression, thrust President Herbert Hoover and the Republican party from control of the government yesterday, elected Franklin D. Roosevelt President of the United States, provided the Democrats with a large majority in Congress and gave them control of many states in the Union."

The historical significance of the Democratic victory was as unprecedented as its scope. Never before had a presidential election so sharply and

(Above, left) President-elect Franklin D. Roosevelt at Campaign Headquarters, Hotel Biltmore, New York City. (Left to Right) James Farley, Campaign Manager; James Roosevelt; F.D. Roosevelt, and Mrs. Roosevelt. (Above, right) By rail and bus, Roosevelt and Speaker John Nance Garner, his running mate, campaigned through the Middle West to swelling popularity. (Bottom) An earlier platform. 1930 New York State Democratic power. (Left to right) Frank Walker, Professor Raymond Moley, James A. Farley, Governor Franklin D. Roosevelt, and Gus Gennerich. (Inset) May 14, 1932. Beer for Taxation Parade, New York City.

Cloudy

DAILY MIRROR

ELECTION EXTRA

VOL. IX. No. 119 • • • New York, Wednesday, Nove... 15. 2 cents ...

ROOSEVELT WINS!

A ROOSEVELT-GARNER VICTORY!—Early returns indicated success for Gov. Franklin D. Roosevelt and Speaker John N. Garner, the Democratic ticket.

ELECTED!—The nation has expressed its will and elected the Democratic standard bearers, Gov. Roosevelt as President, and Speaker Garner as Vice-President.

irrevocably marked the end of one era and the beginning of another. The New Deal, its advent confirmed by this emphatic plebiscite, was to revolutionize many aspects of American life.

Nor was the significance of what had happened confined to the politicians and the philosophers. Three babies, born election night in Brooklyn's Beth-El Hospital, were promptly hoisted toward immortality by perceptive parents who named them Franklin Delano Mayblum, Franklin Delano Finkelstein, and Franklin Delano Ragin.

CHAPTER 5
Interlude
November 1932–March 1933

THE WINTER OF 1932–33 has a very special significance in the history of our times. The four months between the end of the Old Deal and the beginning of the New Deal marked the crest of a historical watershed—a pregnant interlude between dusk and dawn. Much that was familiar and conventional and orthodox in American life would be changed.

What did we think and feel and do and concern ourselves with in this brief but momentous entr'acte? It can be said with certainty that very few had the prescience to regard the period as momentous in any way. It was most of all a period of perplexity, of wait and see, of hoping something good would come out of the political changeover without knowing what to hope for. Adversity had become a part of nearly everyone's life. It was hard, in fact, not to believe that this was the way things would be from here on out. In some this bred bitterness and resentment, in some a sullen cynicism, and in others (a majority probably) apathy and resignation. For just about everyone, however, faith in the maxims and the conventional wisdom of the past was weakened or had vanished, and for most there were no new moorings to tie to.

The universality of hard times had brought some interesting changes in values. There was a leveling of tastes and social priorities that tended to dissolve middle-class distinctions. Families who had grown up to feel that doing one's own housework, or sending one's children to public school, or doing without charge accounts at the stores bore a taint of vulgarity, were forced to adjust to the new circumstances. Many did so with a touch of pride in their stoic virtue. Residents of both sides of the railroad tracks unexpectedly rubbed elbows in the public libraries, museums, and parks. Golf was "democratized" as country-club memberships dwindled and public fee courses proliferated. The social stratification of many churches was erased as their congregations counted the cost of Sunday transportation and switched to churches nearer home. It was far short of universal brotherhood, but a common predicament did cause a new sense of tolerance and human understanding to break down ancient social barricades.

In spite of painful stresses, life in the United States continued to rock along that memorable winter in its accustomed and variegated pattern. Though unemployment pushed beyond the twelve million mark and the economy hit new lows all across the board, not everyone had to stand in a breadline, nor did everyone conspire to bring down the regime. For most people, the primal urge to survive, to prosper, to enjoy, and to compete was undimmed. Accordingly they got into and out of trouble, made asses and heroes of themselves, reached greatness or stumbled into futility, sinned and repented, made love and poetry and music very much as they had always done.

For a decade the popular culture of the nation had focused on the phenomenon of prohibition—its alleged virtues, its manifest evils, and its spin-off of crime, hypocrisy, and instant folklore. In the winter of 1932–33, public fascination with the prohibition issue was at a peak as the drive for repeal of the Eighteenth Amendment mounted toward a climax. On February 20 Congress overwhelmingly approved a repeal resolution, and the Twenty-first Amendment was submitted to the states for ratification.

This was bad news not only for the Anti-Saloon League and the drys but also for the booze barons, who saw their billion-dollar-a-year industry threatened by legitimacy. In spite of the Depression they had ridden a rising wave of prosperity, particularly during the preceding five years as public support of the law dwindled and enforcement slackened. They had invested untold wealth in flashy speakeasies and cabarets, in bribes and graft to corruptible officials, in elaborate "alky" plants and oceangoing rum runners, and in interlocking gangland alliances for supply, distribution, and "protection." The bootleggers' underworld was a part of the life of every city and town—visible to all and supported by the patronage of the best people as well as the worst. It provided a morbidly fascinating backdrop of outlawry, sadistic violations, swashbuckling drama, and even of low comedy that cast a lurid glow on the social landscape of an entire decade.

The newspapers routinely reported incidents like these:

Larry Fay, proprietor of a gaudy speakeasy known as Casa Blanca on New York's West 56th Street was shot down by the doorman of his establishment, who apparently was in league with a rival bootleg gang.

Gangland enemies of rum runner Joseph Weshefsky strangled him to death, stuffed his body into a burlap sack and left it in a stolen automobile in front of New York police headquarters on Centre Street.

Coast Guardsmen patrolling the beach near Truro, Massachusetts, surprised a party of twenty men in the act of burying 1,000 cases of Canadian whisky just unloaded from an innocent-looking fishing trawler standing a mile off shore.

Frank Nitti, righthand man to Chicago's gang lord, Al Capone, was gunned down by a city detective who, in turn, was designated "gangland enemy Number One" by the Capone syndicate and marked for extinction.

College students on a midwestern campus roughed up and put to flight a squad of prohibition agents seeking to confiscate a shipment of moonshine whisky destined for the school's midwinter prom.

Not all of the extraordinary crime and violence of that winter was traceable to the bootleg trade. The kidnaping and murder of the infant son of Colonel and Mrs. Charles A. Lindbergh, in March 1932, had triggered a series of repetitions in many parts of the country. The kidnaping toll during the next year was the greatest on record. Among the more prominent victims who made the headlines were Charles Boettcher, Denver; Peggy McMath, Harwichport, Mass.; Mary McElroy, Kansas City; William Hamm, Jr., St. Paul; John ("Jake the Barber") Factor, Chicago; Jackie Russell, Brooklyn; Charles Urschel, Oklahoma City.

One of the most celebrated manhunts of the decade reached its climax in January 1933, when Tom Crawford, who had been on the FBI's elite roster of "most wanted" criminals for three years, was shot down by police and Federal agents at Cape Girardeau, Missouri. Other high points in crime that winter: In Seattle, Julian Marcellino, a Filipino, ran amok on the streets with two bolo knives in his hands, killing six persons and seriously injuring fifteen others; a murder charge against lustrous torch singer Libby Holman in the death of her tobacco-heir husband, Smith Reynolds, Jr., was *nolle prossed* by a court in North Carolina; Winnie Ruth Judd, condemned to the electric chair in Arizona for chopping up the bodies of two women she suspected of stealing the affections of her husband and shipping them in a trunk to Los Angeles, was granted a stay of execution in February and later committed to a mental institution for life.

The most shocking crime story of the winter was the attempted assassination of President-elect Roosevelt at Miami on February 15. He had come ashore late that afternoon at the end of a vacation cruise and was being welcomed by a crowd of 10,000 at Bay Front Park. As he sat in an open car talking with Chicago's Mayor Anton Cermak, standing nearby, a swarthy little man climbed on a box in the midst of the crowd and fired six shots from a revolver in Roosevelt's direction. Cermak, struck in the chest and shoulder, slumped to the ground. A Secret Service man was grazed on the hand by one of the bullets. Roosevelt doubled up in his seat but called out strongly, "I'm all right! I'm all right!" The enraged crowd converged on the gunman and pummeled him to the ground. He was Guiseppe Zangara, thirty-two, an unemployed bricklayer from Paterson, New Jersey. His only motive seemed to be a hatred of the rich and powerful. "I hate all Presidents," he told police, "no matter from what country they come." The unconscious Cermak was rushed to a hospital in Roosevelt's car. He died on March 6. Zangara was indicted for murder on the same day. He pleaded guilty and was electrocuted in the Florida state prison at Raiford on March 20.

In the somewhat more sophisticated fields of felony, these events made top-head news during the winter: The courts at Athens, Greece, refused a request by the United States for the extradition of Samuel Insull, wanted here on charges of mail fraud in the collapse of his huge utility empire. . . . In another extradition case, the Governor of New Jersey refused to turn over to the Governor of Georgia an escaped convict named Robert Elliott Burns, who had achieved fame as author of the best-selling *I Am a Fugitive From a Georgia Chain Gang.* . . . "Puddler Jim" Davis, onetime Secretary of Labor in the Hoover Cabinet was indicted for running an illegal lottery for the Loyal Order of Moose. Of $2.2 million raised, it was charged, a scant 10 percent reached its intended beneficiary, the fraternity's orphanage at Mooseheart, Indiana. Davis was not convicted. . . . A Polish émigré, Henry F. Gerguson, alias Prince Michael Alexandrovitch Dmitry Obolensky Romanoff, one of the most amiable and successful high-society impostors in a generation, was picked up on a New York Street street by immigration officers for deportation. As he had done in the past, and would so often do again, "Prince Mike" talked himself out of the law's grasp. . . . . In North Carolina, Colonel Luke Lea and his son, convicted of bank frauds totaling nearly $1 million, fled from arresting officers to the Tennessee mountains, where they holed up for two weeks in

February with a small army of hired gunmen. . . . Appearing before the Senate Finance Committee in Washington, Charles E. Mitchell, president of New York's National City Bank and an authentic Wall Street superman during the boom years, confessed to elaborate stock manipulations that led to his later indictment and trial for evading more than half a million dollars in income taxes. He was subsequently acquitted.

If the forces of evil were rampant that winter, so were the forces of righteousness. To many impressionable people the suffering and perplexities of the Depression appeared to be the hand of God raised against a wicked society. Aflame with that conviction, prophets had arisen in many quarters to point the way to redemption and salvation.

In established churches, membership was on the rise that winter (as it had been for several years), but so was membership in unorthodox sects and cults of various hues. The Salvation Army, with its cornets and tambourines and curbside gospel, was a familiar part of the night scene in every large city. Its combination offer of soup and prayer found many takers. Tent evangelists flourished as never before in the small towns of the South and Middle West, and in larger cities throughout the country even some of the more fashionable churches caught the fever for extended and well-publicized revivals. Evangelists Billy Sunday and Gypsy Smith were among a score of renowned itinerant preachers who regularly filled auditoriums and ball parks with their fire-and-brimstone exhortations. In Los Angeles the exotic Aimee Semple McPherson cast her spell from the floodlit pulpit of Angelus Temple, and in more lurid fashion in the columns of newspapers and magazines.

Turbaned swamis, barefoot faith healers, mystics, and self-proclaimed messiahs in almost infinite variety hung out their shingles on vacant storefronts or declaimed to the jobless from street corners. In the mountain hollows of Appalachia and the red-clay barrens of the Deep South, foot washers and snake handlers sought in primitive ways to propitiate a primitive God. The Oxford Group (forerunner of Moral Rearmament), led by Dr. Frank Buchman, made spectacular gains among the traditionally resistant members of the urban upper middle class. In a nationwide poll, Mary Baker Eddy, the founder of Christian Science, was picked as the outstanding woman in a century of American progress. On Christmas Eve, Pope Pius XI broadcast to the world a proclamation designating 1933, the nineteenth centenary of Christ's death, as a Holy Year for all members of the Catholic faith.

In the area of the arts and entertainment, the winter was not without its merits. Established romantics among the novelists and playwrights, such as Ellen Glasgow, Booth Tarkington, and John Drinkwater, had already been pretty well displaced by members of the new school of realists, which included such now-formidable names as Sinclair Lewis, Eugene O'Neill, Pearl Buck, and Ernest Hemingway. The runaway best seller of the winter was *Mutiny on the Bounty*, by Charles Nordhoff and J. N. Hall, destined to become a minor classic among adventure stories of the sea. Other popular American novels of

(Top and middle) Mildred "Babe" Didrikson, winner of 2 Gold Medals and a Silver in Track and Field in the 1932 Olympics, was purported also to swim, shoot, ride, row, box, and play tennis, golf, basketball, baseball, football, polo, and billiards. A New York reporter asked the Texas Babe, "Is there anything at all you don't play?" "Yeah," she said, "dolls." (Bottom) Bill Carr, U. of Pennsylvania, took the 400-meter Gold Medal in the record time of 46.2 seconds. (Bottom right) Stamp for the Xth Olympiad, Los Angeles, 1932.

UNITED STATES POSTAGE

XTH OLYMPIAD·LOS ANGELES·1932

3 CENTS

At left: The demise of the Heavyweight Championship! Primo Carnera and trainer doing roadwork at Dr. Bier's Health Farm, Pompton Lakes, New Jersey, 1933, in preparation for his title fight with Jack Sharkey, then champion. "Da Preem" took out Sailor Jack in 6 with a punch that has yet to be seen, probably owing to gangsters Owney Madden and Big Frenchy DeMange in Carnera's corner and Detroit's *Purple Gang* backing Sharkey. Sharkey (bottom right) had an erratic and gangster-backed career which included a "foul" victory over "Phainting Phil" Scott and a 1930 loss of the championship to Max Schmeling, fouled and flat on his back.

Following spread: Paul Muni in *I Am a Fugitive from a Chain Gang.* Directed by Mervyn LeRoy for Warner Brothers, 1932.

1) Joan Blondell/*Gold Diggers of 1933.* 2) Garbo & Barrymore/*Grand Hotel.* 3) Harlow & Gable/*Red Dust.* 4) Jean Harlow. 5) W. C. Fields. 6) Richard Barthelmess/*Heroes for Sale.* 7) Kate Smith/*Hello Everybody.* 8) Lillian Roth. 9) Chico & Harpo Marx /*Horse Feathers.*

JACK SHARKEY

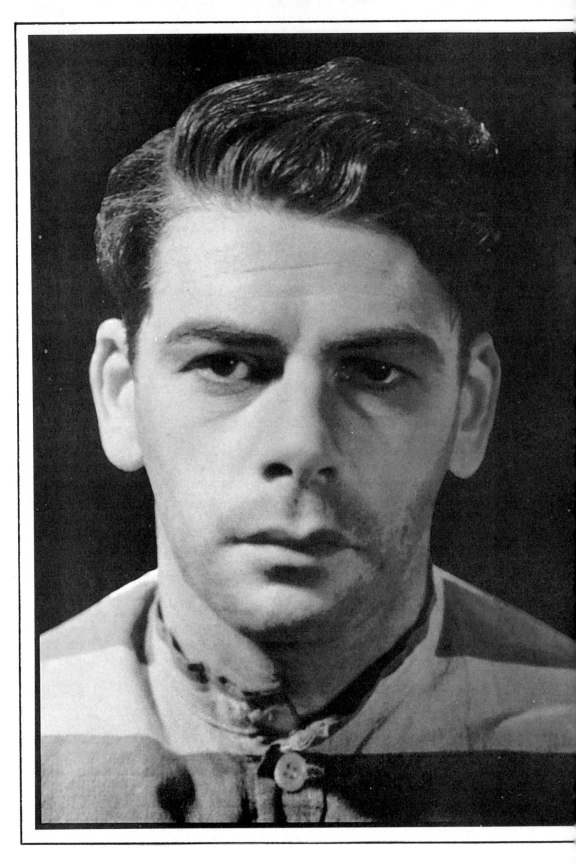

(Microphone, clockwise) 1) Russ Columbo. 2) Rudy Vallee. 3) Ethel Waters. 4) Mildred Bailey. (Center) Bing Crosby and The Boswell Sisters

Opposite page: (top) Playboy Tommy Manville and wife #3, the former Yvonne Taylor, at the Central Park Casino, and Winnie Ruth Judd (leaning on elbows), condemned murderess, at sanity hearing in Florence, Arizona, 1933. (Below) Libby Holman, Blues singer and exonerated murderess of husband and tobacco heir Zachary Smith (Skipper) Reynolds, and Giuseppe Zangara in Miami cell after assassination attempt on President-elect Roosevelt. (Inset) Evangelist Aimee Semple McPherson rising from the waves: a composite photograph hawked at the time of her disappearance, 1926. (Above) A decade later, Evangelist McPherson, with popularity dimmed by the '20's kidnapping hoax, was still attired in satins, silks, and chiffons to do battle with the Devil; and another Evangelist, the Reverend Billy Sunday, was still saying that someday "Hell will be forever for rent." (At left) 15-year-old violin virtuoso, Yehudi Menuhin.

Brunswick
U. S. PAT. 1,637,54.

Comedienne with Orchestra

LOVE FOR SALE
From the Musical Comedy
"The New Yorkers"
Porter—
LIBBY HOLMAN
6044
N

THE BRUNSWICK-BALKE-COLLENDER COMPANY
REG US PAT OFFICE — M DE F MARCA INDUSTRIAL REGISTRADA
MADE IN U.S.A.

Cloudy

DAILY MIRROR

FINAL

MUrray Hill 2-1000

Copyright, 1932, Daily Mirror, Inc.
Registered U. S. Patent Office

Entered as second class matter
Post Office New York, N. Y.

Vol. VIII No. 218

New York, Thursday, March 3, 1932

2 cents IN CITY
Elsewhere

COPS TRAIL LINDY BABY KIDNAP CAR TO NEWARK!

Story on Page 3

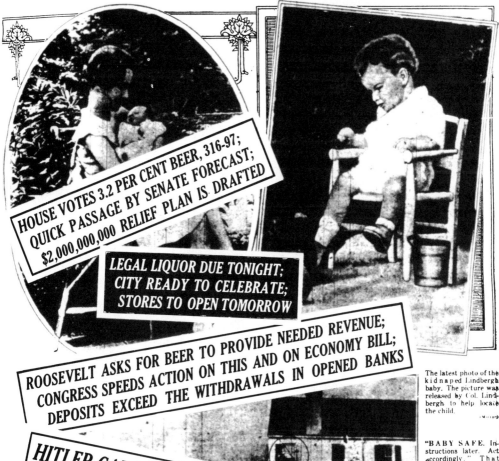

HOUSE VOTES 3.2 PER CENT BEER, 316-97; QUICK PASSAGE BY SENATE FORECAST; $2,000,000,000 RELIEF PLAN IS DRAFTED

LEGAL LIQUOR DUE TONIGHT; CITY READY TO CELEBRATE; STORES TO OPEN TOMORROW

ROOSEVELT ASKS FOR BEER TO PROVIDE NEEDED REVENUE; CONGRESS SPEEDS ACTION ON THIS AND ON ECONOMY BILL; DEPOSITS EXCEED THE WITHDRAWALS IN OPENED BANKS

HITLER CABINET GETS POWER TO RULE AS A DICTATORSHIP; REICHSTAG QUITS SINE DIE

The latest photo of the kidnaped Lindbergh baby. The picture was released by Col. Lindbergh to help locate the child.

"BABY SAFE. Instructions later. Act accordingly." That was the terse and hope-bearing message on a post-card addressed to "Lindbergh" and found in a Newark letter box. Immediately a police cordon was thrown about a 12-block area in Newark. Thirty-five planes of Lindy's buddies, the "Quiet Birdmen," waged search from the skies, even as police did down below.

Col. Henry Breckenridge at window (circle) of Lindy home through which the baby was kidnaped.

the season included *And Life Goes On,* by Vicki Baum; *God's Little Acre,* by Erskine Caldwell; *The Last Adam,* by James Gould Cozzens; and *Rip Tide,* a novel in verse by William Rose Benét. Among the outstanding imports that shared in the 1932 Christmas book trade were *Night Flight* by Antoine de Saint-Exupéry, *Black Mischief* by the English satirist Evelyn Waugh, and the first approved (and slightly bowdlerized) American edition of that perennial British shocker, *Lady Chatterley's Lover.*

More emphatically than for the previous twenty years, Broadway was the center of the theatrical world as hard times and the advent of sound movies closed down vaudeville and legitimate theaters in most other cities. The result was a financially disastrous overproduction in New York, where, during the 1932 Christmas week, theatergoers had a choice of thirty-six new plays and musicals to choose from at top prices ranging from $3.30 to $4.40. Among the better offerings that week were Walter Hampden in the title role of the grotesque and tragic lover in Rostand's *Cyrano de Bergerac*; Eugenie Leonto-vich in *Twentieth Century,* a comedy produced by the popular writing team of Ben Hecht and Charles MacArthur; Virginia Stevens, starring in *The Little Black Book*; and Osgood Perkins in *Goodbye Again.* A major January open-ing brought Noel Coward, Alfred Lunt, and Lynn Fontanne together in Coward's elegantly risqué farce *Design for Living.* A few weeks later Katharine Cornell was presented in Sidney Howard's moody folk-piece, *The Alien Corn.*

The musical stage was supplied by such hardy perennials as "Earl Car-roll's Vanities" (which endured the aesthetic affront of having to put bras-sieres on its topless chorus girls upon express orders of Mayor Joseph McKee); the all-Negro revue "Shuffle Along of 1933"; and George White's "Music Hall Varieties," with comedian Bert Lahr and dancer Eleanor Powell. The Gershwin brothers, George and Ira, collaborated on a popular hit called *Pardon My English,* and Cole Porter wrote the music for *Gay Divorcée,* fea-turing Clare Luce and Fred Astaire.

For more serious music lovers, the Metropolitan Opera Company opened its fiftieth season in November with Verdi's unfamiliar *Simon Boccanegra,* with tenor Tito Schipa in the leading role. Doubts that a full season could be run in the Depression were largely dissipated when the opening night audience, conspicuously deficient in white ties and diamond tiaras, produced a gratifying gate of $15,000. Early in January the Met gave the world pre-miere of *The Emperor Jones,* an experimental venture based on a play by Eugene O'Neill, which critic Olin Downes of the *Times* acclaimed "an instant and sweeping success." In San Francisco a new opera house was opened that winter with beauteous Lily Pons in the title role of *Lucia di Lammermoor,* supported by an obscure young basso named Ezio Pinza. The Chicago Opera Association launched an experiment at about the same time in "pop" opera by putting on *Aida* in the hangar-like Chicago Stadium at a $1.50 top and drew an opening audience of 10,000. The country's leading symphony orchestras, reduced to less than a dozen, managed to open their seasons but mostly with reduced personnel and curtailed schedules. The country's most exciting musical prodigy of the day, the fifteen-year-old Yehudi Menuhin, won a new laurel leaf for his crown when, appearing in London's Albert Hall before a capacity audience, he played the solo part of Elgar's violin concerto with the London Philharmonic, as Sir Edward Elgar, the seventy-five-year-old dean of British composers, conducted.

Although the movies enjoyed a steady patronage throughout the Depression (they were everybody's escape hatch), Hollywood had fallen into deep financial difficulties by the winter of 1932–33, and the effects were visible in the anemic quality of the output. The industry's ailment was due to rampant overexpansion during the boom years of the twenties, to the tremendous outlays demanded by the shift to sound (a process begun in 1927), and to the meagerness of box office returns. Thirty-five cents was about the average admission charge for the general run of movie houses, and even the plush Paramount in New York seldom dared to push its fee to a dollar. In consequence, producers concentrated on low-budget pictures with a frothy, mass appeal—Westerns, honky-tonk musicals, slapsick, war adventures, and myriad hackneyed variants of Cinderella and boy-meets-girl. People with a full quota of problems of their own wanted only light entertainment.

There were a few exceptions to the general run of cinematic mediocrity. One was Cecil B. De Mille's somewhat pretentious *Sign of the Cross*, whose cast included Fredric March, Elissa Landi, Claudette Colbert, and Charles Laughton. Another exception was *A Farewell to Arms*, whose cast included Gary Cooper, Helen Hayes, and Adolph Menjou; it was a sweetened-up version of the novel that sent author Ernest Hemingway into a profane and scornful rage. In other above-average releases bug-eyed Eddie Cantor showed up as an improbable matador in *The Kid from Spain;* Marlene Dietrich wrought her usual glandular havoc on male audiences with her portrayal in *Blonde Venus;* and the screen's two leading voluptuaries, Jean Harlow and Clark Gable, chose a far-off place called Saigon for their love-making in *Red Dust*. In a notable innovation, Walt Disney released his first *Silly Symphony* in technicolor and said he could not decide whether, in future color releases, his principal star, Mickey Mouse, should be a white mouse with red eyes or just a black mouse. Thousands of fans wrote offering their suggestions.

An evening ritual in millions of homes across the nation was getting dinner over in time to gather around the family radio to hear "Amos 'n' Andy," the most durable pair of blackface comedians of all time. Introduced by an incongruously sedate waltz melody, "The Perfect Song," the nightly untangling of the dilemmas of the proprietors of the Fresh Air Taxicab Company and their friends was far and away the most popular network program on the air. In spite of the Depression, radio had had a phenomenal growth since its commercialization in 1922 and was now on the threshhold of its "Golden Age." It attracted top stars from the entertainment world, famous orchestras, and concert artists. If its choices from the field of journalism were meager, its regular and special newscasts had become a staple in the field of communication. Newspaper publishers were so terrified of radio competition that many refused to carry program listings except as paid advertisements.

Then as now in the mass-minded world of electronics, humor was valued above all other modes of expression, with popular music as its prop and closest competitor. Thus, the simpering vacuity of Ed Wynn, the "Texaco Fire Chief," rated close to "Amos 'n' Andy" in popularity, along with the garrulous spinsters "Myrt and Marge" and the nonsensical team of "Stoopnagle and Bud." Among the many variety programs offered, Eddie Cantor's "Chase and Sanborn Hour" was widely rated as the best, closely followed by "The Lucky Strike Hour" with the memorable "chant of the tobacco auctioneer" as its signature, the "A & P Gypsies," and similar groups.

The ubiquity of radio made name bands and their music famous in the remotest hamlets. Paul Whiteman with his magnificent brass choir playing at the Biltmore in New York, Ben Bernie at the Edgewater Beach Hotel in Chicago, Glen Gray and his Casa Loma Orchestra, and Ted Lewis asking seductively, "Is everybody happy?" were as familiar to the boondocks as to the Great White Way. Although there were no disk jockeys to pick the ten top tunes in 1932–33, there were indisputable hits, such as "Dancing in the Dark," "Goodnight Sweetheart," "When the Moon Comes Over the Mountain," which seemed to be the exclusive property of Kate Smith, Bing Crosby's distinctive rendition of "When the Blue of the Night Meets the Gold of the Day," "Night and Day," which was one of Cole Porter's best, and, as a sort of topical commentary, "Brother Can You Spare a Dime."

Serious music was much in vogue, both on the networks and over individual big city stations. Thus, in one typical January week listeners in New York were offered live broadcasts by the Metropolitan Opera Company, the New York Philharmonic, the Boston Symphony, Lily Pons, Lawrence Tibbett, Josef Hofmann, Sigrid Onegin, and, for good measure, a reading by Edna St. Vincent Millay of some of her own poems. Critics on the big newspapers gave almost as much serious attention to a broadcast program by a Heifetz or a Stokowski as to a personal appearance by them at Carnegie Hall.

In the field of sports, the New York Yankees, with a pair of sluggers named Babe Ruth and Lou Gehrig, were the inevitable world champions. Notre Dame, tops in collegiate football (professional football was in its infancy in the winter of 1932–33), suffered an unexpected 13–0 defeat in a post-season game with the University of California at Berkeley. Yale gave Harvard its worst defeat in fifty-one years of football rivalry, 19–0, in a downpour of rain in the Yale Bowl. Groton took a drubbing from St. Marks Prep, 7–0, in spite of standout performances by Franklin D. Roosevelt, Jr., as right tackle, and John A. Roosevelt as assistant manager and waterboy. In December an angry controversy erupted among sports enthusiasts when Babe Didrickson, the "wonder girl of sports" who broke four Olympic track records in 1930, was briefly deprived of her amateur standing on charges (later disproved) that she had been paid for a commercial endorsement. In February, Ernie Schaaf, a Boston heavyweight, died after a bout in Madison

Square Garden in which he was knocked out in the thirteenth round by Italy's mountain-sized Primo Carnera.

Who else and what else made news during that historic winter? The first issue of Bernarr Macfadden's new (and short-lived) magazines, *Babies, Just Babies*, reached the newsstands with this introductory comment by editor Eleanor Roosevelt: "Babies! Can you think of anything more wonderful?" . . . A vogue for "Hoovercart Rodeos" got its start in Goldsboro, North Carolina, and soon swept the country: the back half of an old Model T Ford hitched to a team of mules and raced over an obstacle course. . . . A contingent of 637 spry but aged Civil War veterans showed up at Springfield, Illinois, for the 66th annual reunion of the Grand Army of the Republic. . . . A coal mine explosion in Moweaqua, Illinois, two days before Christmas, killed fifty-four miners. Two days later an earthquake in Kansu Province killed an estimated 70,000 Chinese. . . . Evidence that hard times were universal was supplied by the news that the government of Chile had decided to beach its navy for a year, and that the Shah of Persia was seeking a buyer for his solid-gold Peacock Throne, valued at $19.5 million. . . . In Rome, Guglielmo Marconi, "the father of radio," predicted that worldwide radio-telephone service would soon be a reality (it was more than twenty years coming), and the picturesque Swiss scientist Auguste Piccard, on a lecture tour in the United States, predicted that cosmic rays would soon provide mankind with an abundant and virtually cost-free source of energy (it hasn't come yet). . . . The convention of the American Federation of Labor at Cincinnati in December was thrown into a brief uproar as a group of "Red" sympathizers led by Louis Weinstock sought to force through a resolution calling for diplomatic recognition of the Soviet Union. . . . A price war within the tobacco industry forced the price of most popular brands of cigarettes down to ten and twelve cents a package. Other bargains, as recorded in the advertising pages of *The New York Times* during post-Christmas sales, included the following: large turkish bath towels, 34¢; double cotton sheets, 84¢; men's all-wool sweaters, $1.95 and $2.65; ladies' black Persian coats, $95; men's overcoats, $16; men's derbies, $2.75, and women's and misses' corsets marked down from $69.50 to $19.50. What one saved on cigarette and corset bargains might profitably have been invested in winter travel bargains. There were eight pages of travel advertisements in the *Times* for Sunday January 15, 1933, including a sixteen-day Caribbean cruise by the Italian Line for $205 and a round-trip to Boston via the Fall River Line for $7.50, plus $1 for a stateroom. . . . On January 23 Missouri ratified, and thus made effective, the Twentieth Amendment to the Constitution which set the inauguration of future Presidents (excluding FDR) up from March 4 to January 20. In the same week, Congress overrode President Hoover's veto of a bill promising independence to the Philippines in twelve years, and the Senate dug in for a historic filibuster by the rambunctious freshman Senator from Louisiana, Huey "Kingfish" Long. . . . Former President Calvin Coolidge, undoubtedly thankful to the end for having said four years earlier, "I do not choose to run," died of a heart attack at his home in Northampton, Mass., on January 5. His will, leaving his $400,000 estate to his wife, was, characteristically, but seventy-five words long and was written in longhand on White House stationery.

News from abroad made little impact on our consciousness in those Depression years. "Isolationism" was a state of being rather than the partisan doctrine it would become later. However, even the most casual newspaper reader became aware during the winter of 1932–33 that storm clouds were building up along distant world horizons—clouds that were casting portentous shadows in the direction of the United States. . . . Long-seething unrest among liberal and left-wing masses in Spain erupted into civil war in the southern provinces early in January; martial law was declared, and pitched battles were fought between rebels and government troops in Valencia. . . . Late in November, 1932, Japan rejected mediation efforts by the League of Nations to halt its two-year aggression against China, sent its warships into the Yellow Sea, and in the following January opened a massive drive to seal off Jehol Province and thus complete its conquest of Manchuria. . . . On January 30 Adolf Hitler became Chancellor of Germany and two days later dissolved the German Parliament. When the Reichstag building was destroyed by fire on February 27, he forced from the faltering hand of President von Hindenburg an emergency decree suspending all constitutional guarantees respecting personal property and individual freedom. Nazism, which during the next dozen years would come close to destroying Western civilization, had found its power base.

CHAPTER 6
Inaugural
1932

SATURDAY, MARCH 4, 1933, was a raw, blustery day in Washington with dark clouds scudding overhead and sporadic gusts of cold rain slashing through the bare trees and across the glistening pavements. Along Pennsylvania Avenue from the foot of Capitol Hill to the White House half a million people wrapped in blankets and overcoats huddled in open bleachers or pressed against the ropes strung along the curb, waiting for the inaugural parade to begin. Other thousands pressed shoulder to shoulder in the great plaza before the Capitol, where the inaugural platform had been erected. The city was alive with flags and the sound of music, but the holiday spirit of the people seemed to have been damped out by the weather and by the somber significance of the event they had come to witness. "The atmosphere," one observer wrote, "was comparable to that which might be found in a beleaguered capital in wartime."

Unheralded that morning, Roosevelt had summoned members of his own family and of the families of his principal aides and Cabinet officers to join him in private religious services at old St. John's Church across Lafayette Square from the White House. It was a solemn and moving occasion. "If ever a man wanted to pray and wanted everyone to pray for him, that was the day," Frances Perkins, who had been chosen as Secretary of Labor, recalled. "It was impressive. Everybody prayed, it seemed, as Dr. [Endicott] Peabody read out the prayers for grace and help for 'Thy servant Franklin, about to become President of these United States.' We were Catholics, Protestants, and Jews but I doubt that anyone remembered the difference." [1]

Shortly before noon the President and the President-elect set off in an open car from the White House for the ceremonial procession to the Capitol. It was a cheerless journey, made uncomfortable by the tensions of personal dislike and resentment between the two men. For Herbert Hoover it was the last, cruel mile in a long distinguished public career now ending in failure and rejection. For Franklin Roosevelt it was the beginning of a test as severe as that faced by Lincoln.

They had sparred warily for the last three months as Hoover tried to involve Roosevelt in policy decisions affecting the crisis, and as Roosevelt stubbornly refused to be encumbered by a predecessor's commitments and mistakes. They rode grim-faced and silent to the Capitol, barely acknowledging the sporadic cheers of the damp crowds along the way.

Within the great domed Capitol all was turmoil. Roosevelt was wheeled past pushing throngs of Congressional clerks and other spectators into the privacy of the Military Affairs Committee room while John Nance Garner took the Vice Presidential oath in the Senate chamber. Then there came the strains of the U.S. Marine Band playing "Hail to the Chief" as President Hoover walked from the rotunda out to the columned inaugural stand built above the steps of the east portal. Moments later, the President-elect followed. Supported on the arm of his son James, he walked stiffly down the long carpeted aisle to the waiting, black-robed figure of Chief Justice Charles Evans Hughes. A shout went up from the massed spectators below—the first genu-

The Inaugural Committee

requests the honor of the presence of

to attend and participate in the Inauguration of

Franklin Delano Roosevelt

as President of the United States of America

and

John Nance Garner

as Vice President of the United States of America

on Saturday the fourth of March

one thousand nine hundred and thirty three

in the City of Washington

Please reply to Ray Baker
Chairman Committee on Reception of Governors of States
and
Special Distinguished Guests
Washington Building Washington D.C.

Cary T. Grayson
Chairman, Inaugural Committee

This great Nation will endure as it has endured, will revive and will prosper. So, first of all, let me assert my firm belief that the only thing we have to fear is fear itself—nameless, unreasoning, unjustified terror which paralyzes needed efforts to convert retreat into advance.

First Inaugural Address
Washington, March 4, 1933

Section 1

"All the News That's Fit to Print."

The New York Times.

LATE CITY EDITION
WEATHER—Fair today and tomorrow; temperature unchanged.
Temperatures Yesterday—Max., 43; Min., 34

Section 1

Copyright, 1933, by The New York Times Company.

VOL. LXXXII....No. 27,434. Entered as Second-Class Matter, Postoffice, New York, N. Y. NEW YORK, SUNDAY, MARCH 5, 1933. F Including Rotogravure Picture, Magazine and Book Sections. TEN CENTS | TWELVE CENTS Beyond 200 Miles, Except in 7th and 8th Postal Zones.

ROOSEVELT INAUGURATED, ACTS TO END THE NATIONAL BANKING CRISIS QUICKLY; WILL ASK WAR-TIME POWERS IF NEEDED

PLAN TO USE SCRIP HERE

Bankers Ready to Issue Clearing House Paper at End of Holiday.

WILL MEET WOODIN TODAY

Eastern Financiers to Join Parley at Capital on Plans to Permit Reopenings.

STOCK EXCHANGES CLOSED

Drain on the Gold Reserve Is Halted—Cash Being Set Aside to Meet Payrolls.

The Banking Situation.

The New York Clearing House Association prepared to print and issue certificates to be used by the public as substitute money.

In every State of the nation, including the District of Columbia, banking was wholly or partly suspended.

In London, Paris and other European capitals, dollar transactions were suspended.

Bankers from New York and other financial centres will confer with Secretary of the Treasury Woodin on remedial plans for presentation by the President to this afternoon's legislative conference.

Scrip Being Rushed.

Clearing house certificates will be used instead of currency in New York when the banks reopen on Tuesday after the two-day holiday proclaimed by Governor Herbert H. Lehman, according to present plans of the New York Clearing House Association, it was learned last night.

This was confirmed by Mortimer N. Buckner, president of the New York Clearing House Association and chairman of the board of the New York Trust Company, following a meeting of the clearing house committee at the clearing house, 77 Cedar Street.

Bankers from New York and other centres have been called to Washington to confer with William H. Woodin, Secretary of the Treasury, at 10 o'clock this morning on plans for meeting the emergency. George W. Davison, chairman of the Central Hanover Bank and Trust Company and head of the Clearing House Committee, left for Washington yesterday afternoon; and George L. Harrison, governor of the Federal Reserve Bank of New York was scheduled to go last night. Charles S. McCain, chairman of the board of the Chase National Bank, was in Washington yesterday and it was thought likely that he would remain for the conference.

In the event that the discussions of the bankers with Mr. Woodin develop a plan which can be put into effect through Congressional action, the proposals will be laid before President Roosevelt this afternoon and presented by him to a conference of legislators. It is expected that the results of the conference may have a bearing upon how quickly the new Congress is called into session.

In addition to the New York bankers, representatives from the banking communities of Philadelphia, Chicago, Baltimore and Richmond are expected to attend the conference.

Act to Meet Payrolls.

It was indicated last night that arrangements would be made whereby payrolls due yesterday or tomorrow would be met by the withdrawal from the banks of sufficient amounts of currency to pay all or part in cash. Concerns accustomed to paying by check would be permitted to withdraw cash, it was predicted, or the banks would make special provision for cashing pay checks. Governor Lehman is expected to give his approval to a payroll plan being worked out by the banks and business houses.

The banking holiday ordered by Governor Lehman in a proclamation issued at his apartment, 820 Park Avenue, at 4:20 o'clock yesterday morning, was effective yesterday, and will expire at the

Continued on Page Twenty-five.

Checks Still Accepted Here For Federal Income Taxes

Collectors of Internal Revenue in New York City were still accepting checks yesterday in payment of Federal income taxes, and it was said that checks would continue to be accepted during the bank holiday.

No consideration was yet being given to possible postponement of payments, due on March 15. This could only be granted by the Secretary of the Treasury or Commissioner of Internal Revenue in Washington, although the law allows individual applications for extension of time.

Walter E. Corwin, Collector in Brooklyn, said clearing-house certificates would not be accepted, if issued as a medium of exchange. The law permits payment in cash, checks, Treasury notes or Liberty bonds.

VICTORY FOR HITLER IS EXPECTED TODAY

Repression of Opponents Held to Make Election Triumph for Regime Inevitable.

FIRES BLAZE ON BORDERS

Nazis Light Them as Sign of "Reawakening"—Imperial Flag to Be Restored.

By FREDERICK T. BIRCHALL.

Special Cable to The New York Times.

BERLIN, March 4.—In a countrywide blaze of bonfires and torchlight parades the allied National Socialist and Nationalist parties tonight closed the electoral campaign, which tomorrow is expected to entrench them securely in power not only throughout Germany as a result of the Reichstag elections but throughout Prussia, where the electorate will vote simultaneously for a separate State ticket.

Tonight, on every eminence along Germany's borders, not excluding the Polish Corridor, a bonfire flamed to signalize the Nazi ideal of an awakening nation. In Koenigsberg, East Prussia, Chancellor Adolf Hitler himself made his closing appeal to aroused patriotic fervor.

In every city and every town of considerable size uniformed Nazis marched to some centre, where amid the blare of brass bands playing partiotic songs, in which the whole assemblage joined, Nazi orators proclaimed the dawning of a new day.

In Berlin alone there were twenty-four parades to an equal number of meeting places, where through loud-speakers the voice of Herr Hitler was heard and acclaimed.

No Counter-Demonstrations.

There were no counter-demonstrations from the opposition. They were "verboten," for this is a one-way election. Nor, late tonight, despite the dire predictions sent to the outside world, had any serious disturbance been reported. All that is over, for what is the use of inviting inevitable and overwhelming reprisals when all the authority and all the weapons are monopolized by the other side?

In Thuringia, the only State in which a few Socialist newspapers remain unsuspended, they were all compelled by the Nazi State government today to reprint Chancellor Hitler's recent speech against "Marxism" on the front page.

The utmost left for those opposed to an all-Nazi régime is to vote against it silently and secretly tomorrow—if they dare—and to hope for the best.

So confident today are the government leaders of a verdict in their favor that even before the polls are open they are already announcing the first act of the new Reichstag. It will be to retire the Republican flag of black, red and gold under which Germany has fought her way out of the difficulties in which the World War left her and to replace it with the black-white-red banner of the former imperialism.

"We shall be happy to get rid of that emblem of 'Marxism,'" declared Captain Hermann Wilhelm Goering, Minister Without Portfolio and the spokesman of militant na-

Continued on Page Twenty.

READY TO CALL CONGRESS

President Probably Will Summon Extra Session for Wednesday.

WORKS ON LEGISLATION

Cabinet Ordered to Meet With Him Today to Draft Banking Reform Measures.

AID LIKELY IN A WEEK

Steps Considered Include Deposit Guarantee, Use of Scrip and Tax on Hoarded Gold.

Special to The New York Times.

WASHINGTON, March 4.—President Roosevelt plunged immediately into the banking situation tonight by summoning members of his Cabinet and leaders of Congress to meet tomorrow afternoon to decide upon a program to deal with it.

As soon as the program is agreed upon, Congress will be called into special session, probably on Wednesday, and it is the expectation of administration advisers that legislation will be enacted within another week.

The White House issued the following statement at 7:20 P. M.:

"Respecting the date for the extra session of Congress, no decision has been reached tonight, but probably will be by tomorrow night.

"The Secretary of the Treasury will begin tomorrow a series of discussions called at the request of President Roosevelt, looking to prompt action in the banking situation. He is calling a number of individuals and Reserve Bank officials to Washington. Some have already been invited and more will be called tonight."

Bankers from New York, Philadelphia, Chicago, Baltimore and Richmond were invited to the conference with Secretary Woodin at 10 o'clock tomorrow morning.

After they have discussed the banking situation, whatever plan may be adopted will be transmitted to President Roosevelt for presentation to the legislative conference in the afternoon.

Four Proposals Advanced.

While President Roosevelt was reviewing the parade from the stand in front of the White House this afternoon, members of his Cabinet and two former Secretaries of the Treasury, David F. Houston and William G. McAdoo, were engaged in discussion of a program which will be laid before the conference tomorrow.

The main points advanced but not finally decided upon at this informal conference, in which Secretary Woodin participated for a few minutes, were:

1. The organization of a corporation to which banks must subscribe to guarantee bank deposits.

2. The issue of scrip, as was resorted to in the banking emergency in 1907, to be put out by the banks to the amount of frozen deposits.

3. A tax on hoarded gold, as high as 15 per cent.

4. Other measures to protect our gold holdings.

Secretary of State Hull said, however, that a tax on hoarded gold did not seem practicable, and probably would not be resorted to in the hope of raising any considerable amount of money, but merely as a move to force hoarders to put gold into circulation and restore confidence in the banks.

These suggestions with others will come before the conference tomorrow and the new administration leaders were confident tonight that a program could be agreed upon for submission to and prompt action by Congress by the middle of next week.

Problem Is to Allay Fear.

"The main thing right now," said Secretary Hull, "is to allay the unreasonable and unreasoning fear in the public mind. That in itself would be a long step in the direction toward restoration of confidence. Nothing right now is more unjustifiable than attempts to hoard money."

Former Secretary of the Treasury

Continued on Page Twenty-four.

THE NEW PRESIDENT TAKING THE OATH OF OFFICE.

Franklin D. Roosevelt, With Hand Raised, Being Sworn by Chief Justice Charles Evans Hughes on the Rostrum in Front of the Capitol at 1:08 P. M. Yesterday. At the Right Are His Son, James Roosevelt, and Former President Hoover.

HOOVER, AS CITIZEN, HERE ON WAY HOME

Spends Evening in Seclusion in Hotel After Seeing His Successor Take Office.

SEEMS GLAD TO GET AWAY

Bids Genial Farewell to Old Friends in Capital After Morning of Heavy Cares.

By RUSSELL OWEN.

Herbert Hoover entered private life yesterday after a day of foreboding, in which his successor addressed the nation as though it were entering upon a war. With downcast eyes and a diffident manner, Mr. Hoover went to the Capitol to see Mr. Roosevelt inaugurated as President, and left hurriedly, as if glad to throw from his shoulders the mantle of responsibility for the affairs of a country desperately distressed.

Immediately after the ceremony he left the Capitol and drove to the railroad station to take a train for New York, where he arrived at 8:50 o'clock last night. He went to the Waldorf-Astoria and spent the evening in seclusion, avoiding visitors.

Until half an hour before he stepped into the automobile that was to bear him and President Roosevelt to the inaugural ceremonies in Washington, he was busy with affairs of state. As no other man who has stepped from the office of Chief Executive, he was beset with complex problems until the end of his term. The last bills he signed were those to aid the country through the present crisis. He signed them grimly, with a grave face, realizing to the full the difficulties which he was bequeathing.

Raises Hat Only Once.

The drive from the White House to the Capitol was through lines of people who watched with serious, rather than enthusiastic faces. A sense of depression had settled over the capital so that it could be felt. The two men, side by side, were looked upon as symbols of a government trying to cope with dangers which were as subtle as they were treacherous. The few cheers were for Roosevelt rather than Hoover. He realized that, and only raised his hat once during the trip, although the new President smiled and doffed his hat frequently in response to the faint cheers from the stands and sidewalk.

But once in the railroad station to take the train to New York after the inauguration, Mr. Hoover came into his own again. There were people who firmly believed in him,

Continued on Page Four.

Text of the Inaugural Address; President for Vigorous Action

"This Is Pre-eminently the Time to Speak the Truth," He Says, in Demand That "the Temple of Our Civilization Be Restored to the Ancient Truths."

Special to The New York Times.

WASHINGTON, March 4.—President Roosevelt's inaugural address, delivered immediately after he took the oath, was as follows:

President Hoover, Mr. Chief Justice, my friends:

This is a day of national consecration, and I am certain that my fellow-Americans expect that on my induction into the Presidency I will address them with a candor and a decision which the present situation of our nation impels.

This is pre-eminently the time to speak the truth, the whole truth, frankly and boldly. Nor need we shrink from honestly facing conditions in our country today. This great nation will endure as it has endured, will revive and will prosper.

So first of all let me assert my firm belief that the only thing we have to fear is fear itself—nameless, unreasoning, unjustified terror which paralyzes needed efforts to convert retreat into advance.

In every dark hour of our national life a leadership of frankness and vigor has met with that understanding and support of the people themselves which is essential to victory. I am convinced that you will again give that support to leadership in these critical days.

In such a spirit on my part and on yours we face our common difficulties. They concern, thank God, only material things. Values have shrunken to fantastic levels; taxes have risen; our ability to pay has fallen; government of all kinds is faced by serious curtailment of income; the means of exchange are frozen in the currents of trade; the withered leaves of industrial enterprise lie on every side; farmers find no markets for their produce; the savings of many years in thousands of families are gone.

More important, a host of unemployed citizens face the grim problem of existence, and an equally great number toil with little return. Only a foolish optimist can deny the dark realities of the moment.

Yet our distress comes from no failure of substance. We are stricken by no plague of locusts. Compared with the perils which our forefathers conquered because they believed and were not afraid, we have still much to be thankful for. Nature still offers her bounty and human efforts have multiplied it. Plenty is at our doorstep, but a generous use of it languishes in the very sight of the supply.

Charges "Money Changers" Lack Vision.

Primarily, this is because the rulers of the exchange of mankind's goods have failed through their own stubbornness and their own incompetence, have admitted their failure and abdicated. Practices of the unscrupulous money changers stand indicted in the court of public opinion, rejected by the hearts and minds of men.

True, they have tried, but their efforts have been cast in the pattern of an outworn tradition. Faced by failure of credit, they have proposed only the lending of more money.

Stripped of the lure of profit by which to induce our people to follow their false leadership, they have resorted to exhortations, pleading tearfully for restored confidence. They know only the rules of a generation of self-seekers.

They have no vision, and when there is no vision the people perish.

The money changers have fled from their high seats in the temple of our civilization. We may now restore that temple to the ancient truths.

The measure of the restoration lies in the extent to which we apply social values more noble than mere monetary profit.

Happiness lies not in the mere possession of money; it lies in the joy of achievement, in the thrill of creative effort.

The joy and moral stimulation of work no longer must be forgotten in the mad chase of evanescent profits. These dark days will be worth all they cost us if they teach us that our true

Continued on Page Three.

500,000 IN STREETS CHEER ROOSEVELT

Their Spirits Are Lifted by His Smile of Confidence as They Watch Parade.

MANY ON ROOFS, IN TREES

Throng Waiting for Ceremony Is Solemnly Silent Until New President Appears.

Special to The New York Times.

WASHINGTON, March 4.—The quadrennial pageant which traditionally accompanies the inauguration of a new President was enacted here today with all the pomp and panoply of more prosperous years and with all solemnity.

Before the august Capitol, in an inadequate and windswept forty acres, 100,000 of his countrymen saw Franklin D. Roosevelt swear on the ancient Bible of his Dutch fathers to cherish and defend the Constitution of his country.

Five hundred thousand others saw his reassuringly confident smile as he rode from Capitol to White House at the head of a parade of 18,000 marching men and women, among whom were such of his formidable rivals for the nomination as Alfred E. Smith and Governor Albert C. Ritchie of Maryland.

Mr. Roosevelt became the thirty-second President of the United States on a day that was cloudy and chill, with an occasional ray of sunlight piercing the clouds below which rode majestically the navy airship Akron and ninety-six military airplanes from Bolling and Langley Fields.

Flags flew at half-staff on the Senate and House Office Buildings in memory of Senator Walsh, who was to have been Attorney General in the new Cabinet.

Over the vast throngs there hung a cloud of worry, because of the economic and business outlook. The new President's recurrent smile of confidence, his uplifted chin and the challenge of his voice did much to help the national sense of humor to assert itself.

Reviews Parade for Three Hours.

Again, standing throughout the afternoon while legions of men of all degrees and colors marched past his glass-enclosed reviewing stand in the Court of Honor, the new President, advocate of a new deal, set an example of resolute fortitude and cheerfulness as he doffed his hat in deference to the colors and in greeting to old friends and supporters.

He stood between Admiral William V. Pratt, Chief of Naval Operations, and General Douglas Mac-

Continued on Page Two.

100,000 AT INAUGURATION

President, Grim, Terse, Pledges 'Adequate but Sound Currency.'

SCORES 'MONEY-CHANGERS'

In Fighting Speech He Demands Supervision of Credits and Investments.

STICKS TO CONSTITUTION

Calls on People and Congress to Follow Him as Leader in War on Depression.

By ARTHUR KROCK.

Special to The New York Times.

WASHINGTON, March 4.—With solemn mien, Franklin D. Roosevelt of New York took the oath of office and became the thirty-second President of the United States on the main steps of the Capitol at eight minutes after 1 o'clock this afternoon.

A deep consciousness of the task before him was patent in his unusual demeanor as, his face stern, his voice grave, he repeated after Chief Justice Hughes the historic words of the oath. This realization animated also the inaugural address which Mr. Roosevelt then delivered in the presence of at least a hundred thousand persons who gathered in the Capitol grounds.

The sense of the administration's burden was apparent, too, in the manner and speech of Vice President Garner, who, an hour before the President took the oath, laid down his gavel as Speaker of the House of Representatives and was inducted into his new office in the Senate chamber, where he will henceforth preside.

Keeps Pledge of Action.

"Action" was the promise of Mr. Roosevelt's speech, and action was immediately forthcoming. The first moment after the ceremonies were over, the President swore in his Cabinet, summoned the party leaders to a Sunday conference to work out the plan for banking relief and arranged to call an extra session of the Seventy-third Congress, probably on Wednesday, to legislate the plan into law.

"This nation asks for action, and action now," he said on the steps of the Capitol. Within a few hours, he acted.

The President had consistently maintained his attitude that he would not accept responsibility without power in the period between his election and his inauguration. Powerful and subtle suasions could not move him. But when authority came he moved at once as he had said he would.

Atmosphere Is Grim.

Though the city was gay with flags and lively with the music of bands and cheers for the marchers in the inaugural parade which followed the oath taking, the atmosphere which surrounded the change of government in the United States was comparable to that which might be found in a beleaguered capital in war time.

The President in his address told the people that they were at war with the forces of depression and offered them leadership and action in the new campaign to be waged against these forces.

In words that burned and scourged he denounced the financial leaders of the nation, declared that these "money changers" should be driven from the temple and that they should not be allowed to return to their high places. No more, he declared, should those entrusted with other people's money be permitted to misuse it.

The inaugural address was a Jacksonian speech, a fighting speech, implicit with criticism of the lack of leadership and the philosophy of government which the President imputed to his predecessor, who sat there, listening. He would lead, he said, as the people expect, within the confines of the Constitution, and he will demand that Congress follow this leadership.

But if his present powers prove insufficient to win the war to which he pledged his full mind and

Continued on Page Three.

At right: March 4, 1933. President-elect Franklin Delano Roosevelt and a dour Herbert Hoover on the way to the Inauguration.

inely spontaneous demonstration of the day, according to one observer—and then subsided as the solemn ceremonies of the oath-taking began.

This was the scene as described in the next day's *New York Times* by Arthur Krock:

With solemn mien, Franklin Delano Roosevelt of New York took the oath of office and became the thirty-second President of the United States today on the main steps of the Capitol at eight minutes after one o'clock.

A deep consciousness of the task before him was patent in his unusual demeanor as, his face grave, he repeated after Chief Justice Hughes the historic oath of office.

This realization animated also the inaugural address which Mr. Roosevelt then delivered in the presence of at least 100,000 persons who gathered on the Capitol grounds.

All across the nation on that memorable Saturday, millions sat thoughtfully and silently by their radios and listened as the strong, confident voice of the new President summoned them out of their lethargy and despair:

This is a day of national consecration, and I am certain that my fellow Americans expect that on my induction into the Presidency I will address them with a candor and a decision which the present situation of our nation impels.

This is preeminently the time to speak the truth, the whole truth, frankly and boldly, nor need we shrink from honestly facing the conditions in our country today. This great nation will endure as it has endured, will revive and will prosper.

So first of all let me assert my firm belief that the only thing we have to fear is fear itself—nameless, unreasoning, unjustified terror which paralyzes needed effort to convert retreat into advance. . . .

As Roosevelt spoke from the windswept steps of the Capitol, a faint radiance of sunlight broke briefly through the cold March sky.

Some, at least, of the millions who heard his voice that day felt a quickening of hope within their troubled spirits.

CHAPTER 7
The Hundred Days
March–June 1933

THE FIRST WEEK OF Franklin Roosevelt's Administration produced a palpable lifting of the fog of despair that had hung over
the nation for three years. His great inaugural speech cut like the
blast of a clear and certain trumpet through the confusion and anxiety
of men's minds to bring them their first sensation of hope. His resolute promise of "action—and action now" had the ring of truth about
it, and before Inauguration Day came to a close, he was to show
that there was substance behind the promise. As the last floats of the inaugural
parade passed the reviewing stand in the gathering dusk before the White
House, his Cabinet was sworn in and immediately went to work.

In the days that followed, the Washington scene was abruptly transformed
from the quagmire of torpor and bewilderment that had gripped it for the past
six months into an arena of spirited activity. Men with unfamiliar names and
faces scurried purposefully in and about the White House and the executive
departments. The President was in constant consultation with a succession of
aides and dignitaries whom he had called to his side. Conferences went on
almost around the clock, not only at the White House but at the Treasury
(particularly the Treasury), the State, and the Commerce Departments, and
in private suites at the Carleton, the Mayflower, and other hotels. Congressional leaders pushed into and out of these assemblages; so did bankers and
lawyers and labor leaders and politicians and college professors. The Washington press corps, electrified by this sudden deliverance from the Hoover
doldrums, laid siege to the obvious news centers and used guerrilla tactics to
keep up with what was going on at a score of ever-changing outposts. They
poured millions of words of gossip and speculation and some exciting hard
news onto the news wires for a public that had suddenly developed an insatiable curiosity about what was going on in Washington. And a lot was
going on.

I

The Roosevelt Administration's fabled "Hundred Days"—probably as
crucial a brief epoch as any in the nation's history—had started. They were
to dissipate the panic of the Depression even if they would not break the
back of the Depression itself. In virtually his first official act in office, initiated
within hours of taking the oath, the President decreed a national bank holiday, shutting down every financial institution in the land, and called a special
session of Congress to convene within four days. Simultaneously, a dozen
task forces were at work drafting one of the most revolutionary legislative
programs ever essayed by any President. Between March 9 and June 16
Roosevelt would propose and Congress would pass fifteen "emergency" acts,
which, in their totality, would drastically affect the nation's social and political orientation far into the future. Some of these laws were temporary stop-
gaps and some would in time be struck down by the courts, but fully half of
these "emergency" enactments remain embedded in the statute books today.
Never before had such a legislative miracle been wrought in so short a time.

"Whatever laws the President thinks he may need to end the depression,"

Senator Burton K. Wheeler of Montana said on Inauguration Day, "Congress will jump through a hoop to put them through." His prophecy was fulfilled.

Many urged the President to request—or to seize—the powers of a dictator. "The President's program demands dictatorial authority," the Boston *Transcript* editorialized toward the end of the first week. "This is unprecedented in its implications, but such is the desperate temper of the people that it is welcome."

All across the country there was a sudden upsurge of support and enthusiasm for the new President. At last, people told one another, *something* was being done: the perilous drift toward ruin and revolution was being checked. Even the closing of the banks, as bad as it was for many, was a welcome break in the suspense of not knowing what would happen next. It appeared that whatever the new President decided to do, the people were ready to go along with him. They deluged him with messages of fealty and good wishes. Some 14,000 letters and telegrams poured into the White House mailroom during the first week alone. The New York *Daily News,* which had not backed Roosevelt in the election, grudgingly conceded it might have been wrong and said, "This newspaper pledges itself to support the policies of FDR for a period of at least one year; longer if circumstances warrant." And Alfred M. Landon of Kansas, who was to loom large in the life of Roosevelt four years later, affirmed: "If there is any way in which a Republican governor of a midwestern state can aid the President in the fight, I now enlist for the duration of the war."

FDR was quickly revealed as a man of action, and as a man of warmth and feeling as well. Hoover, a mirthless man under the best of circumstances, had, under the most trying of circumstances, cast a pall of cheerless austerity over the White House. This evaporated instantly as the big, garrulous family of Roosevelts, with their gaiety and informality, moved in. The mood projected itself to official Washington and to the world beyond. The President attacked his job with zest and enthusiasm. At his first press conference he stunned the hundred-odd reporters who crowded into his office by his friendly, relaxed manner, the first-name intimacy with which he addressed many of them, and the candor and liberality with which he answered their questions. "The most amazing performance of its kind in the White House ever seen," is the way a correspondent for the Baltimore *Sun* described this encounter.

President Hoover had dourly told Roosevelt that "a President calls on no one." But FDR found an hour during that crowded week to call at the home of retired Justice Oliver Wendell Holmes on the occasion of the great jurist's ninety-second birthday.

On the evening of Sunday, March 12, as the finale of his first week in office, Roosevelt opened a line of communication directly to the people themselves. It was an intimate way of talking to a vast radio audience—the fireside chat, which he made uniquely his own. These radio "visits" by the President of the United States into the American living room were a triumph of the dramatic art that no other public figure has ever matched. So deftly were they done, so subtle were their histrionics and so free of pretensions or obvious guile, that one could feel the presence of Roosevelt as one listened to his words. In this first fireside chat he spoke as a wise friend speaks to his neighbors, telling them in simple, believable words why their banks were closed and what was being done to get them open again. He did not patronize his listeners with platitudes and false promises. The banking system was truly in a bad way, he said, and some people were going to be hurt before the damage could be repaired. But there would be far fewer victims now than if the crisis were allowed to run its course, and when the banks would reopen in a few days they would be stronger than before.

It was a masterful performance. It helped to restore the people's confidence and built a bridge of intimacy between them and the President. "Never was there such a change in the transfer of a government," wrote Arthur Krock. "At the end of a week so swift-moving and momentous that it contained as many major events as have occurred in the entire administration of some Presidents, Mr. Roosevelt was strong, cheerful, more than hopeful. The feeling is spreading that the 'leadership' which was promised, and for which so many people voted, has arrived."

Charles Michelson, the talented Democratic party "ghost" who helped write the first fireside chat (also many more to come) said: "They were ready to believe FDR could see in the dark."[1]

II

The whirlwind of activity in those early weeks—the outpouring of special messages to Congress, the proclamations, the public statements and appointments—was described at the time as a masterwork of improvisation. This was only partially true. The impression resulted from the urgency for fast action, especially in the banking crisis, and from the sudden decision to press basic new legislation through the special session of Congress while its mood was still pliant. The broad outlines of the New Deal program had been spelled out by FDR in his campaign, and he brought to Washington not only a sizable portfolio of policy papers and legislative proposals but also a corps of aides and experts capable of putting his plans into effect.

The nucleus of this corps was the "Brain Trust,"* a small team of scholars and technicians who had gravitated to Roosevelt during his 1932 campaign to help him formulate his program. The involvement of scholars instead of the familiar priesthood of business and finance on such a high political mission was, in itself, a significant innovation that would distinguish the New Deal from most Administrations of the past. Their field was ideas not votes: how to preserve the capitalist system from collapse and give it a surer footing than it had had. Like disciples of a latter-day Messiah, their dedication to Roosevelt became, for the time being a least, complete. His goals and theirs merged into a single vision of a great reformation, and they came eagerly to Washington to share in its fulfillment. The Brain Trust

* The orgin of this phrase is commonly attributed to John Kieran, an Albany reporter for *The New York Times*. Raymond Moley claims credit for having first applied the New Deal label to the Roosevelt program.

quickly acquired legendary colors and proportions in the poular mind. It was viewed alternatively as an intellectual powerhouse or as a sinister cabal; it was admired, sneered at, or feared depending on the viewer's bias. It lived on in the folklore of the time long after the group itself had dissolved. But its influence during he formative phase of the New Deal was profound and very nearly indispensable.

The key man in the group was Raymond Moley, a professor of government and public law at Columbia University. He was a man of great intellectual energy, a pragmatic liberal whose political philosophy was rooted in the progressivism of Cleveland, Theodore Roosevelt, and Woodrow Wilson. For years he had interspersed his teaching career with frequent writing and with serving on a variety of governmental boards and commissions. It was during one such tour of duty for the State of New York in 1930 that he came to know Governor Roosevelt. Their relationship was fed by mutual respect and a wide base of common political belief. Moley became a sort of unofficial adviser to the Governor in such fields as governmental organization and the administration of justice. It was necessarily a part-time occupation (he was still on the faculty at Columbia), but he soon found himself on an almost equal footing at Albany with Louis Howe, Roosevelt's secretary, and Samuel I. Rosenman, the Governor's counsel. When FDR formally announced his candidacy in January 1932, these three (along with Jim Farley) became a general staff for the candidate.

Farley and Howe concerned themselves exclusively with the political side of the campaign. Moley, Rosenman, and Basil O'Connor (FDR's law partner, who was also enlisted) were concerned with issues and with helping the candidate to formulate a coherent national program for the administration he sought to establish. Old clichés and tired nostrums would not work. Reliance on them had brought the country to its present sorry plight. What was needed were fresh ideas geared to the realities of the times, and the place to find them was, predominantly, in the universities. With Roosevelt's consent (given somewhat dubiously at first), Moley and his colleagues made an inventory of issues demanding attention and then combed over the lists of available experts in each field.

One of the most critical areas of national concern was agriculture. This sector of the economy seemed to be in the throes of a terminal illness for which all the familiar remedies had proved useless. One expert who had done original thinking on the farm problem was Rexford Guy Tugwell, an associate of Moley's at Columbia. Tugwell was a photogenic and marvelously articulate young professor of economics who had written extensively on the ills of agriculture. "Rex was like a cocktail," Moley said of him later. "His conversation picked you up and made your brain race along." Moley and Rosenman, without disclosing the full scope of their intention, invited Tugwell to go up to Albany with them one evening to "meet" FDR.

The testing-out process employed in the case of Tugwell was followed in the ensuing weeks with a dozen other candidates for this elite inner circle. The group would arrive at Albany or Hyde Park in time for an informal dinner with the Roosevelts. Afterward they would adjourn to the Governor's library or study, and the conversation would be steered to the selected subject of the evening and the specialty of the visitor: tariffs, monetary policy, business regulation, whatnot. For two or three hours the guest was subjected to an intensive but friendly third degree to determine what he knew and could contribute and how congenial a companion he would be for the journey ahead.

"The amount of intellectual ransacking that Roosevelt could crowd into one evening was a source of constant astonishment to me," Moley said.

Tugwell made an instant hit with Roosevelt, and Roosevelt in turn virtually mesmerized the young economics professor. He happily enlisted for the duration of the campaign, although neither he nor any of the others could hope to collect even out-of-pocket expenses for their part-time labors.

Another important early recruit was Adolf A. Berle, at the age of thirty-eight a kind of intellectual *enfant terrible,* who had graduated with honors from Harvard College at seventeen and had taken his LL.B. at the Harvard Law School at twenty-one. He was both a successful practicing corporation lawyer and a member of the Columbia University law faculty (and also a registered Republican) when Moley and Rosenman initiated him into the Roosevelt fold. An account of him published at this time said: "Berle's short and slender figure is a concentrate of nervous and intellectual energy. Among the members of the 'Brain Trust' he is the brilliant lawyer, the most thorough analytic economist, a master of prose, and a bit of a moralist."

A dozen other scholars and experts moved in and out of this select company. But the really authentic Brain Trusters of the campaign and post-campaign period were these five: Moley, Rosenman, O'Connor, Tugwell, and Berle. Rosenman dropped out after the Democratic Convention, when Roosevelt named him to the State Supreme Court. A new face was added at about the same time: the volcanic Gen. Hugh Johnson, who was later to be the mastermind of the NRA (the National Recovery Administration).

Moley was, by FDR's choice, the captain of the team. The planning sessions of the group were held evenings in his cramped office on the Columbia campus. There was a certain excitement in the atmosphere as they labored late into the nights, arguing and speculating and writing long memorandums about economic theories and social phenomena in a world suddenly turned upside down. Assignments were parceled out among them for special lines of inquiry, and each man in turn enlisted the help of other scholars and specialists of his acquaintance. Their output was prodigious.

The end product of all this labor was not a set of firm New Deal blueprints and policies. What the session did, Moley has since recalled, "was to make us pull ourselves together and put down on paper a good many of the notions we had been batting around in conversation with the Governor. At last we could see in black and white the outlines of the national program we had been sketching out in talk. We could take note of the holes in our thinking and get to work filling some of them up."

Three basic postulates that came off this intellectual production line are worth noting because they underlay some particularly significant New

FINAL

MUrray Hill 2-1000

SUNDAY MIRROR

Registered U. S. Patent Office.

Copyright 1933 Daily Mirror 235 East 45th St. New York, N. Y.

New York, Sunday, March 5, 1933

5 CENTS
PAY NO MORE

ROOSEVELT ASKS DICTATOR'S ROLE

—Story on Page 3

ROOSEVELT INAUGURATED! READY FOR WAR-TIME POWERS—Here is the scene on the inaugural stand at the Capitol, in Washington, as Supreme Court Justice Hughes (1) swore Franklin Delano Roosevelt (2) into the office of the Presidency. Among the onlookers are ex-President Herbert Hoover (4) and James Roosevelt (3), the new Chief's son. In his inaugural words, Roosevelt electrified the nation by his stated readiness to ask Congress for war-time powers to fight the emergency as though we were "invaded by a foreign foe." Almost immediately after the inaugural speech, Congress confirmed the Roosevelt Cabinet with practically no discussion. Swift action was the guiding rule.

Deal policies: First, that the root cause of the Depression was domestic in origin, not international, and that the principal remedies would also have to be domestic. Second, that the regulatory powers of the government should be used not only to correct abuses to the economy but to stimulate and stabilize the economic system for the benefit of all. Finally, that an industrial economy with huge aggregates of productive capacity was here to stay and that the obligation of government was to invest this mighty force with a new measure of social responsibility.[2]

The argument was often made that FDR got his ideas for the New Deal from the Brain Trust; that he, in effect, was but the mouthpiece and front man for a group of wily professors. This was not the case. While Roosevelt had no more than an intelligent layman's command of economic theory, his grasp of national and international affairs in general was enormous. And this knowledge was held within the context of a liberal political philosophy that had guided him most of his adult life and was exemplified repeatedly during his two terms as Governor of New York. He did not choose advisers in order to be provided with a point of view. Rather, he chose men whose point of view coincided with his own. Their job was not to do his thinking for him, but to enlarge and sharpen his thoughts into visible instruments of policy and action.

Thus a great deal of groundwork on the policy pronouncements and the legislation that erupted from the White House during the Hundred Days had been laid before the Hundred Days began. The Brain Trusters were on hand in an exhausting race against the clock and the calendar to whip their proposals into shape for final consummation. Moley was lodged in the State Department, Tugwell at Agriculture, and Berle at RFC. A few others were deployed elsewhere in the bureaucracy. When that first big legislative push ended in June, the Brain Trust, as such, ceased to exist, but its shadow and its memory remained a fixture of the New Deal scene for years. Moley withdrew from the government entirely in September.

The Cabinet was sworn into office *en masse* at dusk on Inauguration Day. This first Roosevelt Cabinet shone with a good deal less luster at the time than the Brain Trust. "So far as I could see," said Moley, who had been FDR's agent in feeling out many of the prospective appointees, "there was neither a well-defined purpose nor underlying principle in the selection." They were a mixed bag of liberals, conservatives, and neuters. Only one or two had had a leading part in the shaping of the programs they were to administer, or brought any special expertise to their jobs. This was the roster in their order of precedence:

State: Cordell Hull, sixty-two, Democratic Senator from Tennessee. Tall gravely dignified, moderately liberal in outlook, he was a leading advocate of lowered tariffs but otherwise undistinguished in the field of foreign affairs. He was greatly admired by Louis Howe and had backed Roosevelt's cause at Chicago.

Treasury: William H. Woodin, sixty-six, New York industrialist. Shy, small of stature, with a whimsical sense of humor, he was a bundle of paradoxes —a poet and musician at heart, an authentic "captain of industry" with a sizable personal fortune, and a devout supporter of FDR as Governor and presidential candidate. He was chosen after Senator Carter Glass of Virginia, properly suspicious of Roosevelt's fiscal orthodoxy, had declined the appointment.

Justice: Homer S. Cummings, sixty-three, lawyer and Democratic leader from Connecticut. His was an "emergency" appointment to fill the void created two days before the inauguration by the death of Senator Tom Walsh, Montana, the original designee for Attorney General. Cummings remained in the post until 1939.

War: George H. Dern, sixty-one, a mining engineer and two-term Governor of Utah.

Navy: Claude Swanson, seventy-one, a chairman of the Senate Naval Affairs Committee, former Governor of Virginia, and the only leading political figure of that state to support FDR in the campaign.

Post Office: James A. Farley, who was also, of course, chairman of the Democratic National Committee.

Interior: Harold L. Ickes, fifty-nine, a Chicago lawyer and self-confessed curmudgeon. He was active in Bull Moose and Progressive Party politics before turning to the Democrats in 1928. FDR met him for the first time in February 1933, "liked the cut of his jib," and invited him on the spot to join the Cabinet.

Agriculture: Henry A. Wallace, forty-six, a native of Iowa. He was not only the inheritor of a great family tradition in agriculture (his father had held the post of Secretary under both Harding and Coolidge) but also, in his own right, an agronomist and a dirt farmer of considerable renown. Tugwell brought him to FDR's attention and met little resistance in urging his appointment.

Commerce: Daniel C. Roper, sixty-six, a native of South Carolina and a successful Washington lawyer. He was Commissioner of Internal Revenue under Wilson and had long been active in Democratic politics.

Labor: Frances Perkins, fifty-two, a one-time social worker whom Governor Roosevelt had appointed New York State Industrial Commissioner in 1930. She was the first woman ever named to the Cabinet and the first Secretary of Labor not to be drawn from the hierarchy of organized labor, which induced more furor over her appointment than over any other. However, she went the full course (as did Ickes), remaining in her post until Roosevelt's death in 1945.

The New Dealers who poured into Washington with the new Administration were not all wild-eyed radicals by any means, but nearly all were liberals in one sense or another and certainly in terms of the Tory bureaucrats whom they replaced. But beyond that, they represented many different political sects and prejudices, and their clashing viewpoints lent motion and color to the scene. Lewis Douglas, a hardheaded young former Congressman from Arizona was named as Director of the Bureau of the Budget. His views of government finance were about as orthodox as they come; he was a devil's advocate within the Administration for economy and a balanced budget until he broke irrevocably with FDR in 1934. Donald Richberge of Chicago, a one-time Bull Mooser and the attorney for the Railway Brotherhoods, was made second in command at the National Recovery Administration as its general counsel. Harry Hopkins, the lanky, dyspeptic Iowa-born social worker from New York, was to become a leading symbol of the New Deal as director of its vast work relief programs. Professor Felix Frankfurter of the Harvard Law School declined appointment as Solicitor General but turned his versatile mind to the needs of the New Deal and his good friend Roosevelt from an unofficial observation post on the periphery. Jerome Frank, a friend of Frankfurter's and a successful New York corporation lawyer with wide-ranging and liberal interests, was put next to Wallace and Tugwell at Agriculture.[3]

There were a score of other equally luminous personalities who helped make the history and the news and the plentiful gossip of the day. And about each one there revolved a constellation of "bright young men" set free by the Depression from law offices and college faculties or drawn to Washington by the excitement and challenge of the New Deal. "A plague of bright young men, each with a mission to save the Republic, has descended on the city" was one observer's description of the invasion.

And an invasion it unquestionably was. The New Dealers and their bright young men—called "Felix's Happy Hotdogs" in recognition of Frankfurter's prowess as a recruiter—swarmed in by the dozens and then by the hundreds to take over the main operating posts of government. They were easily distinguished, by their Ivy League outfits from the stiff-collared civil servants of the old regime in the noon-day crowds along Pennsylvania Avenue. They brought new life and prosperity to restaurants around Farragut Square and on the smelly fish wharves along the riverfront, and they patronized the handful of nightclubs that came suddenly to life in some of the old mansions on Connecticut Avenue. They set up "digs" in the little period houses of Georgetown and Foggy Bottom, gave noisy parties, and held loud disputations far into the night. They worked at their jobs with exuberance and passion, for they were part of a Grand Design, hazy in detail but exhilarating in concept, to bring light to a darkened world. They were full of ideas, full of talk, and full of their own egos. They transformed Washington, Ray Tucker wrote admiringly in *Collier's,* "from a placid Southern town into a gay, breezy, sophisticated metropolitan center. It is exciting and educational to be in Washington these days."

III

It was no empty play to the grandstand that led Roosevelt to break precedent by having his Cabinet sworn in as a group at the close of his first half-day in office. The nation's banking system had collapsed. If the disaster were to be kept from spreading, if a financial panic were to be averted, he had to act swiftly. He needed the full resources of his Administration, even in its incomplete and skeletal form, behind him.

President Hoover had made numerous attempts—the latest on the afternoon of Friday, March 3—to have Roosevelt join him in some form of proclamation reassuring the public that the banks were fundamentally sound. He believed that a part of the mood of panic was due to public distrust of Roosevelt's as yet undisclosed fiscal policies, and he hoped, by means of his suggested proclamation, to bind the incoming President to "sound money." In addition, he still had an abiding faith in the soothing qualities of exhortations from on high. Though they had failed conspicuously in his case, he seemed to feel that a call for "confidence" by his successor would evoke the needed magic. Roosevelt distrusted the power of such incantations and was opposed to committing himself to any program of action until he had the power to act. He refused all of Hoover's entreaties.

Meanwhile, however, Woodin and Moley had been deeply immersed in the practical aspects of the fiscal problem. Ever since their arrival in Washington on Thursday, they had been meeting with Hoover's chief fiscal officers, Ogden L. Mills and Arthur Ballantine, Secretary and Under Secretary of the Treasury, respectively. There was substantial agreement among these four men that the only immediate prospect of salvation lay in a temporary closing of all banks to provide a breathing space. Woodin and Moley knew that Roosevelt was committed to such a course of action by federal decree once he had the authority, but Mills and Ballantine were deterred by Hoover's known objections to such an exercise of federal power. The need grew more imperative as reports continued to pour into the Treasury on Friday of further bank runs and closings in different parts of the country. The reports revealed that during the week another quarter billion dollars in gold had been drained out of the system and gone into hiding, and that the cash reserves in all the nation's operating banks had dwindled to a mere $6 billion against some $41 billion of liabilities in deposits.[4]

It was clear to the men in the Treasury that the American banking system had now reached the point where it could not stand the strain of another business day. If a national bank shutdown could not be ordered over President Hoover's objections, then the only alternative was to achieve the same end through action by the governors of the individual states. Already twenty-two governors had decreed either total or partial suspension of banking activities in their states. On Friday evening Treasury officials began calling the other governors urging them to take similar action before daylight. The last such arrangement, with Governor Herbert Lehman of New York, was not nailed down until 4:30 on Saturday morning.

Thus it was that as the control of government changed hands on the Capitol portico at a little after noon on Saturday, March 4, 1933, the financial heartbeat of the greatest capitalist nation on earth had come virtually to a stop.

That same night, after the Cabinet had been sworn in, the new President sat down in the unfamiliar surroundings of the White House with Woodin,

(Above, left to right) Harry Hopkins, Henry Wallace, Cordell Hull, and Dean Acheson. (Bottom, left) The informality of a Roosevelt Press Conference. (Bottom, right) Rexford G. Tugwell and Harry Hopkins, "trouble shooters" of the New Administration.

(Oval, at left) President Roosevelt's First Cabinet. Seated, L. to R.: Secretary of War Dern, Secretary of State Hull, President Roosevelt, Secretary of the Treasury Woodin, and Attorney General Cummings. Standing, L. to R.: Secretary of Agriculture Wallace, Secretary of the Interior Ickes, Secretary of the Navy Swanson, Postmaster General Farley, Secretary of Commerce Roper, and Secretary of Labor Perkins.

Moley, Cummings, and a handful of other advisers and made a series of momentous decisions that were to set the Hundred Days off from any similar period in American history. (Those present at the meeting attended none of the evening's inaugural festivities. FDR was represented by Mrs. Roosevelt, who gaily led a troop of family and friends from one function to another.) The first decision was to go through with the plan of declaring a national bank holiday; the second, to call Congress into special session to deal with the bank crisis; and the third, to summon a group of leading bankers to Washington immediately for any advice they could give in the emergency.

Putting these plans into effect meant another grueling night of labor for men who were already near the point of exhaustion. Mills, Ballantine, and other top Treasury officials of the Hoover regime had agreed to stay on the job temporarily in order to help their successors over the hurdles. Most of that night and all day Sunday they worked with Woodin and Moley to draft a bank holiday proclamation, including an embargo on any traffic in gold and silver. They also devised a set of temporary procedures and standards for deciding which banks could reopen at the end of the four-day holiday (it later was extended to eight days). Then the question arose of whether the twelve regional Federal Reserve banks should also come under the ban. Eugene Meyer, Chairman of the Federal Reserve Board, argued that there was no legal authority anywhere to close these banks, desirable though it was under the circumstances. When the pros and cons of this had been explored futilely for half an hour, Moley exploded: "Look, if two Secretaries of the Treasury and the Governor of the Federal Reserve Board can't order the Reserve banks closed, who in God's name can?" The question of including these banks in the ban was decided affirmatively.[5]

Late Sunday the weary conferees returned to the White House with the final text of the bank holiday proclamation. Woodin, meanwhile, had assured the President that, come what may, he would have the draft of an emergency bill to govern the reopening of the banks ready for Congress within four days. Turning to half a dozen Congressional leaders who had been brought in, Roosevelt asked if a special session of Congress could be convened on Thursday to handle the bill. They agreed that it could.

By ten o'clock that night the necessary proclamations and orders were issued (thoughtfully postdated 1:00 A.M. Monday to avoid profaning the Sabbath). Effective immediately, every bank in the nation was closed for four days, the shipment of gold and silver was embargoed, any violation of the banking order was punishable by a fine of $10,000 or ten years imprisonment, and Congress was under orders to convene at noon on Thursday, March 9.[6] With stunning speed and decisiveness the New Deal had moved to fulfill its leader's promise of "action—and action now."

Imagine what it would be like *today* to wake up one morning to discover that the government had shut every bank in the nation; that all the money you could lay your hands on was what you had in your pocket, and that you couldn't get any more when that was spent. Would hysterical mobs go screaming through the streets, storming the banks with crowbars and dynamite, looting the stores for food and weapons? Would the well-to-do rush to bury their jewels and family plate under the cellar floor, and farmers sit with shotguns across their laps to repel invasion by hungry city mobs?

Well, nothing of the sort happened on that historic Monday more than three decades ago. Some individuals probably did panic; some rushed in disbelief to their banks to find if the news was really true; some housewives took all the change they could scrape together and converted it into a hoard of salt meat and canned goods at the grocery store. But they were the exception. Among the people as a whole the reaction was just the opposite. The shutting of banks snapped the bonds of tension and uncertainty that had bound them for weeks. Suddenly the agony of fear and waiting was over. Something that everybody could understand had happened, something as clear and unequivocal as a clap of thunder at midnight. There was a sense of relief, the kind of euphoria that comes with a sudden release from pain. Grim, even tragic, though the provocation was, people could laugh and make jokes about their common dilemma—at the outset at least.

The experiences that people endured in a moneyless society were immensely varied, some of them painful and comic. Salesmen stranded in cities away from their homes hawked the contents of their sample cases in hotel lobbies—shoes, jewelry, patent medicines, wearing apparel—to get money for train fare. Businessmen met their payrolls with postdated checks, promisory notes, company-backed scrip, merchandise from their inventories. Hotels and restaurants went on an all-credit basis; so did grocers, dairies, drugstores and gasoline stations for their regular customers. Soon the most critical shortage became not money per se but currency in usable denominations and in coins. With only a twenty-dollar bill in your wallet you were as bad as broke if you wanted to buy cigarettes or ride in a taxi. Shopkeepers cruised the streets looking for newsboys and apple vendors who would sell them 80 cents worth of change for a dollar bill. New York commuters drained the ready cash reserves of the Long Island Railroad by cashing in their commutation tickets. Patronage at movie houses fell almost to zero. The promoters of a boxing tournament at Madison Square Garden accepted any kind of usable barter for tickets, including, it was said, a pair of ladies' silk panties. In Miami the American Express Company put a $50 limit on the amount of a vacationer's checks it would redeem, and a hotel in the Chicago Loop discovered that under its benevolent "stay-now, pay-later" plan it was playing host to a number of denizens of the nearby skid row.

For many millions the novelty and the humor of the situation was a pretty thin veneer that quickly wore through. Few wage earners could afford to miss a single payday without encountering distress. Few had even a blocked bank account on which they could draw checks, nor did they have credit beyond the needs of a day or two at the corner grocer. Raising carfare to get to and from work or school or a source of charity was a family problem. Relief applications soared. Thousands began to suffer from hunger and cold. In Detroit, where the bank holiday was in its fourth week, business activity was off 60 percent. Some municipal workers, with uncashable pay checks in their pockets, fainted on the job for lack of food.

Scrip showed up in different forms in scores of cities. It was issued to employees in lieu of real wages by municipalities and by private concerns. The city of Cleveland circulated thousands of scrip "dollar bills" signed by the mayor and treasurer. A three-cent stamp had to be affixed each time a scrip changed hands. When a bill had acquired thirty-six stamps, the city promised to redeem it for $1.08 in "real" money. A resort hotel in Pasadena printed its own scrip, which the railroads accepted to get the hotel's guests back to their homes. The _Daily Princetonian_ printed scrip in 25-cent denominations for the use of its student subscribers. Telephone slugs, postage stamps, bus and subway tokens, foreign coins, and even cigarette coupons all played a vital role in this "funny money" epic of the great bank holiday.[7]

When Congress convened in special session at noon on Thursday, March 9, Secretary of the Treasury Woodin had ready for it the draft of an emergency banking bill. It had been written and rewritten, cut and trimmed and pasted together through many hours of arduous labor during the preceding four days. What it did, in effect, was to validate the President's bank-closing proclamation of Monday, including the penalties for hoarding or using gold. It gave the Treasury power to grant or withhold licenses for the reopening of banks and to appoint "conservators" for the shakier ones, and it authorized the issuance of Federal Reserve notes if necessary to replenish the currency supply.

There was not time enough to have the bill printed. The half-dozen typewritten copies that were rushed to the Capitol the morning of March 9 still bore marginal notes and corrections scribbled in pencil. In the House of Representatives there was no pretense of committee consideration. Only a few of the leaders had even seen the text. As the House reading clerk finished reading the one copy available in that chamber, cries went up from the floor, "Vote, vote!" Thirty-eight minutes later the bill was passed by acclamation. The Senate was slightly more deliberate. It listened to three hours of debate, most of it stimulated by Huey Long's clamorous pleas in behalf of "the little state banks at the forks of the creek," before passing the bill 73 to 7. At 8:37 that night, FDR, with newsreel cameras focused on his desk in the White House, signed the first legislative enactment of the New Deal.

The psychological impact of this swift, bold stroke was enormous. Its first manifestation occurred the next day, Friday. Gold hoarders by the thousands queued up before the regional Reserve banks in New York and elsewhere to get rid of the yellow treasure, which had suddenly become contraband. It was "a gold rush in reverse," said _The New York Times_, "unlike anything in the memory of the downtown banking community." Expensively dressed men and women, some of them carrying packages and valises filled with gold coins and certificates, stood patiently in line to convert their hoards to legal tender. An armored truck drove up with the $6 million in bullion said to have been the nest egg of an unnamed but obviously jittery corporation. Housewives and teenagers and grandparents joined the line to push personal coin collections through the tellers' wickets. (Small, sentimental holdings such as these were later omitted from the ban.) By Saturday night the Federal Reserve System had recovered $300 million in gold—enough to back up the issuance of $750 million in new currency.

Under the emergency legislation, controlled reopening of the banks was to be permitted beginning on Monday, March 13. Treasury officials had divided the nation's banks—about 5,000 national banks, members of the Federal Reserve System, and about 14,000 nonmember state banks—into three categories of relative solvency. Class A banks, numbering about 2,400, were adjudged to be in sufficiently good shape to reopen at once. Class B banks would need some sort of shoring up before they would be permitted to reopen. Class C banks numbering about 900, would have to remain closed for the time being at least, under a "conservator," appointed by the Treasury.

The men at the Treasury worked furiously that week at the formidable task of grading and licensing some 19,000 individual banks. (The strain broke Woodin's frail health; he resigned in November and died within a year.) One of the most feared imponderables was whether, when the banks did open their doors again, still panicky depositors would withdraw their money and start the lethal bleeding process all over again. Roosevelt's fireside chat on Sunday night was designed to avert just such a reaction, though there was no assurance that the remedy would work.

But by noon on that critical Monday it was clear that the panic was over. All but nine of New York City's 140 banks reopened for "business as usual" at 9 A.M., and there were openings in similar proportions in other cities up and down the eastern seaboard and westward. There were uncommonly long lines at the tellers' windows, but the majority of customers were putting more money into their accounts (putting it *back,* possibly) than they were taking out. In New York City alone, deposits exceeded withdrawals that day by $10 million, and this pattern was repeated in major banking centers all across the country. At the end of the week approximately 75 percent of the Nation's banks were back in business.* The New York Stock Exchange and the Chicago commodity markets—unleashed along with the banks—had one of their best weeks since September 1932. And an $800 million refinancing offering by the Treasury, which most officials had anticipated with dread, was oversubscribed two and a half times.

---

* When the Hundred Days were over, some 2,000 banks had disappeared, either through merger or through permanent closing, and approximately $5 billion in deposits remained frozen. (Raymond Moley, *The First New Deal* [New York: Harcourt, Brace & World, 1966], p. 198.)

One day at midweek hundreds of stock tickers in brokers' offices around the country carried this greeting from an exuberant Wall Street teletype operator: "Happy Days Are Here Again." Most people agreed.[8]

IV

Senator Wheeler had said that Congress would "jump through a hoop" to pass any legislation the President asked for. It had originally been Roosevelt's intention to send Congress home once the emergency bank bill was passed, because he thought that his new Administration needed a chance to get the feel of its job and to devote a lot of care to the drafting of the legislative program. But the momentum and good will generated by his swift handling of the bank crisis was too valuable an asset to be wasted. Tugwell urged him to push for passage of the farm bill while he still had Congress in his hand, and Lew Douglas urged with equal vigor that now was the psychological moment to strike a blow for economy and fiscal "soundness." Roosevelt, aglow with optimism and impatience, said "Why not?," and picked up Senator Wheeler's option.

The legislative leaders had come to the White House on Wednesday night to be briefed on the emergency banking bill, which they would receive on the following day. When this part of the discussion was over, the President went on in a disarmingly casual, conversational way, to say that he would have "a pretty important" economy bill for them on Friday. Most of them would agree, he observed airily, that Hoover's extravagance had led the country close to bankruptcy. And he reminded them that the Democratic platform called for a 25 percent cut in federal spending and a balanced budget. Well, he was ready to show the country he meant business on economy, just as he had on the banking crisis. The new bill would call for slashing veterans' benefits almost in half—by $400 million—and for cutting government salaries, including those of members of the Congress, by another $100 million.

The legislators were aghast. The veterans' lobby was one of the most powerful in the nation and had successfully resisted every previous attempt to curtail their pensions and other prerequisites. They were too potent politically, the legislators protested, to be offended in this way at the very outset of the new Administration. And as for the salary cuts, they went on, quite aside from the financial burden it would bring to individual members of Congress, there was a sizable bloc in both houses who felt that such a deflationary measure was just the opposite of what the economy needed.

Roosevelt was unimpressed. He had no strong views of his own on this complex economic issue, but he admired Lew Douglas, to whom this sort of fiscal orthodoxy was the keystone of recovery. He was anxious, too, to reassure the business community that his would be a "sound" Administration, one that they need not fear. This was perhaps the most profound contradiction of the early New Deal. Very shortly FDR would switch to deficit financing on a huge scale as blithely as he now embraced pay-as-you-go.

The economy bill reached Capitol Hill on Friday, while Congress was still spinning from its encounters with the banking bill. As the leaders had prophesied, it caused sparks to fly. Representative Joseph W. Byrns, the new Democratic floor leader, refused to sponsor it in the House. Speaker Henry T. Rainey tried but failed to get a binding vote of support from the Democratic caucus. However, a handful of loyalists rallied the troops, arguing that the President would know by their votes "whether the members of his own party were willing to go along with him in his fight to save the country." Though the bill passed 266 to 138, it was a closer shave than the score indicted. Ninety-two Democrats deserted their leader, but sixty-nine Republicans swung over to sustain him. Without those Republican votes the Hundred Days might have been fatally foreshortened then and there.

Even more trouble was expected in the Senate, which planned to take up the economy bill on Monday. Discussing the outlook with a small group of friends at dinner Sunday evening, FDR was seized with a sudden inspiration. "You know," he said, tilting his cigarette holder skyward, "this would be a good time for beer." He sent for a copy of the Democratic platform, snipped out the plank on Prohibition, and wrote a seventy-two-word message calling for the immediate legalization of light beer and wine.

The message, totally unexpected, went to Congress on Monday. Its effect was like that of the carrot on the stick to get a balky donkey in motion, just as Roosevelt had intended it to be. That day the economy bill won a 60 to 20 test vote in the Senate. On Tuesday the House passed the beer bill 316 to 97. On Wednesday the Senate cleared the economy bill 62 to 13, and the next day it passed the beer bill.[9]

"What the country needs if we are to shake off the torpor of fear and hopelessness," said *Editor & Publisher* in an editorial a few days before the inauguration, "is a series of blinding headlines proclaiming action, resolute leadership, a firm grip at the controls. The President must work rapidly and openly, speaking his mind in plain terms, if he is to succeed in creating the psychology that is so desperately needed."

Roosevelt did precisely that. He created not only the "series of blinding headlines" but a national psychology of expectancy and enthusiasm. (There was a modicum of resentment and apprehension, but it was limited to a sullen handful of Hoover's Old Guardsmen.) People eagerly snatched each fresh edition of their newspapers and listened hourly to the radio news broadcasts to learn what new surprises were being unveiled in Washington. The magician's hat seemed never to run out of rabbits. Sometimes they would appear two at a time, as one Presidential message to Congress piled on top of the one before it. Often the bills were hastily and inexpertly drawn, for careful drafting had given way to the more exigent consideration of striking while Congress was hot, and of extracting the last ounce of advantage from the tidal wave of public opinion on which the New Deal was riding.

After the banking and economy acts, other major programs came into existence in quick succession during the Hundred Days. Most of the programs are examined in detail in later chapters, but their substance is indicated in the following list. It is an incredible catalogue of bills submitted to, and enacted by, the Congress. In each case, the introductory date in the listing is the date of submission to Congress:

March 16. *Agricultural Adjustment Act* (enacted May 12). The draft presented to Congress was a composite of several plans, old and new, for raising farm income and reducing surpluses. Essentially, it offered subsidies to farmers who agreed to restrict their planting of certain basic crops. Subsidies were to be derived from a processing tax paid by manufacturers (e.g., flour millers), a provision that later proved to be the legal undoing of this statute. The bill included an important amendment giving the President wide authority to bring about inflation by reducing the gold content of the dollar and by issuing greenbacks.

March 21. *Civilian Conservation Corps* (enacted March 31). The CCC was an original idea of FDR's, stimulated by his longtime interests in forestry and conversation. He proposed to take 250,000 unemployed young men off the streets and welfare rolls and give them jobs at $30 a month plus keep for doing useful work in forests and national parks. This work program for youths was the first and most widely approved of a variety of work relief programs that were to follow. Within a week after enactment the first CCC camp opened near Luray, Virginia, with an enrollment of 2,500.

March 21. *Federal Emergency Relief Act* (enacted May 12). Roosevelt asked for an appropriation of $500 million for a direct assault on unemployment and drought through loans and grants to the states. The act creating the Federal Emergency Relief Administration was soon followed by further laws providing jobs for the unemployed on public works: the short-lived Civil Works Administration (CWA), the Works Progress Administration (WPA), and the longer-ranged, slower-paced Public Works Administration (PWA). Harry Hopkins, whose name would become as nearly synonymous with the New Deal as Roosevelt's, was named FERA Administrator. (PWA shortly came under the jurisdiction of Harold Ickes.)

March 27. *Farm Credit Administration.* By Executive Order, the President established the FCA, a single agency combining activities of half a dozen agencies dealing with farm credit: the Federal Farm Board, Federal Land Banks, the Agricultural Credit Corporation, etc. The purpose was to centralize in one place all farm credit services. Legislation was enacted June 16 to complete the merger. Henry Morgenthau, Jr., was appointed FCA Governor. (Later he succeeded William H. Woodin as Secretary of the Treasury.)

March 29. *"Truth in Securities" Act* (enacted May 27). In submitting this bill to Congress, FDR said: "This proposal adds to the ancient rule of *caveat emptor* the further doctrine, 'Let the seller also beware.' " The bill required the seller of securities to disclose fully all pertinent information about them; empowered the Federal Trade Commission to block the sale of misrepresented securities; and imposed stiff penalties for violators. The name "Truth in Securities" of this act is a synonym for the Securities Act of

1933, which was only half the legislative package dealing with securities; the regulatory half was provided in the Securities Exchange Act of 1934.

April 10. *Tennessee Valley Authority Act* (enacted May 18). In one bold stroke FDR resolved a controversy that had raged between liberals and conservatives for a decade. He asserted the government's right to own and operate for the public good the huge hydroelectric and manufacturing facility at Muscle Shoals, Alabama, built during the World War at a cost of more than $165 million. It had stood idle while the advocates of public and private power battled for its possession. FDR not only came down on the side of public ownership but vastly enlarged the scope of the under-taking to make it the world's outstanding example of regional conservation and economic development.

April 13. *Home Owners Loan Act* (enacted June 13). The provisions of this act did for the urban homeowner what the Farm Mortgage Act did for the farmer: it averted foreclosures and the eviction of tens of thousands of families unable to keep up existing mortgage payments. With a revolving fund of $2 billion raised through the issuance of bonds, the Home Owners' Loan Corporation refinanced individual home mortgages up to $14,000 at 5 percent interest for a maximum of fifteen years.

April 19. *Abandonment of the Gold Standard* (by Executive Order). The pressure for inflation—to get more money in circulation—had become so intense by mid-April, particularly from Congress, that Roosevelt was faced with the choice of either submitting to it or managing it. He chose the latter. His Executive Order *permanently* embargoed all exports of gold (a tem-porary embargo had been ordered on March 6), which left the dollar free to find its level among the other devalued currencies of the world.

May 4. *Railroad Coordination Act* (enacted June 16). The nation's railroads, most of them afloat on Reconstruction Finance Corporation loans, were in as depressed a condition as any segment of industry. The bill submitted on May 4 represented an effort, tentative at best, to enforce economies by consolidation and rate-making reforms, with the ultimate view (never realized) of creating a coordinated transportation system. Joseph B. Eastman was moved from the Interstate Commerce Commission to be Federal Coordinator of Transportation.

May 17. *National Industrial Recovery Act* (enacted June 16). The NIRA was the crowning legislative achievement of the Hundred Days and one of the most conspicuous, if least durable, monuments of the entire New Deal. A patchwork of many schemes and ideas, it vested in the President unprecedented peacetime powers to manage the business life of the nation down to the smallest unit. The National Recovery Administration (NRA), established under the NIRA, gave the nation business "codes" with the force of law, the thirty-hour week, minimum-wage rates, the symbolic Blue Eagle, Gen. Hugh "Iron Pants" Johnson, and almost three years of un-remitting turmoil, excitement, hope, and despair.

May 17. *Glass-Steagall Banking Act* (enacted June 16). This law was not, strictly speaking, a New Deal measure, for it had been gestating in Con-

THE SILVER SPOON.

UNCLE FRANKLIN. "NOW, SAMMY, I WANT YOU TO BE RE-BORN AS A BOUNCING LITTLE BIMETALLIST."

At left: $1 Scrip money used in Canarsie, Brooklyn, during the 1933 Banking Crisis. Local bank deposits guaranteed each dollar of scrip that was used.

Teacher:
"And That Will Be
All the Home Work for Today."

(Above) Brisk business despite Bank Holiday! Motion picture theaters on Broadway accepted personal checks in lieu of cash or scrip money.

(Below) The biggest Gold Rush since '49! Under the new Federal Anti-Hoarding Gold Act, people were required to turn in gold bars, coins, and certificates. By midnight of the fourth day of the Bank Holiday, more than $200,000,000 in gold had poured back into the Federal Reserve Bank.

gressional committees for two years. But it fitted the New Deal pattern of reform, and the New Deal provided the impetus for its ultimate passage. It forced commercial banks to get out of the investment business, and it established, over the loud protest of most orthodox bankers, insurance of deposits in national banks under the Federal Deposit Insurance Corporation.

May 26. *Annulment of Gold Clause in Contracts* (enacted June 5). Most government obligations (bonds, currency, etc.) and many private contracts called for payment in gold—that is, dollars with a specific gold content (23.22 grains). The continued existence of this requirement virtually nullified the President's recently won powers to inflate the currency. Enactment of the measure meant the final breakaway from the gold standard.

V

The 73d Congress, 1st session, adjourned in the early morning hours of June 16, bone weary but jubilant. In ninety-nine tumultous days it had established a record such as no Congress before it or since has matched. In fifteen major legislative enactments it had broken many bonds with the past, had set the nation on a revolutionary course toward new social and political goals, which could be perceived only dimly, and had subdued (though it had not wholly overcome) a crisis of confidence that had shaken the foundations of the Republic. The capitalist system had been "saved"—this was Ray Moley's word for it, reiterated as recently as 1966.* And it is possible that a revolution was averted.

If you were there you will remember the bitterness and disillusionment of those bleak early months of 1933, with some twelve million jobless men walking the streets and farmers with shotguns defying the courts. If, in this situation, the despair had been magnified by a collapse of the national currency through an unresolved banking crisis, who can say that there would not have been rioting and bloodshed in the streets of a hundred cities?

The tide turned with Roosevelt's swift and decisive action as he took office. Despair turned into hope, and faith and confidence reached a peak as the Hundred Days came to an end. The Depression wasn't over, but the fear of it was. That knot in the belly that came from dread of what another day might bring was gone. Things were looking up all over. If you had a job, you now felt reasonably certain of holding on to it. If you didn't have a job, the prospects of getting one were looking better. There were still apple sellers on the streets, and the Chicago schoolteachers still rioted to get their back pay, and the Unemployed Councils still marched on City Halls. But stories in the papers also showed a brighter side: new CCC camps were being opened up; the Civil Works Administration was hiring men to repair the streets and tidy

---

* "I still feel as I did in 1939 when I wrote that 'capitalism had been saved in eight days.' Now, in reviewing the years of the Great Depression, I feel that the decisive event that turned the tide was the brilliantly successful rescue of the banks. Surely nothing so gripped the imagination of the American people and gave them assurance that their nation was sound at heart and capable of providing them once more the means of a good life." (Moley, *The First New Deal* [New York: Harcourt, Brace & World, 1966], p. 208.)

up the parks; and the farmers in Iowa and Wisconsin were bringing their milk to market instead of dumping it on the highways. It was possible to have a good steak for dinner now and then, and you didn't feel extravagant if you spent a quarter to see a movie. Some families even ventured to plan a summer vacation. *The New York Times* for Sunday, July 1, carried three full pages of cruise advertisements.

From the moment the banks began to reopen during the second week in March there was a steady quickening in the pulse of the nation's business life. "Up go the prices of stocks and bonds, adding millions of value," said the *Literary Digest* exultantly. "Up go the prices of wheat, corn and other commodities putting millions into the pockets of depression-harried farmers. Around the world runs a ripple of hope as American business feels this rush of activity."

A graphic illustration of the exuberant response of business to the Hundred Days is shown in two *New York Times* charts reproduced on these pages: The Weekly Business Index, published on March 5, 1933, the Sunday after the New Deal moved in; and the Business Index rise from March to mid-June, published on June 18, the Sunday following the adjournment of the special session of Congress.

Sharp Reaction in Weekly Business Index; Car Loadings, Power and Steel Series Down

INDEX NUMBERS ADJUSTED FOR SEASONAL VARIATION AND LONG-TIME TREND. ESTIMATED NORMAL = 100

March 5, 1933

THE NEW YORK TIMES weekly business index has dropped sharply to within one-tenth of a point of the previous low record established in the two weeks ended Aug. 20, 1932. With business in many sections severely curtailed by banking mor-atoria, freight shipments fell sharply, carrying the adjusted carloadings index down more than 5 points, which was the main factor in reducing the combined index to 52.3 for the week ended Feb. 25 from 54.4 for the preceding week and 61.0 for corresponding week last year.

	Feb.25, 1933.	Feb.18, 1933.	Feb.27, 1932.
Freight car loadings	*52.0	57.3	61.3
Steel mill activity	16.9	17.5	28.9
Elec. power production	63.0	61.5	71.5
Automobile production	31.1	21.2	35.5
Carded cot. cloth prod.	96.4	95.3	96.1
Combined index	*52.3	54.4	61.0

—Week Ended—

* Subject to revision.

Business Index Rises Sharply to Highest Point in Two Years

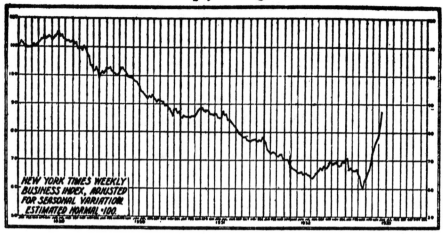

June 18, 1933

With every series registering a gain for the week ended June 10, THE NEW YORK TIMES weekly index of business was lifted to the highest level in more than two years. An advance of nearly 4 points brought the figure to 87.1, as compared with 83.2 in the previous week. The index for the week ended June 11, 1932, stood at 65.7.

	Week Ended		
	June 10, 1933.	June 3, 1933.	June 11, 1932.
Freight car loadings	58.7	58.4	51.9
Steel mill activity	64.5	60.9	23.8
Electric power output	91.7	91.3	85.7
Automobile production	50.4	43.4	45.2
Lumber production	55.0	53.4	39.9
Cotton forwardings	222.7	181.7	58.7
Combined index	87.1	88.2	65.7

On that first weekend in March the nation's fortunes had hit rock bottom. On that third weekend in June they had soared to a two-year high. So had the people's spirits.

Reviewing "the extraordinary course of events at Washington since March 4," *The New York Times* of June 18 said in an editorial that Roosevelt had managed to convert the national emergency into a personal triumph. "That was because he seemed to the American people to be riding the whirlwind and directing the storm. The country was ready and even anxious to accept any leadership. From President Roosevelt it got a rapid succession of courageous speeches and efforts and achievements which inclined millions of his fellow citizens to acclaim him as the heaven-sent man of the hour."

The "corner" that President Hoover had vainly sought for three long years had been turned at last—in Roosevelt's Hundred Days.

CHAPTER 8
Decline
of the Moneymen

The Alderman's Offspring

ONE OF THE LIVELIEST SPECTACLES of the early New Deal was the public unfrocking of the priesthood of High Finance.

For generations The Banker had been a symbol of wisdom, power, and virtue in American folklore—an object of emulation by every right-thinking youth who hoped to make his mark in the world. The Bankers were, in fact, a duling caste in the economic and political life of the nation. Their dicta were listened to with equal respect in the village council and in the President's Cabinet. One financial instution—the firm of J. P. Morgan and Company, with its enormous leverage in domestic and international finance—was the nearest thing to an invisible government that the United States had known in the twentieth century. But the image of The Banker and the whole breed of moneymen had been tarnished in the stock market crash. Now, in 1933 and 1934, their degradation was augmented as the greatest champions among them were forced to confess their fallibility (and often their larceny) in broad public view before a committee of the United States Senate. The spectacle, as it unfolded day after day in the newspapers and the newsreels, had the popular fascination of a witch-burning.

A good deal more was involved than a simple exposition of crime and punishment. As one after another of the most notable Captains of Finance was made to walk the plank, the national mood was prepared for a series of far-reaching reforms in the nation's credit and currency structure. For the most part, the reforms have endured to the pesent time. The moneymen have since regained much of their public luster, but only because they have learned to walk in rectitude with a leash about their necks.

I

The impulse to clean up the capital market was not unique to the New Deal, but it was the New Deal that converted the impulse into action. The previous Administration had grappled warily with the notion for two years and had brought forth the Reconstruction Finance Corporation. As a "bank for bankers" operating on conventional banking principles, its medicine was too weak for the catharsis needed by the patient; it did not get to the source of infection either in the banks or in the securities business. Hoover and his men could not bring themselves to violate the sanctity and prerogatives of the marketplace nor to impede the skill, initiative, and ingenuity of the free enterprisers who operated there. But by the summer of 1932 it was manifest that something drastic would have to be done about the banks, for if the banking system toppled, as it was clearly in danger of doing, the rest of the nation's financial structure would come tumbling down too. There was wide agreement on this in principle if not in detail, and in January 1933 the Senate Banking and Currency Committee undertook to find out what kind of legislative remedies could be devised.

The Committee's mandate included a wide-ranging investigation, not only of the banking system as such but of the capital market as a whole, particularly the issuance and sale of securities. To head the inquiry the Committee picked Ferdinand Pecora, a Sicilian-born New York jurist who, as assistant district attorney of New York County, had won a reputation for uncovering fraud and corruption. With his flashing black eyes and crest of iron-gray hair, he made an imposing figure. Pecora's objective was to expose weaknesses and abuses in the existing system wherever he could find them. To this end he hired a staff of a hundred accountants and investigators, armed them with blank pads of subpoenas, and sent them coursing through Wall Street and its outposts like a pack of bloodhounds.

Spokesmen for the financial community protested this invasion of their preserve. They argued that some reforms might perhaps be in order, but the manner and the timing of the investigation could only further weaken public confidence and so delay recovery. Their protest sounded hollow against the disorderly clatter of events in the financial world that spilled daily onto the front pages of the nation's press. Ivar Kreuger, the "Swedish match king" who had committed suicide in March 1932, was revealed as a $100-million swindler whose fraud had involved the respected American brokerage house of Lee, Higginson and Company. Samuel Insull, whose multimillion-dollar utility empire had collapsed and swept thousands into bankruptcy, was a fugitive from justice aboard his yacht somewhere in the Mediterranean. The RFC had halved the number of bank failures in 1932, but even so, more than 1,400 had gone under that year with $715 million in deposits. And there was the familiar figure of Charley Dawes, who had quit the chairmanship of the RFC and immediately obtained a $90-million loan for his City National Bank and Trust Company in Chicago. *Time* magazine that year introduced the word "bankster" into the vocabulary, to rhyme with gangster.

It was against such a background that Pecora staged his first public hearing in February 1933. The scene was the high-ceilinged Caucus Room in the Senate Office Building. Twelve members of the Banking and Currency Committee were ranged along one side of a huge mahogany table and a crowd of three hundred spectators occupied the available seats or stood along the walls. The first witness was Charles E. Mitchell, the robust and self-assured president of New York City's National City Bank, whose merest scowl a few years earlier could cause stock tickers to flutter uncertainly. National City, and its brokerage affiliate, the National City Company, had been one of the prime generative forces in the stock market boom, and Mitchell's reputation as a mastermind of finance had, like his bank, survived the crash and persisted into the thirties. Pecora demolished him in three days.

Under the skilled prodding of the prosecutor, Mitchell made these admissions: For the years 1927, 1928, and 1929 he received salary and bonuses totaling approximately $1.2 million annually. To avoid paying income tax in 1929 alone, he "sold" 18,000 shares of his National City stock to his wife in such a way that he could report a net loss of $2.8 million for the year. It was not a bona fide sale, and he repurchased the stock from his wife without any money changing hands. In November of the same year, after the market crash, he and other officers of the bank loaned themselves $2.4 million, interest free and without collateral, to protect their personal margin accounts in National City stock. Less than 5 percent of the loans had been repaid at the time he testified before the Committee. Meanwhile, he conceded, several hundred lesser employes of the bank who had bought

National City on margin at around $200, only to see it drop to $40, got no such generous help but were put through the wringer.

As one damaging admission after another was drawn from him, the great banker lost his aplomb. He grew limp and defensive under the revealing lights of the newsreel cameras and the unbelieving stares of the crowded press tables. Reluctantly, hatefully, a veritable Titan of Wall Street was confirming what up to now had been merely Main Street gossip about how the insiders played the game at the expense of the suckers. Messengers clutching sheets of yellow copy paper scurried ceaselessly between the press tables and the Western Union office downstairs with fresh bulletins to top the day's biggest story in the next edition of practically every daily newspaper in the country.

And what about the Peruvian bonds? Pecora asked. Grudgingly, Mitchell told the story. Back in 1927 the National City Company had contracted to underwrite a $25-million issue of Peruvian Government bonds. Its own analysts, sent to make a firsthand study of the economy and political stability of the country, gave a strongly adverse report and said that any succeeding regime would almost certainly repudiate any bonds issued by its predecessor. National City pigeonholed this report, and marketed the bonds at or near par in $500 and $1,000 lots to appeal to small investors. It pocketed a 10 percent commission and, as a further part of the deal, kept the proceeds of the sale on deposit, interest free, in the National City Bank, where they were hired out as Wall Street "call money" at 15 to 20 percent interest. So successful was the original issue that during the next year Peru and National City floated two new issues of $30 million and $35 million each. When the crash came, Peruvian bonds were as worthless as old soap wrappers.

"If it's right to send Al Capone to the Federal penitentiary for income tax evasion," Senator Burt Wheeler said in the Senate the day after the completion of Mitchell's testimony, "some of these crooked bank presidents ought to go too."

Thousands agreed. Mitchell's testimony had shocked the public. Even more shocking was the realization that such refined banditry was quite within the law. Neither Mitchell nor his fellow officers of National City had violated any statute through their scheme to sell worthless securities to the public. Mitchell was tried that summer of having evaded $573,000 in income taxes for 1929, but he was acquitted. The carefully arranged device of a fictitious sale of assets to establish a "loss" for income tax purposes was also within the law and was regularly employed by the nation's richest men—Andrew Mellon and J. P. Morgan among them—as many subsequent witnesses before the Senate Committee were to admit.

"You see, there is a lot of things these old boys have done that are within the law," Will Rogers observed, "but it's so near the edge you couldn't slip a razor blade between their acts and a prosecution."

The inquisition of the moneymen continued almost without letup through the summer and fall of 1933 and into the spring of 1934. Dozens of the nation's leading bankers, brokers, and financiers took the hot seat under

Ferdinand Pecora's baleful gaze and confessed to their faults and iniquities —their own and those of the system of which they were a part. The austerely dignified J. P. Morgan himself and a whole covey of Morgan partners were on the stand for nearly three weeks. Others forced to march across the stage included Richard Whitney, the indignant and unrepentant president of the New York Stock Exchange; A. H. Wiggin, president of Chase National; Otto Kahn, of Kuhn, Loeb and Company; O. P. Van Sweringen, the Cleveland railroad magnate; Harry F. Sinclair, of Sinclair Consolidated Oil Corporation; and Edsel Ford and Clarence Dillon and Winthrop Aldrich, and a score of lesser tycoons.

It was a cast of characters drawn from the Social Register of high finance. Pecora treated them all with cool scorn as miscreants. His prosecutor's manner drew protests of rage from some elements of the press and from some members of his own committee, such as Virginia's Carter Glass, who loudly insisted, "These men are not on trial." But FDR went out of his way to back up Pecora, who continued relentlessly to expose the code of personal greed and social irresponsibility that ruled the financial community. The shocking revelations colored the attitude of a whole generation toward its one-time idol, The Banker. But there were positive benefits as well, as we shall see.[1]

An irreverent folk ballad of the era bespoke The Banker's fall from grace with rare poignancy. "Four Prominent So and So's," with words by Ogden Nash and music by Robert Armbruster, was written for the March 1933 show of the exclusive Dutch Treat Club of New York. By way of various subterranean channels (most publishers were sissies in those days) it soon reached a less exclusive but equally appreciative audience through tavern and parlor singers in many parts of the country. The first and fourth stanzas and the chorus follow:

I'm an autocratic figure in these democratic states,
I'm a dandy demonstration of hereditary traits.
As the children of the baker bake the most delicious breads,
As the sons of Casanova fill the most exclusive beds,
As the Barrymores, the Roosevelts and others I could name
Inherited the talents which perpetuate their fame,
My position in the structure of society I owe
To the qualities my parents bequeathed me long ago.
My pappy was a gentleman and musical to boot;
He used to play piano in a house of ill repute.
The madam was a lady and a credit to her cult,
She enjoyed my pappy's playing, and I was the result!
So my mammy and my pappy are the ones I have to thank
That I'm Chairman of the Board of the National Country Bank!

Chorus
Oh, our parents forgot to get married,
Oh, our parents forgot to get wed.

Did a wedding bell chime? It was always a time
When our parents were somewhere in bed,
Tra la la la, they were somewhere in bed.
Oh, thanks to our kind loving parents
We are kings in the land of the free—
Your banker, your broker, your Washington joker—
Four prominent bastards are we, tra la la la,
Four prominent bastards are we.

I'm an ordinary figure in these democratic states,
A pathetic demonstration of hereditary traits.
As the children of the cops possess the flattest kind of feet,
As the daughter of the floozie has a waggle to her seat,
My position at the bottom of society I owe
To the qualities my parents bequeathed me long ago.
My father was a married man and what is even more,
He was married to my mother, a fact which I deplore.
I was born in holy wedlock, consequently by and by,
I was rooked by every bastard with plunder in his eye.
I invested, I deposited, I voted every fall,
And if I saved a penny, the bastards took it all.
At last I've learned my lesson and I'm on the proper track.
I'm a self-appointed bastard and I'm goin' to get it back.

II

The first major reform growing out of the Senate's investigation of the moneymen materialized while the House of Morgan was still taking its lumps from Ferdinand Pecora. One June 16, 1933, the President signed the Glass-Steagall Banking Act, which (1) provided for the Federal guarantee of bank deposits, (2) ordered the separation of commercial and investment banking, and (3) put a halter on the competition in interest rates on bank deposits. This was less than the purists had hoped for; many favored a complete nationalization of the banking system. But even so, it was a giant step forward in responsible banking, and it struck at some of the worst evils in the existing system.

This supervision of banks was not an innovation of the New Dealers. The father of the act was Senator Glass, who had been fighting for it, minus the provision for the deposit guarantee, for two years. The deposit insurance provision—a controversial feature—was contained in a separate bill sponsored by Representative Henry B. Steagall, chairman of the House Banking and Currency Committee. Conservative and eastern bankers resisted the deposit guarantee as unworkable and likely to penalize the sound banks to the dubious benefit of unsound ones. Roosevelt, at the outset, shared this view. But the combination of circumstances created by the banking holiday and by the exposures of the Pecora inquiry dictated a compromise of opposing viewpoints. Glass and Steagall got together promptly when the special session of

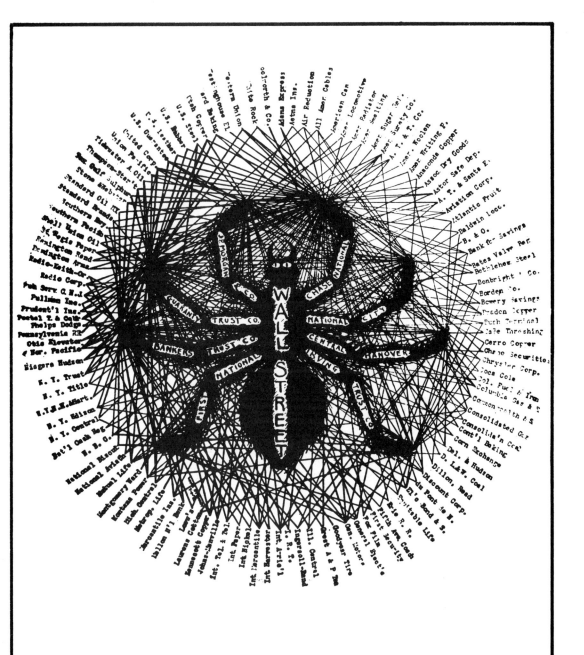

EXHIBIT A OF HECKLERS

The famous *Spider Web of Wall Street* was published in a simplified form by the *New Leader*, Socialist newspaper, five years ago. It was brought to a more interested national attention by Senator George W. Norris, who exhibited a six-foot-high enlargement of it at the last session of Congress. But it looks more sinister than it in fact is. For an aggressive management can and does subordinate its directorate. —Lewis Stanley, July 1st, 1932. Courtesy of Harris & Ewing.

Congress convened, and the combined bill was passed by both houses with overwhelming majorities.

Forcing commercial banks to get out of the investment business and vice versa, wiped out one of the most costly and shameful abuses to which the system had fallen victim. By 1929 the practice of joint banking and investment business was almost universal, and accounted in major part for the epidemic of bank failures that followed the stock market crash. But of more direct importance to the average citizen was the system for insuring him against the loss of the money he had entrusted to the banks. The Federal Deposit Insurance Corporation, created under the Glass-Steagall Act and capitalized jointly by the Treasury and the Federal Reserve System at $300 million, guaranteed him 100 percent protection on the first $10,000 of his deposit and up to 50 percent of the first $50,000. The "run on the bank," that panicky prelude to so many personal and community disasters, was to be a thing of the past.

How much a thing of the past it has become can be demonstrated with a few figures. Bank failures during the decade prior to 1930 ranged from 300 to 700 annually. They soared to 1,352 in 1930, 2,294 in 1931, 1,456 in 1932, and 4,004 in 1933 under the shaking-out process of the bank holiday. From 1935 to 1940 the average dropped to less than fifty a year. Since 1940 the average has been about four a year.[2]

III

The banking bill was but one fork of a two-pronged attack that Roosevelt launched against the domain of the moneymen. Repeatedly in his campaign he had promised to "drive out the money changers," and the Democratic platform of 1932 specifically promised "protection of the investing public" by requiring that securities offered for sale be truthfully represented. Legislation to clean up the stock market was high on the New Deal agenda, and Ray Moley and other members of the Brain Trust had begun work on such a program as early as January 1933.

The motivation for this was not only one of morality and benevolence but also one of hard economic necessity. The most depressed sector of the economy was in durable goods production. Recovery was stagnated there for lack of new capital investment, which in 1932–33, was at its lowest trickle in a generation. And investment was all but blocked by a shattered public confidence in the securities market. A Congressional committee noted in May 1933 that, of $50 billion worth of new securities floated during the decade of the twenties, "fully half have proved to be worthless . . . fraudulent . . . because of the abandonment by many underwriters and dealers in securities of those standards of fair, honest and prudent dealing that should be basic to the encouragement of investment in any enterprise." [3]

The original intention was to include in one legislative package both a "truth in securities" code and government machinery for regulating the stock exchanges. By a series of miscalculations in the White House the drafting job was turned over to two groups, neither of which knew what the other was doing. When the inevitable conflict was exposed, Roosevelt, through Moley, asked his old friend Felix Frankfurter, dean of the Harvard Law School, for help in putting together a truth-in-securities bill alone. This was the simpler of the two parts of the securities package. With time pressing, the regulatory measure would have to wait until later.

Frankfurter sent to Washington two of his former students to do the job under his guidance—a pair whose brilliant minds would become permanent adornments of the New Deal. Benjamin V. Cohen, gentle and withdrawn and with the mien of a scholar, was a superb legal draftsman and a lawyer's lawyer. Moreover, he had learned about Wall Street at first hand by judicious speculation during the twenties. James M. Landis, a member of the Harvard law faculty, was sharp-featured, cool, and precise. His legal perceptions were tinctured with Presbyterian morality (his parents had been missionaries in China). Landis was destined to stay on to administer the truth-in-securities law (and subsequently others as well), and Cohen was to become a sort of floating intellectual troubleshooter for the White House.

The bill they produced, with the collaboration of Moley and others high in the New Deal, was molded in the hot fire of public indignation against the chicanery of the securities business—a fire being fed daily by the revelations of the Pecora investigation. It was the sort of reform—a governmental checkrein on big business—that Frankfurter and others of the so-called Brandeis school of liberalism had long advocated. Wall Street denounced the measure as a stumbling block on the road to recovery. But it passed both houses of Congress by comfortable margins, and the President signed the Securities Act of 1933 into law on May 27 with great acclaim.

The act contained these three main provisions: (1) Every new issue of securities offered for public sale was to be registered in advance with the Federal Trade Commission. (2) The registration statement must contain "every important essential element" about the issuer that a prudent investor would need to know, including both a balance sheet and a three-year profit-and-loss statement showing the condition of the issuing company. (3) Twenty days must elapse between the filing of the registration statement and the offering of the issue for sale. Legal penalties were provided for giving false, misleading, or incomplete information, and the FTC was empowered to block the sale of any issue whose registration statement it deemed inadequate.

This was stiff medicine indeed for an industry where deception had long been tolerated as smart business; where the "insider" with his pools, wash sales, and preferred lists of buyers had an unfair advantage over the multitude of "outsiders"; and where the success of many flotations depended on the issue being snapped up by the gullible in a one-day crash sale. To the angry protests of the moneymen, Frankfurter replied that a corporation offering its securities to the public assumes a public responsibility. "[This] principle of public trusteeship in corporate affairs," he added prophetically, "is bound to receive more and not less recognition."

Upon Frankfurter's strong urging, Roosevelt named Jim Landis to a vacancy on the FTC with special responsibility for administering the "truth in securities" law.[4]

The Securities Act of 1933 was only the lesser half of the far-reaching reform of the securities market contemplated by the New Deal. The other half was to impose regulations and rules of conduct on the market itself—on the stock exchanges, the investment bankers, and the traders and brokers, who had long been accustomed to running this vast public enterprise like a private partnership.

In December Moley and the President turned again to the Cohen-Landis team—this time for preparing the draft of the regulatory part of the securities law. Pecora and Adolf Berle were added to the team, as was another Frankfurter protégé, Thomas G. Corcoran, who was also destined for renown in the hierarchy of the New Deal. "Tommy the Cork," as Roosevelt affectionately nicknamed him, was an ebullient, moon-faced young man of Irish ancestry with a nimble wit and an intuitive sense of politics. He had been one of Frankfurter's brightest law students, had served as clerk to Justice Oliver Wendell Holmes, and was staked out at the moment in the office of the legal counsel of the RFC. His association with Ben Cohen on the securities exchange bill was to ripen into a warm and fruitful partnership on a number of New Deal projects of the highest priority. Though totally disparate in appearance and temperament, Corcoran and Cohen became known as FDR's "Gold Dust Twins."

With a strong message of endorsement from President Roosevelt, the new securities bill was introduced in the House and Senate on February 9, 1934. Picking up where the original act left off, its main provisions were: (1) creation of an agency known as the Securities and Exchange Commission, with wide regulatory powers over interstate traffic in securities, including the licensing of stock exchanges, their members, and brokers and dealers in the over-the-counter market; (2) periodic disclosure by "insiders" (officers, directors, and 10 percent owners) of their position in respect to the stock of any company with which they are affiliated; (3) extension of the registration requirements of the Securities Act of 1933 to *all* listed securities, and the filing by all issuers of securities of periodic financial reports for public inspection; and (4) control over margin requirements (the amount of credit brokers may extend to investors), to be prescribed by the Federal Reserve Board.

It was a drastic, indeed a revolutionary bill—one of the tightest pieces of financial legislation ever drawn. It was so airtight, according to a contemporary comment, "that the Wall Street corporation lawyers, who were accustomed to driving a span of captains of industry through the United States Constitution whenever the banks desired, couldn't find a loophole in it." [5]

The response of the financial leaders was immediate and violent. Such a law, they said, would instantly dry up the capital market; recovery would be frozen in its tracks; Wall Street would "become a deserted village"; the capitalist system would perish. As Congressional hearings on the bill began in March, an intense and highly organized lobbying and propaganda campaign in opposition was launched. Its spearhead was Richard Whitney, president of the New York Stock Exchange, who moved to Washington with a head-quarters staff to direct the effort in person. He was solidly backed by the leading brokerage and investment houses across the nation, and by scores of such powerful industrialists as George Humphrey of Cleveland, president of the Hanna Company, Sewell Avery of the United States Gypsum Company, and Tom Girdler of Republic Steel. Many local chambers of commerce and similar groups joined the crusade, bought newspaper and radio advertising, stimulated wholesale letter-writing campaigns, and pinched the sensitive political nerves of their congressmen and senators where it hurt the most, at the grass roots. The din and the pressure became almost unbearable in Washington. Roosevelt supporters in Congress, even some who were high within the Administration, began to waver.

As the battle approached a climax, the tension was momentarily relieved by a bit of unconscious comedy. Appearing before the House Commerce Committee on March 23, James Rand, Jr., president of Remington-Rand and chairman of the archconservative Committee for the Nation, made the shock-ing allegation that the stock exchange bill was simply one stratagem of a New Deal plot to deliver the nation into the hands of the Communists. The source of this ominous intelligence, he said, was Dr. William A. Wirt, super-intendent of schools in Gary, Indiana, who had it directly from the lips of certain members of the Brain Trust.

The members of the House Commerce Committee and the reporters at the press tables snapped to incredulous attention. Rand was a man of consider-able repute in the business world, and he was deadly in earnest in casting this dire warning before the world. The Committee for the Nation, he said, was even then incorporating Dr. Wirt's "proof" in a pamphlet on the spreading of Communist influence throughout the government. Rand added that he was sure Dr. Wirt would be pleased to tell the Congress what he knew if they chose to call him.

Two weeks later, preceded by a great trumpeting of headlines and alarmed editorial speculation, Dr. Wirt took the stand in the Committee hearing room. He was a stocky, square-jawed man of sixty, slow-spoken and dogmatic. He had achieved a limited fame, both as an educational innovator and as an advocate of unorthodox monetary schemes. In a long and rambling discourse he told the Committee that six months earlier he had attended a dinner party in a Washington suburb at which he had heard a group of "New Dealers and Brain Trusters" describe in detail how, by holding back recovery and crippling business, they were preparing the way for a Communist regime to succeed the New Deal. Wirt was told, he said, that Roosevelt was merely the Kerensky of this revolutionary plot and that Tugwell was its Stalin. He confessed that he had been astounded by these disclosures and that he had pressed his fellow guests at the dinner to explain how they expected to get away with their scheme.

(Clockwise) Joseph P. Kennedy, first head of the Securities and Exchange Commission, and, Financiers in disrepute: J. P. Morgan; Ivar Kreuger, the Swedish Match King; and Richard Whitney, ex- president of the Stock Exchange.

(Clockwise) Judge Ferdinand Pecora of the New York Supreme Court and earlier (bottom) the dynamic investigator for the Senate Banking Committee's hearings on Wall Street malpractice. Ben Cohen, one of the "Gold Dust Twins," and Samuel Insull, Chicago utility magnate, extradited from Turkey to face embezzlement charges.

"We are on the inside," he said they told him. "We control the avenues of influence. We believe we have Mr. Roosevelt in the middle of a swift stream and that the current is so strong he cannot turn back or escape from it. We believe we can keep Mr. Roosevelt there until we are ready to supplant him with a Stalin."

Even before he completed his long and hairy tale of intrigue, it was evident that Dr. Wirt was over his head in fantasy and exaggeration. Under sharp questioning by members of the Committee it turned out that the conspirators around the dinner table who had so alarmed him were, rather than "New Dealers and Brain Trusters," five quite obscure civil service employees far removed from the echelons of power and influence in Washington. One of them had been Wirt's secretary in Gary a few years before. A sixth conspirator, whose presence might have given a modicum of credence to Wirt's concern, was Laurence Todd, and American-born correspondent for Tass, the Soviet news agency. It turned out that few of the sinister designs Wirt attributed to the dinner group had been stated categorically; rather, he had "deduced" them "from the drift of the conversation." He finally admitted that he had done most of the talking that evening himself, expounding his views on monetary reform and other subjects.

Mercifully, the Committee excused Dr. Wirt without bothering to ask him to recant. "The Hoosier school master," said the *Literary Digest,* "has given Washington its biggest laugh since the advent of the Roosevelt administration." And *Time* in its characteristic fashion, asserted: "Flatter than a *crêpe suzette* fell the Red Scare of 1934."

Flat also fell Mr. Rand, the Committee for the Nation, and the organized opposition to the Securities Exchange Act of 1934. It passed both houses of Congress by substantial margins in May and was signed into law on June 6.

But also flattened in the long ordeal was Roosevelt's honeymoon with the business community. It had lasted for a year and had been exciting and fruitful. But now what? To the conservative overlords of industry and finance the stringencies of the Securities Exchange Act with its naked intrusion of government into the marketplace was the finger of destiny writing on the wall. Where would That Man strike next? Having rallied once to oppose him and having failed, this band of diehards determined to stay together and to fight another day. And they did, with gathering fury, to the last days of the New Deal.

After much deliberation, Roosevelt picked Joseph P. Kennedy to be the first chairman of the Securities and Exchange Commission and rewarded Landis and Pecora with seats on the five-man commission. Kennedy's appointment drew loud protests from New Deal liberals; it was, they said, like inviting the fox to guard the henhouse. A tall, energetic, red-headed Irishman from Boston in his mid-forties, Joe Kennedy had made a fortune in steel, movies, and rough-and-tumble speculation in the stock market, from which he had managed to escape before the roof fell in. To many he symbolized the very sort of evil the securities laws were designed to curb. But he bore excellent

Democratic credentials, was a friend and ardent supporter of Roosevelt for the nomination, and was firmly endorsed by Ray Moley. He pleaded with the President to give him a try at the SEC chairmanship. The President reasoned that a knowledgeable insider was a better pilot in these shoaly waters than a crusading idealist, provided his heart was pure, and Kennedy seemed to fit the pattern.

It was a sound decision. Joe Kennedy knew the stock market inside out, but he also recognized its weaknesses and wanted to correct them. Moreover, he enjoyed a certain degree of confidence among his fellow moneymen; at least, he was one of their own and not a "long-haired professor." In his first few weeks in office he helped to thaw out the market for new capital issues, which had been virtually frozen since passage of the 1933 "truth in securities" bill. From a low of $1 billion in that year, the total rose to a modest $4.5 billion level during the next three years and approached close to the 1929 high of $11 billion in 1944. He also set about constructing the body of regulations and administrative law that would, over the years, make the SEC a model among regulatory agencies of the government, respected alike on Wall Street and on Main Street.

Wall Street did not, as so gloomily predicted, become "a deserted village." [6]

IV

In 1932 more than 200,000 homeowners, farmers, and businessmen lost their property because they could not keep up payments on their mortgages. The foreclosure rate in that bottom-of-the-depression year was 221.5 percent greater than in the approximately normal year of 1926. The total of mortgage indebtedness as the New Deal came to power was about $40 billion, of which almost half represented home mortgages and one-quarter represented farm mortgages. [7] Foreclosure was invariably a tragedy for the borrower, and it seldom was a bargain for the lender, since there was virtually no market for real estate, urban or rural. One major element in the convulsion of the banks was the glut of mortgages loans on which they could not collect. Many insurance companies were similarly afflicted. The grinding pressure of this load of debt had already sparked revolutionary mob violence in the farm belt, and by March 1933 it was adding dangerously to the distress and unrest in the cities.

The banker was not the willful culprit of this crisis. His institutional plight was only a little less desperate than the plight of the dispossessed homeowner. It was necessary for the government to get squarely into the mortgage business to save both the banker and his customer from disaster. The Administration's method of doing so afforded an early and illuminating example of the New Deal's affinity for trying to build a welfare state on the foundations of a capitalist society.

Mortgage relief for the farmer and for the urban homeowner came almost simultaneously, in May–June 1933, but in separate legislative and administrative packages. Relief for the farmer was embodied in the omnibus Agricultural

Adjustment Act, and for the town dweller in the Home Owners' Loan Act, which set up the independent Home Owners' Loan Corporation (HOLC). The *modus operandi* was virtually the same for both. For the sake of brevity, it is traced out here in terms of the HOLC, which was the more familiar of the two at that time.

The purpose of the HOLC was to refinance individual home mortgages. If you were facing foreclosure, or were behind in your payments, or were in danger of becoming so and could prove yourself to be a "good moral risk," you could go either to your bank or to any of hundreds of local HOLC offices and apply for relief under the Home Owners' Loan Act. If your application were accepted, the HOLC would buy your mortgage from whoever held it and make you a new loan of up to $14,000 at 5 percent interest for a maximum period of fifteen years, payable in monthly installments. Moreover, if you were also behind in your taxes, you could have a cash advance to settle them added to your loan.

To finance its operations, the HOLC was capitalized initially at $200 million, subscribed by the United States Treasury, and it was authorized to issue up to $2 billion worth of bonds bearing interest at 4 percent. When it bought your mortgage from the bank, HOLC paid for it in an equivalent amount of its own bonds. Here came the most serious rub with the bankers, who in most instances, had been charging you 6 percent for your mortgage money. To the bankers, acceptance of the government's bonds meant a loss in potential earnings of 2 percent. The alternative to *not* trading with the HOLC was, of course, to risk losing the whole bag. So, in due course, and after some legal arm twisting in the Federal courts, the banks came around.

Psychologically, the HOLC was an instant success. Even before it became operative in late summer of 1933 it had had a soothing influence on harassed borrowers and panicky lenders. The rate of foreclosures that had been running during the winter and spring at an average of above 20,000 per month declined markedly after it became known that help was on the way. Local HOLC offices were flung open, often in a vacant storefront with rented desks. Bewildered clerks took care of customers who piled in as if to a fire sale. Fifteen thousand applications were filed in New York City alone when the HOLC opened for business there on August 15. Within a week there were a dozen claimants to the distinction of having gotten the "first" HOLC loan. In some cities racketeers tried to muscle in on the supposed bonanza by offering quick action on loans—for commissions ranging up to 25 percent. Hundreds of impecunious young lawyers began to prosper under the refreshing trickle of fees for title searches, appraisals, and similar services stimulated by the new agency. From the standpoint of legislation for the middle class, the Home Owners' Loan Act probably did more than anything else to cement the bonds between white-collar America and the New Deal.

Substantively, however, the HOLC fell somewhat short of its early billing. Wholesale mortgage lending does not commend itself to execution on a crash basis. In spite of the optimism and high hopes for early relief, the agency had granted only about 6,500 loans up to November 1. At the end of 1934, after eighteen months of operation, the number had risen to 722,000 out of a total of 1,741,000 applications, and the average of all loans granted was a modest $3,024. The high expectations of the morning had given way to grumbling at midday over the slowness and niggardliness of the HOLC operation. "The bankers have taken over," people complained, and they wrote letters to their newspapers and congressmen urging that the Administration "loosen up." Then, slowly, the benevolent eye of HOLC began to harden with a moneylender's glassy stare. The agency said: "Pay up or get out." Defaults had begun to rise alarmingly in 1936; by mid-1938 HOLC had foreclosed on more than 100,000 homes.[8]

On balance, however, HOLC was a boom to the economy and a godsend to most of its clients. It was strictly an emergency operation; its lending authority ran for only three years. But it fathered other forms of federal aid for homeowners to take its place, some of which have continued to the present day. All told, HOLC made 1,017,821 loans, aggregating $3,093,451,321 (its lending authority was doubled in 1934) between June 13, 1933, and June 12, 1936. In the servicing and liquidating of these loans over the next twenty years, it foreclosed on 201,942 individual properties (almost one in five), on which it suffered a net loss of $336,548,215. Most of this attrition came during the sharp recession of 1937–39 when many borrowers lost their jobs. In the end, however it made a profit. When it closed its books for the last time on December 31, 1951, and went out of existence, HOLC had $14,068,588 in surplus net earnings to turn back to the United States Treasury.[9]

V

Roosevelt's ultimate affront to financial orthodoxy was offered in his abandonment of the gold standard and the devaluation of the dollar. He had the deliberate objective of creating inflation as a means of getting the economy going again, but his path to that goal zigzagged bewilderingly around obstacles of ignorance, uncertainty, and improvisation. Along the way he lost some of the stoutest allies of the New Deal, but he picked up some quite improbable recruits as well.

"Sound money" is, or was, one of those fetishes of the classical economists that are supposed to lie untouched and unquestioned as a foundation stone of the capitalist ethic. Disaster may strike the marketplace and turmoil snarl the wheels of progress, but an economy in upheaval must adjust itself to a stable dollar, not the dollar to the economy. This may have seemed to be good doctrine for the owners and renters of capital, but it played hob many times with producers and wage earners. It was this kind of discontent that fed the rise of Populism at the end of the nineteenth century and gave William Jennings Bryan his ringing slogan "You shall not crucify mankind upon a cross of gold." Populism was dead when the Great Depression struck, and "sound money" remained the respectable and dominant point of view. But as the economic crisis deepened, refusing stubbornly to yield to "natural laws," many of the higher disciples of the "sound money" doctrine found their faith waning.

Inflated money is the opposite of sound money. "Inflation," incidentally, had a somewhat different connotation thirty years ago from what it has acquired in more recent times. In 1933 it meant simply employing any of a number of devices to put more money into circulation and to make credit more plentiful, thus "cheapening" the dollar in relation to gold. The result of such inflation is that more people have more money to spend; merchants clear their shelves and place new orders with manufacturers; manufacturers buy new raw materials, and so on along the whole economic pipeline. Prices, and then wages, rise. The trouble with inflation is that too much of it can be as bad as, or worse than, its opposite, deflation. The greater availability of money is more than offset by the decline in its purchasing power. The result: boom, bust, stagnation.

Inflation is said to share a common attribute with pregnancy: It is hard to have just a little of it. Roosevelt decided, somewhat gingerly, to test that hypothesis.

By the beginning of 1933 a strong inflationist bloc had arisen in Congress, mainly among members from the farm states. Their views found substantial backing among some business groups and among some influential members of the New Deal inner circle as well including Tugwell, Moley, Wallace, and Henry Morgenthau, Jr. Roosevelt was also being tempted in this direction by such prominent economic philosophers as Professor Irving Fisher of Yale and Professor George Warren of Cornell, whose unorthodox ideas about a more flexible monetary system had gained a wide following. But on Inaguration Day Roosevelt was still far from being committed. His action embargoing gold as part of his emergency bank decree was aimed at the banking crisis, not at inflation.

The pressure for inflation mounted rapidly during the early weeks of the new Administration. The scarcity of money was aggravated by the freezing of some $5 billion of deposits in still unopened banks. The sluggish farm sector of the economy did not share the sudden surge of activity that occurred in manufacturing and trade. The burgeoning recovery had a disturbingly lopsided look. The clamor for inflation in Congress gained "such formidable strength," Moley was to write later, "that Roosevelt realized that he could not block it, that he could at the most try to direct it." [10]

The opportunity came when a new farm bill, the Agricultural Adjustment Act, was moving toward passage in April. It contained an important amendment sponsored by Senator Elmer Thomas of Oklahoma authorizing a series of drastic steps to inflate the currency. He argued convincingly that such steps were a necessary part of any rescue operation for the farmers. Roosevelt was only partially convinced that Thomas might be right, but he was certain that Thomas had the votes to prevail, right or wrong. He therefore agreed to accept the amendment provided use of its powers were made discretionary with the President instead of mandatory under law. When he casually announced this decision to a group of his advisers at the White House on April 18, "hell broke loose in the room," Moley reported. To the sound money advocates this was capitulation to the "wild men," heresy against sacred laws. Lew Douglas, the Budget Director, bowed his head in agony and called it "the end of Western civilization."

The farm bill, with the Thomas amendment firmly locked in, was enacted on May 3. It put inflationary tools into the President's hands by giving him authority (1) to order the Federal Reserve to conduct open market operations in government obligations; (2) to issue up to $3 billion in greenbacks; (3) to reduce the gold content of the dollar by as much as 50 percent and to fix the monetary ratio between gold and silver; and (4) to buy up to $100 million in silver and to issue silver certificates against the silver thus received. This authority represented a mixed bag of monetary theories owing paternity to, among others, banking orthodoxy (open market operations of the FRB); agricultural Populists tradition (issuance of greenbacks); the Senate silver bloc (silver purchase program); and the advocates of the "commodity dollar" and other forms of managed currency (reduction of gold content). Of the lot, the power to change the gold content of the dollar was to prove the most significant.

The President had already effectively taken the country off the gold standard by making permanent his March 6 embargo on gold and requiring domestic holders of bullion and gold certificates to cash them in at Federal Reserve banks. Early in June he reinforced his order by securing a joint resolution from Congress abrogating the clause in contracts—private and government—requiring payments in gold. Thus, though the currency continued to be based on gold, gold was no longer legal tender. To most "sound money" men, "going off gold" was the moral equivalent of denouncing motherhood or denying *e pluribus unum*. Their protests, like the protest of Lewis Douglas, rent the air. But a surprising number of business and financial leaders applauded the action as a drastic but necessary jolt to the economy. The ultimate benediction was pronounced by J. P. Morgan, who said that it was "the best possible course under existing circumstances."

The President now had at his disposal a variety of tools for inducing inflation, but for the time being he chose not to use them. In part this was due to his absorption in other aspects of his recovery program, which interested him more. He had, as Arthur Schlesinger, Jr., has observed, "a casualness of mind" toward the whole complex subject of finance that often left many of his advisers in despair.

In the spring and early summer of 1933, the economy did not seem to need additional prodding. The upswing since the end of the March bank holiday had been phenomenal. *The New York Times* business index, which stood at an all-time low of 60 on March 18, was up to 74.1 by May 31, the biggest and fastest gain for any like period since 1929. Even with hundreds of banks still closed and thirteen million jobless on the streets, the stock market was beginning to behave like its old self again: merchants were busy, dead factory smokestacks were coming back to life, and people everywhere were happier and more hopeful than they had been for four years. Everywhere, that is, except down on the farm. But in the general state of euphoria that prevailed it was tempting to forget about the farmers.[11]

In the midst of these developments the World Economic Conference to which the United States was a party assembled in London in June. President Hoover, wedded to the belief that the Depression had its roots in European rather than American soil, had been one of its original sponsors. The Conference was called in an effort to palliate an assortment of not always correlative economic ills, which included war debts, trade barriers, international exchange, currency stabilization, and similar problems that seemed to affect all nations indiscriminately. It was an inheritance that Roosevelt viewed skeptically but could not conveniently disavow. Indeed, he left Prime Minister Ramsay MacDonald of Great Britain under the impression that he was in accord with the same objectives that MacDonald sought. But his heart was not in it; nor, it would appear, was his mind, except fleetingly. In the end he brought the Conference down in complete disarray.

The large American delegation was headed by Secretary of State Cordell Hull. No titan at that time in the field of diplomacy, and wholly unversed in the arcane language of international finance, he was surrounded in the delegation by others equally unsophisticated. The President's instructions to the delegates were vague, reflecting his lack of deep concern for the venture on which they were embarking. In consequence, the group had hardly set sail from New York before they found themselves hopelessly at odds with one another on what they were supposed to accomplish, and how. Once arrived at the conference table in London, their confusion was compounded when they ran up against the hardheaded bargainers for the European powers who *did* know what they wanted. Above everything, they wanted stabilization of world currencies based on gold with the dollar as anchor. Granted that, they might then consent to talk about tariffs, silver, or whatever else the Americans wanted.

The dilemma of Secretary Hull and his associates was acute. Stabilization of gold was one thing on which Roosevelt had been emphatic: He didn't want it. To subject the free-wheeling dollar to international control at this juncture, he reasoned, would risk recovery at home on the uncertain gamble that recovery could thereby be induced in other lands. But if the Americans rejected international stabilization out of hand, they would sacrifice other objectives and possibly wreck the conference.

As the Americans strove and maneuvered for a way around this impasse, tensions and conflict within the delegation mounted, and so did the exasperation of the delegates from other countries. One proposed stratagem after another was rejected by Washington—often, it seemed to the distressed Secretary of State, capriciously or out of ignorance. Cables were delayed and garbled, the overseas telephone was erratic, and for more than two weeks Roosevelt was frequently out of reach for days at a time as he cruised the pleasant waters off New England and Nova Scotia. Some embittered members of the delegation threatened to resign; others spilled their resentment and disillusionment to the press. Walter Lippmann, reporting from the scene for the New York *Herald-Tribune,* wrote:

Mr. Roosevelt cannot have understood how completely unequipped are his representatives here to deal with the kind of project he has in mind. For one thing, they do not know what is in his mind. For another, there is not among them a single man who understands monetary questions sufficiently to debate them. For another, they have been so frequently repudiated that they are demoralized. For another, they are divided among themselves. . . . Mr. Roosevelt's purposes may be excellent. He has completely failed to organize a diplomatic instrument to express them.[12]

Early in July the President dispatched Raymond Moley to London with instructions to try to pull the U.S. delegation together and to effect some sort of compromise with Britain, France, and the other leading powers that would allow the conference to expire without a complete loss of face. Such a compromise was eventually worked out over many hard hours of negotiation and semantic nit-picking. It was an innocuous acceptance of the *principle* of stabilization, which committed the United States to nothing while opening the way to substantive agreement on other issues.

Proudly, the draft was cabled to Washington for Presidential approval. Shockingly, the word came back that the President rejected it, root and stock. The World Economic Conference, in Moley's words, had been "torpedoed"— largely, he believed, because Roosevelt failed to grasp the true significance of the face-saving compromise.

The President probably felt that he had saved his fast-paced recovery at home by protecting the dollar from onerous foreign entanglements. But the cost may have been greater than he reckoned, for as the London Economic Conference sank from view (as it soon did), it carried with it the World Disarmament Conference, which had been going on more or less simultaneously in Geneva. Broadus Mitchell wrote:

The decision was probably the most momentous one that Franklin Roosevelt made. One may speculate, with cause, whether in defeating the world's resolution to stabilize currencies and thereby promote trade, President Roosevelt did not contribute heavily to the international economic and political deterioration that led to fresh war. . . . Infatuated with the prospect of rising prices at home, did he hastily condemn others to frustration, discord, and the appeal to arms? There was a lighthearted suddenness in his behavior which spoke of ignorance or certainly of the little knowledge which is a dangerous thing.[13]

Such strictures come with the special acuity of hindsight. But in July 1933 only the unreconstructed "sound money" men were offended by the President's rejection of the currency stabilization move. Others, like John Maynard Keynes in England and Russell Leffingwell of the House of Morgan applauded its wisdom.

Meanwhile the boomlet of the first Hundred Days was coming to an end, and by mid-August it seemed to be in danger of collapse. The stock market turned sluggish, and the Federal Reserve's index of industrial production, which had climbed with such exuberance to a high of 102 in July, slid to 91 in August and to 70 in November. Unemployment had scarcely been dented. The wind had gone out of the sails of recovery, and pressure mounted on the President to put to use some of the inflationary tools given him in the farm bill.

In a radio speech on October 22, Roosevelt made it clear that he would exercise the new monetary powers given him, indicating that he would employ in the process some of the ideas of Professors Warren and Fischer and even a dash of Keynes. As a first step, he said, the RFC was being authorized to buy gold, "at prices to be determined from time to time. . . . My aim in taking this step is to establish and maintain continuous control [over the currency]. This is a policy, not an expedient. It is not be used merely to offset a temporary fall in prices. We are thus continuing to move toward a managed currency."

Thus the value of the dollar (*i.e.,* the price paid for the gold supporting it) would be whatever the President said it was. For weeks he varied it a few cents each day (mainly to confound the speculators) in breakfast conferences at his bedside with Jesse Jones of the RFC and one or two officials from the Treasury. This expedient wasn't quite what Professor Warren had in mind, but it was closer to his cherished "commodity dollar" than he had ever hoped to come.

Notice of this abrupt departure from orthodoxy sent shock waves through the financial community and caused, as well, a number of serious ruptures in the New Deal fabric. Among the monetary moderates who had hung on in the belief that Roosevelt would not go so far, Dean Acheson, Under Secretary of the Treasury, was one of the first to break away. Since September he had been Acting Secretary during Will Woodin's illness. When he told the President he was opposed to the gold-buying scheme on both philosophic and legal grounds, Roosevelt tartly suggested he resign. When Woodin also resigned, primarily because of his health, Henry Morgenthau, Jr., a more pliant convert to monetary reform, was moved over from the Farm Security Administration as Secretary.

On December 21 Roosevelt made another direct application of the inflationary powers given him in the Thomas amendment. Responding to intense pressures from the farm and silver blocs, he issued an Executive Order calling for free coinage of silver on the 16 to 1 ratio made familiar to every schoolboy by Bryan and his political heirs. This produced a bonanza for Western silver producers over the next several years, but in neither its short-range nor its long-range effects did it have any measurable impact in raising prices or general economic recovery. Even under inflationary pressure, silver—in the complicated arithmetic of monetary theory—is a poor competitor with gold as a medium of exchange. "All in all," Mitchell has observed, "the silver program was a fiasco."

In January 1934 Roosevelt took a third and longer stride into the fiscal unknown. He pressed for, and Congress passed, the Gold Reserve Act, which virtually consolidated control of the monetary system in the President's hands. The act made the government the only legal owner of monetary gold in the

United States. Gold was to be reduced to bullion and held solely as a reserve. The act also empowered the President (as did the Thomas amendment) to reduce the theoretical gold content of the dollar, set since 1834 at 23.22 fine grains, to 13.71 fine grains, or 59.06 percent of its old weight. The silver dollar was devalued by the same ratio. This marked the end of Roosevelt's flirtation with the Warren "commodity dollar," which he had initiated in October. Thus the 59-cent "Roosevelt dollar" became the "baloney dollar" of political ill fame, but it immediately enriched the supply of currency in circulation by some $2.8 billion. A reserve of gold was set aside for the balancing of intertional payments, but except for these transactions in hard metal the United States was, in all senses except the most theoretical, to be henceforth on a paper currency basis. It still is today.

The pace of recovery, which had faltered in August and September, had regained much of its forward momentum by the beginning of the new year of 1934. How much of this was attributable directly to the inflationary effects of Roosevelt's monetary policies, and how much was generated by NRA, AAA, work relief, and similar programs, it is impossible to say. However, the New Deal was never to retreat from its mastery of the prime sources of the nation's currency and credit. In fact, it would move in future years to further strengthen its hand in this field.

"Brothers, this talk of unemployment is grossly exaggerated. Every one of us is working overtime."

VI

In less than a year, Roosevelt had done more to democratize the nation's financial and credit structure than any President before him. Arthur Schlesinger has likened his performance to Andrew Jackson's assault on the Bank of the United States, but it is a pallid comparison at best. For Roosevelt did more than merely oust the oligarchy of moneymen who had controlled the country's financial affairs for almost a century. He literally moved the financial center of gravity from Wall Street to Washington. He not only made control of the nation's monetary resources an affirmative instrument of government policy but also asserted the right of the people to fair and reasonable access to the supply of money.

Bankers were denied the temptation to gamble with their depositors' wealth in the stock market, and the safety of individual deposits was put under government guarantee. The captital market—the buying and selling of securities—was purged of its more grievous villanies and subjected to strict government discipline. The little fellow with only a few hundred dollars to invest could play the game with the reasonable assurance that he would get as fair a shake of the dice as the big shot with a million.

The paralyzing load of mortgage debt was lifted when the property of tens of thousands of farmers and homeowners was saved from foreclosure. Millions of ordinary citizens learned that the government could be not merely a remote and faceless institution but a personal benefactor responsive to man's needs and circumstances.

The complexities of the gold standard, of international exchange, and of a "baloney dollar" that was suddenly worth only 59 cents but seemed to be as good as ever, swirled far above the heads of most people. But out of all the propaganda and perplexing headlines, the general public divined that somehow it all added up to a break for the common man. FDR was on their side, and the moneymen were against them, and that, in most cases, was as far as they cared to reason the matter.

Roosevelt did not, as his detractors so loudly complained, seek to "undermine the capitalist system." He sought rather to strengthen it, to protect it from its own worst follies, to impose upon it what it had never had, a working sense of social responsibility. He proceeded not according to a well-laid plan of battle but haphazardly, from one target of opportunity to another. But in the distance there was always one guiding beacon of consistency—namely, that the nation's great financial resources lay in the public domain and not in a private preserve.

Banking and stock market reforms, government mortgage lending, freeing the dollar from gold—all this was class legislation for what Bernard Baruch misguidedly called "a small proportion of the population, the unemployed, the debtor class—incompetent, unwise people." Rather, it was class legislation for the middle class, to which the overwhelming majority of the people belong. And it forged a political bond between them and Franklin Roosevelt that would endure for the rest of his lifetime and beyond.

CHAPTER 9
Almanac
1933–1934

A miscellany of events occurring during the early thirties that engaged our interest and sometimes affected our lives; a random selection among the more engrossing headlines of the period and the stories behind them.

April 4, 1933

(From *The New York Times*)

DIRIGIBLE AKRON CRASHES IN LIGHTNING STORM AT SEA, ONLY 4 OF THE 77 MEN ABOARD ARE REPORTED RESCUED, AIRSHIP IS BELIEVED A TOTAL LOSS, WIDE SEARCH ON

NEW YORK—Trapped at sea in a violent thunder storm, the U.S.S. Akron, largest and finest dirigible airship in the world, crashed off the Barnegat Lightship at 12:30 o'clock this morning with 77 officers and men aboard. Among them was Rear Admiral William A. Moffett, chief of the Bureau of Aeronautics.

Only four of the 77 were known to have been saved at 5 o'clock this morning. At that time the wreckage of the stricken airship was out of sight in the storm and darkness from the German oil tanker Phoebus, which first reported the catastrophe. A northwest wind blowing about 45 miles an hour was blowing the wreckage off shore and made rescue operations doubly difficult.

No hint of the cause of the disaster was contained in the fragmentary and frequently confusing reports received from the Phoebus, but it was considered highly likely that the great airship was struck by lightning. . . .

A rare and always exciting experience during the early thirties was to hear the far-off and unmistakable drone of the engines and to look up and discover one of the huge dirigibles of the day sailing in majestic dignity across the sky. They seemed incredibly big, graceful as a bullet caught in slow motion, and impervious to the laws of nature as they glided sedately through the heavens or hovered in motionless contemplation of the earth below. Far more than the airplane, which was the plaything of daredevils, the airship seemed to be the key to man's ultimate triumph over gravity. The magazines and Sunday supplements wrote glowingly of the early prospect of leisurely overnight journeys across the continent or oceans, of vacationing for a week in celestial splendor miles above the clouds, even a sort of heavenly suburbia with commuters flying tiny airplanes from a stationary dirigible apartment house to the roofs of their earthly offices.

It was a fascinating picture, and a wholly improbable one. The big dirigibles never got beyond the experimental stage, and the crash of the *Akron* was the beginning of the end.

The Germans wrought the evolution of the free balloon to the rigid, propeller-driven, hydrogen-filled airship, and the great Zeppelins that flew over France and England in the First World War rained awe as well as bombs on the cities below. After the armistice, the United States (which had a monopoly on the world supply of noninflammable helium) and the other major Allies busied themselves to duplicate the German's feat. Hard luck stalked their efforts the whole way.

The Navy took the lead in the United States. The airship, with a speed three times that of the fastest destroyer and a range far greater than that of any airplane, would, it was believed, vastly augment the Navy's coastal patrol far out to sea. In 1919 Congress authorized the purchase of the ZR-1 and the ZR-2, built on German designs, and the construction of a base to house them at Lakehurst, New Jersey. The ZR-1 crashed on a shakedown cruise over England in 1922. The ZR-2, christened *Shenandoah,* broke up with a heavy loss of life in a storm over Ohio in 1925.

That looked like the end of the airship, but the Navy refused to give up. After a lot of engineering work and political lobbying, Congress in 1928 gave the Navy the go-ahead for two new airships of greatly advanced design—the *Akron* and the *Macon.* Each was to be 785 feet long (130 feet longer than the Washington Monument), with 6,500,000 cubic feet capacity, and capable of launching and retrieving a complement of five scouting planes housed within its cavernous belly. The *Akron* was commissioned in August 1931. and its twin, the *Macon,* in March 1933. Together they cost over $7 million.

During its brief life the *Akron* was the Navy's most cherished showpiece. She flew several times across the continent, engaged in fleet maneuvers off both coasts, and managed to "show the flag" over many cities across the country, filling the citizenry with awe and pride. If experts grumbled over her cost and extreme vulnerability to attack in wartime, Navy buffs gloated over her immense propaganda value. She was proudly declared *not* to be vulnerable to wind and storm and to be "easier to ride than a battleship."

But it was wind and storm that brought her down while on "routine patrol" in the midnight blackness off Barnegat Lightship in April 1933. The experts concluded that she hit a low pressure area and literally dived into the sea. The death of seventy-three members of the crew made this the worst air disaster on record up to that time. The nation was saddened for weeks as details of the tragedy slowly unfolded. Her sister ship, the *Macon,* launched only a month before, tried valiantly to restore the prestige of the lighter-than-air service, but in February 1935 she too went to a watery grave off Point Sur, California.

By this time England, France, and Italy had experienced similar disasters with airships and had given them up. Only the Germans persisted, led by the stubborn genius of Dr. Hugo Eckener, who had helped develop the wartime Zeppelin. The end came for the last great dirigible when Eckener's *Hindenburg* exploded in a hideous holocaust while trying to dock after its third trans-Atlantic voyage at Lakehurst on May 6, 1937.

At right: U.S.S. *Macon* in flight in 1933. The surety and serenity was lost forever in 1935 as the $4,000,000 airship sank in the Pacific off Point Sur, California, with 83 men and officers lost. (Alongside) First Day Cover for U.S.S. *Akron* Christening, August 8, 1931. (Middle) "*Akron* flying Lakehurst to Philadelphia to Delaware Capes, thence along coast..." then tragedy as the "Queen of the Skies," buffetted by an electrical storm, plunged into the sea off Barnegat Light, New Jersey, claiming the lives of 74 officers and men. (Bottom) First Day Cover, Memorial Day 1933, commemorating the *Akron* Disaster. (Below) Dirigibles *Akron* and *Los Angeles* over Lower Manhattan, 1932.

U. S. S. AKRON
CHRISTENING

U.S.S.   AKRON

AKRON, OHIO U.S.A.
AUG. 8, 1931

April 17, 1933

(From *The New York Times*)

SCOTTSBORO NEGRO IS SENTENCED TO DEATH

DECATUR, ALA.—Judge James W. Horton sentenced one of the Scottsboro Negroes to death today in accordance with the findings of a jury which found him guilty of attacking a white girl two years ago, and postponed the trial of his eight co-defendants indefinitely.

In doing so Judge Horton said that statements issued by opposing counsel since Haywood Patterson's conviction a week ago made an impartial trial of the other defendants here and now impossible. . . .

Throughout the decade of the thirties the case of the Scottsboro Boys was a national *cause célèbre,* played out in one impassioned episode after another, like an endless Greek tragedy. It was a cause that split liberals from conservatives, Notherners from Southerners, white men from black men, and preachers of every faith from one another and from their congregations. At issue was the medieval code of Southern justice for the Negro, and it was set in a web of circumstances designed to inflame the most primitive emotions and prejudices of the day. Adding to the heat of the controversey was the fact that the Communist Party assumed the principal burden of defense and exploited the case shamelessly in its propaganda.

What gave particular moment to Judge Horton's action in sentencing Haywood Patterson to death was that it came virtually on the heels of a Supreme Court decree setting a previous conviction aside. Alabama justice was not to be denied.

The nine youths were arrested at Paint Rock, Alabama, on March 25, 1931, on the complaint of two white women of dubious virtue, Victoria Price and Ruby Bates. They told police that a fight had broken out between the Negroes and three white men with whom they were riding in a boxcar. When their white companions were put to flight, the girls said, several of the Negroes raped them.

Medical evidence did not support their charge of an assault, and months later Ruby Bates would repudiate her accusation in court. Nevertheless, the nine Negroes were lodged in the Scottsboro jail, charged with the most heinous offense a black man in the South can commit. Two weeks later they came to trial in the Jackson County court. The white attorney appointed by the court to defend them publicly protested his assignment as distasteful and called no witnesses in his clients' defense. All were found guilty, and the judge immediately imposed the death sentence upon each.

Had the events taken their normal course, the Scottsboro Boys would have been executed and the case would have disappeared from view as no more than a mutely reproachful footnote in legal history. But the case was rescued from oblivion to become a contemporary counterpart of the Sacco-

Vanzetti case. Chiefly responsible was the Communist-oriented International Labor Defense (ILD), which hired a well-known New York criminal lawyer, Samuel Leibowitz, to take over the defense and to seek a new trial. Other liberal groups joined the effort in time, but the ILD was so aggressively in command that it was able to transform the case into a Left Wing crusade, complete with a riot in Harlem and a march on Washington.

Between April 1931 and October 1937 there were six separate trials in the state courts of Alabama and three appeals to the Supreme Court of the United States. In the end, Patterson and three other defendants were given life sentences, and charges against the remaining five were dropped. Of the four who went to prison, the last was freed on parole in June 1950.

Few criminal cases of the twentieth century have aroused such partisan passions for so long a time as the case of the Scottsboro Boys. Reporters by the score covered the various trials. The boys were immortalized by a host of "proletarian" poets, novelists, and playwrights and by at least one WPA muralist (their likenesses appear in a mural decorating the Department of Justice building in Washington today).

The question of civil rights for the Negro was little more than a pious abstraction to the white generation of the thirties. But the Depression had instilled in many a new and unfamiliar concept of "social consciousness." For some it was a deep conviction, belatedly acquired; for others, a fad. But one could take the side of the Scottsboro Boys and all their kind without being a radical or a "nigger lover." That was an important discovery.

May 27, 1933

(From *The New York Times*)

CHICAGO FAIR OPENED BY FARLEY, RAYS OF ARCTURUS START LIGHTS

CHICAGO—The portals of The Century of Progress Exposition, Chicago's second world's fair, were thrown open to the people of all nations today. Four hours of ceremony reached their climax in Soldiers' Field where Postmaster General Farley dedicated the $37,500,000 exposition and delivered a message from President Roosevelt. . . .

A miraculous moment came at 9:15 o'clock tonight when a beam of light which started forty years ago from the star Arcturus was caught by astronomers and transmitted in augmented volume to delicate lighting mechanisms in the tower of the exposition's Hall of Science.

Instantly upon that contact the grounds, pavilions and waterways of the fair were drenched with light. Thousands of awed beholders burst into cheers. Roaring cannon and bombs, bursting in cloudless sky, released hundreds of American flags. The jubilation blended into the harmony of the National Anthem.

(Below) The Scottsboro Boys under heavy guard from lynch threats outside the Scottsboro, Alabama, Jail, 1931. L. to R.: Ozzie Powell, Clarence Norris, Charlie Weems, Olen Montgomery, Willie Robertson, Roy Wright, Hayward Patterson, Andy Wright, and Eugene Williams. (Inset, left) Negro Protesters parading to the White House to petition President Roosevelt to intervene for the Scottsboro Boys. (Inset, right) Free The Scottsboro Boys, Tom Moody, Edith Berkman, etc. Union Square Demonstration, 1932.

1933

A CENTURY
OF PROGRESS
☰CHICAGO☰

"The Dolly Sisters." Period New York City slang
for two coppers and their 1933 Ford V-8 coupé.

The *first* Airflow. 1934 De Soto.

1934 Lincoln V-12.

At left: (Top) First Day Cover—
Logotype for the Chicago World's
Fair. 1933. (Bottom left) Fan Dancer Sally Rand, shown *modeling*
"ticker tape" for a Los Angeles
Tape Convention, was a "Century
of Progress" unto herself, as she
outdrew rickshaw boys along the
Midway (bottom right), modern
architecture, and the Hall of Science. However, the hard under-
belly of the Fair and all of Chicago, that Depression summer of
1933 was forever etched by Nelson Algren in his first novel *Somebody In Boots.*

On Display Today
The New Ford V-8 Cylinder

Bands. bells, choruses and a | plazas, promenades and pal-
symphony   orchestra   filled | aces with music. . . .

The Caesars who gave their hungry peasants circuses instead of bread were good psychologists. The Chicago World's Fair, which opened at the bottom of the Depression in the summer of 1933, was a gigantic exercise in showmanship—the biggest ever up to that time. It showed something profound about the adaptability of the human spirit. Financed on a shoestring, designed in sleazy opulence to extract dollars from citizenry supposedly plunged in gloom and bankruptcy, it was a smash hit that enlivened the popular culture of the day and paid dividends to its backers. It ran for two full seasons, drew an attendance of over twenty million, gave to a fun-starved world such memorable divertissements as the Sky Ride, the Streets of Paris, the Hall of Science, and Miss Sally Rand, the fan dancer. It ended so comfortably in the black that it contributed $160,000 of left-over profits to the city's Field Museum.

Projected in the lush days of 1928, the fair's managers were barely able to sell enough bonds in the lean days of 1931 to get their project going. Backed by hope and credit, they cleared a vast expanse of marshy lakefront extending some twelve blocks southward from the Loop and gradually transformed it into a modernistic Disneyland of multicolored towers, domes, and pagodas set off by instant greenery and synthetic waterfalls. It was a dazzling mirage that spoke of an improbable tomorrow.

The thematic center was the Hall of Science—a huge, futuristic structure that displayed hundreds of working models and dioramas depicting the wonders of the new age in electricity, chemistry, manufacturing, whatnot. In one great enclave one could view the whole life-sized panorama of transportation—from the pony express, complete with a band of attacking Apaches, to a monstrous sixteen-wheel locomotive with steam hissing from its boiler, and a gleaming airliner capable of carrying twenty-four passengers.

There were a dozen "villages"—English, Irish, French, African— through which the visitor could roam to absorb foreign culture and to buy the overpriced souvenirs of far-off lands. Florida supplied a growing orange grove for its exhibit in the Hall of States. New York countered with an authentic acre of Adirondack mountainside. Tulane University set up a genuine Mayan temple, which its archaeologists had dug out of the jungle of Yucatan. There was the Sky Ride, a monorail with bullet-shaped cars that careened breathtakingly along a hundred feet above the ground. The mile-long Midway offered every fleshly temptation from cotton candy and bingo to a tribe of Zulu warriors and Sally Rand.

The Chicago fair was a "sleeper" that surprised not only its financial backers but just about everyone else. It drew customers by the trainload from every part of the country; clubs, churches, schools often banded together to get reduced rates and accommodations. By some strange alchemy of chance or psychology it seemed to offer just the kind of release that a depression-bogged society needed.

July 23, 1933

(From *The New York Times*)

POST ARRIVES SAFELY IN NEW YORK, CIRCLING WORLD IN 7 DAYS, 19 HOURS

NEW YORK—Wiley Post landed safely in his fleet monoplane the" Winnie Mae" at Floyd Bennett Airfield, Brooklyn, at 11:59½ last night. completing a record-breaking flight around the world.

The aviator who used to be a farmer in Texas and an oil driller in Oklahoma, thus became the first person in history to fly alone around the world. He also established a new speed record in circumnavigating the globe in 7 days, 18 hours, 49½ minutes.

Post beat the record of 8 days, 15 hours, 51 minutes established by himself and Harold Gatty, then his navigator, two years ago by 21 hours, 1½ minutes. The thirty-one year old flier, who has only one eye, is the first person to fly around the world twice. It was the same plane, the purple and white "Winnie Mae," which carried Post and Gatty around the world in 1931.

His course, which took him from New York to Berlin, to Moscow, then over Siberia to Alaska and finally across Canada to Floyd Bennett, covered 15,597 miles. His average [air] speed was a fraction over 127 miles per hour. He made ten refueling stops along the way. . . .

Fliers were the universal heroes of the early Depressions years, and the sound of an airplane overhead almost anywhere in the United States caused people to stop whatever they were doing and look up in wonder and admiration. Young boys of the decade yearned to be aviators instead of cowboys or ballplayers and spent hours gluing up model airplanes that were powered with rubber bands and seldom got off the ground. There was an insatiable fascination with the dangerous art of flying. The efforts to set new speed, distance, and endurance records, and the frequent crackups and fatalities, regularly made the front page of the nation's press.

Since Charles Lindbergh's audacious first solo flight across the Atlantic in 1927, a whole generation of daring young men, and a few daring young women, had risked, and frequently lost, their lives to advance man's conquest of the air. Their planes were terrifyingly fragile affairs. Aerial navigation depended less on science than on luck and good eyesight. The best pilots flew "by the seat of their pants."

The "Winnie Mae," for example, was a high-wing monoplane with a 41-foot wingspread, a single "Wasp" engine of 550 horsepower, and a fuselage crammed with tanks to carry more than 600 gallons of gasoline and 30 gallons of oil. Its equipment included one of the first "robot pilots," which, characteristically, failed to work most of the time. When Post got lost over the

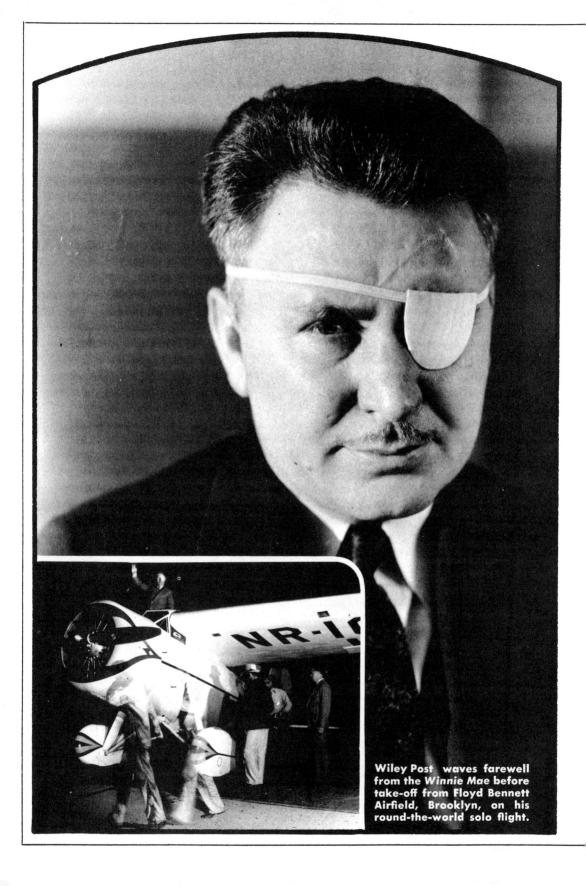

Wiley Post waves farewell from the *Winnie Mae* before take-off from Floyd Bennett Airfield, Brooklyn, on his round-the-world solo flight.

B. Ward Beam's
International
CONGRESS of DARE-DEVILS

MARY WIGGINS

FAMOUS MOVIE DOUBLE

AND·10·OTHER THRILLERS

ONE·DAY·ONLY

CHEMUNG COUNTY FAIR

ELMIRA

SATURDAY

Afternoon Only - 2:30 P. M.

SEP. 15

(Above) Novelist William Faulkner and his 1935 novel *Pylon*, about barnstorming, wing-walking, and parachute-jumping, set in the New Orleans of the early Depression. (At right) Stunt pilots Frank Clarke and Paul Mantz at the Pacific International Air Races, Oakland, California, 1934. (Below) A lady wing-walker, supported by a safety belt and wires, rides upside-down as the pilot does acrobatics at a mid-western county fair.

Russell Boardman and his Gee Bee before take-off in the 1933 Bendix Trophy Race.

1934 Thompson Trophy Race

	Pilot	Aircraft	Av. Speed	Prize Money
1	Roscoe Turner	Wedell-Williams	248.129mph	$4500
2	Roy Minor	Brown B-2 Spec.	214.929mph	$2500
3	Johnny Worthen	Wedell-Williams	208.375mph	$1500
4	Harold Neumann	Howard "Ike"	207.064mph	$1000
5	Roger Don Rae	Keith Rider R-1	205.358mph	$ 500
6	Art Chester	Chester "Jeep"	191.597mph	——

Lee Miles out on last lap. Doug Davis, killed, high speed stall while leading on eighth lap.

Roscoe Turner. "King of the Pylons."

Siberian wastes between Moscow and Novosibirsk (a Michelin road map had been his principal guide from Berlin to Moscow), he landed in a meadow by a road and waited until a party of startled peasants came along. After a heroic dialogue in sign language, they told him in what direction Novosibirsk lay.

Wiley Post's around-the-world flight was the most exciting aerial exploit of the year. At each overnight stop he telegraphed an account of that day's journey to an American news syndicate, and his progress was followed avidly day by day by millions of readers all over the country.

But he was not the only hero in the skies that year. James Mattern had attempted an almost identical flight a month earlier. He crashed and was lost in the icy loneliness of Siberia for three weeks before rescuers reached him. J. R. Weddell set a breathtaking new speed record of 305 miles an hour at the International Air Races in Chicago in September. Also that summer, Frank Hawks set a new nonstop transcontinental record, flying from Los Angeles to New York in the unbelievable time of 13 hours, 25 minutes, 14 seconds. And Colonel and Mrs. Lindbergh spent five well-publicized months trail-blazing a route for future trans-Atlantic airliners by the way of Iceland and the Scandinavian peninsula.

Nov. 17, 1933

(From *The New York Times*)

UNITED STATES RECOGNIZES SOVIET EXACTING PLEDGES ON PROPAGANDA: BULLITT NAMED FIRST AMBASSADOR

WASHINGTON—Official relations between the United States and the Soviet Union were established at ten minutes before midnight yesterday. The fact was announced this afternoon by President Roosevelt, but historically speaking the date was 11:50 P.M., Nov. 16.

The undertakings of the two governments were set forth in eleven letters and a memorandum exchange between the President and Maxim Litvinov, Soviet Commissar for Foreign Affairs, covering agreements and concessions completed in ten days of negotiations.

The United States received the most complete pledge against Bolshevist propaganda that has ever been made by the Soviet government. . . . In a speech last night to the National Press Club M. Litvinov disavowed any claims of the Communist Party in the United States to represent the governing group in Russia. . . .

The President's action put an end to a diplomatic standoff that had existed since 1917, when U.S. relations were broken with the revolutionary Kerensky regime, successor to the Czarist regime. It did not, however, put an end to the intense ideological debate over the issue that had raged in this country for almost a decade. Conservatives and most members of the clergy adamantly opposed giving any aid or comfort to "godless Communism" or its agents, who "stir up discontent among our American workingmen." Liberals and intellectuals, on the other hand, favored greater intercourse with a land where they were sure the wave of the future was gathering, soon to break over the world's political landscape.

But the decisive voice seemed to be that of economists and businessmen, who saw in the huge, awakening Russian peasantry a half-billion-dollar annual market for American cotton, wheat, steel, machinery, and manufactured goods. "We can lick their propaganda any time," it was confidently said, "by sending over a couple of boatloads of Sears Roebuck catalogues." It was never as simple as that, and the hope of an instant trade bonanza bogged down in the intricacies of arranging credits and the settlement of old debts.

William C. Bullitt, whom FDR sent as his first Ambassador to Moscow, was almost the stereotype of the millionaire capitalist. Yet he had been an advocate of recognition since 1919, when President Wilson sent him as a secret emissary to sound out Lenin on the Versailles Treaty. The Russians welcomed him with open arms on his return in 1933.

In spite of Russian assurances to the contrary there was an almost immediate increase in Communist propaganda in this country, and the Communist Party in the United States had its most vigorous period of growth. It is doubtful, however, if either phenomenon was much influenced by the fact of diplomatic recognition. The climate of the times made a growing interest in Communist doctrine inevitable.

Dec. 5, 1933

(From *The New York Times*)

PROHIBITION REPEAL IS RATIFIED AT 5:32 PM, ROOSEVELT ASKS NATION TO BAR THE SALOON: NEW YORK CELEBRATES WITH QUIET RESTRAINT

City Toasts New Era; Crowds Swamp the Legal Resorts But Legal Liquor is Scarce

WASHINGTON—Legal liquor was returned to the United States today with President Roosevelt calling on the people to see that "this return of individual freedom shall not be accompanied by the repugnant conditions that obtained prior to the adop-tion of the Eighteenth Amendment and those that have existed since its adoption."

Prohibition of alcoholic beverages as a national policy ended at 5:32½ P.M., Eastern Standard Time, when Utah, the last of the thirty-six states furnished by vote of the con-

DAILY MIRROR

Copyright, 1933, by Daily Mirror, Inc.
Registered U. S. Patent Office

★ ★ FINAL

MUrray Hill 2-1000

VOL. X. No. 112   New York, Wednesday, December 6, 1933   2 cents IN CITY LIMITS
3 cents IN CITY LIMITS

WEATHER
CLOUDY COLDER

High Tide: 10:14 A. M.
11:31 P. M.

Low Tide: 4:15 A. M.
5:39 P. M.

NRA

Entered as second class matter
Post Office New York, N. Y.

PROHIBITION ENDS AT LAST!

New York got the breaks from Utah. . . . The lid is off! . . . . The 36th and most necessary State to ratify, repeal of the Prohibition Amendment had dillied and dallied yesterday while New York fumed and then "out of consideration for the rest of the nation" . . . New York in particular. . . . the long-dry Mormons opened their hearts and cast their ballots for repeal hours ahead of the time expected. . . . Then the fun began!

Utah can't have a drink until Jan. 1, anyway—because of state laws to be repealed—but they agreed to let us have ours.

And did New York like the idea!

TRUCKS OFF!

Trucks started rumbling.
Retail liquor stores lighted

and hotel proprietors smiled and scurried after a day of worry and gloom.

A moving hand turned the light to one side and there was cheer and gaiety and laughter where there had been gloom for thirteen years, ten months and eight-een days; and in moving the hand turned the light away, from that side where the cheer and gaiety had been and left it in the dark.

For New York in greeting the new era and bidding farewell to the old, said goodbye to the speak-easy, the illegitimate night club and the gilded groggery it has known for these long years

TEARS FOR SPEAKS.

As New York greeted the new era with a cheer and a smile she shed a tear or two, for accompany-ing the voice raised in "greeting" there was an undertone of the clanging shut of iron-barred doors.

It was not farewell to those doors with the peep-holes, it was goodbye. Police Commissioner Bolan had promised that and when the toxin sounded the end of the bootleg era 118,000 men, from the Commissioner down to the newest rookie, went out to see that the promise was kept.

SET AT 8,000.

"The 8,000 speakeasies must close," Bolan said tersely to a gathering of all commanding offi-cers in the department at a meet-ing shortly before noon.

He was questioned about the fig-ure 8,000. Former Police Commis-sioner Grover Whalen, while in office, had put the number at 32,000.

RAIDS PLANNED.

The Commissioner stuck by his figure. Many speaks were closed by the depression. Others failed to get beer licenses and folded be-cause of competition and lack of bootleg beer, he explained.

He was very specific in his in-

Continued on Page 18

(Top and middle) Repeal Celebration along Broadway and, at an earlier date, 3.2 Repeal—a Society Beer Party. (At right) Rudy Vallee's revival hit (formerly *The Drunkard Song* in 1893 and 1911) of the Repeal Era.

vention the constitutional majority for ratification of the Twenty-first Amendment. This new amendment repealed the Eighteenth and with the demise of the latter went the Volstead Act which for more than a decade held legal drinks in America to 1½ per cent of alcohol, and the enforcement of which cost more than 150 lives and billions in money. . . .

* * * *

NEW YORK—Slowly gathering momentum from the time when the news began to spread just at nightfall that national prohibition was no more, the public rejoicing at the end of the long, dry reign was carried out last night with restraint and the absence of undue hilarity. With the city's entire police force of 19,000 men mobilized to guard against over-exuberant celebrants, arrests did not exceed the normal number for any day of the last five years. . . .

All across the country that night the popular reaction to the repeal of Prohibition was less exuberant than might have been expected. A principal reason was that it was anticlimactic. For eight months the nation had watched the "wet" score pile up as state after state, starting with Michigan on April 10, voted overwhelmingly to ratify the Twenty-first Amendment, leaving no more uncertainty about the outcome than which state would win the race to cast the binding thirty-sixth vote. Utah claimed that prize.

Another dampening effect was the lateness of the hour. Trucks and drays loaded with freshly distilled liquor and just-unloaded wines and brandies from abroad were held at the warehouses until the moment arrived when they could legally set out on their cheerful errands. In spite of all the wild scrambling that then ensued, only a handful of the leading hotels and nightclubs could be supplied. Less than a dozen of the hundreds of newly licensed retailers in New York, for example, had anything to put on their empty shelves that night. So, unless you were one of the few thousand revelers who squeezed into the Waldorf or Sardi's or the Palmer House or some other oasis on that historic evening, you were obliged to postpone your toast—it might well be the first legal drink in your lifetime—until the next day.

The occasion was not without its ceremonial aspects. At 5:33 o'clock that afternoon Joe Weber of the comedy team of Weber and Fields was served the first glass of authentic and legal champagne to be dispensed across the bar of the Astor Hotel's Hunting Room in fifteen years. Photographers and reporters duly recorded the event for posterity, and a score of similar "firsts" at other leading bistros. Later, celebrants at the St. Moritz wound in a joyous snake dance to the lake in Central Park to drown Old Man Prohibition, and the Art Students League, conducting a wake for the same at the Roosevelt Hotel, resolved that December 5 should forever be observed as the American equivalent of Bastille Day. But the whoopee was generally restrained. Times Square had only a few more inhabitants than its normal nighttime quota. Dozens of prosperous speakeasies, such as the Stork Club and the Club, suddenly turned legitimate with no discernible interruption in their familiar routines. In New York, as in many other cities, the big alcoholic bash the cops had been preparing for did not come until New Year's Eve.

Whatever may be said of the evils of prohibition—and they were many and lurid—it lent a zest to life in the early thirties that nothing has replaced. It cannot accurately be compared with the preoccupation of the sixties with "pot" or the hallucinatory drugs, because outwitting the law to get a drink of third-rate booze did not imply an addictive weakness nor did it involve, except in the strictest bluenose circles, an intolerable social stigma. Excluding the zealous few who truly believed that the curse of alcohol could be expunged by law, most mature people felt that the Eighteenth Amendment was either a sociological blunder or an infringement of their inalienable rights, and that they could evade the law in good conscience, with whatever dissembling they thought their social standing required.

To those of college age, patronizing the bootlegger and consuming his nauseous wares (the taste of ordinary moonshine is simply indescribable) held an extra appeal. It was a comparatively risk-free route to adventure and tribal status. The purchase always had a touch of cops-and-robbers excitement. It usually involved an after-dark visit to the back room of a pool parlor or a thinly disguised delicatessen on the wrong side of town. As you handed over your money ($2 to $5 for unlabeled domestic stuff; up to $10 for "imported") and received your bottle in a brown paper bag, you had the feeling that you were in league with the underworld. And there was always the off-chance that a nosy cop or prohibition agent might turn up to give you a hard time. But to have the stuff on hand was a social "must," and to show up at a dance, a party, or a football game without a flask marked you as a dud.

Status was also to be had by the quality of one's home brew. Most family kitchens were equipped with earthenware crocks, siphons, bottle cappers, and other paraphernalia for putting down a batch of what, after a week or more of acrid fermentation, would pass for beer. There was much discussion about the merits of different brands of malt and yeast and of how much sugar to put in each bottle to boost the alcoholic content. Too much could trigger a delayed explosion like the blast of a shotgun. The simplest of homemade concoctions was synthetic (bathtub) gin: grain alcohol from the bootlegger, distilled water if available or tap water in a pinch, and any of a variety of juniper drops or other flavoring from the druggist or the grocer.

All such mixtures were offensive to the taste but elevating to the spirit, provided they didn't make you ill. The thumbnail test was said by many to be an adequate guide to the purity of what was offered. You poured a bit of it on your thumb, and if the nail didn't come off the stuff was safe to drink.

Repeal put an end to such follies—and substituted others.

Jan. 8, 1934

(From *The New York Times*)

STAVISKY ENDS LIFE AS POLICE TRAP HIM

PARIS—Alexandre Stavisky, leading figure in the Bayonne pawnshop swindle, shot himself yesterday afternoon in a locked room in a lonely villa at Chamonix, a snow covered

ONE WEEK ONLY

BEG. MON. MAT. APR. 18

BY POPULAR REQUEST

CONNIE'S INN

FLOOR SHOW FAVORITES   RETURN ENGAGEMENT

DYNAMIC BABY COX - BESSIE DUDLEY

PAUL MEERES - ROY WHITE

and   LEONARD HARPER'S UNIT OF

16-CREOLE MADCAPS-16

IN CONJUNCTION WITH OUR REGULAR

BIG DOUBLE

BURLESQUE SHOW

75-BLACK & WHITE FUNSTERS-75

By the early thirties, *Connies Inn*, Harlem night spot, no longer the successful White Tourist Trap of the late twenties, was reduced to vaudeville and burlesque.

Louis Armstrong,
World's Greatest Trumpet Stylist, 1933.

Duke Ellington and His Orchestra were featured in the 1934 Paramount film *Murder at the Vanities.*

Ivie Anderson, Duke Ellington vocalist circa 1933, scored big and predated the naming of an era with *It Don't Mean A Thing (If It Ain't Got That Swing).*

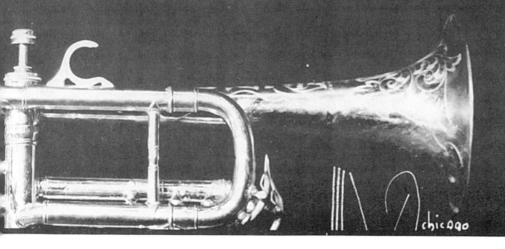

At left: (clockwise) Dick Powell and Ruby Keeler, Warner Brothers song-and-dance team; Kate Smith, back to radio, after flopping in Paramount's 1933 musical *Hello, Everybody*; Ethel Merman in a publicity still from her first film, the 1934 Paramount musical *We're Not Dressing*, starring Carole Lombard, Bing Crosby, Ray Milland, and Leon Errol. (Spread) The chorus line from Earl Carroll's Paramount picture *Murder at the Vanities*.

(Below) Rudy Vallee in *George White's Scandals of 1934*. (Alice Faye is part of the chorus at lower left.). (At left) Carole Lombard and John Barrymore in *Twentieth Century*, directed by Howard Hawks, Columbia, 1934.

(Top left) Gertrude Niesen, dusky-voiced and sultry-looking, rose to airwave and film prominence with such song hits as *Smoke Gets in Your Eyes* and *Harlem on My Mind*. (Top right) Bright Pennies all! Busby Berkeley chorus line from *Gold Diggers of 1933*. (Inset) Crooner Lanny Ross and the chorus line from *College Rhythm*, Paramount, 1934. (Bottom left) Harry Richman's song-and-dance routine from *Puttin' On the Ritz*, United Artists, 1934. (Bottom right) Alice Faye and Walter Winchell (playing himself) in Twentieth Century Fox's *Wake Up and Live*.

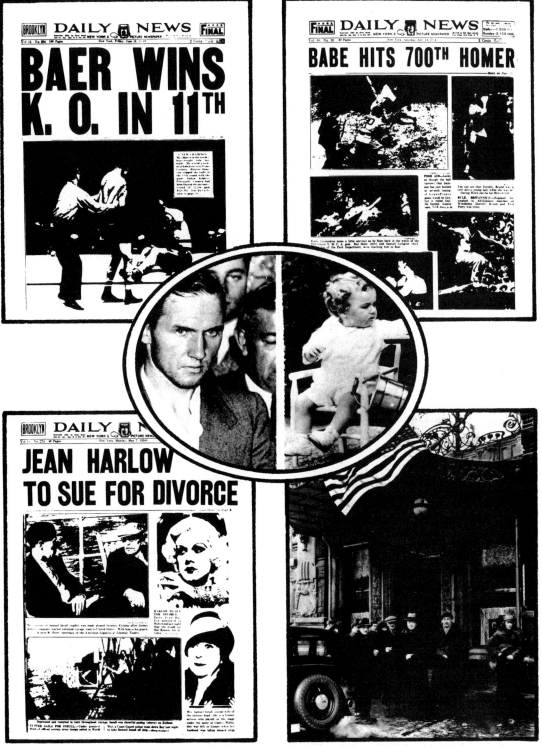

(Top left) Clownish Max Baer won the Heavyweight Title with a TKO in the 11th round as a helpless Primo Carnera was floored twelve times! (Top right) Aging Babe Ruth, New York Yankees outfielder, hit his 700th homer July 14, 1934. (Inset) Abductor Bruno Richard Hauptmann and victim Charles Lindbergh, Jr. (Bottom right) Flag raising in Moscow at the Hotel National for the new American Ambassador, Mr. William C. Bullitt.

town in the shadow of Mont Blanc, while police who had come to arrest him, hammered their way through the door.

In Paris at the time of the shooting the French Cabinet was meeting to decide what must be done in the face of an accusation that at least one of its members was implicated in the gigantic fraud which Stavisky had engineered. . . .

There are many unanswered questions in this case [and] political interests cannot be kept out. . . . It was only two years ago that Andre Tardieu, then Premier, was in a similar position to that of M. Chautemps (the current Premier). He had to defend one of his ministers who was implicated in the Oustric case while the whole Left opposition, now in power, shouted accusations. . . .

The French *do* grace their behavior with a certain style. As Americans began to weary of their daily menu of crime news, the monotonous repetitions of kidnapings, gangland slayings, and larceny by the rich and well-placed—crude and unimaginative felonies for the most part—France supplied the world with a true-to-life mystery thriller of unmatched complexity and dramatic clout.

The "Stavisky affair" had just about everything: a suave, handsome, and enigmatic villain; a beautiful and charming woman who loved him; crooked police and public officials; a bond swindle of majestic proportions; murders that might have been suicides and suicides that might have been murders; riots in the streets of Paris and the fall of a government—all played out in public view over months of deepening suspense. It lacked only two ingredients for perfection in its dramatic genre: a hero and a last-act solution. For almost a year it held a worldwide audience spellbound. *The New York Times* Index for 1934 devoted five closely packed columns to its coverage of one of the most celebrated crime stories of the decade.

Serge Stavisky, Russian-born and French-reared, was forty-eight years old at the time of his death. Over the preceding twenty years he had served two brief prison terms for fraud, had evaded other sentences, and had gained a wide reputation as a gambler, confidence man, and promoter of dubious enterprises. He was wealthy and charming, and he and his glamorous wife, Arlette, traveled in the best Parisian society with ambassadors and cabinet ministers among their intimates.

In 1931, using the alias Alexandre, he set up the Crédit Municipale de Bayonne—a municipal pawnshop—as just another of a string of ventures in which he was openly or covertly involved. Bonds to the value of 200 million francs were put on the market and sold, greatly aided by the public endorsement of Albert Dalimier, Minister of Commerce in the Cabinet of Premier Camille Chautemps. When, in December 1933, the bonds were discovered to be worthless forgeries, Alexandre Stavisky disappeared. There was a huge public outcry, abetted by an intensely partisan press, which suggested that Dalimier and other members of the government were implicated in this and other Stavisky frauds that came to light simultaneously.

"It is not possible," one newspaper protested, "when half the waiters of Paris knew that Alexandre was Stavisky that his friends did not know it also."

When Stavisky was captured at his hideaway in Chamonix, the police said he shot himself when they burst in on him. Mme. Stavisky said her husband was murdered—that he was shot in the right side of the head but that the gun he held was found in his left hand. Volatile French emotions exploded anew over this revelation. The newspapers screamed imprecations, and politicians of the Right and Left hurled insults at one another and dueled with sabers. Crowds surged angrily in the streets. The Chautemps government tottered, Dalimier was forced to resign, the Mayor of Bayonne was jailed. A parliamentary commission was created to investigate the entire affair. Political opponents of Chautemps charged the Premier and dozens of his associates with complicity in the fraud and with conspiring to smother the investigation.

In February a magistrate of the Court of Appeals, Albert Prince, who was reputed to know more of Stavisky's secrets than any one alive, was found mangled to death on the railroad tracks outside Dijon, his feet tied to the rail with rope. His records were missing. The police said he had committed suicide. Others said it was a ritual murder of the Carbonari, a secret sect of Freemasons to which both Chautemps and his brother-in-law, the Attorney General, belonged.

Mme. Stavisky went to prison for refusing to turn over her husband's records to the courts. An inspector of the Sûreté Général who did procure them, with their presumably incriminating evidence, was suddenly taken off the case and demoted in rank. Stavisky's body was twice exhumed for medical examination, but the report of the doctors was suppressed. Rioting broke out in Paris and a dozen other cities, killing twenty-seven and injuring hundreds. Communist-led labor unions called a general strike throughout France. The Chautemps government collapsed, and there was fear abroad that the Third Republic might be pulled down with it.

Month after month the controversy raged without abatement. French passions flamed with anger and suspicion. What was the real scope of Stavisky's swindles? Was he killed by the police to seal his lips or was he a suicide? Who were his protectors in the government? Who ordered the murder of Magistrate Prince? And what became of the incriminating dossier he was supposed to be guarding?

The courts and the parliamentary commission, engulfed in partisan warfare, questioned hundreds of persons and clapped a handful in jail, but they seemed never to get close to any hard answers. They dared not, people said, for too many big names were involved. Every doorman and shopclerk and editor in Paris claimed loudly to know more about the case than the police.

"The truth is," *The New York Times* reported in September, eight months after "l'affaire Stavisky" surfaced, "that the report of the doctors, the report of the police, the report of the magistrates and, probably when it is published, the report of the commission of inquiry do not enjoy the least public confidence. There has been so much lying, so much camouflaging of the truth, such violence of accusation, such insidious insinuations that very few people any longer believe anything that emanates from any quarter in which the hand of politics can be suspected. And the hand of politics is seen everywhere."

The Stavisky affair burned itself out at last as the sensation-hungry French press found other scandals to feast upon. It dropped out of the American press as well. When the parliamentary commission finally released its report in March 1935, an ambiguous document that absolved just about everyone except the dead Stavisky himself, no one cared very much. But the mystery of one of the most colorful and audacious con men of the decade remained as obscure as ever.

February 9, 1934

(From *The New York Times*)

AIR CONTRACTS CANCELED, ARMY TO CARRY THE MAILS McCRACKEN EVADES ARREST

WASHINGTON — President Roosevelt took the troublesome air mail situation into his own hands today, ordered annullment of all existing domestic air mail contracts and ordered the Army to fly the mails during the emergency thus created.

The annullment order, brought by Postmaster General Farley, came at the climax of a day packed with developments involving the air mails, a day which witnessed among other things a continuance of the defiance by William P. McCracken of the Senate's attempt to try him for contempt.

Secretary of War Dern said the Army was equipped to take over the air mail and would carry out the President's order promptly and efficiently. . . .

Roosevelt's abrupt cancellation of the airmail contracts had been intended as a sharp rap on the knuckles of a small but rapacious segment of big business. In the explosive backfire, he suffered a blow to his own prestige that was a long time mending.

In January 1934 Senator Hugo Black opened public hearings, for which he had long been preparing, into the award of subsidies and contracts to the commercial airlines for carrying the mails. Black was a courtly and disarmingly mild-mannered Alabamian, but he was an astute inquisitor and his investigation soon began to make noisy headlines. Moguls of the young but fast-growing aviation industry were forced to admit on the stand to enormous salaries, bonuses, and stock benefits; to intricate holding company and Wall Street tie-ups; and to collusion and preferential treatment in tapping the government's $19-million annual airmail subsidy.

Three large aviation combines, it developed, held an apparently unbreakable monopoly on twenty-four of the existing twenty-seven airmail routes. Many were acquired without competitive bidding. More shocking was the disclosure that these arrangements had been deliberately fostered by two former officials of the Hoover Administration: Walter F. Brown, the Postmaster General, and William P. McCracken, the Assistant Secretary of Commerce for Air.

Mr. McCracken seemed particularly vulnerable, for upon leaving office he had become the principal Washington lobbyist for the airlines. For a few days his defiance of the Black committee stole the spotlight from the main purpose of the inquiry. He refused under subpoena to produce certain of his records, saying they had been destroyed. They *had* been destroyed, but not very well. Government agents seized 300 sacks of rubbish in the basement of the National Press Building, where McCracken had an office, and painstakingly pasted back together several hundred letters and other documents bearing his name which had been hastily torn up.

Furious, Senator Black demanded, and the Senate voted, that McCracken be brought before the bar of the Senate and tried for contempt, a rarely invoked exercise of Congressional authority. Chesley W. Jurney, the sergeant at arms was dispatched to bring the culprit in. Impressively uniformed in gray striped trousers, a black cutaway coat with a red boutonniere, and a black Texas Stetson on his head, Jurney set out in a hired limousine, having no paddy wagon of his own, to get his man. Two hours later, visibly crestfallen, he reported back to the Senate that he had been unable to find him. There followed a week-long "manhunt" rivaling the best slapstick routine of the Keystone Kops, with McCracken at one point camping overnight on the porch of the reluctant Jurney's home, daring the officer to arrest him. In the end, the majesty of the Senate was upheld and McCracken expiated his contempt by spending ten days in the District of Columbia lockup.

The airmail inquiry generated intense feeling throughout the country, and Roosevelt's stern action in canceling the carriers' usurious contracts drew instant applause. The applause swiftly turned to public dismay and then to anger.

The Army Air Corps, it turned out, was embarrassingly inadequate to the task so suddenly thrust upon it. Of its total inventory of 412 planes, only 172 bombers and attack and cargo planes were deemed suitable for mail service. Of these only twenty-two carried radio equipment and other modern devices necessary for long-range operation. Army pilots were largely inexperienced in night flying and in combating bad weather, and they were unfamiliar with the routes and landing fields they were now required to use. As they began their assignment, the whole northern half of the nation was besieged by a long period of intensely cold and stormy weather.

The result was inevitable. Daring young men in helmets and goggles took off heedlessly in sleet and driving snowstorms. They pushed their fragile, ice-laden craft across forests and mountain ranges toward unfamiliar destinations, which they often had to find by visual observation from the murky skies. In the first week of operations there were five crashes in which seven fliers were killed and several wounded. As the bad weather continued and the Army's inexperience became more evident, flights were curtailed and mail schedules went on a "when and if" basis. Still, planes were wrecked and fliers lost their lives; the fatalities would reach eleven before this grim farce ended.

Stalked by Stork

I WANT WORK Now!!

Age **28**
5ft. **7**in.
135lbs.
$ **20.**

8 YEARS EXPERIENCE
ADVERTISING,
SALES PROMOTION,
CONTACT, PUBLICITY, PRINTING, etc.

RESIDENT of BROOKLYN

At left: (Top and bottom) February 4, 1934, 2000 rampaging Taxi drivers, in their third day on Strike, terrorized New York City from Wall Street to Times Square when Mayor LaGuardia was not available for their petitions. (Above) Jean Harlow in her style trademark— satin blouse and high-rise, wide-legged slacks. (At right) the Pickens Sisters— (top to bottom) Jane, Helen, and Patti, popular vocal trio. (Below) Gene Autry, circa early thirties, the first big singing cowboy star in films and on records.

Sincerely Yours
Gene Autry

Arcadia, La., May 23, 1934. Bullet-Riddled front door (Barrow was driving) of 1933 sedan in which Clyde Barrow and Bonnie Parker were killed in a roadside ambush by Texas Rangers and county sheriffs.

DILLINGER SLAIN IN CHICAGO; SHOT DEAD BY FEDERAL MEN IN FRONT OF MOVIE THEATRE

Cummings Says Slaying of Dillinger Is 'Gratifying as Well as Reassuring'

By The Associated Press.

WASHINGTON, July 22.—Smiling in elation, Attorney General Cummings tonight termed the slaying of John Dillinger by Federal agents "gratifying as well as reassuring."

The Attorney General was notified just before he boarded the train for the West, the first leg of a journey to Hawaii. At Union Station he dictated the following statement:

"The search for Dillinger has never been relaxed for a moment.

"He has escaped capture on several occasions by the narrowest of margins.

"The news of tonight is exceedingly gratifying as well as reassuring."

Mr. Cummings said the end of the Indiana bandit reflected great credit on the Chicago office of the division of investigation.

J. Edgar Hoover, chief of the Bureau of Investigation, rushed to his office at word that the desperado had been shot down. He told news men:

"This does not mean the end of the Dillinger case.

"Any one who ever gave any of the Dillinger mob any aid, comfort or assistance will be vigorously prosecuted."

He referred directly to George (Baby Face) Nelson, Homer Van Meter and another gangster. Nelson, named by the department as the killer of Special Agent W. Carter Baum in the Dillinger outbreak in the Wisconsin woods last April, was described by Mr. Hoover as a "rat."

REACHED FOR HIS GUN

Outlaw's Move Met by Four Shots, All Finding Their Mark.

HAD LIFTED HIS FACE

Desperado Had Also Treated Finger Tips With Acid to Defeat Prints.

TWO WOMEN WOUNDED

Agents, Tipped Fugitive Was Going to Theatre, Waited While He Saw Show.

Special to THE NEW YORK TIMES.

CHICAGO, July 22.—John Dillinger, America's Public Enemy No. 1 and the most notorious criminal of

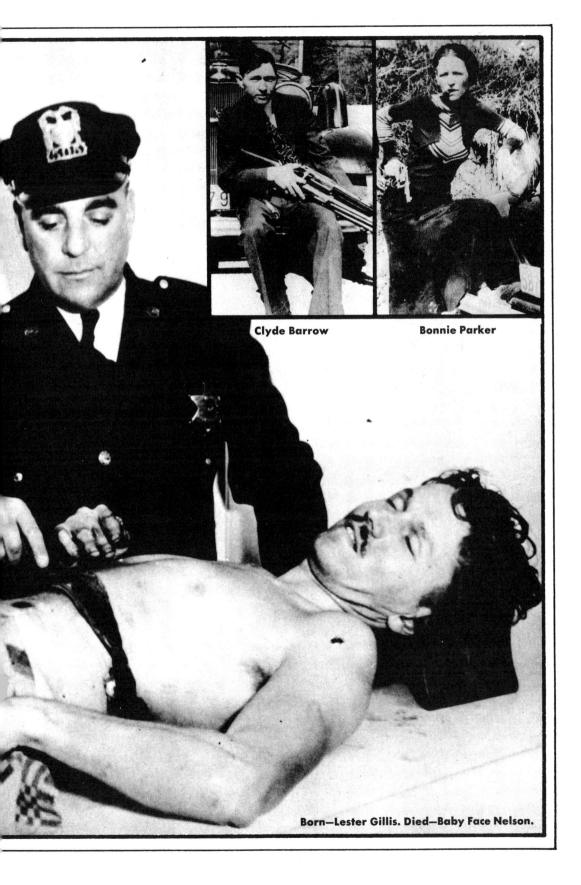

Clyde Barrow

Bonnie Parker

Born—Lester Gillis. Died—Baby Face Nelson.

BROOKLYN

DAILY NEWS

NEW YORK'S PICTURE NEWSPAPER

 FINAL

New York, Thursday, July 26, 1934

2 Cents

NAZIS SLAY DOLLFUSS

ITALY MOBILIZES

AUSTRIA APPEALS FOR POWERS' AID

The Hitler swastika in action
—"Leningradskaia Pravda"
(Leningrad)

VON HINDENBURG DIES AT 86
AFTER A DAY UNCONSCIOUS;
HITLER TAKES PRESIDENCY

END COMES AT 9 A. M.

Reich President Dies at His Home in East Prussia.

MADE A VALIANT FIGHT.

Disappearance of House Flag at Neudeck Announces News to World.

THERE HAD BEEN NO HOPE

He Lapsed Into Coma After Hitler Reached Bedside for Last Meeting.

By The Associated Press
NEUDECK, Germany, Thursday, Aug. 2.—President von Hindenburg died at 9 A. M. today.

The President's death was indicated to correspondents by the disappearance of the house flag from the flagstaff.

Death came to the 86-year-old leader of the German people and former war marshal after a valiant fight against a complication of ailments.

Chancellor Hitler has assumed the Presidency.

Times Wide World Photos.

ENBURG

Mein Kampf

Von

Adolf Hitler

Zwei Bände in einem Band
Ungekürzte Ausgabe

Erster Band:
Eine Abrechnung

Zweiter Band:
Die nationalsozialistische Bewegung

XVIII. Auflage

1933

Popular heroes of the air such as Col. Charles Lindbergh rushed into print to condemn the government's action, and Capt. Eddie Rickenbacker denounced it as "legalized murder." Airline spokesmen bitterly reminded the President, "We told you so!" They were backed up by a mounting frenzy of protest from the public and the press. All but forgotten in the uproar was the prelude that had set this tragic train of events in motion. What mattered was that the blood of these brave young men stained the hands of Roosevelt and his Postmaster General, Jim Farley. (It was, Farley lamented later, "One of my saddest experiences in public life. I cannot think of it now without being stirred by regrets. It was one of the most controversial decisions of the [first] Roosevelt administration.")

There was an end to the unhappy business in May. New contracts with the airlines were negotiated, and the Army, shaken and humiliated, withdrew from the field. Congress meanwhile had enacted new legislation covering both mail and passenger service, which corrected some of the immediate evils. These laws were to evolve five years later into the more comprehensive Civil Aeronautics Act, which is the backbone of today's far-reaching regulatory apparatus.

The airmail contract troubles in the early months of 1934 weakened public confidence in Roosevelt's judgment more than any other event of that first New Deal year. Clearly, "That Man" was not infallible.

May 28, 1934

(From *The New York Times*)

FRAIL MOTHER OF 6 GIVES BIRTH TO FIVE

CORBELL, ONTARIO— Five baby girls, the largest weighing 3 pounds 4 ounces and the smallest a pound less, were born today to Mrs. Oliva Dionne in her farm home two miles from here.

Visitors found the 24-year-old mother and the babies in good condition and the father, seven years older than his wife, busy at his chores. There are six other children in the family, the oldest being seven.

"Well, do you feel proud of yourself?" the father was asked.

"I'm the sort of fellow who ought to be in jail," he answered.

Mrs. Ben Lebell attended the mother at birth and reported all five girls were born between 4:30 and 5:00 A.M. Three of them arrived before the doctor did, she said.

* * * *

CHICAGO—Birth of five children at once, such as occurred today at Corbell, Ontario, is so rare, medical historians here said, that only thirty cases have been recorded in the last 500 years.

Dr. Morris Fishbein, editor of the Journal of the American Medical Association, added that in none of the cases on record have all of the children lived more than fifty minutes.

"If the five girls born to Mrs. Oliva Dionne live longer than an hour or so," said Dr. Fishbein, "then it is truly a rare and noteworthy event."

Few events of the nineteen-thirties excited the compassion of so many people as the birth and progress of "the quints." For months the newspapers and magazines printed every scrap of information about them they could get: their gains in weight ounce by ounce; the tiniest fluctuations in their spirits and appetites; the daily prognosis of their colics, rashes, and sniffles; the tortuous involvement of their parents and guardians in the bewildering web of notoriety in which they were caught. The little four-room farm home in which the Dionnes lived was suddenly besieged by hordes of photographers, writers, broadcasters, and curiosity seekers. When it was learned a week after the birth of the quintuplets that their hard-pressed father, Elzire, had signed a contract to exhibit the babies of the Chicago World's Fair, an audible wave of indignation rolled across Canada and the United States.

Elzire canceled the contract, and gifts of money, food, clothing, toys, and whatnot began to pour into Corbell like a flood. Dr. Allan Roy Dafoe, the modest country doctor who attended the babies, struggled to stem the tide of unwanted attention (not the money) being showered on the quints and to provide a more normal and propitious environment for them.

In June the government of Canada, recognizing that the babies were no less than a national treasure, made them wards of the state, undertook their protection and support, and built a modern home and nursery for them. The King of England bestowed a royal bounty of £5 on Oliva Dionne. Grandfather Dionne set up a flourishing business at a stand just outside the nursery compound, where he sold pictures of the quints and other curios to tourists. Elzire Dionne tried with growing sullenness to keep out of the limelight and to go on with his farming.

Annette, Cécile, Marie, Emilie, and Yvonne were their names. Defying the laws of probability and medical experience, they grew into plump, gravely pretty little look-alikes, whose birthdays, schooling, and everyday life continued to fascinate millions for a decade. Emilie died at the age of twenty in 1954. Yvonne entered a convent, where she remained until 1965. The remaining three sisters married and (gratefully no doubt) disappeared from public view.

Sept. 9, 1934

(From *The New York Times*)

MORRO CASTLE BURNS OFF ASBURY PARK, 200 TO 250 LISTED AS DEAD OR MISSING

Survivors Tell of Leaping Into Sea to Escape Flames

NEW YORK—In one of the worst maritime disasters on record, the liner Morro Castle was swept by fire of unknown origin early yesterday morning off the New

A taste for Mushrooms grows on you

And it's pretty much the same with SPUDS!

1ST TIME

1ST SPUD

10TH TIME

10TH SPUD

CORK TIP or PLAIN

20TH TIME

20TH SPUD

SPUD MENTHOL-COOLED CIGARETTES

15¢

The Morro Castle Disaster: Greatest tourist attraction in Asbury Park's History.

(Below) Ernest Dionne with his 5 baby girls. Born May 24, 1934.

A sick man has no place in business

Jersey coast with heavy loss of life. The scene of the tragedy was not far from where the dirigible Akron was wrecked during a storm off Barnegat Lighthouse last year.

By a strange coincidence Capt. Robert Wilmott, master of the Morro Castle, died of a heart attack about 8:45 o'clock Friday night, nearly eight hours before the SOS went out at 4:23 A.M. New York time Saturday. When the fire started the ship was under the command of Chief Officer William F. Warms, who remained aboard the burning ship until taken off by a Coast Guard cutter late yesterday.

The exact number of dead and missing was not known finally last night but it was believed to be between 200 and 250. . . .

The burning hulk of the ship was beached about 150 feet offshore at the foot of Sixth Avenue, Asbury Park. Fire was plainly visible through the portholes and smoke was still pouring out of the vessel. A crowd of 10,000 gathered on the boardwalk to watch. . . .

If the burning of the *Morro Castle* was not the worst maritime disaster since the sinking of the *Titanic,* it certainly was the most horrifying one for the tens of thousands of spectators along the rain-lashed Jersey coast who watched the flames licking into the dark sky. They ran into the water to help the first terrified survivors ashore, some in lifeboats and others struggling through the choppy seas in life preservers. With daylight the first bodies of the dead were washed up by the surf. Scores of local residents put out in their own small craft to help the Coast Guard and other rescue vessels that had sped to the scene.

The *Morro Castle* was only a few hours out of New York at the end of a seven-day vacation cruise to Havana when disaster struck just before dawn. There were 562 persons aboard—318 passengers and 244 crew. The fire apparently started in the passengers' writing room in midship and raced swiftly through open air ducts to other parts of the vessel. The radio operator broke off his frantic SOS at a little before 4:30 o'clock with the words, "Can't hold out much longer," and was heard from no more.

Minutes after the first on-board alarm sounded, the entire midsection of the ship erupted into an inferno that fused the glass in the portholes and twisted steel beams like tinfoil. Those trapped below decks were incinerated. Chaos reigned topside as crewmen tried with equal urgency to fight the flames and to save their own lives. Fire doors were left open; some fire hoses were not connected; water pressure failed; all the lifeboats on one side of the ship were destroyed in their davits; and none of the life rafts were launched. Screaming passengers milled about the afterdeck in terror. Scores leaped over the rail into the heaving black sea—some couples hand in hand—to drown, to be picked up, or to swim ashore.

The death toll was 124. The inquiry that followed painted an ugly picture of the behavior of most of the officers and crew, but there were accounts of heroism as well, among both crew and passengers. Chief Officer Warms and three fellow officers were convicted of negligence and sentenced to prison in the trial that followed in 1936. On appeal, this verdict was reversed, and the court put the blame for the disaster on the dead skipper, Captain Wilmott.

Sept. 20, 1934

(From *The New York Times*)

LINDBERGH RANSOM RECEIVER SEIZED, $13,750 FOUND AT HIS EAST BRONX HOME, THE MYSTERY SOLVED POLICE SAY

NEW YORK—Charged with being the man who received the $50,000 ransom in the kidnaping of twenty-month-old Charles Augustus Lindbergh, Jr., at Hopewell, N.J., two and one-half years ago, a German alien named Bruno Richard Hauptmann was under arrest last night. He was caught in the Bronx on Wednesday morning but the news was kept secret until yesterday afternoon.

Police Commissioner John F. O'Ryan and Col. H. Norman Schwartzkopf, Superintendent of New Jersey State Police, said that the prisoner had been connected with the actual kidnaping as well as with receipt of the ransom. They declared their belief that the arrest would solve the entire kidnaping.

When Hauptmann was arrested at his home at 1379 E. 222nd Street, the Bronx, a $20 gold certificate of the ransom money was in his pocket. The passing of another of the ransom notes had led to his capture. Later the police found $13,750 of the ransom bills in $10 and $20 denominations in the garage back of his home. They said they also had learned that Hauptmann had $24,000 or $25,000 on deposit with a brokerage house. . . .

The kidnap murder of the Lindbergh baby was not in itself remarkable in the gruesome catalogue of such crimes that were occurring with shocking frequency during the ealy years of the decade. What elevated it to a national tragedy was the heroic stature of the parents—the immortal "Lindy" and his gentle, self-effacing wife, Anne Morrow Lindbergh—and the incredible brutality of the imposters, who, through one hoax after another, sought to cash in on the family's grief and despair. No personal tragedy of the century up to that time stabbed so cruelly into the hearts of so many people or evoked such an outpouring of wrath against the perpetrators.

Sometime between 8:30 and ten o'clock on the night of March 1, 1932, an intruder placed a crude wooden ladder against the side of the isolated Lindbergh home in the Sourland Mountains of New Jersey near the little town of Hopewell. Silently he climbed into a second-story window, took the sleeping twenty-month-old infant. Charles Augustus Lindbergh, Jr., from his crib, and stole out again into the darkness. On a lonely ridge some five miles away he stopped his car, took the child into the woods, bashed in its head, stripped

(Clockwise) Mrs. Helen Wills Moody and Miss Helen Jacobs; George Herman "Babe" Ruth; Joe Di Maggio; Gordon "Mickey" Cochrane; Jerome "Dizzy" Dean and Paul "Daffy" Dean; Knute Rockne, Jr.; Lynewood "Schoolboy" Rowe; "Dizzy" Dean with tuba; John L. "Pepper" Martin; Coach Lou Little; Glenn Cunningham; Al Barabas.

Jerome H. "Dizzy" Dean. 1934 St. Louis Cardinals. Won 30, Lost 7, .811 pct.

off its sleep suit (a useful talisman later), and buried the body in a shallow grave. He left a note behind on the nursery window sill which read:

Dear Sir

Have 50000$ ready 25000$ in 20$ bills 15000$ in 10$ bills and 10000$ in 5$ bills. After 2-4 days we will inform you where to deliver the money. We warn you for making anyding public or for notify the police. The child is in gut care. Instructions for the letters are . . . [Here a symbol of two interlocking circles was drawn.]

News of the kidnaping blazed on front pages and in radio broadcasts in every part of the country the next day. Hordes of police, private detectives, and reporters converged on the Lindbergh home. Known haunts of the New York underworld were combed for clues. Colonel Lindbergh obtained the money as he was instructed to do and waited in an agony of suspense for word from the kidnaper. Days went by in desolating silence. He made a personal appeal by radio to the unknown abductor, promising not only the ransom but immunity from arrest if his child were returned unharmed. He accepted the offer of two well-known New York gangsters to act as go-betweens if the captor would come forward. With the police, he worked to exhaustion, sifting and exploring tips and leads that came in by the score.

The most promising lead came after two weeks from a retired Bronx schoolteacher, Dr. John F. Condon, who was to become familiar under the code name "Jafsie." He had received a mysterious note from one "John," who asserted that he was the kidnaper and that he would accept Condon as an intermediary. Their communication was to be carried on through cryptic advertisements inserted in the newspapers. Secretly and with the consent of the police and Colonel Lindbergh, Jafsie demanded some token of "John's" authenticity. A few days later he received at his home a package containing the baby's sleep suit. This was proof enough. A week later Jafsie held a midnight rendezvous with "John" in an isolated cemetery, handed over the ransom money, and received in return a note saying the baby was aboard a small sailing boat named "Nellie" lying off Martha's Vineyard. The child was in the care of two persons, the note said, "who are inosent."

The "Nellie" was never found, and "John" never again responded to the messages addressed to him in the want ad columns. This hoax, by the kidnaper himself, was the first and the cruelest. Others hoaxes were attempted and some were carried out.

In Washington Mrs. Evalyn Walsh McLean, a wealthy and eccentric widow, was drawn into a liaison with Gaston B. Means, one of the most notorious confidence men of the day, on his assurance that he knew the kidnapers and could make contact with them. She gave him $100,000 in cash to secure the baby's release. Means reported periodically to her on his dark and highly involved "negotiations." His false pretenses amounted to larceny on a grand scale. He knew no more about the kidnaper than Mrs. McLean did.

Another volunteer intermediary showed up in the person of John Curtis, a boatbuilder in Norfolk, Virginia, who said he had been approached by an agent of the kidnapers through a Norfolk bootlegger. He presented a detailed plan for a small-boat rendezvous with the abductors many miles out to sea off the Virginia capes. Lindbergh and Curtis had been cruising for many days without locating their quarry when they learned by radio that the baby's body had been found in New Jersey. Curtis later confessed that he had faked the whole deal.

During all this time, and afterward as well, the police and the FBI were pressing one of the most intensive manhunts in criminal history. Dozens of suspects were picked up in different parts of the country, questioned, and released. False leads by the hundreds were meticulously checked out. Al Capone from his prison cell in the Atlanta Penitentiary offered to have the underworld scoured for the culprit. Serial numbers of the ransom bills had been circulated to all banks in the country. Occasionally one of them would turn up, but the source of these bills remained a total mystery for a little more than two and a half years.

And then one day in September 1934 a Bronx service station attendant was given a $10 gold certificate in payment for 93 cents worth of gasoline by a nondescript customer with a German accent. Since gold currency had recently been proscribed by the government, the attendant jotted down the customer's license number on the back of the bill, just in case there should be trouble with the bank. Bruno Richard Hauptmann, a taciturn, mild-mannered German carpenter with a wife and a young child of his own, was arrested at his home five days later.

Hauptmann was brought to trial at Flemington, New Jersey, on January 3, 1935. It is improbable that a truly impartial jury to try him could have been found in any jurisdiction in the United States, for he was an authentic "enemy of the people." His trial was made grotesque by the stridency of its coverage by much of the press and radio and by the unrestrained theatrics of many of the lawyers, witnesses, and self-proclaimed experts drawn to the little courthouse. For six weeks the country was awash in a steamy tide of bathos and sensationalism such as has rarely been endured in all its history.

The evidence against Hauptmann was overwhelming. He was convicted of first-degree murder on February 14. After exhausting appeals all the way to the Supreme Court, he was electrocuted in the New Jersey state prison on April 3, 1936. To his memory there stands the so-called Lindbergh Law, an act of Congress passed on May 18, 1934, which makes kidnaping across state lines a federal offense.

Nov. 6, 1934

(From *The New York Times*)

NEW DEAL SCORES NATION-WIDE VICTORY

WASHINGTON — President Roosevelt and his New Deal in their first electoral test yesterday won the most overwhelming victory in the history of American politics.

A record number of voters for an off-year election gave the President a clear mandate to proceed with his policies in his own way. And in giving him that mandate they literally destroyed the right wing of the Republican party. . . .

(Above)
Barney Ross,
Welterweight
Champion, 1934

(Above)
Tony Canzoneri,
Lightweight
Champion, 1933

Primo Carnera (left) and Max Baer (right) at weigh-in ceremonies
before their Heavyweight Championship fight, June 14, 1934.

Joe Louis—1934

July	4	Jack Kracken	K.O.	1
July	11	Willie Davis	K.O.	3
July	29	Larry Udell	K.O.	2
Aug.	13	Jack Kranz	WON	8
Aug.	27	Buck Everett	K.O.	2
Sept.	11	Otto Barchek	K.O.	4
Sept.	25	Adolph Wiater	WON	10
Oct.	24	Art Sykes	K.O.	8
Oct.	30	Jack O'Dowd	K.O.	2
Nov.	14	Stanley Poreda	K.O.	1
Nov.	30	Charley Massera	K.O.	3
Dec.	14	Lee Ramage	K.O.	8

FIGURE 152. This is the cover of—not the first comic book, but the first American comic magazine in modern format to be placed on newsstands for sale, independently of newspapers or premium connections. It appeared in May, 1934.

VICTOR
27531-A

For best results use
RCA Victor Needles

I GOT IT BAD AND THAT AIN'T GOOD—Fox Trot
(From the musical production "Jump For Joy")
(Me Ha Dado Malo y Eso No Es Bueno)
(Paul Webster—Duke Ellington)
Duke Ellington and his
Famous Orchestra
Vocal refrain by Ivie Anderson

FULL-RANGE
RECORDING

Vocalion

Fox Trot   Vocal Chorus
(B 16284)   Skinny Ennis

GOT A DATE WITH AN ANGEL
—Grey-Miller-Waller-Tunbridge—
HAL KEMP
and his ORCHESTRA
4652

VICTOR
25012-A

Not Licensed for
Radio Broadcast

THE LADY IN RED—Rumba
(From the First National film "In Caliente")
(La Dama En Rojo) M. Dixon-A. Wrubel
Xavier Cugat and his
Waldorf-Astoria Orchestra
Vocal refrain by Don Reid and chorus

PERFECT

Not licensed for   Fox Trot
Radio broadcast   Vocal Chorus by
(E 36212)   Cab Calloway

MINNIE THE MOOCHER
(THE HO-DE-HO SONG)
—Calloway-Mills—
Cab Calloway and
his Orchestra
15872 A

NOT LICENSED FOR RADIO BROADCAST

Columbia
REG. U.S. PAT. OFF.

Columbia

Fox Trot   Vocal Refrain by
                        Billie Holiday

Your Mother's Son-In-Law
From Lew Leslie's "Blackbirds of 1934"
(Nichols and Hollner)
BENNY GOODMAN & HIS ORCH.

2856-D
(152568)

MADE AND PAT'D IN U.S.A. RE.16588 AND 1702564 © C.A.CO.

Brunswick
MADE IN UNITED STATES OF AMERICA
Not Licensed for Radio Broadcast

(15939)   Vocal with
                          Orchestra

Stars Fell On Alabama
—Parish-Perkins—
JACK TEAGARDEN
6993

BRUNSWICK RECORD CORPORATION

Columbia
REG. U.S. PAT. OFF.

Vocal Orchestra Accompaniment

TONY'S WIFE
(Lane and Adamson)
GERTRUDE NIESEN
2759-D
(152377)

MADE AND PAT'D IN U.S.A. RE.16588 AND 1702564 © C.A.CO.

Brunswick
MADE IN UNITED STATES OF AMERICA
Not Licensed for Radio Broadcast

(105)   VOCAL
                          3-0

INKA DINKA DOO
From "Palooka"
—Ryan-Durante—
JIMMY DURANTE
6774

BRUNSWICK RECORD CORPORATION

PERFECT

Not licensed for   Fox Trot
Radio broadcast   Vocal Chorus by
(B 11923)   Cab Calloway

REEFER MAN
—Razaf-Robinson—
Cab Calloway and
his Orchestra
15872 B

BLUEBIRD
RECORD

MUSIC IN MY HEART
(From RKO film "Make a Wish")
(L. Alter-P. Webster—Oscar Straus)
Bobby Breen
Boy Soprano with orchestra
conducted by Hugo Riesenfeld
B-7158-A

Brunswick
MADE IN U.S.A. US PAT

Not Licensed for
Radio Broadcast
(12735)   Comedienne
                       with Orchestra

EADIE WAS A LADY—Part I
From the Musical Comedy "Take A Chance"
—DeSylva-Whiting-Brown—
ETHEL MERMAN
With Vocal Effects by
"Take A Chance" Octette
6456

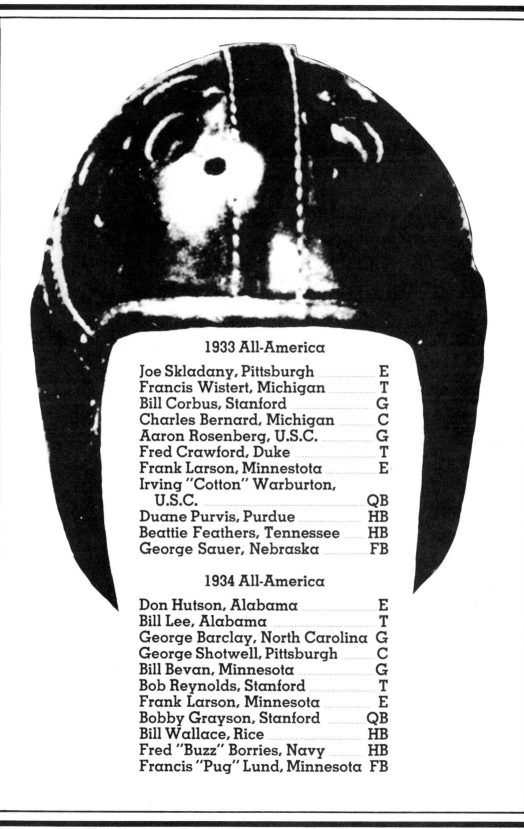

1933 All-America

Joe Skladany, Pittsburgh	E
Francis Wistert, Michigan	T
Bill Corbus, Stanford	G
Charles Bernard, Michigan	C
Aaron Rosenberg, U.S.C.	G
Fred Crawford, Duke	T
Frank Larson, Minnestota	E
Irving "Cotton" Warburton, U.S.C.	QB
Duane Purvis, Purdue	HB
Beattie Feathers, Tennessee	HB
George Sauer, Nebraska	FB

1934 All-America

Don Hutson, Alabama	E
Bill Lee, Alabama	T
George Barclay, North Carolina	G
George Shotwell, Pittsburgh	C
Bill Bevan, Minnesota	G
Bob Reynolds, Stanford	T
Frank Larson, Minnesota	E
Bobby Grayson, Stanford	QB
Bill Wallace, Rice	HB
Fred "Buzz" Borries, Navy	HB
Francis "Pug" Lund, Minnesota	FB

It was a pretty spiritless campaign. On election eve former President Hoover emerged from his retreat at Palo Alto, California, to tell the voters they should elect a Republican Congress, "if our institutions are to survive." But not many were listening. The next day there were more Democratic mayors, state legislators, governors, and congressmen and senators than before. With its top-heavy Democratic majorities, the 74th Congress lined up this way:

House		Senate	
Democrats	332	Democrats	69
Republicans	103	Republicans	25
Progressive	7	Progressive	1
Farmer-Labor	3	Farmer-Labor	1

The explanation for the outcome was fairly obvious. But it was further clarified by this account of what happened in the senatorial race in Missouri as reported in *The New York Times:* "The fact that Sen. Roscoe C. Patterson's record in the Senate has been one of implacable opposition to the New Deal has alienated even members of his own [Republican] party. It is pretty difficult to arouse much antagonism against an administration which has directly or indirectly assisted more than 500,000 persons in Missouri in the last eighteen months . . . [or] to arouse the voters who have seen the Federal government spend approximately $225 million in the state since Mr. Roosevelt took office."

The walk-away winner in that contest was an obscure Jackson County commissioner named Harry S. Truman.

CHAPTER 10
Flight of the Blue Eagle
NRA

THE BLUE EAGLE OF THE NRA—the heraldic symbol of the National Recovery Administration that adorned practically every factory and shop window in America and was emblazoned on every pound of butter, suit of clothes, ton of steel, and whatever else was traded in interstate commerce—soared bravely to its zenith three months after it was hatched and spent the remaining year and a half of its life fighting downdrafts and crash landings. In its brief passage across the sky, where it hung with the distracting glitter of a Fourth of July star shell, it almost obliterated the rest of the New Deal from view.

The NRA was a hastily conceived scheme for a planned economy. Launched with the zeal of a Children's Crusade, it wound up in the shambles of a minor civil war. While it lasted, it was a national spectacular that, in one way or another, involved the energy or emotions of just about everybody, from board chairman to yard hand, from sociologist to housewife.

I

The genesis of NRA within the New Deal cannot be firmly established. Frances Perkins, who had a hand in its formulation, said that in April 1933 Roosevelt's mind "was innocent as a child's" of any such program as NRA.[1] Ray Moley, on the other hand, insists that the Brain Trust had done much preliminary work on programs of this nature many weeks before the inaugural. This seems the more plausible explanation, even though the National Industrial Recovery Act of 1933 in its final form, was hastily whacked together from bits and pieces borrowed from a variety of sources.

At all events, there was a considerable historical and intellectual background for the idea of corralling the business and industrial resources of the nation into a more disciplined force, subduing their anarchic tendencies, and infusing them with a minimal sense of social responsibility. These instincts had found expression some decades earlier in the Sherman and Clayton antitrust acts and in the establishment of the Federal Trade Commission, all aimed primarily at curbing monopoly. President Theodore Roosevelt, in 1906, and Woodrow Wilson, in 1919, had gone further by proposing to license corporations as a means of preventing destructive competition. Under emergency legislation in the First World War, the War Industries Board had done substantially that, exercising its control through quasi-official trade associations. Throughout the decade of the twenties, and particularly during the chaotic early years of the Depression, similar ideas had engaged a number of scholars, political leaders, and even businessmen. Their schemes ran the gamut from outright socialization to simple abrogation of the antitrust laws.

One of the more noteworthy of a dozen books on the subject was Rex Tugwell's *The Industrial Discipline*, published late in 1932, in which he proposed, among other things, the chartering of corporations under Federal rather than State laws. "We possess every needful material for Utopia," Tugwell wrote. "It is a quite simple conclusion in most minds that control ought to be taken out of the hands of people who cannot produce it from the excellent materials at their disposal. . . . Our problem is to liberate technique by good management." [2]

Tugwell, like others of his faith, was a prophet of the economy of abundance. America's capacity to produce, they said, need be limited only by her capacity to consume.

While the very idea of national planning as opposed to laissez-faire was repugnant to most conservatives, by 1933 it was clear to almost everyone that the economic machine could no longer be allowed to rock along without a steering gear. When the recovery bill went to Congress in May, one of its most enthusiastic supporters was Henry I. Harriman, president of the ever-conservative Chamber of Commerce of the United States, who said it marked "a most important step in our progress toward business rehabilitation."

The statistical facts of business life put a hard floor of necessity under these aspirations. Between the high-water mark of 1929 and the low-water mark of 1932, business activity as a whole had been cut just about in half, and nothing but more of the same was in sight to the most astute prophets. The index of manufacturing (using 1923–25 as a base) had tumbled during those years by approximately 55 percent, from 119 to 63; manufacturing gross income, from $68.4 billion to $27.6 billion; and the number of manufacturing entrepreneurs, from 133,000 to 72,300. Hardest hit in the slide were iron and steel, down on the index scale from 130 to 31; autos, 135 to 35; and textiles, 115 to 83. Retail sales had been cut almost in half, from $49.1 billion to $25.0 billion. Building construction had suffered even worse devastation: its volume had slumped from $200.2 billion to $76.1 billion.

Factory payrolls had dropped from $10.8 billion in 1929 to $4.6 billion in 1932, a decline of 57 percent, and hourly wage rates from an *average* of 43.7 cents to 35 cents. Total unemployment, inaccurately and deceptively alleged by the government to be virtually nonexistent in mid-1929 (it actually was 1.5 million, 3.1 percent of the labor force) was 12.6 million in mid-1933, which was 25.2 percent of the labor force.[3]

By 1933 businessmen had come to recognize unemployment as something more than a regrettable social phenomenon. Every fourth wage earner out of a job meant that there were that many fewer customers to buy the goods produced.

When the New Deal came to power, business leaders formed their own breadline in Washington, imploring the new Administration to do something to get business on its feet. Many clamored for an "economic dictatorship," others for a reinstitution of wartime price and production controls, still others for handouts of new working capital from the RFC in exchange for common stocks and a share in management. A delegation of coal operators, according to Hugh Johnson, urgently proposed that the government buy out the industry at its own price and run the mines itself. "Anything to get us out of this mess," they said.

II

In the hectic early weeks of the Administration, the President had given little thought to the immediate needs of business. Two circumstances brought it front and center on the stage of his attention in April. One was the pending enactment of the farm bill designed to give an immediate boost to agricultural income, and thereby to the cost of food. A companion measure was therefore needed to give a comparable boost to urban wage earners, so that they could buy the farmers' produce. The other circumstance was the apparent readiness of Congress to enact a bill sponsored by Senator Hugo Black of Alabama establishing a mandatory thirty-hour week for all workers. The bill was simply a "spread the work" device, but since it contained no provision for maintenance of earning levels, its net effect would be to "spread the poverty." One marginal wage of $12 a week, for example, would be split into two submarginal wages of $6 a week, condemning two families instead of one to the relief rolls.

It was in the shadow of this under-the-gun crisis that Roosevelt told Moley early in April to prepare legislation to do for the city worker what the AAA was expected to do for the farmer—legislation that would at the same time outflank the Black bill. Moley was swamped with work and could not give his immediate attention to this assignment. A few days later, running into Hugh Johnson in the lobby of the Carleton Hotel, he had the sudden revelation that here was just the man to take on the business recovery assignment. A protégé of the most eminent business sage of the day, Bernard M. Baruch, and a veteran of the War Industries Board of a decade and a half earlier, the volcanic ex-cavalry officer had recently become a most useful idea man on the Brain Trust. Johnson snapped at the offer with relish. Moley took him immediately to his own office across from the White House, cleared off a desk for him, dumped before him the material on the subject that had accumulated in his own files, and told him to dig in. Johnson pulled off his coat, unbuttoned his shirt, and went to work as though the next tick of the clock was his deadline.

Hugh Samuel Johnson at fifty-three was the most colorful figure of the early New Deal—an impulsive, outspoken extrovert who sprang from practically nowhere to the center of the stage, and about whom there flared more contention and acrimony, more gossip and tall tales, and, in the end, more personal pathos than about any of his peers. He was perennially rumpled, with his tie sagging two inches below the collar line. He had a squat, thick-chested body and a seamed, leathery face marked by the bulbous nose and puffy eyes that betrayed an aversion to sleep and a fondness for bourbon whisky. He was raucous, profane, as bellicose as a top sergeant, driven by boundless energy and enthusiasm, and subject to sudden surges of sentimentality that could bring tears to his eyes and remembered bits of poetry to his lips. There were only three kinds of people in his world—heroes, buddies, and bastards —and he was forever shifting the labels on those who crossed his path. There was more philosophy than levity in the inscription on the flyleaf of a book he wrote after his NRA days: "Everybody in the world's a Rink-Stink but Hughie Johnson and he's all right." [4]

Apart from his burlesque mannerisms, Johnson had an enormously fertile and versatile mind and command of a wide range of public affairs. He was a facile writer who could summon a phrase from the classics or coin a pungent epigram of his own on the instant. He had written several successful boys' books as a young man, had contributed to important magazines, and had been the principal "ghost" in later years for his patron, Bernard Baruch, on political and economic topics of considerable profundity. In spite of his cavalry nickname, "Ironpants," Johnson spent most of the war years desk-bound, helping to write the draft act of 1917 and to administer the War Industries Board. After the war he had a successful business career as a manufacturer of agricultural implements and later renewed his association with Baruch, whom he regarded with the reverence of a young seminarian for the Pope. Baruch "loaned" him to the Roosevelt Brain Trust in March 1933 to help out with writing the farm bill, and thus set Hugh Johnson's foot on the path to immortality.*

Within a few days Johnson had melded his own ideas for business recovery with a dozen others contained in the files that Moley had turned over to him. He compressed his synthesis into one and a half pages of yellow foolscap. Using the War Industries Board as a model, he proposed to group the main elements of industry into federal licensed trade associations that would set production, price, and wage standards. He also proposed a $3-billion fund for industrial loans and for an extensive program for low-cost housing and military construction.

Meanwhile he and Moley discovered that his plan would have to compete with half a dozen others commissioned by the President without their knowledge. Labor Secretary Perkins had developed a plan expanding the Black thirty-hour work week concept by the creation of government-controlled wage boards to set minimums and correct inequities. John Dickinson, an Assistant Secretary of Commerce, had come up with the idea of organizing trade associations for the single purpose of regularizing wage and hour practices. Henry Harriman of the Chamber of Commerce submitted a long memorandum on a proposal that would virtually abolish the Clayton Act and confer on trade associations the right to limit production by the allocation of quotas. And Senator Robert F. Wagner of New York had evolved a plan for labor-management cooperation through trade associations, coupled with an elaborate program of government-financed public works.

* Baruch had an avuncular fondness for his admiring protégé but a rather limited confidence in his judgment. When told by Secretary Frances Perkins that the President planned to make Johnson administrator of the new recovery program, the sage shook his head ruefully and said: "I think he's a good number-three man, maybe a good number-two man, but he's not a number-one man. I'm fond of him, but do tell the President to be careful. Hugh needs a firm hand." (Perkins, *The Roosevelt I Knew* [New York: Viking, 1946], p. 200.)

In characteristic fashion, Roosevelt called the competing architects to the White House early in May and "locked them in a room" until they could work out a single, acceptable compromise. It was a prodigious labor, but within a week they laid on his desk a draft built mainly on the Johnson and Wagner proposals but borrowing something from most of the others. The draft was submitted to Congress on May 17 with a ringing endorsement from the President. It was debated vigorously, with two main choruses of dissent: Old-time progressives, such as Senators Wheeler and Borah, protested the weakening of the antitrust laws by permitting collusive action through trade associations; and some conservative business spokesmen argued that the liberal labor provisions would bring the industrial establishment down in ruins. But business titans such as E. H. Harriman, Gerard Swope, and Charles M. Schwab, gave the bill their enthusiastic blessing. It passed the House easily but got through the Senate by the relatively narrow margin of 46 to 39. Roosevelt signed it into law on June 16, the day after Congress adjourned. In a public statement issued at the time, Roosevelt said:

The law I have just signed was passed to put people back to work—to let them buy more of the products of farms and factories and start our business going at a living rate again.

In my inaugural I laid down the simple proposition that nobody is going to starve in this country. It seems to me to be equally plain that no business which depends for existence on paying less than a living wage to its workers has any right to continue in this country. . . .

Throughout industry, the change from starvation wages and starvation employment to living wages and sustained employment can, in large part, be made by an industrial covenant to which all employers shall subscribe. It is greatly to their interest to do this because decent living standards widely spread among our 125 million people eventually means the opening up to industry of the richest market the world has ever seen. . . .

This is the principle that makes this one of the most important laws that have ever come from Congress because, before the passage of this law, no such industrial convenant was possible.

I am fully aware [the President went on, like a doctor applying iodine to an open sore] that wage increases will eventually raise costs. But I ask that management give first consideration to the improvement of operating figures and to the greatly increased sales to be expected from the rising purchasing power of the public. This is sound economics and good business. The aim of this whole effort is to restore our rich domestic market by raising its vast consuming capacity.[5]

III

The heart of the National Industrial Recovery Act—the NIRA—was contained in Title I. What it did, essentially, was to set aside the antitrust laws to permit groups of businessmen to write their own rules of competition, production, and marketing—"codes of fair competition," they were called. Theoretically at least, the business groups were not to set price levels, except that price increases were to be restrained, and sales below the cost of production were forbidden. They were required to set uniform maximum hours of labor, varying from thirty to forty per week according to the type of industry, and to establish minimum wage levels ranging, in most instances, from $11 to $15 per week. The goal was to preserve the same earning level for the shortened week that had prevailed under the longer week, which traditionally had run upwards from forty hours to as many as sixty. Each code was also subjected to observance of Section 7(a) of the NIRA (a genuine landmark in this nation's labor history), which guaranteed to the workers in any plant the right to collective bargaining through unions of their own choice, and the right to join or not join a union as they chose.

Title II of the act authorized a $3.3-billion public works program designed for a quick infusion of purchasing power and reemployment into the economic system. Both titles of the act were to expire in two years.

The NIRA was a bold break with the traditional doctrine of laissez-faire, yet it fell considerably short of the genuinely controlled economy sought by the more radical planners. It vested voluntary "code authorities" established by industry with quasi-legal authority to enforce rules of business conduct; it relieved business of certain strictures against collusive action contained in the antitrust laws; and it imposed on business hitherto illegal requirements as to wages and hours of labor. But each code authority was responsive to government as the final arbiter of its rules and conduct and as the guardian of the public interest. The President was empowered to alter a code he did not approve of, and to impose a code on an industry group that could not reach voluntary agreement among its members. Legal penalties were provided for code violations.

The arrangement contained trace elements of a fascist corporate state and of socialist public ownership. As Broadus Mitchell observed, it was a cross between the medieval guild and the modern cartel. Roosevelt described it as a "partnership" between government and business, which it was. But government remained a discreet junior partner throughout the life of the undertaking, and such disciplinary powers as it had it was reluctant to use. This was one of its main afflictions.

Another built-in weakness of NIRA was a want of confidence. Many people (even within the Administration) who favored the objectives of NIRA were doubtful that it could withstand a serious challenge to its constitutionality. The Supreme Court had made clear in the past that it did not regard wages and hours of labor as permissible subjects of legislation under the interstate commerce clauses. But here, wages and hours were in fact being legislated through powers conferred on the President to dictate their inclusion in the industrial codes. It was the snare of constitutionality that ultimately brought the Blue Eagle down.

The most hotly debated feature of NIRA, however, was Section 7(a), the collective bargaining clause. Except in a few large industries, such as railroads, construction, mining, and the garment trades, labor unions scarcely counted as a factor in the industrial life of the nation in 1933. Membership in the American Federation of Labor was less than two million. But to most businessmen the union organizer wore the horns of the devil and carried a communist bomb in his hand. For years they had exhausted themselves emotionally and sometimes financially protecting their workers from the organizer's sinister and seditious doctrines. But now, under NIRA, they were required to throw open the gates to this trouble-making intruder. It was a bitter pill, which many employers resolved to hold under their tongues rather than swallow.

"As they [the businessmen] look at it," Will Woodin told a friend after a visit to his old haunts on Wall Street, "it is going to put the country entirely in the hands of labor."

IV

Enactment of the recovery program was greeted with loud hosannas from coast to coast. Except for the most stubborn skeptics, people believed that Roosevelt had at last found the magic key to unlock the gates of prosperity. As Hugh Johnson, who had been named the NRA administrator, promised first three million, then four million, and then six million new jobs by Labor Day, everyone's hopes soared. The stock market took a new spurt, trade picked up, factories began to call back their laid-off crews. Businessmen congregated noisily in convention and association meetings to talk about codes and how to get around 7(a). Labor leaders fanned out to the coal fields and mill towns and auto factories to organize the unorganized. Pundits gravely proclaimed the NIRA a stroke of genius and saw nothing but clear sailing ahead.

In typical headlong fashion Johnson had swung into action to set up his recovery administration while the legislation was still being debated in Congress. He sustained an early setback when the President decided to lop off the public works program and put it under Harold Ickes' Interior Department. Johnson felt that this was a mortal blow to the program and to his own prestige. He threatened to resign but thought better of it before nightfall the same day. He also resisted, futilely, the creation of separate advisory commitees on labor and consumer interests to guide him in code-making. He felt that businessmen would be guided by the benign light of their own self-interest to provide properly for workers and the public. He was so dazzled by the vision of a great cooperative regeneration of the entire industrial system that he believed everyone must share his revelation. "I regard NRA as a holy thing," he said with emotional solemnity one time. "Perhaps I am a zealot or even a fanatic in this, but I feel it so intensely that I will fight for it." [6]

Organizationally, NRA proliferated almost overnight into a baffling array of divisions and bureaus, chiefs and subchiefs, specialists and experts, lawyers and statisticians, philosophers and pitchmen. They were recruited by the hundreds, many of them partisans of particular schemes and cliques that ranged from Adam Smith conservatism to the proletarian revolution. They turned an entire wing of the new Commerce Department building into an agitated anthill.

Johnson had acquired an able deputy and general counsel in the person of Donald R. Richberg, the Chicago-based lawyer for the Railway Brotherhoods. He had been chiefly responsible for getting Section 7(a) inserted into the recovery bill and defending it against its enemies on Capitol Hill. With an imposing build and high-domed forehead, Richberg was something of an intellectual virtuoso (he was a part-time novelist and song writer) who enjoyed the full confidence of organized labor while not frightening management. He was particularly adept at spotting the legal loopholes and evasions that corporation lawyers wrote into their clients' codes and at arguing them to a standstill. But he was sensitive, high-strung, and ambitious, and he and Johnson were to have an irreparable falling out before many months passed. The same thing was to happen to many of the principal aides whom the impulsive General had clasped so eagerly to his bosom in the early days. Their feuds and infighting gave a special piquancy to the general turbulence that pervaded the NRA headquarters.

Reflecting once upon the fact that Caligula had appointed his horse ("a whole horse") to the Roman Senate, Johnson ruefully conceded, "I have once or twice failed to look to the question of equine entirety in my own appointments." [7]

Throughout that sweltering summer of 1933 (it was one of the hottest on record) there was intense activity in Washington in the drive to get industrial codes written and put into effect. Business delegations converged upon the city in droves, caucused in hotel lobbies and around park benches, paraded in sweaty frustration through the teeming corridors of the Commerce Building trying to find out what to do and whom to see, and relieved their nocturnal tensions in the speakeasies and burlesque shows along Ninth Street. Johnson had been working since May with some of the larger industrial groups—steel, automobiles, textiles, coal mining, construction—hoping to have their codes ready for enactment at the crack of the gun. Such a headstart with a few of the leaders would have had a valuable psychological effect on the others. But he underestimated the complexities of code-making. Only the cotton textile industry was even near the ready mark. Its code, the first, was signed by the President on June 27, with appropriate fanfare. The fanfare was well deserved, for the code cut through a long history of cutthroat competition and sweatshop labor to produced a pattern of stabilized production, uniform wages and hours, and an end to the industry's notorious exploitation of child labor.

But the other big industrial groups, and the lesser ones as well, were bogged in seemingly hopeless contention, among themselves and with the NRA. Little fellows fought the big fellows to keep from being "coded out of business." What was fair competition to one producer was piracy to another. Southern coal operators refused to be bound by any code adopted by the northern operators. Henry Ford said flatly he would have nothing to do with any code. Should the Collar Button Institute be bracketed under "metals" or "men's clothing"? The disputes were endless and acrimonious, but the most aggravated of all revolved around Section 7(a). The businessmen schemed and connived in a hundred different ways to avoid or evade the collective bargaining clause.

V

The success of NRA depended as much on psychological as on substantive factors. It needed a great wave of popular enthusiasm to carry it over the shoals of innovation and reform. But if its fulfillment was to be dragged out for months by haggling over codes, the enthusiasm would dry up and the great impetus to voluntary cooperation would be lost. This haggling soon emerged as a serious threat to the whole program. Johnson's solution was a dazzling exercise in showmanship. He proposed a temporary blanket code to which all businesses would subscribe while their individual group codes were being worked out—a universal, one-shot application of the wage, hour, and other basic provisions of the NRA that would, he believed, produce an instant and electrifying boost to recovery.

The President's Re-employment Agreement, as the device was called, was promulgated late in August. To assure its nationwide adoption, a monster publicity and promotional campaign was launched with all the patriotic fanfare of the first Liberty Loan drive of 1917. Every employer was expected to sign up, and every consumer was expected to boycott any business house that failed to do so. Millions of flags, placards, gummed labels, banners, and other printed devices, bearing the Blue Eagle rampant upon a red scroll proclaiming "We Do Our Part," were rushed to NRA offices across the country —sometimes by Army bomber, to heighten the publicity effect. These emblems were to adorn the offices, shop windows, and merchandise of the cooperators, like a badge of merit or a symbol of social acceptability.

Meanwhile every governor, mayor, chamber of commerce and service club had been enlisted to beat the drum for local compliance with NRA, to push "Buy Now" campaigns, and to organize parades, rallies, or other suitable pulse-raising ceremonies. A million housewives, Boy Scouts, and schoolchildren were organized into a volunteer army to obtain signed pledges from householders promising to patronize only Blue Eagle firms. Labor unions set themselves up as vigilante corps to report on violators of the agreement, and editors and preachers and political stump speakers vied with one another in their patriotic exhortations to "do your part."

New York celebrated "Blue Eagle Day" in mid-September with one of the biggest parades in its history. Grover Whalen marched at its head, Al Smith sat in the reviewing stand with General Johnson, and a Navy blimp floated overhead trailing a one-hundred-foot banner with the slogan, "We Do Our Part." The featured speaker at a big NRA rally in Tulsa was Mrs. Samuel L. Johnson, the General's seventy-seven-year-old mother, who warned: "People had better obey the NRA because my son will enforce it like lightning, and you can never tell where lightning will strike." And on the Boston Common, Mayor James W. Curley led a hundred thousand schoolchildren in this solemn oath of allegiance: "I promise as a good American citzen to do my part for the

NRA. I will buy only where the Blue Eagle flies. I will ask my family to buy in September and to buy American-made goods. I will help President Roosevelt bring back good times." [8]

The ballyhoo and evangelism of the drive had the desired effect. It generated a kind of emotional fervor that found expression in many ways: There was a brisk sale in neckties and ladies' cotton print dresses in which the Blue Eagle was the dominant motif; tattoo artists along the New York waterfront embedded the bird and its slogan imperishably in scores of masculine shoulders and biceps; vaudeville artists wove it into their acts ("That was some pigeon I saw you with last night, Mike. That wasn't no pigeon, Ike, that was my boss's Blue Eagle. He pays me time-and-a-half to walk it for him."). Scores of big industrialists like Harvey S. Firestone wired the President their promise "to adopt and to put your program into effect," and at least one little one, Nathan Schachter of Chicago, bought advertising space in a local newspaper to proclaim:

NRA: Necessities First, Luxuries Last
Fellow Citizens: I, a citizen of the United States and of the City of Chicago, do dare entitle myself a prophet and make the following favorable prediction in reference to the NRA which, when adjusted and properly administered throughout the nation, will relieve human misery, automatically produce an almost permanent employment era and will serve to keep our great nation together. . . . May God help our great President on to victory—ROOSEVELT OR RUIN.[9]

The campaign was something of a thirty day wonder. When the razzle-dazzle had petered out around the end of September, the Blue Eagle had become as familiar an emblem as the American Flag and as compelling a buyers' guide as "satisfaction guaranteed" or "25% off." Johnson proudly estimated that some 90 percent of the nation's business establishments from barbershops to steel mills had taken the NRA pledge, and that 2.7 million "new" jobs had been created (somewhat below his earlier optimistic estimate of six million). Also, the logjam in code-making had been broken. By October, sixty-three approved codes were in operation, including all of the "big six" industries, and 700 had reached the hearing stage. By the end of the year more than 200 would be in force, and by the end of 1934 more than 550.[10]

But the Blue Eagle's robustness was only feather-deep; its congenital frailties were beginning to slow it down. In spite of all the summer's cheers and flag-waving, by autumn recovery was still lagging, production was still sluggish, and unemployment had scarcely been dented.

NRA had been oversold and overcommitted. When it could not deliver, public confidence dried up and opposition stiffened. Labor strife was rampant as workers sought to avail themselves of the collective bargaining rights under Section 7(a) and as employers sought to thwart them with company unions and other dodges. A National Labor Board had been set up under NRA to mediate such disputes, but it lacked the means to enforce its decisions. In December, for example, the Weirton Steel Company flatly refused to permit its workers to participate in a secret election for union representation that

The Blue Eagle was everywhere!

From the White House door of the
Chief Executive . . .

To the Outhouse door of cartoonist O. Soglow.

"The Great American Bank Bubble" by a Banker

REAL
AMERICA

April   25c

The Rise and Fall of
General Hugh S. Johnson
By Hugh Russell Fraser

VE

Orthophonic Recording

"HIS MASTER'S VOICE"

VICTOR

Not Licensed for
Radio Broadcast   24761-A

An extract from a radio address by
PRESIDENT FRANKLIN D. ROOSEVELT
on September 30, 1934,
ON THE NRA.

RCA Victor Company, Inc.
Camden, N.J.

VE

VANITY FAIR

At left: General Hugh S. Johnson was the
cover story for this issue of *Real America*—
a liberal "exposé" monthly of the early
Depression. (Alongside) Johnson, popularly
known as "Old Iron Pants," stumped the
nation as NRA administrator rallying industry to a short-lived but spectacular
phase of the early New Deal. (Below) New
York's NRA parade, 250,000 strong, September 13, 1933.

the Board had called for. Another labor grievance was that the NRA minimum wage was often achieved by slicing the pay of workers in higher brackets, and that the shortened work week was gained by enforced layoffs during the slack hours of the day. Legitimate union membership rose slowly (about a million new members from August to January), but it was an uphill fight marked by 435 bitter and frequently damaging strikes during the five-month period.[11]

Business dissatisfaction with the NRA centered not only on its labor provisions but on the pricing and other policies enforced by the codes. Many companies protested that they were being pushed to the wall in the squeeze between higher labor costs and the freeze on prices. Here and there, exemptions to the ban on raising prices was granted in special "hardship" cases; the steel industry was one such beneficiary. The effect was to creat a clamor from other industries demanding similar concessions. Where they were not granted, prices were often raised anyway, either in devious circumvention or in open defiance of the codes. Small businessmen were particularly vehement in their outcry against the regimentation and injustice under NRA. The code machinery, they complained, was dominated by a handful of big fellows who were using their power to regulate production and prices to drive small competitors out of business. Hundreds of them figuratively tore up their Blue Eagle certificates and publicly proclaimed their return to "free enterprise." Senator Borah received over 18,000 requests for help from small businessmen after a speech in February 1934 in which he accused NRA of fostering the growth of monopoly.

NRA's fair-weather friends among prominent business leaders were also falling away. Henry I. Harriman of the Chamber of Commerce expressed his disillusionment in numerous speeches and called for a total revamping of the program in both concept and administration. Dr. Virgil I. Jordan, a prominent economist, warned a special convocation of the National Association of Manu-facturers in December: "The industries of the United States are faced today by the destruction of the foundations for full development of the industrial arts by a political dictatorship based on extraordinary popular delusions and widely accepted economic falacies." [12] The Hearst newspapers blasted NRA as a "blatant exercise in state socialism," reflecting a sentiment that was spreading rapidly through most of the press.

NRA contributed to its own fading fortunes by its erratic administration and by its reluctance to enforce compliance with the codes. Johnson, characteristically, talked tough but acted timidly in such crises. He threatened violators with "a punch in the nose." In a major speech to an assemblage of code authorities during March 1934 he thundered: "I want to warn non-compliers that we are not only going out to revive public sentiment for the Blue Eagle, but under the specific orders from the President we are reorganizing to enforce the penal sections of the act. I have been too gentle. We deliberately delayed action because of misunderstandings. But if I may lapse into the vernacular —You ain't seen nothing yet!" [13]

For all his tough talk, however, the General had no intention of really getting tough. For one thing, he sincerely believed that NRA could succeed only with the voluntary cooperation of business. For another, the agency had few powers of coercion to get tough with. It had to depend on the Justice Department and the Federal Trade Commission for punitive action in the courts, and both of these agencies were skeptical of NRA's legal under-pinnings and were therefore reluctant to prosecute. Henry Ford continued serenely to sell his automobiles without the Blue Eagle emblem, although, of his own volition, he met the wage and hour standards of the auto code for his unorganized workers.* The one big club that NRA had to swing, the power to impose federal licensing on a recalcitrant industry, was never used.

VI

As it approached its first birthday, the Blue Eagle that had soared so handsomely into the sky at birth had become a sadly clipped, dourly squawk-ing old bird, held aloft on a wing and a prayer. The tension and the agonies of keeping it aloft had taken their toll of everyone concerned, especially of Hugh Johnson. His mountainous zeal seemed never to flag (he apparently preferred to exist without sleep, rest, or bodily nourishment), but his strength and his judgment seemed to falter. He depended more and more on liquor to keep himself going, turned up bleary-eyed and unshaven for meetings, disappeared unaccountably for days at a time. He became more and more impetuous and irascible—a real "Rink-Stink" (a term he had dreamed up in his childhood days in Oklahoma). He abdicated ever more of his respon-sibilities to his pert and efficient secretary, Frances M. Robinson (the in-effable "Robbie," about whom much gossip circulated), who divided her time between administering the NRA and ministering to the personal needs and welfare of her addled boss. Richberg (as well as other top officials) was driven into a frenzy by the chaos and disintegration that had fastened upon NRA. He wrung his hands in desperation and poured out his anxiety to whoever would listen. Johnson *had* to go and NRA *had* to be reorganized, in that order, he said.

President Roosevelt was of like mind. He learned from all sides that NRA was in danger of falling apart, but his loyalty to and fondness for the General stayed his hand. "The President has been trying to lose him [John-son]," Harold Ickes, a less than sympathetic spectator, said, "but he is so tender-hearted that he has not been able to say the final word. Johnson per-sists in staying . . . and goes through all sorts of theatricals with the President in order to hold on." [14] At last, however, in a tense and emotional scene at

---

* Ford's intransigence was an acute embarrassment to Johnson and the whole administration. When a Maryland Ford dealer came up with the low bid on 500 trucks for the Civilian Conservation Corps, in December 1933, Johnson, in a well-publicized gesture of retaliation, directed the purchasing agency to throw out the Ford offer and give the contract to the next highest bidder, Dodge Motors. He was promptly overruled by the Controller General, and Ford had the double satisfaction of winning a good contract and publicly rubbing the General's nose in the dust. (Allan Nevins and Frank E. Hill, *Ford: Decline and Rebirth, 1933-1963* [New York: Scribners, 1963.])

the White House late in September, the General got the message and handed in his resignation. The President accepted it in a heartfelt "Dear Hugh" letter, which said:

I repeat what I have so often said to you—that I am happy not only in our friend-ship and your loyalty, but that in a time of great stress your courage, enthusiasm, and energy were a very potent factor in restarting a stalled machine. More than that it will always be remembered that under you the NRA in over a little more than a year accomplished long overdue reforms in our social and business structures. The elimination of child labor, the recognition of the principles of a fair wage and of collective bargaining, and the first effort to eliminate unfair practices within business—these among others are chalked up to your credit. . . .[15]

At noon on October 1 virtually the entire 4,500-man staff of NRA packed into the Commerce Building auditorium for a sentimental leave-taking of their flamboyant old chief. In spite of his irascibility Hugh Johnson was the kind of leader who evoked as much affection as anger, whose weaknesses were as endearing as his courage, and whose devotion and idealism could transform a function of bureaucracy into a moral crusade. That was just what he had done with NRA, spending his physical and emotional resources lavishly in the process. Many wept unashamedly as the words of farewell and benediction tumbled from his lips. Johnson himself was so overcome that he had to abandon the last few lines of his speech in choked confusion. His sun had not set entirely: He would stage a comeback later as a news-paper columnist, where his verbal propensities would have free play. But nothing would ever match the pride he felt in NRA, nor his hurt in its being taken away from him.

Johnson's departure introduced a new era in both the administration and the concept of NRA. Leadership passed to a five-man National Industrial Recovery Board, of which Clay Williams, president of the R. J. Reynolds Tobacco Company, was chairman, and Sidney Hillman of the Amalgamated Clothing Workers the labor member. Richberg served as chairman of its executive committee, and W. Averell Harriman as its administrative officer. This setup was expected to give a more balanced and coherent direction to the agency than Johnson's often quixotic "dictatorship." At the same time, efforts were launched within the organization to limit and to tighten the cope of NRA's domain, which had proliferated so haphazardly. A principal objective was to abandon the effort to regulate the vast and mutinous army of service trades and family business enterprises—laundry and dry cleaning plants, corner groceries, and the "Mom 'n' Pop" restaurants and filling stations—which had generated almost 90 percent of the charges of noncompliance.* The emphasis would be put on the larger business groups, where enfore-

---

* Running down the alphabetical listing of the more than 500 code authorities that came into being, one encounters a kaleidoscopic variety: Advertising Industry, Anti-Hog Cholera Serum Industry, Corset and Brassiere Industry, Drinking Straw Industry, Funeral Home Industry, Gummed Label Industry, Lightning Rod Industry, Machine Tool Industry, Pretzel Industry, Railroad Industry, Shoe Repairing Industry, Vault (Burial) Industry, etc.

ment would be feasible. Another objective was to take the troublesome wage and hour provisions out of the codes and supplant them by substantive law.

But these and similar reforms were slow in fulfillment, and the NRA continued through the fall and into the new year of 1935 to be wracked by dissension within and mounting opposition from without. When President Roosevelt asked Congress for a two-year extension of the act in February (it was due to expire in June 1935), the dissents and conflicts created a bedlam. Big-business spokesmen favored extension only if the act were rewritten to give the code authorities full power to set prices and regulate production, thus further stifling competition. Liberals urged the government to assume this responsibility, thus coming closer to their dream of a fully managed economy. Labor asked that 7(a) be rewritten to ensure iron-bound guarantees of free collective bargaining. Small business and orthodox conservatives wanted the whole enterprise junked, in order to cut competitive corners and slash labor costs on the one hand, and reinstall the hallowed rule of laissez-faire on the other. For weeks during March and April the halls of Congress reverberated with debates on these demands.

Meanwhile, in the halls of Justice, the denouement of this political drama was quietly being written. Of a score of noncompliance cases that had reached the courts, one of the weakest from the Administration's point of view happened to become the pivotal one on which the fate of the Blue Eagle hung. The Schechter Poultry Company of Brooklyn, which bought and slaughtered poultry for the New York market, was convicted in the U.S. District Court late in 1934 on eighteen specific charges of violating the wage-and-hour and trade-practices provisions of the Live Poultry Code. The conviction was upheld in the Court of Appeals, and the case was then appealed to the Supreme Court.

The Schechter brothers charged in their defense (1) that enforcement of the poultry code represented an unconstitutional delegation by Congress of its legislative powers; (2) that their business was wholly intrastate and thus beyond the reach of Congressional authority; and (3) that the penalties imposed upon them under the code represented a breach of the due process clause of the Constitution. In its argument before the high court the government contended (1) that the code was constitutionally valid when viewed in the light of the national emergency that prompted Congress to authorize it; (2) that in so doing Congress had not wrongfully delegated its law-making powers but had expressed a broad legislative intent and left its implementation up to the President; and (3) that the Schechters were engaged in interstate (as opposed to intrastate) commerce, since some of their poultry originated outside the State of New York.

On May 27, in a resounding unanimous decision read by Chief Justice Charles Evans Hughes, the Supreme Court found for the Schechters in each of their complaints. The NRA was unconstitutional and an improper abdication by Congress of its law-making powers. "Extraordinary conditions do not create or enlarge constitutional powers," the Court said in rebutting the government's principal justification of an emergency. And of the power granted the President to approve or impose codes it said: "Such a delegation of legislative power is unknown to our law and utterly inconsistent with the constitutional prerogatives and duties of Congress. . . . No such plenitude of power is susceptible of transfer."

That was it. The Blue Eagle was dead. Roosevelt thought briefly of trying to revive it in a legally more acceptable form, but then rejected the idea. Publicly he derided the Court for having forced the country back into "the horse and buggy days." But privately he told Frances Perkins: "We have got the best out of it [NRA] anyhow. Industry got a shot in the arm. Everything has started up. I don't believe they will go back to their old wage levels. I think the forty hour week will stick except in a few instances. I think perhaps NRA has done all it can." [16]

Most of the nation's press agreed with him. Editorial reaction around the country varied from a curt "good riddance" to a more tolerant "good try, anyway." The New York *Herald-Tribune* said: "The demise of the Blue Eagle is not exactly startling news. The President was about the only one left in Washington who refused to concede its failure and collapse." The Denver *Post* thought the decision "the most reassuring development the country has experienced in many a year. The decision loosens the bureaucratic brakes which had been clamped on business." In its valediction *The New York Times* echoed the President's feeling when it said: "The recovery program has done its work, the chief benefit of which was to stir the people into hopeful activity. It has now become almost universally regarded as a piece of legislation which is obsolete and ineffective."

Wall Street took unalloyed pleasure in the Blue Eagle's downfall, but some major business leaders expressed concern about the consequences of the vacuum left behind. Most businessmen took the repeal of the NRA as a deliverance from oppression, but for one in particular the pleasure was tinged with regret. Joseph Schechter, the now famous Brooklyn poultry tycoon, said: "The legal battle cost me $60,000, every nickel I had. If I'd known at the start how much this thing was going to cost I probably would have gone to jail" [17]

Most economists agree that it is not possible in retrospect to demonstrate statistically what contribution the NRA experiment made to economic recovery. There was a substantial measure of recovery between 1933 and 1935, but many forces besides NRA were at work—namely, relief and public works payments, aids to building construction, farm price supports, currency reforms, etc. Between those years the gross national product rose from $39.6 billion to $56.8 billion; the index of manufacturing production (Federal Reserve Board) went up from 68 to 87; income from salaries and wages increased from $28.7 billion to $36.3 billion, and so on. But the most formidable index of all budged only slightly: Unemployment decreased by 2.4 million to a still unmanageable total of 10.2 million.[18] There was a reassuring light at the end of the tunnel, but it was still a long way off.

THE EAGLE *STILL* HAS TWO WINGS

. . . as he had in April, 1934, when Fortune first ran his picture. But whereas the Right wing was far and away the stronger in 1934, the Left is now the mistress pinion. The five large primaries on the Left exert more leverage at the moment than all the Right-wing feathers put together. Their push however is somewhat counterbalanced by the tendency of the undifferentiated central tail feather, now grown to enormous size, to steer in aid of the bedraggled Right.

—Cartoon by Harrison, February 1938. Courtesy of Fortune Magazine.

NRA did more for the nation's morale than for its pocketbook. It did create a lively and exhilarating sense of moving ahead, of getting something done. Everyone felt, in one way or another, that he had a part in it. In the closing battle, all chose up sides, "for" or "against." The NRA also made the people aware, in a way they had never known before, that through their government they could strike directly and tellingly at glaring social evils, such as child labor, the sweatshop, the six-day week and the ten-hour day, and the denial of the right to collective bargaining. The NRA moved the country a long step forward in these respects, and there has been no falling back since.

CHAPTER 11
A New Deal for the Farmer

AT NOON ON A HOT FRIDAY near the end of July 1933, William E. Morris, a small cotton farmer of Nueces County, Texas, was ushered into the oval office at the White House to meet President Roosevelt, He was accompanied by his Congressman, Richard Kleberg, who by some act of divination (probably assisted by his alert and efficient young administrative assistant, Lyndon B. Johnson) had established that Mr. Morris was the first farmer in the nation to plow under a part of his cotton crop in accordance with the Administration's new war on agricultural surpluses. The President, beaming happily for the photographers who crowded around his desk, handed Mr. Morris a government check for $517 as his "adjustment payment" for the forty-seven acres of growing cotton (one-quarter of his crop) that he had plowed back into the ground. The President congratulated his visitor warmly and said he hoped other cotton growers would be as cooperative with the new program.

The little ceremony at the White House signaled the launching of as radical a strategy to bring about recovery as any that the New Deal contrived. The plan to plow under a quarter of the standing cotton crop—about ten million acres—was followed almost immediately by a plan for the instant slaughter of seven million little pigs and brood sows. The immediate aim was to avoid adding to the already crushing surpluses in cotton and corn (the corn-hog ratio is an arcane unit of measurement fully understood only by agricultural economists) and to raise the ruinously low prices prevailing for cotton and pork. The long-range aim, as embodied in the Agricultural Adjustment Act of 1933, by which the destruction was sanctioned, was to break the Depression's stranglehold on the American farmer. But such an emergency remedy was harsh indeed and without precedent in this country as a government policy. It shocked not only the sentimental city dweller who felt sorry for the poor little pigs, but more practical realists as well.

To Henry Wallace, the Secretary of Agriculture, the willful destruction of living crops was an obscene and wicked necessity. "These were not acts of idealism in any sane society," he said later. "They were emergency acts made necessary by the almost insane lack of world statesmanship during the period from 1920 to 1932." To Broadus Mitchell, writing about it a generation later, it "marked the extreme irony, not to say imbecility, to which the depression had brought the nation's economy. Millions were hungry and naked while food and fiber were turned back to the clod or fields were left untilled. The economy of scarcity never found franker illustration." [1]

I

The farm economy had been in a state of acute depression since the early nineteen-twenties. As Hugh Johnson put it, "the red flags of distress" were flying throughout the farm states during all the years of the industrial and financial boom. The crash of 1929 simply changed the farmer's plight from desperate to intolerable. Under government prodding he had expanded production enormously during the World War, but in the brief depression that followed the war, his domestic market shrank and his export market virtually disappeared, but out of habit as well as conviction he continued to plant all the tillable acreage he had. The result by the end of the decade of the twenties was vast overproduction—warehouses bursting with unsalable cotton in Georgia and Mississippi, mountains of wheat and corn rotting on the ground along railroad sidings in Kansas and the Dakotas—and disastrous price declines for farm commodities of all kinds.

Wheat, which had sold for $2.94 a bushel at Chicago in 1920, was $1 in 1929 and 30¢ in 1932; choice beef on the hoof dropped from $14.95 per hundredweight in 1920 to $11 in 1929 and to $5.78 in 1932; and cotton skidded downward from 37¢ to 12¢ to 6½¢ per pound at New Orleans. The gross income received by farmers was $16 billion in 1920 and $6.4 billion in 1932, and the "parity index"—the ratio of prices received by the farmer to the prices he paid for what he had to buy, which is a way of comparing his purchasing power with that of the city dweller—sank to the all-time low of forty-nine in February 1933. The government during all these years gave the farmer scant relief. President Coolidge twice vetoed tariff bills that promised to be of some help, and it was only with reluctance and mistrust that President Hoover agreed to the creation of the Federal Farm Board in 1929. The Board's purpose was to buy up a part of the huge wheat and cotton surpluses overhanging the market, but it did nothing to prevent the piling of new surpluses on top of the old. The program was a fiasco and left the individual farmer as deeply in trouble as he had been before. There is little wonder that armed Wisconsin dairymen were hijacking milk trucks and dumping their contents on the road or that Iowa farmers were breaking up mortgage foreclosures with guns and hangman's nooses.[2]

The New Deal's farm program underwent a long period of gestation in the Brain Trust. It was a recurrent theme in Roosevelt's election campaign and was given top priority after the inauguration. Its principal authors were Rexford Tugwell, Henry Wallace, and M. L. Wilson, a professor at Montana State College, who had spent fruitless years trying to get a hearing from Congress and the big farm leaders for his domestic allotment plan as a means of securing voluntary acreage reduction. Tugwell and Wallace embraced Wilson's idea with enthusiasm.

Many schemes for rescuing agriculture were afloat at the time, each with its devout band of advocates in Congress and elsewhere. Many favored the approach of the McNary-Haugen tariff bill, which Coolidge had vetoed. It called for a subsidy to bolster domestic prices by dumping surplus crops abroad. Other schemes called for a cost-of-production guarantee to the farmer; still others sought to cure the farmer's ills (thought to be induced by the eastern money trust) by a wholesale inflation of the currency. Few of the schemes looked to the basic problem of a balance between supply and demand.

The bill that Roosevelt sent to Congress on March 16 was an elaboration of Wilson's domestic allotment idea. Farmers were to be paid to reduce their acreage of four basic crops—cotton, wheat, corn, and tobacco—by "leasing" a portion of their productive land to the government and restricting their output to the remainder. The scale of the reduction would vary from year to year, depending on the government's estimate of probable demand, and each grower would be given his individual acreage allotment accordingly. Minimum prices would be set for the crop so grown; if the market failed to yield such prices, a subsidy would be paid the cooperating grower to cover the difference. To provide for the subsidy, a "processing tax" was to be levied against primary processors such as millers and packers. The processors and distributors would enter into marketing agreements covering prices, production, and fair trade practices. The Secretary of Agriculture would be a party to all such agreements, and the processors would, in effect, be licensees of the government.

A farmer who had carried out his allotment plan and still found himself with a surplus on hand could dispose of it to the government at the established base price (actually in the form of a loan). Participation in the program would be voluntary, and a substantial part of its administration would be handled by county committees elected by the participants themselves. No penalty was to attach to a farmer who decided to stay outside the program, but as a matter of simple economics a participant was likely to make more out of his reduced acreage and price guarantee than a neighbor who insisted on planting right up to the cabin door and taking his chances on the open market.

In its many ramifications, this legislative proposal abounded with staggering implications. It sought in one grand sweep to bring the American agricultural system out of the nineteenth century into the twentieth, to harness the most highly individualistic sector of the nation's economy into a massive cooperative endeavor, and to apply the full leverage of government to raising the financial status of an entire class of the nation's citizens. To achieve these ends it gave to the executive branch of government a range of discretionary powers unmatched except in times of war.

"I tell you frankly," President Roosevelt said in sending the bill to Congress two weeks after his inauguration, "that it is a new and untrod path. But I tell you with equal frankness that an unprecedented condition calls for the trial of new means to rescue agriculture."

Historian Arthur Schlesinger, Jr., appraising the bill a generation later, said: "Probably never in American history had so much social and legal inventiveness gone into a single legislative measure. . . . For another quarter century agricultural policy came up with very little which was not provided for one way or another in the Agricultural Adjustment Act." [3]

The decision to press for enactment of the farm bill during the emergency session of Congress was a hasty one dictated by two compelling considerations: (1) to get the program going before the crop year was too far advanced (cotton was already going into the ground down in Dixie); and (2) to take advantage of the compliant mood of Congress and public opinion, which could be decisive with so revolutionary a measure.

The bill passed the House in four days, but by the time it reached the Senate an alarmed opposition had mustered its forces. Eastern conservatives and spokesmen for business were horrified at the wide powers given the President to impose taxes and to coerce business through marketing and production agreements. Some farm groups opposed enforced crop reduction as violative of good sense and God's will. Others, conceding the necessity of controlling output, demanded in return outright guarantees of the farmer's cost of production. The most powerful dissent came from the inflationist bloc, which saw salvation only in putting more money in the farmers' hands—greenbacks or their equivalent. Milo Reno, the hot-headed leader of the Farmers' Holiday Association, which had shown its muscle on former occasions, threatened to call a national farm strike unless both greenbacks and cost of production were written into the law.

The debate over the bill, fiery and emotional at times, occupied the Senate and the nation's press for weeks. Here and there the Administration gave ground, most notably to the inflationists, but the essentials of the Tugwell-Wallace-Wilson plan were preserved. As it cleared its final hurdle in the Senate 64 to 20 on May 12, the Agricultural Adjustment Act of 1933 was composed of three parts. Title I, the "guts" of the act, contained the domestic allotment plan and its subsidiary arrangements for marketing agreements and the processing tax. Title II incorporated the Farm Mortgage Act (see page 125) for the relief of farm debt. Title III was the Thomas amendment giving the President powers to inflate the currency.

Typical of all such political compromises, the act had something in it for everybody and something that everybody could find fault with. In Tugwell's words: "For real radicals such as Wheeler, Frazier, etc., it is not enough. For conservatives it is too much. For Jeffersonian democrats it is a new control, which they distrust. For the economic philosophy it represents, there are no defenders at all. Nevertheless . . . something has to be done. Also, there is no alternative." [4]

II

It seems strange in retrospect that the staidly conservative Department of Agriculture and its newly acquired appendage, the Agricultural Adjustment Administration, should have become the hottest center of social ferment in New Deal Washington. But such was the case, and the fact was given high visibility by the endless warfare between the orthodox, old-time professionals who had dominated the department and the agricultural establishment for decades, and the theorists and reformers who now occupied the seats of power. And deployed around them, displacing the baggy-kneed civil servants of the Republican ascendancy, was a host of hot-eyed young ideologists from the universities and big city law offices, intent on making over a decadent sector of American society.

The young newcomers were "Felix's Happy Hotdogs," real or putative. They were fertile of mind, glib of tongue, bursting with zeal, and full of a contagious confidence in the coming of a new social order. They worked feverishly in a kind of perpetual brainstorm, and their disputations echoed far into the night, from stately Georgetown dinner tables to shirt-sleeved beer busts in brownstone walk-ups around DuPont Circle. They dismayed elderly congressmen from the boondocks and enriched the prose of columnists and magazine writers. If few of them had been no nearer a farm than the City Market, they were letter-perfect in all the literature on rural deprivation and economic imbalance. A standard joke of the period was about the young AAA executive fresh out of a New York law office who demandd to know if a proposed code for the macaroni industry would be fair to the macaroni growers.

Henry Agard Wallace, Roosevelt's instant choice for Secretary of Agriculture, was highly respected throughout the agricultural community, even if his philosophizing often went over the heads of ordinary farmers. A third-generation Iowan whose father had been Secretary of Agriculture under Presidents Harding and Coolidge, he was editor of the widely influential family-owned magazine *Wallaces' Farmer,* and an agronomist and plant geneticist of considerable repute in his own right. He was huskily built with wide shoulders and strong hands. A shock of dark hair was indifferently parted on the side with a forelock dangling over the forehead. He had rugged facial features and pale blue eyes that seemed at once both troubled and serene. His manner was shy, his speech was hesitant and humorless, and he seemed often to be preoccupied in deep introspection. He was a religious mystic, a social philosopher, and a businessman-scientist all in one. Henry Wallace was a puzzling phenomenon in the politically charged atmosphere of New Deal Washington. No one claimed to understand him (his brief penchant for hurling an Australian boomerang as a recreational pursuit did not help matters), but everyone liked him and most people respected his advanced ideas on the treatment of agricultural problems.

Among Wallace's most ardent admirers was Rex Tugwell, who, in respect to urbanity and sophistication, was his exact antithesis. "We are in the process of making a friendship," Tugwell noted in his diary at an early stage of their association, "and are exploring each other's minds with a sort of delighted expectancy. We have much in common and our minds work in somewhat the same way. We are both over forty and have been exploring the world independently up to now. To know Wallace and [M. L.] Wilson well makes a good deal of sacrifice worthwhile." [5] Having brought Wallace to Roosevelt's attention in the first place, Tugwell was quite willing to take a subordinate position to him as Under Secretary of Agriculture, with Wilson as an Assistant Secretary.

Tugwell's influence on Roosevelt and the New Deal ranged considerably beyond the confines of the farm problem. His intellectual concern embraced the whole condition of man and his contemporary environment. He had absorbed the teachings of Marx as he had of other great social and political philosophers. He was no communist (as his detractors often hinted), nor even an orthodox socialist. His synthesis came down to a managed economy, in which the vitality and incentives of free enterprise would be firmly directed by government control toward the common good. He was skeptical in this of compromises and half-measures, which he felt much of the New Deal to be, knowing that it was all too easy for the owners and managers of wealth to tip the balance of power back in their own favor. He was no shrill dogmatist about his beliefs (his manner was suave, pedagogically detached), but he adhered to them with unyielding conviction. "His famed political ineptitude," Paul Conkin has noted, "often indicated only tenacious honesty and high personal integrity."

To the members of the conservative opposition, the handsome, prematurely gray young professor epitomized what they suspected to be a New Deal revolutionary scheme to subvert the American way of life. His advocacy in 1935 of stronger pure food and drug legislation drew the fire of powerful business interests. He was hectored in the press and pilloried by Congressional committees to the point where his continued presence in Roosevelt's circle of advisers was a hindrance to the formulation of policies and legislation with which he was most concerned. He resigned at the end of 1937, leaving a gap in the Roosevelt Administration that could not easily be filled.

In the choice of an administrator for the AAA, which enjoyed a semi-autonomous status within the Department of Agriculture, Roosevelt went almost to the opposite end of the political spectrum. He chose George Nelson Peek, a crusty counterpart and longtime friend and associate of Hugh Johnson. Sixty and wealthy, Peek was a hard headed conservative who spoke the language of the National Grange and other powerful elements of the agricultural establishment. He saw salvation only in terms of shifting the American farmer's burden to the rest of the world, by means of a high protective tariff against agricultural imports and the wholesale dumping of American surpluses abroad. He had little faith in other new-fangled remedies. The President chose Peek, however, because of his standing with the big farm organizations and in the hope that he could be persuaded to go along with the more advanced provisions of the farm act. Like most conservatives in the movement, Peek abhorred the idea of inducing a farmer *not* to grow as much as he could, and he surrounded himself at AAA with a bureaucracy of like-minded traditionalists. He meant to run his own show.[6]

The tight exclusiveness of this bureaucracy—and of Peek's peace of mind —was ruptured with the naming of Jerome N. Frank, a forty-one-year-old corporation lawyer out of Chicago by way of New York, as General Counsel and third in command (after Chester Davis, the deputy administrator) at AAA. Frank had impressive legal credentials (he had been recommended by Felix Frankfurter), a glittering intellect, and a liberal philosophy that quickly established him as the brightest star of the New Deal's Far Left. A house he and Tugwell shared briefly in the DuPont Circle area was Washington's most envied intellectual salon.

Peek took Frank's appointment as a personal affront. His attitude had been formed years earlier when Frank had helped to liquidate one of Peek's companies for a group of Chicago bankers. On Frank's arrival at the Agriculture South Building on Independence Avenue, where AAA was quartered, Peek hired another lawyer at his own expense as his personal counsel and by-passed the General Counsel whenever he could. Meanwhile, Frank staffed *his* office with a corps of such radical young activists—Alger Hiss, Lee Pressman,

John Abt, Nathan Witt, Charles Kramer, among others — that Whittaker Chambers, scouting the territory for recruits for his communist cell, found at AAA "a bumper crop of incipient or registered Communists," many of whom he allegedly signed on.[7] Other brilliant but less vulnerable stars on the Frank team included Adlai Stevenson, Thurman Arnold, Abe Fortas, and Gardner "Pat" Jackson, who had earned his stripes battling for Sacco and Vanzetti in the twenties.

Such a flammable mixture, human as well as philosophic, was bound to ignite sooner or later. Peek was its first casualty. His open warfare with Frank and his lack of sympathy with much of the new agricultural program caused Roosevelt to remove him in December 1933, and to replace him with Chester Davis. A year later, yielding to the hot winds from Capitol Hill, there was a "purge of the radicals" in Frank's shop. But the AAA, in spite of almost constant turmoil and controversy, established itself as a principal power center of the New Deal. "This gigantic and difficult undertaking," the scholarly Edwin G. Nourse wrote in a report for the Brookings Institution in 1936, "met with a degree of operative success which may well command the respect of students of government administration." And a prominent journalist of the period, John Franklin Carter, wrote: "There are more brains and more real ability per pound of human flesh in the agricultural wing of the New Deal than anywhere else. In spite of the hampering effects for a time of George N. Peek, the agricultural wing is performing its prodigious work with more thoroughness and intelligence than is any other department of the Roosevelt Revolution."[8]

III

If the Triple A managed to comb the hair and wash the face of American agriculture, it still left a lot of dirt behind the ears. True to its promise, the new program moved swiftly to raise farm incomes, to reduce farm debt, and, with a big assist from the drought, to trim most surpluses down to manageable size. All the major indexes on the economists' charts in Washington started moving slowly upwards. It was a most encouraging picture until you took a closer look.

Out in the Dust Bowl, farms were blowing away—literally. The thin topsoil of the Plains States, overcultivated for a generation and baked to a fine silt by three years of drought, was being picked up by the winds in black clouds that turned noon to midnight in places like Huron, South Dakota, and spread a gritty, bronzy pall across the sky as far away as New York. Lorena Hickock, on a field inspection tour for Federal Relief Administrator Harry Hopkins in November 1933, told what it was like:

We started out about 8:30 in the morning intending to drive up into the northern part of the county to see some farmers. We had gone less than ten miles when we had to turn back. It kept getting worse. You couldn't see a foot ahead of the car. It was truly a terrifying experience. Like driving in a fog, only worse because of the wind which seemed as if it would blow the car right off the road. It was as though we were being picked up in a vast, impenetrable black cloud which was hurling us right off the earth.

The street lamps were on when we got back to Huron. By noon it was as black as midnight. You couldn't see across the street. It happened to be the worst dust storm they'd had within memory of the oldest inhabitant, and they've been having these storms, less intense ones, every two or three weeks this fall.[9]

Drought and dust storms not only ate up the farms; they ate up the farmers too. Tens of thousands of them—the second-besters, the Woolhats and Rednecks, Negroes and poor whites, who had barely been able to scrape a living out of their small holdings or tenant's shares in even good times—were driven into a hopeless migration to the cities or, like the Okies and Arkies, toward that dubious Promised Land, California. And if it wasn't the drought and the dust storms that set them adrift, it was other kinds of hard times, including the Triple A.

Throughout the domain of King Cotton, from western Texas across the Mississippi Delta and all the way to the Georgia seabord, other tens of thousands—tenants, sharecroppers, and ordinary field hands, the lowliest of the low—were being pushed off the land. White and black, they were the inheritors of the tradition of Southern slavery, living in virtual peonage and tied to other men's land by debt and ignorance. AAA contracts, which the cotton and tobacco planters signed with the government, were supposed to protect the tenants and the croppers—a measure that Frank and his bright young men had fought for. But enforcement was difficult (not a sharecropper sat on a single AAA county committee in the Deep South), and evasion was rife. The owner who had retired a thousand acres of cropland had no need for the eight or ten families who had worked it and who were perpetually in debt for their "furnish" at his commissary. Contract or no contract, they had to go, and there had better not be any trouble about it.

This was the face of the farm problem that people living in the cities saw. Norman Thomas, that indefatigable troublemaker for the unrighteous, was among the first to reveal the picture to the unbelieving gaze of the city dwellers. In the spring of 1934 he went into Arkansas to help organize the Southern Tenant Farmers Union, a sort of peasant uprising that sent the plantation owners and their sheriff's deputies into fear and angry reprisal. The STFU sought to get a fair share of the government bounty for its people and to halt their eviction from the land. Its organizers were beaten up, thrown into jail, or run out of the state. Armed bands of night riders swooped down on isolated cabins and clearings in the pine woods where clandestine union meetings were held. Thomas organized a holy crusade for the STFU and its people, put some of them on exhibition in New York at fund-raising rallies, and recruited young preachers and social workers in the cities to brave the "reign of terror" in Dixie in their behalf. The terror and the violence spread to the sugar-beet harvests in Colorado, to the lettuce fields of Arizona, to the orange groves of California.

Between 1933 and 1937 the nation's conscience was frequently tortured as reporters and magazine writers by the score, playwrights and novelists, preachers and poets, plumbed the depths of misery afflicting a landless American peasantry. Photographer Margaret Bourke-White's shocking picture book, *You Have Seen Their Faces,* sprang to the top of the best-seller lists.

Wisconsin farmers battle for higher prices by dumping milk in roadside ditches.

Troopers and dairy farmers clash in Milk War, spring, 1933.

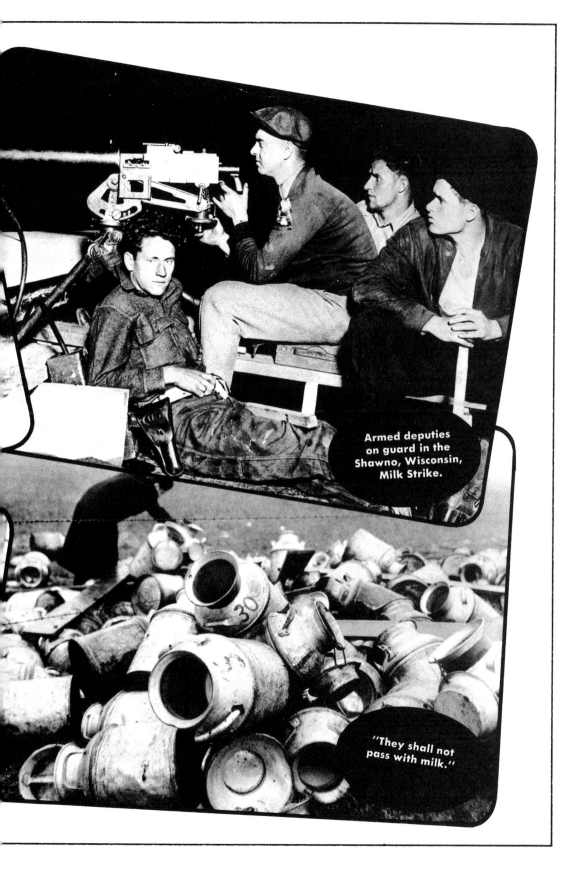

Armed deputies on guard in the Shawno, Wisconsin, Milk Strike.

"They shall not pass with milk."

Preceding pages: (top) Dorothea Lange's *Tractored Out*, Texas Panhandle, 1938. (Middle) Soil erosion in the TVA area, and (bottom) contour farming and terracing to avoid soil erosion, Ventura County, California. (Spread) Arthur Rothstein's *Dust Bowl*, Oklahoma, 1936. (Above) Dorothea Lange's *Hoe Culture*, of Alabama tenant farmer, 1936. At right: (clockwise) Walker Evans' *Sharecropper's Family*, Alabama, 1936; Dorothea Lange's *Sharecroppers*, Alabama, 1937, and *Georgia Tobacco Sharecropper*, 1938; painter and photographer Ben Shahn's *Rehabilitation Client*, Boone County, Arkansas, 1935.

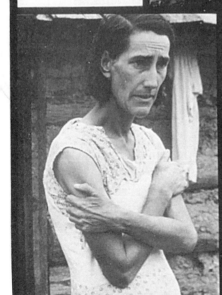

Erskine Caldwell's play *Tobacco Road* had a long run on Broadway and a longer one on the road. Pare Lorentz produced one of the first great film documentaries in *The Plow That Broke the Plains* (1936), and a year later *The River*. Carey McWilliams wrote *Factories in the Field,* while John Steinbeck was honing his anger to a biting edge for his 1939 classic, *The Grapes of Wrath*. The discovery in those years that Pa Lester and the Joad Family and all their countless melancholy tribe were real gave a new and urgent dimension to America's concern for its soul.[10]

IV

Roosevelt's response to the glaring need among destitute farm families (there were at least a million according to official estimates) was the creation in April 1935 of the Resettlement Administration under Tugwell's direction in the Department of Agriculture. It inherited a number of rural programs from the Federal Emergency Relief Administration. In 1937, after the passage of the Bankhead-Jones Farm Tenant Act, its name was changed to Farm Security Administration, but its central purpose remained unchanged. The FSA was empowered to get poor farm families off the relief rolls, to grubstake and hand-carry them, if necessary, until they could achieve self-sufficiency. The RA-FSA was independent of AAA, but in practical terms it was the Triple A's social service arm. It proved to be the New Deal's most daring attempt to create a planned society and the most controversial of all its social experiments.

The program was many-faceted. It provided several types of government loans and grants to enable impoverished but promising farm families to buy and equip small farms outright, or to pay off the debt and upgrade the farms they were already occupying. Their lives meanwhile were to be "programmed" by farm experts and social workers who would show them how to get the best results from their acres, the most nourishment from their food, the greatest mileage out of their dollars.

Many families were literally transplanted, singly or by whole neighborhoods. The FSA simply bought up their worthless land and moved them to where the soil was better and their prospects were brighter. Some ten million acres of marginal farmland was by this process allowed to revert to the groundhogs and jackrabbits and to pass into the national domain.

Many of these families were moved into so-called resettlement communities—clusters of small farms—where they entered into a form of collective society that was totally strange to them, and to most others as well. It was a mixture of Karl Marx and nineteenth-century utopianism, with a subsidy from the national treasury. With government help and government loans, they built their own houses and barns. They formed cooperatives to buy tractors and other heavy equipment for their common use; to operate commissaries and gasoline stations; to market their crops; and to provide prepaid medical services. Startled conservatives said the settlers were being "sovietized."

Another type of community was the subsistence homestead project. It attempted to combine small-scale farming (three to five acres in most instances) with handcrafts and small manufacturing. This project sprang from the romantic vision of tidy little clusters of white cottages set in a scene of rustic repose, each with its kitchen garden, orchard, and cow and chickens, and peopled by a contented peasantry earning its livelihood both from the soil and the machine.

Mrs. Eleanor Roosevelt was so bewitched by the idea that she virtually launched the first subsistence homestead project herself and adopted the program as her own private corner of the New Deal.

That first project was Arthurdale, a fertile tract of 1,200 acres of abandoned farmland with a magnificent setting in the Appalachian highlands of northern West Virginia. The natives living on the hillsides and in the hollows nearby were mostly coal miners who had been stranded and impoverished for years by the closing of the mines. A group of Quakers had begun in a small way to rehabilitate some of the families on small tracts of the good land on the idle Arthur estate and to develop their handcraft skills to provide a minimal cash income. When Mrs. Roosevelt discovered the place in the fall of 1933, she was carried away with the possibility of developing it into a national demonstration of what social idealism backed up by government money could do.

Using her immense zeal and prestige, she badgered various agencies in Washington into taking over Arthurdale from the Quakers and pressing ahead with its development on the double. There would be a hundred or more little houses equipped with plumbing and electricity (luxuries the natives had never known), each on its small plot of ground. A school would be built, a church, a store, and a craft shop, and ultimately a small factory of some sort. Bernard Baruch promised to get a small factory located there as his contribution to fulfilling the great lady's dream. Each family would produce its own food and earn a little cash from weaving, or making hand-sewn bedspreads, or working part time in the factory. After a couple of years they would start paying the government back for its bounty at the rate of $15 or $20 a month.

The happy homesteader, a sympathetic reporter wrote after an early visit to Arthurdale, "would have room, air, fresh food, and a root cellar and a preserve closet for the winter. And he will have opportunity to turn his face to the sky instead of to the earth to watch the long summer wane and the color came to the mountains and the snow fall and pass and the redbuds turn the hills to new splendor instead of being shut away among the slag piles down in the 'holler.' " [11]

There was an unfortunate aspect to such rhapsodies and to Mrs. Roosevelt's enthusiasm for Arthurdale and other homesteads like it that were to follow. They focused the public's attention on the projects and served to magnify the inevitable difficulties encountered in these hastily improvised experiments. Under the glare of critical and often unfair publicity, Arthurdale and its counterparts came to stand as the symbol of the fatuous do-gooder in government.

Arthurdale had problems aplenty, and all of them got into the newspapers. A rush order for the first fifty prefabricated houses resulted in the delivery to the site of fifty frame beach cottages totally inadequate to the sub-zero rigors of a West Virginia winter. Moreover, they did not fit the foundations built for them in advance by local Civil Works Administration workers. Newspapers and magazines delightedly carried pictures of one of the finished houses perched on its foundation with the fireplace and chimney standing nakedly in the open ten feet away from the nearest wall.

Converting the houses boosted their cost from $2,500 to $7,500 each. Squabbles occurred among the tenants, and between the tenants and the project managers, and between the Resettlement Administration (it fell heir to the undertaking in 1935) and the West Virginia authorities. The miners' families had few talents for salable handcrafts; many proved to be indifferent gardeners and had to fall back on county relief for food; and the small assembly plant that General Electric had been induced to set up had jobs for only a handful of the settlers. The plant closed down after a year of unprofitable operations, and another manufacturer had to be found to take its place.

Anti-New Dealers in Congress and the press found Arthurdale and the whole resettlement experiment an inviting target for their jibes. They said it was impractical, wasteful, and even communistic. But Mrs. Roosevelt and her backers in the Administration pressed on dauntlessly. She contributed money earned from her broadcasts and newspaper columns to help equip Arthurdale's community building. She visited the little village frequently, usually with an entourage of reporters, writers, and government officials in tow. She visited in the settlers' homes, bought Christmas gifts for their children, square-danced with them to the tunes of hillbilly fiddlers, and in the summer of 1938 brought her husband out to make the commencement address at the community school.

Arthurdale *had* to succeed, and in a way it did (as did most of the other subsistence projects). After so long a time the settlers began to get the hang of their new way of life, and the misfits and troublemakers were quietly weeded out. They got used to the plumbing and electric refrigerators; their gardens prospered; they added fresh milk and eggs to their diet; and the mask of grime and lethargy disappeared from the children's faces. A hosiery mill moved into the empty factory building, and later a small woodworking plant was added. When the FSA was ordered by Congress to liquidate its interests in the subsistence projects in 1940 (to "sell" them to the residents), Arthurdale had a population of 165 families, or about a thousand persons. All told, the government had spent about $4 million to set them up, and it got back about $200,000, or an average of about $1,800 per house. Thus, it had cost about $20,000 over a six-year period to rehabilitate each family. Whether this was a sound investment, either socially or economically, no one seems to have made a serious effort to discover.

But Arthurdale is still there, a pinpoint on the map. As you swing eastward off State Route 119 between Grafton and Morgantown, there it lies spread out on its rolling, tree-shaded, green plateau. It has not grown or changed perceptibly in more than thirty years. The tidy cottages, each on its spacious plot of ground, look thrifty and well kept. Some have been faced with brick or stone, rooms and porches have been added, television masts have risen from the roofs, and cowsheds have been converted into garages. The residents have long since lost their peculiar identity as homesteaders, as wards of the government. They think and act and make a living just the way their neighbors over the next ridge do. And though most of the "first families" have either died or moved away, Arthurdale still has a lingering flavor, a sort of collective consciousness, of its romantic past.

"I never pass that little white meeting hall without remembering Mrs. Roosevelt—the First Lady—coming in there in a gingham dress and mud on her shoes one night to square dance with the settlers," says James Manchin, who has lived in the neighborhood most of his life. "That was real democracy." [12]

V

The New Deal's agricultural programs—AAA, RA-FSA, and their kindred projects and undertakings—were its boldest and most productive reforms. The Triple A flew in the face of all precedent and tradition to regulate agricultural production at the source and to invoke the power of government to bring about at least a partial redistribution of income for the farmer's benefit. The FSA program, in effect the good conscience of AAA, was a forthright exercise government paternalism toward the individual, a heady foretaste of the welfare state. Both programs came under intense political and ideological fire from the conservative right, but Roosevelt's faith in them did not waver (as it did with NRA), and they survived through many vicissitudes.

By the time AAA was struck down by the Supreme Court in January 1936, the nation's farm economy had made an impressive recovery from the depression trough of 1932–33. Farm prices had risen 66 percent, and farmers' cash income had gone up 58 percent, from $4.3 billion to $6.9 billion. A good part of this affluence was attributable to AAA benefit payments, which aggregated $1.2 billion from 1933 to 1936, and also to the cumulative effects of the drought, which did almost as much as the government to curb overproduction and to raise prices. Farmers in the main adjusted willingly to the regimentation of AAA and, indeed, asked for more.[13]

Not so however with the processors, distributors, and bankers at the business end of the agricultural production line. The AAA was hampering free enterprise, they said, and the farmers' welfare was being paid for out of the profits of the business sector. Scores of suits filed in the courts beginning in 1934 challenged the government's right to regulate agriculture in general and to levy a processing tax in particular. A suit that reached the Supreme Court, *United States* v. *Butler*, involved the Hoosac Mills, Inc., of New Bedford, Massachusetts, which sought the recovery of $86,914 in cotton processing taxes it had paid in 1934, just before going bankrupt.

The Court's affirmative decision, handed down on January 6, 1936, was no surprise; it had been foreshadowed in the case of NIRA. In a six-to-three majority opinion that was remarkable for its narrowness of viewpoint and harshness of language, the Court held that since the Constitution nowhere gave Congress the right to regulate agriculture the imposition of a tax in furtherance of regulation was also unconstitutional. It ordered the restitution

(Above) The way it was! Dorothea Lange's *Ditched, Stalled and Stranded*, San Joaquin Valley, California, 1935. (Inset) Miss Lange's *Damaged Child, Shacktown*, Elm Grove, Oklahoma, 1936. At right: The look of the mid-thirties Deep South. Margaret Bourke-White's tenant shack from *You Have Seen Their Faces.*

of some $200 million in processing taxes. Justice Owen D. Roberts was spokesman for the majority.

In a biting dissent for the minority, Justice Harlan Fiske Stone said that such a "tortured" interpretation of the Constitution would forestall the government's effort in many of its vital areas of operation. There could be no abridgment of the government's right to levy taxes for the general welfare, and the condition of agriculture was clearly a threat to the general welfare. "The suggestion that [the power of the purse] must now be curtailed by judicial fiat because it may be abused by unwise use hardly rises to the level of argument. So may judicial power be abused."

The scuttling of AAA was a smashing triumph for the conservatives. "Perhaps we are witnessing the twilight of the gods of national planning," the Philadelphia *Ledger* gloated. But the triumph was short-lived. Liberals, farm organizations, and the farm bloc in Congress all reacted defiantly. Edward O'Neal of the Farm Bureau Federation said that the six Justices sitting aloof from the world in their new marble palace were "enemies of the people." He urged his constituents to deluge Congress and the press with letters of protest. Senator James F. Pope of Idaho told his colleagues of the Senate: "The

Supreme Court has placed agriculture beyond the reach of Congress. Nature has placed it beyond the power of the states. It seems therefore appropriate to go to the root of the problem, the judiciary, for a solution." He proposed a constitutional amendment to curb the Court's powers—a thought that had already taken shape in a somewhat different form in Roosevelt's mind.[14]

Having anticipated AAA's destruction, Henry Wallace and the President were ready with an alternative. A year earlier Congress had passed the Soil Conservation Act, the aim of which was to check the intolerable wastage of good soil by erosion. It permitted the government to pay farmers either to take endangered cropland out of production or to plant it to nondepleting crops such as grasses and legumes. This act was now dusted off and refurbished as the Soil Conservation and Domestic Allotment Act of 1936, which Congress passed by large majorities late in February. It differed chiefly from the defunct AAA in that the processing tax was eliminated and benefits were paid out of regular Congressional appropriations. The farmer was paid to reduce his acreage *not* as a means of holding down surpluses but to prevent erosion of the land, a fiction that served its purpose quite well for a number of years.

This act of 1936 was supplanted in 1938 with the second Agricultural Adjustment Act, which embodied most of the desirable features of the earlier law and contained, in addition, Wallace's concept of the ever-normal granary (surpluses from times of plenty held against the time of need). Its system of price supports was designed to give the farmer a "parity" income based on the relatively prosperous period of 1909–14. Government protection for the agricultural economy had now been written firmly and irrevocably into the national charter. Today it remains there largely unchanged and in undiminished force.

The FSA had a briefer and more troubled existence, but in terms of human values its record can stand comparison with the Triple A. Up to 1940 it had made short-term rehabilitation loans totaling $475 million (the average was about $500 for each borrower) to 830,000 families, and it had made long-term tenant-purchase loans to 13,600 families. Approximately 15,000 other destitute families had been resettled on 148 community farm and subsistence homestead projects at an over-all cost of $138 million.[15] Happiness and prosperity did not automatically become the lot of all these people. Many were disappointed, dissatisfied. Some were simply incapable of making their own way, or were the victims of too much zeal and too little planning on the part of their government benefactors. In time many slipped back to their previous condition of servitude and dependency. But the majority, it is possible to believe, never went back to Tobacco Road. The FSA gave them a new and reasonably permanent handhold on security and self-respect.

The FSA died a lingering death at the hands of its political enemies. It was condemned for its extravagance, derided for its mistakes and for "coddling" its clientele, and darkly accused of being un-American. Congress directed it to begin in 1938 to liquidate its resettlement projects and to start no new ones. Its appropriations were progressively cut back, and its programs curtailed. In 1944 it was directed to go out of business altogether.

CHAPTER 12
"End Poverty in America"

"People don't eat
in the long run, Senator,
they eat
every day."

—Harry L. Hopkins

ASK ANY MIDDLE-AGED CITIZEN what he remembers most vividly about the New Deal and the chances are that he will say, "The WPA." His memory will have lumped together a number of alphabetized relief and work programs like FERA, PWA, CCC, etc. They were all out of the same bag, but WPA—the Works Progress Administration—was the biggest, costliest, most conspicuous, and most controversial of the lot and came to represent them all in the public mind. A thousand jokes were made about it; a thousand cartoonists penned variations on the theme of the idle "reliefer" leaning on his shovel; and a thousand editorial writers and columnists denounced "boondoggling," "playing politics with relief," and "the weakening of the moral fiber of the underprivileged," which was said to be induced by dependence on "government handouts."

This is a part of the WPA picture that clings today. But many of the middle-aged can embellish the picture with more meaningful detail. To them, WPA also recalls a pleasant park or playground carved out of a stretch of urban wasteland; the first water and sewer lines to be laid in a neglected part of their city; a new brick schoolhouse out in the country; a levee along the riverbank, or murals on the walls of the town library. Such an inventory will evoke for some even more personal experiences, such as six months spent in the forest with the Civilian Conservation Corps; a job with the National Youth Administration that helped them through college; their first exposure to a live theater or symphony orchestra performance, manned by professionals from the WPA rolls; and probably the wages earned on a WPA project when a regular job and steady income seemed as unattainable as riches.

In the seven years from 1933 to 1940 the WPA, with its forerunners and collateral derivatives, became a part of the life of every county, hamlet, and city in the nation. It put nearly $20 billion worth of wages and relief payments into the pockets of the needy. How many people were its beneficiaries will never be known, but they ran to tens of millions. In January-February, 1934, alone, the peak month for the decade as far as government statisticians have been able to figure, there were eight million *households* on the receiving end of this pipeline, which comes out to some twenty-eight million men, women, and children, or approximately one person in six out of the total population. At the low point in the summer of 1937, when things were on the upturn, there still were 4.5 million households getting help. An unduplicated total is impossible to arrive at because people came onto and went off the rolls as fortunes varied and as bureaucratic dictates required. But no one was a stranger to the program. Some families were shielded from it by luck or pride, but many were not. It was a part of daily experience, and it was a major preoccupation of mayors and governors and congressmen and the President. Stories about the program were rarely missing, in one guise or another, in the newspapers.[1]

I

Twelve to fifteen million workers were out of jobs when the New Deal came to power in March 1933. Most of them had been unemployed for as much as a year, and many for three years and longer. Possibly twice that number were subsisting on some form of organized poor relief or charity. About a million youths and men—and some thousands of women and girls—were riding the rails and roaming the highways as migrants; they were flooding into California at the rate of 1,200 day. Their condition was a social catastrophe such as the country had never faced before.

The Hoover Administration had been slow to face up to the realities of unemployment or to attempt anything substantive for its alleviation. This was due less to a callousness of spirit than to a fixation of mind. In the conventional wisdom of that day and generation, destitution was a personal affair, like an accident or sickness, to be dealt with by one's family and friends. A neighbor took a basket of groceries to the unlucky family or paid the rent, and the ladies of the church contributed second-hand clothing and shoes for the children. If there got to be too many of these unfortunates and the local charities broke down, then the city might lend a hand, or even the state. But personal misfortune, however multiplied, was no proper concern of the federal government, and there was the horrifying example of the British "dole" to illustrate what a retreat from that conviction could lead to: erosion of the virtues of self-reliance and a taste for socialism.

"Under our political system," Hoover told Congress in December 1930 in opposing a public works bill, "government is not, nor should it be, a general employer of labor. There are times when private enterprise fails. In such periods society must assume the care of those who are unable to help themselves. The primary obligation is upon the local political division where such conditions exist." [2]

But the notion that joblessness and distress were just a series of local mishaps would not hold. It was everywhere and growing worse. The troubled President, torn between compassion and principle, moved warily to bring relief. In 1931 he launched a prestige-laden President's Emergency Committee on Unemployment to pump new life and urgency into local welfare efforts. With a great outpouring of propaganda, speeches, slogans, and mass meetings the people were urged to double and treble their community chests, or to give a day's salary each month to the local Red Cross or unemployment fund. "Spruce Up," householders were told, by hiring a jobless painter or carpenter, or "Buy Now" instead of laying by for a rainier day.

It was a sincere but futile tugging at the bootstraps, and it yielded next to nothing. As the Depression worsened, more workers were thrown on the streets, more families ran out of savings and credit. Local charities collapsed under the burden of public need, and cities and counties by the score exhausted their revenues and reached the limits of their borrowing power. Families lucky enough to get on the county welfare rolls in Mississippi received as little as $1.50 a week to feed a family of four; in the great city of Philadelphia, families were little better off at $5.50 a week. The veterans' bonus army laid siege to Washington. There were hunger marches in New York and Chicago, and riots in Detroit. Bands of armed miners in Harlan County, Kentucky, plundered company stores to feed their hungry children.

(Top) Cleveland Bonus Veterans commandeer a locomotive after railroad officials refused their request for a freight train for transportation to the Capitol. (Bottom) Father James R. Cox of Pittsburgh, Bonus Army leader, leaving the White House with aides after an interview with President Hoover. (At left) General Douglas Mac-Arthur and his aide (at right) Major Ike Eisenhower were called out by Hoover to take over from embattled Washington Police Chief Pelham G. Glassford, and the Battle of Anacostia Flats was underway. With tanks, infantry, tear gas, and cavalry, Army Chief of Staff MacArthur "pig stuck" the 20,000-strong Bonus Army down Pennsylvania Avenue and out of the city. 7/28/32

(Top) The Bonus Army's "Tent City" along the muddy Anacostia River. (Middle) Bonus Marchers congregate in sight of the White House. (Bottom) Army tanks rumble down Pennsylvania Avenue to help evict Bonus Army squatters from about-to-be-demolished Federal Buildings.

Mount The Barricades

Music by
Carl Sands
(1933)

Dorothea Lange's Gas Station Sign, Kern County, California, 1938.

AIR
AIR
THIS IS YOUR
COUNTRY DONT
LET THE BIG
MEN TAKE IT
AWAY
FROM YOU

(Above) Communist Party members plan White House demonstrations on issues of jobs, fair labor practices, and police brutality. (At left) Hunger Marchers resting on the Capitol grounds after pressing for a $6,000,000 work program. (Below) Marchers pause for a hot *dole* on way to Washington, D.C. (Bottom, left) Writers John Dos Passos and Theodore Dreiser with lawyer Samuel Ornitz after having viewed the Harlan County, Kentucky, Riots.

(Above) Hunger. Demonstra-
tion. And Police Brutality!
New York City, 1930. (Be-
low) Band accompanying
Hunger Marchers pauses in
Baltimore on way to the
Capitol.

By the beginning of 1932 it was clear that private charities and local governments were incapable of meeting the crisis. Only the federal government, with its greater resources and wider taxing powers, could stem the slide into chaos. But how? Panaceas by the score were advanced in the press and in Congress. Some were frightening in their implication and simplistic plausibility. Upton Sinclair was winning thousands of converts in California and elsewhere to his "production for use" platform, which was a virtual abandonment of capitalism for socialism. Huey Long, the Louisiana Kingfish, was inflaming the masses with his bellicose crusade to "share the wealth" and make "Every Man a King." The Hearst newspapers were demanding a bond issue of a mind-boggling $5 billion to finance relief and public works, and a dozen variants of this scheme were gathering momentum in Congress.

Harrassed and troubled almost beyond endurance, Hoover yielded at last, though cautiously, to the heresy of making the federal government an almoner of human needs. In June he signed legislation authorizing $300 million of RFC loans to the states to be used for relief and public works. It was a mere trickle to quench a conflagration that reddened the whole sky, but it was *something*. And more importantly, it was a precedent.

Franklin Roosevelt shared many of Herbert Hoover's misgivings about involving the federal government directly in relief programs for the unemployed. It went against all the doctrines and customs he had grown up with, and it could lead no one knew where. Blithely he had promised in his campaign to balance the budget and to cut government expenditures: this was the conventional remedy for a sick economy, and quite probably he meant it. But without batting an eye (except in pride, since it was his own idea) he launched the CCC during his first few weeks in office to take a quarter million jobless young men off the streets and to pay and support them at government expense to work in the forests and national parks. With only slightly less aplomb he would agree a little later to the inclusion of a $3-billion public works fund in the legislation creating the NRA.

His first unemployment relief bill—sent to Congress in March and signed into law on May 12—created the Federal Emergency Relief Administration and appropriated $500 million for direct grants—not loans—to the states to be used for the jobless and destitute. One half the sum was to be matched by the states on a three-for-one basis, the other half was for outright, no-strings-attached gifts where state resources were too badly strained to meet the matching requirement. Before that first day ended, Harry Hopkins, whom Roosevelt had designated Federal Emergency Relief Administrator, had preempted a desk and telephone in a corridor of the RFC building and "given away $5,000,000," as one impressed reporter wrote for his paper. The federal government was now in the relief business, about ankle deep; within a year it would be up to its knees, or higher.[3]

II

"People don't eat in the long run, Senator, they eat every day." Harry Lloyd Hopkins, a lanky, casually dressed man in his early forties with a long dished face, prominent probing eyes, and the slightly sardonic manner of a bored police court judge who has heard it all before, summed up in that comment his passion for getting on with what had to be done rather than wasting time in analyzing and rationalizing. With an arm slung carelessly over the back of the witness chair at an appropriation hearing, he said, no, he did not think it wise "in the long run" to hold back a part of the relief funds in the hope that employment would soon pick up. The unemployed are hungry and miserable *now,* he insisted, and business statistics aren't going to fill their bellies tomorrow or pay next week's rent.

Harry Hopkins had seen enough of poverty in his lifetime to know what it was. He was born in Grinnell, Iowa. His family was a large one and poor but managed to put him through the hometown college. He fell into social work almost by accident the summer after graduating, with a job at New York's Christadora House, and made a lifetime career of it. During the World War he was a regional director in the South for the Red Cross. He came back to New York to direct a succession of charitable and philanthropic enterprises. In 1932 Governor Roosevelt picked him as director of New York's Temporary Emergency Relief Administration. He had a hand, inevitably, in shaping the New Deal's relief program, and when it became law in May 1933 Roosevelt put him in charge.

Hopkins had the zeal of a reformer, but he refused to wear the hair shirt. He envied the rich and the well-born, enjoyed their attentions, and would have liked to emulate them if he could afford it, which he never could on his government salary. With hundreds of millions of dollars flowing through his hands, he complained once to a reporter about his inability to buy his wife a new winter coat or to move his family out of their drab little rented house in Georgetown. His one extravagance and principal relaxation was betting on the horses. With a handful of his aides, he was a frequent visitor to the race tracks in nearby Maryland and invariably found it administratively necessary to go on an inspection trip to Louisville around the time of Derby Day or to Miami when there was a big card at Hialeah.

But his zeal to fight poverty and hunger seldom relaxed, even at the race track. It was not his job but a cause that relentlessly drove him and the like-minded men and women he brought in to help him: Aubrey Williams, Howard Hunter, Corrington Gill, Ellen Woodward, Jacob Baker, among others. Like him, they were professional social workers or at least oriented in that direction; and also, like him, they were pragmatists who suddenly had the means to do something about destitution on a scale such as had never been dreamed of. To hell with the hand-wringing and the red tape; get on with the job! Hopkins was contemptuous of bureaucratic formalities. He told a visitor from the Budget Bureau that he didn't have time to bother with drawing up an organization chart for FERA, that if the Bureau wanted one it could prepare its own. He kept his headquarters force in Washington to less than two hundred during the first year, housing them in a shabby office building back of the Corcoran Art Gallery—the Walker-Johnson Building, whose doors were warped and whose pervasive odor was that of an insecticide used in a losing battle against an indomitable population of cockroaches. Hopkins' office on the top floor, no larger than a sizeable hotel room, was bleak and untidy, with a collection of hand-me-down government-issue furniture.

Hopkins' blunt speech and occasional bursts of sarcasm soon made him a favorite of the Washington press corps. Asked at a news conference one day if he planned to close down a white-collar relief project in New York, which a newspaper had criticized as a "boondoggle," he snapped:

Why should I? They are damn good projects. You know, dumb people criticize something they do not understand, and that is what is going on up there. God damn it! Here are a lot of people broke and we are putting them to work making researches of one kind or another where the whole material costs 3%, and practically all the money goes for relief. They can make fun of these white collar and professional people if they want to. I am not going to do it. They can say, let them use a pick and shovel to repair streets, when the city ought to be doing that. I believe every one of these research projects are good projects. We don't need any apologies! [4]

On another occasion, when Governor Gene Talmadge of Georgia complained in the newspapers that relief wages were undermining the supply of farm labor in his state, Hopkins fired back: "All that guy is after is headlines. He doesn't contribute a dime, but he's always yapping." He was not intimidated by rank and self-importance.

"Harry has taken Washington by storm although he has offended a lot of politicians and the Tory group is out for his scalp," John Franklin Carter wrote of him in 1934. "He is a man of the deepest human sympathies and one of his chief concerns is to prevent relief work from falling heir to a dull and undiscerning bureaucracy, just as he has insisted that it be kept free of political influence. For he is one of the men who really understands the American experiment and belongs with that select band of men and women who *are* the New Deal." [5]

This was an apt description. Hopkins outlasted nearly all his peers in the New Deal hierarchy, his intimacy with and influence upon FDR growing steadily over the years. With the relief job all but done, he moved into the Cabinet in 1939 and then into his final role as confidential adviser and roving wartime ambassador for the President. Next only to Roosevelt's, no other name evokes so powerfully the turbulent years of the New Deal as his. [6]

III

In Roosevelt's optimistic view the FERA was aptly labeled an emergency operation. He counted on it only to tide the jobless and destitute over until recovery took hold. The principal engines for that were AAA and NRA with a booster in the form of the $3-billion public works appropriation attached to (and shortly to be detached from) NRA. Hopkins and others in the New Deal were less sanguine. Such a massive weight of unemployment could not be caused to evaporate in a season. In fact, he doubted that it ever could be dissipated entirely. Modern technology, he believed, made inevitable a permanent residue of some five to seven million unemployed even with a

revived economy. For years to come the government would have to provide
support for these rejects in one form or another. The simplest and most
conventional means was direct relief, such as that being dispensed by the states
under FERA, which could never be much more than a dole, barely sufficient
to avert acute suffering. But a dole tended to destroy whatever spiritual
resources the recipient had, left him hopeless and resentful, and made him an
object of contempt to his fellows. "Those who are forced to accept charity,
no matter how unwillingly, are first pitied and then disdained," Hopkins said.
"You can pity six men, but you can't keep stirred up over six million." [7] The
solution as he and most other professionals in the field of social service saw
it was work relief—giving the unemployed the opportunity to earn their relief
payments in the form of wages on public work projects.

By midsummer of 1933 it was becoming clear that neither the Blue
Eagle nor any other magic was going to produce recovery and jobs for the
jobless before another winter set in. The economic upsurge that had accompanied the emotional upsurge of the Hundred Days was running out. The
stock market broke precipitously in July, and manufacturing production
turned disappointingly downward. It was also obvious by now that the public
works program was too slow-paced to bring any measurable results before the
following spring. Almost daily there issued from Ickes' office fresh announcements of Public Works Administration projects that had been approved:
great bridges, dams, major highway construction, and the like. He noted with
pride in his diary one day that it had been "a great day for public works."
He had authorized the purchase of 100,000 tons of rails for the nation's railroads and simultaneously approved an $80-million project to complete elec-
trification of the Pennsylvania Railroad between Washington and Wilmington. [8]
What he failed to mention was that many months would pass before these
complex undertakings would be translated into jobs for the unemployed; also,
their ratio of material cost to manpower was so high as to make their impact
on the mountain of unemployment relatively weak. Harold Ickes was a prudent
man with a dollar. In his view PWA was meant chiefly to prime the pump of
the capital goods market, and benefits to the jobless would come as a by-
product. It would take time, and it was "sound," and other prudent men agreed
with him.

Harry Hopkins was unschooled in economics and government finance,
but he knew enough about poverty to have no faith in what he called the
"trickle-down theory" as a palliative for mass destitution. He believed in a
"trickle-up theory": Put money in the hands of the poor and it will quickly
soak upward and nourish the roots of the whole economic structure.

As autumn waned and winter approached—a winter that would turn
out to be as savage as any in history—Hopkins went to Roosevelt with a
staggering proposal. He wanted to put four million unemployed men and
women to work immediately for wages to be paid entirely out of the federal
treasury. They would be employed on public projects that could be organized
quickly: repairing roads and streets, refurbishing run-down schools and other

public buildings, teaching the illiterate and the unskilled, working as helpers in public offices, etc. They would be paid regular wages for their work instead of being given a relief handout. Hopkins was passionate and persuasive. He was armed with facts and figures and the opinions of experts. He handed the President a yellowed newspaper clipping to prove that organized labor would back away from its doctrinal objection to large-scale government works: Samuel Gompers, the patron saint of the working man, had proposed just such a program during the "panic" of 1898.

Roosevelt was impressed, at least to the extent of trying the experiment through the winter. He picked up a pencil and doodled briefly on a pad. "Let's see," he said, "four million people—that means roughly four hundred million dollars. I guess we could take that out of the public works fund and not have to ask Congress for a separate appropriation." Hopkins left the White House an hour later, "fairly walking on air," as he said. He put in a call for Aubrey Williams, who had helped to devise the plan, and interrupted him in the middle of a speech he was making in New Orleans to tell him the good news.[9]

On November 9, a little more than a week after his talk with Hopkins, Roosevelt issued an Executive Order setting up the Civil Works Administration. Its working capital was the $400 million transferred from PWA plus $80 million of left-over FERA funds. At the same time governors and mayors were invited to Washington for a briefing on the new program. They showed up a few days later almost a thousand strong. The CWA, it was explained, would be virtually an all-federal program with communities putting up about 10 percent of the project costs for material. FERA was all but suspended, and state and local relief administrations would in most instances be transferred to federal jurisdiction to run CWA. Quotas would be allowed to each state, depending upon need. Roughly half the four million jobs were to go to persons already on relief, and half to those unemployed who were in need but had managed to stay off the relief rolls. Wage scales for a thirty-hour week would range from 40¢ to 50¢ an hour for unskilled labor, from $1 to $1.20 for skilled labor, and from $12 to $18 weekly for white-collar workers. (This was a cut above the minimums set in most NRA codes, a fact that was to cause trouble later.) The aim, Hopkins said, was to put four million people to work before Christmas. It was up to the governors and mayors to hustle up useful projects for them to go to work on.

The instant reaction of state and local authorities to CWA was almost wholly favorable. For most of them unemployment was their worst dilemma. They had seen at first hand the misery of their own people—the slow erosion of pride and spirit as they lined up for relief checks and grocery orders. Now the federal government was about to move against this quagmire of despair in a more meaningful way. Lights burned late in city halls and statehouses all across the country as officials worked feverishly to put the new program into effect.

"The striking thing about this employment program," a correspondent wrote in *The New York Times* from Omaha in late November, "has been the alacrity of the response by local communities to submit projects and the speed with which they have been approved and men put to work. The rate at which working gangs are being organized makes it a certainty that by the end of this week at least 6,000 of Nebraska's quota of 27,750, and 10,000 of Iowa's 50,000 quota, would be on the payroll." Another correspondent reported from Dodge City: "The sudden shift of 40,000 men and women from pauperism to employment at a living wage has transformed the relief situation in Kansas."

The reaction was the same almost everywhere. As the word went out to the unemployed that paychecks instead of relief checks were the new order of the day, they descended in droves on the employment centers to apply for work. Many who had fought against going on relief now applied for it in the belief that this would improve their chances of being picked for a CWA job. Schoolteachers, bank tellers, shoe clerks, or craftsmen who had not drawn a salary for a year or more competed with bricklayers, truck drivers, and laborers for whatever the CWA had to offer.[10]

Most of what it had to offer was pick-and-shovel work or its equivalent. There was no time to devise and engineer projects efficiently nor to match the skills of workers to available jobs. But there were potholes aplenty in the streets and highways that needed fixing, sewers that were clogged or overloaded, leaky roofs on county buildings, parks that had been surrendered to underbrush and decay, and, yes, leaf-raking even where there weren't many leaves to be raked. "Leaf-raking" entered the vocabulary for a time as a derisive synonym for time-wasting, put there by people who were out of sympathy with CWA. They were the same ones who wrote indignant letters to the editor when they saw fifty-man work gangs grading a stretch of road with hand shovels and wheelbarrows while bulldozers and other power equipment that could have done the job faster and cheaper stood idle.

CWA was, indeed, a massive exercise in improvisation, a mad race with the weather and the clock. There were boondoggles aplenty. A research team in New York delved into the history of the safety pin. A hundred-man squad in Washington patrolled downtown streets with toy balloons on long strings to frighten away the vast flocks of starlings that had for years roosted noisily and untidily on the ledges of government buildings. But there were solid accomplishments as well. Over 250,000 miles of roads and streets were repaired, over 1,000 airfields built or improved, some 50,000 teachers put into understaffed schools, and adult education programs established. Millions of old public records and documents were rescued from the hazards of fire and decay, cleaned up, and catalogued. Thousands of artists, actors, and musicians were hired to put their talents on free public display. Critics scoffed at the makeshift arts program, but Hopkins was not moved. "Hell, they have to eat just like other people," he said.

CWA was forbidden to make improvements on private property, but one conspicuous exception was granted. Under the sponsorship of the Public Health Service 150,000 outdoor privies, conforming to the most modern specifications for such structures, were erected in backyards all through the rural South, where plumbing was a rarity and typhoid and like diseases were endemic. A rustic comedian of the day, one "Chic" Sale, achieved a rich but fleeting fame with a booklet called "The Specialist," in which he discoursed upon the mechanics and social advantages of one design as against another.

Even as CWA won plaudits for its boldness and speed in aiding the unemployed, charges that the program was shot through with corruption and politics mounted. A project supervisor in Washington was jailed for taking kickbacks from his staff; another, in Pennsylvania, went to trial for taking commissions from suppliers of materials. In Los Angeles a grand jury was impaneled to investigate charges of fraud. In hundreds of communities there were complaints that local officials were screening job applicants according to their political loyalty. Congressmen and senators protested to the White House and to Democratic Chairman Jim Farley that they were being ignored by Hopkins in the appointment of administrators and other top officials in their states. Hopkins conceded that there was a disturbing incidence of graft and corruption in a program so hastily thrown together, and that his own investigators had uncovered many examples. In February he sent fifteen such cases to the Department of Justice for prosecution. But he angrily denied there was any politics as far as the headquarters organization was concerned, and wherever it did exist it had been injected against his instructions by local officials.

CWA not only met but exceeded its job goal. A million men had been put to work in the first two weeks of operation. The total reached 4,264,000 by mid-January 1934. The sudden expansion of buying power in some poorer communities left shoe stores and grocery shelves almost bare. One hundred eighty thousand projects were approved. The program was scheduled to end February 15, for that was as far as its original grant of money would take it. But the prospect brought cries of protest from local officials, and the unemployed organized mass meetings and sent delegations to their mayors and governors pleading for CWA to be continued. These arguments were bolstered by the weather. The winter of 1933–34 was one of the most brutal on record. In February a vast wave of arctic air blanketed most of the nation, and deep snows blocked highways and railroads as far south as Georgia. The temperature plummeted to sixteen degrees below zero in Chicago, fourteen below in New York, eight below in Washington. Cattle on the Western range froze into icy statues, and forty persons died of exposure. Millions still lived in poverty too acute to afford adequate clothing or fuel to heat their homes.

Roosevelt asked Congress for $345 million to extend the life of CWA to April, and Congress responded with alacrity. The job program was to be tapered off by that time, and relief under FERA resumed. For this purpose the appropriation bill included $500 million.

In spite of its blunders and the knocks it had accumulated, CWA had been a stirring and valuable experience for the nation. "When the history of the New Deal is written," the *Literary Digest* observed late in March, "one of the most amazing chapters will be about the CWA. A billion dollars was thrown headlong into every part of the country. The permanent improvements it bought are to be seen in the thousands of miles of improved roads and bridges, the parks and schools. . . . It was a courageous experiment on a heroic scale."

Looking at it in retrospect some years later, Hopkins said:

The whole story of CWA can never be written. Set up to cover local and unique situations, it had infinite variety. Minor details of the problems or of the inventiveness which they were dealt with adhere to the minds of those widely scattered persons who participated in that winter's program. It touched actively between twenty and thirty million people who followed its ambitions, its successes, failures and gossip with pride and anxiety. . . .

For awhile it was the habit to ask about CWA, was it a success or wasn't it a success? In the relief business where our raw material is human misery and our finished product nothing more than amelioration, effectiveness has to be measured in less ambitious terms than success. That word applied better to marginal profit, material or otherwise. Relief deals with human insolvency.[11]

IV

No one was particularly pleased in the spring of 1934 by the return to the old system of the dole and the free market basket. Recipients who had had a taste of earning their keep were made resentful, and the communities got little in return for what they paid out. Friction between Washington and the state capitals over money, policies, and politics took on a sharper, angrier note. When Illinois legislators refused to appropriate $3 million monthly to match FERA grants, Hopkins shut off the federal spigot and threw the state's relief program into temporary paralysis. He charged Governor Martin L. Davey of Ohio with shaking down relief contractors and suppliers for political contributions and fired the top men Davey had put in control of the state's relief program. Davey retaliated by suing the FERA administrator for criminal libel. Hopkins fought with Governor Talmadge of Georgia and others in the South over their contention that relief scales were upsetting the farm labor market, which they were indubitably doing in a system where cotton field hands were traditionally paid five and ten cents an hour. There was a parallel clamor froom the urban North: employers of household and common labor complained they could not entice workers away from the relief rolls. "Some of these guys just can't stand to see other people making a decent living," Hopkins said contemptuously.

Relief was getting a bad name all across the country. It was reflected in cartoons and editorials and political speeches. The economy had picked up again and was moving slowly forward. Businessmen, no longer fearful that the roof would fall in, sternly demanded that the government withdraw its hand and stop wasting the taxpayers' money. The newly formed Liberty League, with its roster of gilt-edged reactionaries, was denouncing the heresies of the New Deal at expensive dinners and in large newspaper advertisements. " 'That Man' is bleeding the country white" was a safe conversational opener among the country-club set in almost any community. Republicans began to take heart that they might start their party back on the road to solvency in the November elections. And Democratic leaders like Jim Farley and Vice President Garner were urging the President to ease up on New Deal reforms and spending "to give the country a breathing spell."

It seemed to be an unpropitious time to try to launch the Administration on another huge attack against unemployment, but that was the risk Hopkins took. Backed up by such influential colleagues as Ickes, Morgenthau, Tugwell, and Perkins, he sketched out the scheme on a visit in November to the President at Warm Springs, where FDR was vacationing. The goal, he explained, was to replace relief by a permanent works program, which was to be a return to the CWA concept but strengthened in scope and substance by adaptation of some of the PWA standards. The federal government would provide jobs for as long as they were needed to three or four million *employ-ables* on the relief rolls, and turn back to local authorities responsibility for the one or two million *unemployables* (the aged and others who could not work). Fulfillment of the program would involve practically all of the construction and emergency job-giving resources of the government: highways, dams, rural power lines, soil conservation, and public housing—in other words, public works both large and small, including projects for women and the white-collar classes. It was a revolutionary proposal in that it formally recognized unemployment as a durable and not a transitory phenomenon, and its cost was to be reckoned in the billions of dollars, not millions.

Delbert Clark of *The New York Times,* getting wind of what Hopkins and his colleagues were cooking up, wrote that the program was of such a magnitude that it might properly be labeled "End Poverty in America" (EPIA), an acknowledged steal from Upton Sinclair's "End Poverty in California." But the framers resisted the temptation. It would be thirty years before another President would acknowledge reaching out for so ambitious a goal.

Roosevelt was impressed. He was in an expansive mood, for the New Deal had just won a substantial vote of confidence at the polls in the Congressional elections. He was of a mind to spit in the eye of the Liberty League and other counselors of caution. He told Hopkins to get all of his ideas down on paper in readiness for Congress in the new year. Back in Washington Hopkins exulted to Williams and Gill and other intimates at FERA: "Boys—this is our hour. We've got everything we want—a works program, social security, wages and hours, everything—now or never. Get your minds to work on developing a complete ticket to provide security for all the folks of this country up and down across the board." [12]

Hopkins' elation was not misplaced. Roosevelt's State of the Union Message delivered to Congress on January 4, 1935, was a rousing affirmation of the social objectives of the New Deal. In an industrial society, he said, security for the individual becomes an obligation of government which must be secured by pensions for the aged, unemployment insurance, and jobs instead of charity for workers made idle by conditions over which they have no control.

"The federal government must and shall quit this business of relief," the President declared. "I am not willing that the vitality of our people be further sapped by the giving of cash or market baskets, of a few hours of weekly work cutting grass, raking leaves or picking up papers in public parks. We must preserve not only the bodies of the unemployed from destitution but also their self-respect, their self-reliance and courage and determination."

Roosevelt's plan called for the liquidation of FERA and the lumping of all emergency work activities within a single agency. He asked a staggering $4.8 billion to put the plan in operation but was sketchy on the details of how it was to be used. He had asked, in fact, for another "blank check," this one of unprecedented size, and the Senate balked in angry, wordy rebellion. Neither Hopkins nor Ickes, called to testify before the Appropriations Committee, could shed much light on what specific priorities the President had in mind. If FDR himself knew at that point, he had not shared the knowledge with the two men who presumably would be his chief deputies in the matter. After more than two months of wrangling, however, the Emergency Relief Appropriation Act of 1935 was passed on March 23 by substantial and skeptical majorities.

The structure of the new agency to administer the works program was an unbelievably clumsy one. Roosevelt had set the overall design. He wanted a super works agency through which all of the government's emergency construction and work relief efforts, including public housing and the newly created Rural Electrification Administration, would be channeled. Ickes and Hopkins were then called on to fill in the details. By this time they were secretly working at cross purposes with one another. Each sought ascendancy in the program, not only personally but for their widely differing ideas of how the program should work.

Ickes, a man who valued a dollar and had almost a fetish about the public trust, favored conventional, large-scale public works from which the government would realize at least a partial return on its investment. Such works would stimulate industry, from whence the benefits would flow downward and outward to create both "primary" and "secondary" employment. He reckoned that one new man put to work on a dam in Colorado would mean the hiring of another steel worker in Pittsburgh, a coal miner in West Virginia, and, say, a railroad section hand in Illinois. That was the scheme of the Public Works Administration; it was economically sound; and it had "never been touched by scandal." He defended it stoutly.

Hopkins, the social worker, was distrustful of this kind of reasoning. Big public works were all right as far as they went, he reasoned, but it took too long for the benefits to trickle down to where they were most needed, and too much was drained off along the way for materials and overhead. The most that PWA had claimed to date in direct employment was 800,000, and Hopkins was skeptical about the alleged three-to-one secondary benefits. He wanted the principal emphasis put on a multiplicity of small, flexible projects that could be spotted where the unemployed were and would put most of the cost directly into their pockets as wages.

The difference in outlook between these two stubborn and opinionated advocates was, in essence, whether to lance the patient's boil first or to give him some medicine to purify the bloodstream. In consequence, the separate recommendations they turned in to the President were sprinkled with innocent-looking loopholes and deceptive bypasses. What emerged in synthesis was a cumbersome, top-heavy bureaucracy of hopeless ambiguity and dubious effectiveness.

The President sat at the top of a pyramid called the National Works Authority. Next below him was a Division of Application and Information, to which all proposals for expenditures out of the works fund (a score of different agencies were entitled to a bite at it) were sent for initial "screening." Its chief was the genial onetime Postmaster General Frank W. Walker, presumed to be a neutral in the works controversy. From here the proposals were routed to an Advisory Committee on Allotments (an unwieldy seventeen-man board with Ickes as Chairman) for further study; those approved by the committee were recommended to the President for acceptance. Finally, a Works Progress Division (later changed to Administration), with Hopkins as its chief, was charged with a vague assortment of reporting, recommending, and advisory functions and, almost incidentally it seemed, the right to "recommend and carry out small useful projects designed to assure a maximum of employment in all localities." Here was a major Hopkins loophole that Ickes had failed to close. In short order Hopkins would widen that WPA loophole to make it look like the big front door.

The feud that now developed between Harry Hopkins and "Honest Harold" Ickes was one of the longest and lustiest of the New Deal. Both were strongly opinionated chip-on-the-shoulder scrappers. Each was jealous of the other's proximity to the President. Ickes, almost twenty years older than Hopkins, had won his stripes as a liberal battling for reform in Cook County, Illinois, and in the national arena as a Bull Mooser and LaFollette Progressive. He turned Democrat to support Al Smith in 1928 and went down the line for Roosevelt at Chicago in 1932. He was a moderately successful Chicago lawyer, once a partner of Donald Richberg, but reform politics had absorbed as much of his time as the law. Roosevelt took an instant liking to him the first time they met, which was early in 1933, and asked him on the spot to be his Secretary of the Interior.

Ickes was Pennsylvania Dutch by birth and temperament. He was a bit under medium height, compactly built with a large head set on wide, slightly stooping shoulders. His expression was dour, unsmiling, with eyes peering skeptically over the top of rimless spectacles, and he looked every inch the "Self-made Curmudgeon"—an epithet he applied to himself in a sort of reverse vanity. His speech was pungent, to the point, and often laced with a dry, bucolic humor. He had a sort of Calvinist morality that abhorred pretense and elevated the virtues of caution and frugality. After an early inspection tour of his new domain at the Interior Department he issued a general order that no pencil stub longer than three inches was to be discarded. Hunched unsmilingly over his desk with his fingers entwined imperturbably before him, he looked very much like a small-town banker who wanted to know only one thing: How good is the collateral? These qualities endeared him to FDR and to most of his colleagues in the New Deal, who, at the same time, were often irritated by them.

In the controversy over the works fund Hopkins found him wholly exasperating, and Ickes returned the compliment. "He is stubborn and righteous, which is a bad combination," Hopkins said of his adversary. "He bores me." And Ickes, confiding to his diary, fumed: "I am thoroughly convinced that he [Hopkins] is a lawless individual bent on building up a reputation for himself as a great builder [through WPA] even at the expense of the President and the country. I think he is the greatest threat today to the President's reelection."[13]

The Hopkins-Ickes feud was a popular year-round spectacle in Washington. Reporters attending their frequent press conferences could nearly always trigger a barbed comment or two to spice up a dull day's news. The same reporters covered both men (the two officers were within shouting distance of one another at the intersection of Eighteenth Street and New York Avenue), and they acted unashamedly as talebearers between the two. The feud was becoming an annoyance and political embarrassment to the President. A showdown was not long in coming.

The central goal of the program from the outset had been to put 3.5 million men to work at once. By September something less than two million jobs had been created by all the participating agencies combined, including PWA and WPA. Clearly, the goal would not be reached at this pace before another hard winter set in. The creaking administrative machinery was mainly to blame, but, while it creaked and groaned indecisively, Hopkins was able to scoop off a sizable share of the project approvals for WPA, about $750 million worth all told. PWA had done less well, partly because Hopkins had managed to have some 2,000 of its applications rejected because of the high ratio of the cost of materials to labor costs. While wages were approximately the same for workers under both programs, it cost about $330 to produce a man-month of employment under PWA as against an average of only $82 under WPA.

In mid-September the President at last called the warring fractions together at Hyde Park. After a long day of scratch-pad arithmetic it was discovered that of the original $4.8 billion appropriated for the works program, only $1.2 billion remained unallocated. How best to use this to provide a year's work for the remaining 1.5 million jobless? With little hesitation Roosevelt gave the lion's share—$1 billion—to Hopkins and $200 million to Ickes. With its previous commitment, WPA thus got by far the largest slice of the pie—$1.7 billion—and PWA's slice was a modest one of less than $500 million.

Ickes was crushed. He was "sore and discouraged," he said, and "didn't leave Hyde Park in a very pleasant frame of mind." Hopkins was delighted. WPA had come out top dog, and he meant to keep it that way.[14]

V

WPA was an astonishingly vital, vulnerable, many-faceted operation. It was more than just a New Deal device to make jobs for the jobless. It was a major phenomenon—the symbol and principal engine of the New Deal social revolution. During the last few years of the decade, as the dynamic of reform slowed down and the focus of political concern turned outward toward the troubled horizons of Europe and Asia, the WPA stood as a still viable token of what the New Deal had been all about, an unwelcome but indispensable reminder that the Depression was still upon us. And its head, Harry Hopkins, was now firmly established in the top rank of the New Deal hierarchy. He was not only a trusted adviser to the President, as Moley and Louis Howe had been, but also enjoyed the warm friendship of Franklin and Eleanor Roosevelt. He was a frequent drop-in guest in the family quarters of the White House.

WPA quickly became one of the biggest bureaucracies in government, its arms reaching into every state capital and practically every country courthouse in the land. It was the biggest spender, and each day it touched directly and personally the lives of more people than any other agency of government, save only the postal system! Its political potential was formidable. Its familiar red, white, and blue project signs were everywhere—along the roadside, in a schoolyard, at a street excavation, outside a public health clinic, maybe in an alcove of the city library. The people who worked *for* it (the administrative personnel) and the people who worked *on* it were a cross section of any middle-class neighborhood. They were not on relief, and that was a gain. There was a certain social acceptability about WPA, and the wages might be just as good as on a comparable job in private employment.

Not everybody approved of it. Some wondered why, with conditions getting better all the time, it was necessary for the government to put out all this money—"taxpayer's money." Wasn't it possibly true that a lot of these people were just loafers getting a free ride? That many of the projects were trifling, inefficient boondoggling? That the politicians had their hands in it all the way up to the elbow? That was what the papers said, most of them anyway, and there was lot of talk about it, pro and con, over a beer at the tavern or at the dinner table. But like it or lump it, most people recognized that if there were no WPA something very much like it would have to be invented.

WPA was patterned after the CWA, but with a number of modifications —some good, some bad. Ninety percent of its workers had to be employables from the relief rolls. (Or so the regulations read. Many local officials palmed off their unemployables on WPA, thus cutting down the county's relief bill, and left the employables to shift for themselves.) The result was a generally inferior work force. About three-fourths of the workers were unskilled or semi-skilled.

They were paid (acording to regulations that were frequently evaded) a "security wage" based roughly on wages prevailing in the community for comparable work. With a maximum thirty hour week, this averaged out nationally to between $50 and $60 a month, about 20 percent above the old relief level. By contemporary standards this was a living wage in most communities (if the family wasn't too big), "good money" in others.

Local sponsors (public bodies) were required to put at least 10 percent of a project's cost, as under CWA, but standards of performance and utility were generally tightened. Bigger, better-planned projects were favored, but leaf-raking could not be wholly eliminated. There were provisions for a number of federally sponsored projects that could be operated uniformly across state lines.

Hopkins vastly enlarged his headquarters staff (it overflowed three sizable buildings), installed a regional organization to speed up administration, and instituted a series of research and statistical studies into the phenomena of unemployment. As with CWA, state and local WPA administrators were on the federal payroll and answerable to Washington. This was a reach for good management, but it netted almost as much political grief as administrative efficiency.

Hopkins was a good if unorthodox administrator considering the complex and inherently chaotic domain over which he presided. He brought in scores of competent deputies to assist him—engineers, economists, lawyers. Though the social impulse of WPA remained dominant, the social worker atmosphere disappeared from the Walker-Johnson Building. He attracted the intense loyalty of the people around him, down to messengers and stenographers; they felt bound together in a common cause that was tinged, for some at least, with the emotional excitement of a crusader.* He tried conscientiously to keep his program immune to political interference. When he found that it could not be done (the deck was stacked against him by 1936), he played the game with the subtle craftsmanship of an expert.

From the summer of 1935 to the end of 1940 WPA spent over $10 billion, about 80 percent of it in wages. It provided jobs for an average of 2,112,000 persons in each of those years, hitting a peak of 3,330,000 in November 1938, and a low of 1,450,000 in September of the previous year. Altogether, about 8,000,000 persons—one-fifth of the nation's labor force—worked on WPA projects at one time or another in that period. Of the thousands of individual projects approved, some 75 percent were for construction, and 25 percent in the community service category.[15]

Their variety was infinite: airports, sewing rooms, schoolhouses, outhouses, flood control, dry land irrigation, and the construction or improvement of parks, roads, streets, bridges, sewers, and water lines. WPA workers built LaGuardia Airport in New York and the elaborate municipal recreation center in San Francisco's Aquatic Park; salvaged the riverfront in St. Louis; sealed thousands of abandoned coal mines in Kentucky and West Virginia to prevent the seepage of sulphuric acid into the creeks and rivers; excavated

*The writer worked in the Press Section of WPA and for a time as information director for the National Youth Administration between 1936 and 1939. Previously he had covered relief and similar activities in Virginia as a reporter for the Richmond *Times-Dispatch.*

Indian mounds in Georgia and New Mexico; took over the entire municipal function of the bankrupt and desolated city of Key West, Florida. WPA workers taught illiterates to read, served hot lunches to schoolchildren, cared for the indigent sick at home and in clinics, re-bound books for libraries, tidied up old tax and land records. They wrote and published the monumental *American Guide* series, gave a wholly new impetus to the dissemination and popularization of American art, created dozens of concert and symphony orchestras, and infused the American theater with new blood and ideas.

The record was marred by many failures and blunders. Some road jobs disintegrated with the first freeze, bridges buckled, sewers were laid upgrade, playgrounds were built where there were no children to use them, buildings were botched by incompetent mechanics, surrealistic paintings and "salacious" plays offended prim local sensibilities. There was leaf-raking in many guises. The plentiful boondoggles were assiduously tracked down and exploited for all they were worth by anti-New Deal newspapers and politicians. Congressional committees probed for evidence of waste and inefficiency, and the House Un-American Activities Committee combed the professional projects for subversive influences. "Now this [Christopher] Marlowe," the Hon. Joe Starnes of Alabama asked Hallie Flanagan, director of the Federal Theater Project, in the course of one such inquiry, "is he a communist type too?"

The charge of "politics" cast an even more damaging and more credible blemish on the WPA record. Much of it was spiteful exaggeration of isolated occurrences, much of it simply was not true, but enough of it was true to keep the New Deal constantly on the defensive. Here and there local Democratic bosses did dispense WPA jobs as patronage, extorted political contributions from the workers, or monopolized the administrative jobs and supply contracts for their relatives and friends. Time and again newly paved roads reached only as far as the county commissioner's gate; obscure park projects turned out to be private landscaping; job training programs carried out with a "cooperative" local plant owner were used as a blind to thwart unionization. WPA "scandals" became daily newspaper fare as the political climate heated up during and after the 1936 election.[16] Thomas L. Stokes, a greatly respected political columnist for the Scripps-Howard newspapers, won a Pulitzer prize in 1938 for a series of stories on how the reelection of Kentucky's Senator Alben Barkley was "bought with WPA votes."*

Hopkins did what he could to squelch petty politicking at the expense of the ordinary WPA worker. He reminded the workers often, in public statements and in notices attached to their paychecks that their political beliefs were their own business, that no one had a right to tell them how to vote or to solicit them for political contributions. He reprimanded or fired scores of minor officials for infractions of his no-politics rules. During

---

*The Hatch Act of 1939 was a direct outgrowth of these occurrences. It forbade federal employees to participate in any form of political activity for elective offices.

his FERA and CWA days he had been equally severe with governors, mayors and other high level politicos. They owed him nothing, he owed them nothing; he could tell them to go to hell with impunity. But the potentialities for spoils in WPA were too vast and too tempting to be long denied. Governors wanted their own men in the top jobs, and a bigger say in how things were run in their states. They complained to their senators and to Jim Farley. "The WPA is still impossible to local Democrats," a party leader in Michigan wrote Farley in 1936. "For months they have been going over the heads of local committeemen making appointments of Republicans." Farley passed the letter to Hopkins with a reminder that, along with good works, the New Deal also had to win elections.

If Hopkins could give the brush-off to governors and mayors, he could not behave so cavalierly to senators and congressmen. He was locked into this accommodation by an amendment to the 1936 appropriation act that called for Senate confirmation of all appointees earning $5,000 or more. This meant that the state administrators and most of their chief deputies were drawn under the patronage blanket. To get and keep the kind of men he wanted in those jobs—indeed, to get the kind of appropriations and administrative freedom he needed—called for some expert wheeling and dealing on the part of the onetime social worker. He made the transition with less difficulty and distaste than he anticipated.

"I thought at first I could be completely non-political," he told a friend later. "Then they told me I had to be part non-political and part political. I found that was impossible, at least for me. I finally realized there was nothing for it but to be all-political."[17]

Hopkins' politicking within WPA was of the strategic variety such as men wise in the art have always employed and secretly respect. If a key member of the Appropriations Committee wanted an airport in his district as his price for a favorable vote, he was likely to get it. If there was a choice of candidates for a salaried post, the Democratic senator's nephew could be considered a shoo-in. If the launching of a big new project in Buckeye County could be timed to coincide with the reelection announcement of Buckeye's friendly Congressman, it probably would be done. The reciprocal favor subtly rendered, Hopkins was quick to learn, is the best lubricant of political intercourse.

Hopkins was painted black—and occasionally Red—by the Republican opposition and the gentry of the Liberty League. But all things considered, he ran his huge, sprawling program with a firm and efficient hand. WPA did not cure unemployment (it took a war to do that), nor did it "end poverty in America," but it did greatly alleviate the distress of poverty.

Time has obliterated most of the monuments WPA left behind, or at least the awareness of why and by whom they were built. Its more enduring epitaph might be that it preserved an immeasurable share of the nation's human resources—the skills, the self-respect, even the loyalty of some millions of American men and women. Measured against its background of crisis, it performed superbly.

In 1939 Harry Hopkins was named Secretary of Commerce. The Works

Progress Administration, its name changed to Work Projects Administration, was incorporated into the new Federal Works Agency, which was headed by Howard O. Hunter. The Federal Works Agency's activities and importance dwindled after 1940 as war preparations speeded up and industry began to absorb the unemployed. It was abolished by act of Congress in 1942.[18]

The Public Works Administration under Harold Ickes played a secondary role throughout its history in providing work relief, but its contribution to the national inventory of public structures was substantial. From 1933 to 1939 its grants and loans helped to build some 70 percent of the nation's new schools, 65 percent of its new courthouses and city halls, 35 percent of its new hospitals. It made possible the construction of Manhattan's Triborough Bridge, the completion of Boulder Dam, and the development of the port city of Brownsville, Texas. It gave the Navy the aircraft carriers *Yorktown* and *Enterprise,* rehabilitated a score of Army camps, and built more than fifty military airports. In the end Ickes surmounted his frustrations with Hopkins and was justly proud of the relatively trouble-free record of PWA.[19]

VI

The National Youth Administration (NYA), an important adjunct of WPA, was set up to meet the educational and economic needs of young people whose careers had been blocked by the Depression even before they could get a start. A needy youngster looking for work in the nineteen-thirties was constantly confronted by this exasperating paradox: You can't get a job without experience, and you can't get experience without a job. Young people were coming into the labor market at the rate of 1,750,000 a year. More than two-thirds of them went a year or more without finding a job. In 1935 those in the sixteen to twenty-four age bracket (some three to four million) represented about a third of the total unemployed. Unable to continue their education, they haunted employment offices, loafed disconsolately about their impoverished homes and on street corners, or took to the road as migrants.*

The Civilian Conservation Corps offered an escape for male youths who were physically and temperamentally adaptable to life in the forest. CCC enrollment was limited, averaging about 300,000 in most years. It offered a little something in job training, but considerably less for the continuation of formal education. It was, of course, closed to girls.

NYA was authorized in the Emergency Relief Appropriation Act of 1935. It had a semi-autonomous status under the WPA. Its national director was Aubrey W. Williams, Hopkins' chief deputy. Williams was a tall, rawboned Alabamian with a seamed and kindly face and the confidence-inspiring

---

*It is interesting to note that college enrollment did not decline during any of the Depression years, it rose steadily from 924,275 in 1930 to 1,350,905 in 1938. In part this is attributable to normal population increase and in part to a general lowering of tuition and other costs. It is also probable that many young people, despairing of getting a job after high school, made an extra effort to go to college to avoid idleness. The largest increase occurred between 1935 and 1938, which may reflect the influence of the NYA student aid program.

manner of a small-town family doctor. He started out to be a preacher after college and two years in the American Expeditionary Forces, but he became a social worker instead. His blunt honesty in speaking out against the social ills of the day made him almost as bright a target of the political right as Hopkins.

The principal thrust of NYA was to help young people from relief and near-relief families to complete their education, and to keep them off the overcrowded labor market as well. Under its Student Aid Program a variety of part-time jobs were created for them in their schools and colleges, where they did administrative chores, worked in libraries and laboratories or as research assistants and teaching aids, or engaged in building maintenance. The pay was meager, but in most cases it meant the difference between staying in school and dropping out, or going on to college and perhaps a graduate degree instead of settling for a high school diploma. Thus, high school students could earn $6 a month, college students $10 to $20 a month, and graduate students up to $30.

For those not in school there was a work program of light construction and similar projects not unlike those of WPA, for which the pay ranged between $20 and $30 monthly. Persons under twenty-four were ineligible for WPA employment, and NYA jobs were generally limited to cases where the small supplemental income was critical to a family's welfare. As far as possible, the projects were aimed at teaching the young workers a trade, so that they might acquire at least a modicum of experience with which to compete in a labor market that was heavily stacked against them.

Up to the end of 1940 approximately 1.5 million youths had drawn their pittances from NYA, about two-thirds of them in the form of student aid. This depression-born program for disadvantaged young people has a close parallel in the Job Corps of the government's poverty program of the nineteen-sixties. It may also be relevant that the state director for the NYA in Texas was a coming young politician named Lyndon B. Johnson.[20]

VII

The following is excerpted from a story appearing in the *Washington Daily News* of January 8, 1968:

1 IN 8 AMERICANS GET
SOCIAL SECURITY BENEFITS

The mammoth social security enterprise called Social Security has grown from slender beginnings in 1937 to a level where, in 1968, it expects to pay out $25.2 billion to some 23.8 million Americans.

In 1967 Congress enacted into law revisions of the 31-year-old system which will provide for the largest total benefit increase to the elderly and others in the system's history. The average increase in benefits is in the range of 13 percent.

The new law also modified Social Security's important Medicare offshoot to enlarge and improve hospital insurance protection and to make it easier for those who elect to buy the supplemental insurance to handle [their] doctor bills.

(Below) Senator Huey Pierce Long, the Louisiana "Kingfish," arrives in New York and strikes a fistful pose for the press. (Inset) Back home in "Kingfish Country" the Senator is serenaded with a little "Beautiful Louisiana." At right: (top) CCC group doing roadbuilding through Angel Forest, Lancaster, California, 1937; and (below) a guitar-playing recruit and his buddies on the way to Missoula, Montana.

BOY AND GIRL TRAMPS OF AMERICA

THOMAS MINEHAN

(Upper left) Kid tramps and young migrants, journeying from coast to coast seeking work, make the East St. Louis, Illinois, Salvation Army Headquarters a favorite food and rest stop. (Above) Dorothea Lange's *Cabins*, U.S. Highway 99 between Tulare and Fresno, California, 1939. (Below) Dorothea Lange's *Gasoline Station*, Kern County, California, 1939.

TVA
ELECTRICITY FOR ALL

Social Security was the most profound and the most enduring of all the New Deal's social reforms. Unlike most other experiments of those days to improve the human condition, this one sought to cure rather than to palliate a chronic cause of distress, namely to lay by in days of plenty a store against the days of need. In most of western Europe social insurance in one form or another had existed for a generation before 1930. In the United States it was still a novel idea, repugnant to many as being inimicable to the virtue of self-reliance and as bearing the dreaded tinge of socialism. A man (or woman) who had been so imprudent as to reach old age without financial resources could look only to his children for support, to private charity if that failed, and *in extremis* to the public poorhouses. Pauperism among the aged was regarded simply as one of the unfortunate but inexorable vicissitudes of life, like bad weather and poor crops.

But that stiff and ungenerous philosophy began to soften under the grinding realities of the Depression. Need, it was realized, was not merely a consequence of personal dereliction. Destitution was a national illness, and the most helpless of its victims were the old and infirm. Every family had its own tragic evidence of that truth. The defenselessness of the aged made it easy to dramatize their plight. Serious scholars as well as demagogues made their cause their own. The rationale was as often economic as humanitarian. A plan for the establishment of a social security system occupied a foremost position on the agenda the New Deal brought to Washington. It was slow in fulfillment. Legislation was not enacted until 1935, but once achieved the program was secured for all time. Social security expanded cautiously over the years (its only radical enlargement did not come until 1965–67). It is now fastened to the bedrock of American life.

Roosevelt's tardiness in confronting this problem was a matter of weighing priorities rather than a lack of concern. He had promised Frances Perkins when she accepted his offer to become Secretary of Labor that he would do something about social insurance. In its given context, the term meant "workers' insurance" against both unemployment and old age. But the various relief programs initiated during the Hundred Days appeared to take care of the most immediate problems in this area, and there were many other things to occupy the President's mind.

Meanwhile, however the pressure for decision was building up in other quarters. Unemployment insurance appealed to students as the soundest antidote to the periodic downswings of the business cycle. Senator Robert Wagner and others had pressed for legislation to this end as early as 1931. After the 1932 election the movement got some unwanted help from more radical sources, including the Communist Party. In 1934 Congressman Ernest Lundeen, from the far-left fringe of Minnesota's Farmer-Labor Party, offered a bill promising full pay indefinitely for all unemployed workers. The cost to the government was estimated at $10 billion annually. The proposal was not taken seriously on Capitol Hill, but it got noisy support from the left wing, and it had the effect of making more moderate advocates raise their own antes. The trend became worrisome to the White House.

At the same time an "old folks" lobby was pressing assiduously for a system of old-age pensions. The arguments were that this was not only an urgent social necessity but an economic stimulant as well, since regular pensions would take older workers out of the labor market, thus easing the crunch of unemployment, and the spending of those pensions would vitalize the channels of commerce. The population was getting older, it was warned, and the problem of old-age dependency would increase with the years. There were already 6.6 million people sixty-five and over—5.4 percent of the population. The ratio would double by 1980, when, it was predicted, the total population would reach 150 million.*

Abraham Epstein of the American Association for Old-Age Security and Professor (later U.S. Senator) Paul H. Douglas of the University of Chicago were among a score of prominent leaders who had proselyted long and earnestly for a universal, federally-sponsored pension system. By 1933 they were beginning to make some headway. But the greatest evangel of this new faith was a frail, mild-mannered sixty-six-year-old family doctor from Long Beach, California—Francis E. Townsend. His plan had the virtue of grade-school simplicity: Give every person in the country sixty and over $200 a month on the stipulation that it should be spent within the month, the program to be financed by a general sales tax of 2 percent—not enough to hurt anybody.

From its hospitable seedbed in California, the Townsend Plan spread with stunning swiftness to every part of the country. Townsend Clubs sprang up in every city and small town, often with highly prestigious local elders among the sponsors. They held regular meetings in church basements and school auditoriums, peppered the newspapers with letters to the editor, petitioned their representatives in Congress, and attracted the interest of ambitious politicos who were too young to join their ranks but wise enough to sniff their power. A large national organization with a substantial treasury and an efficient public relations arm emerged. It published a weekly newspaper, manned an active lecture circuit, and put the good doctor himself repeatedly on national radio networks. When the 1934 election returns were in, it could claim a dozen converts to its cause in Congress. As a political tour de force the Townsend Plan had just about everything, including a touch of the old-time religion.

By the summer of 1934 Roosevelt faced the alternative of seizing the initiative on both unemployment and old-age insurance or of being confronted with legislation he might not like. Secretary Perkins, Harry Hopkins, and Congressional leaders urged him to act, warning at the same time that the path to an effective social insurance program was strewn with technical and legal pit-

*There was a general belief in the 1930's that the population curve had flattened out, probably for good. The reasons: decline of immigration, urbanization, lessened economic opportunity through mechanization, etc. The belief did not prove out. U.S. population hit the 150-million mark in 1950. The 1968 projection for 1980 is 250 million, with 9.2 percent of this total in the sixty-five and over age.

falls. Congress was about to adjourn, so Roosevelt publicly announced his commitment to such a legislation in the coming year and then created a specially staffed Cabinet committee to study the subject and come up with recommendations. Secretary Perkins was its indefatigable chairman, and she and her corps of experts put in many hours during the fall and early winter thrashing over alternative plans and details. What they were grappling with was a totally new structure in American life, which could be neither so grandiose as Congressman Lundeen had proposed nor so beautifully uncomplicated as Townsend had dreamed up. Roosevelt became absorbed in the study and quite carried away by its possibilities.

"You want to make it simple," he told Miss Perkins at one point, "so simple that everyone will understand it. The system ought to be operated through the post offices. Just simple and natural. . . . The rural free delivery carrier ought to bring papers to the door and pick them up after they are filled out.

"And what's more," he mused on in fascination at the prospect unreeling in his mind, "there is no reason why everybody in the United States should not be covered . . . [not] just the industrial workers. Everybody ought to be in on it, the farmer and his wife and family. I see no reason why every child, from the day he is born, shouldn't be a member of the social security system."

He was writing a pretty large order, Miss Perkins murmured in mild reproach.

"I don't see why not," Roosevelt answered stubbornly. "Cradle to the grave—from the cradle to the grave they ought to be in a social security system." [21]

But so elaborate a tapestry could not be woven out of the tangled legal, technical, actuarial, fiscal, and political threads with which the Cabinet committee had to work. Should the system be all federal, all state, or federal-state? Should the cost be borne by the workers, by their employers, or by both, and in what proportion? Would payroll taxes to support the program stand up under a Supreme Court test? What effect would the accumulation of a multibillion dollar reserve fund have on the nation's fiscal health? Since not everyone could be covered, who would be excluded? And could a provision for compulsory health insurance be sustained against the violently proclaimed objections of the American Medical Association? To that last question, the committee's answer was an emphatic if reluctant No. The political power of the AMA was such that it was feared the doctors' lobby might scuttle the whole package in order to block "socialized medicine."

What emerged was a pragmatic blending of many conflicting ideas, less ambitious than Roosevelt had hoped for, but in any event a historic leap into the welfare state. In his State of the Union Message in January 1935 the President asked Congress for laws to create (1) a system of unemployment insurance under joint control of the states and the federal government; (2) a system of old-age annuities to be under federal control exclusively; and (3) a permanent and regularized program of federal grants to the states for aid to dependent children and the blind and for the enhancement of public health services. "We pay now," Roosevelt said, "for the dreadful consequences of economic insecurity—and dearly. This plan presents a more equitable and infinitely less expensive means of meeting those costs. We cannot afford to neglect the plain duty before us."

On the day of his message to Congress, identical bills to effect his purpose were introduced in the Senate by New York's Robert Wagner and in the House by Representatives David J. Lewis of Maryland and Robert L. Doughton of North Carolina. Committee hearings began promptly. Speed was essential, Roosevelt warned, since forty-four state legislatures were meeting that year and should enact enabling legislation to put the program into effect in their states.

The reaction to the program, in general, was almost universally favorable. Dissent, such as it was, focused mainly on details and methods. "Unless the members of Congress are almost unanimously ignorant of the national state of mind," Arthur Krock commented in *The New York Times*, "people who would destroy or seriously damage the economic security program offered by the President today would simply be letting the country in for calamitous alternatives. If senators and representatives accurately describe the feelings of their districts, the defeat or extreme dilution of the Roosevelt proposals will mean the ascendancy of the ideas of Huey P. Long, Dr. Townsend, or both. The country is determined somehow to be cushioned through old age, unemployment, [sickness] and against a repetition of the experience of millions of people during this depression."

(As if to give tooth to this warning there appeared on the front page of the same edition of the *Times* a brief dispatch from California under the headline SACRAMENTO ARMS TO MEET RED REVOLT. The story said that a 600-man citizens' army had been mobilized to repel an expected invasion "by 2,000 western Communists" to protest the trial of seventeen of their comrades on charges of criminal syndicalism in advancing the "class struggle." A violent upshot of the class struggle seemed not improbable to a great many people in the thirties.)[22]

In spite of the wide popular support, Congressional labors on the social security bills were protracted. The subject was extraordinarily complex and invited a great deal of technical and legalistic hair splitting. Nor was political dissent wholly stilled. The Townsendites, sensing the doom of their $200-a-month windfall, resisted stubbornly. For a like reason, Huey Long tied the Senate up in a filibuster while he extolled his doctrine of "Share the Wealth" and the virtues of Bible reading and Louisiana gumbo. Liberty League spokesmen said that the law would destroy the moral fiber of the working man and kill the instinct for frugality. Every stalwart American citizen, others said, would be humbled by having to wear a dog tag around his neck with his social security number. Predictably, the New York *Sun* labeled the whole scheme "socialistic." And Secretary Perkins was interrupted in her testimony at a Congressional hearing by a woman in the audience loudly proclaiming that an almost exact counterpart of the social security plan could be found on page eighteen of Karl Marx's *Communist Manifesto*, which she waved threateningly in her hand.

But the broad outcome was never in doubt. The bill passed both houses by large majorities and became law with the President's signature on August 14, 1935. The scope of the program was slimmed down in the process. Participation in both unemployment and old-age insurance was restricted to about one-half of the total work force of 48.8 million by a number of categorical exclusions—for example, farm and domestic labor, business with fewer than eight employees, professionals, and the self-employed. Unemployment insurance was established as a joint federal-state system to be financed by a payroll tax progressing from 1 percent to 3 percent in 1938. Benefits would become available beginning in 1937. The old-age assistance program was established as an all-federal system funded by both an employer's payroll tax and an employee's earnings tax progressing from 1 percent to 3 percent in each category by 1949. Benefits were not to exceed $85 monthly nor drop below $10 monthly for persons sixty-five and over, depending upon the beneficiary's earning record. Annuities were to begin in 1942 to allow for the accumulation of a suitable trust fund, but eligible persons reaching sixty-five in the interim were to receive benefits out of funds specially appropriated by Congress. Formulas were established for grants to the states for aid to dependents and the blind, for public health services, and for vocational education. It was estimated that during the first full year of operation benefits would go to 1,543,500 old people, 1,473,900 dependent children, and 51,400 blind persons at an overall cost of $128 million. Over the succeeding years these programs have been substantially broadened and liberalized, most notably by the addition of Medicare in 1965.

Ever since the creation of the Social Security system, many experts have complained that it was too timidly conceived and too parsimonious in execution to meet the needs of American society adequately. Too many people were for years excluded from its coverage; its benefits have rarely equaled minimal needs of the recipients; and standards that were subject to state manipulation have been erratically enforced. Thirty years passed before care for the indigent sick was broadly encompassed. Britain, France, and the Scandinavian countries are still, in the late sixties, far ahead of the United States in the sophistication of their social insurance programs. Be that as it may, the Social Security Act of 1935 was one of the greatest landmarks in the social history of the United States, perhaps the most important single legacy of the New Deal. It *has* ended poverty for some Americans, and greatly mitigated it for others.[23]

CHAPTER 13
Almanac
1935–1937

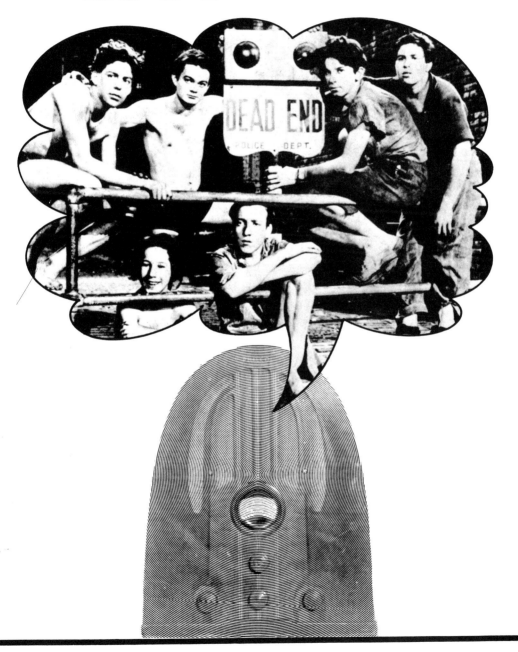

A miscellany of events occurring during the middle thirties that engaged our interest and sometimes affected our lives; a random selection among the more engrossing headlines of the period and the stories behind them.

Jan. 6, 1935

(From *The New York Times*)

AUTO SHOW OPENS TO RECORD CROWD

NEW YORK—Mayor La-Guardia officially opened New York's 35th annual automobile show at the Grand Central Palace yesterday afternoon.

The doors were scheduled to open to the public at 2 P.M., but by 1:45 the lines outside were so long that police asked officials to open the doors so that the sidewalks could be cleared. It was said to be the largest opening day attendance in the history of the show.

"Let us hope," the Mayor said, "that this is not only the opening of another automobile exhibition but also the starting of a new era of prosperity."

The exhibition hall, decorated in silver and burnished copper on the main floor, presented a brilliant setting for the gleaming array of cars. A large sign, "Motordom on Parade" welcomed the visitors. . . .

In 1935 there were twenty-two million motor vehicles of all types and vintages on the road and every second family owned a car—often a quite dilapidated one that had been nursed beyond its normal life expectancy.* In the Depression years the automobile had not attained quite the rank of indispensability that it occupies today, but it was even more highly prized as a luxury and as a mark of social and economic status. Acquiring a car, particularly one's first, was likely to be a momentous and exciting occasion approached over a long period of yearning, speculation and painful budgeting. Thus, the annual auto show, a week-long spectacle in almost every city, was an eagerly awaited event.

The 1935 New York show marked the opening of a banner year for the auto industry. That was the year Detroit "turned the corner" and began to pull away from the Depression trough. Dealers sold 2,743,908 of the new models, which was two and a half times their sales at the bottom of the market in 1932, and 44 percent above sales for 1934.

Many innovations had been added to the 1935 models to spur the public's appetite. Streamlining was the designers' vogue that year, with sloped radiators and windshields and back-swept fenders to give an impression of

*Total registration in 1968 was 99.9 million; 78.6 percent of all families owned at least one automobile and every fourth family owned two or more. (U.S. Bureau of the Census and Public Roads Administration)

lightness and speed. Auburn unveiled a flashy, torpedo-shaped "supercharged eight" with gleaming chromium exhaust pipes sweeping out from under the hood and a claimed speed of one hundred miles per hour. General Motors introduced the "turret top," an all-steel construction that would, it was delicately suggested, enable one to survive a roll-over crash. "Knee action"—independent front-wheel suspension—was another highly touted improvement said to produce a smoother ride and to eliminate front-wheel shimmy. "Fingertip" gear shifts, "syncro-mesh" transmissions, automatic "overdrive," and hydraulic brakes were among other allurements offered the buyer.

But even more alluring than the gadgetry was the price of the new cars, low even by Depression standards. A new Chevrolet "business coupe" (a style that, along with the "roadster," has become obsolete) could be bought for $465, f.o.b. Detroit, and for another $50 a rumble seat would be added. Ford and Plymouth each had competitive models at approximately the same price. Higher up the scale, the Hudson 8 began at $760 and various models of the Nash ranged from $895 to $1,240. The aristocratic Pierce-Arrow, somber as a hearse and half again as big, was in the $2,000 range. At the pinnacle of the price pyramid was that lonely super-aristocrat, the Cadillac V-16, priced at $3,500 without extras. But there were not many takers for these opulent models in 1935. Ninety-five percent of the year's output was priced below $750 wholesale, and the average retail price of all new cars sold was $580.

In spite of great engineering progress and refinements in design, cars of the mid-thirties were, by today's standards, sluggish, noisy, and undependable. Self-starters were by then standard equipment, but each new car came with a hand crank tucked unobtrusively under the front seat, just in case, and also a kit of tire tools. When you had a flat you generally had to change the tire, not the wheel. Seventy miles per hour was about the top speed attainable in all but the more expensive models, cruising range was about fifty (if road conditions permitted it), and long hills had to be negotiated in engine-boiling second gear. Highways, too, left something to be desired. Duals were virtually unknown, and even three-lane stretches were rare. Of the 507,000 miles of two-lane roads that made up the nation's highway system in 1935 only 358,000 miles were paved.

Two hundred models, under twenty-five manufacturers' trade names, were put on exhibit at the 1935 auto show in New York. Most of the names that are still familiar a generation later were represented, but many others have since passed into nostalgic limbo: Pierce-Arrow, Hupmobile, Reo, Terraplane, Graham, Packard, Stutz, Studebaker, Willys, and, for connoisseurs of foreign class, Duesenberg. The process of attrition and mergers that has reduced the once wildly proliferated auto industry into a monopoly by the "big four" was already under way in 1935.

(Below) The 1937 Cord, Model 812 Westchester Convertible: styled by Gordon Buehrig, with a Lycoming V-8 engine developing 125 b.p.h. at 3500 r.p.m., front-wheel drive with 125 inch wheelbase; curb weight 3500 lbs.; top speed 112 m.p.h.; $1995 f.o.b. New York; Auburn Automobile Company, Connersville, Indiana. Roland Young and Constance Bennett were "seen" in one in the MGM film *Topper*, 1937.

At right: (clockwise) 1935 Auburn Straight-Eight 4-door sedan; the Edsel Ford designed 1937 Lincoln Zephyr V-12; 1936 La Salle 2-passenger Coupé; 1937 Ford 4-door sedan; 1935 Ford Deluxe V-8 2-passenger Coupé; 1936 Plymouth 4-door sedan; 1937 American Bantam Business Coupé, $335 f.o.b. Butler, Pa.; 1937 Buick 4-door sedan.

April 20, 1935

(From *The New York Times*)

DIMES FLOOD MAIL IN CHAIN LETTERS

Federal Inquiry Begins

DENVER — "Send a dime" chain letters are pouring into the post office here in a new scheme which has sprung up almost overnight.

Postal Inspector Roy E. Nelson pronounces the letters a violation of the lottery laws and the laws prohibiting the use of the mails for fraud, and threatens to arrest the organizers of the scheme if they can be found. . . .

Many stories about the chains are current. A poor seamstress is reported to have received enough to purchase a sewing machine. A widow is reported to be paying off burial expenses for her husband. A mother is said to have paid off hospital expenses for the birth of her child and to have had enough left over to buy a baby carriage. None of these reports are confirmed.

The letters have multiplied so rapidly in the last few days that almost every family in the city has received one or more. . . .

The chain-letter craze that swept the country during the spring of 1935 was the daffiest get-rich-quick scheme since the South Sea Bubble. No one got hurt very badly by it, nor did anyone make a killing, but millions of people worked up such a lather of expectancy over it that the national sanity seemed to be coming unstuck.

It worked like this: You received a letter in the mail with six names and addresses at the bottom. You were urged to send a dime to the person at the top of the list, scratch his name, add your own at the bottom, and send copies of the letter to five friends. Through five such progressions (provided no one broke the chain) your name would reach the top, and you would be happily bowled over by an avalanche of 15,625 dimes— $1,562.50 on a ten-cent investment. It was mathematically sound, beguilingly simple, and dirt cheap. Even if it was preposterous on the face of it, what the hell, why not give it a whirl? Millions did—clerks, housewives, bookkeepers, society matrons, businessmen, schoolchildren, relief workers, pensioners, everybody.

Beginning about March (how and where no one knew), the scheme ballooned in a few weeks into a national mania, clogging the mails, disrupting schoolrooms and business offices, and monopolizing thought and conversation. Post offices in scores of cities were swamped and thrown behind schedule as much as twenty-four hours. One of the worst hit was Denver, where, during one week in May, the normal mail volume more than doubled and ninety additional clerks and letter carriers had to be hired. As the craze snowballed to a climax in Iowa, banks in Des Moines had to send to the Federal Reserve in Chicago for fresh supplies of dimes.

Racketeers quickly moved in to get their share of the take. *Time* magazine called them "chainsters." One enterprising combine in Cleveland mailed out 30,000 letters with their own names attached, ensuring that if anyone made money on the deal it would be they. Others organized chain "clubs," with such enticing names as "Pot of Gold" and "Over the Rainbow," and sold profit-sharing memberships. As the boom grew bigger and daffier the ante was boosted in many cases from a dime to a dollar and as much as five dollars. Some ambitious plungers went in for $5 chain telegrams to get around mail fraud charges.

Springfield, Missouri, went through an incredible two-day binge when the business life of the city came virtually to a standstill while the chain-letter pitchmen took over. They offered a new gimmick—the "guaranteed" chain letter selling for from $1 to $5 with the buyer's signature officially notarized. Operating from a score or empty offices and downtown storefronts, with stenographers and notaries public on hand and salesmen combing the streets, the scheme caught on like a brush fire, and was as quickly over. Somehow or other the notary's seal was supposed to make the letter foolproof. It did nothing of the sort, of course, but one promoter was reputed to have cleaned up more than a thousand dollars in twenty-four hours, and some buyers of the letters had winnings of a few hundred dollars each.

No part of the country was immune to the chain-letter frenzy, nor was any name too big to be put on the sucker list. Several hundred letters were addressed to President and Mrs. Roosevelt. Al Smith received an average of fifty a day for more than a month. Catholic bishops, prominent philanthropists, gangsters, ballplayers, and movie and radio stars were inundated. The Post Office Department strove mightily and futilely to stanch the flood, invoking the laws against lotteries. So did some state and municipal authorities, and fines were actually levied in a few instances.

It was not the gambling laws but the law of diminishing returns that finally took the steam out of the chain-letter fad. As it slowed down it took a number of aberrant twists. You were urged by the "Liquid Assets Club" to send a pint of whisky to the top man on your list. Some letters asked for an elephant, a kiss, a brass collar button. Dr. H. E. Coakley of Denver conceived the bale-of-hay chain letter and was rewarded with a 50-pound bale of the stuff deposited on his waiting-room floor.

By mid-June the madness was over. Everyone agreed it was a silly business from the start, but it was fun while it lasted, except for the mailmen.

May 10, 1935

(From *The New York Times*)

PRESIDENT WELCOMES BYRD HOME AS GUNS BOOM SALUTE TO EXPLORER

WASHINGTON—Setting foot on the soil of the United States mainland for the first time in 19 months, Rear Admiral Richard E. Byrd received an enthusiastic welcome when he landed with his crew late this afternoon on his return from his second Antarctic expedition.

Guns roared, whistles screeched, aircraft soared, bands played, flags waved, soldiers and sailors drilled and crowds cheered in a mass salute to the homecoming explorers as a background for the official reception.

The highpoint came at 5 o'clock this afternoon when Admiral Byrd and his men came ashore for a Presidential reception. President Roosevelt went to the Navy Yard to welcome them home on behalf of the nation. Governor George Peery of Virginia welcomed Admiral Byrd as a fellow Virginian, and a Congressional delegation and many members of the Cabinet took part in the tribute.

As the *Bear of Oakland* approached the Navy Yard this afternoon a 13-gun salute boomed in the Admiral's honor. The flashes from the cannon on one side of the river were matched by flashes of lightning on the other. The weather had been alternately clear and rainy all day. . . .

Richard Evelyn Byrd, Rear Admiral, USNR, was the most renowned national hero of the decade, shading even the idolized Lindbergh in the reach and durability of his popularity. He was forty-seven years old and at the peak of his fame as he stepped ashore on that rainy afternoon in May 1935 to receive an extraordinary personal welcome by the President. He was the only man in history to have flown over both the North and the South Pole and his daring explorations in those unknown wastes had for years awed and exhilarated millions of chair-borne adventurers. His latest discoveries had made him something of a latter-day Columbus, and his ordeal of surviving alone through six months of an Antarctic winter had cast him in the heroic mold of Scott and Amundsen. His modest bearing and decorous behavior, and his aristocratic lineage going back to colonial Virginia, completed a picture of romantic dimensions. But he was real enough, as the newspapers and the newsreels constantly attested, and the string of his exploits seemed never to run out.

On his 1928-29 Antarctic expedition he had made his historic first flight over the South Pole. The expedition that began in 1933 and ended in 1935 was soundly based on geographical and meteorological objectives. By air and by dogsled he and his party surveyed vast stretches of the mysterious continent, mapped hundreds of miles of its coastline, identified mountain ranges and other topographic features never known previously to exist. Great mineral wealth was believed to lie in the primeval soil hundreds of feet below the endless ice sheath. But of more immediate concern to Byrd and the scientific community was the influence of the raging Antarctic climate on the weather of the rest of the world. Byrd and his fellow explorers established instrumented weather stations at a few widely scattered locations linked by radio to the expedition's base at Little America on the ice shelf of the Ross Sea.

To supplement this inadequate system Byrd appointed himself an on-the-spot weather observer through the bitter darkness of an entire Antarctic winter. He erected and provisioned a small weatherproof shack 125 miles inland from Little America and dug in. As 100-miles-an-hour gales tore at the tiny structure and temperatures settled to a paralyzing fifty and sixty degrees below zero, Byrd's only contact with the land of the living was an erratic and sometimes blacked-out radio link with his main base. Had he fallen ill (which he did, from the fumes of his stove) or found his life of isolation unbearable, there was no way for help to reach him until the worst of the winter had passed. He experienced alternate spells of despair and ecstasy, of fruitful meditation and relentless boredom. He later recounted his experiences in a book called, simply and appropriately, *Alone*.

"Dick" Byrd was the younger brother of Harry Flood Byrd, Jr., Virginia's onetime Governor and at this time U.S. Senator. He graduated from the U.S. Naval Academy in 1912 and after sea duty during the World War went into Naval aviation. He developed an immediate ambition to fly the first airplane across the North Pole but could arouse little interest for the project in the Navy. In 1926 he secured enough private financing to make the flight possible. With Floyd Bennett as copilot he set out from a base at Spitzbergen, Norway, on May 9 of that year and in a 1,360-mile flight circled the Pole and returned safely to land sixteen hours later. The whole world cheered the daring young airman.

Byrd was also ambitious to be the first man to fly the Atlantic, a field in which there were already a number of aspirants. Again with private financial backing he made the effort, but with bad luck he placed third in the race behind Lindbergh and Clarence Chamberlain. When he finally did take off with a three-man crew on June 29, 1927, he encountered storms and fog the whole way and crash-landed on the French coast short of his destination, Paris. Within the year he was busy organizing his first expedition to the Antarctic, and on November 29, 1929, a tensely waiting world learned that he had added man's first flight over the South Pole to his list of achievements.

Thereafter the South Polar Continent drew irresistibly upon Byrd's dreams and imagination. He led three more exploratory expeditions there—in 1933, 1939, and 1946—and became the world's leading authority on the region. In 1954 he headed the Navy's elaborate Operation Deep Freeze to set up the first permanent Antarctic base at McMurdo Sound. When

At left: (top) The French luxury liner *Normandie* arriving New York on her maiden voyage, June 3, 1935. (Alongside) The "Chain Letter" craze tied up many a U.S. Post Office in the Spring of 1935. (Bottom) Followers of Father Divine on parade, Harlem, 1937. (Alongside) Gossip columnist and sometime "sob sister" Walter Winchell with Broadway chorus girls, 1935. At right: (clockwise) Admiral Richard E. Byrd having a lonely meal in the Antarctic, *Second Little America Expedition*, 1933–1935; Spring floods paralyzed New England in March, 1936, when Connecticut River overflowed; Kate Smith and Babe Ruth "mugging" over CBS radio. (Spread) The *Queen Mary* arriving in New York on her maiden voyage, May 27, 1936.

members of the party went to look for Little America, Byrd's original base, they found only the tip of a 75-foot radio mast projecting above the ice and drifted snow.

Admiral Byrd, last of the great explorers, steadfast hero to a whole generation of real and would-be adventurers, died at his home in Boston on March 11, 1957.

Sept. 8, 1935

(From *The New York Times*)

DOCTOR SHOOTS HUEY LONG IN LOUISIANA STATE CAPITOL: BODYGUARD KILLS ASSAILANT

BATON ROUGE, La.—Senator Huey P. Long was shot through the stomach and gravely wounded tonight as he walked from the chamber of the Louisiana House of Representatives where he had been directing the passage of bills aimed at strengthening his grip upon the politics of the state and to fight the New Deal and Roosevelt policies.

The would-be assassin, shot and killed instantly by three members of the Louisiana State Police acting as bodyguards for the Senator, was identified as Dr. Carl A. Weise, of Baton Rouge. He was 29 and the son-in-law of Judge B. H. Pavy of Opelousa, a leader of the anti-Long faction of St. Landry Parish.

One of the bills considered at this special session of the legislature was designed to gerrymander Judge Pavy's judicial district so that his re-election next January would have been well-nigh impossible. . . .

Hollywood, if it were seeking to cast the Great American Demagogue, could never in its wildest imagining have improved upon the genuine article, Huey Pierce Long, the Louisiana Kingfish. In real life he was the perfect caricature of the type. He was as flamboyant as a carnival pitchman, crude in speech and manner, and with the defiant arrogance of the total egotist. In private or public he adopted the mood that suited his purpose, changing it as easily as he changed his florid neckties. He was alternately the clown, the evangel, the imperious martinet, the vengeful zealot. In whatever role he chose, whether leading the cheers from the sidelines at a Louisiana State University football game, haranguing the United States Senate, or striding through the streets of New Orleans surrounded by his gun-toting bodyguards, his presence was overwhelming. But with all his uncouth theatrics he was as shrewd as a fox, with an intuitive and insatiable sense of power. For a few incredible years he ruled the State of Louisiana as a fiefdom and rattled the political underpinnings of the Roosevelt Administration. He was, said *Time* magazine, "a cross between an unscrupulous Bryan and a political Barnum, a realist as well as an exhibitionist."

Huey Long, born in 1893 of a poor family, was already something of a legend in the South when, at the age of thirty-nine he promoted himself from the governorship to the U.S. Senate in 1931. He had discovered his political talent as a traveling salesman peddling baking powder in the small towns and forks-of-the-road settlements of his native Louisiana. With only seven months study he became a lawyer in 1915, later won appointment to the State Railroad Commission, and began to build a personal political machine. He was elected Governor in 1928, narrowly fought off impeachment his second year in office, and upon this victory built himself a one-man dictatorship as impregnable as any this nation has ever seen.

His strength lay with the great inert mass of rural poor whites, the "Wool Hats" and "Red Necks" who live along the creeks and bayous of the Mississippi Delta and till the cotton and sugarcane fields to the north. He championed their cause against the rich folk of the cities, tripled the state debt, and piled ruinous taxes on the railroads and oil companies to build hard-top roads, new schools, and free hospitals. He purged the state bureaucracy of his enemies to put his own men in power and made it worth their while—and their political lives—to stay in his favor. He ran the office of Governor and the legislature with high-handed disdain. During Assembly sessions, he strode about the chamber, preempted the Speaker's dais, and dictated bills and amendments off the top of his head. He was no less contemptuous of the judiciary; he hired and fired judges as the whim struck him. A Long henchman standing up in a Baton Rouge court to be sentenced for assault and battery against a foe of the machine heard the judge out ("sixty days in jail") and then smilingly pulled from his pocket a reprieve executed and signed by the Governor in advance.

When he came to the U.S. Senate in 1931, Huey left the statehouse in the hands of a subservient stooge, Governor O. K. Allen, and continued to run a one-man show in Louisiana from his base in Washington. He was a vociferous supporter of Roosevelt at the beginning of the New Deal but quickly became his most vituperative critic. The rub was that Long could not get control of the vast expenditures of federal relief and work funds in his state. One of a package of laws he whipped through the Louisiana legislature in his closing days made a state offense of any violation of the Tenth Amendment, which safeguards the rights of the states in these words: "The powers not delegated to the United States by the Constitution, nor prohibited by it to the States, are reserved to the States respectively, or to the people." Thus he sought to jail federal relief and other officials whom he caught trespassing on his domain. His attacks on Roosevelt broadened out to include virtually the whole range of New Deal programs, and he was the Senate's most tireless filibusterer. His periodic tirades regularly filled the Senate galleries and brought millions of listeners to their radios on his many speaking excursions around the country. He was thoroughly disliked by his Senate colleagues and feared by most of them.

Huey made the most of his reputation as the national hobgoblin. "I wanted those folks to think I was somebody," he once said, "and they by God did." Next only to the President, he was the most photographed, cartooned, and talked-about man of his day. Citations of news stories about him in *The New York Times Index* for 1935 fill six and one-half columns for the eight months before his death, as against only four columns for the entire year for the Senate's most distinguished member, Borah of Idaho.

By 1935 most thoughtful people had written him off as a paranoic buffoon and as Louisiana's problem. But they could not dismiss so easily the political gale he had stirred up in many parts of the country. His Share-the-Wealth program picked up at the intellectual fringes of the Townsend old folks' crusade and produced a sort of frenzy among sub-literate masses all over the country. It was a hazily devised scheme to liquidate large fortunes and to give every poor family a house, a car, a radio, a college education for their children, and a pension for the aged. "Every man a king," he said. Five years of grinding depression had made the country ripe for any sort of economic magic. Long deftly channeled this yearning into a crusade and recruited the Reverend Gerald L. K. Smith, a hell-fire evangelist of Shreveport, to give it a religious overlay. By mid-1935 there were more than 25,000 Share-the-Wealth clubs in business with a claimed enrollment of ten million.

Long announced that he would himself run for the Presidency if Roosevelt did not adopt his program in its entirety in 1936. He even wrote a book, *My First Days in the White House,* detailing with grandiose illogic how he planned to make the country over. When he flirted openly with Townsend and Father Coughlin, each with an enormous following of his own, the prospect of such a coalition created a frightening political specter for the New Deal. A secret poll conducted by the Democratic National Committee in the summer of 1935 indicated that Long at the head of a third-party ticket might collect from three to four million votes and cost the party the electoral votes of a number of crucial states.

"Long was the most formidable of the then-current array of demagogues," Jim Farley said later. "It was conceivable that his third party movement might constitute a balance of power in the 1936 election. What he might have done in 1940 is difficult to conjecture. He was high in our political thoughts." [1]

It seems almost inevitable that a man of such violent impulses should have come to a violent end. After the assassin's bullet struck him down that Sunday night in the capitol rotunda at Baton Rouge, he was rushed to a nearby hospital. He subsisted on massive blood transfusions for thirty hours and then died. His state funeral rivaled in pageantry that of a medieval potentate. The Long machine survived in Louisiana for many years. Huey's brother, Earl, served a number of terms as Governor, and his oldest son,

Russsell, has been a United States Senator continuously since 1948. But Huey Long's national influence was decisively snuffed out that night of September 8, 1935.

Less spectacular than Huey Long but fully his match as a political agitator was Father Charles E. Coughlin, the Detroit "radio priest." This short, unprepossessing man in his early forties, who wore spectacles and a clerical collar, was the most effective spellbinder of his time. His resonant, passionate voice, with just a touch of Irish burr, rang with zealous conviction. Those within its range were caught up in a sort of hypnotic trance, eager as penitents to be taught and led.

What Coughlin taught was an undigested religio-economic doctrine that promised instant salvation on earth and in heaven as well. It contained elements of Catholic humanism, Marxian socialism, Populist monetary theories, traces of fascist discipline, and an occasional bitter dash of anti-Semitism. Capitalist greed, he believed, stood in the way of the earthly fulfillment of Christ's promise of the abundant life, an abundance both material and spiritual. The chief malefactors in this conspiracy were the international bankers. Among many other things, Coughlin called for a centralized banking system under government control, a guaranteed annual wage, a stabilized cost of living, and the shifting of the tax burden from the middle class to the owners of personal and corporate wealth.

His agenda was pretty sophisticated compared to the meat-and-potatoes logic of Huey Long's Share-the-Wealth. For this reason its appeal went several cuts higher on the cultural scale. White collars and even starched ones usually outnumbered blue collars and no collars at Coughlin rallies. On a Monday or Tuesday, after one of his broadcasts, you could hear all sorts of people, high and low, talking earnestly about it. But even for those who could not fathom the complexities of the Coughlin polemics, he seemed to be promising a better life for the downtrodden here and now. Coughlin's enemies were *your* enemies, for you wouldn't expect a priest to lead you on a wrong path. Few Pied Pipers ever played a more seductive tune.

Coughlin began his crusade modestly enough in the middle nineteen-twenties when he was named pastor of a small and impoverished parish in Royal Oak, a Detroit suburb. He took to the local radio on Sunday evenings in an effort to build up his congregation. He deftly laced his Catholic theology with political commentary, targeting on the rags-and-riches disparities that so blatantly mocked the Coolidge and Hoover prosperity. The response from listeners was astonishing. His audience quickly outgrew the single local station, and within a couple of years he had been picked up by a national network. By the turn of the decade his popularity rating matched that of such top-flight entertainers as Amos 'n' Andy and Rudy Vallee. Twenty to thirty million people tuned in regularly each Sunday evening for his exhortations from the Shrine of the Little Flower. One broadcast alone was reported to have brought in more than a million letters

THE ROOSEVELT RED RECORD AND ITS BACKGROUND

FELIX FRANKFURTER
NORMAN THOMAS
REXFORD TUGWELL
EARL BROWDER
LENIN
BRANDEIS
ROGER BALDWIN
LA FOLLETTE
EUGENE V. DEBS
STALIN
KARL MARX

ELIZABETH DILLING

(Above) Dust jacket for Elizabeth Dilling's "smear" of President Roosevelt, citing Communist affiliations and Radicalism. At right: (top) "Golden Hour of the Little Flower." Radio ad placement by Father Coughlin. (Alongside) Father Coughlin Apology after he had referred to President Roosevelt as a "liar" and a "double-crosser." (Below) An alignment of home-grown demagogues (left to right) Dr. Francis E. Townsend, Reverend Gerald L.K. Smith, and Father Charles E. Coughlin.

An Open Letter of Apology
To President Roosevelt

Excellency:

In the heat of civic interest in the affairs of my country and in righteous anger at the developments that, it is my conviction, have contributed largely to want in the midst of plenty, I addressed to the President of the United States, in a speech at Cleveland, Ohio, July 16th, the word "liar."

For that action I now offer to the President of the United States my sincere apology.

It has been implied, both in the large section of the public press and elsewhere, that my action on July 16th was due to the fact that promises allegedly given to me in person by the President of the United States were not carried out. My reference was not to such an action.

Specifically, I had in mind the **recorded** promises held out to a nation during 1932 by a candidate for the presidency. I had in mind the noble inaugural address delivered by that candidate-elect on March 4, 1933; and had in mind an oath of office to uphold the Constitution of the United States of America.

Historical record since March 4, 1933, is responsible for the fact that in my Cleveland address on July 16th I did not pussyfoot.

The money changers have not been driven from the temple. Those who "abdicated" their high places have been restored and their places made more secure. There is a greater and far more serious concentration of wealth today than existed in 1932 and 1933.

The President of the United States is on record as having encouraged the Congress of the United States not to take too seriously the Constitution of the United States. That action did not have the effect of upholding the Constitution.

I am conscious that the President of the United States is reported to have made the following declaration on May 14, 1935:

"**As you know, a great many of the high and mighty—with special axes to grind—have been deliberately trying to mislead the people who know nothing of farming by misrepresenting—no—why use a pussyfoot word?—by lying about the kind of farm program which this nation is operating today.**"

I am conscious that the President of the United States has not pussyfooted when attacking either those with whom he is in disagreement or his political enemies.

I was one of the first, and not one of the least, to help you attain the presidency. My assistance was based upon your Excellency's ability to perform. As my President, I still respect you. As a fellow citizen and as a man, I still regard you highly; but as an executive, despite your Excellency's fine intentions, I deem it best for the welfare of our common country that you be supplanted in office. To that end, in a gentlemanly and courageous manner, I shall strive, always willing to admit my mistakes—including those of good judgment and to apologize even publicly when confronted with them.

In conclusion, I wish to state for the record that my remarks and criticism delivered in Cleveland were directed at a candidate for the greatest political office within the gift of the people.

Respectfully,

Charles Coughlin

from listeners all over the United States and Canada. In 1935 he claimed a signed-up membership of 7.5 million for his National Union for Social Justice, the vehicle for his political program. On his frequent personal appearances at such places as Madison Square Garden in New York and the Chicago Coliseum, hundreds of extra police were put on duty to handle the crowds and the traffic jams.

Like Huey Long, Father Coughlin greeted the advent of the New Deal with enthusiasm. "The New Deal is Christ's Deal," he proclaimed extravagantly after visiting President Roosevelt at the White House in the summer of 1933. But his ardor cooled as he saw that the Administration was more interested in propping up the existing capitalist structure than in building a new one according to his blueprints. "This plutocratic capitalist system must be constitutionally voted out of existence," he roared to a screaming New York audience in the summer of 1935. His attacks on the New Deal mounted in vehemence. He called Roosevelt a "liar" and "the great betrayer." Many of Coughlin's superiors in the Catholic hierarchy were shocked by his violent language and reckless politicking, but he was too powerful to be disciplined. Moreover, he had the full support of his own Bishop Gallagher of the Detroit diocese.

Father Coughlin resisted the temptation to weld his National Union for Social Justice into a political party; instead he looked upon it as a powerful "people's lobby." He threw in his lot with the presidential candidacy of Representative William Lemke and the Union Party in 1936, promising to deliver nine million votes from his followers to help unseat Roosevelt. The hapless Lemke polled fewer than a million votes, while Roosevelt achieved the greatest landslide in history. That all but finished Coughlin. He folded his Union for Social Justice, withdrew from the air, and turned back to the obscurity of being a parish priest. He reemerged briefly to trumpet the cause of isolationism in 1939–40 and to say a good word now and then for the pro-Nazi German-American Bund, but not many were listening. His style of demagoguery had burned itself out.[2]

October 2, 1935

(From *The New York Times*)

BIG ITALIAN FORCE INVADES ETHIOPIA, MUSSOLINI RALLIES 20,000,000 ITALIANS ROOSEVELT TO KEEP U.S. 'UNENTANGLED'

ADDIS ABABA—The Ethiopian frontier has been invaded by Italian troops in the neighborhood of Assab, the Ethiopian government announced today. . . .

ROME — Premier Mussolini

threw down the gauntlet to the world this evening. While an enormous crowd of Black Shirts filling the Plaza Venezia shouted themselves hoarse, the Premier let it be known that hostilities are about to begin.

"We have been patient with Ethiopia for 40 years—it is enough now," he cried. . . .

SAN DIEGO—A policy of keeping the United States "unentangled and free" was announced here today by President Roosevelt in his first public utterance recog- nizing the gravity of the threat of war abroad. . . .

ASMARA (Oct. 3)—The general advance of the Italian armies from Eritrea has be- gun. At dawn today 20,000 men in four columns crossed the Mareb River which forms the Ethiopian boundary. Groups of light tanks operat- ing ahead covered the cross- ing. Airplanes hovered over- head and long range guns fired occasional shells to dis- courage opposition. Italian planes bombed Adowa and Adigrat. . . .

Mussolini's invasion of Ethiopia was an international tragedy with overtones of *opéra bouffe*. The strutting, barrel-chested dictator wanted "a place in the sun" as a modern Caesar. He also wanted to be a Caligula whose scourge would transform the easygoing Italian peasantry into a race of conquerors and strike terror into the rest of mankind. Ethiopia, a backward feudal kingdom lying in an economic wasteland, would be his first, easy stride toward empire. He conquered it with brutality and military might, thereby earning not world renown but contempt and loath- ing. His maneuvers drove him into the arms of his political rival, Hitler, a more accomplished despot.

The world of October 1935 was less than startled by news that Fascist armies had marched across the Ethiopian frontier. The event had been foreshadowed for weeks. Mussolini had repeatedly ignored timorous warnings of the League of Nations and defied its threats of economic sanctions. With great fanfare he had dispatched troop and supply ships from Italian ports to bases in Eritrea and Italian Somaliland bordering Ethiopia. In tones of patriotic frenzy he had summoned "Italians all over the world, beyond the mountains, beyond the seas," to remember their heroic heritage. "Rise to your feet! Let the cry of your determination rise to the skies, reach our soldiers in East Africa. It is the cry of Justice and of Victory!"

What did shock the world was the scale and barbarity of the Italian onslaught. It opened with a bombing raid led by Il Duce's son-in-law, Galeazzo Ciano, on the small city of Adowa—a collection of a few hun- dred mud huts where Italian forces had met a humiliating defeat at the hands of semiprimitive Ethiopian soldiers thirty-nine years earlier. In ritualistic revenge, Ciano's bombs reduced Adowa to dust and left half its inhabitants dead. Behind the bombers came columns of tanks, artillery, trucks, and infantrymen armed with the most modern weapons. The Italian force numbered over 200,000 white soldiers and 100,000 fully trained native Somalis. It was the greatest modern army Africa had ever seen.

Haile Selassie, the diminutive, bearded "Lion of Judah"—Emperor of Ethiopia—could summon half a million tribal warriors to his support. Less than half of them carried firearms of any kind. Their equipment included a few thousand rifles captured from the Italians nearly half a century ago, some antiquated machine guns, and, according to Laurence Stallings, who was on the scene for *The New York Times*, "a few dozen cannon of the sort one expects to see in a military museum." Still other warriors, shrouded in billowing white robes, fought with spears, swords, and knives. There was no Ethiopian air force, no air defense, no munitions industry, no transport save donkeys and camels.

With all their awesome might, however, the Fascist legions were unprepared for the rigors of the Ethiopian terrain. Their truck trains bogged down in the trackless sand and mud, their tanks foundered on the rocky mountain slopes, their soldiers suffered for lack of water and fresh food. The enemy harassed them savagely from ambush with sniper fire and lightning guerrilla raids by tribesmen wielding swords and razor-sharp spears. The Italians retalliated with flame throwers, poison gas, and strafing and bombing from the air. In this unequal contest, the defenders were slaughtered in droves. When the war ended, some 28,000 Ethiopians were dead as against less than 1,500 Italian soldiers. But the Ethiopians had slowed the invaders down from what had been planned as a triumphant march to a humiliating crawl. It was May 1936 before General Badoglio entered Addis Ababa, the capital, and proclaimed Ethiopia a vassal of the Italian crown.

There had been a time when Benito Mussolini enjoyed a certain admiration from some observers in the United States. For all his posturing and buffoonery he had put some stiffening into the volatile political life of his people. He had trampled on their liberties, but he had "made the trains run on time." To some Americans, frightened by the prolonged Depression and its anxieties, the gains of Fascism seemed to outweigh its faults. But such as there was of this approval it was washed out by the dismal record of Mussolini's Ethiopian adventure. Haile Selassie, on the other hand, in pathetic exile in England, symbolized the world's outraged conscience.

Western diplomacy was another casualty of the Ethiopian war. Leaders in the United States as well as in France and Britain had buckled in capitulation to Mussolini's bluster. President Roosevelt invoked a strict rule of neutrality. He embargoed arms as well as economic asssistance impartially—to Italy, who did not need it, and to Ethiopia, who did. The United States was not, of course, a member of the League of Nations, but Britain and France were, and these two countries collaborated at Geneva to vitiate any meaningful sanctions against Italy beyond condemning her as an aggressor. This turned out to be the death knell for the League. Vanished was the last hope of collective security in a world already staggering toward a second World War.[3]

Nov. 22, 1935

(From *The New York Times*)

CHINA CLIPPER OFF ON FIRST MAIL TRIP ACROSS THE PACIFIC

ALAMEDA, Calif., Nov. 22 —The China Clipper, first of a fleet of giant airliners to speed the Far East trade, hopped off from here today for Manila to open trans-Pacific air mail service amid the cheers of thousands who lined the shores and other vantage points.

The giant flying boat went into the air with the heaviest payload ever to rise from an American airport, more than 100,000 letters in first class and official mail. Though its pouches alone weighed 1,879 pounds, the plane rose from the waters of the Oakland Estuary with an ease and grace that marked the clipper ships of other days, one of the last of which, the Star of New Zealand, was anchored nearby to bid it godspeed. . . .

It took off at 3:42 P.M. and soon after was lost to sight over the horizon. At the controls was Edwin C. Musick, captain of the China Clipper, a veteran airman and Pan Am's foremost pilot.

The maiden scheduled flight of the China *Clipper* on November 22, 1935, was a historic landmark not only in commerical aviation but in human mobility as well. It began the process by which the terrors of the ocean barriers would shrink to insignificance and put all the capitals of the world within commuting distance of one another. In the nineteen-thirties Japan was fifteen days away by fast steamer and Rome ten, and "going abroad" was usually a luxury reserved for the very rich. In 1935 there were just over a million arrivals and departures at all United States ports. A generation later, in the nineteen-sixties, you could fly from San Francisco to Tokyo in thirteen hours and from New York to Rome between dinner and breakfast, and the flights had fewer of the very rich, more businessmen, more secretaries, and more schoolteachers on a "club charter." The total two-way traffic across the oceans in 1965 was close to ten million, nine-tenths of it aboard the swift and opulent successors to the lumbering China *Clipper*.

The China *Clipper* (soon joined by the Philippine *Clipper* and the Hawaii *Clipper*), built by the Glen L. Martin Company for Pan American Airways, was the biggest aircraft ever built in the United States up to that time. It was a four-engine, Duralumin flying boat eighty-nine feet long and 130 feet wide from wing tip to wing tip. It weighed twenty-five tons, had a range of 2,400 miles with a one-ton payload, had space for thirty-two passengers and a crew of six, cruised at 130 miles per hour (less than the safe-landing speed of a modern jet), and cost $1.2 million.

Her trailblazing flight out of Alameda that bright November afternoon in 1935 was a spectacle to remember. Thousands of excited spectators

(Top) The Sikorsky S-43, 2-engine Flying Boat of Inter Island Airways. (Bottom) Pan American Airways' *China Clipper*, on her shake-down flight, passes over the unfinished Golden Gate Bridge, San Francisco, November, 1935. At right: (clockwise) Air Mail Stamps: Trans-Atlantic and Trans-Pacific commemoratives (actual size); the "Aerial Dinner," circa 1936. Gone the cold fried chicken and paper cup of the early thirties; the revolutionary Boeing 247, first all-metal, low-wing, twin-engined transport. (Inset) A group of United Air Lines "sky girls" of 1935.

DECEMBER 1935
PRICE 35 CENTS

THE CONDÉ NAST
PUBLICATIONS, INC

(Clockwise) Society playboy-pilot Dick Merrell (left) and crooner Lanny Ross (right), 1936; Airport Dedication button honoring Colonel Roscoe Turner; Mrs. Gladys O'Donnell, one of a handful of women pilots who competed on equal terms with men; Jacqueline Cochran prepping for the 1938 Bendix Trophy Race in a Seversky SEV-S2. She finished 3rd in a Staggerwing Beechcraft in the 1937 coast-to-coast Bendix; First Day Cover, Special Delivery Air Mail Stamp, 1936.

SPECIAL DELIVERY
AIR MAIL STAMP

crowded into and around the docking area and lined the promontories and rooftops around the bay. Millions all over the country listened to news broadcasts on their radios and later watched the proceedings on the motion-picture newsreels. A host of dignitaries, led by Postmaster General James A. Farley, stood under flags and bunting at the dock, as Pan Am President Juan Trippe went through the impressive ritual of checking the readiness of the far-flung way stations along the route by shortwave radio. Then, over the loudspeakers, he addressed Capt. Edwin C. Musick, tight-lipped veteran of 11,000 hours in the air, now sitting in the cockpit with his engines idling.

"China Clipper, are you ready?"

"Standing by for orders, sir," came the response.

"Captain Musick, you have your sailing orders. Cast off and depart for Manila in accordance therewith."

A band playing The Star-Spangled Banner was almost drowned out as the four great propellers revved up and the China *Clipper* pulled majestically away from her mooring at 3:42 o'clock. Slowly gaining speed amidst a foaming cloud of spray, she lifted heavily from the water, just barely cleared the menacing cables of the San Francisco–Oakland Bay Bridge (*Time* magazine said that Captain Musick in desperation ducked *under* the bridge when he could not get over it), and disappeared into the brilliant horizon beyond the Golden Gate. Six hours later Captain Musick radioed that the *Clipper* was 595 miles out over the Pacific, flying 120 miles an hour against a light head wind at an altitude of 9,000 feet, and that all was well.

The route of the China *Clipper* was a tortuous one. She landed at Honolulu at 8:30 o'clock (Hawaiian time) the next morning, approximately on schedule. With a one-night layover there and at each subsequent stop, she moved on the next day to Midway, then to Wake, then to Guam, and so to Manila late in the afternon of the fifth day out. Elapsed flying time for the whole 8,000-mile journey was 59 hours 48 minutes. Two days later she turned around and retraced her course. As her two sister ships were put into service, Pan Am inaugurated a twice-a-week airmail schedule over the Pacific route.

In October of the following year regular passenger service was begun on a slightly improved schedule. The hardy pioneers who paid $799 for a one-way ticket ($1,438.20 round trip) were given rather primitive overnight accommodations at Wake, Midway, and Guam, where the airline had developed its radio and maintenance bases at a cost of more than $2 million. There were no jams at the ticket counter. These early Clippers often made the trip half full. Commercial flying had come a long way by 1935, but long hops over the trackless seas still called for more daring and resolve than most travelers could muster.

Pan American pioneered in international air travel for the United States. It held a monopoly on the business into the nineteen-forties. When the China *Clipper* went into service over the Pacific, the company already had well-established routes fanning out from Miami and covering the Caribbean and South America. In 1939 it inaugurated the first mail and passenger service across the Atlantic, with Lisbon as its European terminus. The flagship of this fleet was the Yankee *Clipper* (built by Boeing), a bigger and speedier version of the China *Clipper*. But she was the last of the big flying boats. Air travel was becoming safe enough and routine enough for travelers to trust the faster and more luxurious land planes, even for night-long journeys across the oceans.

Domestic air service in the United States also made spectacular progress between 1935 and 1940. The number of companies involved dropped from 23 to 19 as they merged to form bigger units, but scheduled routes linked virtually every important city in the country. The coast-to-coast time dropped from about 20 hours with five intermediary stops to 18½ hours with only three stops. Total miles flown almost doubled—from 55 million in 1935 to 109 million in 1940—and the number of passengers went up fourfold, from 746,000 to almost 3 million. Riding in an airplane still smacked of adventure in 1935, even in one of those impressive DC3s everybody was talking about, but it was beginning to become commonplace.[4]

March 13, 1936

(From *The New York Times*)

FLOOD TOLL TO 29, NEW ENGLAND LOSS PUT AT $50,000,000

BOSTON—Twenty-nine dead, upwards of 30,000 persons thrown out of work by the enforced closing of water-powered mills, and property damage which probably will exceed $50,000,000 was the flood toll counted in New England tonight.

Flood waters born of a seven-inch rainfall on three to five feet of snow in northern New England reached the lower sections of the region's great rivers tonight and began inundating the larger mill cities and towns, which have yet to feel the full force of the waters.

Northampton, Holyoke, Springfield and Hartford were expected to feel the full effect of the Connecticut River flood waters tonight, while in eastern New England the Merrimac River, swollen close to an all-time high, was beginning to inflict heavy damage at Manchester and Nashua, N.H., and at Lowell, Lawrence and Haverhill in Massachusetts.

Washed out bridges, highways, railroads and power and telephone lines left many communities cut off from all forms of communication. . . .

For brutish, man-killing, soul-destroying weather the years between 1934 and 1938 probably cannot be matched in the climatological annals of the United States. At one time or another during those five years virtually every part of the country suffered record-breaking extremes of winter cold and summer heat. Prolonged drought dried up millions of acres of farmland and pasturage between the Appalachians and the Rockies and dust storms of unprecedented violence darkened the skies from the Texas Panhandle to the New York harbor. Disastrous floods roared down nearly every major drainage basin across the continent, and hurricanes and tornadoes spread havoc through the Middle West and the eastern seaboard.

The toll in lives and property damage from these natural disasters can only be guessed at, but the records of the American Red Cross give a clue to their immensity. Floods and windstorms alone during that period took 3,678 lives, injured 18,791, and destroyed or damaged 559,164 buildings. The Red Cross spent $37.7 million for disaster relief, and local and governmental outlays must easily have been twice as great.

The flood that inundated the usually peaceful river valleys of New England in the spring of 1936 actually afflicted the whole northeast quadrant of the United States (southward to the Potomac, westward to the Ohio) with death and destruction of near record-breaking levels. Layer upon layer of snow had piled up on the slopes of the Alleghenies, the Adirondacks, and the Berkshires during the preceding hard winter, and the intense cold had frozen the ground many inches deep in a hard, impenetrable glaze. Then had come a sudden thaw early in March, and drenching week-long rains pushing up from the Gulf of Mexico.

As billions of tons of water slid off the frozen slopes, creeks became rivers and rivers became raging torrents. Houses were smashed and trees uprooted, bridges crunched like dry straw, railroads and highways twisted into grotesque piles of rubble. Most railroads, such as the Pennsylvania and the Baltimore and Ohio, canceled their west-bound trains for days. Airlines were crippled by flooded runways and by power failures that blacked out airports and radio beacons. A Trans World Airlines plane carried some 5,000 telegrams from New York to Chicago for transmission beyond the flood zone. Small craft from New England fishing fleets cruised many miles inland in Massachusetts and Connecticut to rescue stranded families and their cats and dogs and an occasional cow from rooftops. Pittsburgh, its Golden Triangle under eight feet of water, was without lights or heat and fearful of an epidemic. Boilers in some of the city's steel mills, engulfed when hastily built dikes caved in, exploded in sheets of steam and flame. Manhole covers in the streets of Portsmouth, Ohio, shot skyward, and geysers of muddy water erupted house-high as sewer gates in the 40-foot floodwall were opened to prevent the river from rushing over the top. The Potomac spread out in a mile-wide lake below the Georgetown bluffs, and WPA workers threw up sandbag barricades around the Lincoln Memorial and the Washington Monument in case the waters would reach that far (they did not). Then, as the Connecticut and the Susquehanna and the Ohio crept grudgingly back to their banks in early April, tornadoes erupted in western Georgia and blasted a zigzag path through parts of Mississippi,

Tennessee, and North Carolina, leaving approximately 200 persons dead. Damage to property amounted to hundreds of millions of dollars.

Nineteen thirty-six stands at the top of the curve in this five-year cycle of natural disasters. "The year was marked by extremes in both temperature and precipitation," the U.S. Weather Bureau noted in its prosaic fashion. "Unparalleled long periods of sub-zero temperatures in many states in the early months of the year were followed by unprecedented drought conditions during the summer months."

It was the coldest January and February ever experienced in the upper Midwest and in parts of the Northeast as well. New York, Boston, Cleveland, Chicago, and most other cities in the region shivered through many successive days of below-zero temperature. There was acute suffering particularly among people on relief rolls.

The following summer, thermometers ran amuck in the opposite direction. The heat wave of July and August was one of the worst on record. Arizona, Kansas, Oklahoma, and Texas had peaks of as high as 120 degrees, and day-after-day readings that never dropped below 100. The torrid air spread upward to the Great Lakes and eastward to engulf the Atlantic seaboard as far north as Boston in its sweltering grip. It was the fourth unbroken year of drought over the Plains States. The rainfall in the American breadbasket was 70 percent below normal. Seed could not germinate, and crops that did push above ground withered and died. The government bought 2.5 million head of cattle doomed to starvation, and slaughtered and processed them for free distribution to the poor. Meanwhile the relentless hot winds swept millions of tons of powdery topsoil out of the Dust Bowl, piled it in roof-high drifts against barns and farm homes, and dropped it in gritty showers on cities hundreds of miles distant.

Another bitter winter followed, storing snow in the mountains and ice in the rivers. In February 1937 the worst of all U.S. floods, exceeding in violence the floods of previous years, roared down the Ohio and lower Mississippi valleys, spreading desolation from the West Virginia panhandle to Louisiana. And again, in March and April, the dust blew all the way from eastern Colorado and Kansas to turn the skies to bronze over New Jersey.

The New Deal for all its presumed magic could do nothing about the weather's vagaries, but it could do something about their human and material toll.

For decades conservationists had been warning that the rape of the land through overcultivation and deforestation would bring dire consequences if it were not halted. The flat and semiarid prairies had been tractored bare of their protective cover of vegetation and planted to grain from horizon to horizon. Farther west, the grassy rangelands had been stripped by unrestricted grazing. Upland forests and woodlands, in the South and East particularly, had been lumbered over and left to die. The roots that held the soil in place and the leaves and other organic litter that slowed the flow of rainfall to the creeks and valleys were gone from millions of acres.

Now, in the mid-thirties, the dire prophecies were proving true. The unchecked floods and dust storms were eating away an irreplaceable national asset—some three million tons of topsoil annually—and creating additional havoc. In a landmark report in January 1935 the National Resources Board asserted the premise that conservation of the soil was a national, not an individual or local, obligation and that it demanded emergency application.

The report gave immediate impetus to work that was already going on in a somewhat haphazard way among a number of government departments and agencies: Agriculture, Interior, the Army Engineer Corps. In 1936 the public's interest was engaged by the widespread showing of a remarkable documentary film, *The Plow That Broke the Plains,* produced for the Farm Security Administration by Pare Lorentz. Its equally impressive companion, *The River,* came out in 1938. Conservation, long a cult, became a national preoccupation.

The gears of government had already begun to mesh. The moribund Soil Erosion Service was given new stature and vitality when it was wedded to the program of farm benefit payments under the Soil Conservation and Domestic Allotment Act of 1936 (successor to the original Agricultural Adjustment Act).

Good conservation practices became mandatory for those receiving crop support payments, and demonstration projects were established to instruct farmers in contour plowing, crop rotation, the building of check dams, and other means of conserving and improving their soil. The FSA and AAA bought up thousands of parcels of eroded, submarginal farmland and turned it back to trees and underbrush. Federal grazing laws were strengthened to curtail destruction of western rangelands. The Forest Service, with the help of CCC and WPA, began work on the Shelter Belt, where it planted some 127 million trees in miles-long windbreaks staggered across the Dust Bowl and the Plains States; and it began the process of reforestation in cutover watersheds. PWA stepped up work on many projects for water conservation and hydroelectric power, such as the Grand Coulee dam in the State of Washington, the Fort Peck dam in Montana, and the Norris dam in Tennessee. Tens of thousands of WPA workers labored at levee construction, river-bank development, and other aspects of local flood control. Millions of dollars and man-hours of labor continued to be poured into the biggest and most spectacular conservation and reclamation project of all time: TVA, the Tennessee Valley Authority. It was proudly noted that the Tennessee River, which had been a bad actor all its life when spring freshets came, was a tamed and disciplined watercourse throughout the great flood of 1937.

The years from 1935 to 1940 were a period of historic achievement (in a sense, a beginning) in systematic land and water conservation in the United States. Floods and droughts and windstorms (but not dust storms!) continue to plague us, as presumably they always will. But we have learned much about how to cope with them and to combat their annual toll in human lives and suffering.[5]

May 1, 1936

(From *The New York Times*)

KARPIS CAPTURED IN NEW ORLEANS BY HOOVER HIMSELF

Desperado Put on Plane to St. Paul

NEW ORLEANS—Alvin Karpis, No. 1 bad man of the United States, was captured tonight without resistance by officers led by J. Edgar Hoover, chief of the Federal Bureau of Investigation.

A few hours later the man who succeeded John Dillinger as the country's most wanted criminal, heavily guarded and manacled, was put aboard an airplane for a destination believed to be St. Paul, Minn.

Without a shot being fired, though Karpis was armed, he was taken into custody along with Fred Hunter, 37 years old, a suspect in the $34,000 Garrettsville, Ohio, mail robbery, and a woman known only as "Ruth," as they emerged from an apartment building about half a mile from the center of the business district.

Mr. Hoover made the announcement with the simple statement: "We have cap-tured Alvin Karpis, generally known as Public Enemy No. 1. He was taken without the firing of a shot. Karpis never had a chance. There were too many guns on him."*

Karpis is under indictment for the $100,000 kidnaping of William A. Hamm, Jr., St. Paul brewer, on June 13, 1933, and the $300,000 kidnaping of Edward G. Bremer, Sr., St. Paul banker, on Jan. 17, 1934. He is also wanted on a charge of murder in connection with the slaying of Sheriff C. R. Kelley at West Plains, Mo., on Dec. 19, 1931.

Mr. Hoover said the FBI had known that Karpis had been in and out of New Orleans for the last several months. He, himself, had come here several days ago to direct the manhunt. Between 15 and 20 men took part in the capture. . . .

It was in the mid-thirties that the G-Man suddenly rose to stardom in the pantheon of national folk heroes, a role that has been only slightly eroded with the passage of time. He was the fearless crime fighter and public defender— cool, steely-eyed, fast on the draw and deadly of aim. He was also a paragon of modesty, incorruptibility, and manly virtue. Almost overnight he became the *beau idéal* of a generation of teenagers, whose taste in heroes had run heavily to prohibition-vintage gangsters and outlaws, and of their parents as well.

Whenever he made the front pages of the newspapers, which was fairly

---

*A clumsy gaffe marred this drama at its climax. As Hoover grabbed Karpis and covered him with his gun, he barked to his agents, "Put the cuffs on him!" But no one had thought to bring handcuffs along. One of the agents then pulled off his necktie and bound Karpis' hands behind him.

(At left) A popular hero for his part in leading FBI agents in the John Dillinger ambush, Melvin Purvis quit the Bureau and went to work promoting Melvin Purvis Junior G-Men Clubs for Post Toasties. For 25¢ and Post Toasties box tops you received a badge, fingerprint kit, and magnifying glass, which, along with James Cagney's hero role in the film *G-Man*, made it romantically popular now to be the "cop" in the childhood derring-do of "cops and robbers." (Below) J. Edgar Hoover, FBI chief (left), and his assistant, Clyde Tolson, enjoying a holiday on the Atlantic City Boardwalk. At right: (top) The Palace Chop House, Newark, New Jersey, October 23, 1935: Beer Baron Arthur (Dutch Schultz) Flegenheimer slumps mortally wounded over a table as henchman "Lulu" Rosenkrantz, "Abbadabba" Berman, and Abe Landau were surprised by the Murder Inc. "hit" by Charles "The Bug" Workman. Lepke Buchalter of Murder Inc. ordered the assassination because the Dutchman planned to rub out racket-buster Tom Dewey. (Below) "Mother is the best bet and don't let Satan draw you too fast" —somewhere between O. Henry and Robert W. Service, the delerious and dying words of Dutch Schultz in Newark City Hospital.

Louisiana in September, 1935
"The Senator from Louisiana yields"
—Seibel in Richmond Times-Dispatch

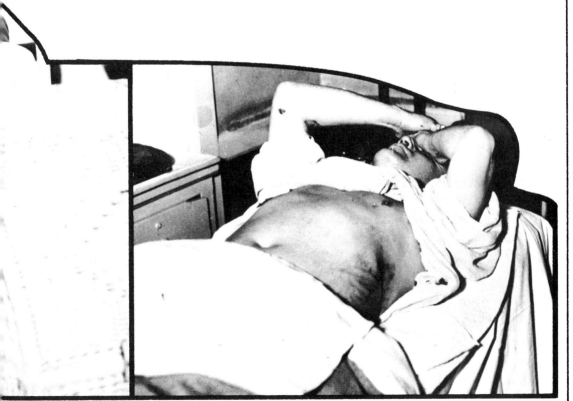

frequent, it usually was in some slam-bang confrontation with a notorious bank robber or kidnapper, with the law triumphant. (When the G-Man missed, not much was said about it.) He generated a booming literature in pulp magazines, comic strips, and sanguinary radio serials, and Hollywood poured forth a prolific succession of B-grade chillers built around his real or imagined exploits: *G-Man, Let 'Em Have It, Men Without Names, Hero No. 1*, and so on. The mystique built up to a point where congressmen and politicians and newspaper pundits were captivated by it. The FBI shield (the G-Man carried it modestly in his wallet instead of pinned to his shirt) became in the popular fancy the shield of the nation.

But the real-life G-Men were, indeed, "men without faces," as they have largely continued to be. Collectively they bore the indomitable, bull-dog visage of their chief, J. Edgar Hoover. The names of individual agents rarely appeared in print, their pictures almost never, and when the FBI spoke it was the voice and the image of Director Hoover that were projected. This was due less to vanity than to smart stage management. Discipline, loyalty, and iron-fisted leadership have been unchanging ingredients of the FBI story. These traits are essential, it is argued, for operational efficiency and good public relations. In both spheres the FBI has built up a nearly matchless record, dating from the time in 1924 when the twenty-nine-year-old Hoover took over a demoralized and thoroughly discredited arm of the Department of Justice and set about its rehabilitation.

The FBI had a clean face but not much muscle when the New Deal came along. Its agents had no guns, no automobiles, no powers of arrest, and very limited jurisdiction with which to combat the wave of kidnappings, bank rob-beries, extortions, and other forms of aggravated lawlessness that had been sweeping the country for years. Most such crimes were state offenses, and the FBI's role, if any, was one of assisting the local cops. The proffer of aid was often received more grudgingly than appreciatively. Moreover, big-time crime had become interstate. A state's police powers stopped at its borders, but the criminals did not stop there. When Charles F. Urschel was kidnapped in Oklahoma City in July 1933, his abductors took him to Texas for safekeeping. The ransom note was sent from Joplin, Missouri, and the ransom money paid in Kansas City, at the other end of the state. A part of the loot was spent in Minneapolis, the rest of it hidden in Texas. One of the kidnappers was cap-tured in California; others were captured in Tennessee, Minnesota, Texas, and Illinois. The map of the crime thus covered seven states and seven separate jurisdictions; the manhunt, sixteen states.

In 1934, under pressure from Senator Royal S. Copeland of New York and Attorney General Homer Cummings, the FBI got its Magna Carta. Con-gress enacted a package of six major anticrime bills that struck away many of the legal shackles that had kept the Bureau more or less impotent. It became a federal offense to kidnap and hold a person for ransom, to rob a national bank, to assault a federal officer, to use the mails for extortion, to engage in interstate racketeering, to transport stolen goods across state lines, to flee across state lines to avoid prosecution, and much more. At the same time, FBI agents were authorized to carry guns, to use armored automobiles, and to make their own arrests of federal offenders. Director Hoover was given funds to enlarge his fingerprint files and his crime laboratory, and to establish a National Police Academy for the training of promising members of local police organizations in modern techniques of crime detection.

From this takeoff point the G-Man soared to fame. Hoover compiled a list of 6,000 gangsters and other interstate evil-doers whom he proposed to run down, and he elevated a chosen few to the elite hierarchy of Public Enemies. At the top of the list, Number One, was desperado John Dillinger, who had a string of ten murders, four bank robberies, and three jail-breakings on his record. He was cut down in a blaze of gunfire on the night of July 21, 1934 outside a Chicago movie theater, where a squad of G-Men had trapped him. (Ironically, the only federal charge against Dillinger at the moment was taking a stolen car across state lines, but the public's outrage over the crime wave was such that any reasonable pretext for apprehending a dangerous outlaw was acceptable.)

As time went on, the intrepid G-Men tied other notable scalps to their belt: "Baby Face" Nelson, "Terrible" Roger Touhy, "Pretty Boy" Floyd, the aforementioned Karpis, "Machine Gun" Kelley (credited with coining the sobriquet "G-Man," meaning "Government man"), Louis "Lepke" Buchalter, and others of their discreditable breed. Meanwhile, of course, the FBI had a lot of knitting to attend to that rarely got into the newspapers. It was responsible for getting evidence against violators of a whole range of quite prosaic federal statutes, from the antitrust laws to the Migratory Bird Act. In 1936 President Roosevelt gave the FBI a mandate to seek out communists, fascists, and other subversives deemed to be threatening the national security. With the approach of war in 1940, counterespionage on the home front was added to the Bureau's duties.

The FBI was given more muscle to do a bigger job, and Congress soon fell into the habit of appropriating whatever funds Director Hoover said he needed. Between 1935 and 1940 he built up his staff of Special Agents from 625 to nearly a thousand. (There were 6,500 on the payroll in 1968.) Under pressure from this augmented force of federal lawmen, kidnapping just about went out of style, bank robberies dropped off so steeply that insurance rates were cut 30 percent (there was a sharp reversal of this trend in the mid-sixties), and recoveries in interstate thefts almost doubled. The conviction rate in FBI cases pushed up to and held at around 80 percent.

The G-Men of the nineteen-thirties did not abolish crime, of course, but they took much of the profit out of it and fragmented some of crime's mightiest empires. They laid the foundation, meanwhile, for something of an empire of their own—an intelligence empire of such scope and secrecy as to alarm some later-day libertarians and political philosophers. But in most eyes the FBI stood, and still stands, as the world's most efficient and glamorous law enforcement agency.

The Philadelphia Tribune

VOLUME 52, NUMBER 50   THURSDAY, OCTOBER 29, 1936   6c in Philadelphia; 10c Elsewhere

Southern Dems Denounced for Lynch Indifference by Jesse Owens

Sweepstakes Money Hopes High In City

One Holds Ticket On Horse Rated 50-One Chance

LIST IS PO...

Roxbury, Mass.
Declared Win...
$2,900 Prize

As the running of...
Sweepstakes appr...
adelphians wait...
they hope w...
some of th...
lars of...
be

"SANTA CLAUS" CAME EARLY FOR THIS GIRL - - $2,900 CHECK!

Olympic Champion Stampedes Audience In Denunciation Of F. D. R. Lynching Indifference

Lynching Is Theme Of Rousing Meeting At Which, Civic, Political Leaders Join In Attack

...NT   F. D. R.   EVASION

By EDGAR W. ROSTER

...balloting less than a week away, the presidential
...is forging to a furious finish, with...me, de-
...oseveltian assurances of confide...
...t Philadelphia is one of the pi...
...e will to a large extent determ...
...as evident by two demonstr...
...ights, and held in the sa...
...in a two-fisted,
...linking the Demo...
...g of humanity
...of which E...
..., spons...
...low...
...D...

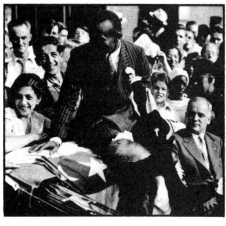

At left: The Gold Medal winning 400-meter relay team: (left to right) Jesse Owens, Ralph Metcalfe, Foy Draper, and Frank Wykoff. (Above) Owens Uber Alles! Jesse Owens soaring to the Olympic Record in the broad jump—26' 5⅜''. (Top, right) Winner of 4 Gold Medals in the 1936 Olympics, Owens returned home to Cleveland a conquering hero. (Below) Program cover for the XI Olympiad.

Tune in on the
BIGGEST MATCH YET!

JOE LOUIS vs. MAX SCHMELING

(Above) Matchbook promotion for the first Max Schmeling–Joe Louis Heavyweight contest, June 19, 1936, sponsored by Buick, with play-by-play and color by Clem McCarthy and Edwin C. Hill. (right) "Der Max" in a training pose at the Napanoch Country Club, Ellenville, N.Y. (Bottom) Louis and Schmeling at the Madison Square Garden weigh-in. Louis, a hot favorite, was battered and bleeding when the end came on a Schmeling KO in the 12th round.

Joe Louis—1935

Jan.	4	Patsy Perroni	WON	10
Jan.	11	Hans Birkie	K.O.	10
Feb.	21	Lee Ramage	K.O.	2
Mar.	8	Red Barry	K.O.	3
Mar.	29	Natie Brown	WON	10
Apr.	12	Roy Lozier	K.O.	3
Apr.	22	Biff Bennett	K.O.	1
Apr.	25	Roscoe Toles	K.O.	6
May	3	Willie Davis	K.O.	2
May	7	Gene Stanton	K.O.	3
June	25	Primo Carnera	K.O.	6
Aug.	7	King Levinsky	K.O.	1
Sept.	24	Max Baer	K.O.	4
Dec.	13	Paulino Uzcudun	K.O.	4

Joe Louis—1936

Jan.	17	Charley Retzlaff	K.O.	1
June	19	Max Schmeling	K.O. by	12
Aug.	17	Jack Sharkey	K.O.	3
Sept.	22	Al Ettore	K.O.	5
Oct.	9	Jorge Brescia	K.O.	3
Dec.	14	Eddie Simms	K.O.	1

Joe Louis—1937

Jan.	11	Stanley Ketchell	K.O.	2
Jan.	27	Bob Pastor	WON	10
Feb.	17	Natie Brown	K.O.	4
*June	22	James J. Braddock	K.O.	8
Aug.	30	Tommy Farr	WON	15

*Won Title

103 MORRIS BERG
Catcher   Boston Red Sox

Born: New York City   March 2, 1903
Bats: Right   Throws: Right
Height: 6' 1"   Weight: 185 lbs.

Moe Berg is regarded as the most educated man in baseball, having graduated from Princeton, Columbia, and the Sorbonne, France. Berg has been a major-league ball player for 18 years, starting in 1923. He is known as one of the smartest catchers in the game, because of his ability to handle young pitchers. He started with Brooklyn as a shortstop, later shifting to catcher, and has seen action with the Chicago White Sox, Cleveland Indians, and Washington Senators, as well as the Red Sox. Moe spends his off-seasons practicing law, and globe-trotting, having been around the world several times. He also speaks fluently eight different languages.

PLAY BALL — *America*

This is one of a series of 250 pictures of leading baseball players. Save to get them all.
GUM, INC., Philadelphia, Pa.   *Printed in U. S. A.*

Joseph M. "Ducky" Medwick,
St. Louis Cardinals,
NL. 1937 Triple Crown Winner
—31 HR; 154 RBI; .374 BA.

Below: (clockwise) President Roose-
vent opening the 1936 Subway
World Series as Managers Bill Terry
(Giants) and Joe McCarthy (Yankees) look on; "Prince Hal" Schu-
macher, Giant right-hander, warm-
ing up during 1936 World Series;
Slugger-to-be Rudy York and Slug-
ger Hank Greenberg on deck in Detroit Tigers training camp, Lake-
land, Florida, 1937; Carl Hubbell
(left), screwball wizard of the New
York Giants, and Bob Feller, rookie
18-year-old Cleveland Indian fire-
baller, about to face each other in
winter camp, New Orleans, La.,
1937; Joe DiMaggio, rookie outfielder of the New York Yankees,
1936; "the high, hard one" of May-
or Fiorello LaGuardia, opening day
at Yankee Stadium, 1935; (center)
Ernesto "Ernie" Lombardi, Cincinnati Reds catcher, 1937.

Melvin T. Ott. "Master Melvin,"
"Ottie." New York Giants,
NL. HR leader—1936 (33); 1937 (31).
RBI leader—1934 (135).

111. VAN LINGLE MUNGO
Pitcher   Brooklyn Dodgers

Born: Pageland, S. C.   June 9, 1911
          Bats: Right   Throws: Right
          Height: 6' 2"   Weight: 185 lbs.

Van Lingle Mungo started his major-league
career with the Brooklyn Dodgers in 1931, after
two years in the minor leagues with Fayette-
ville in 1929, Winston-Salem in 1930 and Hartford for part of 1931. In 1934 he led the National
League pitchers for innnings pitched with 315 in
45 games. Two years later, in 1936, he was
crowned the "strikeout king" of the National
League, when he struck out 283 batters, equal-
ling a league record on July 25th by fanning
seven successive Cincinnati batters — a feat
accomplished only three times before in 60
years of baseball. In 8 years of major-league
baseball Mungo has pitched 1637 innings in 261
games, striking out 983 batters.

PLAY BALL— *America*

WHO'S WHO
in the MAJOR LEAGUES

REG. U.S. PAT. OFF.

PHOTOS, STORIES AND RECORDS
OF EVERY PLAYER IN THE
AMERICAN AND
NATIONAL LEAGUES

CARL HUBBELL

"LEFTY" GROVE

PAUL WANER

LUKE APPLING

5TH. EDITION

BY HAROLD (*Speed*) JOHNSON

25¢

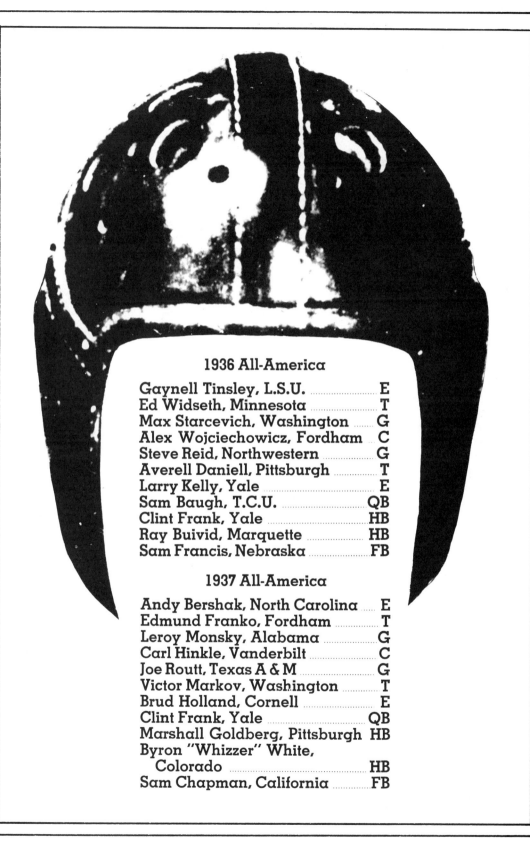

1936 All-America

Gaynell Tinsley, L.S.U.	E
Ed Widseth, Minnesota	T
Max Starcevich, Washington	G
Alex Wojciechowicz, Fordham	C
Steve Reid, Northwestern	G
Averell Daniell, Pittsburgh	T
Larry Kelly, Yale	E
Sam Baugh, T.C.U.	QB
Clint Frank, Yale	HB
Ray Buivid, Marquette	HB
Sam Francis, Nebraska	FB

1937 All-America

Andy Bershak, North Carolina	E
Edmund Franko, Fordham	T
Leroy Monsky, Alabama	G
Carl Hinkle, Vanderbilt	C
Joe Routt, Texas A & M	G
Victor Markov, Washington	T
Brud Holland, Cornell	E
Clint Frank, Yale	QB
Marshall Goldberg, Pittsburgh	HB
Byron "Whizzer" White, Colorado	HB
Sam Chapman, California	FB

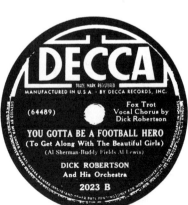

DECCA

TRADE MARK REGISTERED

MANUFACTURED IN U.S.A. · BY DECCA RECORDS, INC.

(64489)

Fox Trot
Vocal Chorus by
Dick Robertson

YOU GOTTA BE A FOOTBALL HERO
(To Get Along With The Beautiful Girls)
(Al Sherman-Buddy Fields-Al Lewis)

DICK ROBERTSON
And His Orchestra

2023 B

At left: (clockwise) Marshall Goldberg, 1937 All-America Halfback and climax runner for Jock Sutherland's Pitt Panthers; "Dandy" Dick Todd of Texas A & M, the most dangerous halfback in the Southwest Conference; Larry Kelly, 1936 Yale All-America end; The Four Horsemen of the Thirties! Pitt's 1937 dream backfield of (left to right) Harold Stebbins, Jack Chickerneo, Marshall Goldberg, and Dick Cassiano; Triple-threat soph flash Sidney Luckman made Columbia fans forget the Rose Bowl heroics of Al Barabas; Clinton E. "Clint" Frank, Yale All-America Quarterback, 1936–1937; J.H. "Brud" Holland, 1937 Cornell All-America end.

Sam "Slinging Sammy" Baugh.
Texas Christian University.
Captain, Quarterback, Safety Man, Punter.
Led nation in passing
and punting, 1935.
Grantland Rice, 1936 All-America Quarterback.

June 30, 1936

(From *The New York Times*)

BOOKS OF THE TIMES

by Ralph Thomson

Margaret Mitchell's "Gone With the Wind" (Macmillan, $3) is an outstanding novel of Civil War and Reconstruction days in Georgia. It is, in all probability, the biggest book of the year: 1,087 pages. I found it—well it is best to delay the verdict for a few paragraphs.

Scarlett O'Hara is growing up on the family plantation, a magnificent place. In April, 1861, she and her sisters wear hooped skirts, their scores of Negro slaves are loveable and happy. Yams drip with butter, plates overflow with golden fried chicken. Young men who come to call are furnished with mint juleps and bear such given names as Stuart and Ashley and Boyd. They wear riding boots, their faces are sunburned. . . . Of course there is a war. Stuart and Brent and Ashley and Boyd rush off and Scarlett weeps. . . .

"Gone With the Wind" is an historical novel . . . not far removed from the motion picture, Birth of a Nation. Miss Mitchell becomes pretty outspoken at times. There is in her story a certain vigor and modernity; she allows her characters to vomit, utter oaths and allude to bodily functions. Scarlett, the heroine, is a vixen and a baggage; Brett, the hero, is alternately a bounder and a gentleman. There is no happy ending. . . .

Any kind of first novel of over 1,000 pages is an achievement, and for the research involved, and for the writing itself, the author of GWTW deserves due recognition. I happen to think the book would have been infinitely better had it been edited down to say 500 pages. . . .

Gone With the Wind was probably the greatest literary smash hit of all time. It was the author's first and only published work. It was an instant success in the bookstores and in two years brought her more than a million dollars in royalties and movie rights and a Pulitzer Prize for distinguished fiction. It has since been translated into thirty languages, and its total sales in all editions aggregate more than thirteen million copies. The publisher reports that there was still a brisk demand for it as late as 1968.

When the movie version came out in December 1939, another wave of excitement and acclaim was loosed. The production cost was an unprecedented $4 million. The film was a full year in the making, the leading roles included such stars as Vivien Leigh, Clark Gable, Leslie Howard, and Olivia de Haviland. Running time in the original, uncut version was just over four hours, with a one-hour dinner intermission. In splendor and panoramic scope it easily outshone such Gargantuan cinema classics of the past as *Birth of a Nation* and *The Four Horsemen of the Apocalypse*. It has enjoyed three major revivals in the thirty years since its release, which seems also to be something of a record.

Margaret Mitchell was as much stunned by her success as anyone else. She had been a reporter on the Atlanta *Journal* for about four years, which was the full extent of her writing exeperience. She began writing the book "for her own amusement" in 1926, when an injured ankle caused her to give up her reporter's job. When a Macmillan editor, who was combing the South for new writers in 1935, asked to see it, she at first declined. It wasn't finished, she said; she had started at the end and worked backward, and had never written an opening chapter. What's more, she didn't really think it was publishable. The editor finally overcame her reluctance. He bought an extra suitcase in which to carry the manuscript she turned over to him back to New York. The publishers never had a second thought about the value of their find, all 460,000 words of it, even though Miss Mitchell thought it was "pretty terrible."

Her book brought her overnight fame, but she did not want to be drawn into the limelight. She continued to live the quiet life of an Atlanta housewife. So far as is known she never tried to write anything else. She died in 1949.

Reviewer Ralph Thompson of the *Times* was not alone in taking a somewhat diffident attitude toward what was to prove to be an all-time best seller. Malcolm Cowley, writing in the *New Republic,* said that in spite of its "triteness and sentimentality" the book has a "simpleminded courage that suggests the great novelists of the past." Peter Quennel, reviewing the book in Britain for the *New Statesman and Nation,* found it "extremely banal . . . never distinguished, but rarely dull." Most Southern critics praised it lavishly as a great document of the Confederacy, although some were prudishly offended by its explicit language and imagery. But the consensus seemed to be expressed by historian Henry Steele Commager, writing in *Books,* who proclaimed: "What is remarkable about this book is not the philosophy, so explicitly set forth, or even the historical authenticity of it all, but the richness of texture, the narrative vigor, the sweep and abundance and generosity of incident and drama . . . the ability to create characters and give them animation and reality. The story . . . is endlessly interesting."

Whether *Gone With the Wind* launched a trend or merely happened to be in the vanguard of a trend, the fact is that over the next decade and more there was a flourishing revival of literary interest in the Civil War period. Miss Mitchell's book, whatever its literary worth, remains the preeminent classic of its genre.[7]

October 23, 1936

(From *The New York Times*)

BURLINGTON ZEPHYR SETS NEW SPEED RECORD, 1,017 MILES, CHICAGO TO DENVER, IN 12 1/5 HOURS

DENVER — Streaking 1,017 miles across four states from daylight to dusk, the Burlington's stainless steel Denver

Zephyr established a world's long distance speed record for railway trains today by pulling into the city at 8:12½ P.M. (Eastern standard time), 12 hours and 12½ minutes out of the Chicago Union Station.

Soon after crossing the Colorado state line the train reached a top speed of 116 miles per hour.

The Zephyr averaged 83.3 miles an hour for today's dash as compared with the old record of 77.4. Aboard the train were 120 Chicago railroad executives, bankers, and businessmen thoroughly enjoying the experience of traveling a thousand miles at a faster clip than passengers have ever traveled before.

The airplanes of the nineteen-thirties bespoke daring and thrills. The new trains of that day—gleaming, streamlined monsters that flashed across the countryside with an imperious roar—signified luxury and glamour, the lure of distant cities and romantic landscapes.

"Thundering across the prairies at night in a flash of silver, white tablecloths and crystal gleaming at the dining car windows, they gave the people of lonely towns a sense of the wealth and power and romance of America and stirred among small boys the restless American's dream of faraway places," Russell Baker wrote in 1968, in a nostalgic lament for the demise of the great passenger trains. He continued:

Scheduled to give the passengers daylight views of some of the world's most spectacular scenery, it [the California Zephyr] crosses the Continental Divide on the second day out of Chicago, snakes through the Rocky Mountain peaks, then runs along the bed of the Colorado River through a fantasy of canyons and gorges until at dusk it comes down into the prehistoric red desert of eastern Utah and roars through the purple sunset toward Salt Lake City.

Next morning it enters the Feather River Canyon through the California Sierra, and for three hours shows the traveler an America more beautiful than is ever dreamed of at 30,000 feet with seat belts fastened, shades drawn and Charlton Heston on the movie screen. Then into the lush, green California valleys with snow peaks for walls and grass as green as April, oranges on the trees, white blossoms on the orchards. . . .

[The Zephyr and its likes] which ought to be preserved as one of America's most precious unnatural resources, is probably going to die. It is a pity. There are organizations to conserve a few of our natural wonders—forests, canyons, rivers —but nothing to save our man-made resources from the hard law of economic necessity.

The nineteen-thirties marked the crest of splendor and fortunes of the luxury train. The Depression had put most of the lines into or close to bankruptcy. With the glimmer of returning prosperity under the New Deal, rail magnates plunged boldly into modernization programs to lure customers back to the ticket windows. High-speed diesel engines began to supplant the smoke-belching old coal burners, and some lines, like the Pennsylvania, went in heavily for electrification. Streamlining gave a sleek, low profile, and the strings of glistening, stainless steel cars with their wide windows and "astrodomes" slid sinuously along the rails like some giant metallic serpent out of science fiction. Speed was up and also comfort. Mile-a-minute schedules on long runs became fairly common. The New York Central Railroad's fabled "Twentieth Century Limited," long rated as one of the fastest on the tracks, clipped forty-five minutes from its New York to Chicago schedule in 1935. And the following year the Union Pacific, with its diesel-powered "M-10001," sliced its fifty-four-hour running time, Chicago to Portland, by eighteen hours.

Disappearing along with the cinders and the clackety-clack were the stiff green plush seats, the double-deck berths, the stench-filled smokers, and the common dressing rooms of the older day coaches and Pullmans. A reclining coach seat on a spotless new streamliner yielded about the equivalent in comfort to a chair in the old-fashioned parlor car and cost no more. The old-styled berths, with their heavy green curtains that kept out the air but not your neighbor's snores, gave way to compact little compartments and roomettes with plumbing and privacy. Snack bars (in addition to diners), cocktail lounges, and roomy club cars made their appearance. Most important of all, the railroads invested heavily in air conditioning for both their old and new equipment.

The railroads sold glamour as well as speed and comfort. They gave many of their trains bewitching names: "Broadway Limited" (Pennsylvania); "Flying Yankee" (Boston and Maine); "Silver Meteor" (Atlantic Coast Line); "Chief" and "Super-Chief" (Union Pacific); "Sunset Limited" (Southern Pacific); and several varieties of "Zephyr." They spent lavishly to advertise the scenic wonders, the up-to-date luxuries, and the elegant company one would encounter on their trains. They publicized the goings and comings of movie stars and other celebrities over their routes. For status, one traveled on the "right" trains and made certain that the home-town society columnists knew it.

The railroads reached their crest of excellence somewhere between 1937 and 1939, but the effort stalled and began slowly to run down. The cost of modernization had been prodigious—in the hundreds of millions of dollars—but the payoff never matched the payout. There were 108 lines in receivership in 1940 as compared with eighty-seven in 1935 and only thirty in the first year of the Depression. Passenger revenue, though spurting temporarily in 1937, never during the decade regained the 1930 level of $730 million. But other modes of travel were booming. Airline traffic, infinitesimally small in 1930, doubled and redoubled to carry 2.8 million passengers in 1940. Travel by private auto increased steadily, and interurban bus lines ate heavily into the railroads' short-haul business. There was a resurgence of rail travel during the war years, but it was not sustained. By the decade of the sixties the railroads had all but given up. Many lines were deliberately discouraging passenger traffic and maintaining only the minimum service required of them by the regulatory agencies. All but a handful of the great glamour trains were gone, and they too, as Russell Baker observed, seemed doomed.[8]

"Come on—we're going to the Trans-Lux and hiss Roosevelt."

At left: (top) Peter Arno's "loving" and witty cartoon of the Roosevelt Era. (Alongside) Destruction from the sky! One of the frequent tornadoes that wrought destruction in Oklahoma, Nebraska, and Kansas in the mid-thirties. (Below) The diesel-powered, stainless-steel beauty of the *Burlington Zephyr* on its record run, October 23, 1936.

DAILY  NEWS

FINAL ★★★

net paid circulation
for May exceeded
Daily ---1,700,000
Sunday -3,000,000

Copyright 1937 by News Syndicate Co Inc. Reg. U S Pat. Off.   **NEW YORK'S** · **PICTURE NEWSPAPER**   Entered as 2nd class matter Post Office, New York N. Y.

Vol. 18. No. 297   New York, Tuesday, June 8, 1937*   56 Main + 4 Special Harlow Pages   2 Cents IN CITY LIMITS | 3 CENTS Elsewhere

BEAUTIFUL
JEAN HARLOW DIES

——Story on Page 3

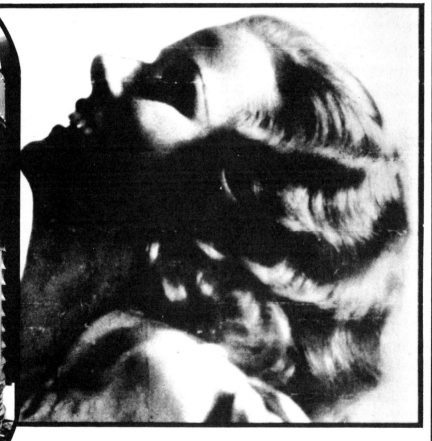

N: Mar. 3, 1911, Kansas City, Mo.   DIED: June 7, 1937, Hollywood, Cal.

Page Harlow Picture Section In Center Fold

Dec. 10, 1936

(From *The New York Times*)

EDWARD VIII RENOUNCES BRITISH CROWN, YORK WILL SUCCEED HIM AS GEORGE VI, PARLIAMENT IS SPEEDING ABDICATION ACT

LONDON—Sometime Saturday morning, perhaps even as soon as tomorrow night, Edward VIII will cease to be King and Emperor. He has made his choice between a woman and a throne and the woman has won.

Today at Fort Belvedere, his country home near Windsor Castle, and in the presence of his three brothers, the Dukes of York, Gloucester and Kent, the King signed a message to his Ministers announcing his determination "after long and anxious consideration" to renounce the throne to which he had succeeded on the death of his father. This, said the message, is "my final and irrevocable decision."

The message was carried by Prime Minister Stanley Baldwin this afternoon to a crowded session of the House of Commons and there read, not without emotion, by the Speaker. . . .

[This] momentous session of Parliament was best described by [the] Prime Minister himself when he said near the close of his narrative of the crisis: "The House of Commons today is a theater which is being watched by the whole world."

Never since the first British Parliament was called by Simon de Montfort 672 years ago had it been the theater for such an impressive tragedy as that enacted today. . . .

And thus, in circumstances that will arouse wonder and pity as long as history continues to be written, ends the brief reign of Edward VIII. It has lasted ten months and twenty-two days before this strange storm that love of woman created has brought it to a close. . . .

At 10 P.M. London time, on Friday, December 11, 1936, millions of people all over the world listened to a memorable radio broadcast from London. Through the crackling static there came, first, the somber, deep-throated tones of Big Ben striking the hour. Next, a strained, reverential voice announced, "This is Windsor Castle. His Royal Highness, Prince Edward." Then came the voice—firm but vibrant with tension—of the man who, only hours earlier, had voluntarily renounced the throne of Britain. He said:

At long last I am able to say a few words of my own.

I have never wanted to withhold anything, but until now it has not been constitutionally possible for me to speak.

A few hours ago I discharged my last duty as King and Emperor, and now that I have been succeeded by my brother, the Duke of York, my first words must be to declare my allegiance to him. This I do with all my heart.

You all know the reasons which have impelled me to renounce the Throne. But I want you to understand that in making up my mind I did not forget the country or the Empire which, as Prince of Wales and lately as King, I have for twenty-five years tried to serve. But you must believe me when I tell you that I have found it impossible to carry the heavy burden of responsibility and to discharge my duties as King as I would wish to do without the help and support of the woman I love.

And I want you to know that the decision I have made has been mine and mine alone. This was a thing I had to judge entirely for myself. The other person most nearly concerned has tried up until the last to persuade me to take a different course. I have made this, the most serious decision of my life, upon a single thought of what would in the end be best for all.

And now we all have a new King. I wish him, and you his people, happiness and prosperity with all my heart. God bless you all! God save the King!

Whatever allegiances and prejudices the millions who heard these words of abdication may have had, scarcely anyone turned away from his radio without a lump in his throat or perhaps the sting of tears in his eyes. For this had been one of the great romantic climaxes of all time—the playing out in real life of a classic plot of poetic drama. The scene was laid against a background of intense controversy and political intrigue, but at the denouement the vast stage was empty save for the solitary figure of a man alone with his heart. "Take all the great speeches of history," Lowell Thomas, the American radio commentator said that night, "and there is nothing approaching in poignancy that of the man who today spoke to the Empire for the last time."

Edward David Windsor, the Prince of Wales and heir apparent to his father, George V, had for a quarter of a century captivated the romantic fancy of the civilized world. Slender, lithe, and youthfully good-looking, he presented a subtle blend of shyness and raffishness, of sedate royalty and man-of-the-world sophistication. He had served creditably in the World War, applied himself dutifully to the ceremonial tasks of his station, traveled the world as a showpiece of the Empire. He had also established himself as a personality in his own right—one who was gregarious, fun-loving, and socially adept. His political attitudes were somewhat "advanced" beyond the nineteenth-century conservatism of other members of the ruling British establishment. His travels had brought him to the United States three times during the twenties. He was fascinated by the country and its people, and they, in turn, were charmed by him.

The Prince was forty-four when, upon the death of his father, he was proclaimed King in January 1936. His accession caused some trepidation within the ruling hierarchy, particularly to such staunch old Tories as Stanley Baldwin, the Prime Minister, and Geoffrey Dawson, that implacable thunderer of orthodoxy who ran the London *Times*. For one thing, Edward had long shown a disturbing streak of intellectual independence. He chafed under the enforced desuetude that was the lot of modern royalty, and occasionally poked his nose into affairs of state and the condition of the working classes, with which he had no business. For another, his way of life did not fit the Victorian proprieties so scrupulously observed by his esteemed parents. He had not

GERMAN SHIP SENDS LAST SOS

Story on Page 3

WEATHER
RAIN
and Colder.
N. Y. Temperatures:
High, Low
1 P.M. 34 1 A.M. 31

DAILY MIRROR

SAVE A LIFE DRIVE SAFELY

PAYOFF EDITION

Vol. 13. No. 119   New York, Monday, November 9, 1936   2 Cents IN CITY LIMITS / 4 CENTS Elsewhere

MRS. SIMPSON TO WED IN PALACE

—Story for this headline on Page 3

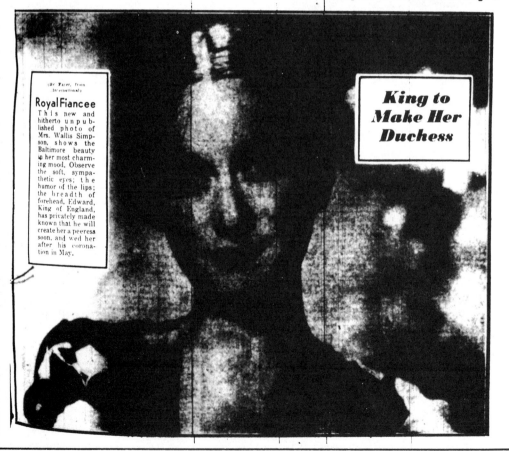

(By Fayer, from International)

Royal Fiancee
This new and hitherto unpublished photo of Mrs. Wallis Simpson, shows the Baltimore beauty in her most charming mood. Observe the soft, sympathetic eyes; the humor of the lips; the breadth of forehead. Edward, King of England, has privately made known that he will create her a peeress soon, and wed her after his coronation in May.

King to Make Her Duchess

(Below) In a most memorable and poetic broadcast—December 11, 1936—Edward VIII, Prince of Wales, renounced his year-old throne of England for the woman he loved.

married and settled down, and he had been known to bow early out of a royal reception at Buckingham Palace and turn up later with a group of rollicking friends at popular London nightclubs. He seemed to have an unregal fondness for polo, for Biarritz, for dancing, and for the company of attractive young women whose families could not be traced in Burke's. There were no shocking indiscretions, presumably, but his goings and comings were common topics of gossip and speculation, particularly in the irreverent American press.

This was no proper image for a British sovereign, Baldwin felt, but there was little he could do about it except grumble fitfully in the privacy of his Cabinet.

Edward first met Mr. and Mrs. Ernest Simpson at a country house-party in November 1930. Simpson was an expatriate American who had taken British citizenship shortly after the war. He was a starchily successful business executive. Mrs. Simpson was also American, the former Wallis Warfield of Baltimore and the onetime wife of a U.S. naval officer, Win Spencer, whom she had divorced some years earlier. Wallis Simpson was tall, vivacious, intelligent, and outspoken. The Prince was instantly captivated by her charm and sophisticated conversation; she had traveled, she read the newspapers, and she had opinions about things. From that time onward the Prince and the Simpsons were often in one another's company. The couple was invited to Belvedere, Edward's modest castle, for dinners and weekends, to other house-parties, and to cruises and receptions, which Edward, too, attended. If Mr. Simpson happened to be away on business or was otherwise occupied, as came increasingly to be the case, Mrs. Simpson showed up without him. London hostesses soon caught on that the way to get the Prince to their parties was to invite Mrs. Simpson.

As the years rolled on, "Wally and the Prince" became more and more an obsessive preoccupation for columnists, magazine editors, and cameramen. In the United States the developing romance was reported and watched with unflagging fascination. Interest leaped to even greater intensity when Edward became King. Would he make Wally—the commoner, the "poor little girl from Baltimore"—his Queen? How would Baldwin and the royal family react? And what had happened to *Mister* Simpson? Did he really say, as reported, "I regret that I have but one wife to lay down for my country"? The King's Mediterranean cruise in the summer of 1937 aboard the yacht *Nahlin,* with Wallis Simpson among the guests, did more for the development of the telephoto lens than Eastman.

The Prime Minister's uneasiness was jolted into near panic when it was learned that Mrs. Simpson had quietly instituted divorce proceedings against her husband. This could mean only one thing: The King planned to marry her and make her his Queen. An unconscionable affront to the royal tradition! Baldwin easily persuaded Dawson and Beaverbrook, Britain's other great press lord, to impose a virtual censorship on the affair. But they could not muzzle the intransigent American press, whose sales in England immediately soared with sensational accounts of the developing "scandal." As news and gossip about the affair percolated tantalizingly from pub to club and to Mayfair drawing rooms, the British public chose up sides. The "best people," or most of them, were indignant; the working classes, or most of them, took a more tolerant view of their King's dilemma.

Communications between a King and his Prime Minister are rigidly circumscribed by protocol. Baldwin, driven to desperation, cut through the barriers late in October to have a secret and highly confidential face-up with Edward. His worst fears were substantiated: the King said flatly he proposed to marry Mrs. Simpson. Baldwin attempted to dissuade him, picturing the frightful disruption to British prestige at home and abroad that would ensue. The King was adamant. At subsequent meetings alternatives were discussed. If Parliament would not consent, as Baldwin asserted, to accepting the commoner as Queen, would it, Edward asked, consent to her becoming the King's wife—his consort—without the title and prerogatives of Queen? No, said Baldwin; he had secretly polled the members of his Cabinet and also the Prime Ministers of the Dominions on just such an alternative, and this, too, was inadmissible. Then, said Edward with finality, there was no recourse for him but to abdicate, and this he intended to do.

As these scenes in the unfolding drama were piling toward a climax, Mrs. Simpson received a temporary decree of divorce in November and, at Edward's insistence, fled to Cannes to escape the bombardments of publicity. The self-imposed censorship in the home press, battered by its American competitors, was coming unstuck. The King talked with her almost nightly by telephone. When he told her, during the first week in December, that his decision to give up the throne was irrevocable, she tried, in what apparently was a stormy session, to dissuade him. Nor could he then dissuade her from issuing a statement to the press of her willingness "to withdraw from a situation which had been rendered both unhappy and untenable."

"Go ahead and issue it," he said at last. "It won't make any difference."

The agony of both principals during the final hours of this tragic episode was intense according to Brian Inglis' excellent book, *Abdication*. Mrs. Simpson was in a state bordering on nervous collapse at the villa she was visiting in Cannes. The King, Inglis says in his book, "had been under constant strain. After Wallis' departure for France, Beaverbrook recalled, it begun to tell on him. 'He smoked incessantly, sometimes a cigarette, sometimes a pipe . . . sometimes he would sit with his head in his hands, [wiping] the perspiration from his brow with a folded handkerchief.' " Not even with the brother who would succeed him, the Duke of York, could Edward steel himself to utter the final and irretrievable word of commitment until the day before the deed would be done.

That day was Tuesday, December 8. At an informal dinner at Belvedere attended by Baldwin, by the Dukes of York, Gloucester, and Kent (Edward's brothers), and by a few friends in government who had remained loyal to him, the King laid on the line his determination to give up the throne immediately. Baldwin, with a sincerity that Edward was always to doubt, made a last but futile attempt to have him change his mind. A brief proclamation was prepared and, in accordance with law, cabled in code to the Dominion Prime Ministers and circulated among members of the Cabinet. The news dam

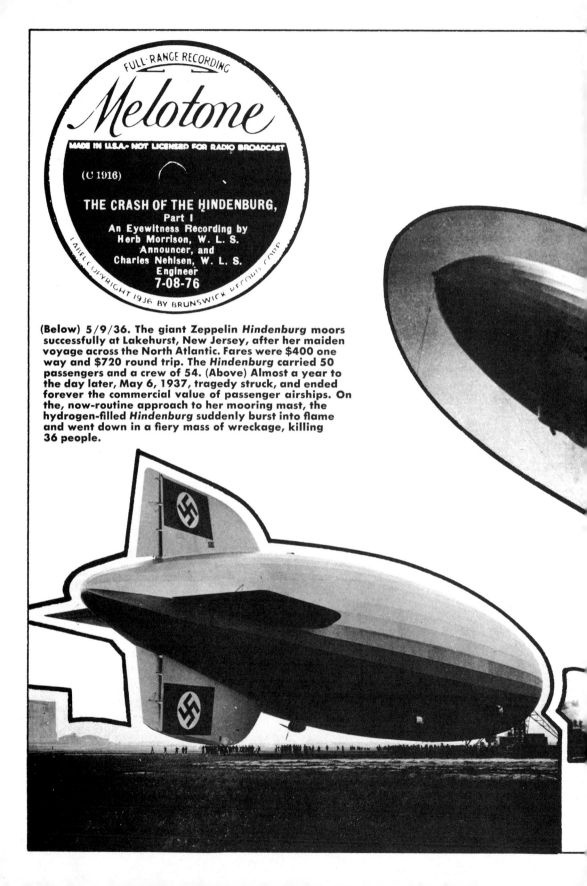

FULL·RANGE RECORDING

Melotone

MADE IN U.S.A.· NOT LICENSED FOR RADIO BROADCAST

(C 1916)

THE CRASH OF THE HINDENBURG,
Part I
An Eyewitness Recording by
Herb Morrison, W. L. S.
Announcer, and
Charles Nehlsen, W. L. S.
Engineer
7-08-76

LABEL COPYRIGHT 1936 BY BRUNSWICK RECORD CORP

(Below) 5/9/36. The giant Zeppelin *Hindenburg* moors successfully at Lakehurst, New Jersey, after her maiden voyage across the North Atlantic. Fares were $400 one way and $720 round trip. The *Hindenburg* carried 50 passengers and a crew of 54. **(Above)** Almost a year to the day later, May 6, 1937, tragedy struck, and ended forever the commercial value of passenger airships. On the, now-routine approach to her mooring mast, the hydrogen-filled *Hindenburg* suddenly burst into flame and went down in a fiery mass of wreckage, killing 36 people.

At left: Benny and Maxine Howard, with their *Mister Mulligan*, were leading the 1936 Bendix Transcontinental Air Race when, suddenly, *Mister Mulligan* threw a propeller blade and crashed into the Arizona desert. Howard and wife survived to fly again and again. (Below) Amelia Earhart and her navigator Frederick J. Noonan, lost somewhere in the South Pacific on a round-the-world flight, were the subjects of the most intensive air-sea rescue search of the decade.

WARSHIP'S PLANES START SEARCH FOR MISS EARHART; NO DEFINITE SIGNAL HEARD

COLORADO IN ACTION

Director of Hunt Says Fliers' Fate Should Be Known Monday

104,000 SQ. MILES COVERED

Itasca, Swan Have Scanned Area North of Howland— Lexington Speeds West

PUTNAM STILL HOPEFUL

and of Lost Flier Believes
May Be Found in Area
w Howland Islands

ssociated Press.

S. COLORADO,
nes catapulted
Colorado
erial search
round-the-
ut returned
ort no trace
g flier and
ick J. Noo-

g off How-
hat was the
ane after it
New Guinea,
2:05 P. M.,
:05 P. M.,
. The planes
M. (12:26
ern daylight

Continue
Press.

—Weak car-
rier wave signals, possibly from the
radio of Amelia Earhart's missing
monoplane, were reported heard
again today by the Coast Guard
just as hope for the safety of the
foremost woman flier sank to its
lowest point since she disappeared

Racing enthusiast Howard Hughes alongside Jimmy Doolittle's 1931 Bendix Trophy winning monoplane, the Laird *Super Solution*, 1935.

RED SAILS IN THE SUNSET

Provincetown Follies

DECCA
TRADE MARK RECORD
MANUFACTURED IN U.S.A. - BY DECCA RECORDS, INC.
(DLA 1167)
Fox Trot with
Vocal Trio
DREAMY HAWAIIAN MOON
From Paramount Production "Cocoanut Grove"
(Harry Owens)
HARRY OWENS
And His Royal Hawaiian
Hotel Orchestra
1798 A

DECCA
REG. U.S. PAT. OFF.
MANUFACTURED IN U.S.A. - BY DECCA RECORDS, INC.
(DLA 722)
Album No. 140
(12 sides-3)
Vocal
with Instrumental
Accompaniment
SWEET LEILANI
From Paramount Picture "Waikiki Wedding"
(Harry Owens)
BING CROSBY
With
Lani McIntire and His Hawaiians
1175 A

VICTOR
Not Licensed for
Radio Broadcast
25349-A
ON THE BEACH AT BALI-BALI - Fox Trot
(En la Playa de Bali-Bali)
(Sherman-Meskill-Silver)
Tommy Dorsey and his Orchestra
Vocal refrain by Edythe Wright
RCA Manufacturing Co., Inc.

DECCA
TRADE MARK REG. U.S. PAT. OFF.
NOT LICENSED FOR RADIO BROADCAST
(DLA 581)
Vocal
Fox Trot
TO YOU, SWEETHEART ALOHA
(Harry Owens)
LOUIS ARMSTRONG
with The Polynesians
914 B
MANUFACTURED IN U.S.A. BY DECCA RECORDS, INC.

Brunswick
FULL-RANGE
RECORDING
Fox Trot
(LA 1569)
Vocal Chorus
Tony Martin
THE MOON OF MANAKOORA
From "The Hurricane"
-Loesser-Newman-
RAY NOBLE
AND HIS ORCHESTRA
Featuring Tony Martin
8079

ARMAMENTS
&
MUNITIONS

WHAT DEPRESSION?
JULY 1, 1935

At left: Escapism in the midst of the Depression reached a peak with John Ford's 1937 South-Sea-Island epic *The Hurricane*, starring Jon Hall and Dorothy Lamour. (Above) "Germany Awake!" read the signs of Hitler's National Socialist Party's Jamboree in Brunswick, Germany, 1935. (At right) Dust jacket for exposé of Nazi spy and *Fifth Column* activity in the U.S., 1936.

THE BOOK THAT FRIGHTENED EUROPE!

THE BROWN NETWORK

BANNED IN HOLLAND AND GERMANY

THE THOROUGHLY DOCUMENTED EXPOSE OF THE ACTIVITIES OF THE NAZ SPIES & TERRORISTS IN THE UNITED STATES & OTHER FOREIGN COUNTRIE

broke, and the word was out in glaring headlines in all the papers. At noon
on Thursday the Prime Minister went before a packed and expectant Commons and in a moving (and some thought a self-serving) speech asked that
the Act of Abdication be acknowledged.

On Friday Edward summoned his old friend Winston Churchill to Belvedere and asked his help in putting the final touches to the farewell he would
deliver to the people of the Empire over the radio. That evening he had a last
dinner with his grieving mother, Queen Mary, and other members of the

family, at the royal lodge. He then went to Windsor Castle, where radio
cables had been strung and where Sir John Reith, chief of the British Broadcasting Corporation, awaited him. At the proper moment, Reith made the
introduction. Edward, inadvertently kicking a table leg with a loud and disconcerting bang, moved to the microphone, and in a voice that quavered but
was strong and unhurried spoke his memorable lines: "At long last I am able
to say a few words of my own. . . . "

Edward, Duke of Windsor, left England that night for a period of seclusion in Austria. Later he had a decorous rendezvous with Wallis in Italy. In
May 1937 her divorce from Ernest Simpson became final. A month later she
and Edward were married at their newly acquired Chateau de Cande, in

FULL-RANGE RECORDING

Vocalion

Fox Trot
(17003)

Vocal Chorus
Wingy Mannone

THE ISLE OF CAPRI
- Kennedy-Grosz -
WINGY MANNONE
and his ORCHESTRA
4464

BEGIN THE BEGUINE

COLE PORTER

ARTIE SHAW'S

HARMS

DECCA
MANUFACTURED IN U.S.A. BY DECCA RECORDS, INC.

(64482)

Fox Trot
Vocal Chorus by
Jimmy Lewis

LAMBETH WALK
From "Me And My Girl"
(Noel Gay-Douglas Furber)
RUSS MORGAN
And His Orchestra
"Music In The Morgan Manner"
2009 A

VICTOR

Not Licensed for
Radio Broadcast

25075-A

MY VERY GOOD FRIEND THE MILKMAN
(Mi Muy Buen Amigo El Lechero)
(Johnny Burke-Harold Spina)
"Fats" Waller and his Rhythm
Vocal refrain and piano by "Fats" Waller

RCA Manufacturing Co., Inc.

DECCA

Vocal with
Orchestra

CHOC'LATE SOLDIER MAN
(OPPENHEIM-RICH)
MAE QUESTEL
(The Betty Boop Girl)
With Victor Young and his
Orchestra
447 A

DECCA

Fox Trot
Vocal Chorus by
Mike Reilly

THE MUSIC GOES AROUND
AND AROUND
(REILLY-FARLEY)
EDDY-REILLY and their
"ONYX CLUB BOYS"
578 A

FULL-RANGE
RECORDING

Brunswick
MADE IN U.S.A. NOT LICENSED FOR RADIO BROADCAST

(LA 1211)

Vocal with
Orchestra

SLUMMING ON PARK AVENUE
From "On The Avenue"
-Irving Berlin-
ALICE FAYE
Orchestra Under Direction
of Cy Feuer
7825

Brunswick
MADE IN UNITED STATES OF AMERICA
Not Licensed For Radio Broadcast

(LA 325)

Vocal with
Orchestra

LULLABY OF BROADWAY
From "Gold Diggers of 1935"
-Dubin-Warren-
DICK POWELL with
Jimmie Grier and
his Orchestra
7374

Red River Valley

with
UKELELE CHORDS
GUITAR CHORDS
and
SPECIAL HAWAIIAN
GUITAR CHORUS

V 241

PRAIRIE RAMBLERS
Over W. L. S. Chicago

CALUMET MUSIC CO
201 EAST 21ST STREET
CHICAGO

DECCA

(62117)

Vocal and
Trumpet Solo by
Louis Armstrong

DARLING NELLY GRAY
(B. R. Hanby)
LOUIS ARMSTRONG and
THE MILLS BROTHERS
1245 A

DECCA

(DLA 587)

Vocal Duet with
Orchestral
Accompaniment

THE WAY YOU LOOK TONIGHT
From R-K-O Picture "Swing Time"
(Jerome Kern-Dorothy Fields)
DIXIE LEE CROSBY and
BING CROSBY
with Victor Young and his
Orchestra
907 B

SHOE SHINE BOY

Connies
HOT
CHOCOLATES
of 1936

Music by
SAUL CHAPLIN

TEDDY BLACKMAN

MILLS MUSIC

Monts, France. It was a small but brilliant social event, as notable for those who did not attend (none of the royal family, for example) as for those who did. Edward's heresy and Wallis' presumption had left a scar on the escutcheon of British aristocracy. The obscure Church of England vicar who had gone cross-channel to marry them was very nearly unfrocked for his daring. As the onetime King and his "woman I love" departed for their honeymoon, they implored the international press to "give them that measure of consideration and privacy which they feel is now their due." But even so, the Duke and Duchess of Windsor, "Edward and Wally," were to remain for many years in the bright glare of notoriety, surrounded even in old age by the fading fragrance of a storybook romance.[9]

September 1937

(From *The New York Times*)

PARALYSIS STRIKES 19 MORE IN CHICAGO

24-Hr Record Brings Prediction of 1,200 More Cases in Ill. before Epidemic Ends

CHICAGO, Sept. 8 — With the report of 19 new cases of infantile paralysis in Chicago alone in the last 24 hours, officials of the State Department of Health at Springfield predicted that the epidemic in the state would reach an all-time record of 1,200 cases.

Today's total reported here has set an all-time record for any 24-hour period. Of the new cases, 16 were persons under 16 years of age, two were 18 and one was 22. This brought the total cases reported within the city limits since the beginning of the present outbreak to 205, with 17 deaths.

Dr. Herman S. Bundesen, president of the City Board of Health, said he could not predict how long it would be before it would be safe for city and parochial schools to open. . . .

WILMINGTON, Del., Sept. 8—Five-year-old Donald Richards died last night from infantile paralysis. He was the second of three Wilmington children to contract the infection in the last week. . . .

HARRISBURG, Pa., Sept. 8 —The Pennsylvania Health Department announced today that 20 new cases of infantile paralysis had been reported this week, raising the statewide total since Aug. 1 to 55. . . .

WINNIPEG, Man., Sept. 12 —Inez Woollman, 23 years old, of Boniface, Man., struggled past the 65-hour mark today without her "iron lung" because another Manitoba child suffered infantile paralysis of the respiratory organs. Afflicted since September 26, 1936, Miss Woollman gave up her place in the lung last Monday night when six-year-old Marilyn Roe, of Bissett, was brought here by airplane in critical condition. . . .

News stories such as these, recurring relentlessly year after year, spread fear and anxiety throughout the nation during the thirties, as they did for two previous decades. Epidemics of infantile paralysis (properly, poliomyelitis; also called polio) were an annual scourge, appearing usually in the late summer and fall. The incidence was not high in terms of the total population. The average for the decade was about 7,500 cases a year, with fluctuations ranging from almost 16,000 (1931) to less than 2,000 (1938), and fatalities were only about one in ten. There were more prevalent and more fatal diseases, but none was more feared than polio. It struck in waves that were unnoticed until they broke. It was an elusive, faceless destroyer, before which medical science was all but helpless. Its principal victoms were children and the young. Those whom it did not kill were maimed for life.

There was no preventive and no cure. The invisible virus was believed to enter the system through the respiratory tract. A variety of inoculations and nose sprays were tried without beneficial results. One such experiment permanently destroyed the sense of smell in a large group of southern schoolchildren. The safest precaution seemed to be to avoid those who might be carriers. Many people wore gauze masks whenever they stepped out of their homes during the polio season. Families who could afford it sent their children to summer camp to get them away from city crowds. Movies and other closed assemblies were shunned. Public swimming pools emptied at the first hint that the infection was at large in a community. Schools were shut or their openings delayed. Prayer seemed as good a precaution as any.

Polio victims were subjected to a variety of therapies: hot packs, cold packs, massage, manipulation, water treatments—all usually without lasting results. Many of those who survived were permanently paralyzed in some part of the body, or condemned to metal leg braces or a wheel chair. Where the breathing muscles were affected, there was the iron lung to breathe for them —an expensive and cumbersome apparatus requiring constant professional attention. Fred Snite, a Chicago youth, achieved an unenviable fame during the thirties by living for more than two years immobilized in such a mechanical cocoon.

The paralysis could not be cured, but it could, with patience and courage, be surmounted. The shining symbol of this hope was President Roosevelt, full of vitality and cheerfulness though paralyzed from the waist down since 1921. Years before coming to the White House he had established, with the help of a few friends, the Warm Springs Foundation at a sleepy little resort in rural Georgia. Here, on a quite limited budget, research went on to try to discover some useful rehabilitative therapy. Such treatment as was available was given to a handful of polio sufferers from the region. The President was a frequent visitor at Warm Springs for rest and relaxation. On many occasions news stories emanating from "Poolside, Warm Springs, Ga.," with pictures of a grinning FDR cavorting in the water, spun the wheels of national and intertional policy. The stories also had a side effect: they rekindled the hopes of thousands of polio sufferers and their families across the country.

The 1937 epidemic was a bad one (though not the worst), with 9,511 cases spotted in clusters in almost every state and a higher-than-usual death toll of 1,461. These figures were about twice as high as for the previous year, but at the same time a glimmer of hope was beginning to tint the medical horizon. New knowledge was proliferating in many areas. The latest "wonder drug," sulfanilamide, was performing fresh miracles almost monthly, bringing such common and critical infectious diseases as pneumonia and tuberculosis under control. Was it possible that polio might yield to some such discovery? The quest was high on the priority list of the United States Health Service and many private research laboratories. Perhaps a massive increase in research would bring results.

Since 1934 the Warm Springs Foundation under the leadership of President Basil O'Connor (he was Roosevelt's former law partner) and scientist Paul de Kruif had been raising more money than it knew what to do with by sponsoring a "President's Birthday Ball" in many cities each January 30. The first ball had been an eye-opener. O'Connor had modestly hoped to raise around $100,000; instead, the net take had been an astonishing $1,016,443. The next three balls had been almost as productive. Most of the proceeds were left in the local communities to buy leg braces and iron lungs for indigent polio patients. Why not direct this great source of emotional and financial energy toward finding a cure for the disease?

On September 23, 1937, while the current epidemic was at its height, President Roosevelt announced the creation of the National Foundation for Infantile Paralysis, whose goal was to raise at least a million dollars a year exclusively for polio research. The annual appeal was to be broadened beyond the society-page clientele of the birthday balls: Everybody from schoolchildren up was to be urged to "send a dime to the White House" to help fight polio. Comedian Eddie Cantor, a member of the organizing committee, was the first to call it "The March of Dimes," and the name stuck. When the first "march" was staged in January 1938, the influx of dime-bearing letters disrupted the White House mailroom for a week, when more than two million letters yielded $268,000. With proceeds of the birthday balls added, the total intake for the Foundation's first year was $1,823,045.

The money continued to roll in year after year, and the Foundation underwrote scores of research projects. But final victory over polio was a long time coming. It was April 1955 when the first Salk vaccine was introduced, and August 1961 before the improved Sabin oral vaccine became available.* Menwhile, polio epidemics had grown to frightening proportions during the war and postwar years. More than 57,000 cases were reported in 1952. But once the new vaccine was put to wide use, the incidence of the disease began to fall off abruptly; by the mid-sixties it had almost reached the vanishing point, on the order of about a hundred cases a year.[10]

*The ultimate credit for the discovery of an effective polio vaccine probably belongs to Dr. John F. Enders of Harvard, who, in 1954, received a Nobel Prize in physiology and medicine for his pioneering work on the poliomyelitis virus. But popular acclaim was bestowed on Drs. Jonas Salk and Albert Sabin, whose vaccines were the first to reach the public. (*Parade* magazine, March 24, 1968.)

CHAPTER 14
Popular Culture – Highbrow

AT 7:30 O'CLOCK ON CHRISTMAS NIGHT, 1937, Arturo Toscanini, standing poised on the podium of a large broadcasting studio in New York, gave a gentle flick to his baton, and the majestic first notes of Vivaldi's *Concerto Grosso* swelled out onto the airwaves and into millions of living rooms across the United States and in Canada. This performance was the premiere of the National Broadcasting Company's "Symphony of the Air"—a landmark of sorts in the cultural history of the nation. This was not, of course, the first time that serious music was heard on radio. Far from it. The Philharmonic and other big orchestras had been on the air scores of times. The Metropolitan Opera had been filling a regular Saturday afternoon slot on Columbia for several years, and a famous concert artist could be heard almost any week on one or more of the big commercial programs. But now a major network had created a first-rate symphony orchestra of its own, had engaged the world's most distinguished conductor as its leader, and had set it up as a permanent part of its corporate inventory along with such popular successes as "Major Bowes" and "Information Please." * NBC gambled on the hunch that the American public's taste for classical music had developed to such an extent that an alert entrepreneur could make it pay, and the hunch was right. It probably would not have been right ten years earlier.[1]

I

Cultural revolutions have to be viewed through a sorcerer's glass, and the sorcerers themselves often disagree about what, if anything, they behold. To a nonsorcerer, however, the nineteen-thirties, seen in retrospect, were a time when the cultural and intellectual landscape of the United States heaved and rumbled and tossed up some interesting new contours. Wars are supposed to be the great catalysts of change, but it is doubtful if either of the World Wars of this century created the intense intellectual and social stresses, the disillusionment and discovery, that prevailed during the decade of the Great Depression, when the exposure to stress was longer (eight to ten years) and was more universally felt then in the war years. The Depression attacked not merely a person's material underpinnings but also his faith and confidence in the familiar verities.

The generation that was of age, or came of age, during the thirties was not wholly naive about or unprepared for the experience. The World War of 1914-18 had knocked out its quota of idols and stereotypes, and it is not just idle rhetoric to speak of the "Flaming Twenties" or the "Lost Generation." The mores and cultural patterns that had survived from the late nineteenth century, Victorian in essence, were rudely shaken in the irreverent postwar decade. Intellectual agnostics like Veblen and Mencken were thumbing their nose at the old tribal gods. Realists like Dreiser and Lewis and Fitzgerald were stripping the novel of its old romantic patina. Sex came boldly out of the

---

*The "Symphony of the Air" outlasted both these hardy radio features; it was discontinued only in 1954, when Toscanini retired. Financially it was no bonanza for NBC, because commercial sponsors footed only a fraction of the orchestra's cost. But as an investment in goodwill and corporate prestige it was immensely successful.

closet, and even "nice" girls necked in the back seats of automobiles and knew more about birth control than was generally suspected. Jazz smote the air, the "Charleston" and the "Black Bottom" shook ballroom rafters, bootleg gin and "moonshine" were common social lubricants, the Ziegfeld Follies showed gorgeous chorus girls with bare breasts, and the movies made heroes of crooks and gangsters. War profits and the Harding-Coolidge "normalcy" had created a brash new aristocracy, which, since it could not break into Newport and Palm Beach, took over Miami and the Catskills. Rotary, Kiwanis, and salesmanship flourished, and the creed of "success" assured any youngster who would put his mind to it that he could make a million dollars. The war had made America aware of Europe, and the automobile and radio were making it aware of what lay across the state line. The old provincialism of mind and custom as well as of geography was crumbling. "Sophisticated" was what the youngsters of the twenties thought of themselves.

The winds of change that blew across the cultural landscape of the twenties rose to gale force in the thirties. They obliterated many familiar landmarks, altered others beyond recognition, and in the end left some new landmarks standing above the debris. The Depression had leveled not merely man-made institutions—banks and factories, homesteads and savings accounts, Sunday schools and country clubs, jobs, careers, and "a stake in the future"—but also the faith and dogmas, the very theology on which these institutions rested. To the generation of the thirties, the collapse of the economic society in which it had been reared was like seeing one's ancestral mansion suddenly cave in and discovering that it can't be put up again because the foundations are faulty, the beams are rotted, and the design hopelessly out of date. A new house will have to be built. But how? Theirs was the dilemma of Housman's Shropshire Lad:

> And how am I to face the odds
> Of man's bedevilment and God's?
> I, a stranger and afraid
> In a world I never made.

One can only generalize about so ephemeral a subject as a nation's moods and introspections, and the documentation can only come out of one's experience. But it is safe to say that a conspicuous attribute of the collective temper of the thirties was the cynicism, particularly among the young, toward the conventional wisdom and the shibboleths and beliefs of the past. Faith was a casualty: faith in religion, faith in moral precepts, faith in the institutions of government and commerce. The old maxims about thrift, frugality, and rewards for had work had been punched full of holes. Capitalism was sick, maybe dead. Long live . . . what?

"Conservative" was a bad word, "liberal" a good word, "socialist" an even better word in many circles. "Communist" was a daring word that, like strong drink, could lead to trouble. But many were tempted by it. For the white-collar type, a bit of the communist dialectic in his speech tagged him perhaps an intellectual.

Above: (clockwise) Alec Templeton, blind pianist and composer, 1938; Dr. Walter Damrosch conducting the NBC Symphony, 1936; "The Music Appreciation Hour" with Dr. Damrosch instructing from the piano; Metropolitan Opera star Grace Moore was one of the first to enter the lush-sounding "pop" classic field; Paul Robeson in 1930. Later in the decade, Robeson had a resounding hit with his recording of "Ballad for Americans"; Lily Pons with André Kostelanetz conducting over CBS. At right: Arturo Toscanini.

That was a good word, too, "intellectual." A new vogue for ideas and ideologies could be found in the most unexpected company, and ordinary discourse often veered off into flights of philosophic fancy. Ph.D.'s were joyfully accepted down in the arena where the conflict between myth and reality was going on, and both big business and big labor hired them to elucidate a rationale for their diverse goals. Theorists and "long-haired professors" manned the levers of government. "The nation's cerebral cortex," to use Dixon Wecter's phrase, was lifted bodily from Manhattan and Wall Street and transplanted to Washington. The voices of the old orthodoxy—Arthur Brisbane, Mark Sullivan, Bruce Barton, Roger Babson among them—still thundered in the public prints, but in diminuendo against the rising chorus of the prophets of a new time—writers and commentators like Walter Lippmann, Heywood Broun, Raymond Clapper, John T. Flynn, Stuart Chase, Thurman Arnold, and others. Usually these new writers fell into more discord than unity, but they were in common agreement that the old verities were dead and that new ones had to be found.

This ferment of ideas and attitudes naturally found its most tangible expression in the arts, in literature, and on the stage. The old forms and the old practitioners were not abandoned. They continued to dominate the scene, in fact, and to scoop up whatever money for such diversions as was lying about. But a vigorous new impulse, born out of the suffering and disillusionment of the Depression, made its appearance early in the thirties and soon was commanding respectful and even fascinated attention. A toughened realism had emerged —a focusing on life as it is rather than as it might or ought to be. Younger writers and painters identified themselves with the social conflict and became political partisans in the class struggle. They saw themselves as puncturers of middle-class illusions and prophets of proletarian "truth." Art for art's sake, in whatever medium, was subordinated in their views to art as a social function.

Many in their newly found political zeal adopted or openly favored Communism as their faith. The American Writers' Congress, first convened in 1935, and later the League of American Writers, which included many of the better-known novelists and playwrights of the day, was generally recognized as a communist front. Some of the members were candidly revolutionaries and propagandists; others espoused varying degrees of proletarianism and disenchantment with the existing order. There was a substantial falling away in the ranks of the Marxists late in the decade, when Stalin made common cause with Hitler. But the rebellious zeal that had caused their defection in the first place gave a verve and glow to artistic expression of all kinds. It has remained as a distinctive intellectual hallmark of the thirties.[2]

II

Nowhere was this *Zeitgeist* more conspicuous than in the theater. Howard Taubman in his history of the theater writes: "With the profit system's promises in tatters in the early thirties, its very foundations came under attack. Some of the blows were as wild as they were naive, but it was an exhilarating epoch in the American theater—the most provocative and exciting, in my judgment, that this country has ever known . . . never were there so much passion and commitment in the theater." [3]

The thirties dealt Broadway a double dose of hard times. The Depression dried up its capital and revenues, and Hollywood, with the advent of talking pictures, raided its supply of talent. There were 240 openings in New York during the 1929-30 season. The next year the number was down to 190, and in a couple of years more even that was cut in half. Big producers like the Shuberts, Arthur Hammerstein, and A. H. Woods went into receivership, and a score of once-proud playhouses either boarded up their fronts or converted to movies. In 1932 the Shuberts brought in the government as a partner, via a loan from the Reconstruction Finance Corporation, to stage a series of sure-fire revivals, such as Gilbert and Sullivan operettas, *Blossom Time* and *The Student Prince*, but the revivals failed to spark. Gangland money was used to back a new musical, *Strike Me Pink,* starring the redoubtable Jimmy Durante, but it flopped after a short run, and the mobsters left Broadway for more fertile terrain.

Here and there hits and near-hits were recorded: Marc Connelly's *The Green Pastures*, a gently patronizing fable out of Negro folklore (which probably would be verboten on the contemporary stage) was launched in February 1930, on a run that was to last eighty weeks, gross $2 million, and win a Pulitzer Prize. Three years later Erskine Caldwell and Jack Kirkland's *Tobacco Road* made its shaky debut. Brooks Atkinson, the *Times* drama critic, called this depiction of a dissolute and lecherous family of Georgia crackers "one of the grossest episodes ever put on the stage," but not without a measure of reluctant admiration for its artistry. *Tobacco Road* was a social document of sorts, with bitter spicing of profanity and incest, and it ran for over seven years to establish a new longevity record in the theater.

Plays of lesser stature and durability, and a fair complement of economy-packaged revues and musicals, managed to pay their way during the early years of the decade, and some were memorable. There was Katherine Cornell in the tenderly romantic *Barretts of Wimpole Street*; Robert Sherwood's *Reunion in Vienna,* a dazzling Continental romp; the incomparable team of Lynn Fontanne and Alfred Lunt in Noel Coward's sophisticated comedy *Design for Living*; a lively musical satire by George S. Kaufman, *Of Thee I Sing,* which poked fun at presidential politics; Cole Porter's sparkling tunes in *Gay Divorcée*. These are a sampling from the top cream of the period.

But many offerings failed to make the grade, and many a good script never got beyond the reader's desk. Never had Broadway, and the entire American theater, been in more dire straits. There were prophets who solemnly declared, "The theater is dead." To thousands of actors, directors, technicians, and other stage people the theater *was* dead. Twenty-two thousand listed their availability with Hollywood casting offices in 1932 alone. The luckless majority went on relief or took jobs as clerks, salesmen, and laborers when they could get them.

Palliatives of every kind were tried: cut prices, low-budget revivals of old favorites, cooperative ventures in which authors, actors, producers, and

SAM S. SHUBERT THEATRE

CENTRAL THEATRES LEASING & CONSTRUCTION .CO.

THE · PLAYBILL · PUBLISHED · BY · THE · NEW · YORK · THEATRE · PROGRAM · CORPORATION

BEGINNING
MONDAY EVENING,
SEPTEMBER 24, 1934

MATINEES
WEDNESDAY AND
SATURDAY

MAX GORDON

presents

WALTER HUSTON

in

SINCLAIR LEWIS'

DODSWORTH

Dramatized by SIDNEY HOWARD

Directed by ROBERT B. SINCLAIR

Settings by JO MIELZINER

CAST
(In the Order of Their Appearance)

SAMUEL DODSWORTH	*Played by*	WALTER HUSTON
A SALES MANAGER	" "	ARTHUR UTTRY
A PUBLICITY MAN	" "	NOLAN LEARY
A SECRETARY	" "	BETTY VAN AUKEN
HENRY E. HAZZARD	*Played by*	ALFRED KAPPELER
FRAN DODSWORTH	" "	FAY BAINTER
THOMAS J. PEARSON, called "Tubby"	" "	HARLAN BRIGGS
MRS. PEARSON, called "Matey"	" "	ETHEL JACKSON
EMILY McKEE, Dodsworth's Daughter	" "	ETHEL HAMPTON
HARRY McKEE	" "	MERVIN WILLIAMS
TWO TRAVELING GENTLEMEN	" { "	NICK ADAMS / WILLIAM E. MORRIS
CLYDE LOCKERT	" "	JOHN WILLIAMS
AN AMERICAN LADY	" "	BEATRICE MAUDE
ANOTHER AMERICAN LADY	" "	MARIE FALLS
A PASSENGER	" "	BERT GARDNER
HIS WIFE	" "	LUCILLE FENTON
EDITH CORTRIGHT	" "	NAN SUNDERLAND
A STEWARD	" "	CHARLES CHRISTENSEN
ANOTHER STEWARD	" "	JOHN ROBERTS
A BARMAN	" "	JAY WILSON
A. B. HURD	" "	HAL K. DAWSON
RENEE DE PENABLE	" "	LEONORE HARRIS
ARNOLD ISRAEL	" "	FREDERIC WORLOCK
KURT VON OBERSDORF	" "	KENT SMITH
A CASHIER	" "	J. H. KINGSBERRY
AN AMERICAN MOTHER	" "	MARIE FALLS

(Above) Walter Huston and Fay Bainter as "Sam and Fran Dodsworth," 1934. At right: (top) James Barton (center) in Jack Kirkland's *Tobacco Road.* (Middle) "The daring young man..." at his peak—William Saroyan, 1939. (Bottom) William Saroyan's Pulitzer Prize and Drama Critics' Circle Award winning *The Time of Your Life,* starring Eddie Dowling and Julie Haydon, 1939.

Clair Luce as "Curley's Wife" in
Of *Mice and Men.*

THE MUSIC BOX

SAM H. HARRIS AND IRVING BERLIN
MANAGERS

THE · PLAYBILL · PUBLISHED · BY · THE · NEW · YORK · THEATRE · PROGRAM · CORPORATION

BEGINNING
MONDAY EVENING,
FEBRUARY 14, 1938

MATINEES
THURSDAY AND
SATURDAY

SAM H. HARRIS
presents

OF MICE AND MEN

by

JOHN STEINBECK

Staged by George S. Kaufman   Settings by Donald Oenslager

CAST

GEORGE	*Played by*	WALLACE FORD
LENNIE	" "	BRODERICK CRAWFORD
CANDY	" "	JOHN F. HAMILTON
THE BOSS	*Played by*	THOMAS FINDLAY
CURLEY	" "	SAM BYRD
CURLEY'S WIFE	" "	CLAIRE LUCE
SLIM	" "	G. ALBERT SMITH
CARLSON	" "	CHARLES SLATTERY
WHIT	" "	WALTER BALDWIN
CROOKS	" "	LEIGH WHIPPER

FORREST THEATRE

DIRECTION . . . . KIRKLAND AND GRISMAN

THE · PLAYBILL · PUBLISHED · BY · THE · NEW · YORK · THEATRE · PROGRAM · CORPORATION

BEGINNING
MONDAY EVENING,
AUGUST 23, 1937

MATINEES
WEDNESDAY AND
SATURDAY

ANTHONY BROWN

PRESENTS

JAMES BARTON

IN

TOBACCO ROAD

A PLAY IN THREE ACTS
BY
JACK KIRKLAND

Based on the Novel
by
ERSKINE CALDWELL

Directed by Mr. Brown

Settings by Robert Redington Sharpe

THE BOOTH THEATRE

CENTRAL THEATRES LEASING & CONSTRUCTION CO.

THE · PLAYBILL · PUBLISHED · BY · THE · NEW · YORK · THEATRE · PROGRAM · CORPORATION

BEGINNING
MONDAY EVENING,
DECEMBER 25, 1939

It is urged for the comfort and safety of all, that theatre patrons refrain from lighting matches in this theatre.

MATINEES
THURSDAY AND
SATURDAY

First production of the Twenty-second Subscription Season

THE THEATRE GUILD, INC.
in association with
EDDIE DOWLING

presents

THE TIME OF YOUR LIFE

a New Play by
WILLIAM SAROYAN

Directed by EDDIE DOWLING and WILLIAM SAROYAN

Settings by WATSON BARRATT

Production under the supervision of THERESA HELBURN and LAWRENCE LANGNER

CAST

(In the order of their speaking)

NEWSBOY	Played by	BLACKIE SHACKNER
DRUNK	" "	JOHN FARRELL
WILLIE, a marble maniac	" "	WILL LEE
JOE	Played by	EDDIE DOWLING
NICK, owner of Nick's Pacific Street Saloon, Restaurant and Entertainment Palace	" "	CHARLES DE SHEIM
TOM, Joe's admirer, stooge and friend	" "	EDWARD ANDREWS
KITTY DUVAL	" "	JULIE HAYDON
DUDLEY, a young man in love	" "	CURT CONWAY
HARRY, a natural born hoofer	" "	GENE KELLY
WESLEY, a colored boy who plays the piano	" "	REGINALD BEANE
LORENE, an unattractive woman	" "	NENE VIBBER
BLICK	" "	GROVER BURGESS
ARAB, an Eastern philosopher and harmonica player	" "	HOUSELEY STEVENS, SR.
MARY L	" "	CELESTE HOLM
KRUPP, a waterfront cop	" "	WILLIAM BENDIX
McCARTHY, a longshoreman	" "	JACK HARTLEY
KIT CARSON, an old Indian fighter	" "	LEN DOYLE
NICK'S MA	" "	MICHELETTE BURANI
SAILOR	" "	JACK ARNOLD
ELSIE	" "	CATHIE BAILEY
A KILLER	" "	EVELYN GELLER
HER SIDE KICK	" "	MARY CHEFFEY
A SOCIETY LADY	" "	EVA LEONARD BOYNE
A SOCIETY GENTLEMAN	" "	AINSWORTH ARNOLD
FIRST COP	" "	JACK ARNOLD
SECOND COP	" "	JOHN FARRELL

At left: Helen Westley (center), June Walker, and Franchot Tone in *Green Grow the Lilacs*, 1931. It later became the basis for the hit musical *Oklahoma*. (Bottom, left) Glenn Anders, Phyllis Povah, Franchot Tone, and Earle Larimore in the Theatre Guild production of Philip Barry's *Hotel Universe*, 1930. (Bottom, right) Maxwell Anderson's Drama Critics' Circle Award, *Winterset*, with Margo and Burgess Meredith, 1935. At right: Burgess Meredith and the "smile of the theatre in the middle thirties.

THE BOOTH THEATRE

CENTRAL THEATRES LEASING & CONSTRUCTION CO.

THE · PLAYBILL · PUBLISHED · BY · THE · NEW · YORK · THEATRE · PROGRAM · CORPORATION

BEGINNING		MATINEES
MONDAY EVENING,		WEDNESDAY AND
SEPTEMBER 27, 1937		SATURDAY

SAM H. HARRIS

presents

YOU CAN'T TAKE IT WITH YOU

A farcical comedy by
MOSS HART and GEORGE S. KAUFMAN

Setting by Donald Oenslager

CAST

PENELOPE SYCAMORE	..........Played by........	JOSEPHINE HULL
ESSIE	" .."	PAULA TRUEMAN
RHEBA	" "	RUTH ATTAWAY
PAUL SYCAMORE	" "	FRANK WILCOX

THEATRE ⟨ GUILD ⟩ PROGRAM

AH, WILDERNESS!

BY EUGENE O'NEILL

WITH GEO. M. COHAN

at the

GUILD THEATRE

JED HARRIS
presents

OUR TOWN

A PLAY BY
THORNTON WILDER

with

FRANK CRAVEN

Production by Mr. Harris
Technical Direction by Raymond Sovey
Costumes Designed by Helene Pons

THE CAST

(In the order of their appearance)

Stage Manager	Frank Craven	Lady in the Box	Aline McDermott
Dr. Gibbs	Jay Fassett	Simon Stimson	Philip Coolidge
Joe Crowell	Raymond Roe	Mrs. Soames	Doro Merande
Howie Newsome	Tom Fadden	Constable Warren	E. Irving Locke
Mrs. Gibbs	Evelyn Varden	Si Crowell	Billy Redfield
Mrs. Webb	Helen Carew	Baseball Players	Alfred Ryder / William Roehrick / Thomas Coley
George Gibbs	John Craven		
Rebecca Gibbs	Marilyn Erskine		
Wally Webb	Charles Wiley, Jr.	Sam Craig	Francis G. Cleveland
Emily Webb	Martha Scott	Joe Stoddard	William Wadsworth
Professor Willard	Arthur Allen	Assistant Stage Managers	Thomas Morgan / Alfred Ryder / William Roehrick / Thomas Coley
Mr. Webb	Thomas W. Ross		
Woman in the Balcony	Carrie Weller		
Man in the Auditorium	Walter O. Hill		

People of the Town: Carrie Weller, Alice Donaldson, Walter O. Hill, Arthur Allen, Charles Mellody, Katharine
Raht, Mary Elizabeth Forbes, Dorothy Nolan, Jean Platt, Barbara Brown, Alda Stanley, Barbara
Burton, Lyn Swann, Dorothy Ryan, Shirley Osborn, Emily Boileau, Ann Weston, Leon Rose, John
Irving Finn, Van Shem, Charles Walters, William Short, Frank Howell, Max Beck, James Malaidy.

The entire play takes place in Grover Corners, N. H.

CREDITS
Music arranged and organ played by Bernice Richmond. Electrical Equipment by Century
Lighting. Costumes executed by Helene Pons Studio. Hosiery by Jessie Zimmer.
Animal effects by Willard Cary

Production owned and operated by J. H. D. H., Inc.

EXECUTIVE STAFF FOR JED HARRIS

Thomas Bodkin	Company Manager	Alfred Ryder	Asst. Stage Manager
Robert Reud	Press Representative	Joe Eisele	Master Carpenter
Jane Broder	Casting Director	Thomas Connell	Master Electrician
Edward P. Goodnow	Stage Manager	Robert Whittet	Master of Properties
Thomas Morgan	Stage Manager	Ernest De Wolfe	Assistant Electrician
		John Davis	Assistant Electrician

HENRY MILLER'S THEATRE

NATIONAL THEATRE

SHUBERT THEATRE CORPORATION, LESSEE
DIRECTION MESSRS. LEE AND J. J. SHUBERT

PROGRAM · PUBLISHED · BY · THE · NEW · YORK · THEATRE · PROGRAM · CORPORATION

BEGINNING MONDAY EVENING, DECEMBER 29, 1930	MATINEES WEDNESDAY, THURSDAY, FRIDAY AND SATURDAY

HERMAN SHUMLIN

(IN ASSOCIATION WITH HARRY MOSES)

PRESENTS

"GRAND HOTEL"

A PLAY BY VICKI BAUM

Adapted From the German by William A. Drake

DIRECTED BY HERMAN SHUMLIN

Settings Designed by Aline Bernstein

CAST

SENF	Played by	WALTER VONNEGUT
PREYSING	"	SIEGFRIED RUMANN
FLAEMMCHEN	"	HORTENSE ALDEN
SUZANNE	"	RAFFAELA OTTIANO
BARON VON GAIGERN	"	HENRY HULL

At left: Leslie Howard as the wayfarer in Robert Sherwood's *The Petrified Forest*, 1935. (Above) Howard comforts Peggy Conklin and Humphrey Bogart (right), as "Duke Mantee," looks on. (Below) One of the big hits of 1934—Lillian Hellman's *The Children's Hour*—with (left to right) Aline McDermott, Katherine Emery, and Florence McGee.

stage hands divvied up the receipts equally. Storefronts and barns were used as theaters. Here and there a provincial repertory company was formed and took root. Robert Porterfield, a young actor just beginning to make his mark on Broadway when the Depression struck, took a dozen of his destitute colleagues to his hometown of Abingdon, in the far southwest corner of Virginia, and set up an acting company in a movie theater that had gone broke. With a bill alternating mainly between Shaw and Shakespeare, folks from the countryside trooped in regularly for this new kind of entertainment, leaving a slab of bacon, a sack of potatoes, a jar of homemade preserves, or whatever, at the box office in lieu of scarce cash. The Barter Theater survived the Depression to become a permanent and professionally respected fixture on the nation's theatrical map.

The most impressive offshoot of the cooperative experiment was the New York Group Theater, which attracted some of the most promising younger theater people whom Broadway had set adrift and provided them with a producing company of their own and a minimum guarantee of room and board. Among the original members (the total was thirty-one) were Harold Clurman, Lee Strasberg, Cheryl Crawford, Stella and Luther Adler, Franchot Tone, Elia Kazan, John Garfield, and Clifford Odets, all of whom either had achieved, or soon would achieve, impressive professional stature. The political orientation of the Group Theater was, naturally, leftward, and most of its productions carried a social message. Thus, it made its first bow, in 1931, with Paul Green's *House of Connelly,* a Chekhovian examination of decadent aristocracy in the South; and its second with John Howard Lawson's *Success Story,* which presented capitalism as the heartless villain. Both plays had a modest financial success, and the Group Theater stood confidently on its own two feet for the next seven or eight years, and then dissolved in the sweet juices of a reviving capitalist prosperity. Of the many fine plays (and a few flops) it offered, perhaps the most outstanding artistically was Odets' *Waiting for Lefty,* a taut drama of labor strife played on a bare stage with Elia Kazan in the leading role. Brooks Atkinson called it "one of the most thorough, trenchant jobs in the school of revolutionary drama."

The most exhilarating development in the theater of the thirties was the creation in 1935 of the WPA Federal Theater Project. Its program coupled the sociological doctrine that actors have as much right to be fed as ditchdiggers with the political notion that government should help foster the arts. It was estimated that 5,000 members of Actors Equity were on relief in New York City alone, and that in the country as a whole between twenty and thirty thousand stage people of varying degrees of professionalism were jobless. To permit this great reservoir of talents to wither away would be an extravagant waste of an important national resource.

WPA Administrator Harry Hopkins turned to a onetime Grinnell college mate of his, Hallie Flanagan, who was then head of the experimental theater at Vassar, to whip the new program into shape. (She was also a friend of Eleanor Roosevelt's, which gave her some extra leverage for the difficult job ahead.) With a first year's allocation of $7 million, she set out to create a nationwide theatrical enterprise: a "people's theater" that would give jobs to 12,000 at wages ranging from $30 to $103.40 a month (meager by any standard but better than the breadline). There were to be five regional centers based in New York, Boston, Chicago, Los Angeles, and New Orleans.

The dream was that the cultural glow would spread from these centers to other nearby states and cities. This dream never fully materialized. Inevitably, New York, where the lion's share of the talent was concentrated (Elmer Rice was the first local director), became the hub of the project.

Mrs. Flanagan faced a host of difficulties. Production costs were limited to 10 percent; the rest of her budget went into wages. Her payroll, screened through local relief offices, was heavily cluttered with has-beens, second-raters, and over-confident amateurs. Commerical producers sniped at her for cutting in on their emaciated business and blocked her access to plays of proved popularity. Politicians denounced the project as an expensive boondoggle and as a haven for radicals and subversive propaganda. In spite of such obstacles the FTP pushed ahead and soon won a comforting measure of both critical and public support. Its fare varied from ancient classics to the most modern experimental plays, from operas and musicals to pageants and puppet shows and even a circus. In its brief history it mounted approximately a thousand different productions. Admission prices were scaled from a dollar downward; many productions were staged free in public parks and school auditoriums. Some were given in foreign languages for the benefit of ethnic neighborhood groups; others were staged by all-Negro casts, a gesture of considerable boldness at the time.

One of its most important innovations was the Living Newspaper, which combined the technique of the radio drama and the newsreel. Developments of current prominence in the news were succinctly and vividly dramatized on the stage. Among the more notable editions were *Triple-A Plowed Under*, which took a harsh look at the social effects of the Supreme Court's destruction of the New Deal farm program; *Power,* a paean for the TVA and public power; and *One Third of a Nation*, which took its text from a Roosevelt speech deploring the existence amidst plenty of the "ill-fed, ill-housed, ill-clothed." The Living Newspaper drew Republican lightning because of its propaganda. The point was well made: the stage offerings were propagandistic but scarcely more subversive than the daily pronouncements by the oracles of the New Deal.

Orson Welles was one of the most brilliant theater craftsmen brought to light by the FTP. His imaginative production of *Macbeth* in the setting of Haiti at the time of the Negro Emperor Henri Christophe, with an all-Negro cast except for himself in the title role, was a minor sensation both in New York and on tour. Later he won still more notoriety when he teamed with John Houseman, a member of the FTP, to stage Marc Blitz-

BELASCO THEATRE

(OWNERSHIP AND MANAGEMENT OF HAZEL L. RICE, INC.)

115 W. 44th St.

FIRE NOTICE: The exit indicated by a red light and sign, nearest to the seat you occupy, is the shortest route to the street.

In the event of fire or other emergency please do not run—WALK TO THAT EXIT

JOHN J. McELLIGOTT, Fire Chief and Commissioner

THE · PLAYBILL · PUBLISHED · BY · THE · NEW · YORK · THEATRE · PROGRAM · CORPORATION

BEGINNING
TUESDAY EVENING
FEBRUARY 19 1935

MATINEES
THURSDAY AND
SATURDAY

THE GROUP THEATRE INC

presents

THE GROUP THEATRE ACTING COMPANY

in

"AWAKE AND SING!"

By CLIFFORD ODETS

"Awake and sing, ye that dwell in dust."—Isaiah 26:19

Production directed by HAROLD CLURMAN

Setting by BORIS ARONSON

CAST

(In the order of appearance)

MYRON BERGER	*Played by*	ART SMITH
BESSIE BERGER	" "	STELLA ADLER
JACOB	" "	MORRIS CARNOVSKY

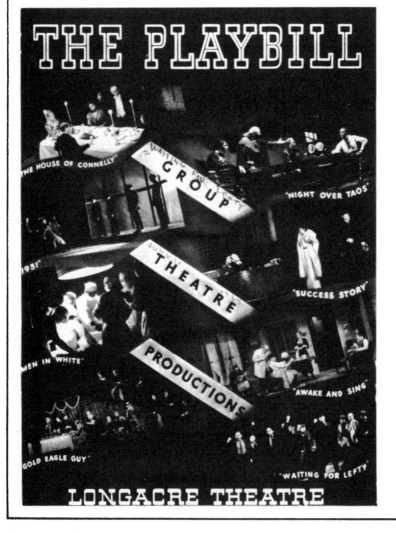

GROUP THEATRE PRODUCTIONS

The House of Connelly	Men in White
1931—	Gentlewoman
Night Over Taos	Gold Eagle Guy
Success Story	Awake and Sing!
Big Night	Waiting for Lefty
	Till the Day I Die

———

The
GROUP THEATRE ACTING COMPANY

Stella Adler	Alexander Kirkland
Luther Adler	Tony Kraber
Margaret Barker	Lewis Leverett
Roman Bohnen	Bob Lewis

Phoebe Brand	Gertrude Maynard
J. E. Bromberg	Sanford Meisner
Morris Carnovsky	Paula Miller
Russell Collins	Ruth Nelson
Walter Coy	Clifford Odets
William Challee	Dorothy Patten
Jules Garfield	Herbert Ratner
Elia Kazan	Art Smith

Eunice Stoddard

———

DIRECTORS

Harold Clurman	Cheryl Crawford

Lee Strasberg

Secretary—Claire Leonard

THE PLAY

'Waiting for Lefty' and 'Till the Day I Die,' a Double Bill by Clifford Odets.

TILL THE DAY I DIE and WAITING FOR LEFTY, two one-act plays by Clifford Odets with the former staged by Cheryl Crawford. Produced by the Group Theatre. At the Longacre Theatre.

TILL THE DAY I DIE.

Karl Taussig	Walter Coy
Baum	Elia Kazan
Ernst Taussig	Alexander Kirkland
Tillie	Margaret Barker
Zelda	Eunice Stoddard
Detective Poppe	Lee J. Cobb
Martin	Bob Lewis
Another orderly	Harry Stone
Captain Schlegel	Lewis Leverett
Adolph	Herbert Ratner
Zeltner	David Kortchmar
Schlupp	Russell Collins
Edsel Peltz	William Challee
1st Storm Trooper	Samuel Roland
2d Storm Trooper	Harry Stone
3d Storm Trooper	Gerrit Kraber
4th Storm Trooper	Abner Biberman
Boy	Wendell Keith Phillips
Old Man	George Heller
Other prisoners	Elia Kazan, David Kortchmar, Paul Morrison
Major Duhring	Roman Bohnen
Frau Duhring	Dorothy Patten
1st Detective	Gerrit Kraber
2d Detective	David Kortchmar
Secretary	George Heller
Arno	Samuel Roland
Stieglitz	Lee Martin
Julius	Bernard Zanville
Women	Ruth Nelson, Paula Miller

WAITING FOR LEFTY.

Fatt	Russell Collins
Joe	Lewis Leverett
Edna	Ruth Nelson
Miller	Gerrit Kraber
Fayette	Russell Collins
Irv	Walter Coy
Florrie	Paula Miller
Sid	Herbert Ratner
Clayton	Bob Lewis
Agate Keller	Elia Kazan
Henchman	Abner Biberman
Secretary	Dorothy Patten
Actor	William Challee
Reilly	Russell Collins
Dr. Barnes	Roman Bohnen
Dr. Benjamin	Clifford Odets
A man	George Heller

Voices Sam Roland, Lee J. Cobb, Wendell Keith Phillips, Harry Stone, Bernard Zanville.

By BROOKS ATKINSON.

After acquiring a prodigious reputation in special performances during the Winter, "Waiting For Lefty" has settled down to steady work at the Longacre, where it was played last evening. This is the one-act play about the taxi strike which has been written by Clifford Odets, author of "Awake and Sing" and poet laureate of the Group Theatre. During the Winter it seemed like one of the best working-class dramas that have been written. On second sight, it is, and it is also one of the most dynamic dramas of the year in any department of our theatre. For Mr. Odets strikes hard. Most of the miniature scenes that sketch in the background of labor insurrection are direct, compact and stinging with reality.

In the new cast, which has been recruited from the ample ranks of the Group Theatre, Mr. Odets appears as the surgeon flung off a hospital staff because of Jewish blood. Although the second cast is in minor details inferior to the first, "Waiting for Lefty" is still a play so full of excitement that it keeps playgoing on the alert. In both the writing and the playing it is centrifugal; the characters are right off the city pavements; the emotions are tender and raw, and some of them are bitter. This column dislikes the egregious office of giving advice, but it does not hesitate to recommend "Waiting for Lefty." People who want to understand the times through which they are living can scarcely afford to ignore it.

Since "Waiting for Lefty" consumes only an hour of playing time, it is preceded by another one-act Odets drama, "Till the Day I Die," which is an anti-Nazi item based on a letter printed in The New Masses. Using a similar device of brief scenes, Mr. Odets has attempted to show how persecution by Nazi terrorists makes the Communists more grimly zealous than ever. "Till the Day I Die" is inferior to both the other current Odets dramas. The characters are less firmly grounded; the point of view is less solid, and Mr. Odets's communistic devotionals are pitched in a key best suited to the party ear.

If you want to register an emotional protest against Nazi polity, Mr. Odets requires that you join the Communist brethren. Even with these reservations "Till the Day I Die" is unmistakably the work of a man indigenous to the theatre. He has a sense of pliable theatre form; he can communicate the pulse and beat of a highly wrought story and his dialogue has the tang of dramatic speech.

In association with the Group Theatre, which has never been in finer fettle, Mr. Odets continues to be our most promising new dramatist—on the vivid evidence of "Waiting for Lefty" and Awake and Sing."

(Above) Brooks Atkinson's rave review of *Waiting for Lefty* in *The New York Times*, March 27, 1935. **(Above, right)** Playwright Clifford Odets, 1935. **(Bottom)** Jules Garfield, Stella Adler, and Phoebe Brand in Odets' *Awake and Sing*, giving the playwright three productions on Broadway for the 1935 season. **At right:** A "broadside" ad protesting the suppression of *Waiting for Lefty.*

FIGHT CENSORSHIP!

Boston, New Haven & Philadelphia Theatres forbidden to go on with their plays on Trumped-Up Charges!

Nationwide protest aroused!

"WAITING FOR LEFTY"

PRIZE - WINNING PLAY BY CLIFF ODETS (AUTHOR OF "AWAKE AND SING" AND "TILL THE DAY I DIE") SUPPRESSED IN BOSTON AND NEW HAVEN ON TRUMPED-UP CHARGES OF "OBSCENITY AND BLASPHEMY" DESPITE THE FACT THAT IT IS NOW BEING PRODUCED ON BROADWAY AND HAS BEEN POINTED OUT AS ONE OF THE MOST SIGNIFICANT PLAYS OF THE YEAR BY LEADING DRAMATIC CRITICS...FOUR MEMBERS OF THE BOSTON CAST ARE OUT ON BAIL...AND DESPITE THE FACT THAT THIS PLAY WON THE YALE DRAMA TOURNAMENT LAST WEEK NEW HAVEN AUTHORITIES REFUSE TO PERMIT THE PLAY TO BE PERFORMED IN THAT CITY.

● **PROTEST NOW!**

● **FIGHT FOR A FREE STAGE!**

● **DEFEND AMERICAN RIGHTS OF FREE SPEECH!**

Write, or wire; The Mayor, Philadelphia Pa.- Police Chief Philip Smith, New Haven Conn. and, The Clerk, District Court, Roxbury Mass. protesting the ban on these plays and demand all charges be dropped.

PHONE OR WRITE TO:

Committee Against Theatre Censorship

(Temporary Address) 114 W. 14 St., N. Y. C.

CHelsea 2-9523

BELASCO THEATRE

DIRECTION SAM H. GRISMAN

THE · PLAYBILL · PUBLISHED · BY · THE · NEW · YORK · THEATRE · PROGRAM · CORPORATION

BEGINNING
MONDAY EVENING
DECEMBER 20 · 1937

MATINEES
THURSDAY AND
SATURDAY

THE GROUP THEATRE
presents

GOLDEN BOY

By Clifford Odets

Direction: Harold Clurman

Settings: Mordecai Gorelik

CAST
(In order of speech)

TOM MOODY	*Played by*	ROMAN BOHNEN
LORNA MOON	" "	FRANCES FARMER
JOE BONAPARTE	" "	LUTHER ADLER
TOKIO	" "	ART SMITH
MR. CARP	*Played by*	LEE J. COBB
SIGGIE	" "	JULES GARFIELD
MR. BONAPARTE	" "	MORRIS CARNOVSKY
ANNA	" "	PHOEBE BRAND
FRANK BONAPARTE	" "	JOHN O'MALLEY
ROXY GOTTLIEB	" "	ROBERT LEWIS
EDDIE FUSELI	" "	ELIA KAZAN
PEPPER WHITE	" "	HARRY BRATSBURG
MICKEY	" "	MICHAEL GORDON
CALL BOY	" "	BERT CONWAY
SAM	" "	MARTIN RITT
LEWIS	" "	CHARLES CRISP
DRAKE	" "	HOWARD DA SILVA
DRISCOLL	" "	CHARLES NIEMEYER
BARKER	" "	KARL MALDEN

At right: Elia Kazan and Frances Farmer. (Below) Morris Carnovsky as "Mr. Bonaparte." (At right) Carnovsky and Jules Garfield as "Siggie."

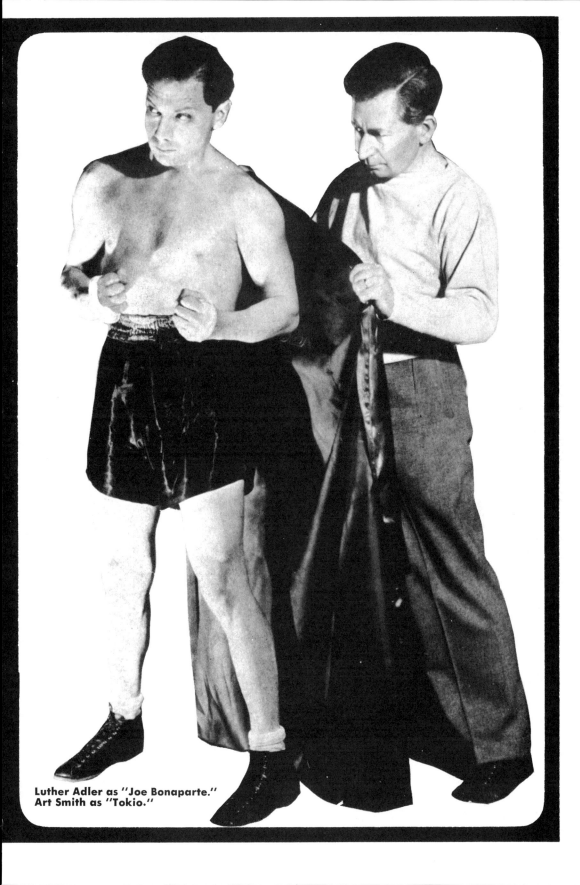

Luther Adler as "Joe Bonaparte."
Art Smith as "Tokio."

Luther Adler and Frances Farmer

Joe: No more fighting, but where do we go?

Lorna: Tonight? Joe, we ride in your car. We speed through the night, across the park, over the Triboro Bridge—

Joe *(taking Lorna's arms in his trembling hands)*: Ride! That's it, we ride—clear my head. We'll drive through the night. When you mow down the night with head-lights, nobody gets you! You're on top of the world then—nobody laughs! That's it—speed! We're off the earth—unconnected! We don't have to think!! That's what speed's for, an easy way to live! Lorna darling, we'll burn up the night! *(He turns and as he begins to throw his street clothes out of his locker)*

Medium Fadeout

20-year-old Orson Welles as "Lamont Cranston,"
The Shadow, on radio, 1935.

At left: Opening night of the John Houseman—Orson Welles Federal Theatre Production of *Macbeth*, Lafayette Theatre, Harlem, 1936. (Middle) Maurice Ellis (left) as "Macduff" and Wardell Saunders as "Malcolm" in a scene from the all-Negro *Macbeth*. (Bottom) At left, Welles as "Brutus" in the first Mercury Theatre production—*Julius Caesar*, 1937. A year later, Orson Welles again as "Captain Shotover" in Bernard Shaw's *Heartbreak House*. Welles was now 23 years old. At right: (top) A scene from the Federal Theatre's "Living Newspaper" unit of 1935. (Bottom) *Triple A Plowed Under*—a scene from another edition of the Federal Theatre's "Living Newspaper."

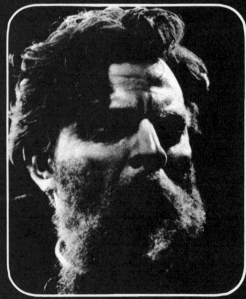

Walter Huston as "Peter Stuyvesant" in the Maxwell Anderson–Kurt Weill musical *Knickerbocker Holiday*, 1938.

WINTER GARDEN

1634-1946 BROADWAY REALTY CO., INC

FIRE NOTICE: The exit indicated by a red light and sign, nearest to the seat you occupy is the shortest route to the street.

In the event of fire or other emergency please do not run—WALK TO THAT EXIT.

JOHN J. McELLIGOTT, Fire Commissioner

THE · PLAYBILL · PUBLISHED · BY · THE · NEW · YORK · THEATRE · PROGRAM · CORPORATION

•   Matinees Wednesday and Saturday

OLSEN AND JOHNSON

present

THE NEW

HELLZ APOPPIN

The Screamlined Revue

Designed For Laughing

with

OLSEN AND JOHNSON

BARTO AND MAN   CHARLES WITHERS   THE RADIO ROGUES   HAL SHERMAN

WALTER NILSSON   THE CHARIOTEERS

BETTYMAE AND BEVERLY CRANE   THEO HARDEEN

Cyrel Roodney and June Winters, Reed, Dean and Reed, Shirley Wayne, Bergh and Moore, Stephen Olsen, Billy Adams and 100 others.

Book by OLSEN and JOHNSON
Music and Lyrics by SAMMY FAIN and CHARLES TOBIAS
Production staged by EDWARD DURYEA DOWLING

Dances Arranged
by GAE FOSTER

Costumes Designed
by JOAN PERSONETTE

NEW AMSTERDAM
THEATRE

DIRECTION
NAMSTERDAM REALTY CORPORATION

THE NEW AMSTERDAM THEATRE PLANNED AND DESIGNED BY
F. RICHARD ANDERSON AND A. L. ERLANGER

BEGINNING
MONDAY EVENING,
MAY 14, 1934

MATINEES
WEDNESDAY AND
SATURDAY

MAX GORDON

Presents

A New Musical Comedy

"ROBERTA"

Adapted from ALICE DUER MILLER's Novel, "Gowns by Roberta"

Music by
JEROME KERN

Book and Lyrics by
OTTO HARBACH

Conductor, Max Meth
Gowns Designed by Madame Tafel   Settings Designed by Carl Robinson
Furs Designed by Max Koch

CAST
(As They Speak)

BILLY BOYDEN, the Hoofer........*Played by*	GEORGE MURPHY	
JOHN KENT, the Fullback........... "	RAYMOND MIDDLETON	
SOPHIE TEALE, the Debutante....... "	HELEN GRAY	
HUCKLEBERRY HAINES' ORCHESTRA .... "	CALIFORNIA COLLEGIANS	
HUCKLEBERRY HAINES, the Crooner. "	BOB HOPE	
MRS. TEALE, the Mother .... "	JANE EVANS	
AUNT MINNIE (Trade Name, ROBERTA), the Modiste .... "	FAY TEMPLETON	
STEPHANIE, the Manager at Roberta's.. "	TAMARA	
ANGELE, the Assistant .... "	BOBETTE CHRISTINE	
LORD HENRY DELVES, the Friend of Roberta .... "	SYDNEY GREENSTREET	
MME. NUNEZ (Clementina Scharwenka), the Star Customer .... "	LYDA ROBERTI	
LADISLAW, the Doorman .... "	WILLIAM HAIN	
MME. GRANDET, the Fitter .... "	MARION ROSS	
LUELLA the Model .... "	NAYAN PEARCE	
MARIE, the Stylist .... "	MAVIS WALSH	

THE MUSIC BOX

SAM H. HARRIS AND IRVING BERLIN,
MANAGERS

PROGRAM · PUBLISHED · BY · THE · NEW · YORK · THEATRE · PROGRAM · CORPORATION

BEGINNING
MONDAY EVENING,
JANUARY 11, 1932

MATINEES
THURSDAY AND
SATURDAY

SAM H. HARRIS

PRESENTS

"OF THEE I SING"

A NEW MUSICAL COMEDY

BOOK BY GEORGE S. KAUFMAN and MORRIE RYSKIND

MUSIC BY GEORGE GERSHWIN

LYRICS BY IRA GERSHWIN

WITH

WILLIAM GAXTON   LOIS MORAN   VICTOR MOORE

BOOK STAGED BY GEORGE S. KAUFMAN
SINGING AND DANCING ENSEMBLES STAGED BY GEORGIE HALE
SETTINGS BY JO MIELZINER
ORCHESTRA UNDER THE DIRECTION OF CHARLES PREVIN

CAST

LOUIS LIPPMAN	Played by	SAM MANN
FRANCIS X GILHOOLEY	" "	HAROLD MOFFET
MAID	" "	VIVIAN BARRY
MATTHEW ARNOLD FULTON	" "	DUDLEY CLEMENTS
SENATOR ROBERT E. LYONS	" "	GEORGE E. MACK
SENATOR CARVER JONES	" "	EDWARD H. ROBINS
ALEXANDER THROTTLEBOTTOM	" "	VICTOR MOORE
JOHN P. WINTERGREEN	" "	WILLIAM GAXTON
SAM JENKINS	" "	GEORGE MURPHY
DIANA DEVEREAUX	" "	GRACE BRINKLEY
MARY TURNER	" "	LOIS MORAN
MISS BENSON	" "	JUNE O'DEA
VLADIMIR VIDOVITCH	" "	TOM DRAAK
YUSSEF YUSSEVITCH	" "	SULO HEVONPAA
THE CHIEF JUSTICE	" "	RALPH RIGGS
SCRUBWOMAN	" "	LESLIE BINGHAM
THE FRENCH AMBASSADOR	" "	FLORENZ AMES
SENATE CLERK	" "	MARTIN LEROY
GUIDE	" "	RALPH RIGGS

Photographers, Policemen, Supreme Court Justices, Secretaries, Sight-seers, Newspapermen, Senators, Flunkeys, Guests, etc.:

ALEXANDER
THROTTLEBOTTOM

Victor Moore as "Alexander Throttlebottom" in the Pulitzer Prize musical Of *Thee I Sing*, 1931. Fred and Adele Astaire in *The Band Wagon*, 1931.

Written by Broadway's sharpest wits—George S. Kaufman, Moss Hart, and Lorenz Hart—and starring George M. Cohan, *I'd Rather Be Right* featured a ribald burlesque of the President of the U.S., his family, his Cabinet, and the Supreme Court, all by name.

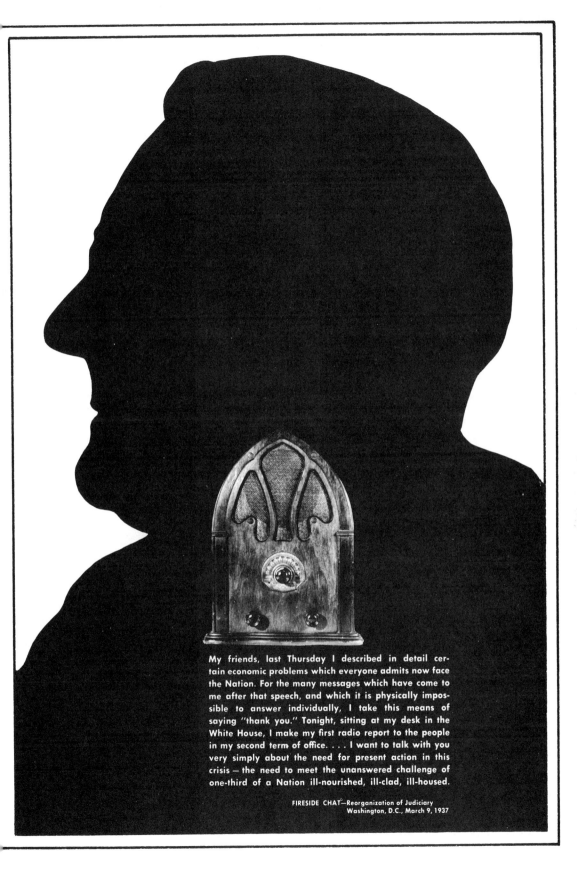

My friends, last Thursday I described in detail certain economic problems which everyone admits now face the Nation. For the many messages which have come to me after that speech, and which it is physically impossible to answer individually, I take this means of saying "thank you." Tonight, sitting at my desk in the White House, I make my first radio report to the people in my second term of office. . . . I want to talk with you very simply about the need for present action in this crisis — the need to meet the unanswered challenge of one-third of a Nation ill-nourished, ill-clad, ill-housed.

FIRESIDE CHAT—Reorganization of Judiciary
Washington, D.C., March 9, 1937

stein's *The Cradle Will Rock,* an abrasive satire on labor conditions in the steel industry. When, on dress-rehearsal night, with a hand-picked audience filling the Maxine Elliott Theater, Washington headquarters vetoed the performance, Welles and company led their guests through the streets to an empty theater nearby and put on the play in defiance of authority. Howard Taubman recalls the scene:

The performance was an incomparable amalgamation of split-second timing and improvisation. Alone on the stage at the piano sat Blitzstein, not certain as he began whether any actors would adopt Welle's suggestion to sit in the auditorium and come in on cue. Blitzstein began the first song and the words were seized from his mouth by the actress in a loge. An actor took up his theme from a place in mid-orchestra. Abe Feder, in charge of lighting, caught each performer in a spot. Not all the company were prepared to risk their meager Project salaries, but most did. The piece moved forward irresistibly, and the audience seethed with excitement, Archibald MacLeish rushed backstage to hail the new day of the participating audience and was asked to top the occasion with a curtain speech.[4]

That was the end of the formal relations of Welles and Houseman with the Federal Theater Project. They pulled out to set up their own group, the Mercury Theater, with *The Cradle Will Rock* as their first hit.

The FTP's most notable *coup* was to gain Sinclair Lewis' permission to stage, without royalty, the dramatization of his popular current novel *It Can't Happen Here,* a biting denunciation of dictatorship. Hallie Flanagan decided to mark the event appropriately: The opening took place simultaneously in twenty-two FTP theaters in seventeen states, including New York, on the evening of October 27, 1936. Some of the performances were undeniably scratchy, but the event taken as a whole was stunning, and critics heaped it with praise. Its aggregate run added up to 260 weeks. Lewis' generosity, incidentally, was quickly matched by other prominent dramatists, including Eugene O'Neill and George Bernard Shaw, who gave the FTP permission to produce any of their plays royalty-free.

Like any theatrical enterprise, the WPA theater had its full quota of misfires and disasters. However, it was ultimately brought down not by its failures but by its successes—it's incisive and sometimes reckless adventures into left-wing ideology and its bold experimentation with dramatic techniques. These gave it artistic distinction but cost it its political life. It became a favorite target of the House Committee on Un-American Activities and of such die-hard economizers as Representative John Taber of New York. Congress cut off its funds in 1939, and the FTP disbanded.

Even in the most desperate Depression years the commercial theater preserved much of its familiar character and variety, if on a greatly reduced scale. Traditional plays were by no means drowned out by the rash of experimentalists, and the old pros continued to assert their mastery. Along with the good was the usual admixture of the tawdry and banal. Such popular revues as George White's *Scandals* and *Earl Carroll's Vanities* glittered forth anew each year. As the general economy began to pick up around 1936, the theater picked up with it. By 1940 its confidence was restored and it had gained some important new faces and new ideas.

Some of the more memorable Broadway productions of the latter half of the decade were Sidney Kingsley's *Men in White* (1935); Maxwell Anderson's *Winterset* (1936) and *High Tor* (1937), both of which won awards from the newly formed Drama Critics' Circle; Robert E. Sherwood's *Idiot's Delight* (1936), with the Lunts at their best, and his monumental *Abe Lincoln in Illinois* (1939) starring Raymond Massey, both of which received Pulitzer awards; Thornton Wilder's *Our Town* (1938); Moss Hart and George S. Kaufman's *You Can't Take It With You* (1937); George Gershwin's ambitious near-opera, *Porgy and Bess* (1935); the incredible sleeper *Pins and Needles* (1937), a musical put-on by a garment workers' union that turned into a smash hit; Olsen and Johnson's crazy-house revue, *Hellzapoppin* (1938), in which some startled member of the audience was likely to find himself the winner of a fifty-pound cake of ice, delivered on the spot into his lap; *The Hot Mikado* (1939), a jazzed-up steal from Gilbert and Sullivan, with an all-Negro cast headed by dancer Bill "Bojangles" Robinson. A happy innovation of 1940 was *It Happened On Ice,* the first of the durable line of ice shows.[5]

III

The intellectual ferment that churned the theater to a froth during the thirties also affected the field of letters. If anything, the surge of social protest was even more marked in literature than on the stage, since visibility was easier to achieve through the medium of books and magazines than through the limited outlet of the stage. There was a great outpouring of novels and short stories with a sociological cast. And there appeared a relatively new genre that can best be described as documentary journalism: books about America and its people that said, often with more passion than objectivity, "Look, this is the way it *really* is." The camera became an important literary tool in this area. There was a marked increase, too, in the publication of books on popularized economic, social, political, and philosophical subjects, many of which sold by the tens of thousands in cheap paperback editions. The thirties may not have witnessed a full-blown renaissance, but millions of people whose complacency about the world had rarely led them beyond the daily headlines were driven by bewilderment and anxiety to try to discover through the printed page what had happened to their world and the pillars of their faith. Thousands of writers leaped to their typewriters to try to supply the answer.

The literary surge of the thirties was, in effect, a continuation and enlargement of what had been most distinctive about the writing of the twenties. It was realism toughened and refined by an admixture of naturalism; an eagerness not only to portray life in its actual dimensions but to include as well its crudities and cruelties—to present, as Malcolm Cowley put it, "a verifiable picture of society." The writers who gave the twenties its characteristic flavor—Hemingway, Fitzgerald, Dreiser, Sinclair Lewis, Dos Passos among them—extended their output and their influence into the new decade. They made the transition to the evolving mode with varying degrees of completeness. Even in the thirties, Scott Fitzgerald continued to be obsessed with the World War's "lost generation," which he first defined in 1920 in *This Side of Paradise*. Ernest Hemingway, until late in the decade, continued to use European settings for his taut novels of postwar disillusionment. Of this select group, only John Dos Passos fully bridged the gap between the decades. He widened his focus from the sad young men who had lost their way in war's wake to a sad society that had lost its way in the cataclysm of depression. His was a dominant figure in the literature of social protest throughout the thirties.

It is futile to try to fit the nuances of literary expression into tidy categories, but as one looks back upon the literary scene of the Depression decade some natural divisions with rather hazy outlines show up on the map. The topography in general is characterized by an introspective social consciousness, a concern for the breed of man rather than for man as an individual. "The tragic 'I'," as Alfred Kazin put it, becomes "the inclusive tragic 'we' of modern society." Within that broad landscape, one area is clearly delineated as belonging to the school of stark, rebellious proletarianism; another, as belonging to a school of awakening nationalism. The nationalist writers of the period probed critically into their land and its sociopolitical institutions, as if for the first time. Another group of writers—the uncommitted, though not necessarily unconcerned—went about their accustomed way buffeted only lightly or not at all by the ideological currents of the day.

The most pronounced color coordinate of the literary thirties is Red. Younger writers in particular, feeling the anger and despair of betrayal, looked upon the old capitalist society and its genteel mores with loathing. The new vision in American life, the essence of the new society, was the class struggle, and the writer who valued his soul had to be not merely an observer but a participant in the conflict. Above the smoke and chaos of the battlefield there shone one clear beacon of order and rationality: Marxism. Its positive and plausible dogma, its confident prophecy of a materialistic Utopia, seemed the only relevant faith left in a demoralized world. Hundreds of writers, known and unknown, took off for the new Promised Land, some bearing banners aloft, others in a speculative frame of mind. Malcolm Cowley, who, in his role as literary editor of the *New Republic,* went at least as far as the bridge with the leftward migration, summed up the phenomenon retrospectively:

We might say that the age was Marxian in a broad sense, but here and there qualifications are to be made. Even the left-wing writers of the time were not much interested in Marx as a philosopher or in Marx as an economist (whatever did he mean by surplus value?) or Marx in his favorite role as a scientist of revolution. Instead, they revered him as a prophet calling for a day of judgment and a new heaven on earth. Sometimes they mentioned dialectical materialism but without trying to understand the Marxian or Hegelian trinity of thought. . . . They bisected and bifurcated, either-ored: either light or darkness, Socialism or Fascism . . . either the glorious (Communist) future or a return to the Dark Ages[6]

Not many of the dedicated revolutionists survived long in the competitive literary struggle. Many were simply deficient as cratfsmen. They were pamphleteers at heart, who, when they had uttered their slogans, could find nothing else to say. From the transitory eminence of having published one or two books, they sank slowly from sight as occasional polemecists for the *Daily Worker, New Masses,* and similar partisan periodicals. The effusions of such intense radicals as Albert Halper, Grace Lumpkin, Michael Gold, and Albert Maltz, for example, though they stirred one's blood at the time, seem as dated and indigestible a generation later as Harold Bell Wright must have seemed to them in the thirties.

Among those who did survive, Dos Passos stands preeminent. His great trilogy on the collapse of the American dream, *The 42d Parallel, Nineteen Nineteen,* and *The Big Money*, published between 1930 and 1936 and combined the following year in a single volume, *U.S.A.,* was an enduring contribution in both substance and style to the American literary heritage. Dos Passos was a fiery Marxist in those days, and some chapters of his books were first published in the *New Masses*, the Communist literary weekly, but his faith began to wane as the decade came to an end.

Close to Dos Passos in both zeal and artistry stands James T. Farrell, creator of *Studs Lonigan*, whose battleground against capitalist wickedness was the industrial canyons of depression-blighted Chicago. Others of the far-left proletarian school include Robert Cantwell, whose principal contribution was *The Land of Plenty*, a novel about labor strife; Jack Conroy, with his delineation of a working class family in *The Disinherited*; Richard Wright, one of the few recognized Negro writers of the period, who produced *Black Boy* and *Native Son*; Ruth McKenney, who wrote with passionate communist conviction about the Akron rubber workers in *Industrial Valley* at the same time that she was turning out crisp and amusing short stories for the upper-class readers of *The New Yorker*. John Steinbeck did not wear a Marxist label, but he wrote one of the most profound and durable proletarian novels of the period, *The Grapes of Wrath* (1939).

"It was not for nothing," Alfred Kazin has pointed out, "that the documentary and sociological prose of the depression period often proved more interesting than many of the new social novels." He calls that particular prose "one of the most remarkable phenomena of the era . . . a vast body of writing that is perhaps the fullest expression of the experience of the American consciousness after 1930, and one that illuminates the whole nature of prose literature in those years as nothing else can." [7]

This documentary prose arose out of the compulsion of the writer to find the cause and the human reality of a social catastrophe greater than any that had happened before. And when he did find the human reality, or shreds and

Left-hand page: (clockwise) Langston Hughes; Ernest Hemingway; Sinclair Lewis receiving the 1930 Nobel Prize; F. Scott Fitzgerald; William Faulkner; Sinclair Lewis. At left: (clockwise) Thomas Wolfe; James T. Farrell; Stork Club, 1935: Gene Tunney, Bernard Gimbel, Ernest Hemingway, Jack Dempsey; F. Scott Fitzgerald; Richard Wright; Erskine Caldwell.

THEY SHOOT HORSES, DON'T THEY?

BY HORACE McCOY

SIMON AND SCHUSTER
NEW YORK
1935

(Above) Horace McCoy's novel, *They Shoot Horses, Don't They?*, was published in 1935 and written during and about the depression depths of 1932. The first American Existentialist novel, and pre-dating Albert Camus' *The Stranger* by almost a decade, it sold 3000 copies (good for a depression first novel) but soon disappeared from the literary scene only to appear in France as a major "enthusiasm" of Existentialists Sartre, Camus and De Beauvoir. Unrelenting in its pessimism and brutality, the novel centered around the tawdry and *danse macabre* (below) aspects of the Marathon Dance and a subsequent boy-girl "mercy killing." A powerful structural device were the typographic chapter openings (below) in which, the ineffectual hero, Robert Syverten, tells his story between pronouncements of the court. McCoy, along with Nathanael West and Nelson Algren truly tapped the bitterness, brutality, and insane competitive aspects of the early days of the depression.

"THE PRISONER WILL STAND....IT IS THE JUDGMENT AND SENTENCE OF THIS COURT...THAT FOR THE CRIME OF MURDER IN THE FIRST DEGREE... YOU, ROBERT SYVERTEN, BE DELIVERED...BY THE SHERIFF OF LOS ANGELES COUNTY TO THE WARDEN OF STATE PRISON...TO BE BY SAID WARDEN...EXECUTED AND PUT TO DEATH ...UPON THE 19TH DAY OF THE MONTH OF SEPTEMBER, IN THE YEAR OF OUR LORD, 1935...IN THE MANNER PROVIDED BY THE LAWS OF THE STATE OF CALIFORNIA AND...MAY GOD HAVE MERCY ON YOUR SOUL...

OF MICE AND MEN

a novel by
JOHN STEINBECK
AUTHOR OF 'TORTILLA FLAT'

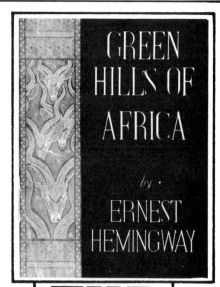

GREEN HILLS OF AFRICA

by
ERNEST HEMINGWAY

A NOVEL
THE BIG MONEY
JOHN DOS PASSOS

APPOINTMENT IN SAMARRA

by
JOHN O'HARA

A COOL MILLION

The Dismantling of Lemuel Pitkin

BY

NATHANAEL WEST

COVICI · FRIEDE · Publishers

NEW YORK

STUDS LONIGAN

A TRILOGY BY
JAMES T. FARRELL

This Volume Contains,
Complete, the Three Novels:

YOUNG LONIGAN
THE YOUNG MANHOOD OF STUDS LONIGAN
JUDGMENT DAY

"A trilogy that is one of the powerful works
of modern American fiction . . . a work of art."
—John Chamberlain in *The New York Times*

traces of it, the creative imagination of the artist became less relevant in the telling than the observant eye of the reporter. The two talents—imagination and reporting—were frequently mixed, but in the best examples of the genre the passion was inherent in the subject matter and spoke its own authentic lines.

The result was to create not only an eye-opening inventory of defeat and suffering and decay spreading across the map of America, but also paradoxically, a new awareness of America as a land and as a nation imbued with strength and beauty and opportunities still not exhausted. It was a literature of national self-discovery—told sometimes with despair, sometimes with pride. It grew from the same roots of disillusionment as the social novel.

Nathan Asch, the novelist son of Sholem Asch, boarded a bus in New York in the summer of 1935, rode all the way to the West Coast and, three months later, back by way of Texas and Georgia. In *The Road: In Search of America*, he reported on what he had seen and experienced—the breadth of America, its beauty and its decay, its stores of grain and its hungry men and women. Edmund Wilson went exploring to write *American Jitters* and *Travels in Two Democracies*. Louis Adamic's *My America*, James Rorty's *Where Life Is Better*, and Sherwood Anderson's *Puzzled America* were a few of many in the same vein—despair and reproach mixed with wonder and hope.

The camera in a few skilled hands became an equal partner in this literary labor. Margaret Bourke-White's pictures in *You Have Seen Their Faces*, probably the most profound documentary on rural deprivation ever assembled, are as impressive as Erskine Caldwell's prose. Photographer Walker Evans collaborated with novelist James Agee to produce *Let Us Now Praise Famous Men*, and with Dorothea Lange and Paul S. Taylor to publish *An American Exodus*. Poet Archibald MacLeish combed the picture files of the Farm Security Administration for illustrations to go with his book *Land of the Free*, and described it as "a book of photographs illustrated by a poem." Pare Lorentz adapted the technique to cinema in producing *The Plow That Broke the Plains* and, more notably, *The River,* a poetic sociologic travelogue down the Mississippi River basin.

The WPA Federal Writers Project gave enormous impetus to the development of this documentary literature. Set up like the Federal Theater Project on a nationwide basis to rescue writers from the relief rolls, it gave jobs to about 6,500 persons at its peak in mid-1936. Possibly a quarter of these writers were professional, with recognizable by-lines. Of 286 persons on the New York project in 1936, ninety had published at least one book or were established magazine writers, but the ratio probably was lower in places like Richmond or Kansas City. Some were jobless newspaper reporters, aspiring poets, novelists and short-story writes, teachers of English and history, research scholars, or just people who could persuade their local relief office to assign them to the project. The national director of the FWP was Henry G. Alsberg, who had worked on the New York *Post* and *The Nation*. His was the task of channeling this reservoir of mixed talents and volatile temperaments into practical and productive employment, and of finding qualified state directors to help him.

Fiction was ruled out at the start as being too hard (and too hot) to be handled as a government commodity. What remained, then, was to write about the common heritage of America, the land and the people. Few realized at the time what an enormous vacuum this represented, how little we really knew about ourselves as a community. The primary result was the series of fifty-three state and regional guides, called the *American Guide* series—the product of millions of hours of travel and original research into the remotest corners of the American landscape, American history, and American folklore. An authoritative critic, Alfred Kazin, has made this appreciative comment:

The guides went so far and so deep into every corner of the American land that they uncovered an America that nothing in the academic histories had ever prepared one for, and very little in the imaginative writing. Road by road, town by town, down under the alluvia of the industrial culture of the twentieth century, lay an America that belied many of the traditional legends about itself. For here, under the rich surface deposits of the factory and city world lay the forgotten stories of all those who had failed rather than succeeded in the past, all those who had not risen on the steps of the American dream from work bench to Wall Street, but had built a town where the railroad would never pass, gambled on coal deposits where there was no coal, risked their careers for oil where there was no oil. . . .

And here, too, was the humorous, the creepy, the eccentric side of the American character; the secret rooms and strange furtive religions; the forgotten enthusiasms of heresies and cults; the relics of fashion and tumbling mansions that had always been someone's folly. Here . . . was a chronicle not of the traditional sobriety and industry and down-to-earth business wit of the American race, but rather of a child-like, fanciful, impulsive and absent-minded people.[8]

The guides were guidebooks in the traditional sense too. They gave the history and ecology of the state and its principal cities and regions; extolled its native heroes, shrines, scenery, and economic resources; and laid out tours covering the principal points of interest. If the writing was seldom brilliant, it was usually literate and concise and remarkably free in most instances of mawkishness and boosterism.

Many of the state FWP state directors fought running battles with chambers of commerce and other political powers in the defense of literary and historical integrity. Governor Curley of Massachusetts, for example, threatened to block publication of his state's WPA guide because of the treatment the writers had given the famous case of Sacco and Vanzetti and the Boston police strike of the nineteen-twenties. The politicians held a whip hand, since the guides had to be sponsored in each instance by a state agency and published on a shoestring by commercial publishers. In spite of such handicaps, the WPA state guides won the almost universal applause of critics and scholars, and they have stood through the decades as a unique and valuable addition to the nation's cultural storehouse.

What was equally important was that the FWP, like the other WPA

NRA
by Louis Nizer

"Mr. Nizer has undertaken a very interesting and useful review of the development and operation of the Code of the Motion Picture Industry. Each industry has its own problems and for a full understanding of the possibilities and accomplishments of the National Recovery Administration it is necessary to understand how the codes of the major trades and industries have been formulated and how they are being administered. Mr. Nizer's book is a valuable contribution to this public understanding."

DONALD R. RICHBERG
Executive Director of The National Emergency Council

The 42ND
PARALLEL

By JOHN DOS PASSOS

HARPER & BROTHERS PUBLISHERS
NEW YORK AND LONDON   1930

SERENADE

JAMES M. CAIN

ALFRED A KNOPF
NEW YORK
1937

BY WILLA CATHER

Death comes for the
Archbishop

ALFRED A KNOPF   NEW YORK

SAVE ME
THE WALTZ

ZELDA FITZGERALD

TO HAVE AND
HAVE NOT
By
ERNEST
HEMINGWAY

NEW ORLEANS CITY GUIDE

Written and compiled by the Federal Writers' Project of the Works Progress Administration for the City of New Orleans

ROBERT MAESTRI, MAYOR OF NEW ORLEANS, CO-OPERATING SPONSOR

Illustrated

HOUGHTON MIFFLIN COMPANY · BOSTON
The Riverside Press Cambridge
1938

DEATH IN THE AFTERNOON

by

ERNEST HEMINGWAY

P. F. Collier & Son Corporation
PUBLISHERS . NEW YORK

CITY OF NEW ORLEANS
OFFICE OF THE MAYOR

ROBT. S. MAESTRI
MAYOR

January 14th, 1938.

The New Orleans City Guide is the first major accomplishment of the Federal Writers' Project of Louisiana. More than a conventional guidebook, this volume attempts to describe the history and heritage of New Orleans, as well as its numerous points of interest.

As Mayor of New Orleans, I am greatly pleased that this publication is being made available to the public.

Mayor of New Orleans.

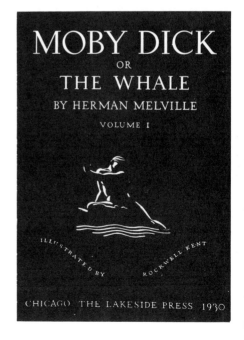

MOBY DICK
OR
THE WHALE
BY HERMAN MELVILLE
VOLUME I

ILLUSTRATED BY ROCKWELL KENT

CHICAGO THE LAKESIDE PRESS 1930

projects, helped to preserve and even to improve, the talents of some scores or hundreds of writers. Their talents might have withered away or never have developed in the arid climate of the Depression. Among the many memorable names from the project roster are those of Vardis Fisher, Conrad Aiken, Richard Wright, John Cheever, Vincent McHugh, and Maxwell Bodenheim.

Nor was the *American Guide* series the project's only output. There were several excellent tour books such as *The Oregon Trail, The Santa Fe Trail, U.S. One,* and a considerable miscellany (about 150 titles all told) on various facets of American life and folklore. The Historical Records Survey rescued thousands of public documents from crumbling obscurity in damp courthouse cellars and fire-prone attics and preserved them for the historians. In all these ways the FWP gave a powerful lift to America's rediscovery of itself. The findings were to have a marked literary influence far beyond the nineteen-thirties.

The sociological impulse provided the dominant trend in the writing of the thirties, but the trend did not turn the whole stream of literature around by any means. Most people continued to read what they wanted to read and not what they thought they ought to read. Few of the more devout Marxians, if we except such writers as Dos Passos, Caldwell, Farrell, and a few others, ever got very high on the best-seller lists. Hemingway, whose stature in both artistic and popular terms towers over the period, was little affected by the trend. His *To Have and Have Not* (1937), which he based on Key West, was set more in the mold of the lost generation than of the universal class struggle. His *For Whom the Bell Tolls* (1940) was a little nearer the mark, but its locale was the civil war in Spain. The same detachment was true in a broad sense of many other major writers of the decade: William Faulkner's depictions of a leached-out Mississippi gentry, as in *Sanctuary* (1931) and *Absalom, Absalom!* (1936); Thomas Wolfe's brooding autobiographical novels, such as *Look Homeward Angel* (1929), *Of Time and the River* (1935), and *You Can't Go Home Again* (published posthumously in 1940); John Steinbeck's *Of Mice and Men* (1937). In fact the three biggest sellers of the decade were historical novels that were alien in both time and mood to the contemporary social trend: Margaret Mitchell's *Gone With the Wind* (1936), Hervey Allen's *Anthony Adverse* (1933), and Nordhoff and Hall's *Mutiny on the Bounty* (1932).

As good a guide as any to what was popular rather than what was profound during the Depression years—the kind of books people spent their scarce cash for—can be gleaned from the catalogue of the Book-of-the-Month Club (which got its start in 1926 and prospered modestly all through the Depression). Here are some well remembered titles, fiction and nonfiction, picked at random from its pages: *The Crusaders* (Harold Lamb), *Lives of a Bengal Lancer* (F. Yeats-Brown), *Grand Hotel* (Vicki Baum), *The Good Earth* (Pearl Buck), *Van Loon's Geography* (Hendrik Willem Van Loon), *The Last Adam* (James G. Cozzens), *Native's Return* (Louis Adamic), *Heaven's My Destination* (Thornton Wilder), *The Seven Pillars of Wisdom* (T. E. Lawrence), *Vein of Iron* (Ellen Glasgow), *The Last Puritan* (George

Santayana), *Drums Along the Mohawk* (Walter D. Edmunds), *The Yearling* (Marjorie Kinnan Rawlings), *The Fight for Life* (Paul de Kruif), *Benjamin Franklin* (Carl Van Doren), *Captain Horatio Hornblower* (C. S. Forester), *Not Peace But a Sword* (Vincent Sheean), and *The Nazarene* (Sholem Asch).[9]

There was a great vogue, too, during these hard-luck years for self-improvement books. Life is just a matter of good salesmanship, Dale Carnegie told a hundred thousand credulous purchasers of *How to Win Friends and Influence People*, and Walter B. Pitkin banished the fear of growing old with *Life Begins at Forty*. In a more substantial vein, many readers sought self-improvement through the reading of history and biography, in which there was a marked revival of interest. Charles and Mary Beard published their impressive *The Rise of American Civilization* (the first volume was published in 1927) in a one-volume edition in 1930 and followed it in 1939 with *America in Midpassage*. Claude Bowers produced *Jefferson in Power*, Douglas Southall Freeman his four-volume *Robert E. Lee,* Carl Sandburg his great work *Abraham Lincoln: The War Years,* Van Wyck Brooks his literary history *The Flowering of New England,* Marquis James his *Andrew Jackson,* and Mark Sullivan his *Our Times*, a six-volume journalistic *reprise* of the first two decades of the tewntieth century. Along with the chroniclers of the past were the explainers of the present and the future: lawyers, economists, and engineers. Stuart Chase, David Cushman Coyle, John T. Flynn, Thurman Arnold, Lewis Mumford, and others turned to writing as elucidators of the tangled skeins of a modern society. Such popular treatises as *The Economy of Abundance* (Chase, 1934) and *The Folklore of Capitalism* (Arnold, 1937) took an irreverent view of some of the old orthodoxies and enjoyed brisk sales and wide acclaim.

So the literature of the thirties was not all of a piece. It could equally nourish a John Dos Passos and a John O'Hara, produce *Gone With the Wind* and *Let Us Now Praise Famous Men*. But in retrospect it has a collective characteristic that sets it apart. Frederick Lewis Allen called it "a golden age of literary sociology." Through some strange alchemy it blended the Marxian revolutionary class struggle and Walt Whitman's sense of American oneness. The zeal of the Marxists cooled in the late years of the Depression under the shock of the Stalin-Hitler pact, and for the same reason the sense of nationalism was enhanced. But the trend toward a kind of made-in-America proletarianism survived. It is this that makes the thirties an important epoch in American literary history.[10]

IV

One day in May 1933, young Nelson Rockefeller ordered the Mexican muralist, Diego Rivera, down off his scaffold in the main lobby of New York's gleaming new Rockefeller Center, handed him a check for $14,000 to wind up his contract, and had workmen cover the half-finished fresco with tar paper. Mr. Rockefeller thus put "art" on the front page of every newspaper in the land and launched a heated politico-aesthetic hassle over

At right: Mural (detail), *Workers of the World Unite!*, New York City, 1933

Self Portrait, Raphael Soyer

Portrait, Moses Soyer

At left: Mural (detail), Diego Rivera, New York City, 1933. (Above) Mural (detail), Diego Rivera, New York City, 1933

Threshing Wheat, Thomas Hart Benton

Bartolomeo Vanzetti and Nicola Sacco,

High Yaller, Reginald Marsh, 1934

Arts of the South,
Thomas Hart Benton

*Loews—Sheridan
Square,*
Edward Hopper

Eggbeater, V,
Stuart Davis, 1930

Breadline,
**Reginald Marsh,
1932**

the rights of artistic expression. Rivera, a good communist, had painted a likeness of Lenin looking down with disapproval on a scene in which obviously American police were breaking up a group of obviously American strikers. When he refused to take Lenin out, the Rockefellers fired him.

The incident was symptomatic of the intellectual ferment then sweeping through the art world. The impact of the Depression on the visual arts was closely akin to what it was on literature. Artists felt a sudden upsurge of social consciousness, and many proclaimed themselves revolutionaries and communists. They experimented with new art fads and styles in which social and esthetic impulses were blended, and they rediscovered the American scene as a source of artistic inspiration. At the same time an unprecedented intrusion by the federal government in fostering the creation and appreciation of art led to a democratization of art. No longer confined to cloistered museums and Bohemian attics, art emerged into the ordinary light of Main Street. That was one of the significant cultural achievements of the decade.

Artists and would-be artists, an impecunious fellowship under the best of circumstances, were, like everyone else, hard hit by the Depression. In their mission as molders and mirrors of social thought, they turned their ire toward the system that had thrown their generation on the waste heap. Many American students of art in Europe had fled homeward from the destitution of Paris and Rome only to find life equally bleak and unpromising in the United States. They poured their resentment onto their canvasses and sculptures—bitter caricatures of capitalist bosses and tycoons; stolid, muscular workers being ground to death by omnivorous machines; the pinched, hopeless faces of the jobless trapped in their gloomy slums, and indecipherable montages of harsh color and angularities that bespoke inchoate anger and frustration. Familiar sights of the period were the impromptu outdoor ateliers—in New York's Greenwich Village, around Washington's Dupont Circle, on Rush Street in Chicago's Near North Side—with artists squatting nearby to offer their wares for whatever the strolling market would bring or to produce while-you-wait crayon and charcoal portraits for a quarter. In a study of the art of that period, John I. H. Baur wrote:

Not all American art of the 1930's was socially conscious, but very nearly all reflected the trend toward increasing realism which came in the wake of the depression. The romantic realist movement reached its peak in this decade, partly because it broke the bounds of its earlier, conventional subject matter and explored new aspects of the American scene. . . . In the Middle West a militant regionalism sprang up.[11]

As the abstract and expressionist painters in the East—Ben Shahn, George Gross, Max Weber, Jack Levine, among others—were involving themselves in the industrial class struggle, a great many others were looking for social significance elsewhere. They found it in the machinery and gadgetry of the factory, the laboratory, and, indeed, the kitchen; in the geometry of bridges and empty streets and cemeteries; in the bucolic aridity of an Iowa farm, a village barber shop, a Kiwanis luncheon; in the brooding faces of

Indians and Negroes and Swedes and the places where they lived. The work by this realist school strayed less from conventional patterns than did the work of the expressionists. Much of it had a social, proletarian context, but it was plausible and identifiable. Among its representative practitioners during the thirties were Grant Wood, Thomas Hart Benton, Andrew Wyeth, Reginald Marsh, and Alexander Brook.

Works of art, particularly contemporary works of art, are among the more dispensable human needs when times are hard and money is short. The Depression quite literally obliterated the source of income for all but a handful of American artists and threw a barrier across the path of most young people seeking a career in art.

The New Deal came more promptly to the aid of artists than to the aid of writers and actors. George Biddle, already a painter of distinction and an old friend of Franklin Roosevelt's, proposed to the President in the summer of 1933 that the new Administration should interest itself not only in the plight of hungry artists but in the esthetic hunger of government buildings, which had long been caverns of austere, institutional bleakness. Several large new federal structures were even then under construction or on architects' drawing boards. Why not hire the unemployed artists to enliven these buildings with murals, sculpture, and other ornamentations, Biddle asked.

Roosevelt was immediately receptive. One prompt result was the establishment within the Treasury Department, which at that time was responsible for most government construction, of what ultimately became known as the Fine Arts Section. It was funded initially with a grant of $1.4 million from the Federal Emergency Relief Administration. Edward Bruce, a prominent lawyer as well as a prominent painter, was put in charge. Bruce was a man of great zeal and good taste. One of his earliest targets was the new Justice Department building on Pennsylvania Avenue, then nearing completion. It was a handsome limestone structure of relatively modern design with many inviting interior wall spaces. George Biddle was among the artists chosen to decorate these walls. One of his striking murals is in the high-vaulted fifth-floor main lobby, hard by the Attorney General's sumptuous suite. A face peeking inconspicuously from the background of this painting is unmistakably that of the artist's brother, Francis, who a few years later was to become master of the premises as Roosevelt's fourth Attorney General.

The experiment with government-in-art under Bruce at the Treasury was quite successful and received wide commendation. Scores of new and existing federal courthouses, post offices, hospitals, and other buildings were brightened with murals and easel paintings, and the tradition for such artistic enhancement became firmly established. Only incidentally was the program geared to unemployment relief; most of its works were commissioned in the usual professional manner. Meanwhile thousands of the nation's artists were still subsisting on street sales and elbowing their way in the breadlines.

The WPA Federal Art Project was launched simultaneously with the projects for actors, writers, and musicians in late 1935. Functionally, it followed much the same pattern. Its primary purpose was to provide jobs for artists wherever they were, and the cultural dividends were secondary. The director of the project, Holger Cahill, was not an artist but a museum administrator; he brought wide knowledge and a liberal viewpoint to the task. Much of traditional art appreciation and reverence for the Old Masters was, he believed, snobbish and ritualistic, and had little relevance for the mass of people. "It is not solitary genius that counts," he said, "but a sound general movement which maintains art as a functioning part of a cultural scheme." On this democratic principle he developed the Federal Art Project along the broadest possible line. It gave free rein to artists of every fad and discipline, set up hundreds of public art centers all across the country, and sent scholars and researchers into museums, warehouses, and attics to seek out the forgotten sources of indigenous American art.

At its peak in 1936 the FAP had 5,300 artists and allied workers on its rolls and was operating in all but four states. Over the next six years (the project closed down in 1942) it produced some 4,500 murals, 19,000 sculptures, and more than 450,000 paintings and prints for the adornment of everything from one-room schools and country courthouses to state capitols. About six hundred art centers were established, some functioning mainly as neighborhood art schools, others as community galleries and museums, which were enriched from time to time by traveling exhibitions and loans from the big metropolitan galleries. A number of these community art centers won financial support from town or state governments and continued to flourish long after the demise of the WPA. (The handsomely housed Virginia Museum of Fine Arts at Richmond is an example.) A unique contribution of FAP to art scholarship was its Index of American Design—meticulously detailed renderings of hundreds of examples of early American manufacturing and handcrafts in such mediums as textiles, furniture, ceramics, metalwork, wood carving. This great collection is preserved at the Library of Congress, where it is in constant demand by both artists and industrial designers.

Much of the output of the FAP was of mediocre quality, and some of it offended both aesthetic and political tastes of the times. Like Rivera's mural at Rockefeller Center, a WPA mural in the Administration building at Floyd Bennett Airfield in New York was ordered to be obliterated because of its stridently communistic flavor. Such departures from conventional tastes were inevitable, given the project's primary mission of providing unemployment relief. Some of the work, on the other hand was of enduring quality, as scores of murals, paintings, and sculptures still on display in public buildings in every part of the country testify.*

*Many of these murals have disintegrated or been destroyed, and thousands of paintings and sculptures have simply disappeared. The Fine Arts Section of the Smithsonian Institution, in Washington, is the official custodian of what remains of these federal works of art but admits it knows very little about what is contained in the vast number of crates marked "WPA Art" stacked in various government warehouses. An effort to locate and inventory the accumulation was undertaken in 1967 by Professor Francis V. O'Connor of the University of Maryland, under a grant from the National Endowment for the Arts.

But the most important aspect of FAP was its salvage of the artistic talent of a whole revolutionary decade. The undeniable shoddiness and mediocrity of much of the work, as Baur points out,

was a small price to pay for what the Project accomplished. Some of our best and most famous artists, men like Stuart Davis, Yasuo Kuniyoshi, and Marsden Hartley, could not have continued without its aid. Great numbers of our promising younger artists—Levine, Breinin, Graves, Bloom, MacIver, and scores of others—whose careers were just starting in the early 1930's might well have been forced to give up painting without its encouragement.

The loss to the creative forces in American life which was averted by the Federal Art Project and the allied program of the Treasury's Section of Fine Arts would indeed have been a serious one.[12]

V

During the nineteen-thirties serious music broke out of its highbrow cloister to become the property of all the people—or more of them in any event than had ever known it before. What the intellectual trigger was will probably never be known. Maybe hunger and deprivation and anxiety *do* send the human spirit a-questing after aesthetic antidotes, as some scholars hold. But the mechanics of that gratification are fairly clear.

The radio played a very important role. By the middle of the decade, good music programs such as the NBC "Symphony of the Air," the Metropolitan Opera broadcasts, and the "Ford Sunday Evening Hour" (Detroit Symphony) had acquired a weekend audience estimated by a contemporary analysis at 10,230,000 families. Nor were these all highbrow listeners. It was not unusual to hail a taxi on a Saturday afternoon and hear a live broadcast of *La Tosca* or *Rigoletto* from the "Met" over the driver's radio. Toscanini's first broadcast for NBC drew hundreds of appreciative fan letters from towns and cities a thousand miles distant from New York. Big independent stations in cities like Pittsburgh, Cincinnati, Chicago, and Los Angeles all offered serious music as a regular part of their weekly programs. It was a poor night when a finicky listener could not pick up a famous orchestra or concert artist somewhere on his dial.

Improvements during the decade. in phonographs and recording techniques sent record sales soaring. "Swing" fans were responsible for the greater part of this business but the new devotees of Brahms and Beethoven created an unprecedented market for the classics. Some big merchandisers offered classical albums, one record at a time, as a bonus for buying their brands of soap or cigarettes, thus laying the foundation for many a low-budget private record collection. Famous bandleaders like Paul Whiteman and Benny Goodman and pianist Oscar Levant helped to bridge the gap between popular and serious music by skillfully blending the two modes in their repertoires. Composer George Gershwin achieved a similar end in his *Piano Concerto in F* and in his opera *Porgy and Bess*. And finally, the government lent a hand to the democratizing process through its unemployment relief program for jobless musicians.

The WPA Federal Music Project put some 15,000 of these idle musicians back to work. The original director of the project was Nikolai Sokoloff, who for fifteen years had been conductor of the Cleveland Symphony. Under his guidance thirty new symphony orchestras were created in as many cities across the country along with scores of smaller orchestras, bands, ensembles, and choral groups. Over the six-year life of the project these groups gave an estimated 225,000 public performances before audiences totaling 150 million persons. Some 20,000 of these performances were symphony concerts, many of them rendered in parks, school auditoriums, firehouses, and similar locales where "live" music of such caliber had never been heard before. The New York City Orchestra moved into Carnegie Hall in 1938 for a regular Sunday night series that attracted capacity audiences at prices ranging from 28 cents to $1.10.

The emphasis of the FMP was on performers rather than composers, but special attention was given to American composers. Music critic Deems Taylor wrote in 1938 that this devotion to the works of American composers probably exceeded that of all symphony orchestras in the country combined over the preceding ten years.

In addition to *making* music, the project sought to enhance the public's understanding of music. Like the Federal Art Project, the FMP set up a hundred or more instructional centers where music lessons were given for those who could not afford to pay for them. At one point half a million students were enrolled in these courses. The project's most interesting innovation was the Composer's Forum and Laboratory. Here the composer of a contemporary work went on public trial, so to speak, before both the orchestra members and the audience to explain and answer questions about his composition. Roy Harris, Virgil Thompson and William Shuman were among a number of native composers who submitted to this artistic inquisition and all claimed to find it stimulating. Shuman, for example, after such a dissection of his first symphonic work, decided to rewrite it and said he had "gained ten years of experience." Another of the project's innovative endeavors sent musical researchers poking into the backwoods and creek hollows to dig out authentic American folk music. This invaluable collection was placed in the custody of the Library of Congress when FMP was closed out in 1941.[13]

VI

Scholars will debate how valid and how durable was the cultural upsurge that occurred in the thirties. But what cannot be gainsaid is the popularization of things cultural that stemmed from it. Whether or not America's aesthetic tastes improved, its aesthetic appetite grew prodigiously. Government nourished that growth on humanitarian rather than cultural grounds, and pulled out when the humanitarian need had been met. A whole generation would pass before government again interested itself in the arts (and that timidly) as a part of its responsibility to the nation's cultural welfare rather than to its poverty.

CHAPTER 15
Popular Culture
–Middlebrow

Vic and Sade, Pepper Young's Family, Ma Perkins, Little Orphan Annie, Uncle Don, Bobby Benson, Renfrew of the Mounted, Amos 'n' Andy, The Lone Ranger, Lum and Abner, Hollywood Hotel, March of Time, Backstage Wife, Romance of Helen Trent, Just Plain Bill, Molly of the Movies, Dick Tracy, Jack Armstrong, Tom Mix's Adventures, The Goldbergs, Your Hit Parade, Rubinoff and His Violin, National Barn Dance, Myrt and Marge, Captain Tim's Adventure Stories, Boake Carter, Singin' Sam, Jungle Jim, Easy Aces, Don Winslow of the Navy, Let's Pretend, Fibber McGee and Molly, Life Can Be Beautiful, Lux Radio Theatre, The Answer Man, Grand Central Station, Hop Harrigan, Bulldog Drummond, The Joe Penner Show, Chandu the Magician, Major Bowes' Original Amateur Hour.

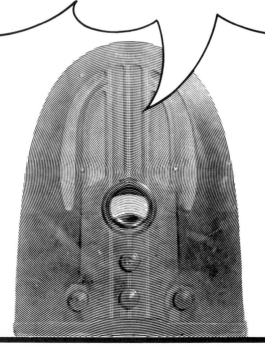

A TYPICAL MIDDLE-CLASS FAMILY of 1935 that was not on relief probably consisted of two adults and 1.6 siblings living in a rented 6.4-room house or a 4.5-room apartment on a gross annual income of $1,348. That is a part of the profile devised by the Bureau of Labor Statistics (BLS) for blue-collar and white-collar city families during 1934-36 in which at least one member was regularly employed. The average is weighted a little more heavily on the side of the lower-middle-class wage earner's family than on the upper-middle-class salaried man's family, but it is the best yardstick available. Not a great many people would have been affected by the slight difference in their scale of living in any event. About 10 percent of all families in the country were bracketed within that $1,348 average and fewer than 2 percent could be described as well-to-do (upper-middle-class) at $5,000 and above.

A typical factory worker earned $19.91 a week in 1935 and a foreman or supervisor somewhere in the neighborhood of $40. White-collar jobs paid only a little better. A typical office worker could count on an average $20.76 weekly, for example, and an insurance salesman $24.99, while an executive in retail trade got $49.16 and the editor of a medium-sized newspaper about $75. Salaries and wages tumbled about 40 percent between 1929 and 1933 (they climbed back slightly by 1935), but living costs came down by only 25 percent, which made plain middle-classlings of a good many people who had always thought of themselves as "upper." Middle-classness was, in fact, a quite prevalent state of being during the Depression, and it lost much of its social stigma.

What did such a family spend its money for in the thirties? Again, the BLS supplies a statistical picture of the average city family's budget based on an annual income of $1,348. To make the picture a little more meaningful it is shown in the accompanying table along with roughly comparable figures for 1960—"roughly" because the methods of compiling the data changed over the 25-year interval. The percentage that each category of expenditures represents of the total budget is included to indicate some rather interesting shifts in consumer tastes and priorities.

	1935*	%	1960†	%
Average annual income	$1,348		$5,368	
Food and alcoholic beverages	472	35.4	1,406	26.0
Housing, heat, utilities, furnishings, etc.	456	33.3	1,584	29.5
Clothing	136	10.2	550	10.4
Automobile purchase and operation	73	5.5	696	13.0
Medical care	53	4.0	345	6.6
Recreation, reading, tobacco	72	5.4	—	—
Recreation, reading, education	—	—	326	6.0
Taxes	5	.4	666	12.0
Miscellaneous expenses	5	.4	118	2.2

*From "How American Buying Habits Change," U.S. Department of Labor, p. 44.
†From "Handbook of Labor Statistics, 1968," U.S. Department of Labor, p. 283. Some minor interpolations and extrapolations have been made by the author.

Luxuries obviously played a very small part in the life of most middle-class families during the thirties. The basic necessities—food, shelter, and clothing—absorbed at least three-quarters of the budget, and this involved a lot of corner-cutting, doing without, and maneuvering with one's creditors. Only about 3 percent owned their own homes. Repairs and improvements were postponed and tenants haggled with their landlords to fix the roof or scale down the rent. Consumption of red meat went down; and fish and poultry, which were cheaper and could often be bought from street vendors, went up. Margarine replaced butter; Jell-O entered its golden age as the cheapest all-purpose dessert; and corn, tomatoes, and pole beans sprang up in backyards and vacant city lots.

About one in every two families owned an automobile. It probably was either a holdover from better days or a second-hand one bought for about $300. Somebody in the family was likely to be enough of a mechanic to grind the valves, change the oil, patch the tires, and do most of what was needed to keep it in running order. The alleged mechanical genius of the American male undoubtedly owes much of its validity to the do-it-yourself vogue of the Depression.

Movies and the radio were the most common diversions. The most popular sport was baseball. Just about every self-respecting community in the land was tied into either a professional or a semiprofessional league of some sort and gave its team the same proprietary oversight that Brooklyn lavished on the Dodgers. But for every fan who went regularly to the ball park, dozens became sweating, cheering participants themselves in the newest sports craze: softball. Teams sprang up everywhere. They were sponsored by business firms, unions, Sunday Schools, or Scout troops, and sometimes organized spontaneously within a neighborhood. The numerous all-girl teams, uniformed in bright jerseys and shorts, played as lustily and expertly as their menfolk. Golf ceased to be the exclusive pastime of the rich, and roller-skating was no longer restricted to children. Indoor rinks, usually in abandoned warehouses, flourished and even bred "derbies." Public recreational facilities of every kind were vastly expanded under the WPA, as were adult education classes in everything from bead-stringing to ancient history. You didn't *have* to sit at home and mope; those few recreational dollars in your Depression budget could buy quite a variety of fun and entertainment.

I

For a close-up view of middle-class family life during the thirties, let's examine briefly a reasonably typical and authentic case history. Our subjects are the familiar John and Mary (not their correct names) who were in their mid-twenties when they were married in 1930. John's salary was $50 a week, out of which they paid $65 a month for a furnished one-bedroom apartment in a good neighborhood of a large mid-western city. When his company and his job collapsed the following year, they wound up in a single "light house-keeping" room (that meant a two-burner gas stove and a tiny icebox crammed into the clothes closet, and a common bath at the end of the hall) in a dilapidated old brownstone near the slums. The rent was $7 a week (in advance) and food came to about $5, which meant that each dime spent for a pack of cigarettes, or each quarter for a movie, was likely to hurt. After a year of fruitless job hunting, and with their savings gone, they headed for the home of John's parents in the East—Mary by bus with such belongings as were salvageable and John by way of a succession of erratic and inhospitable freight trains. John tells the story in his own words:

We moved in on my family at just about the time that my father's business failed. My brother and his wife moved in too; it seemed that everybody we knew was doubling up the same way. He had gotten his law degree the year before, but the town seemed to be running over with lawyers whose briefcases bulged with nothing of greater portent than a sandwich for lunch and the morning paper. Our house was a modest one in a modest neighborhood. It had eight rooms, one bath, and a tiny yard, but six people and three families crowded it physically and emotionally. In-laws were never meant to live together. Every so often we had to draw up a truce.

The economics of our existence for the next year are still vague in my mind. My father was cleaned out when his business failed, but he managed a few months later to get a job with a former competitor at about $30 a week. My brother picked up a few dollars from time to time by hanging around the courts. I did about as well peddling brushes, magazine subscriptions, and what-not door to door, and as a part-time helper in a warehouse. My first regular job came late in 1933 when the NRA 30-hour week caused one of the local papers to hire a couple of extra reporters. The pay was $15 a week, which was $2.50 less than the warehouse offered me to go on full time. It was a hard choice to make but I opted for the newspaper.

Out of our combined resources we had to pay something on the mortgage, taxes, insurance, and so forth. Our food budget for the entire household was $15 a week, and that took a lot of scrounging and corner-cutting. One horrible memory is of rabbit. A family friend who had been hunting gave us eight of them, which we dressed and put on ice. You can get damn sick of rabbit after the fourth straight meal, and I think a fifth would be fatal. There were no labor-saving gadgets in our house. Bread was toasted in the gas oven, dishes were washed in the sink, housecleaning was done with a broom or carpet sweeper, the ice man delivered a 50-pound cake of ice every other day to the ponderous refrigerator, and the laundry was returned "rough dry" to be ironed with "sadirons" heated on the stove. After the gas heater blew up one summer we had to fire up the coal furnace twice a week to get water for baths and dishwashing. This made the house unbearable for hours.

There was one car in the family, a six-year-old Hupmobile with chronically weak tires. We didn't dare take it on trips out of town. For reading matter we depended on the *Saturday Evening Post,* the *Literary Digest,* the local papers, and the public library. Our wind-up Victrola offered a limited Red Seal choice between Caruso, John McCormack, Lily Pons, and the gospel hymns of Homer Rhodeheaver, and a miscellany of current jazz and comics. We pooled resources to buy a family radio for Christmas, 1934. It was a "super heterodyne" (what was that?) table model that cost about $40. My brother and I strung the aerial chimney to chimney, on the roof.

My parents kept up their church attendance, and we went along occasionally to keep them happy. My parents had never been more than moderately well off but the experience of suddenly finding themselves "poor as church mice," as my mother put it, was hard for them to take. It was a blow to their faith and to their pride, and they tended to withdraw and to brood. It was less of a spiritual wrench to the younger members of the family; for them it was more a cause of exasperation and an occasional outburst of nerves. In our natural optimism we were sure that there was a way out of the trap and that sooner or later we would find it. Most of the friends in our age group felt the same way, and it created an extra bond of intimacy. There was a lot of visiting back and forth in the evenings, games of penny ante poker, monopoly, and bridge, sampling the newly legal beer and whiskey, going on picnics, discovering golf at a nearby country club which had opened its course to all-comers at one dollar greens fee. And we spent hours in noisy confabulation, most of it off the top of our heads, about politics, morality, philosophy, and the frustrations and occasional joys of job hunting. But we weren't depressed, really; we all had a sort of insouciant optimism—things couldn't get any worse, they could only get better—and we managed to enjoy ourselves in the way young people always do.

Things began to break a little better for Mary and me in 1936. We moved into our own apartment but continued to help out our parents financially. We were still "poor as church mice" and living pretty shakily with borrowed furniture, make-do clothes, and an awesome pile of debts. But I was now making $25 a week and Mary was making about $15. We felt that the trap which had held up for five years had at last been sprung, and, as it turned out, it had.[1]

II

The movies, not religion, were the opiate of the masses during the Depression. It was the common diversion for young and old, and to attend once a week did not suggest a far-gone addiction. For a quarter, more or less, you could buy a brief respite from the drabness and monotony that were your lot and frolic with the nymphs and fauns in a castle in the sky. Going to the movies was more than just an indulgence; it was an escape from the dispiriting realities of a world gone cockeyed, and the lingering narcosis seemed to make the next set of hurdles down the track somehow less formidable.

In the popular culture of the day Hollywood was not thought to be a suburb of anything. It was the opulent capital of a real land of make-believe, peopled by gods and goddesses, a place where the Cinderella miracle (waitresses transformed overnight into starlets) was commonplace. The lives of the stars were better known than the lives of the saints, and their influence was infinitely more pervasive. The number of tall girls who hoped they looked like Ginger Rogers remains uncounted. Jean Harlow's platinum-blonde hair set thousands of girls experimenting in the bathroom with peroxide and other bleaches. When Clark Gable stripped down in *It Happened One Night* to reveal himself as a no-undershirted man, the men's underwear trade was said to have suffered a slump. Most communities in the thirties could count one or two of their progeny who had made the hopeful pilgrimage to Hollywood. If they showed up on the local screen in even a bit part, the communal chest swelled with pride.

In the ten years between 1925 and 1935 the motion picture industry made tremendous technical strides, which was reflected in the improved qual-

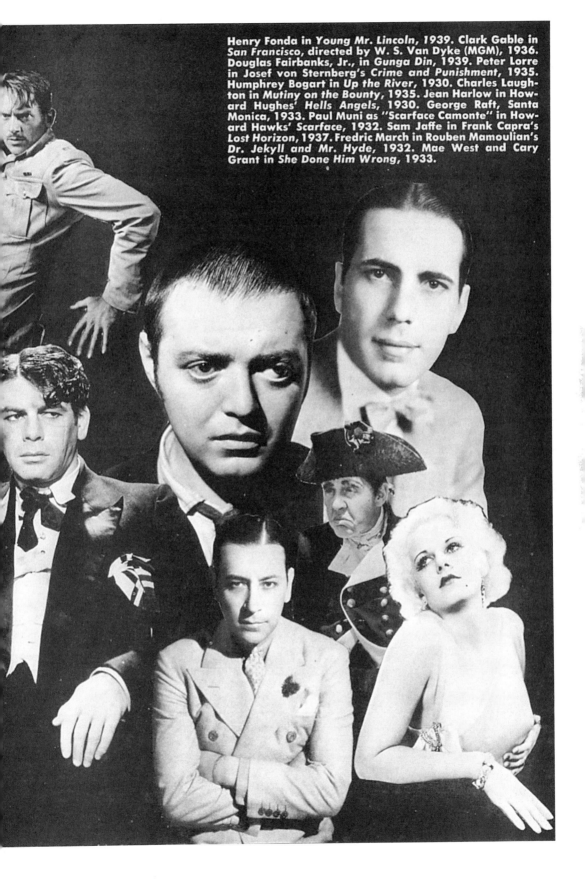

Henry Fonda in *Young Mr. Lincoln, 1939.* Clark Gable in *San Francisco,* directed by W. S. Van Dyke (MGM), 1936. Douglas Fairbanks, Jr., in *Gunga Din, 1939.* Peter Lorre in Josef von Sternberg's *Crime and Punishment, 1935.* Humphrey Bogart in *Up the River, 1930.* Charles Laughton in *Mutiny on the Bounty, 1935.* Jean Harlow in Howard Hughes' *Hells Angels, 1930.* George Raft, Santa Monica, 1933. Paul Muni as "Scarface Camonte" in Howard Hawks' *Scarface, 1932.* Sam Jaffe in Frank Capra's *Lost Horizon, 1937.* Fredric March in Rouben Mamoulian's *Dr. Jekyll and Mr. Hyde, 1932.* Mae West and Cary Grant in *She Done Him Wrong, 1933.*

ity of the output. Sound, which had been haltingly introduced in 1927, was perfected. An actor's lips no longer shaped syllables which ludicrously failed to match the dubbed-in words that came over the loudspeaker. The smooth blending of action with speech, sound effects, and music induced in the spectator a sense of reality undreamed of in the old days of pantomime.

Color made its uncertain appearance early in the decade, beginning with the sharp, three-tone contrasts (familiar to comic-page readers) that were used in some of Walt Disney's animated cartoons. The first full-length feature in the new technicolor process came in 1935, *Becky Sharp,* adapted from Thackeray's *Vanity Fair.* The new medium was not a dazzling visual success, and many theaters were not equipped to handle it. Both the state of the art and the availability of equipment were at a peak when *Gone With the Wind* was released in 1939. The burning of Atlanta by the Yankee General Sherman, was so realistic that impressionable members of the audience said they could feel the heat on their faces. Thereafter the black-and-white movie except for some B-grade Westerns and thrillers, gradually disappeared from the distributors' catalogues.

These innovations wrought a revolution not only in the movie industry but also in the popular taste for entertainment. Audiences wanted action on the screen and a coherent spoken script to go with it—a story line, however tenuous. Above all, they wanted the sound of music, preferably with dancers. Hollywood scrambled in all directions at once trying to supply the demand. Production costs shot from $119 million in 1933 to $198 million in 1937. Musicals were turned out by the bagful. Hollywood raided the legitimate theater for "name" actors and actresses. It hired authors by the score to manufacture fresh scripts and to rewrite Dickens and Shakespeare. As in any mass-production industry, it sought the common denominator of popular demand. It wanted no part of the current social ferment to sour its bland souffles. What it wanted, and what it gave the public (with a few notable exceptions) all through the thirties, was an infinite variation on the durable old theme of boy-gets-girl. Turning a sociologist's eye on the scene near the end of the decade, Leo Rosten wrote:

In the recondite naivete of Hollywood movies, life is a simple game between love and understanding, between the pure in heart and the other kind. Optimism is basic, romance is of the essence, crises are rarely more than personal. In the movies, problems are solved by mere love, sheer will, or expiatory gestures; that is, by virtue, luck, or divine intervention. . . .

The movie makers are compelled in many ways to feed a popular diet to a public which is in firm possession of deplorable tastes—tastes derived from sources far older, deeper and more potent than Hollywood. The very success of Hollywood lies in the skill with which it *reflects* the assumptions, the fallacies and the aspirations of an entire culture.

Whether the movies imitate life or life imitates the movies is for others to decide; this writer believes that, like missionaries on a desert island, they begin to convert each other.[2]

There was a great deal of froth and tawdriness in the average week's offerings at hometown movie palaces, little to stir the intellectual embers. In the earlier years of the decade particularly, there was a heavy emphasis on sex and violence—sure winners at the box office but inflammatory to the keepers of middle-class morality. An informal board of censorship set up by the Catholic church in 1934, the Legion of Decency, had a profoundly restraining effect, and the industry itself moved in with a Production Code Authority to police its own operations.

But along with the trash, a good many nuggets of gold and near-gold spilled off the Hollywood production line in those years. Somehow they escaped the blight of banality. For in spite of the moneymakers who ran the business for a profit, some men of imagination and artistic genius—Frank Capra, Lewis Milestone, John Ford, Sidney Franklin, among others—were able to make their weight felt. They were the producers or directors of the "great" pictures of the thirties. Actors and actresses of enduring fame starred in their productions.

Which were the "great" movies of the thirties? Experts have compiled anthologies and written at length on the subject. My own nonexpert cataloguing, full of prejudices and certainly not exhaustive, contains the following entries:

Musicals, the big new "thing" of the decade, were splashy extravaganzas that outdid Broadway's famed *Ziegfeld Follies* and *Earl Carroll's Vanities*, and they were to be seen right down on Main Street at the familiar old Palace or Strand theater. *Flying Down to Rio* (1933) was one of the earlier and also one of the best of the screen musicals. It brought Fred Astaire and Ginger Rogers together for the first time as the most talented and attractive song-and-dance team in show business. Other good entries under this heading included *Top Hat* (also with Rogers and Astaire), *Dames,* and *42nd Street.*

In the field of comedy, the old pie-in-the-face routine of the silents and the burlesque circuit was elevated to new heights of looniness by the Marx brothers: Groucho, the wise-cracking mastermind of their nefarious plots; Chico, the scheming, try-anything expediter; Harpo the lecherous half-wit whose clowning always threatened to gum up the works. Slapstick was already a declining art form when the thirties came along, and the Marx brothers gave it a rousing, hilarious interment. The best of a half dozen pictures they made during the decade was *A Night at the Opera* (1935).

On a less frenetic level of comedy there were some equally good choices. W. C. Fields, the archetype of the boozy old four-flusher, teamed up with Mae West, whose proportions and demeanor were suggestive of the madam of a prosperous bordello, in a series of mildly salacious travesties on virtue, such as *She Done Him Wrong* (1933) and *My Little Chickadee* (1939). Marie Dressler starred as the frowsy old harridan of *Tugboat Annie* (1933) opposite Wallace Beery, who was her match in disreputability. At the opposite end of this particular spectrum were the sleekly sophisticated figures of

(Clockwise) W. C. Fields and Baby Leroy in *The Old Fashioned Way*; Victor McLaglen as "Gypo Nolan" in John Ford's *The Informer*, 1935; Greta Garbo in *Romance*, 1930; Chico Marx, Harpo Marx, and Louis Calhern in *Duck Soup*, 1933; Gary Cooper as "Longfellow Deeds" in Frank Capra's *Mr. Deeds Goes to Town*, 1936; Hedy Keisler (Hedy Lamarr) in *Extase (Ecstasy)*, a Czech import, 1937; Virginia Cherrill and Charles Chaplin in his silent film, *City Lights*, 1931; (center) Strafing scene from Howard Hawks' *The Dawn Patrol*, 1930.

Edward G. Robinson in Mervyn LeRoy's *Little Caesar*, 1931.

Dance director Busby Berkeley rehearsing the chorus for Lloyd Bacon's Forty Second Street, 1933.

Maurice Chevalier in *Folies Bergère de Paris.*
Directed by Roy del Ruth, 1935.

Jack Haley, Judy Garland, and Ray Bolger having their problems on "The Yellow Brick Road" in this scene from *The Wizard of Oz*, 1939.

FRED ASTAIRE
with
RAY NOBLE
and his Orchestra
Fox Trot

CHANGE PARTNERS
From "Carefree"
-Berlin-

Brunswick
Vocal by Fred Astaire
8189

Fred Astaire and Ginger Rogers in *Roberta*, 1935.

Right: (top) Elsa Lanchester in James Whale's *The Bride of Frankenstein*, 1935. In the Prologue to the film, Miss Lanchester plays Mary Shelley, authoress of *Frankenstein*. (Bottom) Boris Karloff, sans make-up, and as the monster in Whale's first effort, *Frankenstein*, 1931. (Above) Bela Lugosi as "Count Dracula" in Tod Browning's *Dracula*, 1931.

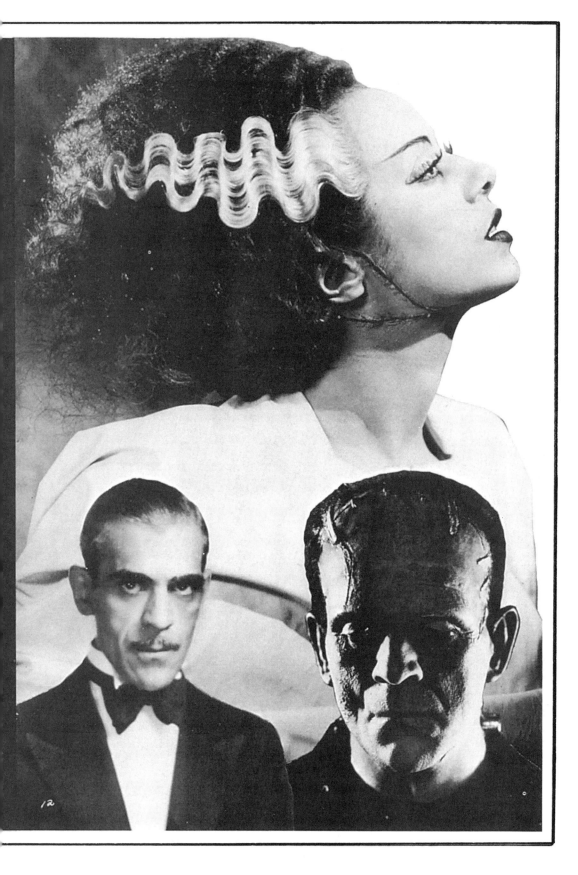

Above: (clockwise) Ernest B. Schoedsack's *King Kong*, 1932. Special effects by Willis O'Brien; Paulette Goddard in Charlie Chaplin's *Modern Times*, 1936; Mickey Rooney and Judy Garland in *Babes in Arms*, 1938. (Center oval) Marlene Dietrich in Josef von Sternberg's *Blonde Venus*, 1932. (Spread) Chaplin and Goddard "on the road" in *Modern Times*, 1936.

Above: (clockwise) Ernst Lubitsch, 1932; Dick Powell in *Shipmates For-ever*, 1935; poster for Tim McCoy in *Man of Action*, 1934; Josef von Sternberg, 1933.

William Powell and Myrna Loy in *The Thin Man* (1934), a murder mystery with laughs. Clark Gable and Claudette Colbert became involved in a hilarious and quite grown-up variant of the boy-gets-girl theme in *It Happened One Night* (1934), which related the predicaments and improbable complications befalling a runaway heiress and a roguish newspaper reporter who find themselves on a three-day bus trip to Miami. A memorable entry under the category of sophisticated comedy was Alfred Lunt and Lynne Fontanne in Molnar's *The Guardsman* (1931); it was their one-shot venture into the tinseled jungle of Hollywood. *Mr. Deeds Goes to Town* (1936), with Gary Cooper as the pixilated protagonist, and *Mr. Smith Goes to Washington* (1939), in which James Stewart played the innocent and bewildered young Senator, showed the maturity of the moviemakers in producing high comedy in a low key.

Horror films gained a spine-chilling new dimension with the introduction of sound. The decade produced some masterpieces of gruesomeness: *Dr. Jekyl and Mr. Hyde* (1932), in which Frederic March, a romantic type, displayed his virtuosity; *King Kong* (1933), the utterly improbable and utterly fascinating saga of a giant ape-god; *Frankenstein* (1931), with Boris Karloff as the hulking, malevolent zombie. These films rated as classics of the genre in the pantheon of the movie world.

How will the experts carve up the decade for movie honors? A substantial clacque insists that the thirties belong to Garbo. This willowy, sensuous, Swedish beauty, with both passion and chastity in her deep-set eyes, was a superb actress in many demanding roles. Off the screen, she managed to surround her life with a quiet dignity and aloofness, which was never disturbed by the shrill clamors of fandom. Greta Garbo was beautiful, talented, and mysterious. She achieved a kind of regal eminence that was unique in the frenetic world of the cinema, and the Garbo cult seemed to number as many women as men. She was usually cast in heroic roles in dramas from the more solid romanticists of the past, but she also skillfully managed a satirical comedy part in a spy thriller, *Ninotchka,* in which she costarred with Melvyn Douglas in 1939. Among other memorable Garbo films of the decade are *Anna Christie* (1930), *Susan Lenox* (1931), *Queen Christina* (1933), *Anna Kerenina* (1935), and *Camille* (1936).

Hollywood managed to provide its audiences with a number of other pictures of genuine merit during the decade. Here is a random sampling of some of the more memorable hits:

All Quiet on the Western Front (1930), based on Erich Maria Remarque's novel of the First World War, with Louis Wolheim, Lew Ayres, and "Slim" Summerville.

The Public Enemy (1931), a quite superior gangster movie, which set Jimmy Cagney on the road to fame.

Strange Interlude (1932), based on the play by Eugene O'Neill, with Norma Shearer and Clark Gable.

A Farewell to Arms (1932), a dramatization of the Ernest Hemingway war novel, with Gary Cooper, Helen Hayes, and Adolphe Menjou.

The Informer (1934), from the Liam O'Flaherty novel about the Irish uprising of the twenties, with Victor McLaglen in a magnificent portrayal of a conscience-stricken turncoat.

Mutiny on the Bounty (1935), the Nordhoff and Hall best seller turned into an impressive screen spectacular, with Clark Gable, Charles Laughton, and Dudley Digges. (A companion piece of the same year was Rafael Sabatini's *Captain Blood,* starring Erroll Flynn and Olivia de Havilland.)

My Man Godfrey (1936), a crackling society farce played by William Powell and Carole Lombard.

The Petrified Forest (1936), Sherwood Anderson's Broadway success transferred to the screen, which was notable, among other things, for giving hard-eyed, tough-talking Humphrey Bogart his first important movie role.

The Good Earth (1937), based on Pearl Buck's Pulitzer Prize-winning novel of the life of a Chinese peasant family, with Paul Muni and Louise Rainer in the title roles.

Lost Horizon (1937), from the James Hilton fantasy, with Ronald Colman, H. B. Warner, and Thomas Mitchell in the cast.

Snow White and the Seven Dwarfs (1938), Walt Disney's magnum opus in animated cartoons. It was a full-length telling of the delightful old fairy tale. Ultimately, it was made with sound tracks in ten languages and was shown in forty-one countries.

You Can't Take It With You (1938), the uproarious antics of a completely fey household presided over by Spring Byington, with Lionel Barrymore, James Stewart and Jean Arthur as members of her daft menage.

Good-Bye Mr. Chips (1939), the tenderly poignant story of an aged schoolmaster played by Robert Donat.

Pygmalion (1939), the first of George Bernard Shaw's plays to be filmed, a satire on British class pretentions, with Leslie Howard as Professor Higgins and Wendy Hiller as Eliza Doolittle, the cockney flower girl. (*Pygmalion* progressed to the musical stage in 1955, and, virtually intact, back to the movies in 1965 as *My Fair Lady,* a classic in its genre.) [3]

III

Radio was certainly the most pervasive and probably the most profound cultural influence of the thirties. The broadcasting industry was born in 1922, reached a stage of precocious maturity along about 1927, and by 1930 was entering its golden age. The business flourished and expanded all through the Depression. In 1929 about 12 million families owned receiving sets, which cost, on the average, around $100. By 1939 the price had been halved, and some 28 million families were owners, representing more than 85 percent of the national population. The social impact of the radio craze was enormous. The magic of sound projected through the "ether" into one's living room was still new enough to have the appeal of novelty. But

Top row: (left to right) Tommy Dorsey and his Orchestra over NBC for Kool and Raleigh cigarettes, 1938; Edgar Bergen and Charlie McCarthy; CBS's unsponsored "The Columbia Workshop" was radio's finest dramatic fare. Orson Welles is at the extreme right in this production of "Terror by Night"; Mellow-voiced Boake Carter rose to stardom with his accurate coverage of the Lindbergh kidnapping; Tony Wons was the early morning heart-throb with his "Tony Wons' Scrapbook"—poetry read-ings and wise "chatter." Bottom row: (left to right) George Burns and Gracie Allen, 1934. Patient George and scatterbrained Gracie (she was always searching for a lost brother) had a large and loyal following in the 1930s; Paul Whiteman (with baton) and his Swing Wing do some impromptu "Gold Fish" swallowing, 1938; Agnes Moorehead and Phil Baker, 1935; Frances Lang-ford, singing co-star with Dick Powell on "Hollywood Hotel," an hour-long variety show of the 1935–1936 season; Kate Smith, "The Songbird of the South," 1935.

wonderment took second place to dependence. People depended on it for news and weather reports and the baseball scores; for music and entertainment, night or day; for guidance on how to bake a cake or to mark a ballot or to find God. Radio leveled the barriers of regionalism and narrowed the cultural gap between the city slicker and the country bumpkin. The teenagers of Busted Forks, Iowa, were as hep to the music of Guy Lombardo or the latest Jack Benny wisecrack as their peers in New York and Chicago, and the homely wisdom of Mary Margaret McBride or "Ma Perkins" was the daily palliative of bored housewives almost everywhere. Even more than the movies, radio was the great homogenizer of middle-class tastes. If the level was distressingly low most of the time, it sometimes ventured into the realm of excellence.

Radio in the thirties occupied a place in the routine of family life comparable to that of television a generation later. The set, often an imposing console wrought with decorative moldings in the Grand Rapids manner, had a position of prominence in the living room. In general, programming was arranged to appeal to the housewife during the daylight hours. She was offered a mixture of melodrama, packaged culture, and helpful discussions on the whole spectrum of feminine interests, from fashions to baby care. In the late afternoons came a variety of children's programs, ranging from the most innocuous fairy tales (wasn't there an "Uncle Wiggly" who read things for tiny tots?) to the hair-raising adventures of "The Lone Ranger" or "Superman." The prime evening hours were, naturally, for the top-rated newscasters, comics, variety shows, and other offerings of a meatier texture.

Radio, having only a single dimension, that of sound, may seem to the uninitiated an inadequate vehicle for shows of any kind. Studio photographs showing the cast of "Hamlet" or of "Allen's Alley" standing around the microphone in their street clothes reading from hand-held scripts while a sound-effects man with his crude gadgetry hovers in the background, suggests a pretty static performance, lacking in illusion and imagery. Nothing could be farther from the truth. The listener himself supplied the other necessary dimension—imagination—to fill the stage richly with life, color, and action. As a result, the characters and the situation and the background scenery portrayed on radio were as convincing an illusion as one might gain from a good book.

Radio was believable. Helen Trent, the fictional heroine of one of the more durable soap operas, was once showered with several bushels of get-well cards when the script required her to be in the hospital for a couple of installments. Most small boys in the know were undisturbed by the discovery that the Lone Ranger's faithful steed, Silver, was just a couple of coconut shells on a soundboard; what counted was that he still bore the Masked Rider of the Western Plains on his sturdy back. And several thousand presumably rational adults were driven out of their minds and out of their homes when Orson Welles invoked an invasion by intruders from

Mars one memorable night in 1938. Whatever its other shortcomings, radio did not suffer from a want of realism.

Radio played a major hand in the revolution of mass communications that has occurred in this century. Unencumbered by edition headlines, it could supply news around the clock and occasionally on-the-spot reporting from the scene of an event—a fire, a city council meeting, an international conference, a ball game or prize fight. This proved to be one of its most attractive features. The volume of news broadcasts doubled between 1932 and 1939. A poll by *Fortune* magazine late in the decade showed that approximately half the people preferred getting their news by radio to reading it in newspapers.

Floyd Gibbons, with his breathless, staccato delivery (his pace was an incredible 217 words per minute) was among the first network news favorites. A "trademark" of some kind was highly prized by many of these early-vintage news stars—for example, the stern voice-of-doom locution of Boake Carter, the hortatory pulpit style of Gabriel Heatter, the tense gravelly monotone of Clem McCarthy recording the jabs and hooks from ringside in Madison Square Garden. As radio news gained status and self-confidence, the way opened for such serious commentators as H. V. Kaltenborn, Raymond Gram Swing, H. R. Baukage, and others of their school who offered not only the spot news but an analysis of its meaning. This type of presentation became increasingly popular as international tensions deepened. In 1938 CBS inaugurated its "World News Roundup," with skilled reporters like William Shirer, Pierre Huss, and Edward R. Murrow reporting from Europe, and Bob Trout from Washington. Another phenomenon of the period was "The March of Time," a hybrid evolving from an uneasy coupling of the newsroom and the stage that was narrated by the martial, awe-inspiring baritone of Westbrook Van Voorhis. At the familiar sign-off, "TIME . . . marches ON!," one could almost envision a column of clocks smartly stepping off in unison toward the horizon.

As vaudeville declined and went into limbo (irrevocably done in by the talking pictures), radio became the refuge for the best of its comedians and variety performers. In fact, the new medium welcomed and rewarded them handsomely, for it had an insatiable demand for mirth-provoking talent to provide something different for each of the prime-time hours that came on relentlessly week after week. The industry divined (correctly in all probability) that what its multimillion audiences wanted above all was belly laughs and gay music, and it devoted its best energies to fulfilling that want.

Like their brethren in Hollywood, the radio moguls shunned any hint of controversy or social protest in their programming, and in this they had the powerful backing of their big industrial patrons, the advertisers. The gag man who ad libbed an impertinence in violation of this orthodoxy was quite likely to find himself out in the street the next day minus a contract. Arthur

WHO'S WHO IN YOUNG & RUBICAM'S 1

1—Jack Benny, 2—Mary Livingstone, 3—Frank Parker, 4—Don Bestor, and Orchestra—for General Foods' Jell-O. 5—Lawrence Tibbett, 6—John B. Kennedy, 7—Wilfred Pelletier, and Orchestra —for the Packard Motor Car Company. 8—The Byrd Expedition, broadcasting from the South Pole—for General Foods' Grape-Nuts. 9—Movie News and previews, 10—Mark Warnow, and Orchestra and Guest Stars, in "45 Minutes in Hollywood"—for the Borden Company. 11—Roxy, 12—Sue Read, with the Roxyaires, Soloists, Mixed Chorus, and Orchestra, in "The Roxy Revue"—for Fletcher's Castoria. 13—Joe Cook, 14—Frances Langford, 15—Donald Novis, 16—Don Voorhees, and Orchestra, in "The Colgate House Party"—for the Colgate Company. 17—Freddy Martin, and Orchestra, with Guest Stars in "Open House at Vicks"—for the Vick Chemical Company. 18—Jane Ellison in "Jane Ellison's Magic Recipes"—for the Borden Company, Eagle Brand. 19—Frances Lee Barton in "The General Foods Cooking School of the Air"—for General Foods.

35 RADIO SHOWS

DANCING TONIGHT

7:00 P.M.
WEAF—Jane Froman
8:30 P.M.
WOR—Jack Berger
9:00 P.M.
WEAF—Harry Reser
WRNY—Willy's Bavarian
9:30 P.M.
WMCA—Harry Garris
WEAF—Leo Reisman
10:00 P.M.
WOR—Roxanne
11:00 P.M.
WEAF—Anson Weeks
WMCA—Jimmy Carr
11:30 P.M.
WABC—G. Lombardo
WMCA—Don Redman
WOR—Jack Denny
WEAF—George Olsen
MIDNIGHT
WABC—Ozzie Nelson
WJZ—Cab Calloway
WOR—Myron Moore
12:05 A.M.
WEAF—Don Bestor
12:30 A.M.
WABC—B. Cummins
WEAF—Vincent Lopez
WJZ—Joe Furst
12:45
WABC—Hal Kemp
1:00 A.M.
WABC—Bud Harrod
WMCA—Charley Johnson
1:30 A.M.
WABC — Roseland
WMCA—Cab Calloway
2:00 A.M.
WMCA—Ted Hill
2:30 A.M.
WMCA—Enoch Light

Godfrey and Fred Allen were among the handful of performers who managed to get away with an occasional sacrilege. Most radio entertainment of the thirties was aimed at the visceral rather than the intellectual levels of middle-class taste. When it was bad it was very, very bad, but when it was good it was quite good indeed.

At or near the top of the mythical "best ten" during most of the decade was Fred Allen, who, with his wife, Portland, and a varied assortment of stooges and straight men, consistently put on one of the funniest and most literate weekly shows in radio. "Town Hall Tonight" was topical comedy that usually found Allen trying to thread his way through an exasperating barrage of gags, nonsequiturs, and verbal pomposities toward some dubious sort of rationality. "Allen's Alley," where Fred sought enlightenment in his later programs, was inhabited by such memorable eccentrics as the voluble Senator Claghorn (the name went into the vernacular as a synonym for "loudmouth"); the wispy, hen-pecked philosopher, Titus Moody; and the resolutely opinionated Mrs. Nussbaum. As a yarn spinner, Allen's mastery of the absurd was prodigal. Telling once what befell one of Portland's brothers who was sent out to the backyard to practice playing the tuba, he climaxed the story with, "Well, sir, you know a high wind swept through town one day when he was out there blowing on that tuba, and it screwed poor Charlie four feet into the ground before anybody could get to him."

An enduring feature of the Fred Allen show was his running feud with Jack Benny, another master of the comic art, whose own show was for years in a seesaw race with Allen's for top rating. Actually the best of friends, the two traded extravagant insults over the air and frequently barged in on one another's programs, bent on adding injury to the score. These encounters were, of course, planned, but both men were adept ad-libbers, and the sessions often degenerated into verbal chaos with cast and audience alike in hysterics. To one of Allen's jabs Benny once snapped back with this memorable riposte: "You coward! You wouldn't say that if my writers were here." When the two promised to meet in actual physical combat on Benny's show on the night of March 14, 1937, the ratings showed that only an FDR fireside chat had ever drawn a larger audience.

Benny, incidentally, is one of the few "old hands" of radio who made a successful transition into the era of television—without, he kept insisting, being a day older than thirty-nine. Allen did not make it.

For sheer durability along with top rating in the field of comedy there probably is nothing to equal the record of "Amos 'n' Andy," the legendary blackface team of Freeman Gosden ("Amos") and Charles Correll ("Andy"), which was on the networks five days a week almost without interruption from 1928 to 1960. A close match would be "Fibber McGee and Molly"—Jim and Marian Jordan in real life, who began their radio career in 1931 and reportedly were still at it in 1959. Theirs, too, was situation comedy, built around the accident-prone menage at "122 Wistful Vista," and Fibber's cocky assurance that there was nothing anybody else did that he couldn't do better. The denouement to these nightly rhubarbs usually went something like this:

FIBBER: Gosh darn it, I'll fix it meself. Where's my hammer? Oh, it's in the closet.

MOLLY (in alarm): Don't open that door, McGee!

A split moment of silence followed while you sat tensed in your chair. You knew precisely what was coming—*Crash! Bang! Rattle! Karoomph!* as dishpans, tin cans, roller skates, crockery, and God knows what all came cascading out on the floor. Fibber McGee's closet routine was, quite simply, funny as hell and produced laughter time after time after time.

A number of other comics had a devoted following during the thirties. A quite popular husband-and-wife team was Burns and Allen—George and Gracie—whose metier was the familiar one of the smart-aleck husband versus the shrewd wife. "Easy Aces"—Goodman Ace and his wife Jane—reversed the formula by capitalizing on Jane's virtuosity as a Madam Malaprop—"and all these years I've been working my head to the bone for you." Fanny Brice was the fiendishly precocious Baby Snooks; Jack Pearl, as Baron Munchausen, challenged the doubter with, "Vas you dere Sharlie?"; and Joe Penner put the nonsensical flippancy "Wanna buy a duck?" into national circulation. In a class all by himself, biologically and in showmanship, was "Charlie McCarthy," the pert, irreverent and slyly salacious ventriloquist's dummy who shot his manipulator, Edgar Bergen, to quick fame and fortune as one of radio's greatest favorites. Charlie's libidinous jousts with such voluptuaries as Mae West and Dorothy Lamour when they visited him occasionally on the "Chase and Sanborn Hour" often inspired a flood of parental complaints to the Federal Communications Commission.

The "Chase and Sanborn Hour" was typical of perhaps a dozen variety shows of merit that graced the radio networks during the thirties. The format of these weekly spectacles was fairly well standardized; it carried over substantially unchanged into the age of television. The programs were usually built around a well-known star as master of ceremonies. They offered a varied menu of singers, orchestras, skits, and comics in infinite guises and a liberal sprinkling of "guest stars." Often a dash of highbrow culture was added by including in the latter category a well-known artist from the opera or concert stage or even (if the producer was particularly daring) a poet to give a reading of his own work. The show usually bore the name of its sponsor: "Texaco Five-Star Theater," "Kraft Music Hall," "A & P Gypsies," "The Fleischman Hour," "Maxwell House Showboat," etc. Some names of shows were merely descriptive, such as "National Barn Dance," "Chamber Music Society of Lower Basin Street," "Hollywood Hotel." The stars in this firmament—singers and orchestra leaders mostly—were an unstable lot; they glowed brightly for a time and then were no longer heard. Among the more durable and noteworthy were Rudy Vallee, Kate Smith, Ruth Etting, Phil Cook, "Whispering Jack" Smith, Bing Crosby, Dinah Shore, Helen Morgan, and, among the band men, Ben Bernie ("The Old Maestro"), Kay Kyser with his "Kollege of Musical Knowledge," and Fred Waring with his "Pennsylvanians." For popular music in the grand style—even a little on the pretentious side—there was Andre Kostelanetz.

Radio Listeners in Panic, Taking War Drama as Fact

Many Flee Homes to Escape 'Gas Raid From Mars'—Phone Calls Swamp Police at Broadcast of Wells Fantasy

A wave of mass hysteria seized thousands of radio listeners throughout the nation between 8.15 and 9.30 o'clock last night when a broadcast of a dramatization of H. G. Wells's fantasy, "The War of the Worlds," led thousands to believe that an interplanetary conflict had started with invading Martians spreading wide death and destruction in New Jersey and New York.

The broadcast, which disrupted households, interrupted religious services, created traffic jams and clogged communications systems, was made by Orson Welles, who as the radio character, "The Shadow," used to give "the creeps" to countless child listeners. This time at least a score of adults required medical treatment for shock and hysteria.

In Newark, in a single block at Heddon Terrace and Hawthorne Avenue, more than twenty families rushed out of their houses with wet handkerchiefs and towels over their faces to flee from what they believed was to be a gas raid. Some began moving household furniture.

Throughout New York families left their homes, some to flee to ──by parks. Thousands of per─── the police, newspapers

and radio stations here and in other cities of the United States and Canada seeking advice on protective measures against the raids.

The program was produced by Mr. Welles and the Mercury Theatre on the Air over station WABC and the Columbia Broadcasting System's coast-to-coast network, from 8 to 9 o'clock.

The radio play, as presented, was to simulate a regular radio program with a "break-in" for the material of the play. The radio listeners, apparently, missed or did not listen to the introduction, which was: "The Columbia Broadcasting System and its affiliated stations present Orson Welles and the Mercury Theatre on the Air in 'The War of the Worlds' by H. G. Wells."

They also failed to associate the program with the newspaper listing of the program, announced as 'Today: 8:00-9:00—Play: H. G. Wells's 'War of the Worlds'— WABC." They ignored three additional announcements made during the broadcast emphasizing its fictional nature.

Mr. Welles opened the program with a description of the series of

Continued on Page Four

Top row: (left to right) Orson Welles during his famous "Martian" broadcast—October 30, 1938; Fred Allen and his wife, Portland Hoffa, 1932; "The Aldrich Family," 1939, (left to right) Katherine Naiht, Ezra Stone, Ann Lincoln House Jamison; Mrs. Franklin D. Roosevelt "on the air" in the Radio City Studio, 1934; Lee Wiley brought an authentic "jazz" voice to the radio of the early 1930s; Fanny Brice as "Baby Snooks" replying to her long-suffering Daddy, played by Hanley Stafford. Bottom row: (left to right) "Wanna buy a duck?" and comic Joe Penner—inseparable!; Jack Benny puts the "Bee" on Fred Allen! The "all-in-good-fun" swipes led to some of radio's most literate repartée of the late '30s; "Easy Aces," written by Goodman Ace and starring wife Jane (at right), was one of the most polished comedy programs on the air; "Myrt and Marge," 1937. Myrtle Vail as Myrt (with comb), and Dora Damerel as Marge (seated) were mother and daughter out of the studio.

"Soap opera" is a child of the radio of the thirties—a sturdy but retarded child, one might say, since it has shown no disposition to grow up or show its age, nor in fact to change in any observable way except to go visual on television. "Helen Trent" was depicted as a settled woman of thirty-five when the serial first went on the air in 1933. "By any mundane reckoning," says radio historian Irving Settel, "she is now in her middle-sixties in 1960 [and] still recapturing romance daily." Several other soap operas, whether still on radio or upgraded to television, have shown a similar longevity with characters, locale and situation unchanged. Regardless of names and script writers, the format has remained stable: simple melodramas of the crises of middle-class family life overlaid with tepid romance and served up with a light dressing of organ music five days a week. These serial melodramas, without beginning or end, had a magical sort of continuity, one episode blending into the next with no jarring interruption to the story line. They inspired a kind of defiant loyalty in their nine-to-five audiences. It was the characters, not the actors (they were largely anonymous), who were the recipients of letters of advice and consolation from their multitudes of fans. Some examples of this venerable art form of the thirties (a few may still be extant) include "One Man's Family," "Myrt and Marge," "Pepper Young's Family," "Just Plain Bill," "Ma Perkins," "Vic and Sade," "Life Can Be Beautiful," "Against the Storm," "Road of Life," and "The Goldbergs."

There were many specialty programs on radio in the thirties. "Major Bowes' Amateur Hour," for example, was a Sunday night must for several million listeners. The unctious Major would spin his wheel of fortune and intone, "Round and round she goes, and where she stops nobody knows," and then bring on a parade of tap dancers, singers, musical saw artists, bazooka ensembles, child prodigies and others in endless variety. The sound of his brass gong spelled doom for the less talented, but those who survived might find themselves rewarded with a paid stint on radio or in a nightclub. Mr. Anthony, on the "Good Will Hour," dispensed advice and somber good cheer to victims of all kinds of personal misfortune whose troubles were anonymously aired on his program. "Take It or Leave It," a progenitor of the popular quiz show, worked up to "the $64 question" in increasing stages of suspense. And in a very hallowed niche in radio's hall of fame is the echo of Lionel Barrymore's gruff and richly dramatic voice giving his annual reading of Dickens' *A Christmas Carol*. For thousands of families all over the country it was as much a part of the holiday ritual as hanging up the stockings or going to midnight mass.

But radio of the thirties was not all froth and gags and sentimentality. Serious music was much in demand, and even good dramatic productions came up on the schedule from time to time, thanks to such programs as the "Lux Radio Theater," "Columbia Workshop," and Orson Welles' "Mercury Theater of the Air." Some of the plays were experimental, written expressly for the new medium of radio; others were familiar old standbys going all the way back to Shakespeare. Indeed, it was possible to make quite a gourmet's choice out of the daily fare. The accompanying illustration shows a *New York Times* list of radio programs for a not untypical week in mid-January, 1936.[4]

RADIO PROGRAMS

LEADING EVENTS OF THE WEEK
(Jan. 19-25.)
(Time Is P. M., Eastern Standard, Unless Otherwise Indicated.)

TODAY.
2:00-4:00—President Roosevelt, Governor Lehman, Mayor La Guardia and Others, at Dedication New York State Theodore Roosevelt Memorial, American Museum of Natural History—WNYC (WABC, WJZ, WMCA, WINS, 2:00-2:30).
3:00-5:00—New York Philharmonic-Symphony Orchestra—WABC.
9:00-10:00—Symphony Orchestra; Gregor Piatigorsky, 'Cello—WABC.
9:45-10:30—Whiteman Orchestra; Susanne Fisher, Soprano—WJZ.
10:00-11:00—Symphony Orchestra; Gladys Swarthout, Soprano—WEAF.

MONDAY.
8:30-9:00—Margaret Speaks, Soprano; Richard Crooks, Tenor—WEAF.
8:30-9:00—"Economic Procedures and Social Objectives," Secretary of Commerce Daniel C. Roper, at National Retail Dry Goods Association Convention. Hotel Pennsylvania—WOR.
9:00-10:00—Play, "A Prince There Was," With Ricardo Cortez and Adrienne Ames—WABC.
10:00-10:30—"Sticking to the Constitution," Dr. Glenn Frank, President University of Wisconsin, at Union League Club of Chicago Founders Day Dinner—WJZ.

TUESDAY.
4:00-4:15—"Serving the Home Owners," George G. Bliss, President Federal Home Loan Bank—WOR.
4:30-5:30—Library of Congress Chamber Musicale; Roth String Quartet; Hugo Kortschak, Viola—WJZ.
8:30-9:00—Lawrence Tibbet, Baritone; Concert Orchestra—WABC.

WEDNESDAY.
9:00-9:30—"The Making of Peace Between Armistice Day and the Signing of the Versailles Treaty," Major Gen. James G. Harbord, Newton D. Baker, Former Secretary of War—WJZ.
9:00-9:30—Lily Pons, Soprano; Concert Orchestra—WABC.
10:00-11:00—Cleveland Symphony Orchestra Concert—WEAF.
10:30-10:45—"Jackson and Roosevelt—The Contrast," James M. Beck, Attorney—WABC.

THURSDAY.
4:30-5:00—Conference on Cause and Cure of War, Washington, D. C.; Discussion, "Peace," Lady Astor, From London; Carrie Chapman Catt, From New York—WEAF.
9:30-10:30—America's Town Meeting: "The Townsend Plan," Dr. Francis E. Townsend, Author of the Plan; Representative Emanuel Celler of New York—WJZ.
10:00-10:30—Robert M. Hutchins, President University of Chicago, at Retail Dry Goods Association Dinner, Hotel Pennsylvania—WOR.

FRIDAY.
5:45-6:15—Los Angeles Philharmonic Orchestra, Otto Klemperer, Conductor —WEAF.
10:30-11:00—"Old Age Pensions," Representatives Joseph P. Monaghan of Montana, John S. McGroarty of California—WEAF.

SATURDAY.
1:45-3:00—"Can America Be Neutral?" George Fort Milton, President Chattanooga (Tenn.) News; Bruce Bliven, President The New Republic, and Others, at Foreign Policy Association—WMCA.
1:55-4:45—Metropolitan Opera, "La Rondine"—WEAF, WJZ.
8:00-9:00—"The Waltz Dream"; Jessica Dragonette, Soprano—WABC.
8:15-9:15—Boston Symphony Orchestra Concert—WJZ.
9:00-10:15—American Liberty League Dinner, Washington, D. C.—WMCA.
(10:15-11:00—Former Governor Alfred E. Smith, John W. Davis, Attorney; Jouett Shouse, President Liberty League—WABC.)
9:15-11:15—Chicago Symphony Orchestra Concert—WOR.

Where there is no listing for a station, its preceding program is on the air.
WMCA..570   WEAF..660   WOR..710   WJZ..760   WNYC..810
WABC..860   WHN..1,010   WLWL..1,100   WED..1,300

IV

In popular music the thirties was the era of "swing." What actually was "swing"? According to Sigmund Spaeth, the encyclopedic musicologist, it was little more than a trivial modification of jazz and not the mystical new medium of sound that its far-out devotees declared it to be. Jazz evolved out of ragtime, which came along about the first decade of the century as antidote to the sentimental waltz tunes and doleful ballads like "Silver Threads Among the Gold" that had been the standard musical fare since the eighteen-eighties. Ragtime added syncopation and a faster beat to pep up the existing musical form. The jazz that reached its peak in the early twenties carried the distortion still further into rhythm and harmony and invited improvisation and virtuosity by individual instrumentalists within a group. The best jazz, Spaeth holds, "has been produced by small groups of instrumentalists who actually arrived at a spontaneous and instinctive polyphony and achieved some of their most astonishing results when honestly improvising. . . . Jazz is not a *kind* of music but a *way of playing*—a new treatment of old and common materials."

Jazz could be either "hot" or "sweet." It became "swing" with the proliferation of the big bands in the early thirties and the commercialization of popular music by the movies and the radio. "Actually," Dr. Spaeth says, "it was nothing more than carefully organized, pre-arranged 'hot jazz,' lacking in spontaneity but impressive as an exhibition of individual and collective skill." [5]

So much for the technicalities. Aesthetically, the popular music of the thirties—"swing" and other forms—was above all gaily melodic; it was meant to be sung, whistled, danced to, remembered. It was usually romantic ("Star Dust"), often sentimental ("When the Moon Comes Over the Mountain," Kate Smith's inimitable signature), and sometimes delightfully and cleverly nonsensical (". . . I press the middle valve down / The music goes 'round and 'round Oh-ho Oh-ho Ho-ho / And it comes out here . . ."). It must have had something, for the best of it still turns up on the air and in nightclubs a whole generation later—not apologetically as "period pieces" but on its own satisfying merits. Much of it continues to be available in phonograph-record reissues, one of the best of which as a sampler of the decade is Frankie Carle's "30 Hits of the Thundering '30s" (RCA Victor LPM-2593).

Many of the "greats" in popular music had achieved their eminence before the thirties began. Bandleaders like Paul Whiteman, Ben Bernie, Wayne King, Meyer Davis, and Ted Lewis, and composers like Irving Berlin, George and Ira Gershwin, Jerome Kern, Cole Porter, and Hoagy Carmichael had substantial reputations from the mid-twenties on. Others won their reputation during the thirties: Benny Goodman, Tommy Dorsey, Hal Kemp, Artie Shaw, and Duke Ellington among the best-remembered bandleaders; and Bing Crosby, Russ Columbo, Frank Sinatra, Ruth Etting, Ethel Merman, Maxine Sullivan, and Billie Holiday among a whole galaxy of singers whose voices became as familiar as raindrops on the roof. Never before had so many musicians had such a huge and voracious audience, thanks to the radio, the movies, and a hundredfold increase in the sale of phonograph records between

1934 and 1939. This was the era, too, in which the jukebox emerged to become a standard adornment in many restaurants and taverns.

Most of the music was for dancing, the vogue for which seemed to ride the same upward popularity curve. The name bands were nearly all based in big hotel ballrooms or supper clubs: for example, Paul Whiteman for many years at the roof garden of the Biltmore, Guy Lombardo and his "Royal Canadians" at the Roosevelt Grill, Tommy Dorsey at the Manhattan Room of the Pennsylvania. But they and many lesser groups also went on tour to play for college "proms" and to make one-night stands in provincial armories and lodge halls, where, among the younger inhabitants at least, their coming had the glamorous aura of a state visit. Dancing styles varied from one region to another, but the standard favorite was the durable fox-trot (subject to infinite interpretations), which had been handed along from the days of the World War. Waltzing was still very much in style. For exotic variations there were the samba and rumba, imported from Latin America; something called the Big Apple, which had a brief vogue around 1937; and the jitterbug, whose acrobatics appealed to the younger and more athletically inclined groups.

The genesis and anatomy of musical hits—and their social implications, if any—are an arcane subject beyond the scope of this work. But it may be helpful both to the serious student of the thirties and the nostalgically inclined survivors of the decade to list a few represenative titles of the period. Dates of publication are comparatively meaningless, for it often took a new song a couple of years to catch the popular fancy. The "Hit Parade," a highly rated weekly radio program advertising Lucky Strike cigarettes, frequently pulled a tune thought dead and forgotten out of obscurity (for one week in 1937 it even resuscitated "Alexander's Ragtime Band," which had had its great day in 1912). The following list is, accordingly, only approximately chronological, covering the years from 1930 to 1939. It is no more than a sample, and, of course, a quite subjective one.

Beyond the Blue Horizon
Ten Cents a Dance
Betty Co-Ed (a Rudy Vallee favorite)
Three Little Words
I Got Rhythm (from the musical "Girl Crazy," which started Ethel Merman
 on her career)
Goodnight Sweetheart (". . . 'til we meet tomorrow")
Life Is Just a Bowl of Cherries
When the Blue of the Night Meets the Gold of the Day (Bing Crosby's theme
 song)
Now's the Time To Fall in Love (Eddie Cantor's theme)
Brother Can You Spare a Dime (a song of social significance that came out
 during the banking crisis)
I'm Getting Sentimental Over You
Night and Day
Easter Parade (one of Irving Berlin's best)
Moonlight Madonna

"Jitterbugs" on the stage
of the Paramount Theater,
New York, 1938.

SWING, MISTER CHARLIE

TRUCKIN' ON DOWN
HARLEM'S LATEST DANCE CRAZE · DESCRIPTIVE DIAGRAMS OF THIS DANCE ON BACK COVER
Words by ARTHUR PORTER
Music by EUBIE BLAKE
WILLIE BRYANT AND HIS ORCHESTRA

ORGAN GRINDER'S SWING
Music by WILL HUDSON
Lyrics by IRVING MILLS and MITCHELL PARISH
EXCLUSIVE

BLUEBIRD
B-10286-A
LITTLE BROWN JUG-Fox Trot
(Arr. by Glenn Miller)
Glenn Miller and his Orchestra
RCA MANUFACTURING CO., INC. CAMDEN, N.J. U.S.A.

VARIETY
The Spice of Music
Fox Trot
(M 156)
Vocal by
Cab Calloway
PECKIN'
From "New Faces of 1937"
-Pollack-James-
CAB CALLOWAY
AND HIS ORCHESTRA
VA 612

Doin' "The Big Apple"
at Glen Island Casino,
New Rochelle,
New York, 1938.

"Lindy Hoppers" at the
Savoy Ballroom, Harlem, 1937.

Benny Goodman, "The King of Swing," 1936.

Artie Shaw, "The New King of Swing," 1938.

"Paradiddle Gene" Krupa, 1939.

COLUMBIA
A Jazz Masterwork
35324
(WC 2824)

DRUMMIN' MAN
Fox Trot - Vocal Chorus by Irene Daye
Krupa-Norman - arr. Norman
GENE KRUPA and his ORCHESTRA
Saxes: Tenor-Sam Donahue; Sam Musiker; Alto-Clinton
Neagley; Bob Snyder; Piano-Tony D'Amore; Guitar-
Remo Biondi; Drums-Gene Krupa; Bass-Biddy
Bastien; Trombones-Al Jordan; Sidney Brantley;
Floyd O'Brien; Trumpets-Tory Halton; Nate
Kazebier; "Corky" Cornelius;
Clarinet-Sam Musiker;

MADE IN U.S.A.
FULL-RANGE
RECORDING
Brunswick
Fox Trot   Vocal Chorus
(WB 24452)   Jack Teagarden

I GOTTA RIGHT TO SING THE BLUES
-Koehler-Arlen-
JACK TEAGARDEN
and his ORCHESTRA
8397

Jack Teagarden, 1934.

Harry James (before Sinatra and after Goodman), 1939.

FULL-RANGE RECORDING

Brunswick

(BW 24514) • Fox Trot

CIRIBIRIBIN
-Dole-Pestalozza-
HARRY JAMES
and his ORCHESTRA
8327

Swing Classic

VICTOR

Not Licensed for
Radio Broadcast

25616-A

FRANKIE AND JOHNNIE—Fox Trot
Bunny Berigan and his Orchestra

Featuring H. Berigan, I. Goodman, S. Lipkins, Trumpets—
M. Samel, S. Lee, Trombones—S. Pearlmutter,
J. Dixon, G. Auld, C. Rounds, Saxophones—
T. Morgan, Guitar—A. Fishkind, String Bass—
J. Lippman, Piano—G. Wettling, Drums

RCA Manufacturing Co. Inc.
Camden, N.J.U.S.A.

VICTOR

His Master's Voice

Not Licensed for
Radio Broadcast

25201-A

THE MUSIC GOES 'ROUND AND 'ROUND–F.T.
(La Música Va en Derredor)
(Hodgson-Farley-Riley)
Tommy Dorsey and his Clambake Seven
Vocal refrain by Edyth Wright

RCA Manufacturing Co. Inc.
Camden N.J.
U.S.A.

VICTOR

Not Licensed for
Radio Broadcast

25523-B

MARIE--Fox Trot
(Irving Berlin)
Tommy Dorsey and his Orchestra
Vocal refrain by Jack Leonard and
male chorus

RCA Manufacturing Co., Inc.
Camden, N. J., U.S.A.

Swing Classic

VICTOR

Not Licensed for
Radio Broadcast

25523-A

SONG OF INDIA–Fox Trot
(Canción India) (Rimsky-Korsakow–Arr by Tommy Dorsey)
Tommy Dorsey and his Orchestra
Featuring T. Dorsey, E. W. Bone, L. Jenkins, Trombones–
B. Cusumano, J. Welch, J. Bauer, S. Lipkins, Trumpets–
F. Stulce, B. Freeman, C. Rounds, J. Dixon,
Saxophones–C. Macwen, Guitar–G. Traxler,
St. Bass–D. Jones, Piano–D. Tough, Traps.

RCA Manufacturing Co. Inc.
Camden, N.J. U.S.A.

At left: (clockwise) Bunny Berigan, 1936, the premier white jazz trumpet of the decade; Perry Como, vocalist with Ted Weems' Orchestra, was often aided by the incidental whistling of Elmo Tanner. Photo of Como, circa 1936. All-girl orchestras prior to the Swing Era were strictly Amateur Hour also-rans. With the advent of the big bands, one-nighters, proms, and the dance craze, the *girl* orchestras got bigger and better bookings. Three of the most successful: Ada Leonard and her All-American Girl Orchestra; Phil Spitalny and his All Girl Orchestra (note the twin harpists and twin accordionists); and the most glamorous of all—Ina Ray Hutton and her Orchestra. (Above) Alto-Saxophonist Jimmy Dorsey lagged behind brother Tommy (at right) as a popular bandleader for many years but finally superseded Tommy with such vocal hits of the early '40s as *Green Eyes* and *Maria Elena*.

At right: (top) The Glen Gray Sax Section, 1936. (Bottom) Bob Crosby and his Orchestra at the Steel Pier, Atlantic City, 1936. (Bottom, right) Charlie Barnet, leader of the most Negro-influenced, "soul" sounding white band, 1936. (Below) "Little Jazz" Roy Eldridge, 1939, the premier Negro jazz trumpet of the decade.

BLUEBIRD
Electrically Recorded
PHONOGRAPH RECORDS

Not Licensed for   Radio Broadcast
THE MILKMEN'S MATINEE—Fox Trot
(Denniker-Davis-Razaf)
Charlie Barnet and his Orchestra
Vocal refrain by Barnet Modern-Aires
B-6593-B
RCA Manufacturing Co. Inc. Camden N.J. U.S.A.

At left and above:
Prez! Lester Young, 1938.
His only *angle*
was the tilt of his horn!
Precursor of the "sound" in
modern Jazz; creator of
phraseology (both played and spoken),
originator of, and model
for, the Hipster of the 1940s.
(Below) Billie Holiday, 1938,
at the time of
her vocal stint
with Artie Shaw.

FULL RANGE
RECORDING

Vocalion

5118
(25297)

LESTER LEAPS IN
Fox Trot   -Young-
COUNT BASIE
KANSAS CITY SEVEN

COMMODORE
CLASSICS IN SWING

S26-A

STRANGE FRUIT

(WP 24403 B)   (Lewis Allan)

Billie Holiday and Her Orchestra

Piano interlude by
Sonny White

Hi-De-Hi! Ho-De-Ho! Cab Calloway, 1936.

Ella Fitzgerald,
featured with Chick Webb
and His Orchestra, 1938

Chick Webb,
"King of the Savoy," 1935.

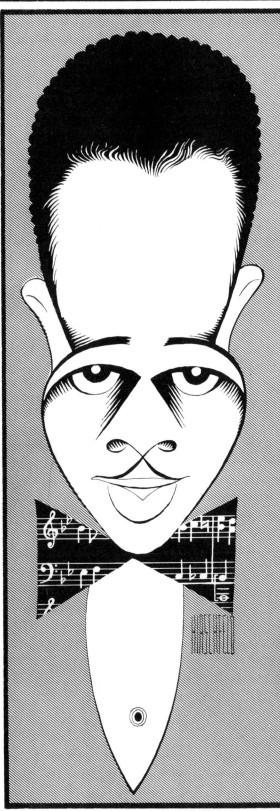

Edward Kennedy "Duke" Ellington, 1934.

Eddy Duchin   Woody Herman and the   Band That Plays the Blues, 1936.

The Ink Spots

The Last Round-up

Bei Mir Bist Du Schoen (Ziggy Elman converted this old Yiddish folk song into a triumph of trumpet virtuosity in a Benny Goodman recording)

Stormy Weather

Smoke Gets In Your Eyes (Spaeth call this "a technically perfect piece of popular music")

La Cucaracha

Solitude (a Duke Ellington original)

Isle of Capri

Anything Goes (Cole Porter at his best)

Wagon Wheels

Love in Bloom (Jack Benny tried and tried and tried)

Begin the Beguine

Alone (a sentimental love song from the Marx Brothers screen riot "A Night At the Opera")

Red Sails in the Sunset

Darling, Je Vous Aime Beaucoup (Hildegarde)

Jockey on the Carousel (Lily Pons in "I Dream Too Much")

The Music Goes 'Round and 'Round

I've Got You Under My Skin

Gloomy Sunday (a real freak, the dirge of a suicide, imported from Hungary. It was rarely played on radio, but the record sales were brisk)

A Fine Romance

Pennies From Heaven (Bing Crosby favorite)

I'm an Old Cowhand

Cheek to Cheek (Fred Astaire and Ginger Rogers in "Top Hat")

Once in a While

Dipsy Doodle

The Donkey Serenade

Loch Lomond (the old Scotch ballad delightfully "swung" by Maxine Sullivan)

Sweet Leilani

Rosalie

Thanks For the Memory

Vieni, Vieni (an old Italian ballad resurrected by Rudy Vallee)

A-Tisket, A-Tasket (Ella Fitzgerald picked this one off the nursery shelf)

Heigh Ho ("heigh ho, its off to work we go," from Disney's "Snow White and the Seven Dwarfs." Also from the same picture was "Some Day My Prince Will Come")

Falling in Love With Love

God Bless America (Kate Smith gave "The Star-Spangled Banner" a hard run with this song. She first sang it on the air on Armistice Day, 1938, although Irving Berlin had written it as long ago as 1917)

Love Walked In

My Heart Belongs to Daddy

September

All the Things You Are

And the Angels Sing

Beer Barrel Polka

South of the Border

Stairway to the Stars

Army Air Corps Song ("into the wild blue yonder" an official song that turned up frequently on "The Hit Parade" and was long a jukebox favorite) [6]

V

The well-stocked magazine rack in a large drugstore or hotel lobby in the nineteen-thirties looked very much as it does today. It had the same glossy, eye-catching covers and the same range of enticement to every level of taste and intellectual capacity. And, by and large, the display showed the same titles and editorial formats that are familiar to the present generation: *Harper's, The Atlantic, Ladies Home Journal, McCall's, Good Housekeeping, Cosmopolitan, True Story, Silver Screen, Saturday Review, Readers Digest, Time, New Republic, The New Yorker,* etc. Among the once-notable titles missing from today's display are *Liberty, Collier's, Literary Digest, Scribner's, American, Youth's Companion, Physical Culture, Ballyhoo,* and others now forgotten. All succumbed, during the Depression decade or shortly thereafter, to incurable economic ailments or to the attrition of time and of changing tastes.

With only a few exceptions their demise was no great loss to the cultural heritage. *Collier's,* which had a sturdy muckracking tradition going back to the first decade of the century, was admired because it was one of the few big "slick" magazines that was in tune with the liberal mood of the times. In articles and editorials it clashed spiritedly week after week with the scolding conservatism of its bigger arch-rival, the *Saturday Evening Post* (which expired at a ripe old age in 1968). *Scribner's,* equally admired, had a solid reputation for literary excellence in its eassys and short stories and had given early recognition to such writers as Ernest Hemingway and Thomas Wolfe. *Liberty,* on the other hand, though professedly as New Dealish as *Collier's* was editorially shallow and undistinguished (its circulation pushed up to the million mark briefly during the decade). The *Literary Digest,* which was essentially a weekly paste-up of news and comment from the daily press, had enjoyed a decades-long renown as the leading news magazine. It expired in 1938, done in not only by the more dynamic editorial and reporting style of its younger competitors, *Time* and *Newsweek,* but also as a result of its egregious polling error that forecast a Landon landslide in the 1936 election. *Ballyhoo,* which had emerged in the late twenties as a purveyor of rather adolescent satire and cartoons, aimed at a slice of the readership then dominated by *College Humor.* Both were victims of the more sophisticated taste in humor developed during the thirties (best exemplified by *The New Yorker*) and withered away.

The most striking innovation of the period was "pictorial journalism"— the wedding of the camera to the typewriter in a union that has endured and strengthened. Publisher Henry Luce (of Time, Inc.) introduced *Life* in 1936, and the Cowles newspaper interests brought out *Look* a short time later. These ventures represented risk-taking of a very high order, for publishing had been put through the wringer by the Depression, and magazine advertising revenues never exceeded 50 percent of their opulent 1929 level during any year of the decade. However, both of the picture magazines survived their early vicissitudes, as did some other new ventures launched at about the same time: *Fortune, Newsweek*, and *Esquire* among them.

In the mass-circulation "family" magazines (there were twenty-eight in

THE SATURDAY EVENING POST

by Franklin

JUNE 17, 1933

BEGINNING IN THIS ISSUE
THE PORTCULLIS ROOM
by VALENTINE WILLIAMS

THE DANGEROUS TRUTH About PETTING

Physical Culture

JANUARY

THE PERSONAL PROBLEM MAGAZINE

25¢

WHO ARE the "HE-MEN" of HOLLYWOOD?
By Adela Rogers St. Johns

CAN STERILITY BE OVERCOME?

HOW THE GIRL WEAKLING BECAME TENNIS CHAMPION
The Story of ALICE MARBLE

CAN SEX IN HUMANS BE CHANGED?

June 27, 1936 THE Price 15 cents

NEW YO

The American
Mercury

Edited by
H. L. MENCKEN

The Impossibility of Education .... E. F. Orr
Chain Department-Stores .... Edith M. Stern
All Dressed Up and Nowhere to Go ...... James T. Farrell
Jonah in the Bible Country .... Charles Lee Snider
Winter on a Mountain Top .... Elizabeth Forsling
Lady Cops in Cap and Gown .... Nelson Antrim Crawford
Songs of a Mountain Plowman .... Jesse Stuart
Bandmaster Gilmore .... George R. Leighton
Casanova .... Carter Brooke Jones
An American Apostle .... H. L. Davis
Crime and Punishment .... Saul Levitt

The Soap-Box and Reviews of the New Books

Alfred A. Knopf, *Publisher*

POPULAR SCIENCE
NOVEMBER 15 cents
FOUNDED MONTHLY
NOW 15¢

SEE PAGE 47

NEW INVENTIONS · MECHANICS · MONEY MAKING IDEAS
HOME WORKSHOP PLANS AND HINTS · 350 PICTURES

LIFE

NOVEMBER 23, 1936 10 CENTS

WILL ROOSEVELT HOLD THE NEXT CONGRESS?
A Revealing Election Forecast

NOV. 3, 1934

NRA CODE

Liberty 5¢

FOOTBALL IS SISSY STUFF
by MEIGS O. FROST

Hearst's International
COMBINED WITH
Cosmopolitan

MARCH · 25

SISTER ACT.. Book-length Novel by FANNIE HURST
A Story of the Private Lives of Quadruplets In Love

the million-and-above bracket in 1935), editorial content ran heavily to fiction as opposed to articles; the ratio was about four to one in such favorites as the *Saturday Evening Post* and *Cosmopolitan*. In the tight competitive situation existing at the time, editors were not much given to taking chances with the tastes and prejudices of their readers, nor, particularly, of their advertisers. With only a few exceptions, editorial policies were cautiously conservative. In both articles and stories, editors were careful to skirt the quagmires of social controversy and unrest. Political controversy was something else, as long as the writer took a soundly commonsense view of things that would comport with the view of, say, General Motors or National Cash Register, which made the New Deal a free target from about 1935 on. But the phenomena of poverty and injustice—or any recognition of the class struggle that might discomfort the generality of right-thinking, tax-paying citizens—were, in most cases, out of bounds. Thus, stories and articles alike tended to sanction the status quo and to uphold the traditional values and conventions of the upper-middle class. Sex was an increasingly attractive and acceptable theme, provided it was held

within contemporary notions of tolerance and good taste. A mild shock to the bluenoses now and then has always been good for business. There is nothing novel about such rubrics in the uneasy world of mass-circulation magazines; the only point to be made is that they were applied with special rigidity in the thirties.

However onerous these editorial caveats may have been to artistic expression (they produced a steady outcry from the intellectual left), American writers enjoyed a wide market for their wares. The demand for short stories was particularly keen. Those writers who could not make the grade with the "slicks" at fees which might run as high as $1,000 for the product of a name writer, might find a taker among the dozens of "pulps" at three or four cents per word. Popular writers of the day were better known, on the whole, for their magazine stories (and occasional articles) than for their novels, although

DOUBLE ACTION

GANG

WHITE WAY
TO HELL!

action-packed novel
of the White Slave
trade, by
E. Hoffman Price

Margie Harris
Norman A. Daniel
Harold Ward

STORIES OF
TRUE GANG
LIFE

ALL STORIES NEW • ALL STORIES COMPLETE

G-8 and His BATTLE ACES

NOW 10¢

AUGUST

VULTURES OF THE
PURPLE DEATH
COMPLETE WAR-AIR NOVEL
By ROBERT J. HOGAN

FREDERICK NEBEL   CHARLOTTE DOCKSTADER   MURRAY LEINSTER
FRANK DEL CLARKE   FRANKLIN H. MARTIN   J. LANE LINKLATER

Black Bat

DETECTIVE MYSTERIES

15¢
5¢
¼

OCTOBER

STAR WESTERN

FUGITIVE LAWMAN
by T. T. FLYNN

DURANGO
VALLEY
RAIDERS
by HARRY
F. OLMSTED

BAEDGER
PEARSOL
KING
SHAW

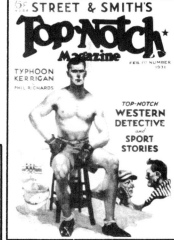

STREET & SMITH'S

Top-Notch
Magazine

FEB. 1st NUMBER 1933

TYPHOON
KERRIGAN

PHIL RICHARDS

TOP-NOTCH
WESTERN
DETECTIVE
and
SPORT
STORIES

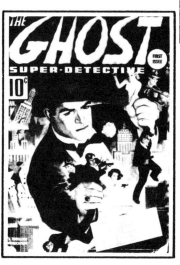

THE

GHOST

FIRST ISSUE

SUPER-DETECTIVE

10¢

SPICY-ADVENTURE
STORIES

TRAITRESS WAGES

their longers works often ran as serials or "complete in this issue." In a typical issue of *Redbook* in 1935, for example, you would have found a complete novelette by Vicki Baum, "Men Never Know"; parts of two serials—"The Spanish Cape Mystery" by Ellery Queen and "Guilty" by Franz Werfel; short stories by Philip Wylie, Alec Waugh, and Edith Wharton; a homily on Lincoln by that inexhaustible apostle of conformity, Bruce Barton; and a chapter of Hugh Johnson's memoirs.

Flip through the pages of half a dozen of the leading magazines of the thirties, and you will encounter most of the names that have since entered the literary hall of fame: Hemingway, Faulkner, Wolfe, Fitzgerald, Willa Cather, Pearl Buck, Alice Duer Miller, to mention a few. But there were many others who, while their fame was less enduring, worked a continuing enchantment upon millions of magazine readers throughout the decade. It is a long roll, but here are a few of the by-lines that were most eagerly looked for on the covers of the big weeklies and monthlies: Mary Roberts Rinehart, Peter B. Kyne, MacKinlay Kantor, Octavus Roy Cohen, Raphael Sabatini, Kathleen Norris, Katherine Brush, P. G. Woodhouse, Rex Beach, Viña Delmar, Borden Chase, Damon Runyan, Corey Ford, Irvin S. Cobb.

One of the most colorful if less estimable publishing phenomena of the time was the Macfadden group of magazines. Bernarr ("Body Love") Macfadden, as *Time* delighted in calling him, was a health faddist and many-faceted eccentric who made a fortune and a fame of sorts out of his fetishes. He launched his first magazine, *Physical Culture,* around the time of the World War. It was dedicated to the proposition that any man could live to be 125 by right living, right diet, and right exercise (Macfadden himself died at the respectable old age of eighty-six in 1955). These doctrines he expounded in great detail both in text and in illustrations of himself and of virile young men and busty young women, all scantily clad, in "classic poses." Some of this early "cheesecake" was as spicey as any to be found in the *Police Gazette* of the same vintage and may have accounted in some part for the modest commercial success of *Physical Culture* and possibly also for Macfadden's subsequent upward progress on the publishing ladder.

In 1919 he came out with the first of the confession magazines, *True Story.* It lured readers with a gimmick: "We offer $1,000 for your life romance." How many of the testimonials were authentic and how many were hack-written in the house is unknown. What is known is that *True Story,* offering the staple elements of romance, infidelity, seduction, and the vicarious pleasures of heartbreak in a frankly middle-class idiom, was an immediaate success. Macfadden had discovered a "secret formula" capable of infinite exploitation. Its application over the next ten or more years produced a dozen new magazines under his imprimatur with such evocative titles as *True Romances, True Experiences, True Ghost Stories, True Strange Stories, True Lovers, Dream World, Movie Weekly, Brain Power, Muscle Builder,* etc., with *True Story* and *Physical Culture* still the bellwethers of the flock. They were a sorry lot by any literary standard—tawdry, banal, often prurient—but they enjoyed an immense patronage among adolescents of all ages.

Macfadden's prolific and profitable stable of magazines was, properly, a product of the booming twenties. But they were conspicuous among the cultural bric-a-brac of the thirties as well, and seemed to reach the peak of their vast popularity about 1935. In that year it was reported that the total monthly circulation of the Macfadden magazines was 7,355,000 copies, which was greater than the circulation of any of the other giants in the field, such as Collier, Curtis, and Hearst. Bernarr Macfadden even thought of running for President, but his grip on his publishing empire was loosened in a stockholders' battle late in the decade, and his flamboyant figure faded gradually from view. But the progeny of his publishing genius (or most of it) survived and spawned countless imitations, which are still to be seen on any well-stocked magazine rack today.[7]

VII

In 1930 the Washington press corps, as measured by Congressional press gallery accreditations, numbered 359 newspaper correspondents and editors. Ten years later the number had grown to 511, an increase just short of 50 percent. This was the largest increase for any like period since the galleries were established almost three-quarters of a century earlier.

This statistic is something more than a straw in the cultural wind that blew across the country during the thirties. It is a firm indication of the rising sophistication of the American middle class; of its concern with public affairs beyond the provincial perimeters of City Hall and the State House; and of the efforts of the newspapers to satisfy the growing appetite to know what was going on in the world of government, politics, and international affairs. Some of this effort may have been inspired by the publishers' fear of competition from radio. Many newspapers were already battling insolvency, with revenues cut in half from 1929 to 1933, and most of them refused for a long time to carry radio schedules except as paid advertisement.* But whatever the reason, the craft of journalism made some salutary adjustments to meet the new demands on it.

One adjustment was to increase on-the-spot coverage of Washington, which had suddenly and urgently become the nation's news center. Nearly all the large city newspapers—some 350—were represented. Three major (and several lesser) wire services—Associated Press, United Press, and International News Service—supplemented this burgeoning Washington daily "file" and also supplied the smaller papers that lacked Washington bureaus of their own. (The AP, for example, almost doubled its Washington staff, from forty

*In 1929 there were 1,944 daily newspapers with a total circulation of 39,425,000. In 1933 the number of dailies had decreased to 1,911, and circulation was off by more than four million. In 1939 there were 1,888 dailies—fifty-six fewer than in 1929—but circulation had climbed slightly above the earlier level to 39,670,000. Robert U. Brown, president of _Editor & Publisher,_ in supplying this information to the author, made the following observation: "You will probably question the relatively small difference between the number of dailies in 1929 and 1939 when the current propaganda is that hundreds of dailies folded during the depression. The answer to that is that the hundreds of dailies that did fold were uneconomically operated, and a lot of others sprang up to take their place in other areas."

to seventy-six during the ten-year period.) Foreign news also received sharply increased attention. In the latter half of the decade—as Hitler, Mussolini, and Stalin churned the political hate mills of Europe—large numbers of American correspondents were sent abroad, and their dispatches competed ever more vigorously with domestic news for front-page positions.

At the same time the character of news coverage began to change. As the news grew in volume and complexity, the reporter's standard formula of "who, what, when, where" (and tell it all in the first paragraph!) acquired a fifth dimension: "why." Readers demanded increasingly to know not only what had happened but what it meant. Major news coverage therefore increased both in breadth and in depth. Cold facts were illuminated with background and interpretation. President Roosevelt inaugurated the custom of regular White House press conferences, and Cabinet members and other officials became available as never before for off-the-record meetings with small groups of reporters under the "Lindley rule" of anonymity (so named for its innovator, Ernest Lindley, bureau chief for the *Herald-Tribune*).

Thus did the "backgrounder" and interpretive news story proliferate. The news magazines *Time* and *Newsweek* also helped to initiate the trend, although they diluted their effort with a good deal of excess rhetorical baggage in the way of overdramatization and verbal slickness. (A contemporary *Time* critic, alluding to its penchant for syntactical involution, wailed, "Where it will all end, knows only God!") Probably the most constructive contribution to this evolution in the reporter's craft was supplied by *The New York Times*. In 1935 it introduced, under the guidance of its Sunday Editor, Lester Markel, its landmark Section IV, "The News of the Week in Review." Here each Sunday major domestic and foreign news events of the week were summarized and brought into sober, understandable perspective by the *Times'* own stable of competent reporters. This style of interpretive treatment was widely copied by other newspapers and in time was to influence the standards of news writing generally.

Another important development of the period was the boom in syndicated columns. This was not a wholly new journalistic phenomenon. It had got its start in the twenties with such pioneers as Frank H. Simonds, David Lawrence, Mark Sullivan, Arthur Brisbane, Frank Kent, and Heywood Broun in the vanguard of the political commentators, and O. O. McIntyre, Mark Hellinger, Louella Parsons, and Dorothy Dix among those serving up a varied fare of big-city and theatrical chitchat, and, in the case of the mythical Miss Dix, advice to the lovelorn. The climate of the thirties caused the breed to multiply rapidly. According to one estimate, upward of 150 new columns sprang to life in Washington alone between 1930 and 1934, many to sink swiftly into oblivion. Those who held on, and the established veterans, served an ever-widening audience.

The *Herald-Tribune's* Mark Sullivan looking as sedate as a Bishop with his crown of white hair, his pince-nez, and his high starched collar, was the generally acknowledged dean of this elite corps. He had been the unofficial "voice" of the Coolidge and Hoover Administrations, and he yielded none of his Republican orthodoxy to the interlopers of the New Deal. He looked upon their "socialistic" antics with Olympian disdain and occasional alarm. No one spoke more vehemently for rock-ribbed conservatism than he, unless it was Brisbane.

Arthur Brisbane was the house oracle of the Hearst newspaper chain. His daily column was usually awarded the off-lead position on the front page. As long as Hearst and Roosevelt were *en rapport,* Brisbane's political commentaries were appropriately restrained. But after 1934 he grew increasingly caustic. He accused the New Deal of leading the country down the road to communism, and of other sins. The Brisbane style was a mixture of pompousness and turgid moralizing, and he could find a parable to underline any point. Thus, noting that the luxurious new liner *Queen Mary* provided special state-rooms for passengers' dogs and that this coddling of the rich had upset some do-gooders, he wrote one day in 1936: "It should comfort the radicals to remember that with all this luxury the dogs are still dogs, just as any man who thinks he can change the world overnight is, after all his talking, still a goose." No one had to guess who "any man" was.

Heywood Broun worked the other side of the ideological street as assiduously as Sullivan, Brisbane, et al, worked their side, but with wit and satire as his chosen implements. He had the proportions and physical grace of an elephant. Dorothy Parker said fondly of him that he reminded her "of an unmade bed." He was on the left of every political controversy that came along, walked in picket lines, and established, almost single-handedly in 1934, the first national labor union for reporters, the American Newspaper Guild. The crusades he conducted in his column "It Seems to Me" were often emotional but never strident. He was at his best, however, when puckishly lancing what he took to be stuffed shirts. For example:

I gather from the jeremiads of Mark Sullivan that most of the dirty work [in Washington] is done at night. It is then that [Rexford] Guy Tugwell sneaks out armed with chalk and writes "Capitalism Must Be Destroyed" on the sidewalks of the town. Mr. Sullivan is convinced that the revolution is not only here but almost consummated. And as I understand it he has two major complaints. He maintains that the upheaval is being carried on secretly and that it is practically painless. When he shakes his head at night and finds that its doesn't roll on the floor you can bet that he is pretty sore about it.[8]

O. O. McIntyre (the initials stand for Oscar Odd) is the best representative of the nonpundits whose columns sought less to excite glandular or cerebral responses than, in one style or another, to beguile with pleasant imagery. His metier was the glitter and glamour of the Big Town—New York, naturally. A small-towner himself from Gallipolis, Ohio (a fact he never let you forget), he adopted the role of the amiable and sophisticated *boulevardier* who was always a little awestruck by the witty and charming celebrities and by the vignettes of human drama that seemed forever to crowd his leisurely peregrinations about Manhattan.

At breakfast M and I were discussing how an invalid so often dominates a household of healthy people. And I recalled how Diego Rivera, the Mexican painter, plucked ants from a plant at Theodore Dreiser's and ate them. And she swished from the table in dudgeon. . . . Nella Webb writes that servants are at a premium in London. All making munitions. . . . Above 14th Street another tragedy of the night. A couple on a doorstep saying goodnight and suddenly a form appears out of the darkness. An outraged woman—likely a wife. In the cold moonlight we thought we saw the flash of a knife. Anyway we heard a scream. . . . One of my favorite people, Lowell Thomas. . . . And so to dinner at Neysa McMein's and there found Robert Sherwood and Bernard Baruch in conspiratorial converse.[9]

There was a good deal of posturing and harmless fraud in all this, but in an age of innocence McIntyre's "New York Day by Day" brought the bright lights of Broadway to the gloom of many an Altoona or Wichita. In 1935, his was the most widely syndicated column in the business, appearing in more than 400 newspapers.

In a class apart was Franklin P. Adams ("F.P.A."), whose daily columns, first in *The World* and later in the *Herald-Tribune*, were a delightful blend of erudition and sophisticated trivia done in the manner of a latter-day Samuel Pepys. The urbane witticisms and sharp but seldom abrasive satire that regularly adorned "The Conning Tower" made Adams one of the most widely quoted commentators of the period.

Among the scores of newcomers who entered the field in the thirties, the most notable were based in Washington. They sprang up in response to the insatiable public urge to get at "the news behind the news," or more responsibly, to find dependable guidance through the tumult of political events. One of the most spectacular successes, judged by readership and financial returns, was Drew Pearson and Robert S. Allen's "Washington Merry-Go-Round." Then as now, it was a lively potpourri of political gossip, conjecture, and second-guessing, with occasional nuggets of solid "inside" news or an exposé that caused some miscreant in public life to wince. (The partnership was dissolved in the forties when Allen joined the Army. Pearson carried on for years alone before acquiring another partner, Jack Anderson.)

It was in this period also that the sage commentaries of Walter Lippmann in the *Herald-Tribune* began to penetrate the reaches west of the Hudson. His syndicated column "Today and Tomorrow" steered a restrained course of intellectual liberalism and soon acquired the status of a national institution. Joseph Alsop began his pundit's career at about the same time, initially with Robert Kintner as a partner. He was abetted by an abundant self-assurance and a close intimacy with the Roosevelt family. The Scripps-Howard papers unveiled three stars of their Washington staff as columnists of national stature: Raymond Clapper, whose reportorial integrity and insight were to become a journalistic tradition; Thomas L. Stokes, who spoke the New Deal creed in the beguiling accents of a fully reconstructed Georgia rebel; and Ernie Pyle, who roamed at large over the country with the eye of a reporter and the ear of a poet. Arthur Krock's "In the Nation" began to appear regularly on the editorial page of the *Times* in 1933. It was not syndicated (the *Times* observed a strict rule of exclusiveness for its writers), but it quickly achieved national prestige for the caliber of its information and insight. There were many other by-lines of the thirties with a vast and devoted following: Paul Mallon, West-brook Pegler, "Bugs" Baer, Walter Winchell, and so on.

The impact of this deluge of syndicated intelligence—some of it sound, some of it half-baked, some of it frivolous and fraudulent—on the popular culture of the thirties was great. It certainly added *something* to the total of knowledge among the middle-class citizenry, and it made them *believe* they were more knowledgeable, whether they were or not, which is a plus of almost the same value. Perhaps the best measure of its effect was taken by Robert and Helen Lynd when they revisited "Middletown" after an absence of ten years:

One dropped back into reading the Middletown papers in 1935 with the sense of picking up a familiar story where one had left off. There is still the morning paper, belonging to a chain . . ., the more independent afternoon paper (both Republican) and the belligerently independent little weekly (Democratic). . . .

The outstanding innovation in Middletown's newspapers is the increased share of signed syndicated features from Washington and New York in the news columns. Whereas Arthur Brisbane's column and David Lawrence's dispatches were the sole features of this sort in the politico-economic field in 1925, Middletown read in its morning paper in 1935 Brisbane's "Today," Drew Pearson and Robert Allen's "Washington Merry-Go-Round," Will Rogers' daily paragraph, Leslie Eichel's "World At a Glance" and Kirke Simpson's "A Washington Bystander"; while the evening paper in 1935 had also entered the field with Walter Lippmann's "Today and Tomorrow," Paul Mallon's "The National Whirligig" and Frank Kent's "The Great Game of Politics." Syndicated columns of a nonpolitical sort include O. O. McIntyre's "New York Day by Day," Walter Winchell's "On Broadway," Dorothy Dix's column on love and marriage, Edgar Guest's "Just Folks," Logan Clendenning's "Diet and Health," Emily Post on etiquette and A. E. Wiggam's "Let's Explore Your Mind." . . .

The presence of more syndicated material in Middletown's papers is working hand in hand with movies, radio, nation-wide fashion services, automobile mobility and many other aspects of its culture to make Middletown identify with the wider America that surrounds it. . . . What one appears to be witnessing is a struggle between the old pride in localism, in being Middletown, and the opposite pride of being *en rapport* with the "newest," the "smartest," the most approved by the "right people" in the big outside world.[10]

What was true for Middletown was true for America as a whole. The gates of "awareness" were opened wider than ever before.

VII

Education was not as badly hurt by the Depression as one might suppose. The big pinch was financial. Colleges and universities suffered a severe falling off in bequests and donations, and in the public schools per-pupil expenditures dropped sharply between 1930 and 1934—from $108.49 to $76.22—but had almost fully recovered by 1938. (The comparable figure for 1967 was $569.) Enrollment in the public schools actually increased a few percentage points faster than the school-age population, and a progressively larger proportion of high school students went on to graduation. There was much the same trend in college enrollments. In 1920 about one in fourteen Americans in the 18–22 age bracket was enrolled in college. In 1930 the ratio had risen to about one in eight, and with only a slight dip during 1932–34 it maintained or slightly improved upon this level throughout the balance of the decade. The lack of jobs for young people undoubtedly had much to do with keeping them in school, but family economic pressures made it necessary for far greater numbers of college students than ever before to make up all or part of their expenses by waiting on table or by whatever part-time employment they could find.[11]

The college generation of the thirties was, accordingly, a considerably more sober and purposeful proup than their predecessors of the twenties. The old rah-rah spirit was largely subordinated to the more pressing business of getting on with studies and earning a degree. Intellectual concerns engaged the students to a greater degree than previously. Campuses became involved in the social and political ferment of the times. Liberal and even communist activity flourished; demonstrations took place at UCLA and a few other large universities for more student participation in administrative affairs; and thousands of students all across the country joined in a variety of pacifist movements. One, such movement, launched at Princeton in 1936 and calling itself Veterans of Future Wars, demanded, with tongue-in-cheek solemnity, immediate payment of a cash bonus of $1,000 plus the increment of 3 percent interest compounded semiannually to 1965 to each prospective soldier of any future war the country might become involved in. The bonus gimmick did not conceal the earnest antiwar intentions of the VFW (to the intense annoyance of the real VFW, the Veterans of Foreign Wars). Within a year the movement was actively at work with its propaganda on some fifty campuses.

But college in the thirties was not all grind and heady idealism. Football and fraternities continued to prosper; deans and preachers bemoaned the high incidence of drinking and sexual promiscuity among students; and somewhere one day in 1938 the first goldfish slithered down a collegiate throat.

In the hard scramble to make a living during the thirties, middle-class America made some striking gains in political and economic sophistication.

From a long heritage of almost total apathy toward government, the Depression made millions of ordinary citizens acutely aware of it—what it was *not* doing for them, what it *was* doing for them, what they thought it *ought* to be doing for them. Taxes were a small part of the average family's worries: they amounted to less than one-half of 1 percent of a year's intake, and most people paid no income tax at all. But government was becoming an increasingly important source of direct income to them—through wages, relief benefits, crop support payments, a veterans' bonus, and so on. Personal income received from the government rose from 8.6 percent in 1929 to 20 percent in 1936. The National Industrial Conference Board reported that the rise in these seven years was as great as the rise in all the preceding 130 years. Suddenly the political process took on a personal dimension. People argued about Roosevelt and the New Deal, about unions and the Liberty League, about payroll taxes and deficit spending, as heatedly and as knowledgeably as they did about crops and the World Series. The 1936 election, whose outcome was never very much in doubt, saw the greatest outpouring of voters in history up to that time—45.6 million, as against 39.8 million in 1932.

A kindred phenomenon of the times was the rapid growth of consumer cooperatives. People became convinced that, in part at least, hard times were due to price gouging, which they believed to be regularly practiced and condoned under the free enterprise system. Two books helped to document their suspicion: *Your Money's Worth,* by Fred J. Schlink, published in 1927, and a sequel, *100,000,000 Guinea Pigs,* by Schlink and Arthur Kallett, published in 1933, which tore into the myths of advertising and exposed many of the chicaneries of merchandisers. The two books combined had sold almost 500,000 copies by 1935 and spawned such a wave of belligerent skepticism among consumers that many businessmen and advertising agencies became seriously alarmed.*

Consumer co-operatives based on the nineteenth-century Rochdale principle sprang up in many parts of the country. They operated in various fields: grocery and meat markets, pharmacies, automobile service stations, and medical clinics. A person could buy a share in a co-op for as little as $5, which entitled him to a year-end rebate based on the volume of purchases. The rebate engendered the smug satisfaction that the profits were coming to you as shareowner and not being spread among a succession of middlemen. Farmers in the United States had experimented with cooperative enterprises of several kinds for a number of years, but the general consumer co-op made little headway until the Depression. There were fewer than 400 in 1929, but by 1939 there were over 4,300 with gross sales of $211.6 million paying annual rebates to 925,000 shareowners and attracting the trade of several million nonmembers. In some circles, being known as a "good cooperator" was a status symbol like membership in a proper club.

Social consciousness was on the rise during the thirties, but it had an anomalous blind spot in regard to racial and ethnic discrimination. Except in urban intellectual settings and the upper reaches of the world of business and finance, Jews remained an alien minority in the middle-class cultural

---

*The alarm of the business community over the consumer movement was well illustrated by *Business Week,* which ran a special 15-page supplement in its issue of April 22, 1939, telling its readers what it was all about. "This is a study in organized discontent," the magazine said. "It is a discontent that feeds upon itself and which business cannot afford to overlook. . . . Time was when it might have been possible to laugh off [these malcontents] as crackpots. But not today. [They] have fomented a movement that has vitally affected the marketing of goods."

The movement was denounced as communist-inspired, and columnist George Sokolsky wrote that it threatened the "American way of life." A national Consumers Foundation was launched with the avowed purpose of coordinating the activities of consumer organizations. It was quickly exposed as a creature of the National Institute of Distribution, a trade organization of big merchandisers who wanted to kill off the co-ops.

complex. They were clustered in particular streets and neighborhoods in most large cities (often indirectly enforced by real estate covenants), had little social intercourse with non-Jews, and were excluded from the "best" clubs and resorts. Their admission to most colleges was regulated by quota. The Gentile's inherent suspicion of the Jew, rooted in the dark recesses of Christian mythology, was exacerbated by the prominence of Jews in radical left-wing activities and by the denunciations of such demagogues as Father Coughlin and Gerald L. K. Smith. But the public conscience seemed to be immune to all save the most blatant expressions of anti-Semitism.

The same was true for discrimination against the Negro. To the great mass of whites the burgeoning concern over civil rights (the popular phrase was civil liberties) had mainly to do with the political and economic rights of labor, not with injustice toward the Negro. His status as a member of an under-privileged class was considered a regrettable but insoluble fact of life. There had been no federal legislation affecting his welfare since Reconstruction. The New Deal, for all its compassion for the "forgotten man," added virtually nothing to the score. Though it did what it could to assure him an even break in the distribution of welfare and work relief benefits (often vitiated at the county level), it approved hundreds of NRA codes that included discrimina-tory wage differentials for Negro workers. To the generality of whites, both North and South, the belief that this was "a white man's country" was a mani-fest article of faith, held without rancor in most instances, but held immutably.

VIII

Summing up, the thirties witnessed a renaissance of sorts in the cultural life of America. The Depression enforced a break with the social postulates and the conventional wisdom that had prevailed at least since the turn of the century. To replace the politico-economic theories that had failed them, the people were driven to explore many new and occasionally radical alternatives, from communism to proletarian art and literature. What they chose in the end was a modest compromise between the old modes and the new, but the net effect was a pronounced liberalizing of the whole spectrum of popular con-ventions and attitudes. The limits of tolerance for what was acceptable were expanded—in politics, in morals, in taste. Along with this change came a dissolving of the old barriers of provincialism—or, put another way, a widen-ing sophistication abetted chiefly by the radio, motion pictures, and the press, in each of which there were significant advances during the decade.

Obviously, the cultural image of the nation was not made anew (some will argue that in the long view it was not even changed for the better) in the span of a single decade. But in no other decade of this century (to midway of the seventh at least) has that image been so much altered as in the thirties.

CHAPTER 16
The Second New Deal

AT SOME POINT IN THE YEARS 1935–36 the First New Deal ended and the Second New Deal began. Scholars still argue over how cleanly and emphatically the switch was made, and whether it was a shift in substance or only in degree. But a change there indisputably was: it could be detected in the mood of the people and in the political climate of Washington.

The ardor and exhilaration of the early New Deal years had cooled. The Good Knight had beheaded the dragon with a flourish, and though its body still quivered and its forked tail still thrashed about menacingly, most onlookers were satisfied that the beast's worst depredations were over. Ten million people were still unemployed, but they no longer sold apples on the street or stood in breadlines. They were out of sight—on WPA projects or on relief. Some six million regular jobs in industry had reopened since the bad days of 1933. Business activity was reviving all across the board (it broke 100 on *The New York Times Index* in May 1936 for the first time in five years). Farm income had doubled from its Depression low. Everywhere the skies seemed to be brighter, and peoples' hopes were on the rise. The zeal for reform, for making a bright new world, for punishing the bad guys and elevating the good, had tapered off. Now the popular urge was to cash in on the gains so far made and not spoil things by pushing too hard. The popular mood had not turned against the New Deal—far from it. Rather, it had come to take the New Deal for granted and was more concerned with harvesting the rewards than with planning new ventures.

I

In terms of program the New Deal had about completed its mission. In the final great legislative offensive of 1935 it got the Social Security Act; the Public Utilities Holding Company Act; reform of the Federal Reserve System; rural electrification; a $3-billion work relief program (WPA, et al), which represented the first overt acceptance of the Keynes doctrine of deficit spending as economic stimulus; a momentous tax bill that aimed at a "redistribution of wealth" but fell somewhat short of the mark before Congress got through with it; and the Wagner National Labor Relations Act, which put the power of the federal government behind labor's right to collective bargaining. The total impact of these enactments was as profound as those that were hammered out in the feverish glow of the Hundred Days, and their effect was more lasting. For while the Supreme Court cut down one New Deal experiment after another from the class of '33, each one from the class of '35 survived the subsequent test of constitutionality.

Philosophically, some of the 1935 programs, such as social security and rural electrification, fit more neatly into the pattern of the First New Deal than of the Second. This distinction is an amorphous one that still divides the historians. Without venturing into the details of this erudite controversy, let us settle for this rather simple distinction: The First New Deal was marked by an exuberant willingness to try anything, conventional or otherwise, to prime a stalled economic engine; the Second New Deal was marked by a determination to rely on conventional primers but to apply them with all the raw muscle needed to make them work.

Roosevelt was strongly influenced in the first years of his Administration by men like Tugwell, Berle, Richberg, and Jerome Frank, who, in one degree or another, favored a fundamental restructuring of the economic system and the jettisoning of its obsolete parts where necessary for modern replacements. A common denominator of their thinking was faith in economic planning, or a strong centralized control of the entire economic mechanism. They won no clear-cut victories, but their theories were visible in the AAA and to a lesser extent in TVA and NRA. Roosevelt had no firmly held economic doctrines of his own; such as he did hold were conventional and conservative, and they were buttressed by such early advisers of a like viewpoint as Ray Moley. But he was willing to experiment and improvise, to try a little of this and a little of that, with an insouciance that sent men like Jesse Jones and Lewis Douglas climbing up the wall. The net result was that the First New Deal was an economic patchwork on a base of traditional capitalism. The profit system was not violated; Roosevelt merely strove to make it more responsive to the common good. In the simplest terms, he sought a mutually agreeable partnership between business and government, with government holding a few extra voting proxies as public trustee.

By the beginning of 1936, however, Roosevelt was persuaded that any meaningful partnership with business was illusory. The brave promise of NRA had been turned into a mockery of evasions and sharp practices. Business leaders, many of them allied with the Liberty League, were growing openly hostile, and "That Man" was the kindest of many epithets they applied to the President. The American Bankers Association seriously debated "boycotting" the federal government until it balanced its budget and mended its spendthrift ways. Rich men, infuriated by "confiscatory" tax policies, talked of bundling up their assets and emigrating to the Bahamas, and a few of them actually did. The Supreme Court, in striking down the NRA and the AAA, gave notice that the road was blocked against any economic remedies applied at the source of infection—within the sovereign boundaries of the states. Labor was being repeatedly frustrated in its efforts to assert its promised role as a partner in the business revival. In spite of that revival, the hard, indigestible lump of unemployment still persisted. The grip of the Depression had been loosened but not broken, and, rationally or not, Roosevelt laid the blame to business.

This viewpoint was strongly reinforced by many in the Administration but nowhere with greater clarity and persuasiveness than in a long, thoughtful memorandum addressed to Roosevelt by Professor Felix Frankfurter in the summer of 1936. He wrote:

The trend toward concentration [in industry] is a very real threat against our traditional competitive system. If that trend is not reversed there is danger of a private socialism in this country as alien to traditional Americanism as state socialism. The backbone of that trend is the creed of greed—that no aggregation of property can be so large as to be beyond the control of concentrated and centralized managers, and that competition is an outmoded, discredited, useless feature of economic life. ... There is no practical way to regulate the economic oligarchy of autocratic, self-constituted and self-perpetuating groups. With all their resources of interlocking directors, interlocking bankers and interlocking lawyers, with all their power to hire thousands of employees and service workers throughout the country, with all their power to give or withhold millions of dollars worth of business, with all their power to contribute to the campaign funds of the acquiescent or to subsidize the champions of the obdurate, they are as dangerous a menace to political as they are to economic freedom. It is necessary to destroy the roots of economic fascism in this country if we wish to remove the dangers of political fascism which engulfed freedom in other lands.[1]

These were the experiences and influences that shaped the President's mood as his first Administration drew to an end and the second began. His first Administration had been conceived in the spirit of consensus; his second would be conducted in a spirit of aggression. Since persuasion had failed, force would be the rule. There were no more rabbits to be pulled from the magician's hat; the emphasis now was on making those that had been produced survive and prosper.

This shift to a more realistic, hard-boiled approach to the achievement of New Deal goals was not made without some severe sacrifices of political support. "The basic conservatism of its economics," Schlesinger says, "was disguised by the aggressive radicalism of its politics." There was a degree of coercion in the second phase of the New Deal that had not been present in the first. The Public Utility Holding Company Act of 1935 demanded that the utility industry abandon its nefarious superstructure of holding companies and return to a more equitable competitive existence. The Tennessee Valley Authority and the Rural Electrification Administration made the government a fighting partisan in the battle of public versus private power. The REA set up a yardstick for measuring the fair market price for electric power, and it offered to finance rural cooperatives who wanted to produce or manage their own power supplies. The Wagner Labor Act told horrified businessmen that they would have to heed the demands of their workers for collective bargaining rights if they wanted to enjoy the fruits of interstate commerce. The Wealth Tax Act reached into corporate (as well as private) treasuries to drain off excess profits and to impose the highest surtax takes in history.

To conservatives generally and to the business community in particular, Roosevelt seemed to be piling one outrage upon another. Their angry fulminations filled columns of newsprint and rocked countless banquet tables. Edward H. Hutton, board chairman of the General Foods Corporation, urged his fellow businessmen to "gang up in a great business and industrial lobby" to go to work on Congress. Robert L. Lund, president of the National Association of Manufacturers, blasted the New Deal for its "contempt for the Constitution" and for "the deliberate firing of class hatred." William Randolph Hearst issued a ukase to his editors that the New Deal henceforth was to be referred to in print as the "Raw Deal."

The sparks from this friction ignited the inherent conservatism of Congress. In spite of the large Democratic majorities, many of the posts of power in the Senate and House were held by Southern Bourbons. Other members of Congress numbered in their constituencies business and financial interests whose wishes could be ignored only at their individual peril. Both the tax and the Holding Company bills strained the President's influence with Congress to the limit and set a number of powerful Democrats, including Vice President Garner, on the path toward permanent disenchantment. The deviators would develop within a couple of years into an informal coalition of Southern Democrats and conservative Republicans capable on given issues of thwarting the President's purpose.

This, then, was the grimmer, less buoyant climate into which the New Deal emerged in its second phase. The excitement of the crusade was over; now came the grubbier tasks of an army of occupation. Ahead lay some momentous and bruising challenges. The pace of recovery would slacken and fall into a recession that would raise all over again questions about the wisdom and efficacy of New Deal reforms. The President would pit his strength against the institution of the Supreme Court and come away with a bloody nose. Industrial strife would reach a new pitch of sustained bitterness as organized labor sought to cash in on the promissory notes the New Deal had given it. The conservative opposition in Congress would stage an impressive breakthrough in the 1938 by-elections, and deal the President a humiliating rebuke in the process. And destined within a short time to overshadow domestic concerns was the towering issue of war or peace, of isolation or intervention.[2]

II

The 1936 election saw the New Deal at the crest of its popularity, but the tide then began slowly to run out. In that contest Roosevelt scored the most one-sided victory since the presidential election of 1820.* He yielded up to his Republican opponent only eight electoral votes, those of Maine and Vermont. At the same time he added to the Democrats' already towering majorities in Congress, leaving the Republicans fewer than one-third of the seats in either chamber. At this moment, too, there was welded together the great Democratic coalition that would make the Democratic party the dominant one in the nation for the next thirty years or more. But in spite of all this, the New Deal was in for a long season of travail.

There was no question but that Roosevelt and Garner would be their party's choice to succeed themselves for a second term. A small *junta* composed of such malcontents as Al Smith, Bainbridge Colby of New Jersey, James A. Reed of Missouri, and a few other diehards within the party's power structure, sought to frustrate this design, but they did not even slow it down. The Democratic convention in Philadelphia in June was a political *mardi*

---

*In the contest of that year John Quincy Adams received only one electoral vote to 231 for James Monroe. There was no popular vote in this and prior elections, the choice being made by electors, who were designated in a number of different ways.

gras, and the preordained candidates were nominated by acclamation. Addressing an ecstatic throng of 100,000 in Franklin Field—and the nation at large by radio—the President gave a rousing acceptance speech that set the terms of battle not only for the campaign immediately ahead but for the oncoming years of his Administration. This nation, he said, "has a rendezvous with destiny" to demonstrate the viability of democracy to a world threatened by dictatorship. He promised unending war against the "economic royalists" at home who for selfish purposes would vitiate his effort. There was a prophecy in that declaration that was lost on many at the time.

The Republican convention, held at Cleveland, was a desolate affair. There was not a remote chance of unseating the New Deal and the Republicans knew it. Their one hope was to mobilize the growing conservative reaction against Roosevelt by creating a better-focused opposition to his "wasteful" and "socialistic" policies, and thus achieve a more effective party stand for their contest of 1940. Senators Vandenberg of Michigan and Borah of Idaho were briefly tempted to seek the nomination but thought better of it before convention time. In the end the choice fell upon Governor Alfred M. Landon of Kansas, a conscientious but blandly ineffectual unknown whose chief political attainment was that he was the only Republican governor elected in 1932 to survive the by-election of 1934. He had another potential virtue that was secretly cherished by some party leaders at the time: He was so guileless and lacking in color that he offered a striking and possibly reassuring contrast to the glib and insouciant FDR. They hoped that this old-shoe quality in their man would galvanize the growing distrust of the sophisticated Easterner. Jim Farley feared that he had committed an irretrievable blunder when, early in the campaign, he derided Landon as "the Governor of a typical prairie state." But for many GOP strategists this was just the sort of homespun, made-in-America image they wanted their man to project. They adopted the sunflower as their symbol and made a campaign anthem out of Stephen Foster's "O Susanna." It went like this:

> The alphabet we'll always have
> but one thing sure is true
> With Landon in, the New Deal's out
> and that means P.D.Q.
> Alf Landon learned a thing or two,
> he knows the right solution,
> And in the White House he will stay
> within the Constitution.

For the Number Two spot on their ticket the Republicans chose Frank Knox, the able publisher of the Chicago *Daily News.* Actually neither Landon nor Knox quite fitted the deep-dyed conservative stereotype that their campaign managers devised for them. Both were at least mildly progressive in outlook and had begun their political careers in the Bull Moose revolt a couple of decades earlier. Landon as Governor had spoken favorably of many New

Deal measures, and that fact was to haunt him more than once during the campaign.

In presidential politics, a candidate often gains office not because he won the election but because the other fellow lost it, as was true in the Truman-Dewey contest of 1948. In 1936 Roosevelt won, affirmatively and overwhelmingly, but (as some contemporary observers pointed out) he might well have lost a couple of more states besides Maine and Vermont had it not been for the clumsy intervention of the American Liberty League on the Republican side. It was the frantic exertions of this "millionaires' union," as Roosevelt called it, that, next to the final vote tally itself, made the election campaign of 1936 exciting and memorable.

The Liberty League in its very nature dramatized the conflict between "wealth and commonwealth" as no amount of New Deal oratory could. It was the brainchild of John J. Raskob, the onetime Democratic chairman, who had become embittered by Roosevelt's nomination in 1932, and R. R. M. Carpenter, a vice president of the DuPont Corporation. At its birth in August 1934 the founders gave it a rational countenance: It would be a nonpartisan forum for the defense of "Constitutional government." It *was* nonpartisan in the sense that both Democrats and Republicans were welcome, but all were partisanly united in the single goal of defeating Roosevelt at the next election and dismantling the New Deal. Its official roster bristled with the names of the captains of industry and finance whom Roosevelt was to denounce so effectively in the campaign as "economic royalists"—the ruling heads of the DuPont empire, of General Motors, of U.S. Steel, and of others of equal caliber and vulnerability. Its one hundred-man executive committee listed seventy presidents or directors of leading corporations and financial institutions. In addition it attracted such disaffected and disappointed Democratic leaders as John W. Davis, Jouette Shouse, and Al Smith. Smith was, in fact, the big gun of its political artillery. When he announced at a huge $100-a-plate white-tie dinner at Washington's Mayflower Hotel in January 1936 that he planned "to take a walk" out of the Democratic party in the upcoming election campaign, the last pretense of nonpartisanship was demolished.

"It is all right with me," the onetime "Happy Warrior" barked to his blue-chip audience, "if they want to disguise themselves as Karl Marx or Lenin or any of the rest of that bunch, but I won't stand for allowing them to march under the banner of Jackson or Cleveland. . . . There can be only one flag, the Stars and Stripes or the flag of the Godless Union of the Soviets. There can be only one national anthem, the Star-Spangled Banner or the Internationale." [3]

What a long way Al Smith had come from the East Side and "Mamie O'Rourke." He had swapped the brown derby for a high silk hat, Charley Michelson said, and now everybody knew it.

For a time in 1936 the Liberty League virtually usurped the function of the Republican National Committee. Its headquarters spread over an entire floor of the National Press Building in the heart of downtown Washington, and its fifty-man staff was twice the size of the Republican Committee's. Its financial resources seemed unlimited, and it poured out a steady stream of pamphlets and other propaganda material (estimated at over five million pieces) that inundated the mails, newspaper offices, and libraries in every part of the country. It found nothing of virtue in anything the New Deal had done. According to its propaganda, the AAA had imposed fascism on a free agriculture; the Holding Company Act was a blow to every citizen who owned a share of stock; relief and social security marked "the end of democracy," and more in the same vein. It waged a form of guerrilla warfare against the Democrats by giving aid and encouragement to any group of defectors within the party's ranks. It was Liberty League money that helped to put "Red Gallus" Gene Talmadge, the fire-breathing white-supremicist Governor of Georgia, into the national spotlight as the guiding genius of the Southern Committee to Uphold the Constitution. The most conspicuous feature of this Committee's great ingathering at Macon in January 1936 was a leaflet prominently displaying a large picture of Mrs. Roosevelt accompanied by two young Negroes and a caption noting that since the Roosevelts entered the White House Negroes had been welcomed at its table and even allowed "to sleep in White House beds."

It seems wholly incredible today that men of stature and talent in the business world could have been such naive blunderers in the political arena. What they had fashioned was a crusade of the rich and powerful to wrest their ancient privileges from the impious hands of the multitude—or so they made it appear, with the hearty assistance of Michelson and the Democratic National Committee. The League never gained any impressive grass-roots support. Its peak membership was 36,055, of whom 26,325 were in the non-dues-paying category, but in millions of minds it lit up the label "economic royalists" in living color. Before the Republican convention opened, Landon implored the League to spare him its kiss of death—an endorsement—which it did. But Al Smith and other Liberty Leaguers stumped actively for him nevertheless.

Roosevelt was confident during the early summer, but not overconfident, that he could take Landon's measure in the campaign. There were many voices and signs around him counseling caution. Harold Ickes was among those who warned him not to regard Landon as "a pushover." Ickes said he could "see the possibility of a Republican victory, although I regard the Democrats' chances as superior." The Gallup and *Literary Digest* polls forecast a Democratic defeat. By the time of the nominating conventions, most New Deal strategists were ready to write off the threat of the Liberty League as such. But they were a good deal less sanguine about the effect on the outcome of the followers of the late Huey Long, of Townsend, and of Father Coughlin. The Dearborn priest was now feeding his huge radio flock a liturgy of vituperation and fear. He denounced Roosevelt as "anti-God," and swore that, just as he had been instrumental in unseating Hoover four years earlier, "so help me God I will be instrumental in taking a Communist from the chair once occupied by George Washington." Coughlin hitched his wagon to the unlikely star of Representative William Lemke's Union Party and promised to deliver nine million votes for it on election day. Some 85 percent of the nation's newspapers joined in the clamor for the New Deal's defeat.

But Roosevelt and Farley had no fears. Wherever the smiling, confident President showed his face during the campaign he was greeted by huge, enthusiastic crowds. One hundred and fifty thousand joined in an impromptu procession to escort him from the railroad station to the Chicago Stadium when he arrived for a major speech in October. A triumphal tour of New England was capped by a delirious mob of half a million that overran the Boston Common. When his campaign train pulled up to a halt at wayside stations in Ohio, Iowa, the Dakotas, or California, jubilant throngs from the surrounding countryside awaited him. They reached out to touch him with their hands, in order to express what was in their hearts. In very truth, Roosevelt was to many the Great White Father who had saved a home or a farm or given a job on WPA or caused a factory gate to open or a union to be organized. Often they watched in choked silence as he made his way painfully up the special ramp provided for him at his railroad car, hoisting himself along by his powerful arms and shoulders. At the top he would turn and wave a cheery farewell, and the silence would be broken by a spontaneous roar of adulation.

Roosevelt had the people with him and he knew it. He ignored Landon during the campaign, and he all but ignored the Republican Party except to equate it with the powers of wealth and special privilege. They were the people's enemies, they were the New Deal's enemies. They were the forces of greed and reaction who would destroy the gains of the last four years, leading the nation back into the gloomy past. He attacked them with the facts and figures of a reviving prosperity—more jobs, better pay, fewer bank failures, fewer mortgage foreclosures. He attacked them with ridicule as frightened sick men who, now that they had been made well, wanted to "throw their crutches at the doctor." His attack had the insolence of a champion who knows the lethal power of his punch. At the concluding rally of his campaign in Madison Square Garden two days before the election, he "called the roll" on those who sought to pull down the New Deal. In a ringing peroration that brought the packed audience to its feet, cheering and stomping, he declared:

Never before in all our history have these forces been so united against one candidate as they stand today. They are unanimous in their hatred for me—and I welcome their hatred.

I should like to have it said of my first administration that in it the forces of selfishness and of lust for power met their match.

I should like to have it said of my second administration that in it these forces met their master.

A NEW LOCHINVAR COMES OUT OF THE WEST

(Below) President Roosevelt winds up his 1936 campaign for re-election with a Fireside Chat from his Hyde Park study. (Bottom, at left) Business, as usual, but on the White House Lawn! A rare picture of Roosevelt and his Cabinet, 1936. (Alongside) President Roosevelt and Vice-President John Nance Garner "munching" words at a Jim Farley Testimonial Dinner.

On the morning of Wednesday, November 4, 1936, newspapers all across the country proclaimed a history-making event, as the *Times* did in this eight-column banner:

ROOSEVELT SWEEPS THE NATION; HIS ELECTORAL VOTE EXCEEDS 500

Roosevelt, said Arthur Krock, had won "the most overwhelming testimonial of approval ever received by a national candidate in the history of the nation." With the largest turnout ever to swamp the polls—some 45 million—FDR had received a plurality of 11 million popular votes. He swept every state in the Union excepting only Maine and Vermont for a total of 523 electoral votes to only eight for Landon.* In Congress the Democrats increased their representation in the House to 333 seats against the Republicans' 103, and in the Senate, seventy-five seats against the Republicans' seventeen.

The magnitude of the sweep created a kind of happy delirium, and conversely a mood of stunned disbelief. Times Square on election night was jammed with an estimated million Roosevelt partisans. When word of Landon's concession was flashed on the moving screen on the Times Tower at 1 A.M., there erupted a noisy bedlam under a cloud of confetti and ticker tape dumped from windows of surrounding buildings. Elsewhere, too, there was a carnival spirit. All the next day, schools were disrupted; office and factory workers celebrated noisily on the bosses' time or took the day off; impromptu victory parades were organized.

The election results, of course, plunged many into despair. "That Man" had been handed a virtually limitless mandate for another four years. To the Liberty Leaguers, Roosevelt's victory was the triumph of "mobocracy" and the advent of an immeasurable disaster. Father Coughlin took to the radio on Friday night to make the bitter confession that he and his Union for Social Justice had been "thoroughly discredited" and that he was withdrawing forthwith from all public contention. (Even with Coughlin's help, Candidate Lemke received fewer than a million votes.) Editors who had been solemnly warning their readers to abjure the tempting seductions of the New Deal gulped in dismay at so resounding a rebuke to their influence. Most newspapers took their medicine manfully, but not the Chicago *Tribune*. In a bitter spirit of "we told you so," it prophesied that Roosevelt would now turn even farther toward the communist left, and it darkly warned: "The results should be apparent in a short time. Millions who voted for Mr. Roosevelt are due for a sharp awakening, and it should not be long delayed."

But at least one presumed foe of the New Deal sounded a contrite note. Joseph Schechter of Brooklyn, whose "sick chicken" had challenged and overcome the NRA's Blue Eagle, meekly asked a reporter: "I wonder if it would be possible to congratulate President Roosevelt through the newspapers and tell him that the sixteen votes in our family were cast in his favor?" [4]

---

*Landon had the meager satisfaction of carrying Roosevelt's home county of Dutchess by 4,406 votes, but that satisfaction probably was canceled out by the loss of his native Kansas to Roosevelt by a margin of 48,000.

III

It was in the 1936 campaign that the so-called Roosevelt Coalition first displayed its formidable might. It transformed the Democratic Party from a loose confederation of feuding chiefdoms into a cohesive popular front that would dominate the political stage for a generation or more. The Democrats had been an ineffectual minority, nationally at least, since the second election of Grover Cleveland in 1892.* But after 1936 the Democratic Party was unmistakably the majority party. It chose the occupant of the White House for all but eight of the next thirty-two years and had effective control of all but three Congresses from the seventy-fifth through the ninety-first. Though it seethed constantly like a houseful of incompatible cousins and in-laws, it was a union of convenience and necessity. In the clutches, all the factions realized there was more to be gained by sticking together than by flying apart.

The base of the Democrats' strength when the New Deal came into power in 1932 lay in two traditional but almost totally disparate strongholds —the solid South and the boss-ruled precincts of the large eastern and a few midwestern cities. The loyalty of the South was cemented by sentiment stemming from the chronic conflict between an agrarian and an industrial society. The loyalty of the city bosses and their organizations was cemented by enlightened self-interest—the pleasant usufructs, so to speak, of patronage and paving contracts. Jim Curley in Boston, Frank Hague in Jersey City, Ed Kelly in Chicago, and Tom Pendergast in Kansas City, to list only a few of this celebrated company, could deliver their cities "like a sack of potatoes" to the Democratic cause on election day, and sometimes with enough heft to swing the rest of the state. The extra heft was supplied in 1932 by hunger and the bitter disillusionment with Hoover and the Republicans. It was supplied in even greater measure in 1936 by the bright promise—and the partial fulfillment of those promises—of the New Deal.

On this base, Roosevelt grafted three additional layers. The most important element was labor. Since the death of Populism at the turn of the century, organized labor—as represented chiefly by the American Federation of Labor—had stood skeptically aloof from national politics. Its chieftains, such as William Greene and John L. Lewis, were mostly Republicans, but the mass of working men were politically unaffiliated and apathetic, and their leaders did little to stir them up. The labor legislation of the New Deal, beginning with Section 7(a) of NRA, and work relief programs under the CWA and the WPA, gave working men and women a stake in national politics such as they had never before enjoyed. The great schism that split the Committee (later Congress) of Industrial Organizations off from the parent A.F.L. in 1935 was motivated at least in part by political restlessness. The split was followed in a few months by the formation of Labor's Non-

*In this context, Woodrow Wilson, a Democrat, was an "accidental" President, his election in 1912 growing out of the Bull Moose revolt that split the Republican Party in two, and his election of 1916 out of the imminence of American involvement in the World War.

Partisan League, with Sidney Hillman of the garment workers and John L. Lewis of the miners at the helm. It was deliberately geared to raising funds and turning out a huge labor vote for Roosevelt's reelection in 1936. The effort succeeded beyond all expectations, and thenceforth the labor wing of the Democratic Party was to be its strongest pinion.

The second important element was the Negro voter. Traditionally, when he voted at all he voted Republican in token of his debt to Lincoln. The vote of Southern Negroes was scarcely measurable in the early thirties, but by that time New York already had the biggest black population of any city in the world, and Philadelphia, Detroit, Chicago, and Los Angeles all had been heavily invaded by migrants from the South. Here and there in the North this voting potential had been mobilized, sometimes by Republican bosses, sometimes by Democratic. But for the most part the Northern Negro felt left out of the political process, and usually *was* left out.

However, the New Deal had much to offer the black man (relief and jobs mainly). Even if it proposed no fundamental improvement in his status, it seemed to care about his condition, which was more than any other Administration had done, and Mrs. Roosevelt obviously did care—openly and sometimes with stirring results. She strove endlessly, with that exuberant energy of hers, to eliminate racial discrimination on WPA and NYA projects and to promote Negro health and education programs. She brought prominent Negroes like Mary McLeod Bethune and Walter White into her quasi-official councils. Secretary Ickes appointed the first Negro, Robert C. Weaver, to a high executive post in the government in more than a generation, and William H. Hastie, professor of law at Howard University, was named Federal District Judge for the Virgin Islands. Negro leaders and editors told their people they had "paid their debt to Lincoln" and that Roosevelt was now their savior. The Democratic National Committee set up a permanent Negro Division to absorb this new reservoir of energy. Negro precincts voted overwhelmingly Democratic in 1936, as they have consistently done ever since.

The third element in the Roosevelt Coalition was the academic and intellectual community. Traditionally the members of this group had been aloof from partisan politics except when excited by an individual issue such as monetary policy or adherence to the League of Nations. But the New Deal was a whole complex of issues—social and economic—wrapped in philosophic controversy and inviting theoretical exploration. Roosevelt himself was a man of wide-ranging intellectual interests. He was not afraid of scholars and "long-haired professors," as evidenced by the influence of the Brain Trust and his reliance on Frankfrurter in staffing many key posts in his Administration. The New Deal created a hospitable climate for intellectuals of every ideological hue and offered an inviting battleground against the Philistines of big business, the courts, and other enemies of "progress." In person or in spirit they flocked to the Roosevelt banner in great numbers. Numerically, their votes did not count for much, but as propagandists and opinion molders they were invaluable. Their allegiance has remained virtually unbroken.

There was manifest discomfort on the part of southern politicians like

Jimmy Byrnes, Pat Harrison, Carter Glass, and "Cotton Ed" Smith at finding themselves making common cause under the banner of the Democratic Party with the likes of labor leader David Dubinsky, Walter White of the NAACP, and radical thinkers such as Rex Tugwell and Harry Hopkins. But the southern politicians were held in line by the most elementary of persuaders—self-interest. The New Deal was giving their region a desperately needed transfusion of economic lifeblood, and only through the continued well-being of the Democratic Party could they preserve this flow and hold on to their vital posts of power in Congress.

For decades political party organizations had been as structured as a tower of building blocks, the lines of force running vertically from precinct to ward to courthouse and on up the scale until once every four years the structure culminated in the national committee. The dynamic of party power was supposed to be in organizaiton and manpower, and in the ability to deliver the vote, precinct by precinct, city by city, when and where needed. Only in extraordinary circumstances did issues count for much in this simplistic calculation. The liberal-conservative dialogue was carried on beyond the reach of the average voter.

The Roosevelt coalition altered the design of the Democratic Party from vertical to horizontal, and it made issues—ideology—its driving force. The liberal impulse of the New Deal to raise wages, provide jobs, tame big business, and redress the imbalance of injustices of the old laissez-faire society had the same gut attraction for the coal miner in Kentucky as for the steel worker in Pittsburgh, for the Negro sharecropper in Alabama and his cousin in Harlem, and, to a substantial but less visible extent, for the small businessman in Chicago and the tobacco grower in the Carolinas. The old mechanics of organization were still essential to get out the vote, precinct by precinct, on election day, but now there was a new and stronger impulse that brought the voters to the polls. In the Roosevelt Coalition, class interest and ideological aims displaced the old narrow parochialism of partisan identification. It transformed the Democratic Party into a truly national party, and so it has remained.

The weakest element in the Roosevelt Coalition was, of course, the South. The first rupture of its solidity occurred in 1948, when four of the eleven states in the region—Alabama, Louisiana, Mississippi, and South Carolina—turned against the Democratic candidate, Harry Truman. The defection was completed in the three-cornered contest of 1968, when only Texas, by a paper-thin margin, cast its electoral vote for Democrat Hubert Humphrey. In spite of the election of Republican Presidents in 1952, 1956 and 1968, the Roosevelt Coalition has remained viable and the Democratic Party has continued to be the majority party.[5]

IV

The most egregious blunder in Roosevelt's political career was his attempt to alter the complexion of the Supreme Court. Its design was devious, it was awkward in timing and execution, and its failure cost him dearly in public esteem and in political support. The crowning irony is that the goal he sought —a more hospitable judicial climate for the New Deal—probably would have been reached whether he raised a finger for its attainment or not. He raised not just a finger but a power-packed fist, and for five months in 1937 the sound of shattering political crockery filled the air.

Roosevelt had cause enough to be angry at the "Nine Old Men" in their impregnable marble fortress across from the Capitol. Of sixteen cases of varying degress of importance to the New Deal that they had adjudicated during the four years ending in 1936, eleven had gone against the Administration. Among the casualties had been the program for business recovery, NRA; the program for agricultural recovery, AAA; the effort to end chaos in the oil industry by regulating "hot oil" shipments in interstate commerce; a pension plan for railway workers; a program for a moratorium on farm mortgages; and a program to regulate wages and hours in the coal industry (the Guffey Act). In addition, the Court had declared unconstitutional a New York State law that was loaded with significance for the New Deal—a law setting minimum wages for women workers in industry.

To the President and his men it was clear that the High Court had set its Olympian face against every meaningful effort of the central government to correct the social and economic afflictions that had brought the nation so perilously close to collapse. It seemed to view the Constitution as a set of static prohibitions, sacred and immutable, impervious to the movement of time or circumstance. "The meaning of the Constitution," one of the Nine, Justice George Sutherland, had said, "does not change with the ebb and flow of economic events." On only two of the major defeats for the New Deal had the Court's opinion been unanimous—the NRA and the farm mortgage moratorium. The other opinions had been by a divided vote. The Court was firmly controlled by a majority of Constitutional fundamentalists, whose understanding of the law and of the social contract had crystallized in the nineteenth century. By the winter of 1935 this august little group of five, sometimes six, Justices had become the last hope of conservative interests in the United States, the last line of defense of those who wished to preserve the doctrine of laissez-faire and the preeminent sanctity of property rights.

The Court's four implacable "Tories" were James Clark McReynolds, Pierce Butler, Willis J. Van Devanter, and George Sutherland. Its three most consistent liberals were Louis D. Brandeis, Benjamin N. Cardozo, and Harlan Fiske Stone. Its two "swing men" were Owen J. Roberts, who sided more often with the conservatives than with the liberals, and the Chief Justice, Charles Evans Hughes, whose bent led him more often than not to the liberal persuasion. Two of the Justices were eighty, four were in their seventies, and three were in their sixties. Justice Van Devanter, a man of gentle disposition but of unshakable convictions, had been appointed to the Court by President Taft in 1910. Justice Brandeis, a profound scholar and the Court's only Jew, and Justice McReynolds, among whose iron-clad prejudices was an emphatic anti-Semitism, had both been appointed by President Wilson, which was the only point of similarity between them. Chief Justice Hughes, a man of awesome dignity and intellect, had served a prior term on the Court, from 1910 to 1916, before being reappointed by President Hoover in 1930. Justice Roberts, who had been named at the same time, brought with him a reputation as a mildly liberal Philadelphia lawyer. At the outset of his career on the High Court, Roberts' liberal instinct had prevailed, but he later came more and more frequently into the orbit of the conservatives. After 1934, whenever an important New Deal case was invalidated in a five-to-four opinion, it usually fell out that Roberts' vote had been the decisive one for the majority.

Roosevelt's reaction to the invalidation of the NRA in 1935 was his memorable outburst condemning the Court for its "horse and buggy" philosophy. Thereafter his frustration and his anger grew with each successive defeat. He discussed with many of his friends and advisers means of overcoming this judicial obstacle. He drew encouragement from most of them, notably from Professor Frankfurter, who told him, "No disinterested student of our Constitutional system and of the needs of our society could view with complacency the impasse created by the blind and stubborn majority of the Court." It was obvious, the Harvard scholar said, that these conservative Justices were harnessing their legal interpretations to their personal predilections and prejudices. He told the President in May 1935 that there was every justification for seeking a drastic remedy by Constitutional amendment affirming the government's power to deal with national economic problems.[6]

But Roosevelt foresaw that the amendment process, requiring ratification by two-thirds of the states, might well drag out beyond the expiration of his term in 1940. Meanwhile, Congress had before it much vital legislation necessary to the fulfillment of the New Deal, chiefly social security and a national labor relations law. He anticipated that the Court as presently constituted would also invalidate these laws. He wanted a quick and direct remedy to forestall such a defeat. The problem was to find an adequate one. But the 1936 election campaign was impending, so he turned the question of what to do about the Court over to Attorney General Cummings.

The President alluded to the Court issue only indirectly during the campaign, but it was never far from the center of his thoughts or of his strategy. His landslide victory at the polls convinced him that any plausible device he adopted would have such massive public support that the conservative opposition would be overwhelmed. To bolster his position, he decided to use the tactics of the "blitz," the sneak attack. Cummings had done his research in the greatest secrecy, taking only three or four of his aides at the Department of Justice into his confidence. Roosevelt himself had kept mum on the subject at the White House. Late in November he and Cummings went over several alternative proposals that the latter had worked up. They made the final choice between them. The President went off on a state visit to Rio de Janeiro, and Cummings got busy preparing a legislative draft and the supporting documents.

All through that December and into January of 1937 these plans went forward with the secrecy of an armed invasion of enemy territory. Not a word was leaked as to what was afoot—neither to the Congressional leaders

Above: A more tractable Supreme Court as it was constituted in 1937. (Seated, left to right) Justices George Sutherland, James Clark McReynolds, Chief Justice Charles Evans Hughes, Justices Louis D. Brandeis and Pierce Butler. (Standing, left to right) Justices Benjamin N. Cardozo, Harlan Fiske Stone, Owen J. Roberts, and Hugo L. Black, Roosevelt's first appointee.

nor within the White House circle. Even such a valued confidante as Frank-furter was kept in the dark. In a letter to his Harvard friend on January 15 Roosevelt yielded up a tantalizing clue, but no more. "Very confidentially," the President wrote at the end of a letter on another subject, "I may give you an awful shock in about two weeks. Even if you do not agree, suspend final judgment and I will tell you the story." [7]

A touch of Gothic drama was intruded into the script. On the night of February 3 all the Justices and their wives (except for Brandeis and Stone, who were indisposed), the Attorney General and his staff, and other leading dignitaries of the bench and bar were guests at the White House for the annual reception for the judiciary. There was dinner and music, the gentle-men in white ties, the ladies in their jewels and long white gloves, the host at his genial and ingratiating best, nourishing his secret with a conspirator's glee. "It was as good as the Duchess of Richmond's ball before Waterloo," an observer said later. "Better, for while the party lacked the advantages of champagne, the military figures, gaiety and bright uniforms, it topped the Duchess' celebrated rout by being given on the eve of a great battle by the commander of one side for the members of the other." [8] It was one of those ironical tableaux such as Roosevelt dearly loved.

Two mornings later, on February 5, Roosevelt dropped his blockbuster on the enemy's lines. The White House staff was called in at 6:30 o'clock to type and mimeograph a set of documents none of them had laid eyes on before—the draft of the Judicial Reform Act of 1937 and its supporting messages. The Cabinet and the legislative leaders were summoned for a meeting at ten o'clock, and a genial, smiling President laid copies fresh from the mimeograph machines before their startled eyes. Unfortunately, he said lightly, he would not be able to discuss the matter with them at any length that morning, since he had a press conference scheduled within a very few minutes, at which the same material was to be given out. With a cheery wave of the hand, he was wheeled out of the room.

Only Homer Cummings in that assemblage knew in advance what those documents said. But the others were quick to sense their import, as the rest of the nation would before nightfall. In essence the proposal gave the Presi-dent the power to put an extra man on the bench for any Federal judge who did not voluntarily retire within six months after passing his seventieth birth-day. The number of such appointments would be limited to fifty for the entire judiciary, with new appointments to the Supreme Court not to exceed six. With rather transparent slyness the substance of the proposal was submerged in explanatory verbiage emphasizing that the purpose of the legislation was to relieve an intolerable burden of overwork that the courts were suffering to the detriment of prompt and evenhanded justice. But it took only a moment for the knowing ones to figure out that the age barrier applied to six of the nine sitting Supreme Court Justices, including the four "Tories," and that the immediate (and probably calculated) effect of enactment of the measure would be to produce a "Roosevelt Court."

Thus, by a legislative stroke, the Judicial branch of the government would be made subservient to the Executive branch—upsetting the trinitarian balance so carefully constructed by the Founding Fathers.

Riding back to the Capitol with his colleagues after the White House meeting, crusty old Hatton Sumners, chairman of the House Judiciary Committee, uttered a dictum that would be heeded by many of his breathren: "Boys, here's where I cash in my chips."

Roosevelt had anticipated that there would be strong conservative objection to his plan, but he had not counted on the magnitude of the outcry nor the corrosive effect it would have on his own party. It did not surprise him to read in the *Herald-Tribune* the next day that his proposal if enacted into law, "would end the American state as it has existed throughout the long years of its life"; or to read in the Boston *Herald*, "It is not a judicial readjustment which he seeks but an enlargement of his own powers." Nor was he surprised when conservative Democrats like Virginia's Carter Glass, or Georgia's Walter George, denounced his scheme as nefarious. But he was shaken as the signs of rebellion mounted during the succeeding days and weeks among Democrats who in the past had been consistently loyal to him.

Summers' expression of disaffection was so widely held in the House that it was deemed prudent to suspend consideration of the bill there until after the Senate had acted. But the temper of the Senate was not much better. During the reading of the President's message, Vice President Garner walked out of the Senate chamber holding his nose in disgust, although he did not publicly withhold his support from the bill. It was apparent to everyone that faithful old Joe Robinson, the majority leader, was measurably distressed although he loyally agreed to lead the fight for passage. A dozen other Administration stalwarts, like Joseph O'Mahoney of Wyoming, Tom Connelly of Texas, David I. Walsh of Massachusetts, and Burton K. Wheeler of Montana, made no mystery at all of their acute displeasure—not so much over the President's goal as over the devious route he was taking to reach it. The irascible, strong-willed Wheeler, in fact, became the leader of a spirited Democratic opposition to the bill. His opposition was so effective that the Republican minority was content to sit back and let the Democrats carry the fight.

Never since he had come to the White House had Roosevelt run into such massive and heated resistance. All the varied elements that had opposed him before, plus many who had always been on his side, joined to defeat his "court packing" plan. They mounted a crusade, adorned in the glaring colors of patriotism, to "save" the Court, the Constitution, Democracy. The Liberty League stumbled back to its feet to get into the procession. The U.S. Chamber of Commerce, the National Association of Manufacturers, and the public utility lobbyists turned their propoganda organs up to full volume. The collective bosom of the Daughters of the American Revolution heaved with mighty indignation.

The mood was contagious, spreading outward and downward. Several state legislatures condemned the plan in formal resolutions. Women's clubs, Kiwanis clubs, and American Legion posts did likewise. A dozen *ad hoc* organizations sprang into being to enlist in the holy cause—things called the Citizens Supreme Court Protective Committee, the Committee to Preserve Our Liberties, Association for America, and so on. One such group packed Carnegie Hall to its standing-room-only capacity one evening in March to hear the President's plan condemned by three prominent Democratic Senators—Walsh of Massachusetts, Copeland of New York, and Burke of Nebraska. Appropriating one of Roosevelt's favorite aphorisms, Burke told the crowd that constitutional democracy was facing "a rendezvous with death." He went on: "I love the President. I think he has done wonderful things. I admire him, but not on this court proposal."

That was the attitude of many of the President's warmest admirers. They urged him to abandon his plan in favor of a more forthright attempt to amend the Constitution; or, at the least, to so modify his proposal as to remove its taint of punitive action against the Supreme Court. Robinson and other Congressional leaders warned him that the bill as written could only be forced through at the risk of a bruising, divisive fight. "I'm not only thinking of the court plan," one of the President's friends told him soberly, "I'm thinking of Franklin D. Roosevelt. I don't want history to record that at the height of his career Franklin D. Roosevelt suffered a bitter defeat at the hands of Congress." This shaft, aimed at the weakest spot in his armor, shook Roosevelt momentarily but he recovered quickly. Having committed himself to this course he would not back down. He was supremely confident that he had the mass of the people with him, and that by the exercise of familiar political pressures he could bring the Congress along too.

This pleasant illusion could not be sustained for long. Events of which Roosevelt did not know were already converging to black it out. Their conjunction would come in separate stages over a period of weeks, so that their full impact could not be measured until they were all put together. Here is how things went:

Back in January, on its first decision day of the new year, the Court unanimously upheld the government's right to levy a retroactive tax on profits gained by speculators who beat the gun on the Silver Purchase Act of 1934. The decision caused little stir; it was not one of the New Deal's blue-ribbon, do-or-die cases. But legal beavers noted that the whole Court had agreed here to reverse an earlier decision, written by the archconservative McReynolds, denying the validity of *any* retroactive tax.

Was this a quiet signal that the Court had decided to change its ways? In all probability it was; it had come a full month before Roosevelt unveiled his plans to "pack" the Court. For the Justices at this very time were also making up their minds what to do about several other cases of vital importance to the New Deal, with results—soon to be disclosed—that were highly relevant to the question.

A second stage, tangential but heavily significant, occurred in mid-March. The Senate Judiciary Committee had opened hearings on the President's bill to enlarge the courts on the tenth, with pro-Administration witnesses leading off. The atmosphere of the Caucus Room of the Senate Office

Building, where the hearings were being conducted, was as charged with tension and drama as a criminal trial. Spectators crowded the ornate old chamber beyond its capacity day after day, and dozens of reporters filed yards of color and verbatim testimony with their newspapers. A majority of the committee was known to be hostile to the bill, and their interrogations were deep-probing and tipped with acid. It was one of those political passion plays unique to the Washington stage but with the whole nation as audience.

There was a fresh surge of anticipation on Monday, March 22, when opponents of the bill were to have their innings. The lead-off man was Wheeler, the lean, saturnine prosecutor a dozen years earlier of the Teapot Dome culprits. Though a longtime New Deal supporter, he now captained the powerful Senate coalition fighting the New Deal's Court bill. By prearrangement, his principal interrogator at the long mahogany committee table led the questioning to the central argument advanced by the bill's supporters: the logjam of uncompleted cases backed up by an under-manned, over-aged Court.

"Well," said Wheeler with contrived casualness, "I have a statement from a man who knows more about the Court than the President of the United Staates, more than the Attorney General, more than I do or any of this committee."

Extracting a paper from his coat pocket, he quietly activated the fuse of his bomb. "I have a letter by the Chief Justice of the Supreme Court, Mr. Charles Evens Hughes, dated March 21, 1937, written by him and approved by Mr. Justice Brandeis and Mr. Justice Van Devanter."

The room was stunned. Not in memory had a Chief Justice stepped so firmly out of the cloister of his Court to take a public stance in a political controversy. Wheeler, who had solicited the letter with considerable misgivings only two days before, now read it into the record slowly, so that its full impact would be registered. Factually and unemotionally, the Chief Justice asserted that the Court was fully abreast of its work, that its members of whatever age were not overburdened, and that the addition of more Justices might, indeed, be an impediment rather than an aid to its performance. As for the proposal that an expanded, fifteen-man Supreme Court might be split into two sections to function independently, he noted with austere logic that such an arrangement would be clearly violative of Article III of the Constitution, which states that "the judicial Power of the United States shall be vested in one supreme Court. . . ." [9]

The Hughes letter wholly demolished the stated rationale of the President's bold plan. Momentarily it seemed to signal a stiffening resistance to the plan's real purpose—namely, a Court more amenable to facing up to the realities of the nation's social and economic imperatives. But this was not the case as the third phase of this dramatic sequence was to disclose.

On March 29, one week after the reading of the Hughes letter, a minimum wage law for the State of Washington that was almost identical with the New York law that had been struck down the year before, was upheld in a five-to-four decision that saw Justice Roberts realigned with his more liberal brethren. On the same day the Court upheld the Railway Labor Act, which for the first time allowed the federal government to leap state boundaries to enforce fair labor standards, and a revised Frazier-Lemke farm mortgage moratorium act—both by *unanimous* decision. Each of these was a "gut" issue for the New Deal, intrinsically and as symbols of its ideology. The White House was immensely pleased, naturally, but skeptical. It did not expect its luck to hold.

There were more surprises in store. On April 10 the Wagner Labor Relations Act was upheld following one of the bitterest legal contests of the decade, again 5–4 with Mr. Justice Roberts siding with the majority. And on May 24 three separate Constitutional challenges to the Social Security Act were set down 5–4, 5–4, and 7–2. Thus, in a span of sixty days the New Deal had won a clean sweep of four major cases of its own pending before the Court, plus a state case in which it had a vital interest.

There was one more relevant episode in the collapsing of the President's fine-spun argument for making over the Court. On May 18 Mr. Justice Van Devanter, eighty years old and an occupant of the High Bench for twenty-five years, announced his retirement. Thus, whether the President's stratagem to enlarge the Court were to succeed or fail, he now had the opportunity to add to it a man of his own choice and to ensure an almost automatic liberal majority.

Had the Nine Old Men seen the light of day at last? Had they read the election returns and decided to "come into the twentieth century"? We cannot be sure what prompted such an about-face in their philosophy, but henceforth they were to follow a much more liberal path. Their capitulation gave Roosevelt the substance of what he set out to achieve while denying him its form and the taste of victory. Many of his advisers urged him to call off the fight, to quit while he was ahead. His good friend, Charles Culp Burlingham, the venerable dean of the New York City bar, wrote him: "Now that the Chief Justice and Roberts have crossed the line and Van Devanter has retired, you have accomplished your real purpose of bringing about a reasonable interpretation and application of the Constitution by the Court. I wish it were in my power to persuade you now to drop so much of the bill as relates to the Supreme Court." [10] But it seemed impossible for anyone to do that. Roosevelt argued that the liberal margin on the Court was too thin for comfort. Moreover, stubborn Dutchman that he was, he had laid his prestige on the line for this piece of legislation, and he meant to have it. He got an undignified comeuppance instead.

On the same day that Justice Van Devanter announced his retirement, the Senate Judiciary Committee voted 10 to 8 in executive session to report out the Court bill unfavorably. Almost a month was devoted to drafting the majority report, with Senator O'Mahoney as the principal architect. It was filed with the Senate on June 14—one of the most devastating rebuffs ever administered a President by a Senate committee dominated by members of his own party. Beginning with a fervent paean to the sanctity of the Constitution and the independence of the three coordinate branches of government, the report enumerated the particular reasons why the bill should be rejected. Its harsh indictment read in part:

It [the bill] was presented to the Congress in a most intricate form and for reasons that obscured its real purpose.

It would not banish age from the bench nor abolish divided decisions.

It would not reduce the expense of litigation nor speed the decision of cases.

It would subjugate the courts to the will of Congress and the President and thereby destroy the independence of the Judiciary, the only certain shield of individual rights. . . .

It is a proposal without precedent or justification.

It is a measure which should be so emphatically rejected that its parallel will never again be presented to the free representatives of the free people of America.[11]

That was the effective end of the Court bill. But Roosevelt still refused to give up the fight, and a small band of loyalists stuck doggedly with him. The *coup de grâce* ultimately fell on July 22, when a motion to recommit the bill to the Judiciary Committee—the parliamentary equivalent of euthanasia —was approved in lopsided fashion by a vote of 70 to 20. The packed galleries broke into cheers and applause, and Vice President Garner in the chair, wearing a puckered smile of smug satisfaction, allowed the demonstration to wear itself out before gaveling for order. As a sop to the President's pride, the Committee came back a week later with a heavily watered-down substitute providing innocuous procedural reforms for the lower courts but wholly ignoring the Supreme Court. Garner jammed it through to passage in fifty-seven minutes. A couple of weeks later Senator Hugo Black, a liberal maverick from Alabama, was named by the President to Van Devanter's seat on the High Court. Before his second term would end, the President would name four additional Justices, making the "Roosevelt Court" an incontestable reality.

So, in a historic period of 168 days—February 5 to July 22—Roosevelt had won his war against the Supreme Court but lost the battle. Indeed, he lost a good deal more. The spin-off from those bruising conflicts was a closing of ranks among anti-New Deal Democrats in Congress and throughout the party at large. In spite of his huge electoral majority only a year before and the spell he still wove on the affection and imagination of the masses of the people, Roosevelt had lost his cloak of political invincibility. Southerners and other conservatives in his own party who had grown restless under his unorthodox fiscal and social policies now had the courage to oppose him openly. From now on the New Deal steamroller would find the going considerably rougher than it had been before.

V

Roosevelt's fight over the Supreme Court was prelude rather than climax. It was the prelude to a decision he had long been formulating in his mind to remake the Democratic Party in the liberal image of the New Deal. Let the Republican Party be the home of the conservatives, most of whom were already lodged there anyway. Conservatism was its tradition. He wanted the Democratic Party to be a homogeneous, dependably consistent instrument for progressive political action that would carry his ideals forward into the future. He had a personal, a visceral, motive for wanting to fulfill this ambition. It was conservatives within his own party who had defeated his Court proposal and now threatened to humble him on other issues, and he meant to avenge himself on them. A case in point was the defeat late in 1937 of a wage-and-hour bill for which he had fought for five months. Passed by the Senate, it was killed in the House 216 to 198, through a coalition of conservative Democrats and Republicans. Roosevelt was "furious" according to one intimate over this "betrayal" by members of his own party on a key issue.

But time was growing short. He would be out of office after 1940 (he almost certainly did not at this time contemplate a third term), and there was no successor in sight on whom he could depend to accomplish his design. Obviously, if he were to do the job himself he must make a beginning in the Congressional elections of 1938. How? By deliberately throwing his immense prestige into the scales on behalf of candidates who met his liberal standards. "The people" were with him; of this he was wholly confident. So how could he lose?

Thus was the climax fashioned—the "purge." Rarely had his political instinct played him more false.

Jim Farley and other party regulars were appalled as Roosevelt's plan slowly unfolded. Twenty-three Democrats were among the thirty senators up for reelection in 1938, along with the entire membership of the House, and the President proposed to intervene, directly or indirectly, in the primary contests of a number of those who had most consistently opposed him. To the devoutly orthodox Farley this was not only political evil but bad strategy: The national party leadership simply did not take sides in state contests to choose a candidate. Its function was to elect Democrats over Republicans, not to tell a state which Democrat should have the honor of combat. Cleveland and Wilson had tried it, with bad results: Resentment over the intrusion of "outsiders" into a traditionally local affair had outweighed any gain from the bestowal of presidential favor. Farley sadly shook his head and tried cautiously to dissuade the President from such a course, but to no avail. (His star was already on the decline at the White House, and Farley sensed it.) He found commiseration among other party stalwarts to whom "regularity" was a prime political virtue.

"The Boss has stirred up a hornet's nest by getting into these primary fights," Jack Garner told Farley one day at the Capitol. "There are twenty men—Democrats—in the Senate who will vote against anything he wants because they are mad clean through. Jim, I think you ought to take exception to the President's attitude. I think you should do it for the benefit of the country."

"John, I just can't do that unless I resign from the Cabinet and the Democratic Committee," the troubled Chairman replied. "I don't like this purge any better than you do, but the situation won't be helped by my breaking with the Boss." [12]

Against such veiled opposition from the regulars, Roosevelt was getting open encouragement from a new breed of political tacticians—younger men, for the most part, who had never bruised their knuckles in political combat but were pretty sure they knew how the battle should be waged. Embittered old Hugh Johnson hung the label "White House Janizaries" upon them and warned the readers of his newspaper column of their sinister intent. They included Harry Hopkins, the WPA boss and now Roosevelt's most intimate counselor; Tom Corcoran and Ben Cohen, the brains-and-muscle twins of the White House inner circle; David K. Niles and the President's son Jimmy Roosevelt, both attached to the White House staff; Secretary Ickes of Interior, a seasoned guerrilla fighter in the political jungles of Midwestern Progressivism; and Joseph Keenan and Robert Jackson, who were high up in the Department of Justice. To them, politics was national and ideological, and the old rubrics of organization and local loyalties were incidental. Early in the year they had lent a hand to secure the nominations of two liberal southerners to the Senate, Claude Pepper of Florida and Lister Hill of Alabama, and this experience emboldened them—and so Roosevelt—to believe that the strategy could be repeated with comparable results elsewhere.

Roosevelt openly disclosed the role he would play in the election in a fireside chat on the evening of June 24. After reviewing the record of Congress, which had just adjourned, he turned to the politics of recovery: the necesssity of regaining the momentum of New Deal reforms. This would be difficult if not impossible, he said, as long as nonbelievers among the Democrats were able to team up with Republicans to defeat his purpose. It was important to have not only a Democratic majority in Congress but a liberal majority. As *President,* he went on, it would be inappropriate for him to try to influence the choice of Democrats to sit in Congress, but—and here he deftly switched hats without so much as a flicker of expression or intonation—"as the head of the Democratic Party, charged with the responsibility of carrying out the liberal declaration of principles set forth in the 1936 platform, I feel that I have every right to speak in those few instances where there may be a clear issue betwen candidates involving those principles or involving a clear misuse of my name."

The "purge" was on. It would be applied in different ways according to individual circumstances, sometimes covertly, sometimes by unambiguous indirection, sometimes by blunt and forthright declarations of preference. The President would not execute all these maneuvers in person, but his imprimatur would be plainly evident in each. Jim Farley had been dragooned into employing the National Committee in the cause; Hopkins and Ickes had the resources of the relief and works programs at their disposal (these would not be used with quite the criminal abandon later alleged by the "purgees," but more than could in decency be condoned); and other agents of the President dispensed blessings or maledictions freely in his name as each case seemed to warrant. It might be a visit and a campaign speech by the President in person; a letter or a statement over his name; the lure of a judgeship or other benefaction strategically poised; or a timely manipulation of the federal pipeline of jobs and work projects.

There were ten members of Congress, all Democrats and many with impressive status and seniority, whom the Presidsent proposed to unseat and replace with other Democrats more to his liking. They were Senators Clark of Missouri, McCarran of Nevada, Smith of South Carolina, Adams of Colorado, Tydings of Maryland, Gillette of Iowa, Van Nuys of Indiana, George of Georgia, and Lonergan of Connecticut; and Representative John J. O'Connor of New York City, who, as chairman of the House Rules Committee commanded the most effective legislative bottleneck in Congress. These ten were the main targets of the purge. In addition, there were a round dozen of senators, congressmen, and governors whom the President aimed to protect by directing the purge at their opponents. In most instances, however, the fate of these men was of secondary importance to that of the leading ten. For in the case of men like George, Tydings, "Cotton Ed" Smith, and Rules Chairman O'Connor, who had stubbornly set themselves across the President's path, there was reserved a special measure of Rooseveltian vindictiveness.

In mid-July Roosevelt embarked on a zigzag journey across the country that took him to many of the selected scenes of conflict. At a great outdoor rally in Marietta, Ohio, he affirmed that if he were a citizen of that state his preference for the next Governor would be "my good friend" Senator Bulkley. Looking on uncomfortably from the rostrum was Democratic Governor George White, a candidate to succeed himself. In Kentucky, Roosevelt heaped praise on Senator Alben Barkley, who was being hard pressed for renomination by the locally popular Governor, A. B. Chandler. The irrepressible "Happy" Chandler almost stole the show from Barkley by his antics on the platform before and after the President's speech, throwing his arms in the air and eliciting shouts of "Hi, Happy!" from the shirt-sleeved multitude. The Presidential cavalcade went on, through Oklahoma, down into Texas, and up through Colorado and Nevada, where the two Democratic incumbents, Senators Adams and McCarran, were given a chilling exposure to the silent treatment. Roosevelt maneuvered to have neither appear with him on the back platform of his train, the indispensable accolade during a Presidential visit. Thence to California, where he publicly embraced the aging Senator William Gibbs McAdoo and relegated his challenger, Sheridan Downey, to outer darkness.

But these encounters were merely the warm-up for the purge. The full treatment was uncorked in August. On his way north from a Caribbean fishing trip, the President stopped over in Georgia. He had once told a friend that if he couldn't get a proper candidate to stand for the Senate there he would run the tenant on his farm near Warm Springs. His agents meanwhile had done a little better: They had induced Lawrence S. Camp, the colorless and relatively unknown U.S. District Attorney for Atlanta, to file at the last minute against that towering eminence of Southern Democratic orthodoxy, Walter

Franklin George, who had served in the Senate since 1922. Governor Gene Talmadge, the tobacco-chewing idol of the semiliterate "crackers," was already in the field and easily outpointing the dignified George in baiting the "communist-led, nigger lovin' " New Deal.

Camp was pushed into the race with virtually no preparation or organization support. There was some hope—a very faint hope—that the two top men might fight each other to a standoff and that Camp would be able to steal home free. But the Roosevelt team failed to calculate the homegrown, inbred quality of southern politics or the nature of its power structure. In Georgia, as in most southern states, control of the Democratic Party was tightly held by a small oligarchy of industrialists, big landowners, and professional politicians whose reach extended through the disciplined ranks of the statehouse bureaucracy down to the county courthouse level. The state party had only the most tenuous ties with the national party; it was an indigenous combine, highly exclusive in its upper echelon, and its primacy was rarely challenged. George and Talmadge had long been kingpins in this structure, but Camp was virtually a stranger to it. The clan could tolerate and even enjoy a scrap between two of its chieftains, but the intrusion of an outsider, particularly one wearing the alien colors of the New Deal, threatened disruption of the clan itself. A Georgia primary was not something to be settled by "the people" rising up in their sovereign might, but something to be marshaled by the cohorts of the Democratic organization. Either the Roosevelt men failed to comprehend this or they overestimated Talmadge's weight against George when they put Camp forward as their champion.

Undismayed, full of confidence and zest, Roosevelt showed up on August 10 at a big oudoor rally in the sweltering little town of Barnesville. On the platform he was flanked by Harry Hopkins. George sat stony-faced behind them, and Camp sat nervously two seats away. The President bluntly asked the voters of Georgia to retire their veteran of sixteen years in the Senate in favor of the younger man whom scarcely any of them had ever seen before. Measuring his words carefully for emphasis, Roosevelt said:

Let me make it perfectly clear that he [Senator George] is, and I hope always will be, my friend. He is beyond any possible question a gentleman and a scholar . . . but with whom I differ heartily and sincerely on the principles and policies of how the government of the United States ought to be run. I am impelled to make it clear that on most public questions he and I do not speak the same language. . . .

Therefore, in answering the requests of many citizens of Georgia that I make my position clear, I have no hesitation in saying that if I were able to vote in the September primary in this state, I most assuredly would cast my ballot for Lawrence Camp.

The sweaty crowd of farmers and townfolk, mixing cries of "Pour it on Mr. President!" with "Hooray for George!," seemed pleased at being at ringside for such a slam-bang battle, Felix Belair, Jr., reported in *The New York Times* the next morning. But the scene on the speaker's stand as the President concluded was one of taut drama. In Belair's words:

It was an occasion that neither the President nor Mr. George are likely soon to forget. Observers who have traveled with the President for years said they could not recall when he had attacked like he did today. By the tone of his voice rather than by the written text of his speech, Mr. Roosevelt exhibited his intense desire to see Senator George retired from the Senate.

As soon as the President completed his remarks, the Senator approached him solemnly, shook his hand and exclaimed: "Mr. President, I regret that you have taken this occasion to question my democracy and to attack my public record. I want you to know that I accept the challenge."

The inevitable result of the President's gesture was to make a martyr of Walter George—a loyal son of the Old South, doing the best he knew for the folks of Georgia and being set upon by communist-tinged New Dealers way off yonder in Washington. George made the most of it in his campaign. When the balloting came in September, he won handily over "Old Gene" Talmadge and left the hapless Camp far behind in third place.

A few days after the Barnesville episode the President gave a repeat performance in South Carolina, with Senator Ellison B. ("Cotton Ed") Smith, an almost unbelievable throwback to the days of the Confederacy, as his target. Later on he stumped in Maryland to bring down the proud and aristocratic Millard F. Tydings. And he put the voters of the Sixteenth Congressional District of New York on notice that he did not want John O'Connor back in the House of Representatives.

On the whole it was an unprecedented performance, an extravagant exercise in Presidential politics, and a disastrous failure. Of the ten principal victims selected for purging, only O'Connor succumbed. George, Smith, Tydings, and all the rest came through with colors flying and their knives resharpened for further mayhem on the New Deal. Of the dozen or so on the periphery whom Roosevelt had sought to help, only Barkley in Kentucky and Thomas in Oklahoma came through as winners. It was a crushing reminder to Roosevelt that personal popularity is a perishable asset on a politician's balance sheet. It was also a reminder that the goals and aspirations that glow with such splendor in Washington are seen uncertainly, as through a haze, in faraway Georgia or Iowa.

The ineptness of the President's performance was emphasized by the outcome of the general elections in November. The Republican Party sprang back to life in 1938 with a surge that astonished the experts and confounded the prophets. Their candidates gained eight seats in the Senate and eighty in the House, and took eleven new governorships. In Congress the party was still in the minority, but with new allies among the growing ranks of anti-New Deal Democrats it was now in a position of dominance.

This was the end of the road for the New Deal. Legislatively it was finished, and even as a popular symbol it had become shopworn and jaded.

CHAPTER 17
A New Deal
for Labor

ORGANIZED LABOR CAME OF AGE in the United States in the mid-thirties. After half a century of frustration, and degradation, it burst the bonds of repression and asserted its right to a share in the national council. Its breakout, marked by rioting and bloodshed, was the closest approximation of class warfare the nation had experienced.

"For the past four and one-half years," the editors of *Fortune* wrote late in 1937, "the United States has been in the throes of a major labor upheaval which can fairly be described as one of the greatest mass movements in our history." And indeed it was. News of strikes, lockouts, and battles on the picket lines, of threats and counterthreats by union bosses and company bosses, dominated the headlines month after month. Debates on the most volatile issue of the day—the rights of labor versus the rights of management—struck sparks in every quarter of society. A new vocabulary was born. Everybody knew what was meant by terms like the stretch-out, the checkoff, horizontal unions, vertical unions. And everybody had opinions about the relative virtues of the open shop, the closed shop, and the union shop. A lot of people who had never linked their destiny to that of the working classes suddenly found it economically feasible and socially acceptable to get into unions themselves: newspaper reporters, schoolteachers, office workers, architects, among others. The picket line became virtually sacrosanct, and the First Lady of the Land set the fashion for regarding it as a moral barricade. In the upsurging cult of liberalism one's credentials were easily established. If you were *for* labor you were a liberal; if *against* labor (or a yes-but equivocator), a conservative.

Out of the turmoil of the years between 1934 and 1939 organized labor reached a pinnacle of numerical strength and of economic and political influence such as had not been dreamed of a decade before.

I

Like American agriculture, American labor was in a badly demoralized state when the Depression struck. That blow reduced it to a shambles. Labor's "house" consisted principally of the affiliates of the American Federation of Labor, the Railway Brotherhoods, and half a dozen other major independents. The concept of craft unionism—organization according to skills and trades—was almost universal among them. But the protective reach of the unions was spotty—limited largely to the fields of mining, transportation, building construction, metals fabrication, printing, textiles, and the garment trades. There were vast reaches of the industrial landscape where no union man had ever set foot.

The prosperity of the twenties not only had passed the labor movement by but, perversely, had bled it of some of the vigor it had acquired during the World War. Industry's wartime experience with unions had alerted American businessmen, many for the first time, to labor's potential power, and in the postwar years they bent sedulously to the task of de-fanging the serpent before it could strike. They were fortuitously aided in this by the "Red scare" of the early twenties, which made it easy to suggest to the gullible that labor unions were the tool of the Bolsheviks. The closed shop, which had long been tolerated, was gradually eliminated from many contracts. Injunctions were freely issued by the courts to combat strikes. Union "agitators" were fired from their jobs and blacklisted, and company unions in deceptive guises were foisted on unorganized workers when they showed signs of unrest.

As wages and employment rates rose modestly in the wake of the "Coolidge prosperity," workers had few incentives to join together for mutual protection. Even in the traditional strongholds, such as the mine fields of Appalachia and the mill towns of New England, the prestige of the labor movement waned and its strength eroded. Between 1920 and 1929 the membership of the A.F.L. skidded downward from 4.1 million to 2.7 million. By 1933 it had lost at least half a million more, and the labor movement as a whole was closer to extinction in this country than it had been in half a century.[1]

II

The National Industrial Recovery Act did for labor what it was supposed, but failed, to do for business—put it on its feet and gave it an infusion of hope and vitality. This achievement was more an inadvertence than a calculated aim. Section 7(a) of the NIRA, which was designed to assure collective bargaining rights for labor under the industrial codes, was written into the law almost as an afterthought and over the objection of Hugh Johnson, the principal architect of NIRA. Johnson regarded inclusion of a bargaining provision as merely a trouble-making caprice. He was certain that the magical benevolence of the Blue Eagle would shine upon the workingman simply in the natural order of things. Frances Perkins, the gentle but doughty Secretary of Labor, was less certain. If businessmen were to be encouraged into collusive action through suspension of the antitrust laws, she argued, workingmen should be granted a compensating opportunity to band together to protect their share of the partnership. What's sauce for the goose is sauce for the gander, she told the President.

Her concern over this was reinforced by a parallel development from another quarter. As the NRA package was being readied for Congressional consideration, Congress was about to pass a mandatory thirty-hour-week bill which had been pushed independently of the Administration by Senator Hugo Black. In the Secretary's view the Black bill promised to do more harm than good. While it might increase the number of jobs, it made no provision for minimum wages to compensate for the reduced working time. The net result, as she saw it, would be a cut in the already dismally low level of the workers' take-home pay, which would, in effect, accentuate the depression spiral. She argued this viewpoint with the President and won his agreement to withhold his support from the Black bill while incorporating a substitute for it in the National Recovery Act.[2]

Thus provisions covering minimum wages and maximum hours for labor were built into the NRA formula. They became basic to each of the industrial codes. To give workers some leverage in enforcing these standards, they were guaranteed under Section 7(a) " . . . the right to organize and bargain collectively through representatives of their own choosing, and they shall be free from interference, restraint or coercion of employers in the designation of such representatives . . . or in other concerted activities for the purpose of collective bargaining or other mutual aid or protection."

Never in the history of capitalist America had the cause of unionism won such a resounding sanction. Liberals hailed it as "labor's Magna Carta" (later they transferred this accolade to the Wagner Act).

The long-dormant labor movement came suddenly to life. From national headquarters of the big unions and on down through the musty, cobwebby warrens of state and city centrals and the hundreds of grimy local union halls, many of which had been boarded up and in disuse for years—an intense activity burst forth. Recruiters and organizers fanned out in every direction, posted themselves at mine tipples and factory gates, called shop meetings and public rallies, and passed out bales of leaflets and membership blanks. Coal miners coming off their shifts in West Virginia and Kentucky had fliers thrust into their hands proclaiming, "The President says you must join the union." Dropouts, holdouts, and those with no present job responded eagerly. Defunct locals came back to life. Shop stewards and walking bosses asserted their authority, and union buttons were openly worn on the job without fear of reprisal.

The results were spectacular. The United Mine Workers claimed to have gained 135,000 new members within three weeks after the signing of the NRA bill. Within a year the International Ladies Garment Workers Union trebled its membership to approximately 200,000. A score of other unions swelled impressively. Between 1933 and 1935 total union membership rose from 2.6 to 3.6 million, and by 1939 it had reached 8.7 million, almost a fourfold increase in six years. The 1939 figure represented 28.6 percent of the entire nonfarm labor force, a level of strength that has not been greatly exceeded since. (It was 35.5 in 1945 and 28.0 in 1966.) Thus, in terms of numerical growth alone, labor made a long leap forward.[3]

This great upsurge created not only an internal turbulence among dissident elements in the unions but also a counterwave of resistance from management. What little most businessmen knew about labor unions in 1933 added up to fear and distrust. For more than twenty years they had devoted a large part of their personal and corporate effort to preventing unions from getting a foothold in their plants. Or, if a union had already made an entry they used every wile to minimize its effectiveness. Now that the New Deal had virtually forced open the door of their nonunion and open shop citadels, they pooled their talents and energies to find ways of neutralizing the hated strictures of Section 7(a). A few followed the lead of Henry Ford, who flatly proclaimed he would not do business with any union that had links outside his own plants, NRA or no NRA. Others dismantled their plants and moved them to the South and to other regions free of union contamination. A greater number sought to head off invasion by the big national unions by quickly devising company unions embellished with group insurance, pensions, and recreational programs but devoid of meaningful collective bargaining rights.

In all substantive ways these company unions were the captives of management. Starting practically from scratch in 1933 (a few had been carried over from the twenties), they proliferated almost as rapidly as the independents and by 1935 had an estimated membership of 2.5 million. They could be made to look legitimate within the meaning of Section 7(a) as long as management could stave off a secret election by employees under the supervision of the National Labor Board, which had been set up for that purpose. And even where the company lost in such a showdown (which they did more often than not), litigation through the courts offered a long and rewarding respite before capitulation became inevitable.

Thus the battle lines were drawn for an historic era of industrial strife. Initially the unions fought chiefly for the right to organize and for recognition as promised them under the NRA. As their flying squadrons of recruiters and organizers collided with sheriff's deputies and vigilantes in the cotton-mill towns of Alabama and Georgia, with armed guards and militiamen at the auto assembly plants of Flint and Toledo, with the stony intractability of a Tom M. Girdler at the gates of the Republic Steel Company, the map of the nation came to resemble a mine field erupting with spasmodic violence.

III

Meanwhile a bitter struggle over strategy and leadership was brewing within labor's own ranks. The A.F.L., presided over by William Green, an earnest and unimaginative former coal miner, was an empire of semi-autonomous principalities coexisting in jealous and often competitive proximty to one another. The empire embraced the constituent national and international unions of carpenters, pipefitters, boilermakers, mine workers, printers, etc., who, collectively, populated about three-fourths of "the house of labor." With the principal exception of the garment trades and the United Mine Workers, each union was stratified according to vertical categories of crafts and skills in its specific industry. Such an emphasis on crafts may have been logical in the developing years of the industrial revolution, but it did not serve the technological revolution that began to transform the face of industry in the nineteen-twenties. Mass production, which Henry Ford had introduced into the making of automobiles, and automated processes of a hundred different kinds were obliterating the need for old skills and long apprenticeships. Mass production required masses of semiskilled workers capable of dealing with great corporate entities spread over many states.

A cry went up for industrial unionism, led principally by John L. Lewis of the Miners. The entrenched chieftains of the craft unions met the proposition coldly. As a compromise, the A.F.L., at its 1934 convention, authorized the establishment of so-called federal unions to sweep in some of the unorganized thousands in such new mass production industries as autos, rubbber, and aluminum. But the compromise turned out to be no more than a stopgap. The new members would in due course be parcelled out among the existing crafts. The stratagem satisfied neither the new unionists, who defected in large numbers from the impotent federal unions almost as rapidly as they were formed, nor the hotheaded revolutionaries who had rallied around Lewis.

As a Hero of Labor, John Llewellyn Lewis stood nine feet tall and could

Barbara Hutton has the dough, parlez vous.
Where she gets it, sure we know, parlez vous.
We slave at Woolworth's five and dime,
The pay we get is sure a crime,
Hinkey Dinkey parlez vous.

Above: (clockwise) "Strike Ends!" The first General Motors sitdown strike at Flint City, Michigan, early 1937; violent death during the Toledo Electric Auto-Lite strike of 1934, one of the 1,856 strikes of that year; February 27, 1937: 110 girls in Detroit's main Woolworth store went on strike for 6 days for higher wages. Result—a 5¢ per hr. wage increase; John L. Lewis addressing Textile workers at Lawrence, Massachusetts, May 24, 1937; (above) "Chicago Memorial Day Massacre," May 30, 1937, of CIO pickets at the Republic Steel Plant. At right: (above) Governor Murphy's executive mansion in Detroit during the General Motors Strike, early 1937; (below) a lull in the Coal Strike, 1933; (at left) a striker shot in the head during the San Francisco waterfront tie-up.

**Above: May Day demonstrations, 1936.
(Top) Dupont, Al Smith, Hearst, and Mellon
attacked as war "profiteers." (At right)
The Suitcase, Bag, and Portfolio Makers'
Union on the march. At right: (top) The
Furriers' Joint Council and "Free Tom
Mooney." (Below) The Communist Party's
farmer–labor float.**

May Day Celebration. Union Square, New York City, 1936

see around corners. He was born in Iowa in 1880, the son of a blacklisted coal miner who had emigrated from Wales. At the age of twelve he went to work in the pits, and from this lowly beginning fought his way into the labor hierarchy. He was a broad-shouldered, beefy man, who moved with the deliberate, purposeful gait of a bull elephant. His massive head was surmounted by a shock of iron-gray hair that fell to the collar line. He wore a perpetual scowl, with an added menace from piercing dark eyes overhung with luxuriant black eyebrows. His voice was a Delphic rumble, and he spoke in the measured cadence of the pulpit, mixing in his rhetoric orotund metaphors of the Scriptures with the blistering scorn of the cynic. His zeal and toughness in behalf of the struggling union movement in the southern Illinois coal fields won him the patronage of Samuel Gompers. His schoolteacher wife nourished his insatiable appetite for learning. In 1920 he became president of the United Mine Workers of America. Intelligent, shrewd, and determined, though suspicious and ruthless toward whoever opposed him, he won the fanatical loyalty of the rank and file in his union. He also acquired the fear, and even the respect, of many of the great coal barons. By 1933, having built the U.M.W. into a position of power within the Federation, he was the most widely known labor leader in the country.

Angered by the rebuffs and duplicity of the conservative craft overlords of the A.F.L., Lewis and his band of revolutionaries made another attempt, at the 1935 convention in Atlantic City, to gain charters for a group of genuinely industrial-type unions. Denied again, they proceeded to defy the parent body. With the U.M.W. as a nucleus, eight unions—representing such fields as the garment trades, automobiles, steel, rubber, oil refining—banded together in November 1935 as the Committee for Industrial Organization. Pooling their resources, they set up an organizing fund of $500,000 and sent hundreds of organizers into the field. Stubbornly, the A.F.L. executive board denounced the Committee for the high crime of "dualism," and demanded that it abandon its program or face suspension. Lewis and his men refused, and in August 1936 the C.I.O. was read out of the Federation.

Meanwhile, the rebel forces had made spectacular progress in recruiting thousands of new members, negotiating contracts, and undercutting the old craft unions in some of their strongholds. The first major target was steel, where the Amalgamated Association of Steel and Iron Workers (A.F.L.) had sunk into virtual senescence while a host of company unions had occupied the field. For over a generation the steelmakers had held out adamantly against every attempt of the national unions to organize their plants, and their open shop policy had stiffened a like resistance in many kindred industries. Lewis put one of his ablest lieutenants, Philip Murray, at the head of the C.I.O. Steel Workers Organizing Committee and raised a separate $500,000 war chest for the assault on steel. On March 8, 1937, the enemy's ramparts fell: President Myron C. Taylor of United States Steel signed a history-making contract with the S.W.O.C. granting it full recognition in all the U.S. Steel plants and providing for the workers a wage increase, an eight-hour day, a forty-hour week, paid vacations, and seniority rights.

This victory gave the fledgling C.I.O. an enormous impetus. ("Little steel"—four companies not affiliated with U.S. Steel—made a different story. Under Tom Girdler's (Republic Steel) leadership they fought the S.W.O.C. on the picket lines and in the courts for two years before capitulating.) The C.I.O. intensified organizing efforts in half a dozen industries, and one big employer after another began to read the writing on the wall. General Motors, when sitdown strikes hopelessly paralyzed its plants in Michigan and Ohio, came to terms with a C.I.O. affiliate, the United Auto Workers. When the C.I.O. held its first national convention in Atlantic City in October 1937 (the A.F.L., bloody but unbowed, was meeting simultaneously in Denver), it claimed over three million members in thirty-two national unions and the execution of 30,000 signed contracts.[4]

IV

Nineteen thirty-seven was the most critical and tumultuous year in the history of labor relations in this country. It was the year in which American industry mounted its last great, concerted assault against union encroachment. That year, too, union labor felt the first full surge of its offensive strength. The destruction of NRA, along with Section 7(a) by the Supreme Court in 1935 gave management the hope that it could undo the iniquities of compulsory union recognition that had been forced on it. But labor had developed too much momentum to be turned aside. The legal vacuum left by the demise of the NRA had been filled in 1935 by new legislation, the National Labor Relations Act (the so-called Wagner Act), which recreated the provisions of Section 7(a) in statutory form. The new law came under immediate attack in the courts as being just as vulnerable to the charge of unconstitutionality as the law it replaced, and employers were widely urged by their lawyers and trade associations to ignore it.

"I won't have a contract, verbal or written, with an irresponsible, racketeering, violent, communistic body like the C.I.O.," hard-nosed old Tom Girdler fumed. "And until they pass a law making me do it, I won't do it."[5] Labor was just as determined to use every weapon it possessed or could lay its hands on to widen the beachhead it had carved out on the enemy's shore. It locked Girdler's Republic Steel and the other "little steel" mills in a bruising, costly, and protracted strike.

In this climate of open hostility and last-ditch defiance, the labor wars of the thirties mounted to a climax. Communists and their sympathizers, who had streamed into the new unions, added to the turmoil. So did labor spies, whom industry hired by the thousands to infiltrate and sabotage the organizational effort. Strikes for recognition multiplied in frequency and violence—some 10,000 of them between mid-1933 and the end of 1937, involving over five million workers. There were more strikes in 1937 than in any previous year—a total of 4,740, costing a record 28.4 million man-days of work. The great General Motors strike, which came in January, spread to six states and pulled 45,000 men off the production lines. The Chrysler strike in March idled 63,000. The "little steel" strike, beginning in May, shut down dozens of plants in seven states and affected 90,000 workers. Tens of thousands of workers in the rubber plants of Akron, the coal mines of Pennsylvania and Illinois, the cotton and rayon mills of South Carolina and Georgia, and the docks of the East Coast and the Gulf ports abandoned their jobs and went on the picket lines. Retail clerks in New York and Philadelphia joined the pickets.[6]

Violence erupted on both sides. Strikers broke windows, smashed machinery, dynamited mine tipples, beat up (or were beaten up by) scabs and strikebreakers. Police, the National Guard, and armed mercenaries hired from the Pinkertons and other professional "security" organizations clashed in bloody hand-to-hand combat with battalions of angry strikers. Dozens of combatants were killed—ten in the bloody "Memorial Day massacre" at South Chicago alone—and hundreds were hospitalized with bullet wounds, cracked heads, and broken bones.

No state and no city, it seemed, was wholly free of violence, or at least the threat thereof, but its epicenter appeared to be Detroit and the surrounding domain of the auto-makers. Here the labor militants perfected their newest and most invulnerable weapon, the sit-down strike. The workers simply shut down their machines and refused to leave the plant. This nonviolent tactic baffled mangement, which could clear the plants forcibly only at the price of itself committing violence. General Motors, facing this dilemma for the first time in January, appealed to Michigan Governor Frank Murphy to send the National Guard to liberate its factories in Flint from occupation by a boisterous, song-singing army of the U.A.W. Murphy refused the troops but intervened as a mediator. Six weeks later General Motors threw in the towel and signed with the U.A.W., granting most of the union's demands. Chrysler followed suit a few weeks later. (Ford held out successfully until 1941.) Of the more than 4,000 strikes called in 1937 the Department of Labor estimated that 82 percent were settled on terms favorable to the unions.

Two other events of 1937 were landmarks in labor's progress toward maturity and power. The Supreme Court upheld the National Labor Relations Act as constitutional in all its parts, and in the summer of that year Congress passed the Fair Labor Standards Act, which gave statutory sanction to the establishment of minimum wages and maximum work-week hours in interstate commerce. The Social Security Act, which had been passed by Congress in 1935 with provisions for workers' pensions and unemployment insurance, was another benefit obtained largely through labor's pressure on the government. American labor had at last pulled abreast of its counterpart in other advanced countries of the world in terms of fundamental guarantees and prerogatives. Indeed, it had something of a bonus in the Wagner Act, for it won certain privileges of collusive action in the prosecution of its demands—privileges that were denied to employers under the antitrust laws. The New Deal had balanced the scales for labor; it in fact, had slightly overbalanced them.[7]

V

Peace was not the happy consummation of these events. Strikes and lock-

William Green, President of the American Federation of Labor; Walter Reuther (left), President of the West Side Local, United Automobile Workers, and Richard Frankensteen, Director of Organization for the UAW, after a scuffle with Ford Motor Company employees, May 27, 1937; A Walter Reuther formed UAW-CIO leaflet distributed during the Ford Strike; Diego Rivera's *Portrait of America* mural (detail), at the New Workers School, New York City, 1933.

Ford Workers

UNIONISM NOT FORDISM

Now is the time to Organize!
The Wagner Bill is behind you!
Now get behind yourselves!

General Motors Workers, Chrysler Workers, Briggs Workers have won higher wages and better working conditions. 300,000 automobile workers are marching forward under the banner of the United Automobile Workers Union.

JOIN NOW IN THE MARCH AND WIN:

Higher Wages and Better Working Conditions
Stop Speed-up by Union Supervision
6 Hour Day, 8 Dollars Minimum Pay
Job Security thru Seniority Rights
End the Ford Service System
Union Recognition

Organize and be Recognized - JOIN NOW!

Union Headquarters for Ford Workers: Michigan Avenue at Addison
Vernor Highway West, and Lawndale

Sign up at Union Headquarters for Ford Workers or at any office of the United Automobile Workers

1324 Clay at Russell	8944 Jos. Campau at Playfair
2141 Milwaukee at Chene	11440 Charlevoix at Gladwin
11725 Oakland at Tuxedo	1343 East Ferry at Russell
4044 Leuschner at Dwyer	3814—35th Street at Michigan
11640 East Jefferson	2730 Maybury Grand at Michigan
10904 Mack at Lemay	4715 Hastings Street
77 Victor at John R.	Room 509 Hofmann Bldg.

Distributed by
United Automobile Workers of America

License No. 4   Printed by Goodwill Printing Co.

outs and battles on the picket lines and angry contentions in the United States Congress and the courts were to continue until the Second World War, with its domestic restrictions, would impose a peace of sorts. Within the divided "house of labor" itself, strife and acrimony persisted between the A.F.L. and the fractious changeling it had spawned, the C.I.O. In 1938 the last tenuous ties between them were severed. (The Committee for Industrial Organization changed its name to the Congress of Industrial Organizations.) The two sides mauled each other in relentless membership raids and jurisdictional warfare. But through all the tumult that marked the closing years of the decade one verity stood out: Labor had won its long, tortuous climb out of the industrial cellar. From now on it would sit proudly, sometimes arrogantly, near the head of the table. It had become a major force to be reckoned with in the economic, social, and political life of the nation.

CHAPTER 18
Up from Isolationism

"FELLOW DIPLOMATS- "
FEBRUARY 27, 1938

LIKE THE SEISMIC TREMORS that preceded an earthquake, world diplomacy during the mid-nineteen-thirties was contorted by the recurrent stresses of nationalist and imperialistic ambitions. Hitler and his Nazi Brownshirts began early in 1933 to turn Germany's clock back toward barbarism. Japan, blinded with the vision of hegemony over all Asia, expanded its conquest of Manchuria into China proper in 1934. In 1935 Italy sent its bombers to rain death over Ethiopia and to seize an African empire. In 1936 a brutal civil war erupted in Spain; it drove a political wedge between the forces of peace and aggression throughout Europe. The League of Nations, man's last frail hope for a disciplined order in international relations, gravitated toward impotence. The Berlin-Rome-Tokyo Axis divided the world into two hostile camps: the belligerent dictatorships on the one hand, and the confused democracies on the other, with the Russian Bear sitting enigmatically on the sidelines. In September 1938 the Munich Pact yielded the hollow promise of "peace in our time."

I

In the United States we strove to persuade ourselves that peace would prevail, or that it could be had for ourselves at least, regardless of what happened in the rest of the world. The nation pursued a course of self-delusion in embracing the doctrine of isolationism. From the halls of Congress, the pulpit, the editorial columns of the press, the lecturers, and the hordes of flag-waving demonstrators in the streets and on the campuses—from the radical Left as from the conservative Right—came demands for the country to stand aloof from all entanglements abroad. The pervasive slogan "No Foreign Wars" rested on the conviction that even if the rest of the world went up in flames our mighty fortress would stand inviolate behind its ocean barriers.

But President Roosevelt, many other statesmen, and a few of the leading newspapers spoke of the danger of remaining aloof. They foresaw the approaching cataclysm and knew that the United States could not escape being involved. They knew that salvation lay not in abandoning the world to destruction but in throwing the enormous weight of this country into the effort to avert it.

Their dissents were a feeble obbligato to the swelling chorus of isolationism. Some voices in that chorus commanded respect: members of the old Progressive bloc in Congress, such as LaFollette of Wisconsin, Norris of Nebraska, Borah of Idaho, Wheeler of Montana, historian Charles A. Beard, the Reverend Harry Emerson Fosdick and other prominent churchmen, and thoughtful liberal journals such as *The Nation* and *The New Republic*. Their opinions had an idealistic basis. But there were others that spoke the language of prejudice and demagoguery: the Hearst and the McCormick press, hundreds of provincial newspapers, and the popular spellbinders, Father Coughlin and the Reverend Gerald L. K. Smith, whose inflammatory oratory over the radio won many adherents. Under such a powerful impetus the crusade for "peace and neutrality" gained a kind of religious fervor that swept reason and caution aside. Schoolchildren and women's clubs were indoctrinated with it. Politicians asked to be elected on their premise to "keep America out of war." The Veterans of Foreign Wars set out to get 25 million signatures to a petition to Congress to pass the Neutrality Act of 1937. A score of organizations— World Peaceways, Fellowship of Reconciliation, National Council for Prevention of War, Womens International League for Peace and Freedom—sprang into existence (or were revived from the days of 1917-18) to mobilize public opinion. Polls and surveys showed that the great majority of Americans favored isolationism. The average American felt, it seemed, that most foreign governments were rotten anyway; that wars were endemic among them; and that the United States, having once before tried at great sacrifice to pull Europe's chestnuts out of the fire, should now leave ungrateful nations to stew in the juices of their own folly.

Today such an attitude seems a self-righteous self-deception, but in the nineteen-thirties it appealed to many as good American common sense. Americans of that generation had been exposed to a kind of "revisionist" history of the First World War and its consequences. A number of writers and intellectual leaders assailed the wisdom and even the patriotic integrity of Woodrow Wilson as a wartime President, and belittled his vision of a world community of nations. Repeated efforts to have this country join the League of Nations failed. Authors of books and articles wrote "exposés" of the chicanery employed by our European Allies to seduce us into the conflict. They called for re-evaluations of the relative guilt of Germany and the Allies for bringing on the war and for the manner of its prosecution. The issue of the unpaid war debts was a further source of exacerbation. "They hired the money, didn't they?" Calvin Coolidge asked caustically. Millions of Americans believed as he evidently did that the British, the French, and the Russians—all except "little Finland"—were simply ungrateful welchers. And many felt with President Hoover that the economic depression that was flattening America somehow had its roots in the mendacity of European statesmen and the corruption of the European character.

In 1934 Senator Gerald P. Nye, chairman of the Special Senate Munitions Investigating Committee, shocked the nation with a series of disclosures tending to show that the war had been brought on through the connivance of international bankers and munitions-makers bent on enriching themselves. Nye stumped the country like a one-man Chautauqua warning convention-goers and women's clubs that these same villains were up to their old villainy. "We didn't win a thing we set out for in the last war," he thundered from one rostrum after another. "We merely succeeded, with tremendous loss of life, to make secure the loans of our private bankers to the Allies." There was hard substance in many of the Nye Committee's disclosures, for some of the armaments-makers had made unconscionable profits out of their war contracts. But there was also a great deal of flimsy melodrama, which did not bother a public eager to believe the worst about the wicked "merchants of death" and the duping of American statesmen. A book addressed to the same theme—

Walter Millis', *The Road to War*, published in 1935—went immediately on the best-seller lists. It made a particular impact on liberals and intellectuals.

Under this kind of conditioning the mood of the thirties developed into a militant parochialism. College students quit their classes in "peace strikes" and took the "Oxford oath" never to engage in a foreign war. Gold Star Mothers held public vigils and sent deputations to Washington. Unions and civic clubs and Sunday School classes adopted pacifist resolutions and proclaimed "America First." Books, magazines, movies, and sermons lent support to the America First theme. The Army, the Navy, and the craft of diplomacy fell into a kind of disrepute, and an innocent expression of patriotic sentiment could evoke the derisive appelation "warmonger." The motives and aspirations that had prompted American policy in the First World War were now distorted by cynicism and the convenient acuity of hindsight. Pacifism became a cult, and isolationism was its political theology.[1]

II

The first New Deal Congresses were less concerned with foreign affairs than with domestic issues. But several bills did reflect the prevailing mood of isolationism. In April 1934 Congress passed the Johnson Act, sponsored by Senator Hiram Johnson of California, whose phobia against all things foreign was notorious. Mirroring the popular resentment over the failure of the Allies to keep up in full their pledged war debt payments, the Johnson bill forbade all sales and purchases in this country of the bonds of the defaulting nations. This move ignored the fact that the economies of Britain and France were even more bankrupt than our own, and it foreclosed one avenue for their eventual rehabilitation. In 1935 the Senate refused to ratify the protocol establishing the World Court, one of the most useful and exemplary instruments of the League of Nations. Every President since Harding had advocated membership in the Court. Roosevelt made a strong plea for it in his State of the Union Message in January 1935. But his advocacy ignited the fires of isolationist prejudice. The Court was a symbol of the League, of internationalism, of "meddling in the affairs of Europe" and inviting Europe to meddle in ours. Propagandists fanned out across the country like Paul Reveres to spread the alarm; the Hearst press rubbed the nerves of chauvinism raw; Father Coughlin turned the airwaves blue with his invective; and more than 200,000 protesting letters and telegrams deluged Congress in the final week of Senate debate. Roosevelt, dismayed by the uproar, withheld at the last a possibly decisive nudge of his influence, and the Senate kept the United States from joining the Court.

Congress now moved to place a heavier restriction on the conduct of our foreign relations. In August 1935 it passed the Neutrality Act, which imposed on the President the duty, when he found a state of war anywhere in the world, of proclaiming an embargo on the shipment of "arms, ammunition or implements of war" to any belligerent, whether aggressor or victim. This act, intended to expire in six months, actually was revised and extended in subsequent years.

Two circumstances favored the easy passage of the law: the triumph of the isolationist lobby in the World Court fight and the imminence of Italy's invasion of Ethiopia. Congress and the isolationists were determined to tie the President's hands irrespective of any considerations of morality, fair play, diplomacy, and even (as it turned out) our own national interest. Thus, an undiscriminating policy of hands-off became the guiding principle of our foreign relations; a principle that made no distinction between friend and foe, between right and wrong.

The Neutrality Act put a straitjacket on the executive branch, severely limiting its field of maneuver in the intricate and devious chess game of world politics. Secretary of State Hull bitterly opposed the neutrality bill in testimony before the committees of Congress. His department had sought to shape an alternative measure that would preserve the principle of neutrality and at the same time preserve enough flexibility to try to avert hostilities before they broke out. But he argued to no avail.

President Roosevelt signed the Neutrality Act with misgivings. He sincerely wanted to avoid war, and was convinced that the course forced on him was the wrong one. Yet he felt powerless to alter it. The rising tide of isolationist sentiment throughout the country made him doubt whether he had the people with him. The Congress, in spite of its large Democratic majorities, had begun to balk at his domestic program, and in the foreign field it was clearly under the control of his opponents. With the 1936 election coming up, and beyond that some legislative and political contests of great importance still to be waged, he hesitated to lay his leadership irrevocably on the line, for he might well wind up with no leadership. "It is a terrible thing," he said to Sam Rosenman, "to look over your shoulder when you are trying to lead—and find no one there."

Roosevelt was subjected to intense criticism from internationalists and nationalists alike—for failure, on the one hand, to act more boldly in the world crisis, and on the other, for scheming deviously to effect the nation's involvement. Retrospectively, most historians of today give him and his Secretary of State generally high marks for their insight and constancy of purpose in confronting an on-rushing catastrophe. Allan Nevins has written:

It may seem strange that a President as popular as Roosevelt, a Secretary of State as beloved as Hull, should be so little trusted in the conduct of [foreign] relations. Actually, it was not strange at all. Roosevelt and Hull had different sources of information than those of Congress—so time proved, much superior sources. They saw the world picture in far broader perspective, with more detail and color; they had to look further ahead and estimate contingent disasters that Congress ignored; they thought of the national interest in an international setting, whereas most Congressmen thought of local interests in a national setting. The Administration was keenly alert to perilous trends that Congress hardly perceived.*

* *The New Deal and World Affairs* (Yale University Press, 1950), p. 77.

III

On the international front, omens of disaster were piling up in formidable complexity. In Japan a war party of young militarists succeeded in displacing such moderates in high places as Prime Minister Okada; they set their goals of conquest beyond Manchuria to all of China, and ultimately toward a "Greater East Asian Co-prosperity Sphere." The island empire was suffering from the growing pains and population pressures of a recently industrialized society. Like Germany and Italy, it demanded space and accommodation from its neighbors to fulfill its "manifest destiny." In November 1935 it sent an army pouring through the Great Wall in a move to detach the five northern provinces from China proper and to set up a puppet government subservient to Tokyo. After two years of guerrilla warfare against surprisingly effective resistance by the Nationalist forces of Chiang Kai-shek, a major battle was fought in July 1937 at the Marco Polo Bridge on the outskirts of Peking. The Japanese broke through after heavy losses on both sides, and they quickly committed the full strength of the Imperial Army and Navy to a full-scale conquest of the vast China mainland. Nanking, Canton, and Hangchow were subjected to repeated bombing attacks, and before long a naval blockade was strung along the whole China coast. In 1936 Japan had joined Germany in an Anti-Comintern Pact designed to instill fear in the still uncommitted Soviet Union, which had armed its Mongolian frontier in response to Japanese activity in Manchuria and China. The Pact between two powerful militaristic nations on opposite sides of the world sent chills of apprehension through the Western democracies.

Secretary Hull protested the Japanese aggression against China in the strongest diplomatic terms, only to be ignored. He called for a "moral" embargo on the export of war matériel from this country to Japan. A partial embargo was effected, but the President refused to invoke the rigid strictures of the Neutrality Act. To have done so would have harmed China far more than Japan. The United States had extensive commercial ties with China, and many thousands of American citizens resided there. Besides, a sentimental attachment to China had developed out of the work performed by several generations of American missionaries and educators. Public opinion in the United States was overwhelmingly sympathetic to the Chinese. American women took to wearing cotton stockings instead of silk as part of a boycott of Japanese goods. But sympathy stopped far short of willingness to take up arms in behalf of the Chinese. Even after the Japanese bombed and strafed the U.S. Gunboat *Panay* in the Yangtze River in December 1937 (for which they apologized with Oriental unctuousness), a Gallup poll showed that 70 percent of Americans favored a complete withdrawal of the handful of our troops stationed about the Far East under long-standing treaty arrangements.

To the men in the White House and the State Department, the prospect (as they then believed) of a swift Japanese take-over in East Asia was a more instant menace to American security than what was happening in Europe. But for most Americans, except those living on the West Coast, the chief focus of their fears lay across the Atlantic, where Mussolini and his Blackshirts were slaughtering defenseless Ethiopian tribesmen, and Hitler was creating a reign of terror against the Jews and transforming the Reich into a land of medieval barbarism.

The Spanish civil war, erupting early in 1936 and escalating rapidly in cruelty and destructiveness, evoked intense partisan reactions in the United States. Liberals and leftists supported the Loyalists, who were seeking (ostensibly at least) to preserve a republican form of government. Americans by the hundreds went as volunteers (the Abraham Lincoln Brigade was the most notable contingent) to fight in the Loyalist ranks; others by the thousands contributed money and intellectual energies. On the opposite side were the Falangists, a fascist party controlled by Francisco Franco. Many Catholics and Americans of Italian or German descent—and political conservatives in general—upheld the cause of Franco and his right-wing rebels. The Falangists had the moral support of the Holy See, and in time the active military support of the Nazi and Fascist dictators, while the Loyalists were aided by disciplined communist volunteers from all over Europe.

Another form of terror was rampant in the Soviet Union, where the Stalin purge was in progress. Tens of thousands of his real or suspected political enemies were executed during 1936 and 1937, after mock trials and extorted confessions of incredible transparency. At the same time Russia was straining its productive resources almost to the breaking point in a huge armament buildup. The great Russian Bear, tormented from within and hateful of all that was beyond its reach, puzzled the outside world. Was the Soviet Union preparing to put its weight on the side of the democracies or on the side of the dictatorships? No one knew, not even the faithful comrades who were strategically deployed in every part of the world.

Other events of sinister portent were underscoring a growing public anxiety. In March 1935 Hitler denounced the Treaty of Versailles, sent his troops to reoccupy the Rhineland provinces, and disclosed that he was building an army and air force second to none in Europe. In 1936 Italy, having completed its conquest of Ethiopia, turned covetous eyes toward Egypt and the Suez Canal. The League of Nations, having failed to secure meaningful sanctions against the Italian and Japanese aggressors, was in disarray and disrepute. Britain and France lamely acquiesced in the outcome of Italy's Ethiopian venture as well as in Germany's march into the Rhineland. Nor did the United States react with any great valor. Being 3,000 miles away and outside the League, its options were fewer: it had permitted vital oil supplies to flow to Italy through a loophole in the Neutrality Act, and it was in no position to confront the Nazis with force in the Rhineland. The Neutrality Act did not apply to the Spanish conflict, but Roosevelt, uneasily supporting the nonintervention policies of Britain and France, imposed a "moral" embargo on war supplies to both the Loyalists and the Falangists.

The Rome-Berlin Axis was forged late in 1936. Initially conceived as a gaudy bit of window dressing (Hitler and Mussolini shared a deep mutual distrust at the time), its long-range implications were not lost on the Foreign

(Below) *Il Duce!* Benito Mussolini addressing and exhorting crowds from Milan to Rome, as (spread) fresh Italian troops depart for Ethiopia.

167 Askari Cavalrymen Advance on Adowa

On October 6, 1935, the Italian forces advanced on Adowa, Ethiopia, taking this city in a sentimental victory, to avenge Italy's defeat in Ethiopia of 1896. Important in this advance was the Askari cavalry, and arm of the native army corps which was cooperating with the national corps. The native riders were accompanied by Italian tanks, well suited to the rough country, and the appearance of these formidable units made quick work of the Ethiopian rout. Despite earlier rumors of fierce fighting on the outskirts of Adowa, later reports suggested that the Ethiopians made no attempt to hold the city in force. Certain Ethiopian chieftains and their men deserted to the Italian side. On October 13, General de Bono entered Adowa and unveiled in the captured city a stone monument made in Florence to the dead of 1896. The picture shows the Ethiopians retreating down a steep slope, pursued by the Askari cavalry.

To know the HORRORS OF WAR is to want PEACE

EYEWITNESS IN
ABYSSINIA

HERBERT MATTHEWS

HOMAGE TO CATALONIA

GEORGE ORWELL

AUTHOR OF "THE ROAD TO WIGAN PIER" ETC.

(Below) To know the HORRORS OF WAR is to want PEACE! Bubble-gum War Cards: a childhood "game" and a childhood "sweet." (Above) Returning members of The Abraham Lincoln Brigade, wounded in Spain in the fight against Franco, give the clenched-fist leftist salute. At right: An international incident: the U.S. gunboat *Panay* bombed and sunk by Japanese planes in the Yangtze River, December, 1937. (Above) Japanese troops going over the Great Wall Of China, 1935.

159 Mistake in Identity Causes Loyalist Slaughter

On January 27, 1938, a strong Loyalist attack on Singra, 24 miles north of Teruel, ended in a mad retreat when a squadron of foreign planes through a mistake in identity bombed and machine-gunned their own troops! The Loyalists in attempting to sever the Teruel-Saragossa highway had thrown four fresh brigades of infantry and three divisions of powerful Russian tanks into the battle. Not long after this action, 16 planes appeared over the front. Under orders to protect the advance from the east the planes mistook the Loyalist forces for the enemy and started to bomb them and strafe them with machine-gun fire. The terrible butchery lasted for a quarter of an hour, completely demoralizing the attacking troops. A whole unit of Loyalist infantry was said to have been wiped out through this awful mistake.

To know the HORRORS OF WAR is to want PEACE

This is one of 240 True Stories of Modern Warfare. Save to get them all and compete for 1000 Cash Prizes. Ask your dealer. Copyright 1938, GUM, INC., Phila., Pa. Printed in U. S. A.

PIECE BY PIECE
JULY 30, 1937

151 Swords and Bayonets Clash in Bloody Fight

Bloody hand-to-hand fighting raged in the barricaded streets of Japanese-army-invaded Taierhchwang on April 1, 1938, with the success of Japan's drive toward the city, Suchow, hanging in the balance. The fight for Taierhchwang was typical of the entire Tientsin-Pukow front. There were disjointed flankings in several places and infiltrations of both Chinese and Japanese lines by independent detachments deprived of organized support, fighting against annihilation. About 10,000 Chinese wielded their ancient broadswords against the less efficient swords and bayonets of about the same number of Japanese in primitive contact fighting. (The inferior quality of Japanese bayonets and swords had been noted early in the year by master swordsmiths sent to China to repair Japanese weapons, and steps were to be taken to eradicate "wicked dealers.")

To know the HORRORS OF WAR is to want PEACE

Offices of Paris, London, and Washington. But democratic governments simply lacked the will and the cohesiveness to interpose their strength against the spread of aggression. Years later Winston Churchill was to describe the temper of England of that time:

Poor England! Leading her free, careless life from day to day, amidst the endless, good-tempered parliamentary babble, she followed, wondering, along the downward path which led to all she wanted to avoid. She was continually reassured by the leading articles of the most influential newspapers, with some honourable exceptions, and behaved as if all the world was as easy, uncalculating, and well-meaning as herself.[2]

IV

Under the impact of alarming news from abroad, a turnabout in the American posture began to materialize in 1937. The adamancy of the isolationist position gradually softened as people read the daily reports of slaughters of the innocent and the inhumanity of the dictators. Ordinary citizens became concerned about foreign affairs as they had not been since 1914. The clouds gathering on the horizon were unmistakably war clouds. The desire for peace increased as its attainment seemed to be receding out of reach. But many began to question whether peace could be ensured merely by prayer and legislative formulas. With the storm breaking over Europe and Asia, could America remain aloof? The aversion people felt toward the aggressors passed from emotionalism to activism. Mass rallies whipped up sentiment for consumer boycotts against dictator-controlled nations, collected funds for medical supplies for the Chinese and the Spanish Loyalists, and urged government aid to get Jewish victims of persecution out of Germany. Even Senator Nye, without renouncing the principles of isolationism, demanded an easing of the unofficial embargo against the Loyalists in Spain.

These activities signified a weakening of the isolationist spirit but not its abandonment. In fact, the mounting sense of crisis inspired in many a toughening determination to withdraw still further from the dangers of contamination by the world's afflictions. Late in April 1937 Congress extended the Neutrality Act, making it permanent and stiffening some of its earlier provisions. As before, raw materials were exempted from the embargo, but now they could be obtained only on a cash-and-carry basis. The arming of American merchantmen engaging in this trade was prohibited; the travel of Americans on the vessels of belligerent nations was forbidden; and private contributions collected for the benefit of either side in a declared war was limited to food and medical services. Congressional debate over the measure was heated, revealing a number of cleavages in isolationist ranks. Again, Roosevelt and Hull sought to substitute a more flexible law, but they could not prevail. Congress had taken the conduct of foreign policy out of their hands. A *New York Times* editorial took a dour view of the situation:

The passage of this mis-named neutrality bill may mark the high tide of isolationist sentiment in this country. Certainly no measure has gone to greater extremes in relying on a policy of isolation to keep the United States at peace in time of war. or ignored so completely the argument that the best hope of maintaining peace lies in concerted action to prevent the outbreak of war itself. . . . There is little doubt that the theories embedded in this bill correspond closely to the prevailing sentiment of a majority of the American people at this time. It need not be assumed, however, that the present mood of the country will last forever.

The mood did not last.

On October 5, 1937, Roosevelt called for a "quarantine" against aggressor nations in a speech delivered before an outdoor gathering in Chicago, where he had gone to dedicate the Outer Drive Bridge, built by the PWA. He warned that the world was moving toward disaster and that this nation could not hope, simply by shutting its mind, to remain immune to catastrophic events.

Apparently, Roosevelt had deliberately chosen Chicago, the capital of isolationism, as the platform for his declaration in order to give it maximum impact. Standing almost within the shadow of the Tribune Tower, the citadel of Col. Robert R. McCormick's powerful newspaper, he spoke with unaccustomed gravity and forcefulness, calling for "concerted action" by the peace-loving nations to pull civilization back from the precipice of self-destruction:

The landmarks and traditions which have marked the progress of civilization toward a condition of order and justice are being wiped away. . . . If these things come to pass in other parts of the world, let no one imagine that America will escape, that it may expect mercy, that this Western Hemisphere will not be attacked and that it will continue peacefully and tranquilly to carry on the ethics and arts of civilization. . . .

If these days are not to come to pass—if we are to have a world in which we can breathe freely and live in amity without fear—the peace-loving nations must make a concerted effort to uphold laws and principles on which alone peace can rest secure. . . .

When an epidemic of physical disease starts to spread, the community approves and joins in a quarantine of the patients in order to protect the health of the community against the spread of the disease. . . . War is a contagion, whether it be declared or undeclared. . . . We are determined to keep out of war, yet we cannot insure ourselves against the disastrous effects of war and the dangers of involvement. We are adopting such measures as will minimize our risk of involvement, but we cannot have complete protection in a world of disorder in which confidence and security have broken down.

Both at home and abroad, the President's speech brought a mixed response. The British press hailed it; Germany and Italy refrained from publishing it in their papers. The extreme isolationist point of view was expressed in a Boston *Herald* editorial, which said that Roosevelt had assumed the mantle of Woodrow Wilson. "But this time, Mr. President, America will not be stampeded into going 4,000 miles across the water to save [Europe]. Crusade if you must, but for the sake of several million American mothers confine your crusading to the continental limits of America." At the opposite extreme, the St. Louis *Post-Dispatch* said, "The President is right, wholly and absolutely right." *The New York Times* lauded the President: "An eloquent voice has expressed the deep moral indignation which is felt in this country against policies of ruthlessness and conquest." In between, the consensus seemed to be, "Maybe he knows something that we don't, but let's not do anything too rash."

Roosevelt had hoped to convert the doubters, but his hopes were not realized. Sam Rosenman thought it was because of poor timing in trying to lead the people "before they had been adequately informed of the facts or spiritually prepared for the event." [3]

Nevertheless, Roosevelt had wrought better than he knew. The speech—his first unequivocal assertion that this nation must join with others for collective security—was his strongest challenge to date to the myth of isolationism. Myths die slowly, but the President's warning had taken root. Within a year, as the Council on Foreign Relations was to find:

Three-quarters of the people in the United States believed that there would be a European war in the near future; an equal percentage admitted that their sympathies in such a war would be on the side of Great Britain and France, and more than half would vote to supply the "democracies" with munitions and war supplies. All this without benefit of twist or wangle from the "merchants of death." [4]

The isolationists were still dominant in Congress and in many parts of the country, but they had yielded up some of their confidence.

V

The year 1937 can be likened to the overture to a great tragic opera in which the principal elements of the story that is about to unfold are suggestively delineated. The next year and a half were like the opening scenes in which the plot begins to take shape and the outline of the eventual climax is intimated. As if following a master script, the characters and forces in this international epic played out the roles assigned to them on the world's stage during 1938 and 1939.

In January 1938 President Roosevelt sent a special message to Congress: "As Commander-in-Chief of the Army and Navy it is my constitutional duty to report to Congress that our national defense is, in the light of the increasing armaments of other nations, inadequate for the purposes of national security and requires increase for that reason." He asked for, and Congress duly approved, a defense budget of $1.042 billion, the largest since 1921, when the lessons of losses in the First World War were still vividly remembered.

The principal goal in the new armaments drive was to build "a navy second to none." Naval construction had been inhibited for more than a decade by various treaty restrictions, but most such obligations had been all but vitiated by 1938—for example, by Japan's denunciation of the London Naval Treaty in 1936. Now the Navy was allotted slightly more than half of the new funds to achieve a 20 percent increase in existing tonnage: from fifteen battleships to eighteen, from thirty-nine cruisers to forty-seven, from six airplane carriers to eight, and from 2,000 naval airplanes to 3,000, with corresponding increases in auxiliary vessels and personnel. The Army, with an enlisted strength of 183,400, was to get the lesser half of the new fund—namely, $459 million—for a nearly comparable buildup that included a goal of 2,300 first-line airplanes (raised the next year to 6,000) for its Air Corps by 1940.[5]

The rearmament program had wide popular support. If other nations were stockpiling weapons and manpower, people reasoned, we had better do so too. Worldwide expenditures for armaments had leaped from $5 billion in 1934 to $12 billion in 1937 and to an estimated $15 billion in 1938. Germany, Italy, and Japan were believed to be spending up to 50 percent of their national income on weaponry; Britain and France, around 25 percent. The level for the United States hovered around 12 percent. A strong army and navy appealed to the most elementary instinct of nationalism. Even most pacifists wanted to be able to defend their country against attack.

But the hard-core isolationists professed to see in the arms program a covert scheme by the White House to join hands with Britain and to prepare the nation for war. "It is, in my opinion, a war bill and nothing else," Congressman George Holden Tinkham of Boston exclaimed in the House of Representatives. "A sinister secret diplomacy is now directing American foreign policy [with] collusive political engagements between the United States and Great Britain." * But the isolationists were outgunned and outvoted on the issue. The arms authorization bill passed both houses of Congress by comfortable majorities and was signed by the President on May 17. It would be substantially enlarged the next year. The program fell far short of "putting the nation on a war footing" (some critics had made such a charge), but it was a significant first step in that direction.

In March, Hitler made patent his imperialistic design on Europe by a ruthless overnight seizure of Austria, annexing it to the German Reich. There was at least a superficial plausibility for such a union. Ethnically, Austria was predominately German but had been separated from the Fatherland at Versailles. Some internal sentiment for Anschluss had been abetted after 1933 by an intensive campaign of Nazi propaganda and subversion. Under the relatively mild dictatorships of Engelbert Dollfuss (he was assassinated during an attempted Nazi putsch in 1934) and then Dr. Kurt von Schuschnigg, a degree of economic and political stability was achieved. In an Austro-German treaty signed in 1933, Germany had benevolently recognized Austria's complete sovereignty. What was not known then but is known now is that at almost the same time Hitler directed the German General Staff to prepare a complete war plan—Operation Otto—for the occupation of Austria when the appropriate moment should come.[6]

---

* Tinkman's irascibility was a many splendored-thing. A formidable figure of a man with wide shoulders, a crisp spade beard, and fierce blue eyes, he rarely said less than he meant. Learning, while on a visit to Geneva in October 1937, that the Administration had decided not to invoke the Neutrality Act in the Sino-Japanese conflict, he shot off a cable to Secretary Hull saying that Congress should "seriously consider the impeachment of the President and yourself for high crime and misdemeanor."

Meanwhile the Fuehrer displayed a puzzling ambivalence toward his small neighbor to the south. He assured the world repeatedly that he had no territorial ambitions in that direction, yet he talked also of the need for "living space" and of uniting all the Germanic peoples. Actually, his intention was anything but ambivalent. In January 1938 he instigated another putsch by his Austrian Nazis, which Schuschnigg effectively aborted, putting many of the plotters in prison.

Now, discarding all ambiguity, Hitler summoned the Austrian Chancellor to his mountain retreat at Berchtesgaden on February 12. There, in the most peremptory and humiliating terms, he demanded that Schuschnigg immediately reorganize his government and install a notorious Nazi collaborator, Dr. Arthur Seyss-Inquart, in the critical Cabinet post of Minister of Interior and Public Security. Schuschnigg was bullied and threatened during the eleven-hour ordeal. While German Generals showed him maps of the disposition of troops along the Austrian border—Operation Otto—Hitler denounced him to his face as a traitor to the German cause. The shaken Schuschnigg returned to Vienna. Three days later, putting the best face possible on the matter, announced the reorganization of his Cabinet around the hated Seyss-Inquart and a general amnesty for some 3,000 imprisoned Austrian Nazis. Paris, London, and Washington felt new waves of anxiety (the widely respected Anthony Eden resigned his post as Foreign Minister in the British Cabinet), but they were not disposed to undertake collective action to ease Austria's plight.

Feeling the iron ring closing remorselessly around him, and with no help visible from beyond his borders, Schuschnigg decided on a last desperate stratagem to ensure his country's integrity. Confident that he could show that Austrians wished overwhelmingly to remain Austrian, independent of the German Reich, he expected to bring the weight of world opinion to bear on Hitler's aims. His decision tripped the time lock on disaster.

On March 9 he proclaimed a national plebiscite on the issue of Anschluss to be held four days later—quickly enough, he hoped, to catch his opponents off balance and to preclude a storm of Nazi propaganda. On March 11 Seyss-Inquart handed him an ultimatum, obviously dictated from Berlin, demanding a delay in the plebiscite. If the demand were refused, German troops would start moving across the border at five o'clock that afternoon. After hours of frantic deliberation, the Austrian leader capitulated. But as he did so, a new ultimatum arrived, this one by air courier directly from Berlin. It demanded Schuschnigg's resignation by 7:30 o'clock that night, the installation of Seyss-Inquart as Chancellor, and the replacement of two-thirds of the Austrian Cabinet by Nazi sympathizers. If these conditions were not immediately met, German troops at the border would begin their advance. At 7:45 o'clock that night, Schuschnigg told the Austrian people by radio, "We have yielded to force. . . . God save Austria!" Within an hour, the swastika banner was flying from the flag mast of the Chancellery, and the Vienna police were giving the Nazi salute. At two o'clock the following morning tanks and cannon and long truck convoys of German infantry were rolling through the Austrian villages and towns. The Austrian state had been wiped from the map of Europe.

The reaction of Great Britain and France was one of acute alarm, and they intensified their mobilization efforts. Mussolini was shaken to discover that his voracious German partner now stared at him across the Brenner Pass. But he preserved a discreet silence before the world.

The news made a lesser impact in the United States. To much of the public it seemed to be just another boiling over of the superheated pot of European power politics. Secretary Hull, concealing the deep concern felt within the Administration, said there was nothing the United States intended to do about the seizure of Austria. But the ominous import of the Austrian debacle was not wholly lost on American public opinion. The influential American League for Peace and Freedom now swung toward the objective of international cooperation to thwart the aggressors by "moral pressure and economic measures." The liberal *Nation* polled its readers and found that 84 percent favored a similar course. Events were moving America toward an overdue recognition of its world responsibilities.[7]

VI

What no reasonably literate citizen of this country could miss was that Hitler's Austrian adventure was not a finale but a prelude. All through the spring and summer of 1937, newspapers and the radio warned that the next scene of action would be Czechoslovakia. Hitler coveted its mines and munitions factories. Most Americans had only hazy notions about Czechoslovakia, a nation that had been pieced together by the Allies in the aftermath of the First World War. But the prevailing impression was that the Czechs were a sturdy and valiant people who were struggling, in their far-off land, toward a democratic way of life. Now it was learned in daily headlines and on-the-spot broadcasts from Berlin and Prague that the Nazi dagger was pressing ever closer to Czechoslovakia's heart. The response to this news was a great outpouring of public sympathy for the Czechs and a mounting concern over their political crisis.

Neville Chamberlain, the British Prime Minister, was destined to play a tragic lead in the Czechoslovak drama. England, like the United States, followed its own course of isolationism. The British Government, in its desire to avoid war, shrank from facing the realities of what was happening on the Continent. Chamberlain, who valued prudence above valor, believed that with a concession here and a compromise there, the frictions that were troubling Europe could be negotiated away. With the French, he had acquiesced in Mussolini's plunder of Ethiopia. He had shut his eyes to the involvement of Italian troops and German warplanes on the side of the Spanish insurgents, and had accepted the swallowing up of Austria as a *fait accompli.*

France was bound by treaty to aid Czechoslovakia in case of attack, and Britain was bound by a parallel agreement to come to the aid of France. Both nations built up their military strength after the Anschluss, but they did not

BEFORE

AFTER

MILITARY
ALLIANCE

Deutsche!
Wehrt Euch!
Kauft nicht bei Juden!

"Don't Buy Jewish Merchandise"

British Prime Minister Sir Neville Chamberlain

At left: (bottom) Fritz Kuhn, head of the German-American Bund, speaking at a pro-Nazi rally at Madison Square Garden, February 20, 1939. (Spread) Clan Rebirth: the Southwestern Michigan KKK in their drive against Communism and Communist tendencies in the CIO. (Above, top) Senator Burton K. Wheeler and Charles Lindbergh at an America First Rally, 1939. (Middle) Isolationist Senator Nye (at right) and wife. (Bottom) "Save Our Sons." Speaker John T. Flynn at an America First Rally.

send aid to Czechoslovakia. Chamberlain called the Czech situation "a quarrel in a faraway country between people of whom we know nothing." He yearned for some positive expression of support from the United States but had to content himself with ambiguities.*

Ethnic Germans made up a quarrelsome minority of about 22 percent of the 15.3 million population of Czechoslovakia. They were concentrated mainly along the western frontier, in the region of the Sudeten Mountains. They and their lands had never been a part of the Reich, but Hitler began early to lavish his solicitude on them and to promise them ultimate "reunion" with the Fatherland. Thus a fanatic German nationalism was engendered, which developed about 1936 into a strong Nazi party led by a trained rabble-rouser and propagandist, Konrad Henlein. The goal was an autonomous Sudeten German state to be carved out of one of the richest regions of Czechoslovakia. This campaign, openly encouraged by Berlin, reached fever heat after the Austrian Anschluss. A stream of propaganda charged oppression and atrocities against the German minority. When, in the summer of 1938, the alarmed Czechs strengthened their western fortifications and held army maneuvers, the Nazi Minister for Propaganda, Joseph Goebbels charged that Germany was threatened by invasion.

The gun at Czechoslovakia's head was cocked at the monster National Socialist rally held September 6 in Nuremberg, where 1,500,000 Nazis shouted deliriously for their Fuehrer. Hitler promised the Sudeten Germans "a party day of their own" by October 15 and an autonomous Sudeten state modeled on Nazi lines and oriented toward Berlin instead of Prague.

September 1938 seemed to move not in a succession of days but in a succession of alarms and crises toward a dreaded climax. Newspaper headlines reflected the mounting tension felt in the United States and Western Europe. The Czechs mobilized their small but powerful army and clamped martial law on the seething Sudetenland. Germany rushed the completion of a double-track rail line leading to the Czech frontier and put half a million labor conscripts to work strengthening the Siegfried Line, which faced France. France strengthened its Maginot Line, which faced Germany, and called half a million men to the colors. Britain put its army and its Mediterranean and North Sea fleets on a war footing, dug air raid shelters, and distributed gas masks to the citizens of London. It sent a mission headed by Lord Runciman to Prague, to try to extract enough concessions from President Benes to satisfy Hitler's demands. The mission was unsuccessful. In the United States, as elsewhere in the West, people were convinced that war in Europe was about to break out—possibly by the end of the month, certainly before winter.

Isolationists clamored for fresh White House assurance that we would not

* For example, FDR's "quarantine" speech and another more to the point delivered at Kingston, Ontario, in August, in which he said that the United States would "not stand idly by" should Canada be attacked by a hostile power. From diplomatic documents and other published sources we know that the President was fully alert to the developing Czech crisis but was retrained by the fetters of domestic politics from essaying a more active role.

become involved. But great numbers of Americans favored a national stand on behalf of the embattled Czechs; they demanded moral, economic, and even armed support for Britain and France. Seldom before had the lines of political, ideological and moral conviction in this country gotten into a more noisome tangle than in that nerve-wracking September.

The denouement in German-Czech relations came swiftly. Prime Minister Chamberlain, taking his pride in his hands, made three hurried pilgrimages to the shrine of the Fuehrer to learn what ransom he would require to lift his siege of Czechoslovakia. The third and decisive visit was on September 29 for a four-power conference at Munich. Hitler had summoned Mussolini to his side. France was represented by Premier Edouard Daladier and Foreign Minister Georges Bonnet. No spokesman for Prague was present.

Hitler reiterated his previous conditions: immediate self-determination for the Sudetenland and a virtually free hand for the Nazis to occupy and control certain other portions of Czechoslovakia. The alternative? His troops, already massed, would strike across the border before the next nightfall. At a little after midnight on September 30, the Munich Accord, granting Hitler substantially all that he asked for, was signed by the four powers. Lord Runciman conveyed the news to President Benes, who, abandoned by his friends, had no alternative but to capitulate, which he did shortly before noon. To satisfy Hitler's imperialistic dream of *Drang nach Osten*, the Republic of Czechoslovakia was, to all intents and purposes, wiped from the map. Its complete liquidation would come in less than a year.

On his return to London, Chamberlain told the crowd gathered in front of the Foreign Office that "there has come back from Germany to Downing Street peace with honor. I believe it is peace in our time." Most of the world heaved a sigh of relief: War had been averted an instant before doomsday. Then, quickly, came a reckoning, and relief was replaced by disgust, humiliation, and guilt. In the United States people spoke of appeasement and betrayal. *The Nation* said: "Everything else that happened during the past week seemed trifling and immaterial beside the stabbing of Czechoslovakia by its British and French bodyguards. Was there ever an occasion that so cried out for mass action, for thunderous denunciation as this?" In New York Rabbi Stephen S. Wise drew loud boos for the British Prime Minister when he told a thousand members of the United Czechoslovak Societies, "Chamberlain has not brought back peace with honor, but dishonor without peace!" Radio commentator Johannes Steel said scornfully: "So they call it peace! They call it peace because the victim, not being able to save itself from its friends, cannot face the enemy alone. They call it peace because the victor received the spoils before, instead of after, the battle." [8]

VII

What had become clear was that Hitler now stood at the head of the most powerful nation in Europe, with conquest in his eye and malevolence in his heart. Twice he had demonstrated that he could bully the democracies into submission and pick off his targets one by one. Now the Balkans, the Ukraine,

Poland—even France and England—lay temptingly before him. His aim to master them menaced Europe, and implied a menace to the United States. This grim fact now penetrated the sophistry of the isolationists. Most Americans held to their abhorrence of war, but they realized that it could no longer be avoided by ignoring its stealthy approach. Two Gallup public opinion polls revealed this awakening. The first, conducted shortly before the Munich crisis, showed that, if a European war came, only 57 percent would favor selling food to Britain and France and only 34 percent would favor selling them arms. The second poll, taken not long after Munich, showed a profound shift in sentiment: 82 percent would sell food to the democracies and 57 percent would send war materials.

Isolationism was not dead. Americans still wanted to keep out of any foreign war, but they now calculated their chances and their options more realistically.

CHAPTER 19
The Days of Peace Run Out
1938-1939

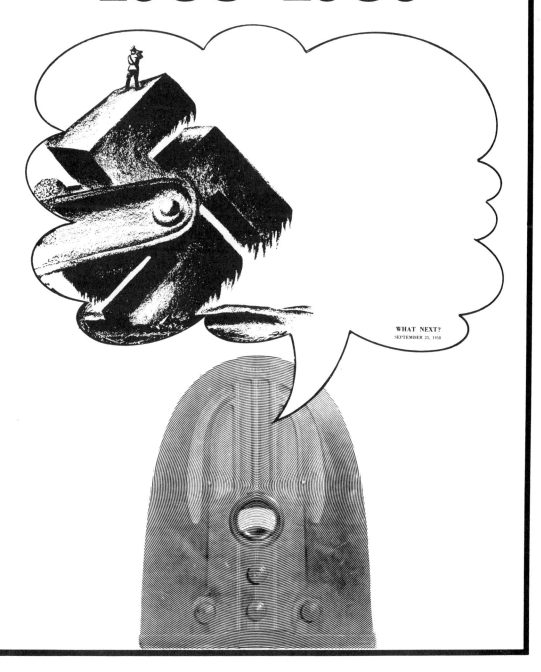

WHAT NEXT?
SEPTEMBER 25, 1938

THE ROAD FROM MUNICH LED in a straight line to the abyss of the Second World War, a short year away. Each milestone marked the civilized world's deepening outrage against the dictatorships and gave new evidence of the helplessness of the democracies to halt the plunge toward disaster.

I

On November 21, 1938, a 17-year-old German Jewish refugee, Herschel Grynszpan, walked into the German Embassy in Paris and unloaded his pistol at the first official he spied. Ernst vom Rath, the third secretary, fell to the floor mortally wounded. Persecution of the large Jewish population of Germany had mounted steadily during the previous four years as a deliberate though unacknowledged aspect of Nazi policy. Herschel Grynszpan's act of retribution unleashed all the furies of Aryan racism. Under the impetus of hysterical propaganda by the state controlled press and radio, a pogrom of unmitigated horror swept over Germany. Brownshirted thugs drove Jews by the thousands from their homes, stripped and beat them in the streets, and subjected them to barbaric indecencies. Synagogues were dynamited and set afire; Jewish shops and homes were smashed and looted. When the mob's violence had spent itself, the state applied another form of torture. By official decree the German Jewish community was required to pay the government an indemnity of one billion marks (about $400 million) for the murder of Vom Rath, and to yield up all insurance payments due for the destruction of their property (estimated at another billion marks). After January 1, 1939, Jews would be forbidden to engage in retail trade and to attend theaters, public schools, or universities.

It was plain to all the world that Hitler was embarked on a plan of systematic destruction of the Jews. President Roosevelt expressed his feeling of outrage: "I myself could scarcely believe that such things could occur in twentieth-century civilization." He ordered Hugh Wilson, his Ambassador in Berlin, home for a first-hand report. Hitler retaliated by recalling his Ambassador in Washington, Hans Dieckhoff. (Both posts were to remain vacant for seventeen years.) Public feeling was so inflamed that police guards were posted at the German Embassy in Washington and the consulate in New York City, to which Mayor LaGuardia assigned a twelve-man all-Jewish detail under the supervision of a Captain Max Finkelstein.

In January 1939 a Falangists force consisting of Italian soldiers and German tanks and warplanes moved on Loyalist positions around Barcelona. This was the last redoubt of the defenders of the Spanish Republic, who had given up virtually all of the rest of the country to the larger and better equipped divisions of Francisco Franco. At Barcelona the Loyalists were overwhelmed, and the Falangists took over. Save for the act of surrender, that was the end of the Spanish Civil War. There was rejoicing in the streets of Berlin and Rome. Mussolini, addressing a throng of cheering Fascists from the balcony of Palazzo Venezia, proclaimed a victory "for our famous legionaries." In Spain the triumphant Franco inaugurated a reign of terror against the Loyalist remnants and their supporters.

This bloody conflict, which had cost one and a half million lives, was a preview in miniature of the greater conflict to come. It was an ideological war between the forces of freedom (however contaminated by communist doctrine) and the forces of repression of an authoritarian state. The forces of repression won.

On March 15 Hitler summoned to Berlin Czechoslovakia's President Hácha, who presided uneasily over what was left of the ravaged nation. Six months earlier, after having absorbed about a third of the Czech population and a quarter of its territory, the Fuehrer had solemnly assured the world that he had no further territorial ambitions in Europe. Now, in a routine that was becoming ominously familiar, he was repudiating his promise. For months Nazi subversion had been at work on the volatile nationalistic rivalries that existed within the truncated little nation's polyglot population—Czechs, Slovenes, Carpatho-Ukrainians, and a few hundred thousand still-unassimilated Germans. Nazi propaganda incited separatist agitations, demands for special ethnic privileges, and political intrigues. On top of everything, Berlin demanded further economic and territorial concessions. Now, confronting Hácha as coldly as he had confronted Schuschnigg and then Benes, Hitler delivered his latest ultimatum: Accept a German "protectorate" over all the remaining provinces of Czechoslovakia or face the immediate bombing of Prague and other cities. Characteristically, the conference was held at 2 A.M. in the Fuehrer's ornate suite at the Reichschancellery. Hácha was given three hours to make up his mind. He fainted twice during the ordeal. Shortly before five o'clock he capitulated. Immediately German troops moved into the surrendered territory (Hungarian and Polish troops were poised on their respective borders, waiting hungrily for their share of the Czech carcass). Late that afternoon Hitler entered Prague like a conquering Caesar.

The annihilation of Czechoslovakia was greeted with public cries of protest and official denunciations. Chamberlain, conceding that appeasement had failed, said that world opinion "has received a sharper shock than has ever been administered to it." In Washington Under Secretary of State Sumner Welles warned that "acts of wanton lawlessness and of arbitrary force are threatening world peace and the very structure of modern civilization." Even from Moscow there came an ominous rumble: "The occupation of the Czech provinces by German troops and the subsequent actions of the German government cannot but be considered as arbitrary, violent and aggressive." Possibly the most poignant lament of all was an unspoken one—an inscription posted on the abandoned Czech pavilion at the about-to-be-opened New York World's Fair, lines taken from Comenius, a seventeenth-century Czech writer and patriot:

AFTER THE TEMPEST OF WRATH HAS PASSED
THE RULE OF THY COUNTRY WILL RETURN TO THEE
O CZECH PEOPLE

On March 21, a mere week after settling "the Czechoslovak question" on his eastern flank, Hitler turned westward to give his attention to "the Polish question." The focus of his attention was the Baltic port city of Danzig, which had been detached from Germany after the First World War along with the so-called Polish Corridor separating East Prussia from the rest of Germany. Danzig was under the protection of the League of Nations as a "free city." It had been sliced away from East Prussia to give Poland a major outlet to the sea. Though politically Polish, it was ethnically and culturally German, and Hitler had long hinted that Danzig must return to the Reich. Now he made his wishes explicit in a note to the Warsaw government proposing (1) absorption of the city by Germany, with a proviso for Poland's use of it as a free port; (2) cession of a fifteen-mile-wide zone across the Corridor to link Germany proper with East Prussia, plus extraterritorial rights for Germans living in the zone; and (3) the extension of an existing nonaggession treaty between the two nations. Coming at a moment when the credibility of Hitler's promises and good intentions were at such a spectacularly low ebb, the Polish government rejected the proposals. With such a dubious ally in control of Danzig and astride the Corridor, Poland could easily be shut off from the sea.

Poland at that time was hardly to be reckoned as a jewel in the diadem of freedom. The government, which was totalitarian in spirit if not in structure, had adopted Nazi tactics toward the country's large Jewish population, and had stood with hands greedily held out while Hitler carved up Austria and Czechoslovakia. But with an excellent army and a passable air force, Poland fitted the category of independent states.

In the after-shock of Hitler's assault on Czechoslovakia, Britain and France offered Poland firm guarantees of military assistance if attacked. The treaty, executed in April, prompted Hitler to cry out against "encirclement." Later he renounced Germany's ten-year nonaggression pact with Poland.

And there, for a few months, "the Polish question" rested, deceptively quiescent as is the nature of a delayed fuse.

On July 11 the Senate Foreign Relations Committee, by a vote of 12 to 11, decided to postpone until the following year all consideration for repeal or amendment of the Neutrality Act. The President, in his State of the Union Message in January, had requested and been granted an additional appropriation of $500 million for national defense, plus another $100 million for the stockpiling of strategic materials such as rubber and certain scarce metals. He had pleaded with even greater urgency for revision of the neutrality laws:

The mere fact that we rightly decline to intervene with arms to prevent acts of aggression does not mean that we should act as if there were no aggression at all. Words may be futile, but war is not the only means of commanding a decent respect for the opinions of mankind. There are many measures short of war, but stronger and more effective than mere words, of bringing home to aggressor governments the aggregate sentiments of our own people.

At the very least we can and should avoid any action, or lack of action, which will encourage or assist or build up an aggressor.

Roosevelt was protesting what had already been starkly demonstrated in the case of Ethiopia, Spain, and China—namely, that the rigidities of the Neutrality Act did more harm to the victims of aggression than to the aggressors. He said that as long as American foreign policy was encased in a hands-off straightjacket, the Hitlers of the world were assured that they had nothing more to fear from the United States than moral preachments. Britain and France, were buying planes and armaments in this country during these terminal months of peace, but with the advent of war they would be cut off.

And that war would come soon, Roosevelt was convinced. "Hitler will march in September unless we pass this legislation," Secretary of State Hull told the Foreign Relations Committee. But the senators put no faith in his words. "There will be no war this year," Senator Borah proclaimed at a White House meeting, adding the startling prevarication: "I have my own sources of information, which are superior to those of your State Department." Representative Hamilton Fish of New York, one of the more strident voices of isolationism, told the House that the practical result of abandoning the arms embargo, "would be to make the United States the slaughterhouse and arsenal for all nations, and particularly for Great Britain." A state visit to Washington during the summer by the British King and Queen stirred a suspicion in the breast of Congressman Tinkham that "an entente of military understanding" had been secretly forged as the two ruling families munched hot dogs at a picnic in Hyde Park.[1]

Roosevelt was frustrated not only by the scaremongering of the isolationists (they still had a vociferous if diminishing following) but also by the decline of his political leadership. His prestige had lately suffered a severe buffeting from his fruitless effort to "pack" the Supreme Court. Of the five Democrats on the Foreign Relations Committee who teamed up with Republicans to pigeonhole action on the Neutrality Act, three had been targets of his ill-conceived "purge" in the 1938 election—Senators George, Reynolds, and Van Nuys.

Another shadow loomed on the political landscape in the summer of 1939: Did Roosevelt plan to break all precedent and run for a third term? The President himself had been enigmatically silent on the question. Those to whom his silence was a bad omen (they included Democrats as well as Republicans) believed that a freer hand to manipulate the levers of war and peace would prove an irresistible temptation to Roosevelt to run again.

Congress adjourned on August 5 without changing its mind about the Neutrality Act.

On August 24 the world was stunned by the announcement from Berlin that Germany and the Soviet Union had signed a nonaggression pact. Up to that moment a basic tenet of Nazi doctrine had been its hatred of Communism —a hatred heartily reciprocated by all Reds. That these antipodal ideologies could ever link hands seemed wildly impossible. Most Europeans and Americans had assumed that the Soviet Union, in the event of war between the democracies and Germany, would either remain neutral or side with the demo-

Douglas "Wrong Way" Corrigan. "Isn't this Los Angeles?" "Los Angeles! This is Dublin!"

At left: (top) New Yorkers acclaim Howard Hughes and his four companions for their record around-the-top-of-the-world flight in 3 days and 19 hours. (Middle) Hughes landing in record time. At right: (top) Howard Hughes being received at City Hall by Mayor LaGuardia after his record-shattering flight, 7/14/38. (Below) Douglas "Wrong Way" Corrigan on his arrival at Baldonnel Aerodrome, near Dublin, after he had accomplished in 28 hours and 13 minutes the first "surprise" crossing of the Atlantic. Without official permission, without passport or visa, with no radio and no parachute, he had flown the ocean alone in a 9-year-old, $900 plane which authorities had described as "not airworthy." Total cost of the flight was $62.26, for gas and oil!

BILLY R

Eleanor Holm

OSE *presents...*

A general view of the New York World's Fair, 1939–1940.   Johnny Weissmuller

Deutsches Reich 25 +10
Internationale Automobil- und
Motorrad-Ausstellung Berlin 1939

At left: Mayor LaGuardia and (behind him) Police Commissioner Valentine on inspection tour of Police Detectives, 1938. (Above) Stamp for the Dr. Ferdinand Porsche—designed "Peoples Car" of Adolf Hitler, a forerunner of the modern-day Volkswagen. (Bottom, left) Abe Reles—V.P. of Murder Inc.—1939. (Center) Brenda Frazier, the season's No. 1 debutante, at a Waldorf Society Cotillion, 1938. At right: Shirley Temple—Typewriter Portrait, 1939.

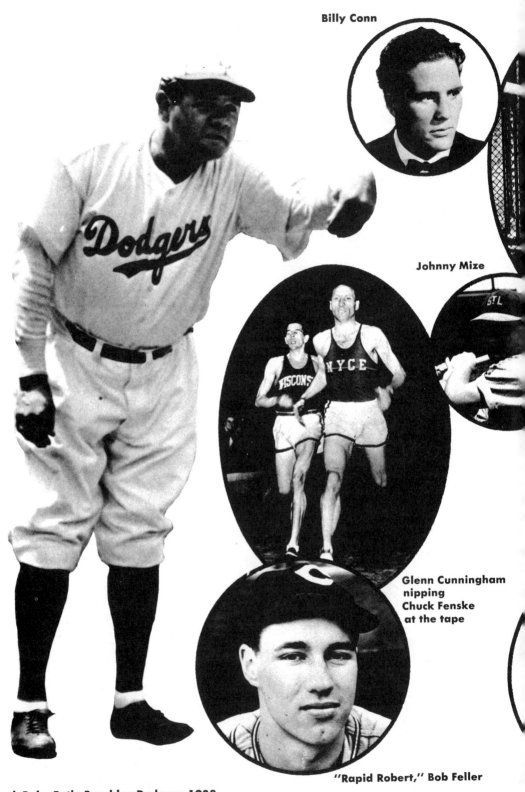

Billy Conn

Johnny Mize

Glenn Cunningham
nipping
Chuck Fenske
at the tape

"Rapid Robert," Bob Feller

Coach Babe Ruth, Brooklyn Dodgers, 1938.

Joe DiMaggio

Willard Hershberger

Babe
Dahlgren

"Big"
Bill Lee

Lou Gehrig

Frank
Cormick

Johnny Vander Meer

Ted Williams

BOXING - WRESTLING - FIGHT FICTION

25 CENTS

MAY

The RING

? LOUIS ● DEMPSEY
WHO WOULD HAVE WON?

Joe Louis—1938 —1939

			Jan. 25—John Henry Lewis		K.O.	1
Feb. 23—Nathan Mann		K.O. 3	Apr. 17—Jack Roper		K.O.	4
April 1—Harry Thomas		K.O. 5	June 27—Tony Galento		K.O.	4
June 22—Max Schmeling		K.O. 1	Sept. 20—Bob Pastor		K.O.	11

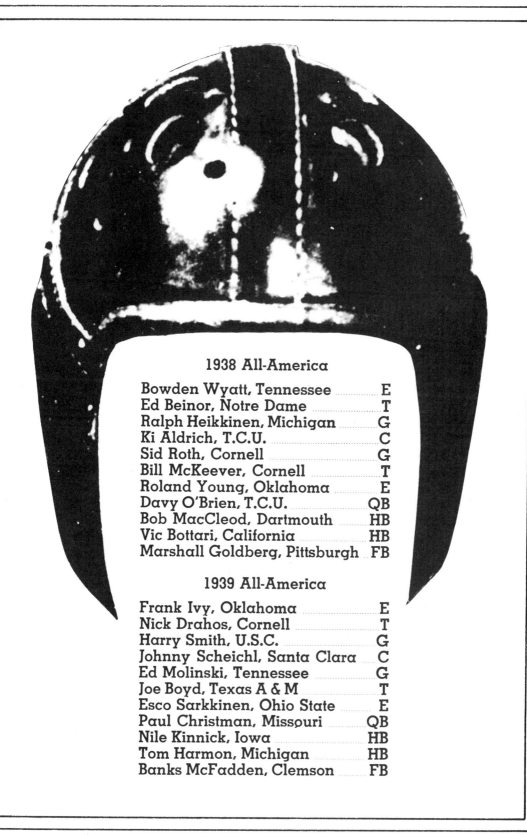

1938 All-America

Bowden Wyatt, Tennessee	E
Ed Beinor, Notre Dame	T
Ralph Heikkinen, Michigan	G
Ki Aldrich, T.C.U.	C
Sid Roth, Cornell	G
Bill McKeever, Cornell	T
Roland Young, Oklahoma	E
Davy O'Brien, T.C.U.	QB
Bob MacCleod, Dartmouth	HB
Vic Bottari, California	HB
Marshall Goldberg, Pittsburgh	FB

1939 All-America

Frank Ivy, Oklahoma	E
Nick Drahos, Cornell	T
Harry Smith, U.S.C.	G
Johnny Scheichl, Santa Clara	C
Ed Molinski, Tennessee	G
Joe Boyd, Texas A & M	T
Esco Sarkkinen, Ohio State	E
Paul Christman, Missouri	QB
Nile Kinnick, Iowa	HB
Tom Harmon, Michigan	HB
Banks McFadden, Clemson	FB

cracies. In fact, a British-French mission, in Moscow at that very time, was seeking to align the Soviet Union in a Peace Front against Hitler. There had been a rough balance of military might and manpower between Germany and her satellites on the one hand, and the countries linked with Britain and France on the other. Now, by a diplomatic lightning bolt, all these comfortable assumptions had been knocked down.

Washington, London, and Paris were not totally unprepared for the blow, for their embassies abroad had sensed that some sort of *rapprochement* between Germany and the Soviet Union was in the works. But the pact itself came as a shock.* The two powers had agreed to "refrain from any act of force" one against the other, and also not to "join any other group of powers" employing such force. That took Russia out of any Peace Front. What was learned later was oven more alarming. By a secret protocol attached to the treaty the two powers agreed to a joint attack on Poland and a division of its territory roughly along the line of the Narew and Vistula rivers, and a partition of the Baltic States. Russia was to get Finland, Estonia, and Latvia, while Germany was awarded Lithuania.

"Stalin and I are the only ones who see the future," an exultant Hitler confided to his General Staff (some of whom were skeptical of the wisdom of his Polish adventure). "So I shall shake hands with Stalin within a few weeks on the common German-Russian border and undertake with him a new distribution of the world." But he added that this would be only a temporary arrangement. At the appropriate time "we shall crush the Soviet Union." [2]

II

In the tense week that followed the signing of the pact, an American diplomat in Berlin wrote: "It is like being in a house where you know someone upstairs is dying. There is relatively little to do and yet the suspense continues unabated." [3] In the United States the radio networks kept their news microphones open on a round-the-clock basis, feeding commentaries and flash bulletins to a news-hungry audience. Day after day *The New York Times* devoted virtually its entire front page, under black headlines, to recording the dips and flutters on the international fever chart: the massing of troops and naval forces from the North Sea to the Danube; the frenetic, mysterious movements of diplomatic agents through chancellery side doors and across frontiers; the emergency meetings of cabinets and war councils; the appeals, warnings, and ultimatums flashing between presidents and prime ministers and dictators. The world seemed to teeter on the rim of a volcano.

And yet, the familiar concerns of a noncrisis world continued to absorb Americans during those late-summer days. New Yorkers wrestled with a milk

*The news also had a shattering effect on the ranks of the radical left. The discovery that their immaculate Socialist fatherland had bedded down with the Beast of Berlin was more than most Marxists and neo-Marxists could stomach. In the United States, communist party hacks stammered their tortured rationalizations. Party leader Earl Browder was rendered speechless for four days. Thousands of converts traded their faith for revulsion, and abandoned the party as well as the creed.

strike. The citizens of Waterbury, Connecticut, hung on the trial of their mayor, charged with a million-dollar fraud of city funds. In San Francisco, longshoreman Harry Bridges, charged with being an undesirable alien (communist), fought deportation to his native Australia. The east coast sweltered in a heat wave. A Gallup Poll showed that Vice President Garner was within a fraction of a percentage point of catching up with Roosevelt's popularity for the next Democratic presidential nomination. Down in New Orleans a federal grand jury indicted Abe Shushan, close political ally of the late Huey Long, for mail fraud. Fashion expert Kathleen Cannell reported from Paris: "Fabulous jewels play an important part in Paris winter fashions. Bigger and better jewelry, and more of it, is literally the style slogan of the season." At Yankee Stadium 29,088 fight fans turned up one night to see Lou Ambers win back his lightweight championship in a bruising 15-round match with Henry Armstrong. Moviegoers were introduced to the delightful revelry of Judy Garland, Mickey Rooney, and Ray Bolger in *The Wizard of Oz.* John Steinbeck's novel *The Grapes of Wrath* was a smash hit with more than 200,000 copies in print, and John Gunther's *Inside Asia* rode at the top of the nonfiction best-seller lists. The Waldorf's "Starlight Roof" offered a double attraction: dance music by both Hal Kemp and Xavier Cugat (cover $1 after 11 o'clock). In Martin's Creek, Pennsylvania, émigré Aleksandr Kerensky, a leading figure in the overthrow of the Russian Czarist regime in 1917 and a fugitive from the Communist dictatorship, was married by a justice of the peace to Lydia Ellen Tritton, an Australian. The twenty millionth customer clicked through the turnstiles at the New York World's Fair. Readers of the New York society pages (on what would prove to be the last Sunday before D-Day) learned that "Tennis Week Draws Many To Newport," " 'Little Season' on North Shore Lists Many Bridals and Debut Fetes," "Mrs. S. M. Rinehart Hostess at Bar Harbor," "Parties at Saratoga Springs Mark Fourth Racing Saturday."

In such fashion did an age of innocence persist up to the moment of its extinction.[4]

<h1 style="text-align:center">III</h1>

How long ago was Munich? Only a year? It had not been a year of days or seasons but of an inexorable procession of nightmares. Hitler had condemned the Jews of Central Europe to extinction. He and his Axis partner Mussolini had collaborated in the destruction of the Spanish republic. He had consummated the total conquest of Czechoslovakia. He had flung a galling challenge to Poland and its allies. He had cynically bought off his enemy Russia, and had observed with scornful satisfaction the impotence of the democracies, including the United States, to lay a restraining hand on him. The ogre of these nightmares was no reckless opportunist. Adolf Hitler was a mad genius in whose pathological conceit there had formed a strategy for the domination of Europe, perhaps of the world. From official documents captured after the war we know that as far back as May 1939 he had told his Chiefs of Staff that he intended to destroy Poland and then to move on against England and France:

Danzig is not the subject of the dispute at all. It is a question of expanding our living space and of securing our food supplies. There is, therefore, no question of sparing Poland, and we are left with the decision to attack Poland at the first suitable opportunity. . . . A German-Polish conflict will [probably] lead to war in the West, then the fight must be primarily against England and France. . . . I doubt the possibility of a peaceful settlement with England . . . it will be a life-or-death struggle. The government must be prepared for a war of ten or fifteen years duration.[5]

At the close of August 1939, a scant year after Munich, the days of peace were running out, fast.

Secure in the knowledge that Russia would not upset his plans, Hitler deployed the bulk of his army along the Polish frontier, sent his warplanes on provocative scouting missions across the border, stepped up his demands for the immediate return of Danzig, and loosed a propaganda barrage charging Polish "atrocities" against Germans living in the Corridor. Polish guns looked out at the Germans across the barricades, Polish planes kept surveillance over the German aerial trespassers, and the Mayor of Warsaw helped dig trenches in the city's parks. The dread of war was everywhere manifest. In London and Paris tens of thousands of civilians streamed out to the countryside in search of safety. Sirens wailed at unexpected hours for air-raid drills, and practice blackouts were held. France closed her border with Germany, suspended telecommunications, and imposed press censorship. The treasures of the British Museum and Westminster Abbey were crated and hauled to safety. Sandbags were piled around London's public buildings.

President Roosevelt cut short a vacation cruise and rushed back to Washington on August 23. Welles had told him the crisis probably would erupt within a matter of days. In a last desperate gesture, the President dispatched notes to Hitler and Polish President Mosciki urging them to refrain from using military force in settling their disputes. To King Victor Emmanuel of Italy he sent a note seeking endorsement of his appeal.[6] (The Italians had kept aloof from the tempest swirling about their Axis partner.) Hitler rejected the proposal angrily without making a formal reply. On the 25th Britain and France proclaimed the signing of a new and firmer commitment to come to Poland's aid in case of attack, and on the 27th they sent special emissaries to Berlin to impress on the German Chancellor the irrevocability of their pledge. There is some evidence that this new toughness by the democracies disrupted Hitler's timetable briefly; that he had been poised to strike on the 27th. At all events, he agreed to receive the Polish Ambassador on the 29th. When the Ambassador called, Hitler presented him with an ultimatum for the immediate and unconditional surrender of Danzig and for agreement to a plebiscite on the Corridor.

The Poles were denied an opportunity to reply. Hitler had already reached his momentous decision. At a few minutes before 5 o'clock the next morning—Friday, September 1, 1939—German planes swooped out of the morning mists to dump bombs and machine-gun fire on the cities of Gdynia, Cracow, and

Katowice, and German troops and tanks smashed across the Polish border from Slovakia on the south and East Prussia in the west.

In the United States millions had been startled out of their beds before dawn by newsboys shouting "Extra! Extra! The war has started!" They turned on their radios and heard the rhythmic chants of *Sieg heil!* as Hitler marched into Berlin's Kroll Opera House, to which he had summoned an emergency morning session of the Reichstag. His voice pitched to hysterical frenzy, he spat out the catalogue of his grievances against Poland and her treaty partners and promised war to the finish. "I have put on my old soldier's coat," he cried, "and I will not take it off until we win victory for the Fatherland!"

Sieg heil! Sieg heil! came the answering chorus.

For Britain and France the die had been cast. There would be no pulling back, no wringing of hands, no offers of appeasement. They put their fleets on war alert, issued ammunition to soldiers, loaded planes with bombs, and took precautions against air raid attacks on cities. Late on Saturday they sent off to Berlin a stiff ultimatum: Withdraw from Poland within twelve hours or face war with its allies. The deadline was 11 A.M. Sunday, September 3 (6 A.M. New York time). At ten minutes past the zero hour, millions of Americans who sat glued to their radios heard above the wavering distortions of the short-wave the sad but firm voice of Neville Chamberlain:

I am speaking to you from the Cabinet Room at 10 Downing Street. This morning the British Ambassador to Berlin handed the German government the final note stating that unless we heard from them by 11 o'clock that they were prepared at once to withdraw their troops from Poland, a state of war would exist between us.

I have to tell you now that no such understanding was received and consequently this country is at war with Germany.

The days of peace had run out. The Second World War had begun.

"All the News That's Fit to Print."

The New Y[...]

Copyright, 19[..] by The

VOL. LXXXVIII...No. 29,805.

Entered as Second-Class Matter,
Postoffice, New York, N. Y.

NEW YORK, FRIDAY

GERMAN ARMY A[...]
CITIES BOMBED, [...]
DANZIG IS ACCF[...]

BRITISH MOBILIZING

Bulletin[...]

[...]LITIES BEG[...]

NAZIS SEIZE AUSTRIA AFTER HITLER ULTIMATUM; GERMAN TROOPS ENTER, INVITED BY VIENNA; SEYSS-INQUART CHANCELLOR; LONDON PROTESTS

Reports Germ[...]
Offensive Moving
Three Objectives

[...], Friday, Sept. 1 (AP).—The H[...]
said today that official French dispatche[...]
indicated that "the Reich began hostilitie[...]
morning."

The agency also reported that the Po[...]
had announced that "Germany violated the[...]
[...]
[...] of pretended violatio[...]

PARLIAMENT IS CONVOKED

Midnight Meeting [...]
Ministers—Nego[...]

FOUR POWERS REACH A PEACEABLE AGREEMENT; GERMANS TO ENTER SUDETEN AREA TOMORROW AND WILL COMPLETE OCCUPATION IN TEN DAYS

NEW RULER OF THE WORLD
OCTOBER 35, 1938

GERMANY A[...]
BIND EACH[...]
HITLER R[...]

rk Times.

Times Company.

THREE CENTS NEW YORK CITY and Vicinity | FOUR CENTS Elsewhere Except in 7th and 8th Postal Zones.

EXTRA
Partly cloudy and somewhat warmer today. Tomorrow generally fair with moderate temperatures.

Temperatures Yesterday—Max., 67 ; Min., 61

TACKS POLAND;
RT BLOCKADED;
PTED INTO REICH

EE CITY IS SEIZED

ster Notifies Hitler of
rder Putting Danzig
Into the Reich

Hitler Acts Against Poland

HITLER GIVES WORD

In a Proclamation He

USSIA SIGN 10-YEAR NON-AGGRESSION PACT;
HER NOT TO AID OPPONENTS IN WAR ACTS;
FFS LONDON; BRITAIN AND FRANCE MOBILIZE

SOURCE NOTES

A principal source material used in the preparation of this work has been the daily and periodical press of the period of the thirties, with chief reliance on the microfilm files of *The New York Times*. So pervasive is the occurrence of this material throughout the text that it is not feasible to cite it except in those instances where it is felt that a reader may wish to consult the source himself.

The many books and individual authorities cited are in every instance those which the author has consulted directly. There is an immense literature covering almost every facet of the decade, but no effort has been made here to present a representative bibliography beyond the limitation mentioned above. More comprehensive listings are to be found in such bibliographic works as *The Harvard Guide to American History*.

Chapter 2

[1] John Kenneth Galbraith, *The Great Crash: 1929* (Houghton Mifflin, 1955), p. 179.

[2] Harold U. Faulkner, *American Political and Social History* (Appleton-Century, 1952), p. 736.

[3] *Statistical Abstract of the United States, 1935* (Government Printing Office), p. 350.

[4] Galbraith, *op. cit.*, p. 71, and *Statistical Abstract, op. cit.*, pp. 285-86.

[5] The stock market quotations are from Frederick Lewis Allen, *Since Yesterday* (Bantam, 1961), p. 264.

[6] Galbraith, *op. cit.*, p. 118.

Chapter 3

[1] The figures used are drawn principally from *Statistical Abstract of the United States, 1935* (Government Printing Office).

[2] There are no precise figures for average family income prior to 1935. The figures used here are based on estimates prepared by the National Resources Committee in 1940. Other sources consulted for this chapter include John Kenneth Galbraith, *The Great Crash: 1929* (Houghton Mifflin, 1955); Arthur M. Schlesinger, Jr., *The Crisis of the Old Order* (Hougton Mifflin, 1957); Broadus Mitchell, *Depression Decade* (Holt, Rinehart, 1966); *World Almanac* for years 1931, 1932, 1933 (*New York World-Telegram*).

Chapter 4

[1] James A. Farley, *Behind the Ballots* (Harcourt, Brace, 1938), p. 63.

[2] *Ibid.*, p. 83.

[3] *Ibid.*, pp. 116–19.

[4] *Ibid.*, p. 134.

[5] *Ibid.*, pp. 147–48; *The New York Times*, July 1, 1932.

[6] *The New York Times*, July 2, 1932. Other sources consulted for this chapter include Raymond Moley, *After Seven Years* (Harper, 1939), chaps. I and II; Samuel I. Rosenman, *Working With Roosevelt* (Harper, 1952), chaps. V and VI; Arthur M. Schlesinger, Jr, *Crisis of the Old Order* (Houghton, Mifflin, 1957), chap. V.

Chapter 6

[1] Frances Perkins, *The Roosevelt I Knew* (Viking, 1946), pp. 139–40.

Chapter 7

[1] The mood and color of the Hundred Days can be gleaned from many sources, including contemporary issues of *The New York Times* and of such periodicals as *Literary Digest, Liberty, Time, Collier's*. One of the best first-hand accounts is Ernest K. Lindley's *The Roosevelt Revolution* (Viking, 1933).

[2] Raymond Moley, *After Seven Years* (Harper, 1939), pp. 18–24; Lindley, *op. cit.*, p. 309.

[3] Sketches of the early New Dealers are found in books by Raymond Moley and Ernest Lindley; also in Jay Franklin Carter, "The Unofficial Observer," *The New Dealers* (Literary Guild, 1934); Samuel I. Rosenman, *Working With Roosevelt* (Harper, 1952); Frances Perkins, *The Roosevelt I Knew* (Viking, 1946); Arthur Schlesinger, Jr., *The Coming of the New Deal* (Houghton Mifflin, 1958).

[4] William Manchester, "The Great Bank Holiday," *Holiday*, Feb. 1960, p. 60.

[5] Moley, *op. cit.*, p. 149.

[6] Lindley, *op. cit.*, p. 82

[7] Details of how the public coped with the bank holiday are abundantly described in Manchester, *op. cit.*, and in contemporary issues of daily newspapers and periodicals.

[8] The banking crisis is covered in detail in Moley, *After Seven Years*, chap. 5, and Moley, *The First New Deal* (Harcourt, Brace, 1966), chaps. 8–15; Broadus Mitchell, *The Depression Decade* (Holt, Rinehart, 1966), chaps. 4 and 5; John T. Flynn, *The Roosevelt Myth* (Devin-Adair Co., 1948), book I, chap. 3; Lindley, *op. cit.*, chap. 3; *Editorial Research Reports*, vol. II, no. 6, April 12, 1933; and contemporary issues of *The New York Times*.

[9] Lindley, *op. cit.*, pp. 87–91; Moley, *After Seven Years*, p. 153.

Chapter 8

[1] "Stock Exchange Practices," Senate Banking and Currency Committee Hearings, 72d Cong., 2d sess., 1933, vols. I–VI, for Mitchell testimony; same, 73d Cong., 1st sess., 1933. vols. I–II for Morgan testimony and vol. V for Wiggin testimony; "The National City Bank Scandal," *The Nation*. March 8, 1933; John T. Flynn, "Other People's Money," *New Republic*, June 7, 1933.

[2] Moley, *The First New Deal*, chap. 26; Lindley, *The Roosevelt Revolution*, pp. 135–46; "Closed Banks and Banking Reform," *Editorial Research Reports*, vol. II, 1933, no. 6. Figures on bank failures from *Statistical Abstract of the United States, 1940* (Government Printing Office), p. 266.

[3] "Securities Act of 1933," House Interstate and Foreign Commerce Committee Report, 73d Cong., 1st sess,, 1933, p. 2.

[4] Felix Frankfurter, "The Federal Securities Act," *Fortune,* August 1933; Ralph F. DeBets, *The New Deal's SEC* (Columbia University Press, 1934); Raymond Moley, *After Seven Years,* pp. 176–84, and *The First New Deal,* chap. 26; "The Capital Market and the Securities Act," *Editorial Research Reports,* vol. II, 1933, no. 11.

[5] Jay Franklin Carter, "The Unofficial Observer," *The New Dealers* (Literary Guild, 1934), p. 321.

[6] DeBets, *op. cit.*; Schlesinger, *The Coming of the New Deal,* chap. 29; Moley, *After Seven Years,* pp. 284-90; Mitchell, *The Depression Decade,* chap. 5; "A 25-Year Summary of the SEC: 1934-1959" (Securities and Exchange Commission).

[7] "Federal Home Loans and Housing," *Editorial Research Reports,* vol. II, 1933, no. 19.

[8] *Ibid.,* p. 357; *Statistical Abstract of the United States, 1935* (Government Printing Office), p. 260; William E. Leutchtenburg, *Franklin Roosevelt and the New Deal* (Harper,1963), p. 165.

[9] HOLC Final Report to Congress, March 1, 1952 (Home Loan Bank Board).

[10] Moley, *After Seven Years,* pp. 156-57.

[11] Lindley, *op. cit.,* pp. 116-24; Schlesinger, *op. cit.,* pp. 195-203; Mitchell, *op. cit.,* pp. 136-39; Burton K. Wheeler, *Yankee From the West* (Doubleday,1962), pp. 302–304.

[12] As quoted by Moley, *The First New Deal,* p. 467.

[13] Mitchell, *op. cit.,* p. 140.

[14] As reported in *The New York Times,* Oct 23, 1933.

[15] Mitchell, *op. cit.,* p. 150.

[16] Extended treatment of the monetary policies during this period is found in Moley, *After Seven Years,* chap. VII, and *The First New Deal,* chaps. 32–38; Mitchell, *op. cit.,* chaps. IV–V; Schlesinger, *op. cit..* chaps. 12–14; James P. Warburg, *The Money Muddle* (Knopf, 1934); and in contemporary issues of *The New York Times,* especially in Section VII of the Sunday editions.

Chapter 9

[1] James A. Farley, *Jim Farley's Story* (Whittlesey House, 1948), p. 46.

Chapter 10

[1] Frances Perkins, *The Roosevelt I Knew* (Viking, 1946), p. 197.

[2] Rexford G. Tugwell, *The Industrial Discipline* (Columbia University Press, 1932); excerpt appears in *The New York Times,* May 4, 1933.

[3] Broadus Mitchell, *Depression Decade* (Holt, Rinehart, 1966), statistical appendix.

[4] Hugh S. Johnson, *The Blue Eagle From Egg to Earth* (Doubleday, 1935), preface.

[5] *The New York Times,* June 17, 1935.

[6] Johnson, *op. cit.,* preface.

[7] *Ibid.,* p. 204.

[8] *Time,* Sept. 25, 1933, p. 12; *Boston Herald,* Sept. 14, 1933.

[9] Franklin D. Roosevelt Library, NRA file.

[10] "Operations of the National Industrial Recovery Administration," report of the Research and Planning Division, 1935, in the Library of Congress.

[11] "Government and Business After the Depression," *Editorial Research Reports,* vol. I, 1934, p. 23.

[12] Annual Report, 1933, National Association of Manufacturers, p. 21.

[13] *The New York Times,* March 8, 1934.

14 Harold L. Ickes, *Secret Diary: The First Thousand Days* (Simon and Schuster, 1953), p. 195.

15 Johnson, *op. cit.,* p. 397.

16 Perkins, *op. cit.,* p. 252.

17 *The New York Times,* May 28, 1935.

18 *Historical Statistics of the United States, 1940* (Government Printing Office). Other sources consulted for this chapter include Raymond Moley, *The First New Deal* (Harcourt, Brace, 1966); Donald R. Richberg, *My Hero* (Putnam's, 1954); Jay Franklin Carter, "Unofficial Observer," *The New Dealers* (Literary Guild, 1934).

Chapter 11

1 *The New York Times,* July 29 1933; Arthur Schlesinger, Jr., *Coming of the New Deal* (Houghton Mifflin, 1958), p. 63; Broadus Mitchell, *Depression Decade* (Holt, 1966), p. 179.

2 Raymond Moley, *First New Deal* (Harcourt, 1966); *A Century of Service: The First 100 Years of the U.S. Department of Agriculture* (U.S. Department of Agriculture, 1963); *Historical Statistics of the U.S., 1789–1945* (Government Printing Office); *Editorial Research Reports,* Aug. 28, 1933.

3 Schlesinger, *op. cit.,* p. 39.

4 Rexford G. Tugwell, Diary 1932-34 (manuscript) in Franklin D. Roosevelt Library.

5 Biographical and related material on Wallace, Tugwell, and Peek is drawn from a variety of sources, including Russell Lord, *The Wallaces of Iowa* (Houghton, 1947); Schlesinger, *op. cit.,* chaps. 2 and 3; Ernest K. Lindley, *The Roosevelt Revolution* (Viking, 1933), chaps. 9 and 10; John F. Carter, *The New Dealers* (Literary Guid, 1934); Moley, *The First New Deal,* and *After Seven Years* (Harper, 1939).

6 Whittaker Chambers, *Witness* (Random House, 1952), p. 334.

7 Edwin G. Nourse, *Three Years of the AAA* (Brookings Institution, 1937) p. 279; Carter, *op. cit.,* p. 75.

8 Hickock, FERA Narrative Field Reports, Hopkins papers, Franklin Delano Roosevelt Library.

9 "The Sharecropper: His Plight Revealed," *The New York Times Magazine,* Apr. 15, 1935; Paul R. Conkin, *Tomorrow A New World* (Cornell University Press, 1959) pp. 184-213; William E. Leuchtenburg, *Franklin D. Roosevelt and the New Deal* (Harper, 1963), pp. 137-42. No history of the STFU has been published. Norman Thomas' role in its activities was described to me in an interview by John Herling, the labor columnist, who was a participant at the time.

10 William E. Brooks in *The Atlantic,* Feb., 1935.

11 Arthurdale is described in some detail in Conkin, *op. cit.,* and in articles in *The New York Times, Time, Saturday Evening Post,* etc., between 1935 and 1937. James Machin, whom I interviewed in December 1967, is a representative in northern West Virginia for the Farmers Home Administration.

12 Nourse, *op. cit.,* pp. 286-89; Moley, *Century of Service,* chap. 8.

13 Basil Rauch, *History of the New Deal* (McClelland, 1944); Moley, *Century of Service.*

14 *World Almanac 1941,* p. 287; Mitchell, *op. cit.,* p. 215.

Chapter 12

1 Federal Works Agency, *Summary of Relief and Federal Work Pro-*

gram Statistics, (Government Printing Office, 1941).

[2] Harry L. Hopkins, *Spending To Save* (Norton, 1936), p. 59.

[3] Raymond Moley, *The First New Deal* (Harcourt, 1966); Searle F. Charles, *Minister of Relief* (Syracuse University Press, 1963); Arthur M. Schlesinger, Jr., *Coming of the New Deal* (Houghton Mifflin, 1958).

[4] Robert E. Sherwood, *Roosevelt and Hopkins* (Harper, 1948), p. 60.

[5] Jay Franklin Carter, "Unofficial Observer," *The New Dealers* (Literary Guild, 1934), p. 181.

[6] An interesting profile of Hopkins was carried in *Fortune,* July 1935. The author of this book worked in the WPA Press Section between 1936 and 1938 and had a reasonably close-up view of Hopkins and his principal aides and their operation.

[7] Hopkins, *op. cit.,* p. 108.

[8] Harold L. Ickes, *Secret Diary: The First Thousand Days* (Simon and Schuster, 1953), p. 115.

[9] Sherwood, *op. cit.,* pp. 51-52.

[10] *The New York Times,* Nov. 26, 1933, and proximate issues of *Literary Digest* and *Time.*

[11] The quotation from *Literary Digest* is from the issue of March 21, 1934. The Hopkins quotation is from *Spending to Save,* pp. 123-25. Some interesting insights into the social impact of CWA is contained in the field reports of Lorena Hickock to Hopkins, contained in the Hopkins papers at the Franklin Delano Roosevelt Library.

[12] Sherwood, *op. cit.,* p. 65.

[13] The quotes are from Charles, *op. cit.,* p. 114, and Ickes, *op. cit.,* p. 434.

[14] Details of the Works Agency setup are described in *Editorial Research Reports,* vol. II, 1935, p. 271. The Ickes *Diary* for this period is sprinkled with illuminating comments on the bureaucratic infighting that was involved.

[15] Federal Works Agency, *op. cit.*

[16] WPA "scandals" are fully explored in published hearings of the House and Senate appropriations committees, and of the House Un-American Activities Committee during the period 1937-39. Many detailed refutations are contained in the file of WPA press releases deposited with the Library of Congress.

[17] Sherwood, *op. cit.,* p. 68.

[18] There is a regrettable lack of published materials on the WPA professional projects—art, theater, writing, and music. One useful source on the theater project is Hallie Flanagan's *Arena* (Bloom, 1965, 2d ed.). The Federal Music Project is treated briefly in two books by John T. Howard, *Our Contemporary Composers* (Crowell, 1941) and *Our American Music* (Crowell, 1954). The artists and the writers left only their works, no histories.

[19] *America Builds: The Record of the Public Works Administration* (Government Printing Office, 1939).

[20] Federal Works Agency, *op. cit.;* Charles, *op. cit.,* pp. 152–54; Mitchell, *op. cit.,* pp. 329–31. A more comprehensive account of the NYA is contained in Betty and Ernest K Lindley's *A New Deal for Youth* (Viking, 1938).

[21] Perkins, *op. cit.,* pp. 282–83.

[22] *The New York Times,* Jan. 19, 1935.

[23] Perkins, *op. cit.,* chapter XXIII; Schlesinger, *op. cit.,* chapter 18; Mitchell, *op. cit.,* pp. 306-308; *Editorial Research Reports,* vol. II, 1936, No. 12.

Chapter 13

[1] James A. Farley, *Jim Farley's Story* (Whittlesey House, 1948), p. 51.

[2] Long's and Coughlin's careers are reconstructed here primarily from news accounts in *The New York Times, Time* magazine, issues of June 24, 1935, and Aug. 16, 1935, and "Paradox in Pajamas," *Saturday Evening Post,* Oct. 8, 1935.

[3] The account of the Ethiopian war is based on contemporary news sources and Martin Gilbert, *The European Powers, 1900–1945* (New American Library, 1965).

[4] Most of the statistical data used here was obtained from *Handbook of Aviation Statistics* (Civil Aeronautics Board, 1962) and *Aircraft Yearbook 1941* (Aeronautical Chamber of Commerce). The state of aviation during the latter part of the decade of the thirties is excellently portrayed in *Fortune,* March 1941.

[5] In addition to contemporary news accounts, material used here was obtained from *Monthly Weather Reports* (U.S. Weather Bureau), vols. 64, 65, and 66; annual and special disaster reports for the years 1934 through 1938 of the American Red Cross and "Soil Conservation and Agricultural Adjustment," *Editorial Research Reports,* Jan. 27, 1936.

[6] Don Whitehead *The FBI Story* (Random House, 1956); annual reports of the Federal Bureau of Investigation for 1935 and 1940; *Editorial Research Reports,* July 10, 1934.

[7] *Digest of Book Reviews—1936* (H. W. Wilson, 1937); *Publishers' Weekly* (R. R. Bowker), June 27, 1936, May 1, 1937.

[8] The descriptive quotation on pp. 564-65 is from the editorial page column of Russell Baker, *The New York Times,* March 24, 1968. Other sources include *Railway Age,* March 17, 1934, Jan. 2, 1937, Jan. 4, 1941; *Forbes Magazine,* Dec. 15, 1936; *Time,* May 13, 1935; *Statistical Abstract of the U.S., 1940* (Government Printing Office).

[10] Much data was supplied directly to the author by the U.S. Public Health Service. The origins of the National Foundation for Infantile Paralysis is contained in a pamphlet, *Four Million Dimes* (National Foundation, 1955).

Chapter 14

[1] Leonard Myers, Music Editor, CBS, in letter to author, June 10, 1968.

[2] The cultural landscape of the 1920s and 1930s has been thoroughly explored by many scholars. The works I have found most useful to supplement my own impressions include Dixon Wecter, *Age of the Great Depression* (Macmillan, 1948); Robert S. and Helen M. Lynd, *Middletown in Transition* (Harcourt, Brace, 1937); Charles and Mary Beard, *America in Midpassage* (Macmillan, 1939); Frederick Lewis Allen, *Only Yesterday* (Harper, 1931) and *Since Yesterday* (Harper, 1940). Throughout this chapter as in most others, I have relied heavily for contemporary color and detail on *The New York Times* and such periodicals as *Time* and *Literary Digest.*

[3] Howard Taubman, *Making of the American Theater* (Coward-McCann, 1965), p. 211.

[4] *Ibid.,* p. 231.

[5] In addition to drawing heavily on *Making of the American Theater,* I am much indebted to Mr. Taubman for a long interview in which he gave me the benefit of his professional experience over a quarter of a century as a drama and music critic. I have also found useful David C. Blum, *A Pictorial History of the American Theater* (Chilton, 1960), and Hallie Flanagan, *Arena: The History of the Federal Theater Project* (Benjamin Blom, 1965, 2d ed.).

[6] *The New York Times Book Review,* Dec. 13, 1964.

[7] Alfred Kazin, *On Native Grounds* (Harcourt, 1942), pp. 368, 485.

[8] *Ibid.,* p. 502.

[9] *The First 40 Years,* issued as a supplement to the Book-of-the-Month-Club News, April 1966.

[10] Two outstanding works on the literature of the 1930s on which the author has drawn heavily are Kazin (*op. cit.*) and Harvey Swados, *The American Writer and the Great Depression* (Bobbs-Merrill, 1968). Much useful material was also found in chap. 10 of Allen's *Since Yesterday, op. cit.*; Daniel Aaron, *Writers on the Left* (Harcourt, 1961), and the annual volumes of *Digest of Book Reviews* (Wilson). There is no concise history of the FWP and the account here is pieced together from a variety of sources, including contemporary articles in such periodicals as *Saturday Review of Literature, Publishers' Weekly,* and *Contemporary Review.*

[11] John I. H. Baur, *Revolution and Tradition in Modern American Art* (Harvard University Press, 1951), p. 8.

[12] *Ibid.,* p. 133. Some interesting examples of art modes that were popular during the 1930s are to be found in Marjorie Longley, Louis Silverstein and Samuel A. Tower, *America's Taste: 1851–1959* (Simon & Schuster, 1960). The government's role as art patron is treated in Ralph Purcell, *Government and Art* (Public Affairs Press, 1956), and by Holger Cahill in his extensive introduction to the *Index of American Design.* Prof. Frances V. O'Connor of the University of Maryland, director of the research project Federal Support for the Visual Arts, gave me valuable assistance through a memorandum and several reprints of articles on the FWAP.

[13] John T. Howard, *Our Contemporary Composers* (Crowell, 1941) and *Our American Music* (Crowell, 1954); "The WPA and the American Composer," article by Ashley Pettis in *The Musical Quarterly,* Jan. 1940. There is no coherent record extant of the FMP.

Chapter 15

[1] The subject of this case history chooses to be anonymous, but the author of this book, being a lifelong acquaintance, can attest that the subject's account is authentic.

[2] Leo C. Rosten, *Hollywood* (Harcourt, Brace, 1941), pp. 358–60.

[3] In addition to Rosten, *op. cit.,* the movie lore of the thirties is generously covered by Bosley Crowther, *The Great Films: Fifty Golden Years of Motion Pictures* (Putnam's, 1967); William K. Everson, *The American Movie* (Atheneum, 1963); Deems Taylor, *A Pictorial History of the Movies* (Simon & Schuster, 1950).

[4] Irving Settel, *A Pictorial History of Radio* (Grosset & Dunlap, 1960) seems to be the only book devoted exclusively to the subject. It gets limited but quite respectful attention in Dixon Wecter, *Age of the Great Depression* (Macmillan, 1948) and Frederick Lewis Allen, *Since Yesterday* (Harper, 1940). The best of all sources, however, is listening to some of the early programs. Highly recommended for this purpose is an album of six long-playing phonograph records, *Golden Memories of Radio,* with narration by Jack Benny, produced by the Longines Symphonette Society, Larchmont, N. Y.

[5] Sigmund Spaeth, *Popular Music in America* (Random House, 1948), pp. 415, 477.

[6] I am greatly indebted to Edward H. Kelly of the Victor Record Division, Radio Corporation of America, for supplying me with an excellent selection of recorded popular music of the thirties, as well as much useful information on the subject from his own experience.

[7] Theodore Peterson, *Magazines in the Twentieth Century* (University of Illinois Press, 1950). Much of the material on the Macfadden empire was drawn from *Time,* Sept. 21, 1936.

[8] *Collected Edition of Heywood Broun,* edited by Heywood Hale Broun (Harcourt, Brace, 1941), p. 306.

[9] This MacIntyre sampler is composed of excerpts from two of his columns, one appearing in the *New York American,* June 1, 1936, the other quoted in *Time,* July 8, 1935.

[10] Robert S. and Helen M. Lynd, *Middletown in Transition* (Harcourt, Brace, 1937), extracted from pp. 374, 379.

[11] *Statistical Abstract of the United States, 1940* (Government Printing Office), p. 108.

Chapter 16

[1] *Roosevelt and Frankfurter: Their Correspondence, 1928-1945,* annotated by Max Freedman (Atlantic-Little Brown, 1967), p. 351.

[2] The transition from the First to the Second New Deal is treated at some length in Raymond Moley, *The First New Deal* (Harcourt, Brace, 1966), chap. 2; Arthur M. Schlesinger, Jr., *The Politics of Upheaval* (Houghton, Mifflin, 1960), chaps. 21, 22; William E. Leuchtenburg, *Franklin D. Roosevelt and the New Deal* (Harper & Row, 1963), chap. 7, and James A. Farley, *Jim Farley's Story* (Whittlesey House, 1948), *passim.*

[3] As quoted in *The New York Times,* Jan. 26, 1936.

[4] The 1936 election was, of course, reported in great detail in the daily and periodical press, from which most of the material in this chapter was taken. Valuable insights into the Democratic campaign are to be found in Farley, *op. cit.;* Samuel I. Rosenman, *Working With Roosevelt* (Harper, 1952), chaps. VII, VIII; Moley, *op. cit.,* chap. 43 and *After Seven Years* (Harper, 1939), chaps. IX, X; Harold L. Ickes, *Secret Diary: The First Thousand Days* (Simon & Schuster, 1953); Stefan Lorant, *The Presidency* (Macmillan, 1951), pp. 597-613.

[5] The Roosevelt Coalition is treated at some length in James MacGregor Burns, *The Deadlock of Democracy* (Prentice-Hall, 1963), chaps. 7, 10, 11; Schlesinger, *op. cit.,* chap 23, and Farley, *op. cit.*

[6] *Roosevelt and Frankfurter,* pp. 381, 272.

[7] *Ibid.,* p. 377.

[8] Joseph Alsop and Turner Catledge, *The 168 Days* (Doubleday, 1938), p. 64. This is the best account extant of the great court fight by two outstanding Washington reporters of the period.

[9] *Ibid.,* p. 125; Burton K. Wheeler (with Paul F. Healy), *Yankee From the West* (Doubleday, 1962), chap. 15.

[10] *Roosevelt and Frankfurter,* p. 399.

[11] Alsop and Catledge, *op. cit.,* p. 232.

[12] Farley, *op. cit.,* p. 137.

[13] The election campaign and attempted "purge" of 1938 are reconstructed here principally from press reports and from Farley, *op. cit.;* Rosenman, *op. cit.* and Thomas L. Stokes, *Chip Off My Shoulder* (Princeton University Press, 1940).

Chapter 17

[1] See Irving Bernstein, *The Lean Years, A History of the American Worker 1920-1933* (Penguin, 1966). Membership figures for A.F.L. are from *Handbook of Labor Statistics, 1968* (U.S. Department of Labor).

[2] Frances Perkins, *The Roosevelt I Knew* (Viking, 1946), chaps. 16, 17; Raymond Moley, *After Seven Years* (Harper, 1939), chap. VI.

[3] Figures on union growth are from *Handbook of Labor Statistics, op.*

cit., p. 360, and Broadus Mitchell, *Depression Decade* (Holt, Rinehart, 1966), p. 272.

[4] This early fight for union recognition is graphically told in "The Industrial War," *Fortune,* Nov. 1937. A highlight of the labor conflict of the mid-thirties was the investigation of industrial espionage by a special Senate Committee on Civil Rights headed by Sen. Robert M. LaFollette, Jr. of Wisconsin. Some of the more dramatic disclosures are contained in Leo Huberman, *The Labor Spy Racket* (Modern Age, 1937).

[5] *Fortune,* Nov. 1937.

[6] "Analysis of Strikes in 1937," bulletin of the U.S. Department of Labor, May 1938.

[7] For an analysis of labor legislation during this period see Milton Derber and Edwin Young, *Labor and the New Deal* (University of Wisconsin Press, 1957).

Chapter 18

[1] The genesis of isolationism and its hold on liberals and intellectuals is well described in Robert E. Sherwood, *Roosevelt and Hopkins* (Harper, 1948), chap. V. See also William S. Langer and S. Everett Gleason, *The Challenge to Isolation, 1937-1940* (Harper 1952), chap. I; Allan Nevins, *The New Deal and World Affairs* (Yale University Press, 1950), chap. III.

[2] Winston S. Churchill, *The Gathering Storm* (Houghton Mifflin, 1948), p. 254.

[3] Some of the considerations that went into the preparation of this speech and comments on the reaction to it are contained in Samuel I. Rosenman, *Working With Roosevelt* (Harper, 1952), pp. 163–68.

[4] Council on Foreign Relations, *United States in World Affairs—1938* (Harper, 1939), p. 20.

[5] *Ibid.,* chap. 5. The figures that follow on world armament costs are from *Editorial Research Reports,* vol. II, 1937, p. 74.

[6] Churchill, *op. cit.,* p. 259.

[7] The developing Austrian crisis was reported day-by-day in *The New York Times* and other leading newspapers and by the radio networks. The events were summarized as of the end of the year in *World Affairs 1938.* An account that benefits from German archives seized at the end of World War II is contained in *Churchill, op. cit.,* chap. 15.

[8] The quotation from *The Nation* is from an editorial in the issue of Sept. 24, 1938; those by Johannes Steele and Rabbi Wise are from *Time,* Oct. 10, 1938.

Chapter 19

[1] Council on Foreign Relations, *United States in World Affairs— 1939* (Harper, 1940), pp. 77-88.

[2] William L. Langer and S. Everett Gleason, *The Challenge to Isolation 1937-1940* (Harper, 1952), p. 182. See also Allan Nevins, *The New Deal and World Affairs* (Yale University Press, 1950); William E. Leuchtenburg, *Franklin D. Roosevelt and the New Deal* (Harper, 1963).

[3] Attributed to Jay Pierrepont Moffat in Leuchtenburg, *op. cit.,* p. 293.

[4] From various issues of the *Times* during last two weeks of Aug. 1939.

[5] Winston S. Churchill, *The Gathering Storm* (Houghton Mifflin, 1948), p. 377.

[6] *Peace and War: United States Foreign Policy 1931-1941* (Department of State, 1943), pp. 67, 75–80. In addition to the foregoing, an excellent account of the developing war crisis as seen from Washington is contained in Joseph Alsop and Robert Kintner, *American White Paper* (Simon and Schuster, 1940).

PHOTO CREDITS

P. 1, Associated Press. P. 6, Paul Parker, New York; (inset) Les Zeiger Collection. P. 1, Ernest Smith Collection; (inset) Les Zeiger Collection. P. 8, (clockwise) Associated Press; Library of Congress; Associated Press. P. 9, (clockwise) Les Zeiger Collection; Theatre Collection, New York Public Library. Pp. 10, 11, Brown Brothers. P. 11, (inset) Courtesy of the *Chicago Tribune*. P. 12, (clockwise) Brown Brothers (3); Times Wide World Photos. P. 13, (clockwise) Brown Brothers; Culver Pictures, Inc.; Les Zeiger Collection. Pp. 18, 19, Photo Files; (insets) Les Zeiger Collection. P. 19, (inset) Mrs. John Held, Jr. P. 20, (clockwise) Brown Brothers (3); Underwood & Underwood News Photos, Inc.; Brown Brothers; Associated Press; Brown Brothers (3). P. 21, Brown Brothers (2). P. 22, (clockwise) Brown Brothers; Photo Files; Brown Brothers; Underwood & Underwood News Photos, Inc.; Brown Brothers (2). P. 23, Brown Brothers (3). P. 24, (clockwise) Les Zeiger Collection; Ernest Smith Collection; Harris Lewine Collection (2). P. 25, (clockwise) Ernest Smith Collection (2); Les Zeiger Collection (2). P. 28, (clockwise) Culver Pictures, Inc.; Courtesy of *The New York Times;* Brown Brothers. P. 29, The Granger Collection. P. 33, United Press International. Pp. 36, 37, (center oval) Brown Brothers; (clockwise) Times Wide World Photos; Brown Brothers; Times Wide World Photos; Brown Brothers (12); Times Wide World Photos. P. 38, (clockwise) Courtesy of *The New York Times;* Les Zeiger Collection (3). P. 39, (clockwise) The Granger Collection; United Press International; Brown Brothers (2). P. 42, The Granger Collection; (inset) United Press International. P. 43, Associated Press; (insets) Associated Press (2). P. 46, (clockwise) Picture Collection, New York Public Library (2); Brown Brothers (2). P. 47, Harris Lewine Collection. P. 48, Picture Collection, New York Public Library. P. 50, (clockwise) Wide World Photos, Inc.; United Press International; Wide World Photos, Inc.; New York Public Library. P. 51, (clockwise) Wide World Photos, Inc.; Culver Pictures, Inc.; Harris Lewine Collection. P. 52, Harris Lewine Collection; (inset) Brown Brothers. P. 53, (clockwise) United Press International; Harris Lewine Collection; Brown Brothers (2). P. 55, Ernest Smith Collection; Photo Files (2); Les Zeiger Collection. P. 57, Brown Brothers. P. 68, (clockwise) Brown Brothers (2); Les Zeiger Collection; Brown Brothers. P. 69, Seidman Photo Service. P. 76, (clockwise) Wide World Photos, Inc.; Associated Press; Seidman Photo Service; Brown Brothers. P. 77, Newspaper Division, New York Public Library. P. 84, (top and middle) United Press International (5); (bottom) Brown Brothers; Harris Lewine Collection. P. 85, Brown Brothers (3). P. 86, Culver Pictures, Inc. P. 87, (clockwise) Photo Files (2); The Granger Collection; Harris Lewine Collection; Photo Files; The Granger Collection; Ernest Smith Collection (2); Photo Files. P. 88, Culver Pictures, Inc., Les Zeiger Collection. P. 89, Les Zeiger Collection (2). Pp. 88, 89, (clockwise) Les Zeiger Collection (2); Photo Files; Les Zeiger Collection; Photo Files; Les Zeiger Collection; Ernest Smith Collection; Les Zeiger Collection; Photo Files (2). P. 90, (clockwise) Brown Brothers; Associated Press; United Press International; Associated Press; (oval) Courtesy of *The New York Times*. P. 91, (clockwise) Associated Press; United Press International; Courtesy of Virginia Fritz; Les Zeiger Collection; United Press International. P. 92, Les Zeiger Collection. P. 93, Newspaper Division, New York Public Library. P. 99, United Press International. P. 101, United Press International. P. 102, Courtesy of *The New York Times*. P. 103, United Press International. P. 105, Courtesy of the Columbus *Dispatch*. P. 111, Newspaper Division, New York Public Library. P. 116, (clockwise) Wide World Photos, Inc.; Bachrach; Brown Brothers. Pp. 116, 117, (oval inset) Brown

Brothers. P. 117, (clockwise) Bachrach; United Press International (2). P. 126 (clockwise) Associated Press; Picture Collection, New York Public Library. P. 127, (clockwise) Associated Press; Courtesy of *The New York Times;* United Press International. P. 131, The Granger Collection. P. 142, (clockwise) United Press International; Irv Haberman; Wide World Photos, Inc. (2). P. 143, (clockwise) Wide World Photos, Inc.; Underwood & Underwood News Photos, Inc.; Wide World Photos, Inc.; Underwood & Underwood News Photos, Inc. P. 153, The Granger Collection. P. 155, United Press International. P. 158, Brown Brothers (2). P. 159, (clockwise) Harris Lewine Collection; Brown Brothers; Harris Lewine Collection; Brown Brothers. P. 162, (inset) Courtesy of *The New York Times.* P. 163, (inset) Associated Press. Pp. 162, 163, United Press International. P. 164, (clockwise) Harris Lewine Collection; Brown Brothers; United Press International. P. 165, (clockwise) Dan List/The Obsolete Fleet; Harris Lewine Collection; Brown Brothers; Ford Motor Company Archives. P. 168, (clockwise) Brown Brothers; United Press International. P. 169, Richard Merkin Collection. P. 170, (clockwise) Brown Brothers; Wide World Photos, Inc. (2); Harris Lewine Collection. P. 171, (clockwise) United Press International; Brown Brothers; Photo Files. Pp. 174, 175, Newspaper Division, New York Public Library. P. 175, (clockwise) Brown Brothers; Les Zeiger Collection; United Press International. P. 178, Richard Merkin Collection. P. 179, (clockwise) Photo Files; Ernest Smith Collection. Pp. 178, 179, Photo Files. P. 180, Photo Files (3). P. 181, Photo Files (2). Pp. 180, 181, Photo Files. P. 182, (clockwise) Photo Files; Culver Pictures, Inc.; Brown Brothers; Ernest Smith Collection (2). P. 183, (clockwise) New York Daily News, Inc. (3); Times Wide World Photos; (inset) United Press International. P. 188, (clockwise) United Press International; Harris Lewine Collection; United Press International (2). P. 189, (clockwise) Photo Files; Ernest Smith Collection; Photo Files. P. 190, (top) New York Daily News, Inc.; (bottom) Courtesy of *The New York Times.* P. 191, Brown Brothers (2). Pp. 190, 191, Brown Brothers. P. 192, New York Daily News, Inc. P. 193, (clockwise) Picture Collection, New York Public Library; Courtesy of *The New York Times* (2); Keystone Press Agency, Inc. P. 196, (clockwise) Harris Lewine Collection (2); Wide World Photos, Inc., Courtesy of The Kellogg Company; (inset) United Press International. P. 197, Harris Lewine Collection (3). P. 200, (clockwise) Brown Brothers; Courtesy of *The New York Times;* United Press International; Times Wide World Photos; United Press International (2); Brown Brothers (3); United Press International (2); Brown Brothers. P. 201, Brown Brothers. P. 204, (clockwise) United Press International; Brown Brothers (2). P. 205, Photo by Nelson. Pp. 206, 207, (top row) Photo Files; Harris Lewine Collection (4). Pp. 206, 207, (middle), The Condé Nast Publications, Inc.; Les Zeiger Collection (2); Photo Files. Pp. 206, 207, (bottom) The Condé Nast Publications, Inc.; Richard Merkin Collection; Les Zeiger Collection; The Granger Collection; Les Zeiger Collection. P. 208, Les Zeiger Collection (11). P. 211, United Press International. P. 222, (top) Brown Brothers; (bottom) United Press International. P. 223, (top) United Press International; (bottom) The Granger Collection. P. 224, (clockwise) Richard Merkin Collection; United Press International; Courtesy of The Condé Nast Publications, Inc.; Les Zeiger Collection. P. 225, (clockwise) Courtesy of *The New York Times;* Courtesy of the *Washington Star;* Courtesy of *The New York Times.* P. 224, 225, Brown Brothers. P. 231, Courtesy of *Fortune* magazine, Time Inc. P. 233, Library of Congress. P. 242, Associated Press; Brown Brothers. P. 243, Brown Brothers (2). P. 244, (clockwise) Library of Congress; United Press International; Orville Logan Snider. Pp. 244, 245, Library of Congress. P. 246, Library of Congress. P. 247, (clockwise) Library of Congress; Courtesy of the Viking Press, Inc.; Library of Congress (3); Courtesy of the Viking Press, Inc. P. 252, Library of Congress (2). P. 253, Magnum Photos, Inc. P. 255, Harris & Ewing. P. 258, (clockwise) Brown Brothers (2); United Press International. P. 259, Brown Brothers (2); (bottom) United Press International. P. 260, Les Zeiger Collection. P. 261, Library of Congress. P. 262, (clockwise) Underwood & Underwood News Photos, Inc.; United Press International (3). P. 263, (top) Wide World Photos, Inc.; (bottom) Associated Press. P. 282, Brown Brothers; (inset) United Press International. P. 283, Brown Brothers. P. 284, Richard Merkin Collection. P. 285, (clockwise) Wide World Photos, Inc.; Library of Congress (2). P. 291, Harris Lewine Collection. P. 294, Harris Lewine Collection. P. 295, (clockwise) Brown Brothers (3); Harris Lewine Collection; Brown Brothers (2); Picture Collection, New York Public Library (2). P. 300, (clockwise) Brown Brothers; United Press International; Brown Brothers; United Press International. P. 301, (clockwise) Times Wide World Photos; Associated Press; Photo Files. Pp. 300, 301, Brown Brothers. P. 306, Richard Merkin Collection. P. 307, (clockwise) Richard Merkin Collection; Wide World Photos, Inc. (2). P. 312, Wide World Photos, Inc.; Brown Brothers. P. 313, (clockwise) Harris Lewine Collection (2); Brown Brothers (2); Courtesy of United Air Lines. P. 314, The Condé Nast Publications, Inc.. P. 315, (clockwise) Irv Haberman; Richard Merkin Collection; Brown Brothers (2); Harris Lewine Collection. P. 322, (top) Richard Merkin Collection; (bottom) Associated Press. P. 323, (clockwise) United Press International; Picture Collection, New York Public Library; Wide World Photos, Inc.

P. 326, (top) Les Zeiger Collection; (bottom) Brown Brothers. P. 327, (clockwise) Brown Brothers (2); Les Zeiger Collection. P. 328, (clockwise) Richard Merkin Collection; Brown Brothers (2). P. 329, Photo by Nelson. P. 330, United Press International. P. 331, United Press International. Pp. 330, 331, (clockwise) Irv Haberman; Brown Brothers; United Press International; Brown Brothers (2); Picture Collection, New York Public Library (W.T. Hoff); Brown Brothers. P. 332, Richard Merkin Collection. P. 334, Les Zeiger Collection. P. 335, Harris Lewine Collection. Pp. 334, 335, (clockwise) United Press International (3); Harris Lewine Collection; Brown Brothers (2); United Press International. P. 340, (clockwise) Courtesy of The New Yorker Magazine, Inc.; Underwood & Underwood News Photos, Inc.; United Press International. P. 341, New York Daily News, Inc. P. 344, Newspaper Division, New York Public Library. P. 345, Les Zeiger Collection; Brown Brothers. P. 348, Les Zeiger Collection; Brown Brothers. P. 349, Brown Brothers. P. 350, United Press International (3). P. 351, Brown Brothers. P. 352, (clockwise) Les Zeiger Collection (6); St. Louis Post–Dispatch; Photo Files. P. 353, (top) Underwood & Underwood News Photos, Inc.; Richard Merkin Collection. P. 354, Richard Merkin Collection. P. 355, Les Zeiger Collection (12); Harris Lewine Collection. P. 359, Alfredo Valente. P. 362, (clockwise) Brown Brothers (3); Les Zeiger Collection; Schomburg Collection, New York Public Library; Photo Files. P. 363, Brown Brothers. P. 366, (clockwise) Theatre Collection, New York Public Library; Culver Pictures, Inc.; Theatre Collection, New York Public Library; Culver Pictures, Inc. P. 367, (clockwise) Theatre Collection, New York Public Library; Culver Pictures, Inc.; Wide World Photos, Inc; Culver Pictures, Inc.; Theatre Collection, New York Public Library. P. 368, Culver Pictures, Inc. (3). P. 369, Culver Pictures, Inc. P. 370, (clockwise) Theatre Collection, New York Public Library (3). P. 371, (clockwise) Culver Pictures, Inc.; Theatre Collection, New York Public Library. P. 372, Vandamm Studio. P. 373, (clockwise) Culver Pictures, Inc.; Harris Lewine Collection; Culver Pictures, Inc. P. 376, Theatre Collection, New York Public Library (2). P. 377, Alfredo Valente. P. 378, Courtesy of The New York Times; Vandamm Studio (2). P. 379, Theatre Collection, New York Public Library. P. 380, Theatre Collection, New York Public Library (4). P. 381, Theatre Collection, New York Public Library. P. 382, Theatre Collection, New York Public Library; Harris Lewine Collection. P. 383, Culver Pictures, Inc. P. 384, (clockwise) Schomburg Collection, New York Public Library; Brown Brothers; Alfredo Valente (2). P. 385 Brown Brothers (2). P. 386, (clockwise) Theatre Collection, New York Public Library (3); Culver Pictures, Inc. P. 387, Theatre Collection, New York Public Library (3); Culver Pictures, Inc. (2). P. 388, Vandamm Studio. P. 394, (clockwise) Schomburg Collection, New York Public Library; Brown Brothers (4); Harris Lewine Collection; Courtesy of The Macmillan Company. P. 395, (clockwise) Underwood & Underwood News Photos, Inc.; Courtesy of the Vanguard Press; Brown Brothers (3); Schomburg Collection, New York Public Library. P. 396, (clockwise) Brown Brothers; Courtesy of Simon & Schuster, Inc. P. 397, (clockwise) Picture Collection, New York Public Library (4); Harris Lewine Collection. P. 400, (clockwise) Picture Collection, New York Public Library; Harris Lewine Collection (2); Gotham Book Mart; Richard Merkin Collection. P. 401, (clockwise) Harris Lewine Collection (3); Les Zeiger Collection. P. 404, Picture Collection, New York Public Library. P. 405, (clockwise) Picture Collection, New York Public Library; L'Elan Galleries (2); Picture Collection, New York Public Library. P. 406, (clockwise) Courtesy of Sheldon Swope Art Gallery; Museum of Modern Art; Metropolitan Museum of Art. P. 407, (clockwise) Courtesy of Sheldon Swope Art Gallery; Museum of Modern Art; The Whitney Museum of American Art; Rehn Gallery; Cincinnati Art Museum. P. 418, (clockwise) Harris Lewine Collection (2); Culver Pictures, Inc.; Harris Lewine Collection; Culver Pictures, Inc. P. 419, (clockwise) Harris Lewine Collection; Culver Pictures, Inc. (2); Harris Lewine Collection; Culver Pictures, Inc.; Harris Lewine Collection. Pp. 422, 423, (clockwise) Culver Pictures, Inc.; Harris Lewine Collection; Photo Files; Harris Lewine Collection; Photo Files; Culver Pictures, Inc.; Harris Lewine Collection; Culver Pictures, Inc. P. 423, Harris Lewine Collection. P. 424, (clockwise) Brown Brothers; Photo Files; Culver Pictures, Inc. P. 425, (clockwise) Les Zeiger Collection; Photo Files. P. 426, The Granger Collection. P. 427, (clockwise) Harris Lewine Collection (2); The Granger Collection. P. 428, (clockwise) Harris Lewine Collection; Photo Files; Harris Lewine Collection. P. 429, (clockwise) Picture Collection, New York Public Library; Harris Lewine Collection; Photo Files; Ernest Smith Collection. Pp. 428, 429, Picture Collection, New York Public Library. P. 432, (clockwise) Photo Files; Underwood & Underwood News Photos, Inc.; Brown Brothers; Photo Files. P. 433, (clockwise) Les Zeiger Collection (2); Photo Files; Courtesy of The New York Times (3). Pp. 436, 437, Harris Lewine Collection. P. 437, Les Zeiger Collection. P. 440, (clockwise) Culver Pictures, Inc.; Underwood & Underwood News Photos, Inc.; National Broadcasting Company; Brown Brothers; Culver Pictures, Inc.; Courtesy of The New York Times (2); Les Zeiger Collection (3). P. 441, (clockwise) Photo Files; National Broadcasting Company; Courtesy of The New York Times (2). P. 446, (clockwise), Brown Brothers; Les Zeiger Collection (4). P. 447, (clockwise) Ernest Smith Collection; Les Zeiger Collection; Ernest Smith Collection; Schomburg Collection, New York Public Library; Les Zeiger Collection (2). P. 448, (clockwise) Les Zeiger Collection; Photo Files. P. 449, (clockwise) Les Zeiger Collection (2); Photo Files; Harris Lewine Collection. P. 450, (clockwise) Les Zeiger Collection; Ernest Smith Collection; Brown Brothers; Les Zeiger Collection. P. 451, (clockwise) Ernest Smith Collection; Les Zeiger Collection. P. 452, (clockwise) Photo Files; Les Zeiger Collection; Photo Files; Harris Lewine Collection; Brown Brothers (2). P. 453, Photo Files; Les Zeiger Collection (2); Photo Files; Les Zeiger Collection. P. 454, (clockwise) Les Zeiger Collection (3); Brown Brothers. P. 455, (clockwise) Photo Files (3); Les Zeiger Collection. P. 456, Harris Lewine Collection. P. 457, (clockwise) Photo Files; Harris Lewine Collection; Photo Files; Les Zeiger Collection. P. 458, Photo Files; Theatre Collection, New York Public Library; Les Zeiger Collection. P. 459, Les Zeiger Collection; Photo Files (2). P. 460, (clockwise) Ernest Smith Collection; Harris Lewine Collection (2). P. 461, Photo Files; Harris Lewine Collection. Pp. 462, 463, Les Zeiger Collection (28); Brown Brothers. P. 466, Culver Pictures, Inc. P. 467, (clockwise) Richard Merkin Collection; Harris Lewine Collection (2); Richard Merkin Collection (3). P. 468, Harris Lewine Collection. P. 469, Harris Lewine Collection. Pp. 490, 491, (clockwise) Brown Brothers; Harry S. Truman Library; Seidman Photo Service; Courtesy of the *New York Herald Tribune;* Harris & Ewing; United Press International; Courtesy of *The New York Times.* P. 491, United Press International. Pp. 498, 499, United Press International. P. 498, Picture Collection, New York Public Library. P. 499, Courtesy of the *Los Angeles Times.* Pp. 516, 517, (clockwise) Brown Brothers; United Press International; Photo: Ritasse; United Press International; Courtesy of The International Ladies' Garment Workers Union; United Press International. P. 518, Brown Brothers (2). P. 519, Brown Brothers (2). Pp. 520, 521, Underwood & Underwood News Photos, Inc. P. 525, (clockwise) Times Wide World Photos (2); Picture Collection, New York Public Library; Print Collection, New York Public Library. P. 527, Courtesy of the St. Louis *Post–Dispatch.* Pp. 534, 535, Brown Brothers. P. 534, Brown Brothers; Richard Merkin Collection. P. 535, Brown Brothers; Harris Lewine Collection; Richard Merkin Collection. P. 536, Associated Press; Richard Merkin Collection. P. 537, (clockwise) Brown Brothers; Richard Merkin Collection; Brown Brothers; Courtesy of the St. Louis *Post–Dispatch.* P. 544, (clockwise) Brown Brothers; Courtesy of the *Los Angeles Times;* Keystone; Brown Brothers. P. 545, Brown Brothers (3). P. 546, (clockwise) Courtesy of the New York *Herald Tribune;* Brown Brothers (2). P. 547, (clockwise) Irv Haberman; Brown Brothers; Irv Haberman. P. 551, Courtesy of the St. Louis *Post–Dispatch.* P. 556, Brown Brothers (3). P. 557, Brown Brothers (2). Pp. 558, 559, Brown Brothers. Pp. 558, 559, Harris Lewine Collection. P. 560, (clockwise) Irv Haberman; Brown Brothers; Irv Haberman. P. 561, (clockwise) Les Zeiger Collection (2); Harris Lewine Collection (2). P. 562, (clockwise) Associated Press; Brown Brothers (2). P. 563, (clockwise) Brown Brothers (2); Associated Press; Wide World Photos, Inc. (4). P. 564, Harris Lewine Collection. P. 570, Courtesy of the St. Louis *Post-Dispatch.* Pp. 570, 571, Underwood & Underwood News Photos, Inc. P. 571, Brown Brothers.

INDEX

1/03   6   11/02